# WEB DEVELOPMENT WITH VISUAL BASIC™ 5

**que**®

# Web Development with Visual Basic™ 5

*Written by Davis Chapman with*

*Robert Amenn • Michael Corning • Loren Eidahl • Steve Elfanbaum*
*Brian Farrar • Dina Fleet • Jeff Gainer • Bill Hatfield*
*Nelson Howell • Rory Job • Lowell Mauer • David Melnick*
*Steve Potts • Bob Reselman • Steve Wynkoop*

# Web Development with Visual Basic™ 5

Library of Congress Catalog No.: 97-65017

ISBN: 0-7897-0811-6

99  98  97      6  5  4  3  2  1

Interpretation of the printing code: the rightmost double-digit number is the year of the book's printing; the rightmost single-digit number, the number of the book's printing. For example, a printing code of 97-1 shows that the first printing of the book occurred in 1997.

Screen reproductions in this book were created using Collage Plus from Inner Media, Inc., Hollis, NH.

# Contents at a Glance

# Table of Contents

## II │ ActiveX Controls

### 3 Building ActiveX Controls with VB 49

## V | Active Server Pages

## 17   Constructing Your Own Server Components   351

## 23 Using Remote Data Objects with the OLEISAPI2 Interface  541

## VIII | Distributed Processing

## Appendixes

# Credits

**PRESIDENT**
Roland Elgey

**SENIOR VICE PRESIDENT/PUBLISHING**
Don Fowley

**PUBLISHER**
Stacy Hiquet

**PUBLISHING MANAGER**
Fred Slone

**GENERAL MANAGER**
Joe Muldoon

**EDITORIAL SERVICES DIRECTOR**
Elizabeth Keaffaber

**MANAGING EDITOR**
Caroline D. Roop

**ACQUISITIONS EDITOR**
Kelly Marshall

**SENIOR EDITOR**
Mike La Bonne

**EDITORS**
Elizabeth Barrett, Kelly Brooks,
Matthew B. Cox, Lisa M. Gebken,
Kate Givens, Nicholas Zafran

**WEB MASTER**
Thomas H. Bennett

**PRODUCT MARKETING MANAGER**
Kourtnaye Sturgeon

**ASSISTANT PRODUCT MARKETING
MANAGER/DESIGN**
Christy M. Miller

**ASSISTANT PRODUCT MARKETING
MANAGER/ SALES**
Karen Kincaid

**TECHNICAL EDITORS**
Nelson Howell
John Smiley

**SOFTWARE COORDINATOR**
Andrea Duvall

**TECHNICAL SUPPORT SPECIALIST**
Nadeem Muhammed

**ACQUISITIONS COORDINATOR**
Carmen Krikorian

**SOFTWARE RELATIONS COORDINATOR**
Susan D. Gallagher

**EDITORIAL ASSISTANT**
Travis Bartlett

**BOOK DESIGNER**
Ruth Harvey

**COVER DESIGNER**
Barbara Kordesh

**PRODUCTION TEAM**
Bryan Flores
Brian Grossman
Lisa Stumpf
Donna Wright

**INDEXER**
Craig Small

Composed in *Century Old Style* and *ITC Franklin Gothic* by Que Corporation.

*To Dore, and the rest of my family, for putting up with me through this entire process once again.*

# About the Author

**Davis Chapman** first began programming computers while working on his Masters Degree in Music Composition. While writing applications for computer music, he discovered that he enjoyed designing and developing computer software. It wasn't long before he came to the realization that he stood a much better chance of eating if he stuck with his newly found skill and demoted his hard-earned status as a "starving artist" to a part-time hobby. Since that time, Davis has strived to perfect the art of software design and development, with a strong emphasis on the practical application of client/server technology. He has been with the Dallas, Texas-based consulting firm B.R. Blackmarr & Associates for the past seven years, and can be reached at davischa@onramp.net.

# Acknowledgments

There are numerous people without whom this book may never have been written. Among these people are all of the coauthors, whose contributions made the size and scope of this book possible. Also deserving credit is Fred Slone of Que, who did his best to put my life on hold for a few weeks, resulting in a much better and encompassing book than what we started out creating. Fred, I've always thought that your contributions are very insightful and help to make a better book, and once again you've proved me right! Thanks to Angela Kozlowski for starting and getting me involved in this project in the first place, and to Kelly Marshall for keeping me involved through the entire second half of the project. Credit needs to go to the entire editing team at Que. I've seen what some of the material you have to work with looks like when it comes in from the authors, and I do not want to trade jobs with any of you. Last, I'd like to thank Microsoft for keeping me on my toes by releasing at least a half-dozen new technologies during the course of writing this book, all of which fell within the scope of the book and had to be included. I'd also like to thank my family for continuing to allow me to put in the work required to produce this book, and for not disowning me in the process.

# We'd Like to Hear from You!

As part of our continuing effort to produce books of the highest possible quality, Que would like to hear your comments. To stay competitive, we *really* want you to let us know what you like or dislike most about this book or other Que products.

Please send your comments, ideas, and suggestions for improvement to:

The Expert User Team

E-mail: **euteam@que.mcp.com**

CompuServe: **105527,745**

Fax: (317) 581-4663

Our mailing address is:

Expert User Team

Que Corporation

201 West 103rd Street

Indianapolis, IN 46290-1097

You can also visit our Team's home page on the World Wide Web at:

**http://www.mcp.com/que/developer_expert**

Thank you in advance. Your comments will help us to continue publishing the best books available in today's market.

Thank You,


The Expert User Team

# Introduction

The Internet and the World Wide Web are the fastest grow-ing and changing areas in computers today. The World Wide Web is also one of the fastest growing areas to open itself to Visual Basic programmers, thanks mainly to the quick change in focus by Microsoft. Up until the day it released Windows 95, Microsoft had little to no interest in getting involved in the Internet, or in the Web. Within three months of releasing Windows 95, Microsoft had completely turned around and was moving head-first into the Internet, and in particular into the rapidly developing Web. The reverberations from this change in direction were felt throughout the computer industry, and will continue to be felt for some time to come.

One of the biggest beneficiaries of this change in direction has been the Visual Basic development community. Just over one year ago, if you were a Visual Basic programmer who wanted to get involved in the World Wide Web, your only real choice was to acquire Bob Denny's original shareware Windows Web server, or one of the early Netscape Web servers that ran on Windows NT, and build WinCGI applications. If you were really brave, you would try your hand at standard CGI programming with one of the other NT-based Web servers. Now, Visual Basic pro-grammers can use their VB skills to build just about any piece of the Web application puzzle.

This book is about all of the pieces of Web application development, and how you, the Visual Basic programmer, can use your programming skills and experience to use building applications on the Web. This is a crucial time for leveraging your existing programming skill and experience for Web application development, because the Web is no longer limited to the Internet. Corporations are putting Web technologies to use in large numbers for building intranet applications, where the Web and other Internet technologies are used on private corporate networks for business application needs.

This book is intended to enlighten the Visual Basic developer on all of the pieces that currently make up the World Wide Web, and show how Visual Basic can be used in each of these situations. Some of these situations are not very pretty, and can look scary to programmers who don't know C or C++ as a complement to their Visual Basic experience; however, most of these areas can be jumped into without looking at another programming language. This book is designed to make sure that you, as a Visual Basic programmer, know full well what is involved when jumping into any of these areas of Web application development. ■

# Who Should Use This Book?

This book was written for the experienced Visual Basic programmer who wants to build Web-based applications. The intentions behind this book are to explain the various aspects of Web application development, and how Visual Basic can be used to build Web applications.

Although there are some new and tricky aspects of Visual Basic programming, this book is not intended as a general programming tome. If you are a beginning Visual Basic programmer, you would be better off purchasing any general Visual Basic programming book from Que, such as *Visual Basic Unleashed*.

This book attempts to walk a fine line between supplying sufficient understanding of the theories fundamental to understanding of how the Web works, showing how the Web can be used as a foundation for building applications, and providing practical examples of how Visual Basic can be used for Web-based application development. The Web is a rapidly growing arena with a large number of new technologies being introduced and added almost weekly. Within this framework, there is a large number of these Web-oriented technologies currently in use, with several more arriving in the very near future. This makes for a lot of ground that this book tries to cover, and some of these areas can and have had entire books dedicated solely to that particular topic. As a result, most of the areas within this book simply provide a starting point, into which you can delve further, depending on which area you are most interested in.

This book takes a more general approach because, without an overall understanding of all of these areas of application development, you might not understand how you need to approach each of these individual areas, and how what you build needs to interact and relate to the other areas involved in Web-application development. One overall fact of Web-application development, is that you, as a programmer, cannot focus solely on the client or server functionality, and ignore all other areas. As a Web-application developer, you need to be aware of and take into account, all areas of Web-application development. If you don't have to work with these areas yourself, you will need to interact with them, and you need to know how to approach them.

Another reason for the approach of this book, is to help you understand all the areas of Web application development. I know of numerous developers who have jumped into Web-application development without really understanding what they were getting into or what was involved. I cannot count how many e-mails and phone calls I have received from developers who read one book that covered only one aspect of Web development, and didn't understand how what they were attempting differed from what they had read about. Because they didn't understand the difference, they had made commitments that they could not meet, all because they had not fully understood the arena into which they were leaping. Too many of these calls came from programmers who didn't know something basic to Web application development such as the difference between the CGI and WinCGI interfaces; the books they had read hadn't differentiated between the two. As a result, just about every one of these programmers were trying to build a WinCGI application with a Web server that didn't support the WinCGI interface.

# What Hardware and Software Do You Need?

The hardware and software needed for building the examples in this book depend a great deal on which examples you want to build. At the very least, you need Visual Basic 5 and a copy of Internet Explorer 3, running on Windows 95. If you are building any of the server-side examples, you will need an appropriate Web server, running on Windows NT. For the CGI example, just about any Web server will work; but, if you want to build and run the WinCGI examples, you will be best off working with O'Reilly's WebSite, or one of Netscape's Web servers, which come with the WinCGI interface as a native interface.

> **NOTE** While Microsoft's Internet Information Server (IIS) does not natively support the WinCGI interface, there is a way to add this interface to your IIS server. In the ActiveX SDK, there is a WinCGI interface included as one of the ISAPI programming examples. You will need a C++ compiler (preferably Visual C++) and will have to tweak a few variables, but it's possible to use this to add the WinCGI interface to an IIS Web server. ■

If you want to build the ISAPI examples, you will need to be working with Microsoft's Internet Information Server or O'Reilly's WebSite Professional. For building NSAPI examples, you will need one of Netscape's Web servers (FastTrack or Enterprise).

For the examples on integrating Visual Basic and other technologies, you might also need to have a copy of the specific tools being discussed in those chapters. When building Internet-enabled Visual Basic applications, you will need to have Microsoft's Inet DLLs to provide the API functions being used in the examples. When using Visual Basic with Java applets, you will need a Java compiler, preferably Microsoft's Visual J++, in order to build the Java examples. For the chapters on Internet Studio, you will need to have a copy of Internet Studio.

# How Is This Book Organized?

This book is organized into six sections, each covering different areas of Web application development. The first section discusses the technologies used in the Web and on the Internet. This section will also discuss some of the drawbacks to programming for both the client- and server-side of the Web. The second and third sections look at each of the programming options for the client-side, and server-side, respectively. The fourth section looks at integrating Visual Basic with other Web-oriented technologies, such as Java and Microsoft's Internet Studio. The fifth section provides a case study in building a typical Web-based application. The sixth section provides reference material for understanding HTML and choosing an appropriate Web server.

## Part I: Visual Basic and the Web

This section is an introduction to Visual Basic as a Web application programming tool. It discusses the features of Visual Basic 5 that are geared toward Web and Internet application programming. Also, it gets your feet wet with a simple, browser-based Web application that will give you an idea of what's to come.

- Chapter 1, "What's New with Visual Basic and the Web," provides an overview of VB Web application development by looking at all of the new features of VB 5 that are aimed at Web and Internet application programming. It also looks at other areas of Web application development using VB that are not necessarily new with VB 5, but still are important topics within the arena of VB Web development.

- Chapter 2, "Up and Running: Browser-Based VB Programming," takes you through building a simple browser-based application that incorporates multiple client-based Web technologies (such as ActiveX controls, VBScript, and ActiveX Documents). This chapter doesn't focus on explaining the technologies used, as they will each be explored in detail in later chapters. This chapter is more to get your feet wet, and give you an idea of what types of applications are possible with VB and Web technologies.

## Part II: ActiveX Controls

This section focuses on building ActiveX controls for use with Web applications. The intention is to take you through various ways of building ActiveX controls, and then end with a discussion on what makes for a "net-friendly" ActiveX control. The idea here is to provide you with a firm understanding of the various options available for creating ActiveX controls—and the issues surrounding them—in order to make the best decisions for creating the controls that will work best for your needs.

- Chapter 3, "Building ActiveX Controls with VB," takes a look at the capability of VB programmers to build their own ActiveX controls by using the new version of Visual Basic. Topics covered in this chapter include providing the required support files to the users of your control (such as the VB 5 runtime DLL and CAB files), placing the control into an HTML document, and so on. This chapter also discusses the options available to the control builder/user for providing initialization information to the control.

- Chapter 4, "Inheriting From and Extending Other ActiveX Controls," focuses on building new ActiveX controls by extending existing ActiveX controls. Topics covered include distribution and licensing issues with the controls that the reader started from, how to make sure that the ancestor control is downloaded with the descendent control, and so on.

■ Chapter 5, "Making an ActiveX Control Communicate with a Server," takes you through building network communications into an ActiveX control, so that it communicates with a server application. This chapter builds on the previous chapter by having the control you build encapsulate the WinSock or Internet ActiveX Controls that are included with VB 5. This chapter includes discussions about network communications, explaining the principles and providing you with a basic understanding of application level networking.

■ Chapter 6, "Making Your ActiveX Controls Web-Friendly," focuses on how to build Web-friendly ActiveX controls. Topics covered in this chapter include portability issues, security, making controls as thin as possible for minimal download time, and code signing with an individual, class 2 certificate (this is also applicable to signing controls with a class 3 corporate certificate), and so on.

## Part III: Scripting

This section focuses on using scripting languages to add functionality to HTML documents and forms. The primary focus will be on VBScript, and how the various HTML elements look and behave like VB Controls, as well as interacting with ActiveX controls and Java applets. Finally, this section includes a brief chapter on using JavaScript (or JScript as MS calls their version) to interact with ActiveX controls.

■ Chapter 7, "Using VBScript to Build HTML-Based VB Applications," introduces VBScript by showing the basics of embedding the VBScript functions and subroutines in the HTML document with the SCRIPT tag. It also shows how the various HTML elements look to VBScript like VB controls by exposing their properties to the VBScript routines, and how the elements events may trigger VBScript subroutines. This chapter builds on your existing knowledge of VB by showing you how VBScript is similar to VB programming, while being sure to point out the differences that you need to know.

■ Chapter 8, "Interacting with ActiveX Controls and VBScript," builds on the previous chapter by adding ActiveX controls into the mix. It takes you through using VBScript to set properties of the ActiveX control, and how to trigger VBScript methods with ActiveX control events.

■ Chapter 9, "Using VBScript with Java Applets," takes you through integrating VBScript with Java applets running in the IE Java VM. It looks at how IE packages the Java VM such that the Java applets look like ActiveX controls to the VBScript (and other ActiveX controls).

## Part IV: Active Documents

This section focuses on ActiveX Document applications, where you can build VB 5 applications that run within a Web browser.

■ Chapter 10, "ActiveX Documents: Serving Up VB in a Web Browser," takes you through the fundamentals of building and running an ActiveX Document Application by using

VB 5. It examines the files produced, and how the .VBP files can be opened in the IE 3 browser, or the Office 95 Binder, and run as a regular VB application. This chapter also discusses the obvious issues surrounding portability and application download size, security, use of ActiveX controls in the VB application, ActiveX Document performance, and so on.

- Chapter 11, "Property Bags and Menus: Extending ActiveX Document Applications," builds on the previous chapter by looking at how property bags can be used to initialize the ActiveX document applications. It also looks at how menus may be added to the application to extend the application further.

- Chapter 12, "Hyperlinks: Extending ActiveX Document Applications over Multiple Windows," builds on the previous two chapters by examining how hyperlinks may be added to the VB ActiveX Document application to take the user to another ActiveX Document application. This chapter covers issues of scope, and how the ActiveX Document applications handle backing up to a previous applet through the Web browser, and how "state" information from the first applet can be passed to the second applet, and so on.

### Part V: Active Server Pages

This section moves over to the server side of the Web, with an in-depth look at Active Server Pages, and how VBScript can be used on the Web server to provide application functionality and interactivity, where all of the script code is located on the Web server, making it difficult for other Web application developers to steal your code. By moving your VBScript code to the server, you also enable your Web applications to be used by a greater number of users, using a wider variety of Web browsers.

- Chapter 13, "Active Server Pages and Server-Side Scripting," delves into the use of VBScript on the server and the IIS Active Server Pages technology, and how it can be used to open up the Web page functionality to build dynamic HTML pages. Topics covered include providing database functionality to Web pages and customizing Web pages to reflect user preferences.

- Chapter 14, "Managing States and Events with Application and Session Objects," dives deeper into a specific aspect of ASP development. This chapter takes a detailed look at some of the objects that ASP provides to enable you to track your users as they move through your Web site.

- Chapter 15, "Building a Foundation of Interactivity with Request and Response Objects," takes a detailed look at the receiving and returning of dynamic data in Active Server Pages. This topic provides the basis for building data-oriented Web applications with ASP.

- Chapter 16, "Enhancing Interactivity with Cookies, Headers, and the Server Object," explores how Active Server Pages enable you to easily use cookies to maintain identification and configuration information on the user's computer by using client-side cookies with Active Server Pages.

- Chapter 17, "Constructing Your Own Server Components," shows how you can use Visual Basic to build your own server-side components that can be used with Active Server Pages to provide additional functionality to your Web applications.

## Part VI: Server-Side Programming

This section is built around the various options and technologies that can be used to provide server-based Web application functionality. Some of these options work very well with and are well suited for Visual Basic. Others are probably best left alone by the Visual Basic programmer, and tackled by using other programming languages.

■ Chapter 18, "The WinCGI Interface and Visual Basic," provides you with an understanding of the WinCGI interface, and how it was designed specifically for use with the Visual Basic programming language. This chapter takes a thorough look at the structure of the WinCGI configuration file, how it is created, how to read it into a Visual Basic application, and how to build the appropriate output file for returning back to the client browser.

■ Chapter 19, "ISAPI, OLEISAPI, and Visual Basic," delves into the ISAPI interface provided with Microsoft's IIS Web server, the OLEISAPI extensions for this interface, how they both work, and how Visual Basic can be used with these interfaces to provide more efficient server-side applications. This chapter also discusses how the OLEISAPI interface can be a potential bottleneck for request processing, and how Visual Basic applications should be written in an efficient manner to minimize the bottleneck potential. This chapter also covers configuring an NT server to allow the IIS server to create COM objects so that the OLEISAPI interface can be used.

■ Chapter 20, "The OLEISAPI2 Interface and the Active Reference Object," discusses the new OLEISAPI2 interface provided as a Visual C++ Active Template Library (ATL) programming sample. It looks at the differences between the implementation of the OLEISAPI and OLEISAPI2 interfaces, and how the VB programmer can work with the OLEISAPI2 interface to provide more functionality to Web applications built using VB.

■ Chapter 21, "Providing an OLEISAPI-Like Interface for Other Web Servers," is for those VB programmers who like the efficiency of OLEISAPI programming, but need to build Web applications running on another brand Web server. This chapter explains what is necessary to build an OLEISAPI-like interface to work with other brand Web servers. For the purpose of illustrating this, the reader will be taken through the actual implementation of an OLEISAPI-like interface for Netscape Web servers. Among the topics discussed are programming for the IDispatch COM interface, looking up the CLSID for a specific ActiveX object, and other ActiveX Automation programming that is normally hidden from the VB programmer (a mini-look under the hood of ActiveX).

## Part VII: Web Database Access

This section focuses on adding database access to Web applications. It looks at several different technologies for adding database access, from the very simple Internet Database Connector, to the point-and-click of Visual InterDev.

■ Chapter 22, "Using Data Access Objects with the WinCGI Interface," builds on Chapter 8 by extending the WinCGI application with database functionality. Topics discussed include approaches and strategies to minimizing the overhead associated with WinCGI database applications from the application startup; and establishment of a database connection along with associated shutdowns and cleanup.

- Chapter 23, "Using Remote Data Objects with the OLEISAPI2 Interface," builds on Chapter 22 by discussing the addition of database access to an OLEISAPI2 Visual Basic application. Among the topics covered are the threading model in VB 5, and how it affects the use of shared resources such as a database connection. This chapter points out how, although the OLEISAPI interface provides much faster response and less overhead than the WinCGI interface, without careful planning and efficient programming the OLEISAPI interface can turn into a Web server killer, by creating a large backlog of OLEISAPI requests waiting their turn in the queue. It also looks at the use of Remote Data Objects (RDO) to bypass the Microsoft Jet database engine in order to go directly to the ODBC datasource, providing the user with less overhead and better performance.

- Chapter 24, "The Internet Database Connector: Providing Database Access on the Web," examines the Internet Database Connector provided with Microsoft's IIS Web server. Although it doesn't directly use any VB programming (though some VBScript may be incorporated into the HTML forms), it does provide you with a simple and somewhat limited way to add database access to a Web application.

- Chapter 25, "Introducing ActiveX Data Objects," introduces the ActiveX Data Objects integrated into Active Server Pages. ActiveX Data Objects make use of the Advanced Data Connector (which is examined in the following chapter), to cache database records on the Web browser, providing the user with the ability to navigate through a set of records without having to retrieve each record from the Web server.

- Chapter 26, "Integrating the Advanced Data Connector into Web Database Applications," looks at Microsoft's new Advanced Data Connector and how it can be used to cache database records in the Web browser. This technology is very similar to that examined in Chapter 24, only providing the user with more dynamic data-interaction.

- Chapter 27, "Building Web Database Applications by Using Visual InterDev," introduces you to Microsoft's new Visual InterDev and takes you through building a Web-based database application by using Visual InterDev. It looks at the use of Web Design-Time controls within the VID environment, and how it is possible to add-in additional controls to extend the VID functionality (this ties into Chapter 33, where you learn how to build your own Web Design-Time controls).

### Part VIII: Distributed Processing

This section deals with building distributed processing applications on the Web by using Microsoft's Transaction Server with Visual Basic in various Web-based situations. It will start by introducing you to Transaction Server, and take you through what Transaction Server does, and the how and why of distributed processing applications. This entire section assumes that you have access to Microsoft's Transaction Server and a Microsoft SQL Server 6.5 database for building and running any and all examples (with certain specific exceptions, such as the SNA chapter).

- Chapter 28, "Microsoft Transaction Server and Visual Basic," examines Microsoft's Transaction Server and how it interacts with Visual Basic, providing distributed processing and transaction functionality to Visual Basic applications, allowing them to scale to handle large numbers of users. This chapter provides you with an understanding of distributed computing architecture.

- Chapter 29, "Multi-Tier Applications and the Web," extends the distributed application begun in the previous chapter, illustrating how an application can be built that integrates several systems into an integrated whole, spread across an entire corporate network. This chapter also examines some of the more advanced programming topics involved with building Visual Basic applications that are integrated with Transaction Server.

- Chapter 30, "Building Distributed Web Applications," takes you through building a small distributed Web application by using IIS, VB, MTS, and SQL Server. This chapter primarily consists of examples, leaving most of the theory and explanations for the previous two chapters. This chapter provides thorough explanations for the decisions made in the design of the application, how to parse off the business rules from the application entry point (Web server), and the database.

- Chapter 31, "Internet Security and Web Applications," discusses Internet security and tools used by various organizations to safeguard their internal networks from external dangers. This chapter also looks at how these tools can affect Web applications, and what can be done to cooperate and coexist with these tools.

## Part IX: Web-Related Topics

This section focuses on taking advantage of functionality of ActiveX controls provided with IE 3.0 and VB 5 to build Web-related applications with Visual Basic. These applications are not Web-based, in that they are not delivered to the user through a Web browser, but instead are standard Visual Basic applications that have various Web functionalities built into them so that they are capable of providing useful tools for building and maintaining Web sites, or providing Web browsing functionality in conjunction with other application functionality.

- Chapter 32, "Web-Enabling Visual Basic Applications," looks at the functionality provided by Microsoft's Internet extensions to the Win32 API, how this functionality has been encapsulated into the Internet ActiveX control provided with VB 5, and how this control can be used to build a Web spider that will check a Web site for broken links.

- Chapter 33, "Building Web Design-Time Controls," examines Microsoft's new Web Design-Time control technology, what these controls do, how they work, and how all Microsoft applications are going to start using and incorporating them. It also takes you through building a Web Design-Time control by using VB 5, and then showing how the control may be incorporated into Visual InterDev (or other Microsoft tools and applications).

- Chapter 34, "Integrating Visual Basic with Java," takes you through integrating Java applets running in the Microsoft Java VM ActiveX Control with a VB application. It looks at how the Java VM control enables the VB programmer to interact with Java applets like ActiveX, calling methods built in Java.

## Appendixes

The appendixes provide you with topics and reference material that, although not directly related to learning how to build the applications discussed in the book, provide valuable information on related technologies and languages.

■ Appendix A, "Standard CGI, WinCGI, and Visual Basic," shows you how the standard CGI interface works, how it is different than the WinCGI interface, what is involved to use Visual Basic with this interface, and why Visual Basic is not the ideal choice for programming tools to use with this Web server interface. All other books in this subject area ignore this subject and can give you the false impression that the WinCGI interface is standard on all Windows-based Web servers. The reality is that the standard CGI interface is the standard on all Web servers, including those running on Windows platforms. The WinCGI interface is implemented on only two or three of the available Windows-based Web servers (O'Reilly's WebSite and Netscape Web servers), with Microsoft's IIS being one of the major Web servers that does not provide the WinCGI interface.

■ Appendix B, "What's on the CD?," takes a brief look at what has been bundled on the CD included with this book, and how the CD has been organized.

# Conventions Used In This Book

This book presents a variety of code, message and HTML text, commands, and response codes. To distinguish these elements clearly from the rest of this book's text, the code, message text, commands, and response codes appear in a special monospaced font. For example, when this book displays a few lines of code, it looks similar to the following:

```
Function AddTwoNumbers(x As Integer, y As Integer) As Integer
    AddTwoNumbers = x + y
End Function
```

However, a more extensive code listing is presented in a formal listing, such as Listing 0.1.

**Listing 0.1   INTRO.BAS—A Sample Code Listing**

```
Function CalculatePercentChange(X As Integer, Y As Integer) As Double
    Dim OnePercent As Double

    OnePercent = X / 100#
    If (OnePercent > 0) Then
        CalculatePercentChange = Y / OnePercent
    Else
        CalculatePercentChange = 0#
    End If
End Function
```

Even though this book contains a large amount of code, you don't have to type it all. The CD that accompanies this book provides all demonstrated code (along with the pieces that aren't shown in the text).

As you read this book, you will come across icons and boxes that mark off separated sections of text. These are notes, tips, and cautions, not necessarily part of the subject under discussion, but related pieces of important information. Some examples of these elements follow.

**CAUTION**

Cautions present information that you want to be aware of to avoid any unnecessary mishaps.

**N O T E** Notes provide additional information about the subject that you are reading about.

 Tips provide important information about using the features that you are reading about.

 Whenever a program is mentioned in this book that is included on the book's CD, you'll see the icon at the right.

# Visual Basic and the Web

# What's New with Visual Basic and the Web

It's still amazing to think about how far the state of Internet and Web technologies has come in such a short time. To think that only one and a half years ago, Microsoft declared a total commitment to building Internet capabilities into all of its applications. This commitment shows in the newest version of Microsoft's flagship development tool, Visual Basic. It's not so much that the Visual Basic development tool is itself Internet capable, but that a lot of work has gone into making it easy to build Internet-capable applications by using Visual Basic.

The ability to build Internet and Web applications by using Visual Basic comes in a number of different flavors, all within the same development tool. You can build ActiveX controls to use in Web pages, or you can build ActiveX document applications that can be run inside a Web browser. You can build Visual Basic applications that communicate over the Internet, or you can build extensions to Web servers in order to provide additional functionality not already built into the Web server. You don't even need to work within the Visual Basic development environment to use VB as your Web development language, taking advantage of Microsoft's push to make VB a primary scripting language, both within Web browsers and on Web servers, through the use of VBScript and

### ActiveX Controls

Visual Basic 5 provides you with the ability to build your own ActiveX controls that can be used in Web pages and Visual Basic applications.

### ActiveX Documents

Visual Basic 5 enables you to build ActiveX Document applications, in which an actual Visual Basic application can be run inside a Web browser, or other ActiveX container such as the Microsoft Office Binder.

### Native Executables and Thread-Safe DLLs

Visual Basic 5 allows you to compile your applications and controls as native executables, providing you with a much faster application. Visual Basic 5 also has the ability to build thread-safe ActiveX DLLs and server applications for use in situations where multiple processing threads may be running simultaneously.

### Internet and Web-oriented controls

Visual Basic 5 comes complete with some Internet and Web-oriented controls, enabling you to build applications that have Internet and Web functionality with minimal programming effort.

Active Server Pages. In all, you have more choices of where and how you use Visual Basic to build applications than ever before. ◼

# ActiveX Capabilities

One thing you'll notice when you first start up Visual Basic 5 is that everything is ActiveX. There's ActiveX DLLs, ActiveX applications, ActiveX controls, and ActiveX documents. This is quite a change from the previous version of Visual Basic. It seems that it was just a little over a year ago that the previous version made the change from VBX controls, to using OLE controls. Now Visual basic has gone through another dramatic change from OLE to ActiveX. Or has it?

## OLE to ActiveX

Microsoft's OLE technologies have built up a reputation over the years as being very sluggish. Applications that use OLE to embed other applications within them require a large amount of memory and generally perform very slowly in comparison to non-OLE applications. For the most part, this is to be expected. When you open up the hood of OLE, and get a good understanding of what it's doing, and of all the functionality that it is providing you, it's only natural that OLE would require a fast machine with plenty of memory to perform at a speed that most users would desire.

Well, when Microsoft decided to leverage its OLE technology onto the Web, and make it much more network friendly, it knew that it would have to come up with a new name to get past the stigma attached to OLE. As a result, OLE became ActiveX. Now everything that was called OLE is called ActiveX. As a result, OLE controls are now ActiveX controls, OLE Documents are now ActiveX Documents, and OLE containers are now ActiveX containers. This name change extends to all OLE (now ActiveX) technologies. That's why everything in the new version of Visual Basic is now ActiveX, and there's no OLE to be found.

In making the change from OLE to ActiveX, Microsoft did more than just place a new name on an old technology; it reworked the internals of ActiveX to make it perform better. Previously, OLE technologies were required to support and implement numerous interfaces, even if the particular application or control did not need some of these interfaces. An example of this was the requirement for all OLE controls to implement all of the OLE interfaces that dealt with how the control displayed itself on the screen while the application was running, even if the control did not have a user interface. With the move to ActiveX, all but the IUnknown interface (which all other OLE interfaces are required to inherit) were dropped from the requirement. Now, a control only has to implement those interfaces that the control needs in order to perform its function. This allows ActiveX controls to be much smaller than their OLE control counterparts, and thus more network friendly (as well as more computer friendly, as they need less memory and computing power to run).

## ActiveX Controls

One of the most publicized features of Visual Basic 5 is the ability to create your own ActiveX controls. These controls can be used in other Visual Basic applications (or any other ActiveX container application), or in Web pages on the Internet. In typical fashion, Microsoft included a couple of wizards to make the task of designing and creating your ActiveX control very easy. Microsoft even updated the Application Setup Wizard to understand VB ActiveX controls, and to know how to package them up with all of the necessary support files that will be needed to use the controls. You'll learn about building ActiveX Controls with Visual Basic in Section II.

## ActiveX Documents

Another type of application that can be built by using Visual Basic 5 is known as ActiveX Document applications. These are full-featured Visual Basic applications that will run only within an ActiveX container, such as the Microsoft Office Binder, or Microsoft's Internet Explorer. This means that you could link an ActiveX Document application to your Web site, and have users download an actual Visual Basic application that will be running within their Web browser. This does not convert Visual Basic into HTML, but is actually Visual Basic running in the browser. You'll learn about building ActiveX Document applications in Part IV.

**N O T E** When building ActiveX Document applications for use within a Web-based application, you will need to make an effort to keep the size of the Visual Basic application as small as possible. The use of ActiveX Document applications on the Web will require a substantial amount of horsepower on the user's desktop computer, not to mention the download time required to send the application from the Web server to the user's browser. This is probably not something that users will want to be encountering if they are connected to the Internet with a 14.4 modem connection. ■

# Internet and Intranet Functionality

Along with the ways that Visual Basic can be used to build Web applications, through ActiveX Controls and ActiveX Documents, Visual Basic now includes several ActiveX Controls that can be used to build standard Visual Basic applications that can communicate over the Internet, and can act as a Web browser. These controls are the Winsock, Internet, and HTML controls.

## Winsock Control

The Winsock control allows you to build Internet applications such as a SMTP/POP3 Mail client or Usenet News Reader without having to delve into the depths of Winsock programming and socket communications. You can also use the Winsock control to build a networked application that communicates with other Visual Basic applications over any network, including the Internet.

## Internet Control

The Internet control enables you to build Visual Basic applications that can interact with HTTP, FTP, and Gopher servers over the Internet, or over any other network. The Internet control eliminates the need to use the Winsock control, or to learn the application protocols for any of these application protocols. If you know the application protocols for any of these three applications, you can take advantage of that knowledge and control the Internet control with a finer degree of precision. The Internet control can be used to download Web pages, or to exchange files with an FTP server. We'll look at how to use this control in Chapter 32, "Web-Enabling Visual Basic Applications."

## HTML Control

The HTML control provides you with a Web browser within your Visual Basic applications. You can pass it an URL, and the HTML control will download and display the Web page that you specified. From here, you can click any links within the page, and the HTML control will navigate to that Web page. This allows you to build your own Web browser with complete functionality, without having to use either the Internet control or the Winsock control.

# Performance Improvements

Along with the Internet and Web-oriented additions to Visual Basic, are a number of performance enhancements made to Visual Basic that also aid in building Internet and Web-based applications. Among these improvements is the option to compile Visual Basic applications and controls as native executables. Another improvement is the fact that it's now possible to build thread-safe ActiveX DLLs and Servers by using Visual Basic.

## Native Executables

Applications and controls built by using Visual Basic 5 have the option of being compiled as a native executable for Windows 95 and Windows NT running on Intel platforms. This capability provides a massive performance boost over the interpreted p-code that has been used for all previous versions of Visual Basic (and is still an option with the newest version of Visual Basic). The Native Executable Compile option was accomplished by plugging the newest Visual C++ compiler into the Visual Basic compiler. This provides Visual Basic applications with a double-speed boost, as there were major performance boosts made to the newest Visual C++ compiler, enabling all applications that are run through it to see significant boosts to their performance, as well as significant reductions in the executable size. You'll see this option used extensively throughout this book in most of the examples.

## Thread-Safe DLLs and Servers

If you are building ActiveX DLLs or ActiveX Server applications that do not have any user interface, then you now have the option of making these elements thread-safe. This means that multiple copies of the methods, subroutines, and functions may be executing at the same time.

This is an important new feature if you are building server components that are likely to be accessed by multiple clients at the same time. This removes a major bottleneck in the building of Web server extensions through the OLEISAPI interface (actually, it also required a revamping of the OLEISAPI interface, but we'll examine this whole area in detail in this book), allowing the use of this interface to Microsoft's Internet Information Server with Visual Basic extensions as a realistic option for busy Web sites that need custom programming.

# From Here...

This chapter provides little more than a brief whetting of the appetite, giving you a brief indication of what lies ahead in detailed examinations of each of the areas of new functionality listed in this chapter. The next chapter will allow you to get your feet wet, by working with a simple browser-based Visual Basic application, using VBScript, ActiveX Controls, and ActiveX Documents. After that, each of the sections in this book will explore an area of Web application development in detail, from building your own ActiveX Controls, to building multi-tier distributed applications on the Web by using Microsoft's new Transaction Server. From here, you might want to get started with one of the following chapters.

- To get your feet wet using client-side Web application technologies, see Chapter 2, "Up and Running: Browser-Based VB Programming."

- To learn how Visual Basic can be used to build your own ActiveX Controls, check out Chapter 3, "Building ActiveX Controls with VB."

- To see how ActiveX Document applications can be built and run inside a Web browser, read Chapter 10, "ActiveX Documents: Serving Up VB in a Web Browser."

- To learn how you can use VBScript on the Web server to build dynamic Web pages, skip to Chapter 13, "Active Server Pages and Server-Side Scripting."

# CHAPTER 2

# Up and Running: Browser-Based VB Programming

When you think of a World Wide Web browser, such as Internet Explorer or Netscape Navigator, your likely inclination is to think of *Surfing the Net*—using browser technology to view sites and documents in cyberspace. However, you can also use a browser to surf your own desktop computer. Also, from a programming and document creation point of view, most of what you can do on the Internet can also be done on your desktop computer. There is a lot of truth to the phrase, "bits are bits, it really doesn't matter where they come from." In other words, with regard to the Internet, the location of data and programs is becoming more and more irrelevant in the work-a-day world. In this chapter, you'll take a look at some new and not so new Visual Basic/VBScript features that allow you to bring the power of browser-based computing to your desktop, regardless your Internet connectivity. ■

**Client-side browsing**

Bring the power of Internet Explorer to your desktop documents and applications.

**Client-side VBScript Programming**

Learn to use VBScript to enhance the power of Internet Explorer, ,regardless of whether you're hooked up to the Internet.

**Using ActiveX controls with VBScript**

Quickly advance VB functionality to your Web pages by using ActiveX controls.

**Using ActiveX Documents**

Bring the power of VB programming to your browser without using HTML or VBScript

# Why Use a Browser?

On the Internet, you can access any data, anytime, anywhere. As such, the notion that you will develop software or content for separate computing environments is fast becoming obsolete. The article that you put on your Web site will be viewed by any number of client environments—Windows, Macintosh, or UNIX. Clearly, it is not practical, and sometimes not even possible, to keep multiple platform-specific versions of content or applications on your Web site. Therefore, it is necessary to have something on the client computer that can "translate" incoming bits and make them understandable to the client's environment.

That's where a browser comes in. Browsers are applications that provide a standardized way for any data, be it content or applications, to behave uniformly on a client computer, regardless of operating system. Browsers act as the "data translator" between your computer and the Internet. Browsers are written to work on a client-specific operating system, yet interpret data delivered via the Internet universally and uniformly.

Eventually as the Internet becomes a more pervasive and integrated feature of work-a-day computing, browsers may become *the environment* to which applications are written.

This is not to say that browsers are useful only when you're using the Internet as the source for content or applications. Quite the opposite is true. In many cases, you can use a browser to view content or use applications that reside directly on your computer's hard drive. The same "interpretation rules" apply, the only difference is the source of the data. To get you more familiar with the concept of client-side browsing, the following sections show you how to use Internet Explorer, Microsoft's browser, to view files, scripts, and custom-designed Visual Basic applications that reside on your computer.

# Viewing Client-Side Data by Using Internet Explorer

As mentioned in the previous section, you can use the browser to view data on your hard drive. However, you must tell the browser what type of data (or file type) you want to view. To find out what file type your configuration of Internet Explorer supports, do the following:

1. Open Internet Explorer.
2. SelectView|Options. (See Figure 2.1.)
3. On the Options property sheet to select the Programs tab.
4. Click the File Types button on the Programs property page. (See Figure 2.2.)

When you click the File Types button on center right of the Internet Explorer Options property page, you see a dialog box that lists the various file types Windows 95/NT supports (see Figure 2.3). This dialog box enables you to configure Internet Explorer to support file types. When you select a file type from the list in the dialog box, if Internet Explorer supports the file type, the MIME file type will appear next to the label, Content Type (MIME). In the case of Figure 2.3, files with the extension .GIF are assigned to the MIME type image/gif.

**FIG. 2.1**

The Options menu provides Internet Explorer configuration information.

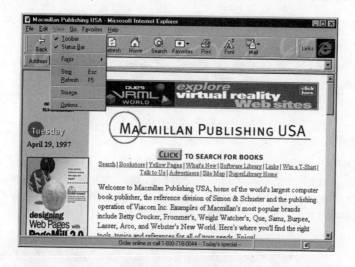

**FIG. 2.2**

You can add or modify file types in the File Types dialog box.

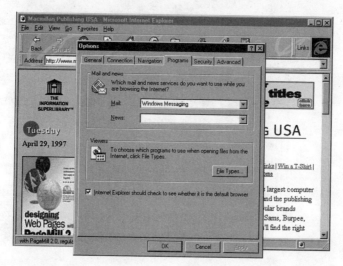

**N O T E**  Multipurpose Internet Mail Extensions (MIME) is a protocol that allows your browser to interpret various types of multimedia data. MIME syntax takes the following form:

type/subtype

where

*type* is data that can be image, text, audio, video, application, multipart, message, or extension-token.

*image* denotes data types that are graphical.

*text* denotes data types that are ASCII text-based.

*continues*

*continued*

    *audio* denotes a data type that is sound.

    *video* denotes data types that are digital video.

    *application* denotes data types that are binary and need another "helper" application to make them viewable.

    *multipart* denotes data that is made up many data types.

    *message* denotes a simple e-mail message.

    *extension-token* denotes experimental data types where the subtype begins with the character x-.

    *subtype* describes details about a specific data type. For example, MIME type, *image/gif* denote an image data type of GIF format. MIME type, *text/plain* is simple ASCII text, such as .BAS code file. MIME type, *audio/x-wav* is a sound data type of the Microsoft audio format. ■

**FIG. 2.3**
Internet Explorer
supports many MIME
data types.

Once your browser is configured to accommodate a file type, you can view it through Internet Explorer regardless of whether the file type resides on the Internet or on your computer's hard drive.

> **N O T E** By default, Internet Explorer can view many file types without any additional tweaking or configuration modification. Some of the file types available for viewing upon installation are audio (.AU, .AIFF), JPEG graphics (.JPG), CompuServe graphics (.GIF), ASCII text (.TXT), and Hypertext Markup Language (.HTML or .HTM). ■

## Browsing Simple File Types

The "smarts" to view different type of files are built right into Internet Explorer. All you need to do is find the file you want to view and bring it into the browser. The simplest way to view a file is to drag and drop one from the Windows Explorer window on to the Internet Explorer window. Figure 2.4 shows the result of dragging and dropping a text file, README.TXT, between Windows Explorer and Internet Explorer.

**FIG. 2.4**

You can use Internet Explorer to view files on your hard drive.

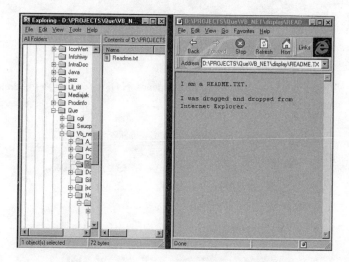

Another way to view client-side files is to use the Open dialog box. To access a file using Open dialog box, do the following:

1. Go to the Internet Explorer menu bar, select File, and then select Open. (See Figure 2.5.)

**FIG. 2.5**

You can open a file or an URL by using the Open menu.

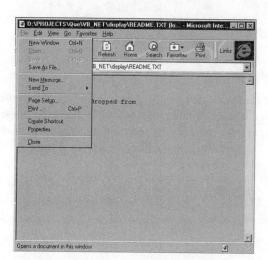

2. The Open dialog box appears. Type in the location of the file you want to view in the drop-down edit box above the Browse button.

3. If you don't know the location of the file you want to view, click the Browse button. (See Figure 2.6.)

**FIG. 2.6**

You can browse your computer by clicking the Browse button.

4. A File Open common dialog box appears. Navigate through the dialog box to the file you want to view. (See Figure 2.7.)

**FIG. 2.7**

The File Open dialog box allows you to navigate your system.

# Browsing Client-Side HTML

Locating and viewing client-side files that use Hypertext Markup Language (HTML) is much the same process you use to locate and view simple, client-side file types. You can drag and drop an HTML file from Windows Explorer to Internet Explorer. You can use the Open dialog box you access from the Internet Explorer File menu. Or, you can enter the URL in the Address drop-down list on the Internet Explorer toolbar.

**N O T E**   An URL (Uniform Resource Locator) can reference an item in cyberspace or on your local computer. However, if you are trying to access a file on your system by typing its location into the Address box of Internet Explorer, you should use *file*, the URL protocol identifier.

The syntax for the file keyword is as follows:

file://hostname/path/file.

Thus, to load the file readme.txt, which is in the \docs directory of your C drive, type the following into the Address box of Internet Explorer:

**file://c:/docs/readme.txt** ■

HTML files usually contain HTML code that references other file types. These file types are usually graphics or sound files. Most often the referenced files are someplace "out there" on the Internet. When an HTML file loads into a browser, the browser has the "smarts" to read the location of a referenced file type (the location is part of the HTML code), go out onto the Internet or the local hard drive, retrieve the file and display it in the browser window. However, the browser's ability to retrieve and display referenced files is dependent on its ability to find these files. If a user's computer is not online, sometimes there can be problems.

Often, users will be offline and try to view a copy of a favorite Web Page they saved on the computer. They're surprised when they see the unable to find graphic file icon where they thought the graphics file should have been. (See Figure 2.8.) The file is "lost" because the computer is offline, but the HTML file is still looking to the Web for its graphic references.

**FIG. 2.8**

Internet Explorer displays this icon if it is unable to find or open a graphics file.

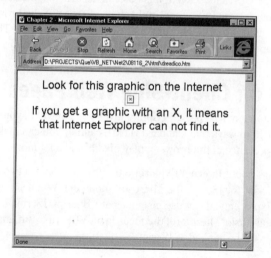

## Browsing Documents

A major innovation of Internet Explorer is the total integration of OLE 2.0 into the architecture of the product. OLE 2.0 permits applications to live inside one another. Operationally, this means that Internet Explorer can *morph* itself when a document made with an OLE 2.0 program is opened into the browser. If Word 95 is installed on your system and you were to take a Word 95 document and open it in Internet Explorer, you would see the Internet Explorer toolbar and menu bar *morph* to accommodate the Word 95 toolbar (see Figure 2.9). When you open a Word document into Internet Explorer, the browser becomes a fully functional instance of Word 95.

**FIG. 2.9**

The Word 95 toolbar and menu bar share the Internet Explorer toolbar and menu bar when viewing a Word document in Internet Explorer.

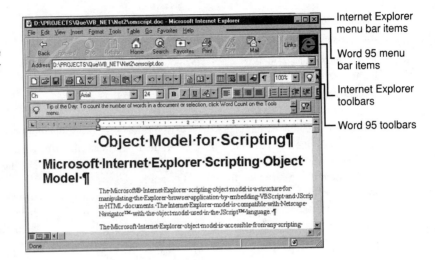

— Internet Explorer menu bar items

— Word 95 menu bar items

— Internet Explorer toolbars

— Word 95 toolbars

The implications of an OLE 2.0-enabled browser are far reaching. As discussed earlier, the world seems to be moving to a browser-based paradigm. Thus, because of OLE 2.0 and its related technologies, COM, and ActiveX, it is possible to write applications that will be able to live within and without Internet Explorer. In this type of scenario the browser becomes nothing more than a consistent, cross-platform container for other applications. Thus, you no longer write programs for operating systems, you write them for browsers.

# Using VBScript on Client-Side Web Pages

Scripting brings life to your Web page. Scripting gives you control of your Web page and your browser's environment in ways that standard HTML cannot. You can make decisions, validate data, change the appearance of the browser, play media, and a lot more.

One of the nice things about Internet Explorer 3.0 is that it supports two scripting languages—VBScript, and JavaScript (or JScript, the Microsoft moniker). When you create your Web pages to run on Internet Explorer, you can use instances of VBScript, JScript, or both. However, this is a book about Visual Basic. Therefore, the focus is on VBScript. But, many of the principals reviewed here can easily be applied to JScript.

## VBScript Is VB!

When you install Internet Explorer on your computer, you have installed a full-fledged Visual Basic programming environment. VBScript is very powerful. Just about anything you want to do with standard Visual Basic you can do with VBScript. And, in cases related to Internet Explorer, some things are actually easier to do with VBScript than with Visual Basic.

VBScript, however, has limitations: It is bound to the interpreter that lives with Internet Explorer; it has data type limitations; it can't do the advanced procedures that Visual Basic does, such as creating custom controls and classes, or accessing the Windows API. Nonetheless, these limitations do not detract from the intrinsic power of the language. The more you use VBScript, the more you'll discover that VBScript is VB!

# The Internet Explorer Object Model for Scripting

To effectively program in VBScript, you need to understand the Internet Explorer Object Model. As with most modern applications, the Internet Explorer is a collection of objects. You can conceptualize them the same way you conceptualize VB controls on a VB form. In VB you have the form which you can think of as a window and on the form you can place other VB objects, a command button, a label, a combo box, and so on. A fundamental parent-child relationship exists between the form and the controls on the form. The same is true of Internet Explorer: You have the basic parent control, the Window. Within a Window Object, you have a Document object, or the Window can be populated with Frame objects. In addition, each Window has a History object, and each Window is viewed through a Navigator object, which is another name for a browser. Table 2.1 gives you an overview of the various objects within the Internet Explorer Object Model. A more detailed account is provided in Part III, "Scripting."

> **CAUTION**
>
> An IE Object Model Navigator object is not to be confused with Netscape Navigator. Netscape Navigator is a value the IE Object Model assigns to the Navigator object. So is Internet Explorer.

When you program with VBScript and Internet Explorer, a good amount of your activity is concerned with not only manipulating data and logic, but also with manipulating the IE Object Model (see Figure 2.10).

**FIG. 2.10**
The Internet Explorer Object Model is a hierarchy of objects.

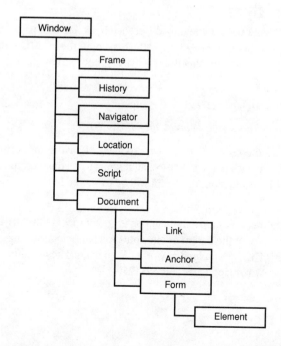

**Table 2.1   The Internet Explorer Object Model**

| Object | Description | Parent |
|--------|-------------|--------|
| Window | Topmost object, Internet Explorer | |
| Frame | A section of a window | Window |
| History | List of visited sites | Window |
| Navigator | Information about browser | Window |
| Location | Provides information about IE's current locations | Window |
| Script | Indicates what script is to be implemented | Window |
| Document | Current page in client area or frame | Window |
| Link | A hypertext link | Document |
| Anchor | An anchor without a link | Document |
| Form | An HTML form | Document |
| Element | An HTML form element | Form |

▶ For more information about the Internet Explorer Object Model for Scripting, see the following location on the Internet:

Chapter 7, "Using VBScript to Build HTML-Based VB Applications,"

**http://www.microsoft.com/vbscript/us/techinfo/vbsdocs.htm**

**http://www.microsoft.com/workshop/prog/sdk/docs/scriptom/**

# Browsing Simple Scripts

From the browser's point of view the only difference between Web pages that contain a script and those than don't is the presence of the <SCRIPT> tag in the HTML of the Web page. A <SCRIPT>... <.SCRIPT> tag indicates that everything between the tags is either VBScript or JavaScript.

The syntax of the <SCRIPT> tag is:

<SCRIPT language = *scripting language*>...</SCRIPT>

When a browser sees the <SCRIPT> tag, it says to itself, "I have some script stuff coming up to consider." And, when it sees the </SCRIPT> tag it stops that consideration. Unless the script is an event handler, sub, or function, the script will be executed in the order in which it is encountered.

Scripts can run from a server on the Internet or from your local hard drive. The browser considers only the structure of the script, not its source. That being the case, you load and run client-side scripted HTML as you load any other Web page. These methods are discussed in the previous section, "Browsing Client-Side HTML."

Listing 2.1 shows a simple script written in VBScript. Figure 2.11 shows the results of that script when executed in Internet Explorer.

---

**Listing 2.1  SIMPLE.HTM—An Example of Using VBScript to Output to an Internet Explorer Window**

```
<!--Simple Script-->
<!--(c)Copyright 1997, Macmillan Publishers-->
<!--By Bob Reselman-->

<HTML>
<TITLE>Script Example: Simple</TITLE>
<BODY>
<SCRIPT language="VBScript">

    'open a document object in the window
    document.open

    'Write an HTML line
    document.write ("Hello World!")

    'Close the document object
    document.close
</SCRIPT>

</BODY></HTML>
```

---

Part

I

Ch

2

Notice that the `<SCRIPT>` element is executed as it is encountered. Upon loading the page, SIMPLE.HTM, the document object is opened, writes a line, "Hello World," and closes.

**FIG. 2.11**

You can use VBScript to output data to the Internet Explorer window.

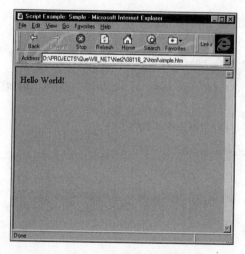

Although Listing 2.1 and Figure 2.11 show how to use VBScript, they don't offer a good argument for using a script in your HTML. You just as easily could have written a simple HTML to output "Hello World" without all the hassle of using a <SCRIPT> object.

However, standard HTML falls short for determining and generating dynamic data—for example, reporting the date and time a Web page is being viewed. Normally, without the use of VBScript, if you access a page off the Internet, you have to use some sort of server-side programming, such as CGI (Common Gateway Interface) or Active Server, to get and generate this information. From a client-side viewing perspective, getting and generating the date and time are nearly impossible, except if you use a scripting language such as VBScript.

Listing 2.2 shows the VBScript for a Web page that reports the date and time a Web page is loaded. Figure 2.12 shows how Internet Explorer displays that script.

**Listing 2.2   SMPLTIME.HTM—You Can Generate Dynamic Data by Using VBScript**

```
<!--Simple Time Script>
<!--(c)Copyright 1997, Macmillan Publishers-->
<!--By Bob Reselman-->

<HTML>
<TITLE>Simple Time Script</TITLE>

<!--Make the background color WHITE-->
<BODY bgcolor=WHITE>

<SCRIPT language="VBScript">
     'open a document object in the window
     document.open

     'Write an HTML line to set the font face and size
     document.write ("<FONT FACE=ARIAL SIZE=5>")

     'Write the date out, converting it to a string
     'with and HTML line break tag, <BR>
     document.write ("This page was loaded on: " + Cstr(Date()) + "<BR>")

     'Write the time out as you did the date
     document.write ("at: " + Cstr(Time()))

     'Close the document object
     document.close
</SCRIPT>
</BODY></HTML>
```

**FIG. 2.12**
VBScript is an excellent tool to use to display dynamic data.

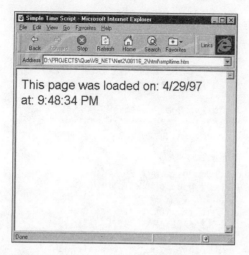

# Browsing Fancy Scripts

Scripts that use line-by-line serial execution are useful but limited, as anybody who has attempted to program in a nonprocedural language can testify. You tend to get spaghetti code that is hard to follow, has limited decision-making capability, and offers little or no reuse. Luckily, VBScript, like its parent predecessor, Visual Basic, is a procedural language that comes loaded with a toolbox full of conditional and loop statements.

**Scripts with Subroutines**   VBScript allows you to write Subs and Functions, just as you do in Visual Basic. Listing 2.3 shows the Web page, time.htm. This page uses a Sub, ReportTime, written in VBScript to respond to the window object's onLoad event.

**Listing 2.3   TIME.HTM—In VBScript You Can Use a Sub to Encapsulate Your Codes Functionality**

```
<!--Simple Script with Sub-->
<!--(c)Copyright 1997, Macmillan Publishers-->
<!--By Bob Reselman-->

<HTML>
<TITLE>Simple Script with Sub: Date/Time</TITLE>

<!--When the page loads, call the VBScript sub, ReportTime-->
<BODY language="VBScript" onLoad="ReportTime">


<SCRIPT language="VBScript">
Sub ReportTime
    '****************************************************
    'Sub:       ReportTime
    '
```

*continues*

**Listing 2.3    Continued**

```
'Arguments: None
'
'Comments:  This sub writes the time and date to two
'           lines in an Internet Net Explorer window.
'
'History:   Created 4/6/97, Bob Reselman
'*****************************************************
    'open a document object in the window
    document.open

    'Set the background color to WHITE
    document.write ("<BODY bgcolor=WHITE>")

    'Write an HTML line to set the font face and size
    document.write ("<FONT FACE=ARIAL SIZE=5>")

    'Write the date out, converting it to a string
    'with and HTML line break tag, <BR>
    document.write ("The date is: " + Cstr(Date()) + "<BR>")

    'Write the time out as you did the date
    document.write ("The time is: " + Cstr(Time()))

    'Close the document object
    document.close
End Sub
</SCRIPT>

</BODY></HTML>
```

Figure 2.12 shows the results of the script in time.htm.

**FIG. 2.13**

Make your code versatile and easy to control by using Subs and Functions.

**Scripts with Loops and Conditional Statements** VBScript comes with all the loop and conditional statements that you find in standard Visual Basic. Take a look at the HTML page, loops.htm (see Listing 2.4). When the page loads, a Sub—loops—is called. The Sub runs a For...Next statement, which makes the beginning part of the even line uppercase. Notice that the effectiveness of this script is not dependent on its source. This script will run the same whether it is being read from an Internet server or from your local hard drive. Figure 2.14 shows the result of the Sub—loops.

**Listing 2.4 LOOPS.HTM—You Can Make Conditional Decisions by Using VBScript**

```
<!--Loop Script-->
<!--(c)Copyright 1997, Macmillan Publishers-->
<!--By Bob Reselman-->
<HTML>
<TITLE>Fancy Script: Loops</TITLE>
<BODY Language="VBScript" onLoad="Loops">

<SCRIPT language="VBScript">
'*************************************************
 'Sub:       Loops
 '
 'Arguments: None
 '
 'Comments:  This sub runs a For...Next loop to
 '           determine even and odd lines. If a
 '           line is even the beginning section is
 '           made upper case.
 '
 'History:   Created 4/6/97, Bob Reselman
 '*************************************************
Sub Loops
     'make a counting variable
     Dim i

     'open a document object
     document.open

     'write out the HTML to make the background WHITE
     document.write ("<BODY bgcolor=WHITE>")

     'Write out the HTML to set the font face to ARIAL
     'and the size to 3.
     document.write ("<FONT FACE=ARIAL SIZE=3>")

     'Run a loop 10 times
     For i = 1 to 10
       'Check to see if the counter is even
       If i MOD 2 = 0 then
         'If it is even, make every thing upper case and write.
         document.write (UCase("I have been through this loop ") + Cstr(i))
```

*continues*

Part
I

Ch
2

**Listing 2.4   Continued**

```
        Else
            'If it is odd. leave things alone and write.
            document.write ("I have been through this loop " + Cstr(i))
        End if

        'end off the string.
        document.write (" times."+ "<BR>")
    Next

    'After looping, close the document object.
    document.close
End Sub
</SCRIPT>
</BODY></HTML>
```

**FIG. 2.14**
You can make a
conditional HTML layout
by using VBScript.

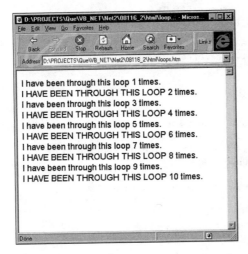

# Browsing Web Pages that Use ActiveX Controls

Using VBScript to manipulate page layout, data, and logic is a very useful addition to your
Internet developer's toolbox. However, you can derive more power and flexibility from your
Web pages when you use ActiveX controls with VBScript.

## Web Pages Can Use Intrinsic Controls

Internet Explorer 3.0 was designed to take full advantage of VBScript. To achieve this goal, not
only did Microsoft enable the language to access the Internet Explorer Object Model, but it
also embedded into Internet Explorer a standard set of controls you can use on your Web
pages. This architecture is similar to Visual Basic, where a standard set of controls are built
right into the runtime DLL. These standard controls are referred to as Intrinsic Controls. They
are built into Internet Explorer. Table 2.2 shows a list of the Intrinsic Controls for Internet Explorer.

## Table 2.2 Intrinsic Controls

| Control | Description |
| --- | --- |
| The HTML Layout Control | Displays HTML <FORM> controls inside Internet Explorer 3.0 by using new (W3C) extensions to HTML |
| Microsoft Forms 2.0 Label | A label |
| Microsoft Forms 2.0 Textbox | A multiline text-display window |
| Microsoft Forms 2.0 Combo Box | A drop-down list of selections |
| Microsoft Forms 2.0 List BoxAllows | A scrollable list of selections |
| Microsoft Forms 2.0 CheckBox | A check box |
| Microsoft Forms 2.0 Option Button | A radio box option |
| Microsoft Forms 2.0 Toggle Button | A multiple state command button |
| Microsoft Forms 2.0 Command Button | A standard button |
| Microsoft Forms 2.0 Tabstrip | A property page tab strip |
| Microsoft Forms 2.0 ScrollBar | A vertical or horizontal scroll bar |
| Microsoft Forms 2.0 Spin Button | A spin button for incrementing or decrementing values |
| The Microsoft ActiveX Image Control | Displays .JPG, .GIF, or .BMP files |
| The Microsoft ActiveX Hotspot Control | Creates transparent hotspots that you can click. |

The benefit of having available and using these intrinsic controls is that you can create Web pages that are actually event driven. Normally, static Web pages allow a user to view some information and maybe input some data to be submitted to an Internet server for analysis or response. However, when you use the Microsoft Form Intrinsic Controls in your Web pages, by default you have available a number of events associated with the Control(s), which you can program as you would an ordinary Visual Basic control. For example, if you use the Microsoft Forms 2.0 Command Button, you'll automatically have available the `CommandButton_Click` event to program.

Listing 2.5 shows a page of HTML using the Microsoft Forms 2.0 Command Button, MyButton, and handling the `MyButton_Click()` for that control.

**Listing 2.5 CLICKME.HTM—You Get the Benefit of Event-Driven Programming When You Use Intrinsic Controls**

```html
<HTML>
<HEAD>
<TITLE>Click Me</TITLE>
</HEAD>
<BODY>
<SCRIPT LANGUAGE="VBScript">
<!--
Sub MyButton_Click()
MyButton.Caption = "No, Click you!"
End Sub
-->
    </SCRIPT>
    <OBJECT ID="MyButton" WIDTH=96 HEIGHT=32
     CLASSID="CLSID:D7053240-CE69-11CD-A777-00DD01143C57">
        <PARAM NAME="Caption" VALUE="Click Me!">
        <PARAM NAME="Size" VALUE="2540;846">
        <PARAM NAME="FontCharSet" VALUE="0">
        <PARAM NAME="FontPitchAndFamily" VALUE="2">
        <PARAM NAME="ParagraphAlign" VALUE="3">
        <PARAM NAME="FontWeight" VALUE="0">
    </OBJECT>
</BODY>
</HTML>
```

Figure 2.15 shows the result when a user clicks the Command Button control, MyButton.

**FIG. 2.15**
Writing Intrinsic Controls event handlers avoids the need to contact a server to handle all user input.

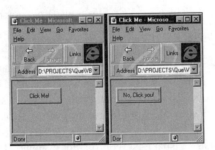

Clearly, an in-depth discussion of the intricacies of every Intrinsic Control and their associated events is beyond the scope of an introductory chapter such as this. The purpose here is to give you a sense of what the controls are and an idea of what you can do with them. You will take a more detailed look at the Intrinsic Controls in Chapter 7, "Using VBScript to Build HTML-Based VB Applications."

**N O T E**  A lot of detailed, error-prone coding goes into writing HTML that uses ActiveX Controls. To make the task a lot easier, you might want to use Microsoft's ActiveX Control Pad. It's a good tool but takes a little getting use to. If you are new to Internet Programming and VBScript, it might take you a little while to get the hang of it. But, after you do, it will save a lot to time and frustration with your VBScript programming efforts. ■

# Web Pages Can Use ActiveX Controls

Not only can you use the Internet Explorer Intrinsic Controls in your Web page, but also you can use ActiveX controls. For client-side programming, all that is required is that the computer upon which your VBScript page is running have the control that your script is calling. Thus, if you write a piece of VBScript that calls an ActiveX control, CoolThing, then CoolThing must be properly installed and registered on the computer upon which you run your script.

You can also write HTML embedded with ActiveX controls and run your pages from an Internet server. However, a little bit more must go on for your code to work. When someone requests your page from an Internet server, Internet Explorer is smart enough to look at the calling client's system to see if the necessary controls are present. If the control is not on the client computer, Internet Explorer will attempt to download that control from the server. If a download is possible, Internet Explorer will also register the control in the Registry of the client computer.

Listing 2.6 shows the VBScript code for a Web page, slider.htm. Embedded in slider.htm is a Windows 95 Slider control and a Label control. The Slider control is an ActiveX control. The Label is an Intrinsic Control. When you move the slider, the value of the tick to which the slider is moved is shown in the Label control, lblMain. Figure 2.16 shows how the code appears in Internet Explorer. This page was made by using Microsoft's ActiveX Control Pad.

**Listing 2.6   SLIDER.HTM—Any ActiveX Control Can Be with VBScript**

```
<HTML>
<HEAD>
<TITLE>Slider Bar Example</TITLE>
</HEAD>
<BODY bgColor = WHITE>
</SCRIPT>
    <SCRIPT LANGUAGE="VBScript">
<!--
Sub MySlider_Scroll()
  'When the slider moves, report the change in the
  'label control, lblMain.
  lblMain.Caption =MySlider.Value
end sub
-->
    </SCRIPT>
Move the slider to see a value change. <BR>
    <OBJECT ID="MySlider" WIDTH=100 HEIGHT=43
 CLASSID="CLSID:373FF7F0-EB8B-11CD-8820-08002B2F4F5A">
    <PARAM NAME="_Version" VALUE="65536">
    <PARAM NAME="_ExtentX" VALUE="2646">
```

*continues*

**Listing 2.6 Continued**

```
        <PARAM NAME="_ExtentY" VALUE="1111">
        <PARAM NAME="_StockProps" VALUE="64">
</OBJECT>
<P>
The result of a slide:
        <OBJECT ID="lblMain" WIDTH=49 HEIGHT=24
 CLASSID="CLSID:978C9E23-D4B0-11CE-BF2D-00AA003F40D0">
        <PARAM NAME="Size" VALUE="1291;635">
        <PARAM NAME="BorderStyle" VALUE="1">
        <PARAM NAME="FontCharSet" VALUE="0">
        <PARAM NAME="FontPitchAndFamily" VALUE="2">
        <PARAM NAME="FontWeight" VALUE="0">
</OBJECT>
</BODY>
</HTML>
```

**FIG. 2.16**

You can mix VBScript, HTML, and ActiveX controls to make effective pages.

With VB5 you can create your own Web ready ActiveX Custom Controls. This is big stuff, no question about it. Before Version 5 of Visual Basic, the world of Custom Controls and ActiveX programming was open only to C++ and Delphi programmers. Now, for the most part, the playing field is a bit more level and all Windows programmers can have their day in cyberspace. For both client- and server-side viewing of VB Custom Controls, the VB5 runtime DLL and the DLLs upon which OLE 2.0 depends must be present on the client. If you access a page from the Internet that uses a VB5 Custom Control that is *not* present on your system, that first download is going to be a whopper. But after the runtime and OLE DLLs are downloaded onto your system, Web pages that use Custom Controls will need to download only the control itself.

Figure 2.17 shows a Web Page, dice.htm. Embedded in dice.htm is a homemade VB5 Custom Control, ccDice, which is on the CD-ROM that accompanies this book. ccDice has no programmable click event. But if you click on the control, the dice will roll.

# Browsing ActiveX Documents

An ActiveX Document is a VB application in which the graphical elements of the application are separated from the "under-the-hood" functionality. This separation relationship is similar to the one between a Word document and the Word executable—the Word executable under-the-hood functions make and show the data contained within the Word document.

You can implement this idea of interface/functionality separation by making a custom control and embedding the custom control in a Web page with HTML and then viewing the page in Internet Explorer. However, this method causes you to be completely dependent upon HTML for delivering, viewing, and using your VB5-created custom control. However, an ActiveX Document can be viewed in Internet Explorer or another container application, such as Microsoft Office Binder, without the need for HTML.

Part

I

Ch

2

## The ActiveX Document Architecture

As mentioned in the previous section, the ActiveX Document architecture separates the viewable interface from the "under-the-hood" functionality of a VB5 application. In a Visual Basic ActiveX Document, the user interface is separated into a file type that ends with the extension .VBD, while the "under-the-hood stuff" is in an OLE Automation Server file that is either an .EXE or .DLL. The Automation Server is intrinsically called by the .VBD file.

▶ For more information about OLE Automation Servers, see Que's *Special Edition Using Visual Basic 5*, Chapter 25, "Using Classes to Create Reusable Objects."

ActiveX Documents are a project type you can choose when you select a New Project from within the VB5 IDE. When you choose an ActiveX Document Project in VB5, you'll create the compiled ActiveX Document (.VBD) and the Automation Server (.EXE or .DLL), the UserDocument (.DOB), as well as the Project Workspace (.VBW).

## Viewing ActiveX Documents in Container Applications

Container Applications are OLE-enabled applications that can display and expose the functionality of any OLE document or ActiveX Document. One of the nice features of making an ActiveX Document with VB5 is that you can make custom OLE document types without having to go through many of the low-level programming intricacies associated with creating them. All you need to do to use an ActiveX Document is to install it and its associated Automation Server on your system by using the Visual Basic Setup Wizard. After the ActiveX Document is installed, you can use a Container Application, such as Internet Explorer or Microsoft Office Binder, to interact with it.

### Viewing ActiveX Documents within Internet Explorer    You can view a client-side ActiveX Document through Internet Explorer, as you would view any other Web page. You can File|Open or you can drag-and-drop the file into the Internet Explorer client area.

On the CD-ROM that comes with this book is an ActiveX Document, ACTDOC.VBD, and Automation Server, ACTDOC.EXE. Go to directory \code\actdoc\setup\ and run the file, SETUP.EXE. This will install the ActiveX document and Automation Server on your system, making the necessary Registry entries and file writes. After the ActiveX Document and associated OLE Automation Server are installed, bring the ActiveX Document into Internet Explorer.

To open an ActiveX Document in Internet Explorer, do the following:

1. Start Internet Explorer.
2. From the File menu, choose the Open menu item (see Figure 2.17).
3. The Open dialog box appears. Type in the location of the ActiveX Document or click the Browse button (see Figure 2.18).

**FIG. 2.17**

You can use the File|Open menu item to open ActiveX Documents into Internet Explorer.

4. If you click the Browse button, the Windows 95 File Open dialog box appears. Navigate through the dialog box to the location of your ActiveX Document. (See Figure 2.19.)
5. Once you locate the ActiveX Document on your hard drive, to insert in into your browser, double-click the .VBD file or select it and click the Open button on the lower right of the Open dialog box.

**FIG. 2.18**

Enter the location of an ActiveX Document in the Open dialog box.

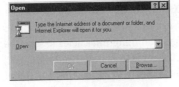

**FIG. 2.19**

When navigating the hard drive to an ActiveX Document, make sure to set the Files of Type drop-down combo to All Files.

▶ **See** Chapter 10, "ActiveX Documents: Serving Up VB in a Web Browser," **p. 201**

**N O T E**  ActiveX Documents can be accessed through the Internet. However, although you don't
embed an ActiveX document in a Web page with HTML to make it viewable, you must load
the ActiveX Document from an Internet Server. You download an ActiveX Document from a Web page by
using an <OBJECT> tag that references a CAB file, which contains the ActiveX Document. This method
is similar to the one used to download an ActiveX Control. ■

**Viewing ActiveX Documents within Microsoft Office Binder**   You can view ActiveX Documents in Internet Explorer and Microsoft Office Binder. To view an ActiveX Document in
Microsoft Office Binder, do the following:

1. Start Microsoft Office Binder.
2. From the Section menu, select the Add from File menu item (see Figure 2.20).

**FIG. 2.20**

You can open an
ActiveX Document
in Office Binder by
dragging and dropping
the document or using
Add from File.

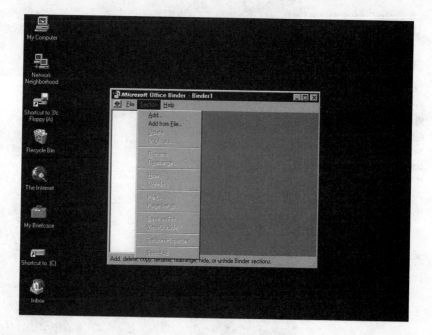

3. From the Add from File dialog box, navigate to the ActiveX Document VBD file on your
   hard drive. Once located, either double-click the file or select it and click the Add button
   on the upper-right of the dialog box. (See Figure 2.21.)
4. Once you select the VBD file, it will be displayed with full functionality in the Microsoft
   Office Binder. (See Figure 2.22.)

**FIG. 2.21**
Make sure you set the Files of Type drop-down combo to All Files (*.*).

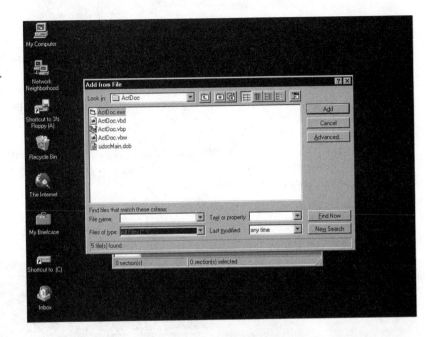

**FIG. 2.22**
ActiveX Documents allow you to use full VB application functionality in a viewable document.

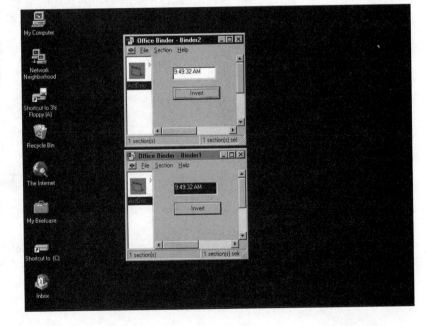

# From Here...

In this chapter, you covered the conceptual fundamentals of client-side browsing. You looked at the role and use of browsers, such as Internet Explorer, for working on the client side. You looked at different file types and how Internet Explorer interprets different file types by using MIME encoding. You saw examples of using Internet Explorer as a container application for, OLE-compliant documents.

You took a look at using VBScript on the client side. Also, you got an overview for using client-side ActiveX controls with VBScript. Finally, you looked at ActiveX Documents as an alternative to HTML Web pages for delivering your VB applications and custom controls to the end user.

For more information on this and related topics, see the following chapters:

- Chapter 7, "Using VBScript to Build HTML-Based VB Applications."
- Chapter 8, "Interacting with ActiveX Controls and VBScript."
- Chapter 10, "ActiveX Documents: Serving Up VB in a Web Browser."

# ActiveX Controls

# CHAPTER 3

# Building ActiveX Controls with VB

One of the most exciting features of Visual Basic 5 is the ability to create your own ActiveX controls. No longer are you limited to using the controls created by C/C++ programmers, if you can dream up a great control, you can build it yourself by using Visual Basic. What's even better, is that you are not limited to using the controls you create in Visual Basic. You can use your controls in any application or development tool that can use ActiveX controls. This means that you have the ability to turn the tables and begin building ActiveX controls in Visual Basic that C++ programmers will be using in their applications. It's a brave new world for the Visual Basic developer.

In this chapter, we'll be taking a look at how you can build your own controls by using the latest version of Visual Basic. We'll be looking at the various approaches that you can take, and some of the issues that you'll need to take into consideration. The information contained in this chapter will be added to in the following chapters, as you learn how to build your own ActiveX controls by extending an existing control that "almost" does what you need your control to do. Later, you'll learn about signing your control by using Microsoft's Authenticode technology so that your control will be usable in Web pages that can be downloaded by any user running Microsoft's Internet Explorer Web browser. ■

## ActiveX control evolution

ActiveX controls have gone through quite an evolution over the past few years. We'll take a look at that evolution and see how ActiveX controls have grown and changed from their earliest incarnation as Visual Basic controls.

## Options for building ActiveX controls

There are three basic approaches for building ActiveX controls by using Visual Basic 5. We'll look at what each of these approaches entail, and some of the issues that you will need to decide when determining which of these approaches to take.

## Building ActiveX controls

You'll build a simple ActiveX control, learning how to expose the control's properties, methods, and events.

## Package the control for Web use

Using the Application Setup Wizard, you can package your ActiveX control for use in Web pages. You'll learn how to prepare your control so that it can be used in Web pages and automatically downloaded by users of Microsoft's Internet Explorer Web browser.

# ActiveX Basics

ActiveX is a technology that was introduced by the Microsoft Corporation in March 1996. It was not really a new technology, but a renaming of Microsoft's OLE technologies. These technologies include the OLE Controls that were introduced with Visual Basic 4 during the previous year. It was the OLE/ActiveX controls that introduced a way to build component objects that can be placed in various applications, including Web pages. This enhanced the ability for programmers to build robust applications quickly with pre-built components.

> **N O T E**   ActiveX isn't just a new name on an old technology. Along with the new name, Microsoft did some significant rearchitecting of the OLE technologies, to make them more "network-friendly." Part of what was done to the OLE control specification was to remove most of the implementation requirements that added unnecessary overhead to the controls, making them larger and slower than the controls really needed to be. Along with the changes to the OLE Control (OCX) specification, Microsoft also introduced several new technologies aimed specifically for use on the Web, including their Authenticode technology for signing controls and applications. In short, Microsoft put a lot of work into making the evolution of OLE into ActiveX a lot more than just a new name on an old technology. ■

ActiveX controls can be used in Web pages to add functionality and greatly improve their appearance. As HTML and scripting languages are fairly limited, ActiveX controls have no limitations. Web page designers can interact with the ActiveX controls on their pages with scripting languages such as VBScript.

ActiveX is the next step of the Visual Basic component technology. Visual Basic component technology was started with VBXs, which were used in 16-bit implementations, and were followed by OCXs, which were used in both 16 and 32-bit implementations.

With Visual Basic 5, you can create an ActiveX control as an ActiveX Control Project. These controls can be used with any container application that supports ActiveX controls. To use an ActiveX control on a Web page, the user's browser must support ActiveX. Microsoft Internet Explorer 3.0 (and 4.0) supports ActiveX controls.

Typical uses of ActiveX controls include the following:

- Assist in Web page navigation
- Multimedia capabilities
- Host emulation
- Communication (for example, a chat room)

The process of building an ActiveX control is simply a matter of following these steps:

1. Determine what you want your ActiveX control to do.
2. Determine what you want your ActiveX control to look like, if you want it to have any appearance at all.
3. Determine what properties, methods, and events your control will provide.

4. Determine if you want to build your control by using the constituent (built-in) controls, or if you will be using other controls as building blocks for your control. When considering other controls, consider licensing and distribution issues.

5. Start a Visual Basic ActiveX control project and draw your control.

6. Add code to enable all the properties, methods, and events you want your control to have. Consider if your control will still be safe for initialization and scripting with the enabling of properties and methods.

7. Create a storage location for your control and all of its supporting files. If you are using a project management system like Visual Source Safe, register your project in it.

8. Build a test project and test your control. Make sure to use all the properties, methods, and events that you gave your control.

9. Compile your control into an OCX.

10. Use the Setup Wizard to build a distributable version including all the supporting files.

11. Test your control on a Web page. Use the HTML page the Setup Wizard made as a starting point. Test all properties, methods, and events from scripting code.

Part

II

Ch

3

# Anatomy of ActiveX Controls

Before you can begin building an ActiveX control, you will need to decide what type of control it will be. Will your control perform all of its functions without using any non-constituent controls? Does the control need another control? Will the control be a visual or non-visual control? These are all decisions that have to be made before beginning your ActiveX control project.

## Two Kinds of ActiveX Controls

There are two basic types of ActiveX control projects you can build: those that you build entirely on your own and those that use other controls, called *constituent controls*, as building blocks.

When Building ActiveX controls from scratch, you start from a plain UserControl object. On this object, you have to perform graphical methods to draw a user interface for the user. For example, if you want to have a control with three round buttons, you have to use the circle method of the UserControl to draw those buttons. Also, you need to use drawing methods to show when this control receives the focus and what the buttons look like pressed down and lifted up. Although building ActiveX controls from scratch can be more difficult, you have complete control of the finished product. Also, when building ActiveX controls from scratch, you do not need to worry about licensing and distributing supporting files as you do when using component objects (to learn about building controls by using component objects, see Chapter 4, "Inheriting From and Extending Other ActiveX Controls").

You can build ActiveX controls by using one or more other controls, called constituent controls. These controls work as building blocks giving you pre-built functionality. This greatly reduces the programming effort for a control. You can expose any properties, methods, or events of the constituent controls that you want. Constituent controls can include any controls supplied with

Visual Basic with the exception of the OLE Container control. Also, most controls that you purchase can be used as constituent controls (see the section "Licensing Issues" later in this chapter).

The constituent controls consist of intrinsic controls and nonintrinsic controls. When using the intrinsic controls, you need not worry about licensing or distribution of supplemental files. The intrinsic controls are built in to the Visual Basic runtime files that you always need to distribute. The Visual Basic intrinsic controls include the following:

```
Label

Textbox

CommandButton

PictureBox

CheckBox

OptionButton

ListBox

ComboListbox

Frame

HScrollBar

VScrollBar

Timer

DriveListBox

DirListBox

FileListBox

Shape

Image

Line
```

# A Quick Example: Build the AXYesNo

In this quick example, you build an ActiveX control that can be inserted on a Web page. The ActiveX control has three constituent controls, two command buttons, and one label. In this example, you toggle the caption of the label by clicking the two command buttons. To build this control, follow these steps:

1. Start Visual Basic 5. If it is already running, choose File, New Project.
2. In the New Project dialog box, select ActiveX Control Project. A new project should start with a UserControl object named UserControl1.
3. Change the Name property of the UserControl to AXYesNo. If the Properties dialog box is not visible, select View, Properties Window. Find the property name property and change it by typing **AXYesNo,** as in Figure 3.1.

**FIG. 3.1**

Set the control name property to "AXYesNo" in the properties window.

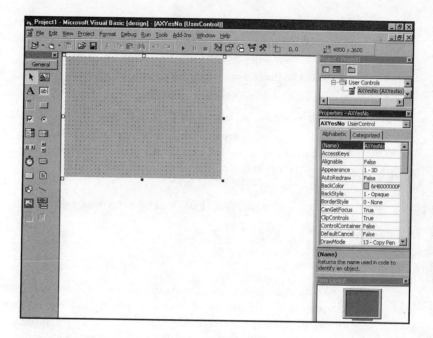

4. Add two command buttons to your UserControl. To add controls to the UserControl, click the CommandButton icon in the toolbox, then click and drag the mouse over the control drawing area, as in Figure 3.2.

**FIG. 3.2**

Draw two command buttons on the control drawing area by selecting the CommandButton icon and then clicking and dragging on the drawing area.

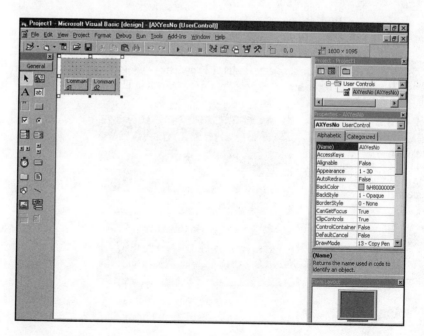

Part

II

Ch

3

5. Position the two CommandButtons so that you can see both of them. To move a CommandButton, click and drag it across your UserControl. You can also resize it by dragging the sizing blocks located on each of its corners.

6. Name one of the command buttons cmdYes and the other cmdNo.

7. Set the caption of cmdYes to Yes and the caption of cmdNo to No.

8. Add a label control to the UserControl object and name it lblDisplay.

9. Add code to the click event of cmdYes to have lblDisplay's caption property say yes. To go to the code window, click cmdYes twice. The cursor should be set in the Private Sub cmdYes_Click() event. Add the code shown in Listing 7.1.

**Listing 3.1  AXYESNO\AXYESNO.CTL  cmdYes Code**

```
Private Sub cmdYes_Click()
    lblDisplay.Caption = "Yes"
End Sub
```

10. Add code to the click event of the cmdNo button to have it change lblDisplay's caption property to No. To navigate between object events inside of the code window, go to the object list and select the cmdNo object. Verify that the event you are looking at in the procedure list is the click event. Add the code shown in Listing 7.2.

**Listing 3.2  AXYESNO\AXYESNO.CTL  cmdNo Code**

```
Private Sub cmdNo_Click()
    lblDisplay.Caption = "No"
End Sub
```

11. Open the Project, Project1 Properties dialog box and name the project AXEYesNo and provide a project description, as shown in Figure 3.3.

**FIG. 3.3**
Use the Project
Properties dialog to
provide the control with
a project name and
description.

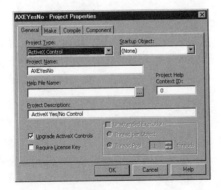

12. Build your control by selecting the File, Make AXYesNo.ocx menu entries.

13. Save your project to its own folder that you name ..\Samples\AXYesNo. Save the UserControl with the name AXYesNo.ctl. Save the project with the name AXYesNo.vbp.

14. Test the control in a test project. Choose File, Add project. From the Add project dialog box, select Standard EXE. Inside Visual Basic, close the UserControl object window. You now see that the user control object you made AXYesNo is now available in the toolbox, as seen in Figure 3.4. Add a AXYesNo to Form1, as in Figure 3.5. You can now test your control by selecting Run, Start. Click each of the command buttons and verify that they work correctly, as in Figure 3.6. Stop the project by choosing Run, End.

**FIG. 3.4**

Once you close the window containing the control you are developing, it will become available in the toolbox for use in another Visual Basic application.

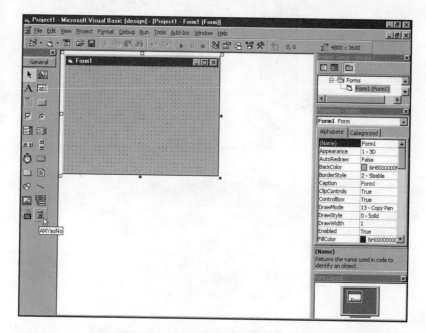

15. Test your ActiveX control from an HTML container by using the Setup Wizard. Close Visual Basic. From the Visual Basic program group on the Start menu, select Application Setup Wizard. On the Select Project dialog box, select ...\AXYesNo\AXYesNo.vbp and check Create Internet Download Setup, as in Figure 3.7.

16. On the Internet Distribution Location dialog box, pick a location where you want your distribution files to become available, as in Figure 3.8.

17. On the Internet Package dialog box, pick Use Alternate Location for runtime components but do not give a location, as in Figure 3.9. A blank will put the files with the other runtime files.

18. On the Internet Package dialog box, click the Safety button. On the Safety dialog box, specify that your control is Safe for initialization and Safe for scripting (we'll explain these settings toward the end of the chapter), as in Figure 3.10.

Part
II

Ch
3

**FIG. 3.5**

The control you have built may be placed on a regular Visual Basic window.

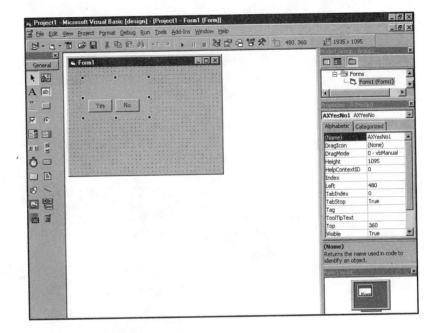

**FIG. 3.6**

When you run the standard Visual Basic project, you can verify that your control works correctly.

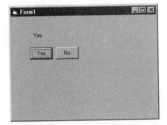

**FIG. 3.7**

To build the necessary files for use in a HTML document, you will need to use the Application Setup Wizard to create an Internet Download Setup.

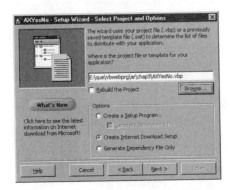

**FIG. 3.8**

You need to specify a location for the Setup Wizard to build the Internet Download files.

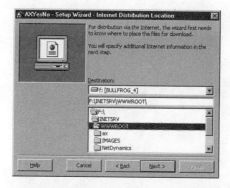

**FIG. 3.9**

You can specify whether the Visual Basic runtime files (and other necessary files) will be downloaded from the Microsoft Web site, the same Web site as your control, or a third Web site.

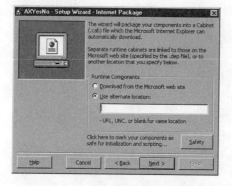

**FIG. 3.10**

By marking your control as safe for initialization and scripting, you are placing your guarantee in your control that it can not harm the user's computer, even if being used in HTML documents that you did not build.

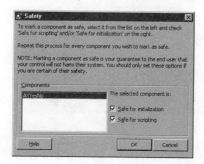

19. Move forward through the ActiveX Server Components dialog box. In the File Summary dialog box, the Setup Wizard will show you a summary of the files that will be included in the package, as in Figure 3.11.

20. Once the Setup Wizard has completed building the Internet Download files, open the AXYesNo.HTM document in Internet Explorer to test your control in a Web browser, as in Figure 3.12.

**FIG. 3.11**
The File Summary dialog box shows you what files will be included in the Internet download files that will be packaged for including on a Web site.

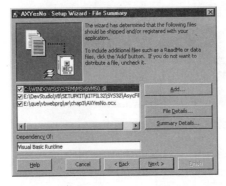

**FIG. 3.12**
Once the Setup Wizard has completed building the download files, it will create a simple HTML file that you can open in Internet Explorer to test your control.

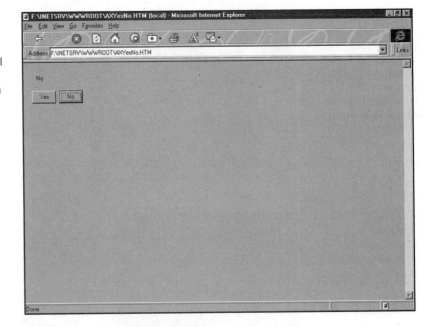

# Exposing Properties, Methods, and Events

You can make properties, methods, and events of your ActiveX controls available to Web designers to increase your controls' flexibility. After properties, methods, and events are exposed, they are available to be manipulated from script code on an HTML page such as VBScript. You can make the native properties, methods, and events of your constituent controls available, or you can make up your own for the special functionality that you are trying to achieve with your control. You need to be careful in what you enable, as it might make your control unsafe (see the section "Marking Your Controls Safe for Scripting and Initialization" later in this chapter).

# Exposing Properties of ActiveX Controls

Properties are characteristics of your controls. By changing properties, you can change the appearance and behavior of ActiveX controls. By exposing your ActiveX controls properties, you can let a Web developer manipulate your control. The availability of your ActiveX control's properties are controlled by property procedures. A property procedure is a public procedure that makes your property available to the outside world. Property procedures allow you to make properties read, write, or read *and* write.

You will need to implement two property procedures for all properties you want to make available to the user of your control. These two property procedures are the Get and Let procedures. The property Get procedure allows the current value of the property to be read by programming code or script, while the property Let procedure allows the current value of the property to be changed by the code. These methods also allow the property to appear in the Properties window when using the control in a Visual Basic application.

In the following example, you are going to make the UserControl object that you made in the first example have a public property named Backcolor, which will be available for read and write.

To make a property of your control available to be read from script make a property get procedure. The name of the procedure is BackColor and it is of type OLE_Color. It returns the value of the UserControl, as seen in Listing 3.3.

**Listing 3.3  AXYESNO\AXYESNO.CTL  Reading the *BackColor* Property**

```
Public Property Get BackColor() As OLE_COLOR
    BackColor = UserControl.BackColor
End Property
```

To make a property available to be changed from script, use a property Let statement, as in Listing 3.4.

**Listing 3.4  AXYESNO\AXYESNO.CTL  Setting the *BackColor* Property**

```
Public Property Let BackColor(ByVal New_BackColor As OLE_COLOR)
    UserControl.BackColor() = New_BackColor
    PropertyChanged "BackColor"
End Property
```

To the Web designer, your ActiveX control should look like one object—although it might be made of many constituent controls. For that reason, a Web designer should only have to change one property to change one attribute—for example, there should only be one BackColor property. You can change multiple objects on your controls properties with one property procedure. For example, if you want the BackColor of the UserControl and the label to have the same BackColor, use one property procedure and have it modify two properties, as in Listing 3.5. This allows you to change both BackColor properties with the single property, as seen in Figure 3.13.

Part
II

Ch
3

**Listing 3.5 AXYESNO\AXYESNO.CTL Setting the *BackColor* Property of Both the *UserControl* and the Label**

```
Public Property Let BackColor(ByVal New_BackColor As OLE_COLOR)
    UserControl.BackColor() = New_BackColor
    lblDisplay.BackColor() = New_BackColor
    PropertyChanged "BackColor"
End Property
```

**FIG. 3.13**

Combining the common properties of the constituent controls into a single exposed property in your control allows you to control all of the constituent properties with a single value.

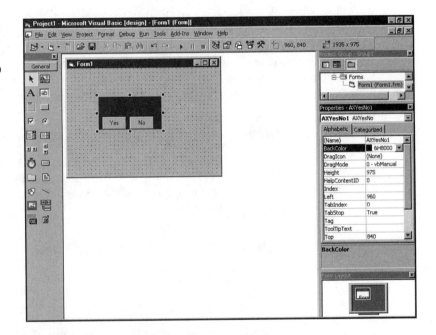

## Exposing Methods of ActiveX Controls

Methods give Web designers the ability to perform actions on the objects of their ActiveX controls. A method is just a function or sub that is declared as public. The function or sub's name associates with the name of a method of an object. For instance, you can add a method to the AXYesNo control to set the label with the code in Listing 3.6.

**Listing 3.6 AXYESNO\AXYESNO.CTL *SetText* Method**

```
Public Sub SetText(Item As String)
    lblDisplay.Caption = Item
End Sub
```

## Exposing Events of ActiveX Controls

By exposing events, you give Web designers the ability to call the code that is associated with those events.

To expose an event, first, declare the event's name in the General Declarations section of your UserControl object. Use the keyword Event and then its name, followed by parentheses—for example, Event Click() declares there will be a Click Event.

Second, create a procedure that uses your new event using the code in Listing 3.7.

**Listing 3.7    AXYESNO\AXYESNO.CTL    Exposing the *cmdNo's Click* Event**

```
Private Sub cmdNo_Click()
    'Change the caption
    lblDisplay.Caption = "No"
    'Raise the Click event
    RaiseEvent Click
End Sub
```

Part
**II**

Ch
**3**

# ActiveX Control Interface Wizard

The ActiveX Control Interface Wizard is a tool for enabling properties, methods, and events of your ActiveX control. The ActiveX Interface Wizard is especially useful in projects with large numbers of constituent controls. It looks and analyzes your ActiveX control, decides what properties, methods, and events are natively available, and lets you enable the ones you want.

To use the ActiveX Interface Wizard to expose properties and methods of your control, follow these steps:

1. From the Add-Ins menu in Visual Basic, choose Add-In Manager.

2. From the Add-In dialog box, choose VB ActiveX Control Interface Wizard and click OK, as seen in Figure 3.14.

**FIG. 3.14**

Before you can use the ActiveX Control Interface Wizard, you will need to enable it by using the Visual Basic Add-In Manager.

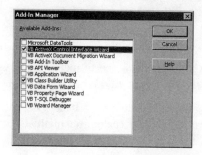

3. From the Add-Ins menu, select ActiveX Control Interface Wizard.

4. As you can see in Figure 3.15, the list on the left shows all the properties, methods, and events available from all the constituent controls in your project. The list to the right shows all the properties, methods, and events you have exposed. The command buttons in the middle move items from one list to the other. After you have selected all the items you are interested in enabling, click Next.

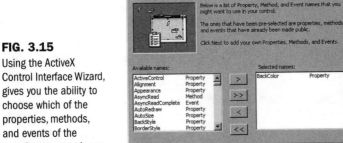

**FIG. 3.15**

Using the ActiveX Control Interface Wizard, gives you the ability to choose which of the properties, methods, and events of the constituent controls you want to expose.

5. If you have any properties, methods, or events that you want to add to the list, add them on the custom members dialog box, as seen in Figure 3.16. When you are done, click Next.

**FIG. 3.16**

The ActiveX Control Interface Wizard allows you to add your own properties, methods, and events to your control.

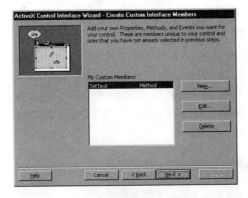

6. On the Set Mapping dialog box, map the property, methods, and events to the controls you want to tie them to, as seen in Figure 3.17. When you are done, click Next.

7. On the Set Attributes dialog box, add descriptions, data types, and any other attribute information that you need to add for your customized methods, properties, and events, as seen in Figure 3.18. When you are done, click Finished.

8. Once you have finished with the ActiveX Interface Wizard, the Wizard will add all of the necessary code to your control to support all of the properties, events, and methods that

you have elected to expose to external control (for example, scripts, application code, properties window, and so on).

**FIG. 3.17**
You can map the exposed properties, methods, and events to the properties, methods, and events of the constituent controls by using the ActiveX Control Interface Wizard.

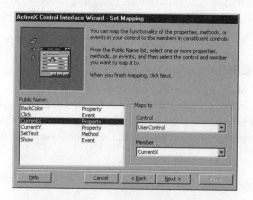

**FIG. 3.18**
You can specify the attributes and add descriptions of the custom properties, methods, and events that you have added to your control by using the Set Attributes dialog box.

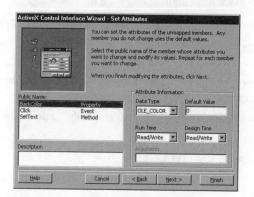

## Testing Your ActiveX Control

A good way to test your ActiveX control is in a control project. To create a control project, add another project to your ActiveX control project. Choose File, Add Project. From the Add project dialog box, select Standard EXE. Inside Visual Basic, close your UserControl object window. You now see that the ActiveX control you have made is now available in the toolbox. Add your ActiveX control to Form1. Add additional elements to test the properties, methods, and events that you exposed in your ActiveX control. You can now test your control by selecting Run, Start.

# Internet Features: Asynchronous Downloading, Navigation with Hyperlink Object

Along with the regular functionality that you need for building ActiveX controls for use in regular applications, Microsoft added a couple of functions intended specifically for use on the

Internet. The first of these functions is the ability to download control configuration and property settings from a Web site, which can be used to download properties such as images, sounds, or other objects that aren't conducive for including in the HTML document. The other of these functions enables your control to navigate the user's Web browser to an URL that you specify.

# Asynchronous Downloading

The AsyncRead method of the UserControl object downloads property values when the object is loaded. Due to varying connection speeds, this can be quick or slow. When the downloading is complete, the AsyncReadComplete event is raised in the UserControl. If you want to cancel after you start an AsyncRead method, you can do so with the CancelAsyncRead method.

The syntax for the AsyncRead method is as follows:

Object.AsyncRead Target, AsyncType [, PropertyName]

The arguments that the AsyncRead method takes are the following:

- Object—An object expression that evaluates to an object in the Applies To list.
- Target—A string expression specifying the location of the data. This can be a path or an URL.
- AsyncType—An integer expression specifying how the data will be presented, as described in Settings.
- PropertyName—An optional string expression specifying the name of the property to be loaded.

Following are the settings for AsyncType:

| | |
|---|---|
| vbAsyncFile | The data is provided in a file that is created by Visual Basic. |
| vbAsyncByte | The data is provided as a byte array that contains the retrieved data. It is assumed that the control author will know how to handle the data. |
| VbAsyncPicture | The data is provided in a Picture object. |

# *Hyperlink* Object of the UserControl

Using the properties and methods of the Hyperlink object, your ActiveX control can request a hyperlink-aware container to jump to a given URL.

The NavigateTo method can be used to jump to a specific URL. For example:

UserDocument.Hyperlink.NavigateTo "http:\\www.microsoft.com"

If your ActiveX document is contained by a hyperlink-aware container, and if the container maintains a history of documents, use the GoBack or GoForward methods to go backwards or forwards through the history list. Caution: If you go beyond the first or last item in the history list, it causes a runtime error. Be sure to use error-checking, as shown in the following code:

```
Private Sub cmdGoForward_Click()
    On Error GoTo TooFar
    UserDocument.Hyperlink.GoForward
    Exit Sub  'if you forget this exit sub you will go too far every time.
TooFar:
    Resume Next
End Sub
```

# Distributing ActiveX Controls on the World Wide Web with the Setup Wizard

The Setup Wizard is a tool used with the Visual Basic Setup Toolkit that aids you in the creation of application setup and distribution. The Setup Wizard sets up distribution of your application across the Internet by using automatic code downloaded from Microsoft Internet Explorer, Version 3.0. The Setup Wizard enables automatic downloading of your object with the initialization of the page that contains it with cabinet (CAB) files. Also, the Setup Wizard analyzes your project and determines what supporting files need to be included with your control.

> **N O T E**  Cabinet files are specially formatted files that contain ActiveX controls along with all of the necessary support files. These files contain information about the control and the necessary support files that tell the Web browser what files need to be downloaded. The Web browser takes the information from the cabinet file and compares it to the files already on the computer to determine if any of the files need to be downloaded. This enables the Web browser to avoid downloading any unnecessary files. ■

# Starting the Setup Wizard

You can start the Setup Wizard by choosing Application Setup Wizard from your Start menu or Setupwiz.exe from the \Setupkit\Kitfil32 directory where you installed Visual Basic.

Then you choose to build an Internet Download package with the Application Setup Wizard, you'll be presented with the following dialog boxes.

## Introduction Dialog Box

The Introduction dialog box makes you aware of the capabilities of the Setup Wizard. The first time you run the Setup Wizard, read the description and then check the Skip the Screen in the Future check box, shown in Figure 3.19. Choose Next to go to the next dialog box.

## Select Project and Options Dialog Box

Type the name of the project file or use the Browse button to find the project file. For the distribution options, select Internet Download Setup, as seen in Figure 3.20. Choose Next to go to the next dialog box.

Part
II

Ch
3

**FIG. 3.19**

The Setup Wizard
Introduction dialog
window provides you
with some basic
information about using
the Wizard to build
application distribution
files.

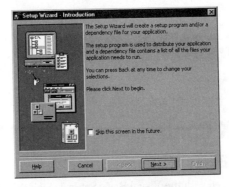

**FIG. 3.20**

To build the necessary
files for use in an HTML
document, you will need
to use the Application
Setup Wizard to create
an Internet Download
Setup.

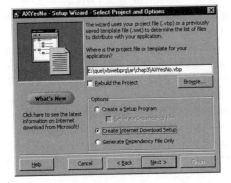

# Internet Distribution Location Dialog Box

Use the file browser to specify where you want your ActiveX control to be placed for Internet
download, as shown in Figure 3.21. Choose Next to go to the next dialog box.

**FIG. 3.21**

You need to specify a
location for the Setup
Wizard to build the
Internet Download files.

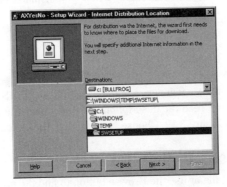

# Internet Package Dialog Box

You must decide where you would like to locate the runtime components of your applications. You can either select your own location on one of your own servers or download runtime components from the Microsoft Web site. Specifying a location on an internal server might be better if you don't have a fast connection to the Internet. By specifying the Microsoft Web site, you guarantee that your users always get the latest copies of the runtime components, as seen in Figure 3.22.

**FIG. 3.22**
You can specify whether the Visual Basic run-time files (and other necessary files) will be downloaded from the Microsoft Web site, the same Web site as your control, or a third Web site.

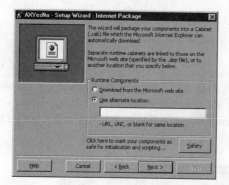

Click the Safety command button to set safety levels for each ActiveX control in your project. If your control is safe for initialization, check Safe for Initialization. If your control is safe for scripting, check Safe for Scripting, as in Figure 3.23. (See the later section "Marking Your Controls Safe for Scripting and Initialization" for more information.) Choose OK on the Safety dialog box, and Next on the Internet Package dialog box to go to the next dialog box.

**FIG. 3.23**
By marking your control as safe for initialization and scripting, you are placing your guarantee in your control that it cannot harm the user's computer, even if being used in HTML documents that you did not build.

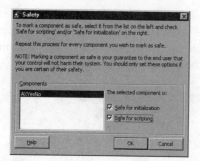

# ActiveX Server Components Dialog Box

The Setup Wizard analyzes your project and looks for any ActiveX controls that you might be using as server-side controls. If your control uses any server-side components, either as local or remote components, add them with this dialog box, shown in Figure 3.24. Choose Next to go to the next dialog box.

**FIG. 3.24**

The ActiveX Server Components dialog box gives you the opportunity to specify any server-side components that your control will need to communicate with.

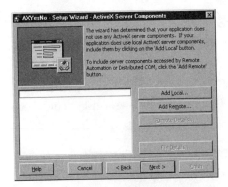

If your control will be distributed to other developers for use in building Web pages, you will need to include the Property Page DLL with your file distribution. This will provide developers with the ability to specify property settings for the control in other, non-Visual Basic development environments. The Setup Wizard will stop and ask you if you want to include this DLL with the setup files, as seen in Figure 3.25.

**FIG. 3.25**

The Setup Wizard will ask you if you want to include the Property Pages DLL with your file distribution package.

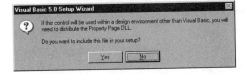

## File Summary Dialog Box

The File Summary dialog box lists all the files that are distributed with your ActiveX control, as shown in Figure 3.26. If there are any other files you want to include with your file distribution, including readme and licensing files, this is where you add them. Use the Add button to add additional files. Choose Next to complete the Setup Wizard.

**FIG. 3.26**

The File Summary dialog box shows you what files will be included in the Internet download files that will be packaged for including on a Web site.

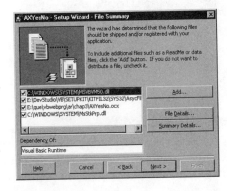

Finally, the Setup Wizard will provide you with the opportunity to save the information you have specified as a template to be used every time you run the Setup Wizard on this same project, as seen in Figure 3.27. Click the Finish button to build your distribution package.

**FIG. 3.27**
The Setup Wizard will allow you to save your setup configuration for use every time you run the Setup Wizard on this same project.

# Viewing Your ActiveX in a Web Browser

The Setup Wizard creates a default Web page that has your ActiveX control inserted on it. This Web page is located where you decide to place your ActiveX control. Open this page with a Web browser that supports ActiveX, such as Internet Explorer 3.0, as seen in Figure 3.28. If you view the source code of the page, you will see a simple HTML document that contains the <OBJECT> element, specifying the Class ID of your control, as seen in Listing 3.8.

**Listing 3.8   AXYESNO.HTM   Source of AXYesNo.HTM**

```
<HTML>
<!--     If any of the controls on this page require licensing, you must create
a license package file.
     Run LPK_TOOL.EXE in the tools directory to create the required LPK file.

<OBJECT CLASSID="clsid:5220cb21-c88d-11cf-b347-00aa00a28331">
     <PARAM NAME="LPKPath" VALUE="LPKfilename.LPK">
</OBJECT>
-->

<OBJECT
     classid="clsid:B7C523AE-6500-11D0-AB01-444553540000"
     id=AXYesNo
     codebase="AXYesNo.CAB#version=1,0,0,0">
</OBJECT>
</HTML>
```

**FIG. 3.28**
Once you have finished building your Internet distribution files, you can open the HTML file that was generated by the Setup Wizard in Internet Explorer to test your control.

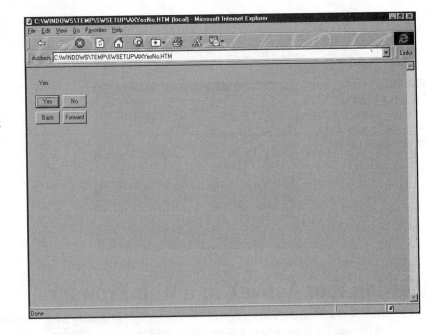

**N O T E**   The Class ID included in the preceding HTML will be different from the Class ID generated in your HTML document. This Class ID is a globally unique identifier automatically generated by Visual Basic when you build your control. You will never generate two matching Class IDs, and the Class IDs generated by Visual Basic to identify your controls will never be the same as any other Class IDs generated by anyone else to identify anyone else's control. This Class ID is automatically registered with your system Registry database, and is used by the operating system to determine whether the control needs to be downloaded from the Web site, or if you already have the control on your system. ■

# Object Definitions in HTML

All object information is defined between the `<Object>` and the `</Object>` tags. The following lists some important tags you should be familiar with:

| | |
|---|---|
| ClassID | The unique ID for this object |
| ID | The name that you use to specify this control in script |
| Codebase | Location of distribution files for your ActiveX control |

▶ For information about accessing your ActiveX control from HTML using VBScript, **see** Chapter 8, "Interacting with ActiveX Controls and VBScript," **p. 165**

# Marking Your Controls Safe for Scripting and Initialization

*Safe for Scripting* means that there is no way to harm a user's computer or obtain information about the user's computer without permission, no matter what commands are scripted to the control.

*Safe for Initialization* means that there is no way to harm a user's computer or obtain information about a user's computer by just executing the control.

If you have not marked your control as *Safe for Scripting* and *Safe for Initialization*, then the user's Web browser will warn the user that the control is not safe, and will not load the control. Only if the user has set the security level on his or her browser to it's lowest and least safe setting will the browser download and run your control.

## Marking Your ActiveX Controls Safe for Initialization

By marking your control safe for initialization, you guarantee users that there is no way to harm their computer or steal information about their computer by loading your control, regardless of the initialization parameters specified in the HTML file. If a user can specify parameters in the <PARAM> tags that accompany the <OBJECT> element that could cause your control to damage or alter the user's system in any way, you should not mark your control as *Safe for Initialization*.

An ActiveX control's initial state is defined by the PARAM statement on the HTML page that calls the object. If your control is safe for initialization, you must verify all properties given in PARAM statements in the controls InitProperties and ReadProperites events.

To mark your control safe for initialization, check the Safe for Initialization check box on the Setup Wizard Safety dialog box. Keep in mind that you are specifying that your control is *Safe for Initialization* by using the honor system. If you have not thoroughly tested your control by using all sorts of corrupt and malicious initialization settings, then you may be dishonestly stating to your users that your control is safe, when it really isn't.

## Marking Your ActiveX Control Safe for Scripting

By marking your control safe for scripting, you guarantee users of your control that there is no way to harm their computer or steal information about their computer no matter what scripting commands are given to your control.

Following are things that are not safe:

- Reading or writing a file from the user's hard drive with a name supplied by script.
- Reading or writing into the Windows Registry using a key supplied by the script. Using a fixed key in the Windows Registry would be OK, especially if it was a key associated with the control itself.

- Calling certain Windows API function.
- Sending commands to other applications.

Be careful when using constituent controls. Many have methods that can be used maliciously. Choose cautiously what properties and methods you make available.

To mark your control safe for initialization, check the Safe for Initialization check box on the Setup Wizard Safety dialog box. Once again, you are specifying this on your honor. You are giving your users your word that your control is safe for their use.

# Control Certification

Users of your control might have never heard of your company and might be skeptical of downloading objects from you. Unlike when you buy a program from the store, there is no accountability when you distribute controls over the Internet, your controls are not shrink-wrapped with your company logo on the package. A programmer who is malicious, or at least not careful, can cause bad things to happen to a user's computer. A poorly written ActiveX control can do the following:

- Delete important files, such as a configuration file
- Find out information about the user's computer and distribute this information without the user's permission
- Make system configuration changes without the user's permission

Digital signatures through third parties give a path back to you in case something unethical is performed with your control. By signing your control with a digital certificate, you are essentially placing your control into an electronic shrink-wrap and placing your company logo on the package, providing your customers with some degree of comfort that they know who built the controls.

▶ For information about using digital certificates to sign your ActiveX controls, **see** Chapter 6, "Making Your ActiveX Controls Web-Friendly," **p. 115**

# Licensing Issues

When you build ActiveX controls with Visual Basic and you use constituent controls to aid in your product development, if the constituent controls that you use with your ActiveX are Visual Basic intrinsic controls, you do not need to include any additional support files with your distribution files, other than the VB runtime DLL. Also, by using the Visual Basic constituent controls, you do not need to worry about any licensing issues.

In most cases, but not all, the authors of programmable objects VBXs, OCXs, and ActiveX controls give you the right to distribute them with your finished project without royalties. However, when you build ActiveX controls that you plan to distribute, you are giving a developer, the Web designer, the ability to create new things with your ActiveX control. Most licensing agreements that come with custom controls do not give you the right to distribute any part of the author's control in a non-finished product form. Also, if the author uses Standard Registry Licensing Scheme, you cannot distribute the author's controls on a Web server.

▶ For information about using other ActiveX controls in your ActiveX controls, and the licensing issues involved, **see** Chapter 4, "Inheriting From and Extending Other ActiveX Controls."

# From Here...

In this chapter, you have learned the basics of building your own ActiveX controls by using Visual Basic 5. You went through the steps of building a simple control, and then packaging it up for use in HTML pages on the Web. In the next few chapters, you'll go more in depth into the various options available to you in building ActiveX controls, and how you can take advantage of functionality provided by other controls, as well as in Visual Basic, to provide your control with additional functionality by writing a minimum of code. You will also learn about Internet security issues surrounding ActiveX controls, and learn how to sign your controls using a digital certificate that you can acquire from a certificate authority like Verisign. From here you might want to check out the following chapters:

- To learn about building ActiveX controls by extending existing controls, read Chapter 4, "Inheriting From and Extending Other ActiveX Controls."

- To learn what's involved in building ActiveX controls that communicate with server-side components, check out Chapter 5, "Making an ActiveX Control Communicate with a Server."

- To learn how to sign your ActiveX controls with your digital certificate, see Chapter 6, "Making Your ActiveX Controls Web-Friendly."

- To learn how you can interact with your ActiveX control in HTML using VBScript, read Chapter 8, "Interacting with ActiveX Controls and VBScript."

# CHAPTER 4

# Inheriting From and Extending Other ActiveX Controls

**Learn why enhancing an existing control is a good control-creation solution**

The second easiest way to build a new Visual Basic ActiveX control is to enhance an existing control.

**Discover how to change an existing control's behavior**

When you change the way a control works, you've actually created a whole new control.

**Find out some tricks for programming a TextBox control**

Visual Basic's TextBox control is the basis for the NumbersOnly control you create in this chapter.

In the previous chapter, you got a quick introduction to two of the ways you can create a Visual Basic ActiveX control. To review, those methods were creating a control from the constituent controls, and enhancing an existing control. There is a third way that you can create an ActiveX control using Visual Basic, and that is by creating a user-drawn control from scratch (but this method is beyond the scope of this book). In the previous chapter, you took a detailed look at the first method, creating a control using existing controls, also called constituent controls. Now, you're ready to tackle the second method. In this chapter, you learn how to enhance already existing controls in order to create a new version of the control. ■

# Advantages of Enhancing Existing Controls

When you decide to enhance an existing control, you gain some of the advantages you did when you created a control from constituent controls. For example, unless you modify the original control a lot, the user will probably be familiar with how the control is used. Also, unlike user-drawn controls, you don't have to worry about drawing the control's user interface. In fact, unless you're an expert programmer who can effectively subclass controls through the Windows API, you're pretty much stuck with the way the original control looks.

Being stuck with the control's appearance can be an advantage or a disadvantage, depending upon what type of control you want to create. Obviously, unless there's an existing control that's already pretty close to what you want, you'll have to go the user-drawn control route. Luckily, Visual Basic provides all the basic types of controls—buttons, list boxes, images, and so on—giving you a wide choice of existing controls from which to choose.

Just as with constituent controls, another advantage of starting with an existing control is that the existing control's basic behavior is already programmed for you. All you have to do is provide the properties, methods, and events you need to make the control act the way you want it to. In this chapter, you'll learn about the mechanics of enhancing an existing control.

# Creating the NumbersOnly Control

Now that you are familiar with some of the advantages of enhancing existing controls, you can get started on a new ActiveX control. This new control will be based on Visual Basic's TextBox control. The control you build in the following sections enables a user to enter only numbers into the text box. As you will see later, this control can be used in a variety of ways. One of the features of the control is to ignore all other keystrokes with the exception of the backspace key.

## Creating the NumbersOnly Project Group

In this first set of steps, you create the basic files and project group for the NumbersOnly control. In succeeding sections, you program the control's enhancements. For now, perform the steps below to create the basic project group:

> **N O T E**  You can find the complete NumbersOnly project in the Chap04\NumbersOnly folder of this book's CD-ROM. ▓

1. Start a new ActiveX Control Project. If you are using the Control Creation Edition of Visual Basic 5, start a new CTLGROUP.
2. Change Project1's name to NumbersOnlyPrj, and give the project the description NumbersOnly Edit Box, as shown in Figure 4.1.
3. If you are not using the Control Creation Edition of Visual Basic, add a standard EXE project by using the File, Add Project menu selections.

**FIG. 4.1**

Use the Project Properties property sheet to name the new control project.

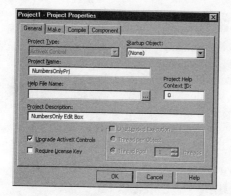

4. Change Project2's name to NumbersOnlyTestAppPrj, and give the project the description Test Application for the NumbersOnly Control, as shown in Figure 4.2.

**FIG. 4.2**

You need to rename Project2, as well.

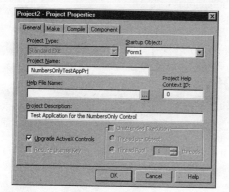

5. Double-click UserControl1 in the Project Group window to display the control's properties in the Properties window, and change the Name property to NumbersOnly (see Figure 4.3).

6. Double-click Form1 in the Project Group window to display the form's properties in the Properties window, and change the Name property to frmNumbersOnlyTestApp.

7. Save the project group's files under the names NUMBERSONLY.CTL, NUMBERSONLYPRJ.VBP, FRMNUMBERSONLYTESTAPP.FRM, NUMBERSONLYTESTAPPPRJ.VBP, and NUMBERSONLYGROUP.VBG.

You've now created the new control's project group, which includes not only the UserControl object for the control, but also a form on which you can build the control's test application.

**FIG. 4.3**

The new control's name is NumbersOnly.

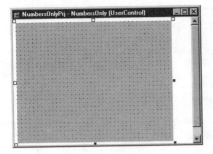

# Building the Control's User Interface

As you know, the control you're building will start off as a Visual Basic TextBox. You'll then modify the TextBox control to give it custom behaviors. First, however, follow the steps below to add the TextBox to the NumbersOnly control:

1. Double-click NumbersOnly in the Project Group window. The new control's designer window appears, and the control's properties appear in the Properties window.

2. Open the Project, Components dialog, and include the Microsoft Form 2.0 Object Library in the project, as seen in Figure 4.4.

**FIG. 4.4**

Add the Microsoft Forms Object Library to the control project.

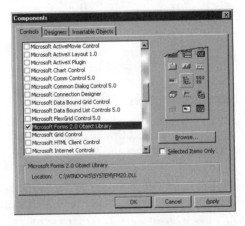

3. In Visual Basic's toolbox, double-click the TextBox control. An instance of the TextBox control appears in NumbersOnly's designer window (see Figure 4.5).

4. In the Properties window, change the TextBox's properties as listed below. The final TextBox should look like Figure 4.6.

| | |
|---|---|
| Name | txtNumbers |
| Height | 285 |
| Left | 120 |
| Text | "" |

| Top | 120 |
| Width | 1215 |

**FIG. 4.5**
This TextBox is the control you'll enhance.

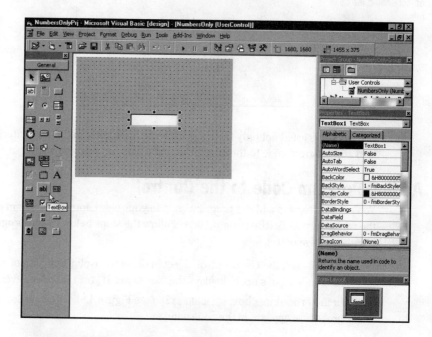

**FIG. 4.6**
The TextBox should look like this after you set its properties.

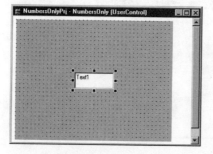

5. Click the UserControl object in order to display its properties in the Properties window. Set the control's properties as listed below. When you're done, the control should look like Figure 4.7.

| Name | NumbersOnly |
| Height | 555 |
| Width | 1455 |

**FIG. 4.7**
The resized UserControl object should look like this.

You've now created not only the control's basic files, but also the user interface. The next step is to add program code to the control so that it acts the way you want it to act.

# Adding Program Code to the Control

You're now ready to add the program code to your new control—program code that changes the way a normal TextBox control acts. Follow the steps below to add program code to the new NumbersOnly control:

1. Double-click the UserControl object in order to display the control's code window. When the window pops up, it displays the UserControl_Initialize() event procedure.

2. In the Procedures box, select Resize (see Figure 4.8). The UserControl_Resize() event procedure appears in the code window.

**FIG. 4.8**
First, you'll add program code that handles the Resize event.

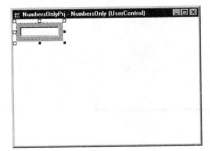

3. Add the lines shown in Listing 4.1 to the UserControl_Resize() event procedure, as shown in Figure 4.9.

**Listing 4.1    LST04_01.TXT—Code for the *UserControl_Resize()* Event Procedure**

```
' Don't let the developer make the
' height of the control too small.
If UserControl.Height < 555 _
    Then UserControl.Height = 555
```

```
' Don't let the developer make
' the control too narrow.
If UserControl.Width < 400 _
    Then UserControl.Width = 400

' Change the width of the TextBox control
' to fit into the resized UserControl.
txtNumbers.Width = ScaleWidth - 200
```

**FIG. 4.9**

Add program to the
*UserControl_Resize()*
event procedure.

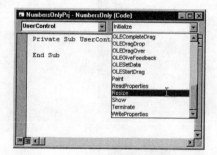

4. In the Object box, select txtNumbers (see Figure 4.10). The txtNumbers_Change() event
   procedure appears in the code window.

**FIG. 4.10**

Use the object box to
select the object whose
code you want to view.

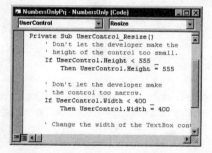

5. In the Procedures box, select KeyPress. The txtNumbers_KeyPress() event procedure
   appears in the code window.

6. Add the lines shown below to the txtNumbers_KeyPress() event procedure, as shown in
   Figure 4.11.

```
If (KeyAscii <> Backspace) And _
(KeyAscii < Zero Or KeyAscii > Nine) _
    Then KeyAscii = 0
```

7. In the Object box, select General. The code cursor moves to just above the
   txtNumbers_Change() event procedure. This is where you place declarations for
   variables and constants used throughout the project.

Part
**II**

Ch
**4**

8. Add the following lines of code where the code cursor is currently positioned, as shown in Figure 4.12.

```
Const Zero = 48
Const Nine = 57
Const Backspace = 8
```

**FIG. 4.11**

Here's the code window showing the new *txtNumbers_KeyPress()* event procedure.

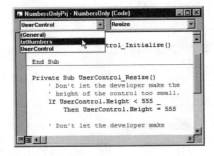

**FIG. 4.12**

You declare global variables and constants in the General section.

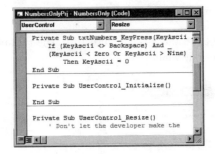

After adding code lines to the project, be sure to save your changes by clicking the Save Project Group button on VB5's toolbar or by selecting the File, Save Project Group command from the menu bar.

> **N O T E** The Change event, which is handled by the Change() event procedure, is common to many of Visual Basic's controls. In the case of the TextBox control, the Change event occurs whenever the contents of the TextBox is changed. This change can occur by the user's typing text into the control. It can also occur programmatically, when your program sets the control's Text property. The KeyDown event occurs whenever the user presses a key that has an ASCII key code. Keys like Ctrl, Alt, and F1 don't have ASCII key codes and must be intercepted in the KeyDown() event procedure instead of KeyPress(). ▓

## Exploring *UserControl_Resize()*

In the NumbersOnly control, the resize event accomplishes much the same task as it did in the Address control. When a developer resizes the NumbersOnly control, you want to be sure that the control's interface remains usable. You don't want the height of the NumbersOnly control to get smaller, because then there would be no room for the standard font. You also don't want the control's width to become too small so that it won't display text the user may type into it.

The first thing `UserControl_Resize()` does is make sure that the control's height doesn't get set to less than 555:

```
If UserControl.Height < 555 _
    Then UserControl.Height = 555
```

Now, if the developer tries to make the control too small, `UserControl_Resize()`sets the height back to where it belongs. The developer can make the control taller, but he can't make it so short that it can no longer hold the default font.

Although you have to be careful about how the developer changes the control's height, the control's width isn't as critical. Because TextBox controls can scroll text, the TextBox doesn't necessarily have to be wide enough to hold the entire line that the user types in. Your new NumbersOnly control can allow the developer to change the width of the NumbersOnly control. Still, you want to limit the width to a sensible minimum amount, like this:

```
If UserControl.Width < 400 _
    Then UserControl.Width = 400
```

This width results in a TextBox that can hold at least a single digit.

Because you never know how the developer has set the NumbersOnly control's size, you need to size and position the TextBox control every time a `Resize` event occurs, like this:

```
txtNumbers.Width = ScaleWidth - 200
```

As you already know, `ScaleWidth` holds the width of the UserControl object's visible area. The previous line sets the width of the TextBox control to 200 twips less than the width of the UserControl object's visible width.

## Exploring *txtNumbers_KeyPress()*

The whole point of creating this custom control is to enable the user to type in only digits. That is, the control should disallow any character except the digits 0 to 9. There is one exception: In order to allow the user to edit what he's typed, the control also must allow the backspace character.

To make the code in `txtNumbers_KeyPress()` more readable, the procedure uses constants to represent the value of the backspace and digit keys. These constants are defined in the lines you added to the project's General code area:

```
Const Zero = 48
Const Nine = 57
Const Backspace = 8
```

The ASCII value for the digits 0 and 9 are 48 and 57, respectively. The ASCII value of the backspace keystroke is 8. By assigning these values to constants, the program lines that need the ASCII values can use the more understandable English words in place of the actual values.

**N O T E** To define a constant in Visual Basic, you use the line Const *name* = *value*, where *name* is the constant's name and *value* is the value you want to assign to the constant. ■

The complete `txtNumbers_KeyPress()` event procedure is shown in Listing 4.2. Notice that the procedure receives two parameters. The first parameter, `KeyAscii`, is the ASCII code of the key that's just been pressed. By analyzing this value, the procedure can determine whether or not to allow the keystroke to make it through to the TextBox control. To do this, the procedure compares `KeyAscii` with the constants that represent the digit or backspace ASCII values. If the keystroke is not a digit from 0 to 9 or a backspace, the `txtNumbers_KeyPress()` event procedure changes the key's code to 0, an ASCII value that will not cause a character to appear in the TextBox control's edit area.

### Listing 4.2   LST04_02.TXT—The Complete *txtNumbers_KeyPress()* Event Procedure

```
Private Sub txtNumbers_KeyPress(KeyAscii As Integer)
    If (KeyAscii <> Backspace) And _
    (KeyAscii < Zero Or KeyAscii > Nine) _
        Then KeyAscii = 0
End Sub
```

# Testing the NumbersOnly Control

You've created your control's interface and added code to handle the `Resize` and `KeyPress` events. You're now ready to put the NumbersOnly control to work by opening the test application's designer window and adding a NumbersOnly instance. Remember that you'll now be acting as an application or Web page developer, using the control just as a developer might. In this role, you ensure that the control performs as it should. To prepare for testing the NumbersOnly control, perform the steps below:

1. Close the control's code window by clicking the close button in the upper-right corner of the window. The window is dismissed from the screen.

2. Close the control's designer window in the same way. The window is dismissed from the screen, and the NumbersOnly control becomes available in VB5's toolbox.

3. Double-click frmNumbersOnlyTestApp in the Project Group window. The test application's form designer window appears.

4. Double-click the NumbersOnly control's icon in VB5's toolbox. An instance of the control appears on the test application's form, as shown in Figure 4.13.

To see `UserControl_Resize()` in action, reduce the width of the NumbersOnly control. When you do, the TextBox control automatically resizes itself to the new control width. If you try to reduce the height of the NumbersOnly control, the control springs back to its minimum size. You can, however, enlarge the control as much as you like. If you reduce the width of the control as far as it'll go, you end up with something like Figure 4.14. No matter how narrow you try to make the control, it'll always stay at least at its minimum size.

**FIG. 4.13**
When you double-click your new NumbersOnly control in the toolbox, an instance of the control appears in the test application's form.

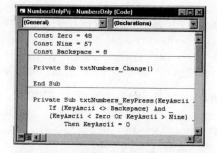

**FIG. 4.14**
This is the test application when the NumbersOnly control is at its minimum width.

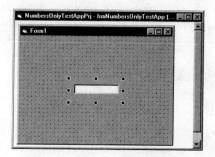

Ensuring that the Resize event is handled properly is part of testing how the control works when the designer is using it to create an application or Web page. But how about the control's behavior when the designer has finished his application and has passed the application on to his users? It would be *very* unwise to create a control that responded differently than what was advertised. To check this important part of the control's behavior, you will have to run the test application.

Press F5 now to run the test application. When you do, the test application's main window appears. Go ahead and type text into the control. (You may first have to click the TextBox to give it the input focus.) You'll discover that the control will accept only digits (see Figure 4.15).

**FIG. 4.15**
You can type letters on your keyboard, but only digits will appear in your new NumbersOnly control.

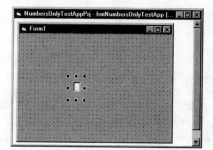

# Compiling the NumbersOnly Control

After you create and test your control, you need to compile it into an .OCX file, which is the stand-alone binary version of the control that you can distribute. When you compile your control into an .OCX file, developers can install the control on their systems and then use the control in their own projects, regardless of whether they're working with a programming language, a Web-page authoring application, or some other development tool. To create a stand-alone .OCX file for the NumbersOnly control, perform the following steps:

1. Double-click NumbersOnly in the Project Group window. The control's designer window appears.

2. Select the File, Make NUMBERSONLYPRJ.OCX in VB5's menu bar. The Make Project dialog box appears.

3. Change the control's file name to **NumbersOnly.ocx**, as shown in Figure 4.16 (you may also need to set the directory to where you want the file to be saved), and click OK. VB5 compiles the new control and writes the .OCX file out to your disk.

**FIG. 4.16**

You can name your control's .OCX file in the Make Project dialog box.

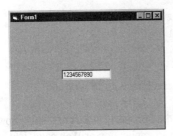

4. Select the File, Remove Project command from VB5's menu bar. When Visual Basic asks whether you want to remove the project, click Yes. (If you're asked to save files, also choose Yes.)

After completing the previous steps, your project group will contain only the test application, frmNumbersOnlyTestApp. However, if you look at Visual Basic's toolbox, you'll see that the NumbersOnly control is again available. Now, however, when you add the control to an application, Visual Basic will use the compiled control rather than the version that was originally part of your project group.

# Packaging the NumbersOnly Control

As you are using the Application Setup Wizard to package the NumbersOnly control for use on Web pages, you will see a couple of new dialog windows that you didn't encounter in the previous chapter. Once you have completed going through the Setup Wizard, and are expecting to be presented with the File Summary dialog, you are presented with the Confirm Dependencies dialog instead. This dialog presents you with the DLL and OCX dependencies for your control, as seen in Figure 4.17. This dialog should contain all of the files included in your project through the Project Components and Project References dialog boxes. By clicking the File Details button, get copyright and version information about the currently selected file, as seen in Figure 4.18.

**FIG. 4.17**

The Confirm Dependencies dialog box presents you with the list of DLLs and OCXs that your control uses.

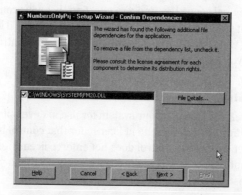

**FIG. 4.18**

The File Details dialog presents you with version and copyright information on the DLLs and OCXs that are used by your control.

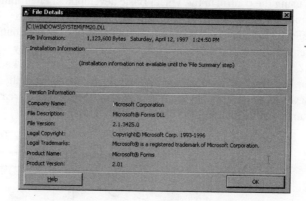

Part

II

Ch

4

Once you finally get to the File Summary dialog box, you will find the dependent files included among the other files that you saw included in the previous chapter, as seen in Figure 4.19.

**FIG. 4.19**

The dependent files that were specified for including in your control distribution will be included in the File Summary dialog.

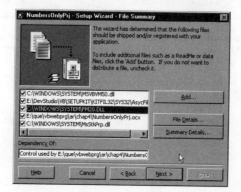

# Licensing Issues

When you use other ActiveX controls as the starting point for creating your own controls, you may have to purchase a special runtime license for the original controls. If you do not acquire a runtime license for the original control, your users may find that your control does not work correctly (assuming that it works at all). To understand why this is, we'll look at how ActiveX controls are licensed, and why you can freely distribute these same controls as part of any Visual Basic applications you have developed.

## ActiveX Control Licensing

When you install an ActiveX control onto your system for use in developing Visual Basic applications, you are given a single-user development license for that control by the control developer. This is an implicit act, even if the control does not enforce licensing. If the control does use licensing, then the control license key is automatically installed into your system registry database by the control install utility.

When you are using the control in the Visual Basic development environment, every time you place the control on a Visual Basic form, or run an application, the control is created using the ActiveX IClassFactory2 interface. This interface creates a copy of the control object each time Visual Basic requests a new copy of the control. Before the control copy is created, the IClassFactory2 interface checks to see if the control requires a license key. If the control requires a license key, the key is retrieved from the registry database. If the IClassFactory2 interface retrieves a valid license key from the registry, the control is created and a pointer to the copy is returned to Visual Basic, as illustrated in Figure 4.20.

**FIG. 4.20**

In the Visual Basic development environment, the control license key is retrieved from the registry database before the control is created.

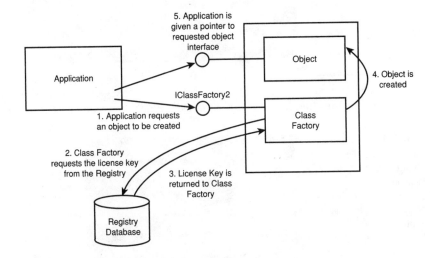

5. Application is given a pointer to requested object interface

Application

Object

4. Object is created

IClassFactory2

1. Application requests an object to be created

Class Factory

2. Class Factory requests the license key from the Registry

3. License Key is returned to Class Factory

Registry Database

When you compile a Visual Basic application, a runtime license for the control is included in the application executable. The Setup utility that you build for your application by using the Setup Wizard does not place the license key for these controls into the user's system registry. As a result, when your application tries to create a copy of the control, the IClassFactory2 interface does not find a valid license key in the registry. At this point, the IClassFactory2 interface turns to the application and requests that the application supply the license key. Because Visual Basic placed a copy of the control license key inside the application when it was compiled, the application is able to supply the requested license key, and the control can be created, as seen in Figure 4.21.

**FIG. 4.21**
When Visual Basic compiles an application, it includes the license key of any controls that require it, so the application is able to supply the license to use the control.

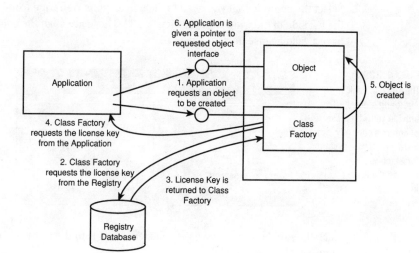

# Licensing and the Web

When you want to use controls on the Web that require license keys, how do you provide the license key for the control? If you embed the license key in the HTML document in which you are using the control, anyone who downloads your Web page will be able to freely use the control. The control developer would not be very happy with you if you did this.

What Microsoft decided to do to prevent this situation was to create a License Manager in Internet Explorer. The License Manager is another ActiveX control that has to be included in your HTML document, before any of the other controls that require runtime licenses. The License Manager requires a single parameter, "LPKPath," which should contain the URL for a license pack that you place on your Web site. The HTML syntax for the License Manager is as follows:

```
<OBJECT CLASSID="clsid:5520cb21-c88d-11cf-b347-00aa00a28331">
    <PARAM NAME="LPKPath" VALUE="MyLicPack.LPK">
</OBJECT>
```

**N O T E** The .LPK file name used in the value for the license pack should be a relative URL. While this won't prevent unscrupulous users from downloading the license pack for their own use, it will make it more difficult. ■

To create a license pack to use with the ActiveX controls on your Web pages, you will need to use the Lpk_tool.exe utility included in the ActiveX SDK and in the Tools directory on the Visual Basic 5.0 CD ROM. Create a license pack by following these steps:

1. Run the Lpk_tool.exe utility using the Start, Run command from the Start menu.

2. Select the controls that you need to include on your Web page from the list of controls on the left side of the window, as in Figure 4.22. These are all of the controls for which you have a valid license on your system.

**FIG. 4.22**

The License Pack Authoring Tool will provide you with a list of controls currently installed on your system for which you can include the license keys in the license pack.

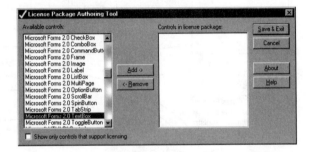

3. Click the Add button to move the selected controls to the right side of the window, as in Figure 4.23.

**FIG. 4.23**

The License Pack Authoring Tool will build a list of the controls that will be included in the license pack.

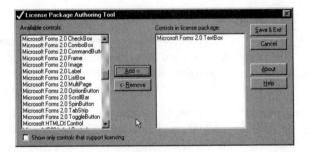

4. Once you have included all of the controls that you will be using on the Web page, click on the Save & Exit button. You will be presented with a Save As dialog, where you will need to specify the .LPK file name to use for the license pack, as in Figure 4.24. This file name will be the license pack name that you use in the LPKPath value in the HTML document.

**FIG. 4.24**

The .LPK file name that you specify will be the name that you need to use in your HTML document as part of the license pack URL.

**CAUTION**

Before including any licensed control in a Web page, or as part of a custom ActiveX control, be sure that you have a valid redistribution license, and that the redistribution license permits use of the control on the Internet. If you do not have a valid redistribution license, you may be opening yourself up to legal action on the part of the component's creator.

# From Here...

Part
II
Ch
4

In this chapter we looked at how to enhance existing controls. We looked at the advantages of using existing controls and how they can be used in our application. We created a NumbersOnly control using existing objects supplied with Visual Basic.

The following chapters will provide additional coverage on creating ActiveX controls:

- To learn what's involved in building ActiveX controls that communicate with server-side components, check out Chapter 5, "Making an ActiveX Control Communicate with a Server."

- To learn how to sign your ActiveX controls with your digital certificate, see Chapter 6, "Making Your ActiveX Controls Web-Friendly."

- To learn how you can interact with your ActiveX control in HTML using VBScript, read Chapter 8, "Interacting with ActiveX Controls and VBScript."

# Making an ActiveX Control Communicate with a Server

**W**insock programming has been perceived as a barrier by many programmers. Development involving TCP/IP networking appeared as an arcane craft known only to initiates of the black arts. For Microsoft to reach their goal of making the Internet and the use of Internet technology for intranets accessible to all, this barrier needed to be removed. As usual, Microsoft did a superb job. One of the tools that Microsoft has provided is the Microsoft ActiveX Winsock Control Version 5.0. This control parks invisibly on a Visual Basic form acting as a client and provides TCP/IP communication with a server program, which also has a Winsock Control. The Winsock API is wrapped in this control and exposed through its properties, methods, and events. If you can write a Visual Basic "Hello World" application, you can create powerful client/server applications that will communicate over a TCP/IP network link.

Use of the Winsock Control is not limited to the Web browser paradigm or to the use of the HTTP or FTP protocols. It lives at a lower level, using the TCP and UDP protocols. There are other Microsoft controls that encapsulate the specifics of the HTTP and FTP protocols.

## TCP/IP communications fundamentals

Ports and friendly names, among other issues, are examined to provide understanding of the requirements of the protocol.

## Properties, Methods, and Events

The Winsock API has been encapsulated in the Properties, Methods, and Events of the Microsoft Winsock Control. Understanding these is essential to effective use of the Winsock Control.

## Building a client application

Moving step-by-step through the development of a client application will provide an understanding of the potential power of the Winsock Control.

## Building a server application

A client without a server is only half the story. You will examine how the server handles the request for service from the client.

## Testing the client/server application and building fault tolerance

Most server applications run unattended. The errors need to be reported to the client for action.

In this chapter, you will explore TCP/IP fundamentals, examine the Microsoft Winsock Control in some detail, and build a working client/server application. Although the example you will build in this chapter is a full Visual Basic application, and not an ActiveX control, it could easily be packaged as a control, without changing anything other than the project type. ■

# Understanding TPC/IP Communications Fundamentals

Winsock is a short name for Windows Sockets. Sockets are a standard programming interface for communications programming with the TCP/IP protocol. The Win32 API includes the Winsock API, which is a fairly straight port of the Berkley Sockets API for Windows. Winsock API encompasses the event-driven nature of Windows programming. Microsoft has added extensions to the Winsock API that are the INetAPI. These extensions are aimed at extending the functionality to include HTTP, FTP, and Gopher.

> **N O T E** A full treatment of TCP/IP is beyond this chapter or book. There are several excellent books on TCP/IP and Microsoft TCP/IP, which is Microsoft's implementation of TCP/IP. In the Microsoft world of TCP/IP, you may also want to explore DHCP (Dynamic Host Configuration Protocol) and WINS (Windows Internet Name Service). The information in this chapter will allow you to use the Winsock Control with little or no problems. ■

## Clients and Servers

Networked applications often use the paradigm of client/server. The client contacts the server and requests information or service from the server application. The server responds by providing the data or service.

In the world of Winsock communications, the important aspect of the client/server relationship is who establishes the connection. The client is always the initiating application. The client sends a request for connection to the server. After the connection has been established, the server can request information from the client and vice versa. Once the connection has been established, a peer relationship exists with either application being able to initiate communication.

## IP Addresses and Host Names

When a system is part of a TCP/IP network, it needs to have an identification address. This address, called the IP or Internet Protocol address is a 32-bit number usually represented as four numbers separated by periods. An example would be 190.137.48.1. These are the decimal representation of four bytes. (This limits the range of the decimal number from 0-255.) This number, when assigned to your computer, is its node address. This is true whether your system is attached to the Internet, attached to your company LAN, or a system of two computers at home that you have attached in a small local LAN as I do.

Because numbers can be hard to remember, a system of "friendly" names has been created wherein each computer has a name called the *domain name*. An example is the Microsoft domain name of www.microsoft.com. In the friendly name system, this represents a node on the network.

**N O T E**   The domain name www.microsoft.com is actually composed of multiple computers reached by the domain name of www.microsoft.com. A system called *round-robining* is used to have multiple computers available to respond to one friendly domain name. As one of the busiest Web sites in the world, it is understandable that one system can't handle the load. ▪

Friendly names are difficult for computers to work with as addresses so a system was devised called the *Domain Name Service*. The Domain Name Service translates the friendly names into IP addresses. The method used to accomplish this is by means of computers on the network that are Domain Name Servers. When you enter a request for service on the World Wide Web, the address is specified as an URL or Universal Resource Locator. Http://www.microsoft.com is an example. HTTP is the protocol being used and www.microsoft.com is the name of a system somewhere on the Internet. The essence of the process is that the www.microsoft.com address is translated by a Domain Name Server into an IP address such as 190.137.12.4. Now the network can work with the address and locate the system to which you wish to attach.

The key factor to remember is that a system on a network may be referred to by either the IP address or the friendly name. If there is a system on the network providing Domain Name Services, the name will be resolved into an IP address. The IP address is the "real" address. The friendly name is an "alias" that is easier to remember.

# UDP and TCP

When data moves across the network with the TCP/IP protocol, there are two choices of method: User Datagram Protocol and Transmission Control Protocol. UDP and TCP are quite different and each has its uses so one is not better than the other. Both are available to you when using the Winsock Control. In general, if you are not sure which one to use, the choice of TCP will always work but it imposes a higher overhead cost.

**UDP**   UDP is somewhat like mailing a letter. When a message is sent over the network with UDP, the message is packaged with a destination address (the IP address of the system to which it is being sent) and the address of the system sending the message (again an IP address). There is a theoretical maximum size for a UDP message of 65K bytes. Many implementations are less than this. A size of 8,192 is the usual smallest maximum size that all implementations will accommodate. If the Datagram exceeds the maximum permissible size for the implementation, the message is simply truncated. Once the message is packaged with the destination and origin addresses, it is sent on a best efforts basis with no guarantee that it will arrive and no checking is done by the protocol to see if it arrived. Any checking must be performed in the application.

This is connectionless communication. There is no checking to see if the destination system is capable of receiving a message.

The UDP message also contains the source port and the destination port number. Ports are discussed later in this chapter.

An example of a service that uses UDP is Simple Mail Transport Protocol (SMTP) for e-mail messages. This is very much like mailing a letter. There is no assurance that it will arrive. This is an unreliable communication protocol.

**TCP**    With TCP, there is no maximum message length. When a message is passed to the TCP protocol, if it is too large to be sent in one piece, the message is broken up into chunks or packets and sent one at a time to the destination address. The TCP packet contains the addressing information as does the UDP message with one addition. The TCP message also contains a packet number and the total number of packets. Because of the nature of the TCP/IP protocol, the packets may travel different paths and may arrive in a different order than sent. TCP reassembles the packets in the proper order and requests the retransmission of any missing or corrupted packets.

Unlike UDP, TCP is a connection-oriented reliable communication protocol. It is somewhat like dialing a telephone and waiting for someone to answer before beginning to send data.

With TCP, the client system sends a request for connection, as discussed earlier.

As with the UDP protocol, the TCP messages contain a destination and origin port number.

## Ports

The TCP/IP protocol is used for communication between computer systems. Port numbers are used for communicating between applications on the two systems. Ports are also called sockets. This is the origin of the Winsock terminology.

When two applications are communicating by using the TCP/IP protocol, the applications use port numbers to identify themselves to the other application. When a server receives a request for a connection, the request will be directed at a particular TCP/IP port. The server will then know which application is being contacted because it has the port number associated with the application.

An analogy might be having two phones in your house, one for business and one for personal use. If the business phone rings, you know when you answer that the communication will be requesting attention from your "business" persona not your "personal" persona.

Servers listen on a particular port and clients send requests to that port. In the everyday world of Internet usage, there are "Well Known Ports." Some of these ports have become standard. The World Wide Web uses port 80 and FTP uses port 21. WWW would function just as well on port 37 but everyone has agreed to use port 80.

This is similar to the use of 911 for an emergency phone number; 919 would have worked just as well, but everyone agreed to use 911.

A particular server application listens on a given port number for requests for connection. If you have a system that is used for both WWW and FTP, it will be listening on both port 21 and

80. If the request for connection comes on port 80 the Web server application will handle the communication.

Having a system work as a server for one application does not prevent it from being a client for another application. A system can be a Web server, listening on port 80, and still communicate with another system on another port for a different application.

An important point to remember is that the client system does not have to send the request for service from the same port on which the server is listening. For example, if the server ABC application is listening on port 239, the client may send its request for service from its port 1593 to the server's port 239. This works because the client tells the server the port number that its request came from so the server will respond to the client by sending the response to port 1593.

The essential parts of the message sent from one computer system to another are:

- Destination IP Address—This is a dotted quartet, for example, 191.187.39.55. This is how the network identifies the node of the network for which the message is bound.

- Origin IP Address—This is also a dotted quartet. This is used if any replies or requests for retransmission are required.

- Destination Port Number—This identifies the socket for which the message is bound. Since sockets or ports are linked or bound to one application, this is the "address" of the application on the system.

- Origination Port Number—This is used for any replies sent to the originating system to identify to the TCP/IP protocol which application is the intended recipient of the message.

- Data—This is the information that the applications are sending to each other.

There are other components of the message, but they are not important for the use of the Winsock Control.

# Examining Properties, Methods, and Events

At the beginning of this chapter, you learned that the Winsock API is wrapped in the Winsock Control. The manner in which the API functions are accessed are through the properties, methods, and events of the Winsock Control. In the next sections, you examine the important Winsock Control properties, methods, and events.

## Properties

Properties can be described by several elements. Some are available to be set at design time, some are read only at runtime and are unavailable at design time, some may only be set at design time and are read only at runtime, and some can be set at both runtime and design time.

Another aspect of the property is the data type of the value. This can be a string, an integer, a long integer, or any other data type.

The third aspect of a property is the Syntax or usage for using the property in code.

**BytesReceived Property**   This property tells you the number of bytes currently in the receive buffer. This property is read-only and is unavailable at design time. The value returned is a long integer. An example of the syntax is:

```
myvar = MyWinsockControl.BytesReceived
```

An example of use would be to determine the size of a display area for the data or to see if there is any data in the buffer.

**LocalHostName Property**   This property returns the name of the local Host system. This property is read-only and is unavailable at design time. The value returned is a string. An example of the syntax is:

```
myvar = MyWinsockControl.LocalHostName
```

**LocalIP Property**   This property returns the local Host system IP address in the form of a string like XXX.XXX.XXX.XXX. This property is read-only and is unavailable at design time. The value returned is a string. An example of the syntax is:

```
myvar = MyWinsockControl.LocalIP
```

**LocalPort Property**   This property returns or sets the local port number. This property is read and write and is available at design time and runtime. The value returned is a long integer. An example of the syntax to read the property is:

```
myvar = MyWinsockControl.LocalPort
```

To set the property, you would use:

```
MyWinsockControl.LocalPort = 1001
```

An example of the use of this property is setting the port before using the Listen Method to set the port number for the application. This allows selection of the port at runtime or design time.

**Protocol Property**   This property returns or sets the protocol of either UDP or TCP. This property is read and write and is available at design time and runtime. (Note that at runtime the control must be closed—see the State Property entry later in this section.) The value returned is 0 or the constant sckTCPProtocol or 1 or sckUDPProtocol. An example of the syntax to read the property is:

```
myvar = MyWinsockControl.Protocol
```

To set the property, you would use:

```
MyWinsockControl.LocalPort = sckTCPProtocol
```

**RemoteHost Property**   This property returns or sets the Remote Host. This property is read and write and is available at design time and runtime. The value returned is a string and can be specified either as an IP address (XXX.XXX.XXX.XXX) or a friendly name such as www.microsoft.com. An example of the syntax to read the property is:

```
myvar = MyWinsockControl.RemoteHost
```

To set the property, you would use:

```
MyWinsockControl.RemoteHost = "192.143.29.47"
```

Setting this property at runtime allows the Remote Host to be selected when the application starts based upon some criteria.

**RemotePort Property**    This property returns or sets the remote port number. This property is read and write and is available at design time and runtime. The value returned is a long integer. An example of the syntax to read the property is:

```
myvar = MyWinsockControl.RemotePort
```

To set the property, you would use:

```
MyWinsockControl.RemotePort = 1001
```

This property can be used to select the application to be contacted at the remote host.

**State Property**    Returns the state of the control as expressed by an enumerated list. This property is read-only and is unavailable at design time. The State property is set by using various methods and events.

The syntax to read the property is:

```
myvar = MyWinsockControl.State
```

The settings for the State Property are:

| Constant | Value | Description |
| --- | --- | --- |
| sckClosed | 0 | Default Closed |
| sckOpen | 1 | Open |
| sckListening | 2 | Listening |
| sckConnectionPending | 3 | Connection pending |
| sckResolvingHost | 4 | Resolving host |
| sckHostResolved | 5 | Host resolved |
| sckConnecting | 6 | Connecting |
| sckConnected | 7 | Connected |
| sckClosing | 8 | Peer is closing the connection |
| sckError | 9 | Error |

Part

II

Ch

5

The State property will need to be checked before state changing methods are used. As an example, attempting to open a closed Winsock Control will result in an error.

# Methods

Methods are predefined functions that perform various tasks on the Control. There are methods that open and close a connection and accept a request for connection. Some of the important methods used with the Winsock Control are discussed here.

***Accept* Method**    This method is used for the TCP server applications only. It accepts the request for connection from a client system. For the Accept method to be used, the control must be in a Listening State. This method is used with the ConnectionRequest event, which is discussed later in this section.

The syntax is shown as:

```
Private Sub MyWinsockControl ConnectionREquest (ByVal requestID as Long)
    MyWinsockControl.Accept
End Sub
```

***Close* Method**    The Close Method is used to terminate a TCP connection from either the client or server application.

The syntax is:

```
MyWinsockControl.Close
```

***GetData* Method**    GetData is the method used to retrieve the current block of data from the buffer and store it in a variable of the variant type.

The syntax is:

```
MyWinsockControl.GetData myvar
```

***Listen* Method**    This method is invoked on the server application to have it wait for a TCP request for connection from a client system.

The syntax is:

```
MyWinsockControl.Listen
```

***SendData* Method**    The SendData method is used to dispatch data to the remote computer. It is used for both the client and server systems.

The syntax is:

```
MyWinsockControl.SendData myvar
```

# Events

Events are the triggers for the methods to be invoked. An example of an event is a mouse click. The events from other objects such as a command button are used to trigger some of the methods listed previously. The Winsock Control generates events that also may be used. Some of these events such as the ConnectionRequest event happen at the server system as a result of an action at the client system. The events generated by the Winsock Control make it possible for an unattended system to participate in a network communications session.

***Close* Event**    This event occurs when the remote computer closes the connection. The event can be used to do cleanup work at the end of a session.

The syntax is:

```
Private Sub MyWinsockControl_Close()
```

***Connect* Event**   This event occurs after the connection with the remote computer has been made.

The syntax is:

```
Private Sub MyWinsockControl_Connect()
```

***ConnectionRequest* Event**   This event occurs when the server receives a request for connection from a client system.

The syntax is:

```
Private Sub MyWinsockControl_ConnectionRequest(requestID As Long)
```

***DataArrival* Event**   This event occurs when new data arrives.

The syntax is:

```
Private Sub MyWinsockControl_DataArrival (ByVal bytesTotal As Long)
```

# Building the Client/Server Application

Building a client/server application is a little like talking to yourself. The client will always initiate the conversation and the server must provide appropriate answers. At any point, if either party does not keep the exchange going, the connection is broken and the conversation ends. If the conversation ends without the proper cleanup, the conversation cannot be reinitiated until the applications have been reset.

The sample application contained in this chapter is a simple form of chat with both the client and server able to send text to the other.

This is a simple application. There is no error trapping so the application is not robust. When an error occurs, both the client and the server must be closed and reopened. This way, you have all of the fun of adding the error trapping. All of the code for this application is on the companion CD and is yours to use.

The project is contained in the Chapter 5 directory. Both the Visual Basic projects and a compiled version of the programs are there.

When the project is started, two controls must be added to the default Visual Basic Tool Box. These are the RichTextBox Control and the Microsoft Winsock 5.0 Control. These are added by choosing Project, Components, and checking the two components in the list presented.

## Designing the Client Application

When the sample client application was designed, the decision was made that users would want to see their message and the reply in two separate test boxes. Rich Text Boxes were selected for the ability to use text formatting. The Rich Text Boxes were designated Inbound and Outbound. A command button was added to be used to initiate the connection.

Part

II

Ch

5

Two text boxes were added to enter the Remote Host name or IP and the Remote Port. This allows the host and port to be selected and set at runtime.

A final text box was added to display the local port number. This local port number can be read before the connection is created and after the connection is made.

Finally, a Microsoft Winsock Control 5.0. This Winsock Control will manage the communications between the client and server systems.

**Laying Out the Form**   The Visual Basic form for the client application at design time is shown in Figure 5.1. When the application is run, the Remote Host name or IP address needs to be entered and the Remote Port number needs to be entered before the Connect button is clicked. Once the connection is established, text may be entered in the Outbound Text box. When entered, it is automatically dispatched to the server application.

**FIG. 5.1**

Notice that the Winsock Control is visible at design time.

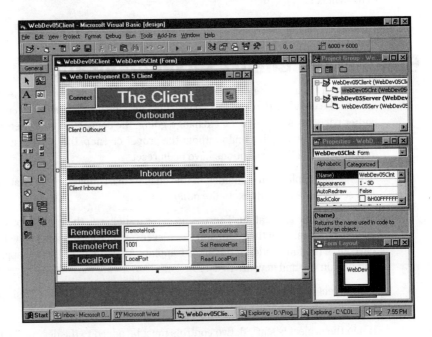

In Figure 5.2, the appearance of the form at runtime is the same as the design time appearance with the exception that the Winsock Control is not visible.

**Adding the Code**   In this section, you examine the code from the client application just as it is in the program. Notice the small amount of code required to create the functionality of the application. The addition of error handling would more than double the code. Here you can see the power of the Winsock Control. In a few lines of code, you accomplish full TCP/IP communication.

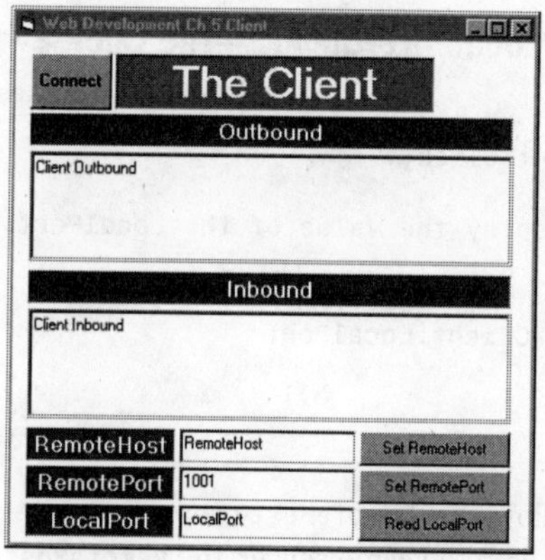

**FIG. 5.2**
The Remote Host and
Remote Port setting
must be entered before
the connection is
attempted in this
example program.

In Listing 5.1, a command button is used to initiate the connection. The Connect method is used. This method gathers the current values in two properties, the RemoteHost property and the RemotePort property, and creates the TCP message that will contact the Remote Host and request the connection. By setting two properties and calling one method, you have accomplished what can require hours or even days of programming to accomplish by using the Winsock API.

---

**Listing 5.1   Sub cmdConnect_Click()—The Click Event that Creates the Connection**

```
Option Explicit

Private Sub cmdConnect_Click()

    'The command button click event is used to create the connection.
    '    The connection request string is sent to the RemoteHost on the
    ➥RemotePort.
    '    The Connect method takes two arguements, in the form of
    '        object.Connect remoteHost, remotePort
    '    If the two properties are blank and the arguments are not supplied an
    ➥error occurs.
    '    The two properties were set in the Form_Load event which occurs
    '    prior to the Command_Click event.

    wskClient.Connect

End Sub
```

---

Part
II
Ch
5

Listing 5.2 shows the sub provided to allow you to see that the Local Port is set to 0 before the connection is made and will be set to a value selected by the system in the process of making the connection.

**Listing 5.2   Sub cmdReadLocalPort_Click()—The Click Event that Displays the Local Port Number**

```
Private Sub cmdReadLocalPort_Click()

    'This will read and display the value of the LocalPort property in
    '   txtLocalPort.Text

    txtLocalPort.Text = wskClient.LocalPort

End Sub
```

Listing 5.3 shows the sub that allows the RemoteHost property to be set at runtime. If the client is always going to communicate with the same server, the RemoteHost property can be set at design time.

**Listing 5.3   Sub cmdSetRemoteHost_Click()—The Click Event that Sets the *RemoteHost* Property**

```
Private Sub cmdSetRemoteHost_Click()

    'This will set the value of the RemoteHost property to the value in
    '   txtRemoteHost.Text

    wskClient.RemoteHost = txtRemoteHost.Text

End Sub
```

Listing 5.4 shows the sub that allows the RemotePort property to be set at runtime. If the client is always going to communicate with the same port number, the RemotePort property can be set at design time.

**Listing 5.4   Sub cmdSetRemotePort_Click()—The Click Event that Sets the *RemotePort* Property**

```
Private Sub cmdSetRemotePort_Click()

    'This will set the value of the RemotePort property to the value in
    '   txtRemotePort.Text

    wskClient.RemotePort = txtRemotePort.Text

End Sub
```

Listing 5.5 shows another method of setting the RemoteHost and RemotePort properties in code.

### Listing 5.5   Sub Form_Load()—The Form Load Event Can Be Used to Perform Initiation Tasks

```
Private Sub Form_Load()

    'The name of the Winsock control for the client is wskClient
    '    This name is the object when setting a property such as
    '    object.property or wskClient.Property

    'The name of the remote host can be set at design time in the
    '    properties dialog or it can be set at runtime in code.
    '    Either the IP address "XXX.XXX.XXX.XXX" or a host friendly
    '    name may be used such as "http://www.microsoft.com"
    '    The RemoteHost property has a data type of string.

    wskClient.RemoteHost = "SomeJunk"

    'The RemotePort property can be set at design time or in code at runtime.
    '    The RemotePort property has a data type of Long Integer.
    '    This is port number on which the Server will be listening.

    wskClient.RemotePort = 1002

End Sub
```

Using the Change event to send the entire contents of a Rich Text Box, as shown in Listing 5.6, is a technique that is quite inefficient since that entire message is retransmitted with each change in the contents. It does illustrate the simplicity of sending data with the SendData method.

### Listing 5.6   Sub rtbClntOutBound_Change()—The Change Event Is Used to Send Data

```
Private Sub rtbClntOutBound_Change()

    'The RichTextBox_Change event is being used to send data.  The contents of
➡the
    '    RichTextBox rtbClntOutBound will be transmitted each time the contents
➡of the
    '    Text property is changed.  The SendData method is used with the argument
➡of
    '    RichTextBox.Text

    wskClient.SendData rtbClntOutBound.Text

End Sub
```

Listing 5.7, is a two-step process of moving the data from the buffer into a variable and then placing the variable contents into the Text Property of the Rich Text Box. It can be placed directly into the Text property of the Rich Text Box.

**Listing 5.7  Sub wskClient_DataArrival(ByVal bytesTotal As Long)—The Data Arrival Event Is Used to Display the Data in a Text Box**

```
Private Sub wskClient_DataArrival(ByVal bytesTotal As Long)

    'The variable strData is declared to hold the incoming data.  It is stored
➥as
    '   a variant.

    Dim strData As String

    'The GetData method takes the data from the incoming buffer and places it in
    '   the strData variable.

    wskClient.GetData strData

    'The strData variable contents are placed in the RichTextBox
➥rtbClntInBound.Text
    '   property

    rtbClntInBound.Text = strData

End Sub
```

The salient feature of the client application program code is its simplicity. You can see the validity of the assertion made at the beginning of the chapter, that if you can write a "Hello World Application," you can use the Winsock Control.

# Designing the Server Application

When the sample server application was designed, its primary function was to service the needs of the client application. The application looks like a mirror of the client application, except that it cannot initiate a connection. Users will see their message and the reply in two separate text boxes. Rich Text Boxes were selected to correspond to the client application. The Rich Text Boxes were again designated Inbound and Outbound.

A text box was added to display the Remote Port number. This allows you to see that the Local Port on the client application and the Remote Port for the Server Application are the same.

Another text box was added to display the State Property of the Server. This changes from 2 (listening) to 7 (connected) as the application is run.

A final text box was added to automatically display the requestID sent by the Client Application or to be able to display the Local Port number for the server.

Of course, a Microsoft Winsock Control 5.0 is added to manage the communications between the client and server systems.

**Laying Out the Form**    The Visual Basic form for the Server Application at runtime is shown in Figure 5.3. When you run the application, the Server Application is in a Listening State. It waits for a connection to be initiated by a client system.

**FIG. 5.3**

There is no command button to initiate the connection on the Server Application form.

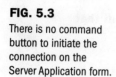

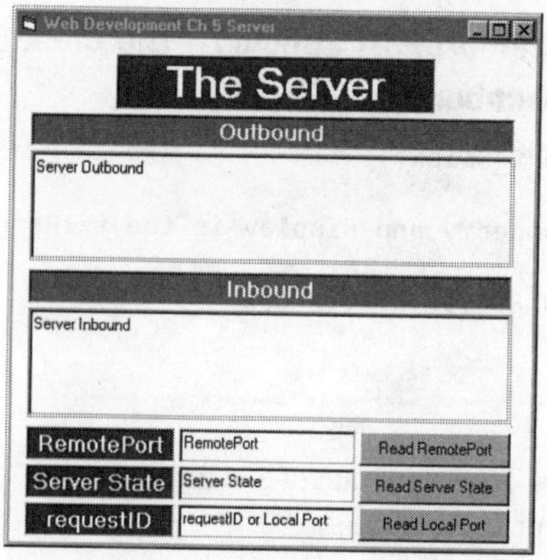

**Adding the Code**  In this section, you examine the code from the Server application. Since this is all of the code, notice the small amount of code that is required to create the functionality of the application. Adding error handling would at least double the total amount of code. Just as with the Client application, little code is required to use the power of the Winsock Control.

In Listing 5.8, a command button click event is used to display the Local Port number. Since this is set by the From Load event, it will read 1001 as set in Sub `Form_Load()` section.

**Listing 5.8  Sub cmdReadLocalPort_Click()— The Click Event that Displays the Local Port Number**

```
Option Explicit

Private Sub cmdReadLocalPort_Click()

    'This reads and displays the LocalPort property.

    txtrequestID.Text = wskServer.LocalPort

End Sub
```

The code in Listing 5.9 displays the remote port number. Display this number before and after the connection is made and you will see that the Remote Port number is set at the time the connection is made.

**Listing 5.9   Sub cmdReadRemotePort _Click()—The Click Event that Displays the Remote Port Number**

```
Private Sub cmdReadRemotePort_Click()

    'Read the RemotePort property and display in the txtRemotePort.

    txtRemotePort.Text = wskServer.RemotePort

End Sub
```

Server state is an enumerated list. A server state of 2 is listening and 7 is connected. The code in Listing 5.10 displays the current server state.

**Listing 5.10   Sub cmdReadServerState_Click()—The Click Event that Displays the Server State**

```
Private Sub cmdReadServerState_Click()

    'Read and Display the current Server State

    txtServerState.Text = wskServer.State

End Sub
```

The Form Load event is being used to set the local port number for the Server Winsock Control and to use the Listen method to place the Server application in a listening state as shown in Listing 5.11.

**Listing 5.11   Sub Form_Load()—The Form Load Event that Is Used to Set Various Properties**

```
Private Sub Form_Load()

    'The name of the Winsock control for the server is wskServer
    '    This name is the object when setting a property such as
    '    object.property or wskServer.Property

    'The LocalPort property can be set at design time or in code at runtime.
    '    The LocalPort property has a data type of Long Integer.
    '    This is port number on which the Server will be listening and must match
    '    the RemotePort property of the Client.

    wskServer.LocalPort = 1001

    'The Listen method is used to start the server monitoring incoming requests
    '    for a connection.
```

```
    wskServer.Listen

End Sub
```

Listing 5.12 shows the Rich Text Box change event being used to send data to the client application.

### Listing 5.12   Sub rtbServOutBound_Change()—The Rich Text Box Change Event that Is Used to Send Data

```
Private Sub rtbServOutBound_Change()

    'The RichTextBox_Change event is being used to send data.  The contents of
➥the
    '   RichTextBox rtbServOutBound will be transmitted each time the contents
➥of the
    '   Text property is changed.  The SendData method is used with the argument
➥of
    '   RichTextBox.Text

    wskServer.SendData rtbServOutBound.Text

End Sub
```

Listing 5.13 shows the ConnectionRequest event being used to open the connection. The Accept method establishes the connection. The request ID is also displayed in a text box.

### Listing 5.13   Sub wskServer_ConnectionRequest(ByVal requestID As Long)—The Connection Request Event that Is Used to Open the Connection

```
Private Sub wskServer_ConnectionRequest(ByVal requestID As Long)

    'Check to determine whether the WinSock Control's state is closed.
    '   If it is not, then close the control before using the Accept method.

    If wskServer.State <> sckClosed Then wskServer.Close

    'The control is now prepared to use the Accept method which will receive the
    '   ConnectionRequest from the Client.
    '   The argument for the Accept method is requestID

    wskServer.Accept requestID

    'The requestID is displayed

    txtrequestID.Text = requestID

End Sub
```

Listing 5.14 uses the DataArrival event to display the data in a Rich Text Box.

**Listing 5.14   Sub wskServer_DataArrival(ByVal bytesTotal As Long)—The Data Arrival Event that Is Used to Display the Data**

```
Private Sub wskServer_DataArrival(ByVal bytesTotal As Long)

    'The variable strData is declared to hold the incoming data.  It is stored
➥as
    '    a variant.

    Dim strData As String

    'The GetData method takes the data from the incoming buffer and places it in
    '    the strData variable.

    wskServer.GetData strData

    'The strData variable contents are placed in the RichTextBox
➥rtbClntInBound.Text
    '    property

    rtbServInBound.Text = strData

End Sub
```

As with the code for the client application, the code required for the server Winsock Control is only a few lines. This is a truly powerful control.

# Running the Client/Server Application

The client/server application can be run on the same system or two different systems on the same network. The application will run on a Windows NT 4.0 or Windows 95 system. The primary requirement is that TCP/IP be installed on the system and that the TCP/IP stack is running. This is usually not a problem on a Windows NT system. Occasionally, you may need to start the TCP/IP stack on a Windows 95 machine. One of the easiest ways to do this is to open a connection to your ISP (Internet Service Provider). This will start the TCP/IP stack on a Windows 95 machine and allow the Winsock Control to be used.

To run the application, go to the Chapter 5 directory on the CD with the Windows Explorer and double-click on both WebDev05Client.exe and WebDev05Server.exe. This will start both programs as shown in Figure 5.4.

When both programs are running, you will need to set the Remote Host name in the client application. This is accomplished by entering the name of the system or the IP address of the system running the Server application in the text box labeled Remote Host and clicking the Set RemoteHost button. The Set RemotePort button also needs to be clicked. Leave the default value of 1001. Now click the Connect button on the client application. A requestID number should appear in the requestID text box on the server system as shown in Figure 5.5.

**FIG. 5.4**

The programs can be run on two systems that are connected on a local network using the TCP/IP protocol.

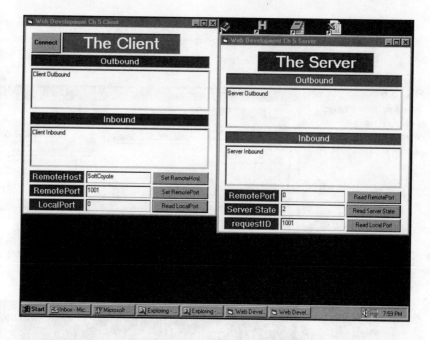

**FIG. 5.5**

The Read buttons at the bottom of the application windows can be used to show various properties.

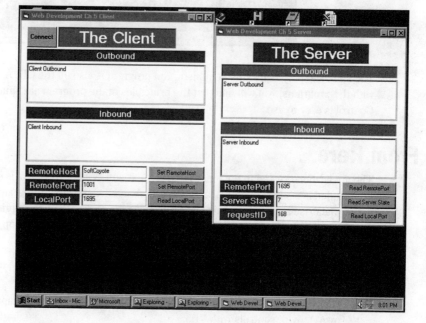

Part

II

Ch

5

You are now ready to use the application for its designed purpose, that is to be a simple chat application. By typing into the Outbound text boxes, you will see the information displayed in the Inbound box of the other application window as shown in Figure 5.6.

**FIG. 5.6**
The information entered is displayed on a character by character basis.

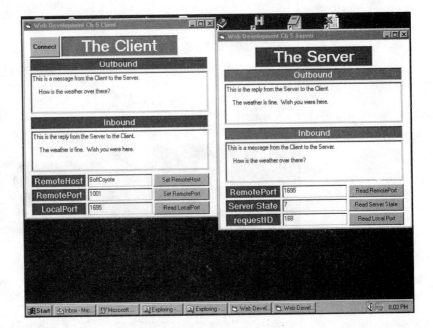

The code and project for this demonstration program is also on the CD. As you experiment with the programs, you will find that the principles of the program are simple. The Winsock Control is easy to use.

# From Here...

The application created to demonstrate the Microsoft Winsock Control is simple. It can easily be included in a VB ActiveX Document, or an ActiveX Control, or integrated with a client/server database application. This powerful application takes the heavy lifting out of TCP/IP programming. As you review the following chapters look for additional opportunities to use the Winsock Control. TCP/IP is now at your fingertips.

- Chapter 2, "Up and Running: Browser-Based VB Programming," explores the array of technologies available for use through a Web browser.
- Chapter 3, "Building ActiveX Controls with VB," examines your capability to build your own ActiveX controls with VB5.
- Chapter 10, "ActiveX Documents: Serving Up VB in a Web Browser," provides information on the use of ActiveX documents as a basis for wrapping Visual Basic Applications in the Internet Explorer Web Browser.

- Chapter 11, "Property Bags and Menus: Extending ActiveX Document Applications," delves into the use of property bags in the initialization of the ActiveX document and adding menus to the ActiveX document.

- Chapter 12, "Hyperlinks: Extending ActiveX Document Applications over Multiple Windows," reviews the use of hyperlinks to link to other ActiveX document applications.

Part
II

Ch
5

# Making Your ActiveX Controls Web-Friendly

**ActiveX security architecture**

Learn the security architecture for downloading ActiveX controls over the Internet.

**Internet component download**

Explore an approach for downloading and verifying executable objects over the Internet.

**Windows trust verification services**

Overview of the `WinVerifyTrust()` API, which provides a framework for certifying downloaded code.

**Sign your ActiveX Controls**

Use the SignCode and ChkTrust utilities to sign your ActiveX controls with your digital signature certificate, enabling the controls to be downloaded from the Web by users of the Authenticode control verification system.

**P**erhaps one of the most pernicious issues affecting the growth and development of Internet-based applications is security. The dynamic document revolution that ActiveX is a part of brings with it the downloadable, executable objects. Unlike when you go to your local software store and buy a shrink-wrapped software package, you can't be sure of the intentions of the software provider on the Internet. One of the greatest things about the Internet is that even the little guy can distribute software to the masses. However, it's harder to know all the little guys well enough to trust the software that their Web sites ask you to download.

The ActiveX framework addresses this more risky environment with an API, tools, and processes that give clients (Web browsers, for instance) the ability to permit downloads from trusted software providers and deny downloads to untrusted or unknown sources. ■

# Internet Component Download

Web browsers, such as Microsoft Internet Explorer 3.0 and other similar client applications, rely heavily on the Internet Component Download process. The WinVerifyTrust API provides the low-level support for these services.

The Internet Component Download specification provides for a safe mechanism to download executable content such as ActiveX Controls into Web browsers. Microsoft defines the Internet Component Download as a process consisting of the following steps:

1. Download the necessary files.
2. Call WinVerifyTrust API before permitting installation.
3. Self-register OLE components.
4. Add entries to the system registry to keep track of downloaded code.
5. Call CoGetClassObject for the appropriate CLSID.

Let's take a few moments with each of these steps and look at a few details.

## Packing Files for Download

In the typical Web browser download scenario, the <OBJECT> tag triggers a request for a downloadable component. The <OBJECT> tag includes a CODE attribute that indicates the location of the component to be downloaded. The Internet Component Download anticipates three different types of downloadable files, as shown in Table 6.1.

**Table 6.1   Types of Files to Download**

| File Type | Description |
| --- | --- |
| Portable executable | A single file OLE control |
| Cabinet file | A multiple file OLE control package with setup instructions |
| .INF file | A text file describing download and installation instructions |

**Working with Portable Executable Files**   The portable executable, or PE, is a stand-alone .OCX or .DLL file. Of course, because the file is itself executable, no additional file compression can be used. This method is used for compact, simple ActiveX Controls.

Note that the Internet Component Download process can rely on the MIME type to determine the appropriate treatment of the PE file. Table 6.2 summarizes the appropriate MIME types.

**Table 6.2   MIME Types for PE Files**

| MIME Type | Description |
| --- | --- |
| application/x-pe_win32_x86 | A portable executable built for Windows NT or Windows 95 on the Intel x86 platform |

| MIME Type | Description |
|-----------|-------------|
| application/x-pe_win32_ppc | A portable executable built for Windows NT or Windows 95 on the PowerPC platform |
| application/x-pe_win32_mips | A portable executable built for Windows NT or Windows 95 on the MIPS platform |
| application/x-pe_win32_alpha | A portable executable built for Windows NT or Windows 95 on the DEC Alpha platform |
| application/x-pe_mac_ppc | A portable executable built for Macintosh on the PowerPC platform |

**Working with Cabinet Files**   Some ActiveX control applications require more than one file. Installation instructions can be somewhat involved. For situations like this, the Internet Component Download process provides for the so-called "cabinet file" (.CAB). Cabinet files must include an .INF information file that describes the installation procedure. Best of all, the cabinet file permits file compression reducing bandwidth requirements during download.

Note that the Internet Component Download process can rely on the MIME type to determine the appropriate treatment of the cabinet file. Table 6.3 summarizes the appropriate MIME types.

**Table 6.3   MIME Types for .CAB Files**

| MIME Type | Description |
|-----------|-------------|
| application/x-cabinet_win32_x86 | A cabinet file built for Windows NT or Windows 95 on the Intel x86 platform |
| application/x-cabinet_win32_ppc | A cabinet file built for Windows NT or Windows 95 on the x86 platform |
| application/x-cabinet_win32_mips | A cabinet file built for Windows NT or Windows 95 on the MIPS platform |
| application/x-cabinet_win32_alpha | A cabinet file built for Windows NT or Windows 95 on the DEC Alpha platform |
| application/x-cabinet_mac_ppc | A cabinet file built for Macintosh on the PowerPC platform |

Part
II

Ch
6

Making cabinet files is really quite simple. If you want to control the building of a cabinet file, the ActiveX SDK includes a utility called DIANTZ.EXE built for just this purpose. Listing 6.1. shows the command-line prototype for the DIANTZ.EXE.

**N O T E**   If you would rather let an automated utility build cabinet files for you, the Visual Basic Application Setup Wizard builds cabinet files for ActiveX controls built using Visual Basic. This process is explained in Chapter 3, "Building ActiveX Controls with VB." ■

### Listing 6.1   Command-Line for the DIANTZ.EXE Application

```
DIANTZ [/V[n]] [/D var=value ...] [/L dir] source [destination]
DIANTZ [/V[n]] [/D var=value ...] /F directive_file [...]

    source          File to compress.
    destination     File name to give compressed file. If omitted, the
                    last character of the source file name is replaced
                    with an underscore (_) and used as the destination.
    /F directives   A file with Diamond directives (may be repeated).
    /D var=value    Defines variable with specified value.
    /L dir          Location to place destination (default is current directory).
    /V[n]           Verbosity level (1..3).
```

Generally, you construct a directive file (with an extension of .DDF) that holds the instructions for creating the cabinet file. Listing 6.2 shows an example of such a directive file.

### Listing 6.2   Directive File for DIANTZ.EXE

```
;----------------------------------------------------------
;-- Directive file for generating Cabinet file
;----------------------------------------------------------
.Option Explicit
.Set CabinetNameTemplate=MyCabinet.CAB
.Set Cabinet=on
.Set Compress=on
MyInfFile.INF
MyActiveXControl.OCX
```

You can try building a .CAB file by taking the following steps:

1. Create a new directory as a temporary working space for creating your cabinet file. The directory \activex\thedisk\NewCh6 was used in this example.

2. Put an ActiveX control file in your temporary working directory. Any .OCX file will do. In this example, a fictitious ActiveX control file called MyActiveXControl.OCX was used.

3. Next, create a file called MyInfFile.INF. Using Notepad or some other text editor, enter the code as shown in Listing 6.3. Save your .INF file.

### Listing 6.3   MYINFFILE.INF—Contents of the MyInfFile.INF File

```
;----------------------------------------
;-- MyInfFile INF file
;----------------------------------------
[Add.Code]
MyActiveXControl.ocx=MyActiveXControl.ocx


;------------------------------------------------
;-- MyActiveXControl.OCX can be found at
;-- the provided URL
```

```
;----------------------------------------------------
[MyActiveXControl.ocx]
file=http://www.somewhere.com/over/the/rainbow/MyCabinet.cab
FileVersion=1,0,0,0
```

4. Next, create a file called MyCabinet.ddf. Using Notepad, enter the code shown in Listing 6.4.

**Listing 6.4   MYCABINET.DDF—A Cabinet Definition File**

```
;------------------------------------------------------
;-- Directive file for generating Cabinet file
;------------------------------------------------------
.Option Explicit
.Set CabinetNameTemplate=MyCabinet.CAB
.Set Cabinet=on
.Set Compress=on
MyInfFile.INF
MyActiveXControl.OCX
```

5. From the command-line, enter the DIANTZ command as shown in Listing 6.5. Press Enter and DIANTZ builds your cabinet file for you.

**Listing 6.5   Starting the *DIANTZ* Command**

```
C:\MSDEV\INETSDK\BIN\DIANTZ.EXE /F MyCabinet.ddf
```

The DIANTZ executable creates two diagnostic files (setup.inf and setup.rpt), as well as a directory called disk1 where the new cabinet file is stored. The setup files show various statistics concerning the cabinet file.

**Working with .INF Files**   The .INF installation file describes which files need to be downloaded or retrieved from the cabinet. This file also provides installation instructions for the files contained in the cabinet.

Note that the Internet Component Download process can rely on the MIME type to determine the appropriate treatment of the .INF file. The MIME type for a stand-alone .INF file is application/x-setupscript.

Take a look at Listing 6.6 which shows a sample .INF file.

**Listing 6.6   An Example of an .INF File**

```
;-----------------------------------------
;-- Sample INF file
;-----------------------------------------
[Add.Code]
MyActiveXControl.ocx=MyActiveXControl.ocx
```

*Part*

**II**

*Ch*

**6**

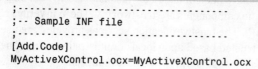

*continues*

**Listing 6.6 Continued**

```
NeedsThis.dll=NeedsThis.dll
mfc40.dll=mfc40.dll


;----------------------------------------------
;-- MyActiveXControl.OCX can be found in the
;-- in the cabinet file at the provided URL
;----------------------------------------------
[MyActiveXControl.ocx]
file=http://www.somewhere.com/over/the/rainbow/MyCabinet.cab
clsid={94EF87GG-634R-929C-23FE-00444ECE293}
FileVersion=1,0,0,0


;----------------------------------------------
;-- NeedsThis.dll can be found in the
;-- in the cabinet file at the provided URL
;----------------------------------------------
[NeedsThis.dll]
file=http://www.somewhere.com/way/up/high/NeedsThis.dll
FileVersion=
DestDir=10


;----------------------------------------------
;-- mfc40.dll must be present, if not the
;-- the installation will fail
;----------------------------------------------
[mfc40.dll]
file=
FileVersion=4,0,0,5
```

Notice the `DestDir` parameter used in the NeedsThis.dll section of the .INF file. This parameter can be set to either 10 or 11. The number 10 indicates that this file should be downloaded to the \WINDOWS directory. If you select the number 11, the downloaded files are placed in the \WINDOWS\SYSTEMS directory.

The other important thing to notice in the .INF file is the `file=` notation in the mfc40.dll section. This entry implies that mfc40.dll version 4.0.0.5 is required to use the downloadable component. However, if this DLL is not available on the local system, the required DLL is not downloaded. Instead, the download operation fails.

Regardless of which type of file you choose to use for your downloaded objects, the download occurs asynchronously.

# Using WinVerifyTrust to Permit Installation

After the proper information and files have been obtained for installation, the next step in the process is to obtain verification that the components are trustworthy. The WinVerifyTrust API is really an extension of the Win32 API. The trust verification services provided are used to determine whether an object can be trusted based upon local administrative policy. The trust model on which WinVerifyTrust is based begins with three basic concepts:

- Trusted authority
- Trust administrator
- Trust provider

A trusted authority is an organization or entity that can be trusted to provide safe objects. For instance, your corporate MIS department would be considered a trusted authority to provide business applications for employees. You might also consider companies that sell shrink-wrapped products to be trusted to deliver safe copies of the products they sell.

A trust administrator holds the decision-making power to determine whether a given organization or entity is considered a trusted authority. The trust administrator can even decide not to trust entities that include digital certificates that guarantee the identity of an entity. Say, for example, a certain software vendor is known to have an infected application in distribution. The trust administrator might decide that local policy prevents software from that vendor to be downloaded and installed.

A trust provider is a software implementation for local trust policy. In essence, a trust provider supplies the logic for determining whether a particular action is permissible via local policy. We discuss this more carefully in a moment.

Trust verification services are actually implemented for "subjects" and "actions." The service evaluates the trustworthiness of a subject based upon the action that's requested using the WinVerifyTrust function. Listing 6.7 shows the declaration of this important function for the WinBASE.h file in the ActiveX SDK.

---

### Listing 6.7   WINBASE.H—Declaration of *WinVerifyTrust*

```
/////////////////////////////////////////////////////////////////////
//                                                                 //
//              Trust API and Structures                           //
//                                                                 //
/////////////////////////////////////////////////////////////////////

WINBASEAPI
LONG
WINAPI
WinVerifyTrust(
    HWND    hwnd,
    DWORD   dwTrustProvider,
    DWORD   dwActionID,
    LPVOID  ActionData
    );
```

---

There are four parameters supplied to the WinVerifyTrust function. If user intervention (and therefore, a user interface) is needed to determine whether trust should be granted, the hWnd parameter is expected to be the handle to the appropriate interactive window. Note that determination of trust is intended to be a largely transparent exercise. Use of direct user interaction should be discouraged. The dwTrustProvider specifies the trust provider is to be utilized to determine whether the subject should be trusted for the requested action. The requested action is specified in the `dwActionID` parameter. The possible values for the `dwActionID` are dependent upon the individual trust provider making the decision. Any additional information required by the trust provider must be passed in the `dwActionData` parameter. The content and meaning of the information passed is determined by the value of `dwActionID` and the individual trust provider.

# Signing Your Controls

When it comes to placing active controls on a user's machine, through embedding them on a Web page so that the controls are automatically downloaded, the issue of security is raised in the minds of lots of users. How do users know that the control is safe to run, and doesn't contain a virus that will wipe out the contents of their hard drive? How can you reassure users that your control won't scan their hard drive, find their online banking records, and upload them to your server? The fact is, they don't know that your control won't cause them any harm, and there's little you can do to reassure them.

ActiveX controls, by their very nature (the fact that they have full access to the computer on which the control is running), have the capability to cause untold damage to a user's computer. A good example of this that has gotten a lot of publicity is Fred McLain's "exploder" control (available from **http://www.halcyon.com/mclain/ActiveX/welcome.html**), which doesn't actually cause any damage to the user's computer, but does shut it down (cleanly). Microsoft's answer to this trust problem is to place signed certificates in each control, as can be seen in Figure 6.1. Unfortunately, as McLain's control demonstrates, the certificate only proves that the control has not been modified or corrupted, not that the original creator did not have bad intent. This issue boils down to whether the user trusts the creator of the control. For large companies like Microsoft, this has little impact; most users still trust controls created by them. But for programmers like Joe Jones, how many users know who he is, much less trust that he writes safe controls?

**FIG. 6.1**

Microsoft Internet Explorer showing the certificate for the WinFrame ActiveX control, which was issued by Verisign. This certificate shows that the control has not been modified or tampered with between the time that the developer compiled it and the time you received it.

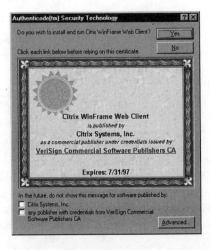

**N O T E** Most of the certificate issuing companies have policies that programmers have to follow to receive certificates for the controls they have created. However, these policies are again a matter of trust. The certificate issuing company does not examine or test your control before issuing a certificate. It is only after the fact, when the company receives complaints, that it takes action, which is limited to requesting that the owner of the control remove it from public accessibility or face possible legal action. There is no way possible for the certificate issuing company to remove the certificate from these controls that have already received certificates. It is up to the programmer to remove the certificate. However, an undocumented enhancement to Internet Explorer 3.1 is to automatically check with the Certificate Authority to determine if a certificate has been revoked. As of the time of this writing, the legal and liability issues surrounding this whole area have not been established, so this remains a murky legal area. ■

**N O T E** Microsoft's position in the issue of signing controls with certificates is that, if users can reliably know who the developer is that developed a specific control, the developer can be held responsible for the control. Because of this heightened level of accountability, Microsoft believes that developers will be very reluctant to build and sign hostile controls. ■

Now that you understand what your browser is doing "behind the scenes" to verify that your ActiveX control is safe to run on your computer, how do you place a certificate on your controls so that users know your controls are safe? When you visit a site that contains ActiveX controls, your browser displays a certificate that tells you who wrote the control, who verified that person or company, and that the control has not been altered or corrupted since it was originally signed. If you visit a site that contains unsigned controls, you are likely to see a window like the one in Figure 6.2, informing you that the control is a potential security risk.

**FIG. 6.2**
If you come across an unsigned ActiveX control, your browser will warn you with a dialog stating that the control is a security risk.

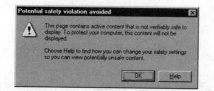

## Getting a Digital Certificate

Getting your own digital certificate is really fairly simple. First, you need to have Internet Explorer 3.0 or higher (the digital ID center at Verisign states that you have to be using the newest version of IE), a credit card, and various other pieces of personal information about yourself. After you have all of this information together, hop on the Web and visit Verisign at **http://www.verisign.com/**. After you are at Verisign's home page, you want to go to its Digital ID Center, shown in the upper-right corner of Figure 6.3.

**FIG. 6.3**

Verisign's home page, showing the entrance to its Digital ID Center in the upper-right corner.

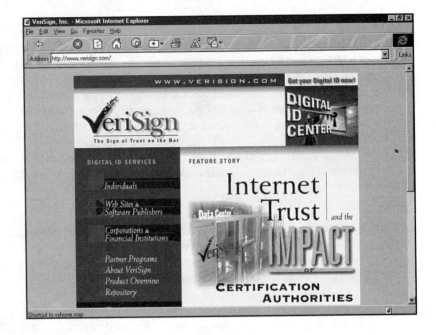

**N O T E**   You need to be running Internet Explorer to apply for a software publishing digital certificate, because the ID process requires certain ActiveX controls to be downloaded to your computer. You also need to be aware that the digital certificate that will be issued to you is tied to the copy of Internet Explorer you are using to acquire the certificate. If you ever reinstall Internet Explorer or switch to a different machine, you need to apply for a new certificate. If you will be signing controls on multiple machines, you need one certificate for each machine. You cannot copy a single certificate to multiple machines. ▪

After you are in the Verisign Digital ID center, you need to choose Enroll and then select Software Publisher. At this point, you are presented with a lot of information about digital certificates and Microsoft's Authenticode technology. This page provides all of the information that you need to be prepared to give while applying for a certificate, as well as the current fees for a certificate (at this time, an individual certificate costs $20 a year). At the bottom of the page is a Continue button, where you start the enrollment process and begin providing information about yourself.

The process of applying for a digital certificate is fairly simple and self-explanatory with everything well-marked. But don't try to rush through the process, as you need to read everything carefully so you know what you are committing yourself to. There are also a couple of steps that take awhile, and you need to be aware of that so you don't quit the process thinking you are stuck. After you have finished the process, Verisign e-mails you an ID serial number, which you use to retrieve your certificate from Verisign's site. The whole process takes some time, but you can get your certificate within a couple of hours.

**N O T E**   At the time of writing this chapter, Verisign is the primary Certificate Authority authorized to issue Authenticode certificates for use in code signing. Another Certificate Authority at this time is GTE at **http://www.gte.com/**. There will probably be even more Certificate Authorities available in the near future. You can get a list of current Certificate Authorities at **http://www.microsoft.com/ workshop/prog/security/authcode/certs.htm**. ■

**TIP**   During the process of applying for a certificate, you generate a public/private encryption key pair. It is not a good idea to keep your private key on your hard drive. If your private key is kept on a floppy drive, it is much more difficult for someone else to steal or corrupt your private key. If someone is able to steal your private key, that person could have the ability to corrupt your signed controls and generate a new hash so that the control looks to users' browsers like it hasn't been tampered with. This would be very difficult to do, but the potential is there.

## Signing a Control

Once you have your digital certificate, you need to download the ActiveX SDK from Microsoft's Web site at **http://www.microsoft.com/workshop/prog/sdk/**. After you have the SDK unzipped and have run the install routine, you find a couple of utilities in the BIN subdirectory where you installed the SDK. These utilities are all intended to be run from the DOS-prompt, so you need to change directory (CD) into the BIN directory to run these utilities.

The first one of these utilities is called SignCode, and it applies your digital certificate to your control. This utility has a large number of options that can be specified on the command line, or you can just run it without providing any information on the command line. If you do not provide any arguments to SignCode, it presents you with a code signing wizard, which walks you through all of the information needed with the following steps:

1. The first information the wizard asks for is the control that you want to sign, the name of the control, and an URL where users can get more information about the control, as seen in Figure 6.4. You need to specify the cabinet file (.CAB) that was created by the Setup Wizard as the control to be signed.

**Part II Ch 6**

**FIG. 6.4**
In the first window in the code signing wizard, you specify the control and the control name.

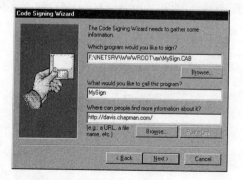

2. The next step asks you to provide your digital certificate and your private key. This step also allows you to choose between two hashing algorithms to be used to verify that your control has not been tampered with. This step is shown in Figure 6.5.

**FIG. 6.5**

The next window in the code signing wizard asks for your digital certificate and private key.

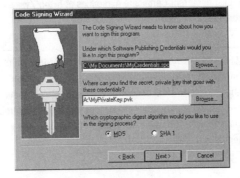

3. This last step asks you to verify all of the information that is used in signing the control, as shown in Figure 6.6.

**FIG. 6.6**

The code signing wizard asks you to verify the information to be embedded in the control before the control is signed.

4. When you are satisfied with all of the information used to sign your control, you select the Sign button on the wizard, and the wizard applies your digital certificate to your control. After the wizard is finished, it informs you that your control has been signed, as shown in Figure 6.7.

**FIG. 6.7**

The code signing wizard informs the user that the control was signed.

**N O T E** If you make any changes or updates to your control, you need to repackage it using the Setup Wizard and resign the control using the SignCode utility.

# Verifying a Signed Control

After you have signed your control, you need to verify that your control was actually signed. You can do this by placing your control (and Web page) on a Web server and trying to download it into a Web browser. That's an awful lot of unnecessary work; however, and it might not work because your computer might determine that the control doesn't need to be downloaded because there is a local copy already on the hard drive. Instead, you can use another utility that is included in the ActiveX SDK called ChkTrust.

ChkTrust does not have a wizard to walk you through, but it's simple enough that it doesn't need one. ChkTrust needs to be run from the command-line, where it requires two parameters to be passed. The first parameter is a flag that informs ChkTrust what kind of file it's verifying—a cabinet file, a PE file, or a Java class file. The flags for these file types can be found in Table 6.4. The second argument is the name of the control file, complete with the path name of where the file can be found. The ChkTrust command looks something like the following:

```
ChkTrust -c F:\Inetsrv\wwwroot\ax\Mysign.CAB
```

### Table 6.4    The File Type Flags for the ChkTrust Utility

| Flag | File Type |
| --- | --- |
| -c | Cabinet file |
| -i | PE file |
| -j | Java class file |

If the control contains a valid certificate, the ChkTrust utility displays the certificate, as shown in Figure 6.8.

**FIG. 6.8**
The ChkTrust utility displays the certificate for the control that it is being used to verify.

# From Here...

In this chapter, you learned about how ActiveX controls can specify any dependent files that need to be downloaded along with the actual control and how those files are packaged such that your Web browser can find and download all of them. You also took a look at how the security mechanism works in ActiveX controls, to verify that they have not been corrupted or altered in any way. Finally, you learned how you can sign your own controls using freely available tools that can be downloaded from Microsoft's Web site.

From here, you might want to enroll yourself with Verisign (or another Certificate Authority), get yourself a digital certificate, and start signing those controls that you have been building so that you can begin placing them in Web pages. This allows you to spice up your Web site with any control that you might dream up. You also might want to check out the following additional subjects:

- To learn how to package up your controls using the Application Setup Wizard, read Chapter 3, "Building ActiveX Controls with VB."
- To see how you can interact with VBScript to extend the functionality of your control to the Web page, check out Chapter 8, "Interacting with ActiveX Controls and VBScript."
- To learn how you can replace a Web page with an actual Visual Basic application, be sure to read Chapter 10, "ActiveX Documents: Serving Up VB in a Web Browser."

# Scripting

# Using VBScript to Build HTML-Based VB Applications

**H**TML elements provide a rich and compelling way for users to interact with Web sites. Sites that can accept user input and provide visual and aural responses are fast becoming the most popular stops on the Information SuperHighway. HTML elements combined with VBScript allow users to extend the scope and functionality of Web pages to include a higher degree of interactivity and control than was previously possible without incurring a lot of client/server transactional overhead. And, when users employ VBScript to bring life into their site, they build upon skills already developed from previous experience programming with Visual Basic.

In the following pages, you'll learn about the most fundamental of all HTML elements—the <FORM> element. You'll look at the essential elements of the <FORM> element. After learning the basics, you'll put it all together and use these HTML elements. Then, you'll learn about the Internet Explorer Intrinsic Controls. You'll extend your understanding of the Intrinsic Controls to include Event Handlers and Procedures. Finally, you'll apply VBScript to HTML elements. ■

**Interactive Web pages**

Learn how to change a static Web page into an interactive, dynamic page by using VBScript and the Internet Explorer Object Model.

**HTML Form Elements**

Learn how to leverage your knowledge of the Visual Basic standard controls to use the HTML 2.0 Form Elements.

**Microsoft Forms Intrinsic Controls**

Learn to go beyond the HTML form elements with the Internet Explorer Instrinsic Controls.

**Writing procedures in VBScript**

Learn to enhance and extend your VBScript with Event Handlers and user-defined Subs and Functions.

# Understanding the HTML *<FORM>* Elements

In its original state an HTML form is used by a Web page to collect and organize data to be returned to an Internet Server. Over time, HTML forms have evolved far beyond their original intention. Although you can still use HTML forms to do standard CGI-based, client/server, and Web-based interactions over the Internet, with the help of a scripting language such as JavaScript or VBScript, you can also use them to analyze and process data on the client side. Thus, you reduce the transactional burdens you place on your server-side programming, making your code more concise and robust.

**N O T E**   The Common Gateway Interface (CGI)is a specification that defines a set of standards by which data enters and leaves an Internet server consistently and predictably. Originally developed for the UNIX environment, CGI is used for Internet-based data processing and decision-making routines such as queries and lookups. Programs that do this sort of server-side processing are called CGI scripts. Usually, they are written in a language such as Perl or C.  n

▶ **See** Appendix A, "Standard CGI, WinCGI, and Visual Basic," for more information about CGI, on **p. 851**

## The *<FORM>* Element

HTML forms begin with the tag, `<FORM>` and ends with the tag, `</FORM>`. The `<FORM>` element takes the format:

```
<FORM ACTION = URL METHOD= post (or get) NAME=aname>
.
.
.
</FORM>
```

Where:

`ACTION` is the server-side Uniform Resource Locator to which the form's data will be passed. Typically, this is a CGI script. However, with the emergence of Microsoft's Active Server Pages initiative, many more URL's are referencing an Active Server Page.

`METHOD` is the way that the data is passed. You can choose from either the `POST` method or the `GET` method. (For a detailed discussion of the `GET` and `POST` methods see Appendix A.)

`NAME` is a user-defined ID that identifies the form. This feature is particularly useful when you have Web pages that contain more than one form.

Thus:

```
<FORM ACTION=http://www.mysite.com/cgi-bin/myscript.exe METHOD=post NAME=myform>
.
.
.
</FORM>
```

denotes a form that will pass its data to a CGI script, `myscript.exe` on the server, `www.mysite.com`. The form will use the POST method. The name of the form is myform.

Forms are parent elements. This means that the information they gather is generated by other HTML elements that live between the `<FORM>` and `</FORM>` tags. An element that lives within a `<FORM>` is called a *child element*. This notion of parent and child elements becomes very important when you work with VBScript or JavaScript and the IE Object Model.

You can have more than one form on a page. The NAME attribute of the form will delineate one form from another. Figure 7.1 shows the HTML for a Web Page with two forms, frmAnimal and frmStooge. Figure 7.2 shows what the HTML looks like when viewed in Internet Explorer.

**FIG. 7.1**
The *<FORM>* element is
the basic building block
for using HTML
elements.

Opening HTML code ——

```
<HTML>
<HEAD>
<TITLE>Form Sample</TITLE>
</HEAD>
<BODY BGCOLOR=#FFFFFF>

<BR><FONT SIZE=5 FACE=TIMES COLOR=#00218C>
Form Sample
</FONT>
<BR>
<HR>
```

Code for frmAnimal ——

```
<FORM ACTION=../cgi-win/animal.exe METHOD=post NAME=frmAnimal>

<FONT SIZE=4 FACE=TIMES COLOR=Red>
Select Animals
</FONT>

<SELECT MULTIPLE NAME="Animals">
<OPTION VALUE="pig">Pig
<OPTION VALUE="goat">Goat
<OPTION VALUE="horse">Horse
</SELECT>
<BR>
<INPUT TYPE=Submit Value="Submit Animal" NAME=Submit>
</FORM>
```

Code for frmStooge ——

```
<FORM ACTION=../cgi-win/stooge.exe METHOD=post NAME=frmStooge>

<FONT SIZE=4 FACE=TIMES COLOR=Blue>
Choose a Stooge<P>
</FONT>

<INPUT TYPE=RADIO NAME=opStoog VALUE=Moe>Moe<BR>
<INPUT TYPE=RADIO NAME=opStooge VALUE=Larry>Larry<BR>
<INPUT TYPE=RADIO NAME=opStooge VALUE=Curly>Curly<BR>
<INPUT TYPE=RADIO NAME=opStooge VALUE=Shemp>Shemp<BR>
<INPUT TYPE=Submit Value="Submit Stooge" NAME=Submit>
</FORM>
```

Closing HTML code ——

```
<HR>
</BODY>
</HTML>
```

Part
**III**

Ch
**7**

**FIG. 7.2**

HTML elements look and behave very much like the standard Visual Basic controls.

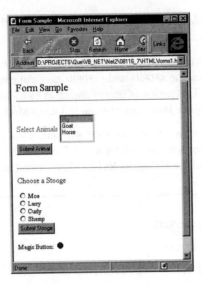

## The *<INPUT>* Element

The <INPUT> elements are what you provide to the user into which they enter form data and trigger a submission of the form's data on to a server on the Internet.

HTML has a standard set of <INPUT> *types* just as VB has a standard set of controls that you adapt to a particular purpose. And, as with VB control properties, each <INPUT> element has attributes that you configure to accommodate a particular layout need.

The <INPUT> element attributes are shown in Table 7.1

**Table 7.1   *<INPUT>* Element Attributes**

| Attribute | Description |
| --- | --- |
| NAME | Defines name of <INPUT>'s data, similar to a variable name. |
| VALUE | <INPUT>'s data, similar to the value of a variable. |
| TYPE | Defines the type of <INPUT> element for example, Text, Radio, Checkbox, and so on. |
| MAXLENGTH | Specifies the maximum number of characters permitted to be entered in an <INPUT>'s field. |
| SIZE | Defines the size (width) of the <INPUT>'s field. Used for Text or Password. |
| CHECKED | Sets a check in a check box or sets a radio to true. |

The <INPUT> element types (see Listing 7.1) are as follows:

**Text**  You use the Text type to allow the user to enter textual data (see Figure 7.3).

---

**Listing 7.1   ELEMENTS.HTM—HTML for *<INPUT>* Type, Text**

```
Name: <INPUT TYPE=Text NAME=txtMain VALUE="Enter your name here"
       SIZE=40 MAXLENGTH=36>
```

---

**FIG. 7.3**
You can set a default value for *<INPUT TYPE=Text>* by setting the *VALUE* to the data you want to show as default.

Name: Enter your name here

**Password**  A Password type (see Listing 7.2) is similar to a Text <INPUT> element type, but the characters that the user enters are masked with asterisks (see Figure 7.4). Though the type does offer some measure of security, the type's security can be breached with little difficulty if you do NOT have a secure transaction.

**N O T E**  A secure transaction involves using a Secure Sockets Layer (SSL) on the Web Server, so that all information passed between the Web browser and Web server is encrypted. ■

---

**Listing 7.2   ELEMENTS.HTM—The Password <INPUT> Type**

```
Password: <INPUT TYPE=Password NAME=pswMain>
```

---

**FIG. 7.4**
Using a Password *<INPUT>* type does NOT necessarily mean total password security.

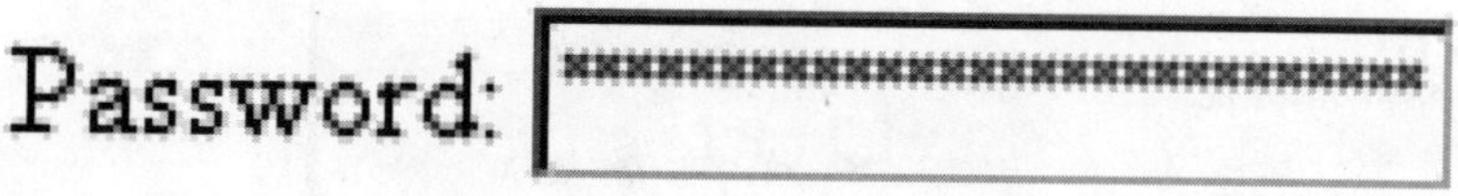

Password: ************************************

**Submit**  The Submit button is the <INPUT> type you use to create a button that, when clicked, will trigger the submission of a form's data to a server on the Internet (see Listing 7.3). The browser will show the caption of the Submit type to be the string, "Submit," unless the VALUE is assigned another string see Figure 7.5.

Part

**III**

Ch

**7**

---

**Listing 7.3   ELEMENTS.HTM—The Submit *<INPUT>* Type**

```
<INPUT TYPE=Submit Value="Submit Profile" NAME=Submit>
```

---

**FIG. 7.5**

You can customize the caption of the Submit <INPUT> type by changing the VALUE= data.

**Reset** The Reset type (see Listing 7.4) creates a button that, when clicked, clears the data (see Figure 7.5) from all fields on an HTML form and returns the fields to their default settings.

**Listing 7.4 ELEMENTS.HTM—The HTML Syntax for the Reset <INPUT> Type**

```
<INPUT TYPE=Reset Value="Clear Profile" NAME=Reset>
```

**FIG. 7.6**

You can custom configure the Reset caption by adjusting the VALUE= attribute.

**Button** This feature creates a button (see Listing 7.5) that can be referenced with VBScript or JavaScript (see Figure 7.6). You can't really use this <INPUT> type in standard, non-scripted HTML.

**Listing 7.5 ELEMENTS.HTM—Creating a Go Back Button Using the Button <INPUT> Type and VBScript**

```
<INPUT TYPE=Button Value="Go Back" NAME=cmdBack
   LANGUAGE=VBScript OnClick=History.Back>
```

**FIG. 7.7**

Button <INPUT> types can be used pretty easily with VBScript or JavaScript.

**Radio** Radio buttons are used to make exclusive choices (see Listing 7.6). They are used much the same way that you use an Option control in VB (see Figure 7.8). The tricky thing about Radio <INPUT> types is to understand that in order to group a set of Radio types to be exclusive of one another, all Radio types to be grouped *must* have the same value attached to their NAME attribute. When you submit the form, only the VALUE of the chosen Radio type will be sent to the server.

**Listing 7.6   ELEMENTS.HTM—A Group of Two Radio <INPUT> Types**

```
<B>Your gender:</B><BR>
<INPUT TYPE=RADIO NAME=opMain VALUE=Male CHECKED>Male<BR>
<INPUT TYPE=RADIO NAME=opMain VALUE=Female>Female<BR>
```

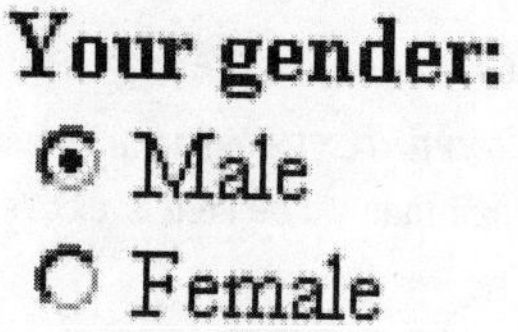

**FIG. 7.8**

If you want to set a default Radio, include the *CHECKED* attribute when you define the *<INPUT>* tag.

## Your gender:

⊙ Male

○ Female

**Check Box**   Check boxes (see Listing 7.7) are used to make inclusive choices. The value of the NAME attribute for each check box must be different. When you submit the form, if a check box is checked (see Figure 7.9), its name-value pair will be sent to the server.

**Listing 7.7   ELEMENTS.HTM—A Group of Four Check Boxes**

```
<B>Have you had:</B><BR>
<INPUT TYPE=CHECKBOX NAME=ckMumps>Mumps<BR>
<INPUT TYPE=CHECKBOX  NAME=ckMeasles>Measles<BR>
<INPUT TYPE=CHECKBOX NAME=ckChickePox >ChickPox<BR>
<INPUT TYPE=CHECKBOX  NAME=ckNone CHECKED>No Disease<BR>
```

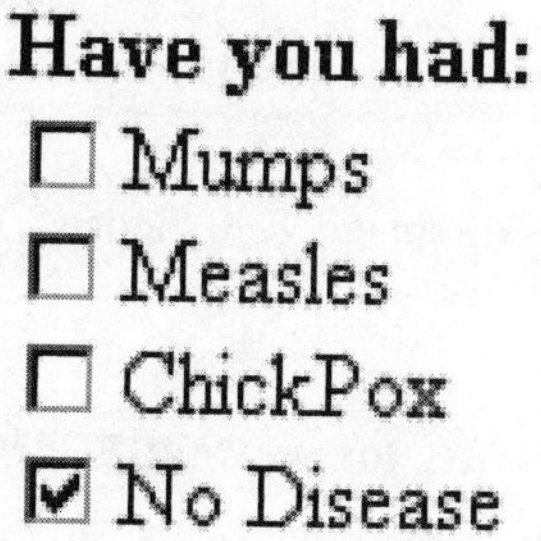

**FIG. 7.9**

If you want to default set a check on a *CHECK BOX*, include the *CHECKED* attribute in the tag definition.

## Have you had:

☐ Mumps

☐ Measles

☐ ChickPox

☑ No Disease

Part

III

Ch

**7**

**N O T E**   When you make an <INPUT> element, you define a TYPE and you assign values to the
NAME and VALUE attributes of the element. When the form's data is submitted to the
server on the Internet, the NAME and VALUE data for the <INPUT> element is sent as a pair associated with the "=" sign. This association is called a NAME/VALUE pair. NAME/VALUE pairs are usually
passed to a server- side CGI Script or an Active Server Page. The server-side script or ASP (Active
Server Page) then parses the VALUE data from the NAME data and acts upon the data as defined in
the script or ASP.

For example:

You create a TEXT <INPUT> element in which the user is to enter a  favorite baseball team. The HTML
syntax is:

```
Favorite Team<INPUT TYPE=TEXT NAME=txtTeam SIZE=40><BR>
```

The user  enters the string, "Yankees" in the <INPUT TYPE=TEXT> element. When the form is
eventually submitted to the server the NAME/VALUE pair that will be sent is txtTeam=Yankees,
where,

**txtTeam** is the value of the NAME attribute

and

**Yankees** is the value of the VALUE attribute.  ■

**Hidden**   Hidden <INPUT> types are well hidden (see Listing 7.8). They're never shown on
the form. They are a good way to send data from the form to the server without the user's
awareness. It's as if you have a piece of data embedded in the form that you can send back to
the server on a free ride basis. In the example in Listing 7.7, the author of the HTML attached
this name to a HIDDEN input type. When the data is sent back to the server, his name will also
be sent to the server without the user knowing about it.

**Listing 7.8   ELEMENTS.HTM—An Authors Name Attached to a HIDDEN
<Input> Type**

```
<INPUT TYPE=Hidden NAME=hidAuthor VALUE="Bob Reselman">
```

**Image**   An IMAGE <Input> type displays a .GIF image  (see Figure 7.10) that has the behavior
of a SUBMIT <INPUT> type (see Listing 7.9).

**Listing 7.9   ELEMENTS.HTM—The HTML for an IMAGE <INPUT> Type**

```
<B>Magic Button:</B><INPUT TYPE=image NAME=imgMain SRC=gifs/gifbut.gif>
```

**FIG. 7.10**
You can give some
artistic variety to your
form with an *IMAGE*
*<INPUT>* type.

# Magic Button: ●

## The *<SELECT>* Element

A <SELECT> element is similar to an <INPUT> element in that it allows users to input data to be submitted to a server on the Internet. However, the <SELECT> element is a little more powerful in that it has the behavior of a Visual Basic listbox or combobox.

The tag begins with <SELECT> and ends with </SELECT> (see Listing 7.10). Within the <SELECT> element you place <OPTION> elements. If you use the attribute, MUTLIPLE, in the tag definition, the element will appear as a list, similar to the Visual Basic listbox. When the element appears as a list, you can submit multiple <OPTION>s to the server. If you omit the MULTIPLE attribute, the element will appear as a drop-down box, similar to a VB combobox, from which you can chose only one <OPTION> (see Figure 7.11).

**Listing 7.10  FORM2.HTM—HTML for Single and Multiple Selection
<SELECT> Elements**

```
<FORM METHOD=post ACTION=../cgi-win/ark.exe NAME=frmArk>

<FONT SIZE=4 FACE=TIMES COLOR=Red>
Select Animals
</FONT>

<!--Allow multiple selections-->
<SELECT MULTIPLE NAME="Animals">
<OPTION VALUE="pig">Pig
<OPTION VALUE="goat">Goat
<OPTION VALUE="horse">Horse
</SELECT>
<P>

<FONT SIZE=4 FACE=TIMES COLOR=Red>
Select a Flower
</FONT>
<!--Allow only one selection-->
<SELECT NAME="Flowers">
<OPTION VALUE="rose">Rose
<OPTION VALUE="lily">Lily
<OPTION VALUE="daisy">Daisy
</SELECT>

<P>
<INPUT TYPE=Submit Value="Submit" NAME=Submit>
</FORM>
```

**FIG. 7.11**
<SELECT> elements are similar to a Visual Basic listbox or combo control.

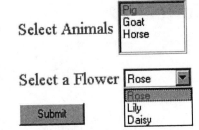

## The *<TEXTAREA>* Element

The <TEXTAREA> element is similar to a TEXT <INPUT> type, the difference being that a <TEXTAREA> element can accept multiple lines of text.

The tag definition begins with <TEXTAREA> and ends with </TEXTAREA> (see Listing 7.11). Any text that appears between the begin and end tag will show up in the field of the <TEXTAREA> (see Figure 7.12).

The <TEXTAREA> element has three attributes (see Table 7.2).

**Table 7.2   *<TEXTAREA>* Attributes**

| Attribute | Description |
| --- | --- |
| NAME | The name of the element (required). |
| ROWS | The number of rows in <TEXTAREA> field. |
| COLS | The width of the field in characters. |

**Listing 7.11   FORM2.HTM—HTML Syntax for a *<TEXTAREA>* Element**

```
<FORM METHOD=post ACTION=../cgi-win/poll.exe NAME=frmComment>

<FONT SIZE=4 FACE=TIMES COLOR=Blue>
Do you have a comment?<P>
</FONT>

<TEXTAREA ROWS=5 COLS=30 NAME=taComment>Enter your comment here.
Don't forget to erase
this message or it will show up in you comments
and that's not something that your would like to
happen.
</TEXTAREA>
<P>
<INPUT TYPE=Submit Value="Submit Comment" NAME=Submit>
</FORM>
```

# The *<SCRIPT>* Element

The <SCRIPT> element denotes a section of script code within a Web page's HTML (see Listing 7.12). The tag definition begins with <SCRIPT> and ends with </SCRIPT>. The element has an attribute LANGUAGE that indicates the scripting language used. Listing 7.12 is a snippet of HTML that shows a <SCRIPT> element that is defining an OnClick event handler in VBScript.

### Listing 7.12   VALNAME3.HTM—HTML Syntax for the *<SCRIPT>* Element

```
<SCRIPT LANGUAGE="VBScript">
<!--
Sub cmdSubmit_OnClick
 Dim TheForm
 Dim i
 Dim MyMsg

 MyMsg = "All field must be filled in. If a field is empty, please type: NONE."

 Set TheForm = Document.frmPurchase

  For i = 0 to CInt(TheForm.Elements.Length) - 1
    If TheForm.Elements(i).Value = "" Then
   Alert (MyMsg)
        Exit Sub
    End If
 Next

 End Sub
-->
</SCRIPT>
```

▶ **See**  Que's *Special Edition Using HTML* (ISBN 0-7897-0758-6), Chapter 21, "Forms and How They Work," on **pps. 489-502**

**FIG. 7.12**
You can use a
<TEXTAREA> element
as a memo field.

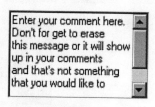

Do you have a comment?

Submit Comment

# Using the HTML *<FORM>* Elements

As discussed in the preceding section, you use an HTML <FORM> element to group, collect, and submit data to a server on the Internet. The type of circumstances that you would typically apply a <FORM> to are situations in which you want to collect personnel data, input sales order information, or get lookup information for an Internet search.

Figure 7.13 shows an illustration of a Web site that uses the HTML `<FORM>` elements, `<INPUT TYPE=RADIO>`, `<TEXTAREA>`, `<INPUT TYPE=IMAGE>`, and `<INPUT TYPE=HIDDEN>` to create a form that allows a user to submit a term or keyword to a server to do a lookup query. Listing 7.13 shows the HTML that's used to create the page.

Notice that instead of using a `<TYPE INPUT=SUBMIT>` element type to create a Submit button, the creator of the this page cleverly uses an `<INPUT TYPE=IMAGE>` that uses a custom illustration to create a unique Submit button. If the user enters the lookup terms **creating VBScript procedures** in the `TEXTAREA`, when the user submits the form's data, the following query string will be sent on to the server

Where,

> `mode=concept` is the `NAME`/`VALUE` pair for the selected Radio
>
> `&` is the chararcter used in HTML to separate `NAME`/`VALUE` pairs
>
> `search=creating+VBScript+prodcures` is the `NAME`/`VALUE` pair that describes that data entered in the `<INPUT TYPE=TEXTAREA>`. The "+" character is used in HTML to indicate a space between words.
>
> `sp=sp` is the `NAME`/`VALUE` pair corresponding to the `<INPUT TYPE=HIDDEN>` element.:

**N O T E** A query string is the string passed on to a server on the Internet when a user clicks a Submit button in an HTML form.

The string is constructed from the `NAME`/`VALUE` pairs of the elements in the form which is being submitted. ■

`mode=concept&search=creating+VBScript+prodcures&sp=sp`

**FIG. 7.13**
Lookup and retrieval
Web pages use HTML
forms.

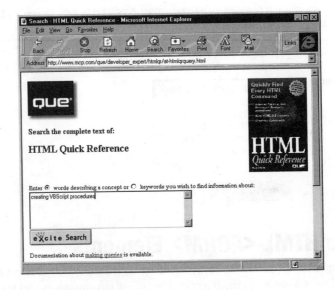

**Listing 7.13   QUE_SRCH.HTM—A Web Page that Uses an HTML Form to Do a Lookup**

```html
<html>
<head>
<title>Search - HTML Quick Reference</title>
</head>

<body bgcolor="#FFFFFF">

<!-- -->
<!-- HEADER -->
<table width=600>
<tr><td width=600>
<IMG SRC="q08671.gif" ALT="book cover" align=right>
<A HREF="/que/"><IMG SRC="../sevb4/que_sq.gif" ALT="QUE" Border=0></A>
<H3>Search the complete text of:</H3>
<H2>HTML Quick Reference</H2>
</td>
</tr>
</table>

<!-- -->
<!-- INPUT FORM (DO NOT CHANGE)-->
<table width=600>
<tr><td width=600>
<FORM ACTION="/cgi-bin/AT-htmlqrsearch.cgi" METHOD="POST">
Enter<INPUT TYPE="radio" NAME="mode" VALUE="concept" CHECKED> words describing a
concept or<INPUT TYPE="radio" NAME="mode" VALUE="simple"> keywords you wish to
find information about:<br>
<TEXTAREA NAME="search" COLS=70 ROWS=4></TEXTAREA><br>
<INPUT TYPE="image" NAME="SearchButton" BORDER=0 SRC="/Architext/pictures/AT-
search_button.gif">
<INPUT TYPE="hidden" NAME="sp" VALUE="sp">
</FORM>
<p>
Documentation about <a href="/Architext/AT-queryhelp.html">making queries</a> is
➥available.
<p><p>
<b>TIP:</b> If you plan on making multiple queries, you might wish to make a
➥bookmark for this page.
<P>
</td>
</tr>
</table>

<HR SIZE=1 NOSHADE align=left width=600>
<!-- -->
<!-- NAVIGATIONAL TOOLBAR -->
<table width=600>
<tr><td align=center>
¦ <A HREF="/que/developer_expert/htmlqr/">Book Home Page</A> ¦ <A HREF="/que/
➥developer_expert/htmlqr/toc.htm">Table of Contents</A> ¦ <A HREF="/cgi-bin/
```

*continues*

**Listing 7.13    Continued**

```
placeorder?express=0-7897-0867-1">Buy This Book</A> ¦
<P>
¦ <A HREF="/que/">Que Home Page</A> ¦ <A HREF="/que/bookshelf/">Digital Book-
shelf</A> ¦ <A HREF="/que/bookshelf/disclaim.html">Disclaimer</A> ¦
<P>
</td></tr>
</table>



<!-- -->
<!-- FOOTER -->
<hr size=8 align=left width=600>
<table width=600>
<tr><td align=center><font size=1>
To order books from QUE, call us at 800-716-0044 or 317-361-5400.
<P>
For comments or technical support for our books and software, select
<A href = "/general/support/index.html" >Talk to Us</a>.
<P>
&#169; 1996, QUE Corporation, an imprint of Macmillan Publishing USA, a Simon
and Schuster Company.
<P>
</font></td></tr>
</table>

</body>
</html>
```

# Using the Internet Explorer Intrinsic Controls

Though HTML forms and <FORM> elements are powerful tools to have in your development toolbox, they are limited. The most fundamental limitation is that the only dynamic interactions you can do with them on the client-side is to submit data to an Internet Server or clear the form. Conceptually, you have only one event—Click, and two operational client-side methods, submit the data and clear the form's data. That's it! Any other validation or modifications that you may want to make have to be done through a plethora of client/server interactions. This is time consuming and incurs a heavy burden of server-side transactions and programming to accommodate those transactions.

N O T E   HTML keywords are not case sensitive, nor do nonwhite space value strings require
        quotation marks. Thus,

```
<INPUT TYPE=RADIO NAME=opFoo VALUE=fooBar1>
```

is operationally the same as:

```
<input type=radio Name=opFoo Value=fooBar1>
```

or

```
<INPUT TYPE=RADIO name=opFoo value=fooBar1>
```

Quotation marks are optional for nonwhite space value assignments but *are* required if you use value assignments with more than one word. Thus,

```
<INPUT TYPE=SUBMIT NAME=submit VALUE=Clear>
```

will work. However,

```
<INPUT TYPE=SUBMIT NAME=submit VALUE=Clear Form>
```

will *not* work. Rather the correct syntax is:

```
<INPUT TYPE=SUBMIT NAME=submit VALUE="Clear Form"> ■
```

**N O T E**    There is lot of variety to HTML coding style in the HTML development community. The important thing to consider when you create your pages is that your code should be consistent, well organized, and easy to read. ■

However, there is a solution to this problem and that is to extend the functionality of standard HTML forms with a scripting language such as VBScript or JavaScript. You'll take a look at this solution in the section "Using VBScript with the HTML <FORM> Elements and Intrinsic Controls," which comes later in this chapter.

## The Internet Explorer Intrinsic Controls

When you install Internet Explorer on you computer, you get more than full multimedia access to the Internet and an OLE container in which you can view documents with full OLE functionality (provided the "maker" applications are installed on your system). You also get a full blown programming environment, VBScript, and the Intrinsic Controls. Just about all the stuff you get with Standard VB, you get with Internet Explorer. You can make programs using VBScript that can use buttons, option controls, check boxes, comb boxes and much more. These controls that are built right into the browser are called Intrinsic Controls. Table 7.3 lists them, with their VB and HTML <FORM> counterparts.

**Table 7.3    The Microsoft Forms 2.0 Controls**

| Microsoft Forms Control | VB Standard Equivalent | HTML Element Equivalent |
|---|---|---|
| CheckBox | CheckBox | <INPUT TYPE=CHECKBOX> |
| ComboBox | ComboBox | <SELECT> |
| CommandButton | CommandButtons | <INPUT TYPE=BUTTON> |

*continues*

Part
III

Ch
7

**Table 7.3    Continued**

| Microsoft Forms Control | VB Standard Equivalent | HTML Element Equivalent |
| --- | --- | --- |
| Frame | None | <FRAME> |
| Image Image | <INPUT TYPE=IMAGE> | |
| Label | Label | none |
| ListBox | ListBox | <SELECT MULTIPLE> |
| OptionButton | OptionButton | <INPUT TYPE=RADIO> |
| ScrollBar | ScrollBar | none |
| SpinButton | SpinButton | none |
| TabStrip | TabStrip | none |
| TextBox | TextBox | <INPUT=TEXT> |
| ToggleButton | none | none |

## Using the *<OBJECT>* Tag to Insert Intrinsic Controls

You manipulate the Intrinsic Controls at runtime by using VBScript. You insert and define these controls at design time by using the <OBJECT> tag. The tag definition begins with <OBJECT> and ends with </OBJECT>. The attributes for the <OBJECT> tag as they pertain to the Intrinsic Controls are shown in Table 7.4.

**Table 7.4    The Attributes of the *<OBJECT>* Tag for Intrinsic Controls**

| Attribute | Description |
| --- | --- |
| ID | Specifies the Object. For Intrinsic Controls and ActiveX controls, this is similar to the Visual Basic Name property. |
| CLASSID | The Globally Unique Universal Indentifier. All ActiveX Controls have unique number by which they can be identified by your system. |
| HEIGHT | The height of the control, similar to the Visual Basic Height property. |
| WIDTH | The width of the control, similar to the Visual Basic Width property. |
| CODEBASE | The server location of the control to be downloaded if the control is not on the client computer. This is not relevant for the Intrinsic Controls because they are built right into Internet Explorer. |

With regard to the Intrinsic Controls, the <OBJECT> tag also has a child tag, <PARAM>. The <PARAM> tag is used to set properties of an Intrinsic Control.

The <PARAM> takes the form,

<PARAM NAME=*PropertyName* VALUE=*PropertyValue*>

For example, if you want to set the Caption of an intrinsic CommandButton with the ID cmdEnter to "Enter", the <PARAM> tag would be:

<PARAM NAME="Caption" VALUE="Enter">

This is the Visual Basic syntactical equivalent of cmdEnter.Caption = "Enter".

Figure 7.14 shows a Web page that uses two Intrinsic Controls, a CommandButton, cmdClickMe, and a TextBox, txtMain. The HTML for the page is shown in Listing 7.14.

**FIG. 7.14**

Intrinsic Controls can interact with one another without the need to incur a lot of client/server transactions.

---

**Listing 7.14  SMPLVB.HTM—Using Intrinsic Controls with HTML**

```
<HTML>
<HEAD>
<TITLE>Simple VBScript</TITLE>
</HEAD>
<SCRIPT LANGUAGE="VBScript">
<!--
Sub cmdClickMe_Click()
  txtMain.Text = "Clicked!"
End Sub
-->
</SCRIPT>
<BODY>
  <OBJECT ID="txtMain" WIDTH=127 HEIGHT=24
    CLASSID="CLSID:8BD21D10-EC42-11CE-9E0D-00AA006002F3">
      <PARAM NAME="VariousPropertyBits" VALUE="746604571">
      <PARAM NAME="Size" VALUE="3329;635">
      <PARAM NAME="FontCharSet" VALUE="0">
      <PARAM NAME="FontPitchAndFamily" VALUE="2">
      <PARAM NAME="FontWeight" VALUE="0">
    </OBJECT>

<P>
```

Part

III

Ch

7

*continues*

**Listing 7.14  Continued**

```
    <OBJECT ID="cmdClickMe" WIDTH=96 HEIGHT=32
  CLASSID="CLSID:D7053240-CE69-11CD-A777-00DD01143C57">
    <PARAM NAME="Caption" VALUE="ClickMe">
    <PARAM NAME="Size" VALUE="2540;847">
    <PARAM NAME="FontCharSet" VALUE="0">
    <PARAM NAME="FontPitchAndFamily" VALUE="2">
    <PARAM NAME="ParagraphAlign" VALUE="3">
    <PARAM NAME="FontWeight" VALUE="0">
    </OBJECT>
  </BODY>
  </HTML>
```

## Handling Events

Having more controls available to readily add to your Web pages wouldn't have much of a payoff unless you had a way to interact with them. Using a CommandButton without having access to the Click event, or a SpinButton without access the SpinDown event, would be a waste of time. Fortunately, this limitation does not exist.

Take a look at the code in Listing 7.14. Notice that in addition to some <OBJECT> tags to accommodate the inclusion of the CommandButton and TextBox controls, at the top of the page you have a <SCRIPT> tag that references a Sub, cmdClickMe_OnClick. This is called an event handler. This piece of VBScript is what will be executed when the user clicks the cmdClickMe button.

An event handler is a Sub. In Visual Basic, event handler code blocks are automatically generated by the Visual Basic IDE (Integrated Development Environment). When using VBScript within HTML, you must create the event handlers yourself.

The syntax for an event handler is:

```
<SCRIPT LANGUAGE="VBScript">
<!--
Sub ControlID_Event
    'handler code
.
.
.
End Sub
-->
</SCRIPT>
```

Where,

> ControlID is the ID of the control whose event you are handling.

> Event is the event to be handled.

Thus, as coded in the event handler, cmdClickMe_OnClick, in Listing 17.14, when the user clicks on the CommandButton, cmdClickMe, the Text property to the TextBox, txtMain, is set to "Clicked!".

Trying to remember all the events and all the event handler syntax that go with any given Intrinsic Control can be a chore. To make programming Intrinsic Controls with VBScript easier, Microsoft created a tool to handle most of the drudgery of these sorts of tasks. It's called ActiveX Control Pad. You can get it by downloading it from the Microsoft SiteBuilder site on the Internet (**http://www.microsoft.com/sitebuilder/**). After you get the hang of it, it will save you a lot of time in your programming endeavors. Figure 7.15 shows the ActiveX Control Pad Script Wizard. Script Wizard is one the many features of ActiveX Control Pad. Script Wizard allows you to write a lot of VBScript with nothing more than a point and a click.

▶ **See** the Que book, *Special Edition Using VBScript* (ISBN 0-7897-0809-4), Chapter 4, "Creating a Standard HTML page," on **pps. 84-98**

**FIG. 7.15**

You can use the ActiveX Control Pad's Script Wizard to code a control's event handler.

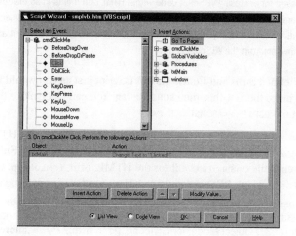

## Subs and Functions

In addition to using VBScript to write event handlers for Intrinsic Controls, you can also use it to write User Defined Subs and Functions, just as you would in standard Visual Basic. The benefit of this is that you can write some fairly complex event handlers, the tasks of which are encapsulated in other Subs and Functions. Using Subs and Functions helps you avoid writing code that has minimal reuse and is hard to read.

**N O T E** The HTML comment tag begins with `<! - -` and ends with `- ->`. Anything that appears between these tags is considered to be a comment and not read by the browser.

For example:

```
<!--I am a comment.
    I am a another comment on another line-->
```

For commenting within a VBScript block, you use the "'" character, just as you would in standard Visual Basic.

*continues*

*continued*

For example:

```
<SCRIPT LANGUAGE=VBScript>
<!--
  'Send out an error message
  Alert "Error Message"
-->
</SCRIPT>  ▧
```

**N O T E** The reason for enclosing VBScript code within HTML comments is so that the VBScript will be ignored by browsers that don't understand or support VBScript. Browsers that do support VBScript understand that any HTML comments within the *<SCRIPT>* element are there for protecting other browsers from the VBScript code.  ▧

You write user-defined Subs and Functions in VBScript just as you would in standard Visual Basic, only you place them within the <SCRIPT> tag. You can place more than one Sub or Function within a set of <SCRIPT></SCRIPT> tags.

Figure 7.16 shows an illustration of the Web page, FORM3.HTM. The HTML for this page is shown in Listing 7.16. This page is an example of using a user-defined Sub to extend an event handler, in this case the OnSubmit event for the HTML form, frmLookup. (The OnSubmit is the method of the Form Object. VBScript considers the <FORM> element to be a Form Object.)

▶ **See** Que's *Special Edition Using VBScript* (ISBN 0-7897-0809-4), Chapter 11, "Using the Internet Explorer 3.0 Object Model," on **pps. 197-199**. For detailed documentation on line about The Internet Explorer 3.0 Object Model for Scripting, go to **http://www.microsoft.com/workshop/prog/sdk/docs/scriptom/** on the Internet.

**FIG. 7.16**
Data validation is a typical use for VBScript.

## Listing 7.15 FORMS3.HTM—The HTML for a User-Defined Sub

```
<HTML>
<HEAD>
<TITLE>Validating a number</TITLE>
</HEAD>
<SCRIPT LANGUAGE=VBScript>
<!--
''''''''''''''''''''''''''''''''''''''''
'Checks a value to see if it looks
''''''''''''''''''''''''''''''''''''''''
like a number
Sub CheckNum(NumToCheck)
  If IsNumeric(CStr(NumToCheck)) Then
```

```
    Alert ("It's a number")
  Else
    Alert ("It's not a number")
  End If
End Sub

Sub frmLookUp_OnSubmit
  CheckNum(frmLookup.txtNumber.Value)
End  Sub

-->
</SCRIPT>

<BODY BGCOLOR=#FFFFFF>
<FONT SIZE=5 FACE=TIMES COLOR=#00218C>
Validating a number
</FONT>
<HR>

<FORM METHOD=post ACTION=../cgi-win/lookup.exe NAME=frmLookup>

<FONT SIZE=4 FACE=TIMES COLOR=Red>
Enter a Number:
<INPUT TYPE=TEXT NAME=txtNumber>
</FONT>

<P>
<INPUT TYPE=Submit Value="Submit" NAME=Submit>
</FORM>
<HR>
</BODY>
</HTML>
```

You'll notice that the event handler, `frmLookUp_OnSubmit` calls a user defined Sub, `CheckNum(NumToCheck)`. `CheckNum` is pretty straightforward. It takes the value to check as an argument and passes that value on to the intrinsic VB function, `IsNumeric()`. (You're probably pretty familiar with IsNumeric. It's been around in VB for years!) If the return is true, the Sub displays an Alert Box containing the string, "`It's a number`." If it's false, the Alert displays, `It's not a number`. (The Alert method is the VBScript equivalent of the VB `MsgBox` statement.)

**N O T E**  A complete illustration and discussion of the VBScript Intrinsic Functions are outside of the scope of this chapter. For the most part, all of the VB functions that are not operating system dependent exist in VBScript. In a few cases, the syntax may be modified a bit.

For a detailed reference of the VBScript Language go to:

**http://www.microsoft.com/vbscript/us/vbslang/vbstoc.htm** ■

The significance of this illustration is that it shows you how to use a user-defined Sub to extend a control's event handler. However, as you read this you might be a bit disconcerted. How can you reference an HTML <FORM> element as you would an Internet Explorer Intrinsic Control? Well, while it is true that a <FORM> is not an Intrinsic Control, it is an Object in the Internet

Explorer Object Model and can be accessed as such. The trick is understanding the Internet Explorer Object Model for Scripting.

# The Internet Explorer Object Model

Many HTML elements can also be treated as Internet Explorer Scripting Objects. In order to work effectively with VBScript and HTML elements and to see how they can intermingle, you need to understand the Internet Explorer Scripting Object Model.

The Object Model is pretty straightforward, if you understand the "object-ness" of Visual Basic. At the top of the IE Object Model hierarchy is the Window object, which is the parent to all other objects. This arrangement is similar to the Form-Custom Control architecture in Visual Basic (see Figure 7.17). Object referencing works the same in VBScript as in VB:

```
parent_object.child_object.property = somevalue
```

Be advised that variable scope and types are a bit tricky. The scope of VBScript variables is described as procedure scope and script scope. What procedure and script scope means is that the variable can be seen only in the sub or function if it is declared inside the procedure. If it is declared outside a procedure, it has script wide scope. A script in this case means an HTML page. All variables in VBScript are of the data type Variant, but you must watch the subtype.

**FIG. 7.17**

The Internet Explorer Scripting Object Model Hierarchy

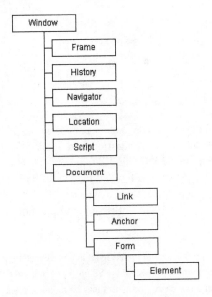

The following sections are a brief description of the objects in the IE Object Model. The files used in the listings can be found in the /HTML directory of this project and on the CD-ROM that comes with this book.

**Window**   The Window is the object at the top of the IE Scripting Object Model. Operationally, it is the Internet Explorer.

**Methods**: alert, confirm, prompt, open, close, setTimeout, clearTimeout, navigate

**Events**: onLoad, onUnload

**Properties**: name, parent, opener, self, top, location, defaultStatus, status, frames, history, navigator, document

---

**Listing 7.16    HELLO.HTM—To Send a Message to a User, You Can Use the Window Object's Alert Method**

```
<HTML><HEAD>
<TITLE>Hello</TITLE>
<SCRIPT LANGUAGE=VBScript>
<!--
Sub window_onLoad
     window.Alert "Hello World"
End Sub
-->
</SCRIPT>
</HEAD>
```

---

**Frame**    The Frame object is similar to and decends from the Window object. Although you can have a collection of Frames, each frame has its own property values and its own document.

**Methods**: See Window object

**Events**: See Window object

**Properties**: See Window object

**History**    The History object holds information about what has been in the window before (see Listing 7.17). It gets this information for the browser's History list (see Figure 7.18).

**FIG. 7.18**
The Internet Explorer's History list in the Go menu.

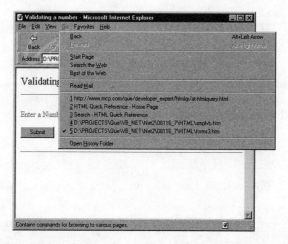

**Methods**: back, forward, go

**Events**: none

**Properties**: length

**Listing 7.17    BACK.HTM—To Go Back to a Previous Page, Use the History Object's Back Method**

```
<HTML><HEAD>
<TITLE>Back</TITLE>
<SCRIPT LANGUAGE=VBScript>
<!--
Sub window_onLoad
     History.back 1
End Sub
-->
</SCRIPT>
</HEAD>
```

**Navigator**    The Navigator object gives you infomation about the browser in use (see Listing 7.18).

**Methods**: none

**Events**: none

**Properties**: appCodeName, appName, appVersion, userAgent

**Listing 7.18    N_GATOR.HTM—To Find Out What Browser Your Client Is Using, Use the AppName Property of the Navigator Object**

```
<HTML><HEAD>
<TITLE>Navigator</TITLE>
<SCRIPT LANGUAGE=VBScript>
<!--
Sub window_onLoad
     Alert Navigator.appName
End Sub
-->
</SCRIPT>
</HEAD>
```

**Location**    The Location Object encapsulates an URL (see Listing 7.19).

**Methods**: none

**Events**: none

**Properties**: href, protocol, host, hostname, port, pathname, search, hash

**Listing 7.19    LOCATION.HTM—To Find the Protocol Being Used by Your Document, Use the Protocol Property of the Location Object**

```
<HTML><HEAD>
<TITLE>Location</TITLE>
<SCRIPT LANGUAGE=VBScript>
```

```
<!--
Sub window_onLoad
     Alert Location.protocol
End Sub
-->
</SCRIPT>
</HEAD>
```

**Script** The Script object (see Listing 7.20) defines the Script used in the Window. Granted, this description is rather vague. At some point Microsoft will probably extend and enhance the utility of this object.

**Document** The Document object encapsulates the document in the current window, as well as the elements in the document, for example, links, forms, buttons, and ActiveX objects. The objects: Link, Anchor, and Form descend from the Document object.

**Methods**: write, writeLn, open, close, clear

**Events**: none

**Properties**: linkColor, aLinkColor, vLinkColor, bgColor, fgColor, anchors, links, forms, location, lastModified, title, cookie, referrer

**Listing 7.20  DOCUMENT.HTM—Write a Line of Code to the Browser by Using the Write Method of the Document Object**

```
<HTML><HEAD>
<TITLE>Document</TITLE>
<SCRIPT LANGUAGE=VBScript>
<!--
     document.write ("I am writing a line.")
-->
</SCRIPT>
</HEAD>
</HTML>
```

**Link** The Link Object (see Listing 7.21) is an encapsulation of an HTML <A HREF...> tag on a given page. It is read-only. Because a Link is a member of the Links collection, (an array of <A HREF...> tags), you need to access a particular link through the Document object's Links property.

**Methods**: none

**Events**: onMouseMove, onMouseOver, onClick

**Properties**: href, protocol, host, hostname, port, pathname, search, hash, target

Part

III

Ch

7

**Listing 7.21    LINK.HTM—To Find <A HREF...> Tabs on a Page, Use the Document Object Property Links. To Find the Text of an <HREF>, Use the HREF Property of the Link Object**

```
<HTML><HEAD>
<TITLE>Document</TITLE>
<SCRIPT LANGUAGE=VBScript>
<!--

Sub window_onUnLoad
   Dim NumOfLinks
   Dim MyAlertMsg
   NumOfLinks = Cstr(document.links.length)
   MyAlertMsg = "There are " & NumOfLinks & " links on this page."
   MyAlertMsg = MyAlertMsg & Chr(10) & Chr(13)
   MyAlertMsg = MyAlertMsg & "The first link is " & document.links(0).href

   Alert MyAlertMsg
End Sub
-->
</SCRIPT>
</HEAD>

<BODY>

<P>
<A HREF="http://www.whitehouse.gov"> Go to the White House.</A>
<P>
<A HREF="http://www.senate.gov"> Go to the Senate. </A>
</BODY>
</HTML>
```

**Anchor**    The Anchor object is similar to a Link object (see Listing 7.22). The difference is that the Anchor object references all <A> tags in a given document as opposed to <A HREF...> objects.

**Methods**: none

**Events**: none

**Properties**: name

**Form**    The Form object represents an HTML <FORM> element in a Document object. You can reference a Form object by either a name or an array index. The Element object is a child of the Form object.

**Methods**: submit

**Events**: onSubmit

**Properties**: action, encoding, method, target, elements

**Listing 7.22  OM_FORM.HTM—A Simple Form Element**

```
<HTML>
<HEAD>
<TITLE>The Virtual Music Store</TITLE></HEAD>
<FORM method=post action=/cgi-win/mycgi.cgi>
Enter your name: <INPUT TYPE=TEXT NAME=yourname>
<BR>
<INTPUT TYPE=Submit NAME=submit VALUE="Enter Name">
</FORM>
</BODY></HTML>
```

**Element**   The Element object is a control placed in your HTML document by using the
<INPUT> tag or the <OBJECT> tag (see Listing 7.23). The former are called HTML elements.
The latter are Intrinsic Controls and ActiveX Controls.

**Methods**: click, focus, blur, select

**Events**: onClick, onFocus, onBlur, onChange, onSelect

**Properties**: form, name, value, defaultValue, checked, defaultChecked, length, options,
selectedIndex

**Listing 7.23   ELEMENT.HTM—To Handle a Click Event of an Element Object
of Type, Button, Code the OnClick Event of the Element Object**

```
<HTML><HEAD>
<TITLE>Element</TITLE>
<SCRIPT LANGUAGE=VBScript>
<!--

Sub btnOK_onClick
     frmMain.btnOK.Value ="Thank you!"
End Sub
-->
</SCRIPT>
</HEAD>

<BODY>
<FORM NAME=frmMain>
<INPUT TYPE=button NAME=btnOK VALUE="Click me">
</FORM>
</BODY>
</HTML>
```

Part
**III**

Ch

**7**

# Using VBScript with the HTML *<FORM>* Elements and Intrinsic Controls

Now that you have gotten a pretty extensive overview of HTML elements, the IE Intrinsic Controls, and the IE Object Model, tie it all together. Listing 7.23 shows the HTML for a customer information registration Web page. This code implements many of the features and techniques that you read about in this chapter.

Notice that the page contains a `frmRegInfo` and that the form is populated with TEXT, PASSWORD, RADIO, SUBMIT, RESET, and BUTTON `<INPUT>` types (see Figure 7.19). However, all the data is analyzed and manipulated by using VBScript. These `<INPUT>` elements are referenced as children objects of the IE Object Model, Form object. Notice too, that the SUBMIT element's default submission behavior (which happens when you press an HTML `<INPUT TYPE=SUBMIT>` element) is modified by using the `OnClick` method of the IE Submit object. Thus, you are able to overcome one of the pivotal shortcomings of HTML elements—the ability to analyze and respond to user input before such input is sent on to a server on the Internet.

To validate that all `<INPUT TYPE=TEXT>` element's VALUEs are not empty, the code takes advantage of VBScript's ability to reference elements as members of a collection, thus averting the need to explicitly query the VALUE of every element by name. This is done by querying each item in the `Form` object's ELEMENTS collection by using a `For...Next` loop and then using a Window object's `Alert` method and `Element` object `Setfocus` and `Select` method if errors are encountered.

**FIG. 7.19**
You can use the *<TABLE>* element to better organize your forms.

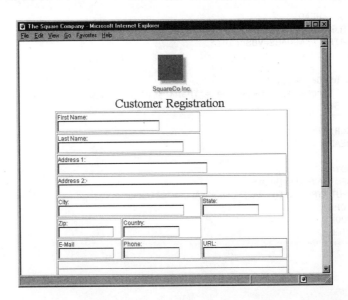

The `History` object's `Back` method (see Listing 7.24) is used within the `OnClick` event of custom-created Return button. This button was created *not* as an IE Intrinsic Control, but rather as an HTML element upon which an event handler has been imposed by using VBScript (see Figure 7.20).

**FIG. 7.20**
You can make a Return button by using HTML elements and VBScript.

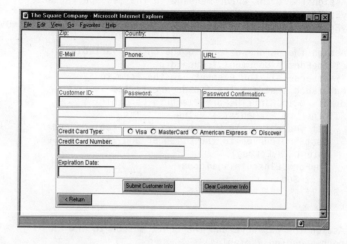

---

**Listing 7.24  CUSTREG.HTM—The HTML for a Customer Registration Web Page**

```
<!--04-20-97-->
<HTML>
<HEAD>
<TITLE>The Square Company</TITLE>
<SCRIPT LANGUAGE="VBScript">
<!--

Sub submit_OnClick
'********************************
'Sub: submit_OnClick
'
'Remarks: This sub checks to make sure that:
'  1. All fields are filled in
'  2. The password matches the password confirmation
'  3. The CC expiration date string is a valid date format
'  It then submits to the form data to the CGI script, TRANSACT.EXE
'  to the "register" CASE.

'Author:  Bob Reselman
'
'Copyright: (c) 1997 MacMillan Publishing
'********************************

  Dim TheForm    'declare a variable for the form object
  Dim i          'declare a counter variable
  Dim MyErrMsg   'declare a variable to hold the error message
  Dim PassWord   'declare a variable to hold the password
  Dim ConfirmWord 'declare a variable to hold the confirmation
```

Part

III

Ch

7

*continues*

**Listing 7.24   Continued**

```
Dim s              'declare a general string variable
'Assign the blank error message to the message variable
MyErrMsg = "All field must be filled in. "
MyErrMsg = MyErrMsg + "If a field is empty, please type: NONE."

'Assign the purchase form to the object variable
Set TheForm = Document.frmRegInfo
'Transverse all the elements in the form to
'make sure that all the fields are filled in.
For i = 0 to CInt(TheForm.Elements.Length) - 1
   If TheForm.Elements(i).Value = "" Then
      'If you get a blank, show the error message and
      'set the cursor to the offender and leave the Sub.
      Alert (MyErrMsg)
      TheForm.Elements(i).focus
      Exit Sub
   End If
Next

'Assign the password and the confirmation to the
'corresponding variables
PassWord = frmRegInfo.txtPassword.value
ConfirmWord = frmRegInfo.txtPassConfirm.value

'Create the password mismatch error message
MyErrMsg = "The password and the confirmation do not match"


'Check to make sure the values match
If PassWord <> ConfirmWord then
   'If you have  mismatch, show an Error message
   Alert (MyErrMsg)
   'Set the focus back to the confirmation textbox
   frmRegInfo.txtPassConfirm.focus
   'HiLite the confirmation textbox
   frmRegInfo.txtPassConfirm.select
   Exit Sub
end if

'Check to make sure that the CC expiration date string is a date
MyErrMsg = "The Expiration Date entry must be in a valid date format."

'Go to the <INPUT TYPE=text NAME=
s = frmRegInfo.txtExpDate.value
If IsDate(s) = 0 then
   Alert (MyErrMsg)
   frmRegInfo.txtExpDate.focus
   frmRegInfo.txtExpDate.select
   Exit Sub
End if

'If you've gotten to here, everything is OK
'Submit the data
TheForm.Submit
```

```
End Sub

Sub cmdReturn_OnClick
'*******************************
'Sub: return_OnClick
'
'Remarks: This sub returns the user to their previous URL
'
'Author:  Bob Reselman
'
'Copyright: (c) 1997 Macmillan Publishing
'*******************************
   history.back 1
End Sub
-->
</SCRIPT>
</HEAD>
<BODY BGCOLOR=#FFFFFF>
<CENTER>
<IMG SRC=gifs/logo.gif>
<BR><FONT SIZE=6 FACE=TIMES COLOR=#00218C>
Customer Registration</FONT>
<BR>

<TABLE BORDER=1 WIDTH=80%>
<FORM NAME=frmRegInfo METHOD=post ACTION=../cgi-win/transact.exe>
<INPUT TYPE=hidden NAME=transaction VALUE= hidRegister>

<!--Name Data-->
<TR>
<TD COLSPAN=2><FONT SIZE=2 COLOR=#840084 FACE=arial>
First Name:<BR><INPUT TYPE=tex SIZE=40 NAME=txtFirstName></TD>
</TR>

<TR>
<TD COLSPAN=2><FONT SIZE=2 COLOR=#840084 FACE=arial>
Last Name:<BR><INPUT TYPE=text SIZE=50 NAME=txtLastName></TD>
</TR>

<!--Address Data-->
</TR>
<TD COLSPAN=4><FONT SIZE=2 COLOR=#840084 FACE=arial>
Address 1:<BR><INPUT TYPE=text SIZE=60 NAME=txtAddress1></TD>
</TR>

<TR>
<TD COLSPAN=4><FONT SIZE=2 COLOR=#840084 FACE=arial>
Address 2:<BR><INPUT TYPE=text    SIZE=60 NAME=txtAddress2></TD>
</TR>

<!--City  State Zip Country-->
<TR>
<TD COLSPAN=2><FONT SIZE=2 COLOR=#840084 FACE=arial>
City: <BR><INPUT TYPE=text SIZE=50 NAME=txtCity></TD>
```

Part
III

Ch
7

*continues*

**Listing 7.24    Continued**

```
<TD><FONT SIZE=2 COLOR=#840084 FACE=arial>
State: <BR><INPUT TYPE=text NAME=txtState></TD>
</TR>

<TR>
<TD><FONT SIZE=2 COLOR=#840084 FACE=arial>
Zip: <BR><INPUT TYPE=text NAME=txtZip></TD>

<TD><FONT SIZE=2 COLOR=#840084 FACE=arial>
Country: <BR><INPUT TYPE=text NAME=txtCountry></TD>
</TR>

<!--E-mail, Phone, URL-->
<TR>
<TD><FONT SIZE=2 COLOR=#840084 FACE=arial>
E-Mail <BR><INPUT TYPE=text NAME=txtEmail></TD>

<TD><FONT SIZE=2 COLOR=#840084 FACE=arial>Phone: <BR>
<INPUT TYPE=text NAME=txtPhone></TD>

<TD COLSPAN=2><FONT SIZE=2 COLOR=#840084 FACE=arial>
URL: <BR><INPUT TYPE=text SIZE=30 NAME=txtURL></TD>
</TR>
</FONT>

<!--Put in a line across the TABLE-->
<TR>
<TD COLSPAN=4>
<HR>
</TD>
</TR>

<!--Customer ID and Password-->
<TR>
<TD><FONT SIZE=2 COLOR=#FF0639 FACE=arial>
Customer ID: <BR><INPUT TYPE=text NAME=custID></TD>

<TD><FONT SIZE=2 COLOR=#FF0639 FACE=arial>
Password: <BR><INPUT TYPE=password NAME=txtPassword></TD>

<TD><FONT SIZE=2 COLOR=#FF0639 FACE=arial>
Password Confirmation: <BR><INPUT TYPE=password NAME=txtPassConfirm></TD>
</TR>
</FONT>


<!--Credit Card-->
<TR>
<TD COLSPAN=4>
<HR>
</TR>
<TR>
```

```
<!--Credit Card Type-->
<TD><FONT SIZE=2 FACE=ARIAL COLOR=#00218C>Credit Card Type:<BR></TD>
<TD  COLSPAN=3 ALIGN=CENTER><FONT SIZE=2 FACE=ARIAL COLOR=#00218C>
<INPUT TYPE=radio NAME=radCcType VALUE=visa>Visa
<INPUT TYPE=radio NAME=radCcType VALUE=mc>MasterCard
<INPUT TYPE=radio NAME=radCcType VALUE=amex>American Express
<INPUT TYPE=radio NAME=radCcType VALUE=disc>Discover
</TD>

<!--Credit Card Number-->
<TR>
<TD  COLSPAN=2><FONT SIZE=2 FACE=ARIAL COLOR=#00218C>
Credit Card Number:<BR><INPUT TYPE=text SIZE=50 NAME=txtCcNumber></TD>
</TR>

<!--Credit Card Expiration-->
<TR>
<TD  COLSPAN=2><FONT SIZE=2 FACE=ARIAL COLOR=#00218C>
Expiration Date:<BR><INPUT TYPE=text NAME=txtExpDate></TD>
</TR>

<TR>
<TD></TD>
<!--Submit Button-->
<TD><INPUT TYPE=button NAME=submit  VALUE="Submit Customer Info"</TD>
<!--Clear Button-->
<TD><INPUT TYPE=reset VALUE="Clear Customer Info"</TD>
<TD></TD>
</TR>
</FONT>

<TR>
<TD  COLSPAN=2>
<!--Return Button-->
<INPUT TYPE=button NAME=cmdReturn VALUE="< Return"></TD>
</TR>

</FORM>
</TABLE></CENTER>
</BODY>
</HTML>
```

Using a scripting language such as VBScript in conjunction with HTML elements is a very flexible, powerful, programming technique. You can use this methodology not only with Internet Explorer by using VBScript, but also with Netscape Navigator. All you need to do to have HTML elements be interactive within Netscape Navigator is to use JavaScript instead of VBScript. If you are reticent about taking the time to learn another scripting language, while it is true that JavaScript is syntactically different than VBScript, they are conceptually similar and Internet Explorer supports JavaScript. It might not be the superfluous use of time that you might think it is.

Part

III

Ch

7

# From Here...

At this point you've taken a look at HTML elements, the Internet Explorer Intrinsic Controls, and the Internet Explorer Object Model. You've seen how to tie them together by using VBScript.

- To see how to use what you have learned on client-side computing, take a look at Chapter 2, "Up and Running: Browser-Based VB Programming."

- To learn how to use ActiveX Controls with VBScript, read, Chapter 8, "Interacting with ActiveX Controls and VBScript."

# Interacting with ActiveX Controls and VBScript

### ActiveX controls and HTML

You can include ActiveX controls with the help of the HTML tag <OBJECT>.

### Setting ActiveX control properties with VBScript

You learn how to set properties of an ActiveX control with VBScript.

### Triggering VBScript subroutines with ActiveX control events

You learn how ActiveX controls and VBScript can act together to accomplish tasks.

HTML pages need to be interesting to the user, as well as functional. ActiveX controls are a great way to make the Web page interesting and still provide a huge amount of functionality that HTML controls do not provide. The average Web user is familiar with a computer environment where functionality is provided with visually pleasing controls such as a tool bar or menu list. While the HTML controls add basic visual support such as the button, it lacks the range of visual functionality that a user is familiar with. By adding common ActiveX controls (or developing their own), users have a sense of a regular computer application and are still able to interact with the Web page.

Currently, the only browser that supports ActiveX controls is the Microsoft Internet Explorer 3.0 (or higher). The HTML standard that describes the inclusion of ActiveX controls can be found at **http://www.w3.org/pub/WWW/TR/WD-object.html**. The HTML tag that supports ActiveX controls is the <OBJECT> tag. ■

# Understanding the HTML *<Object>* Tag's Purpose

The Object tag's original intent was to replace the current tags of IMG, EMBED, and APPLET. These tags all load specific objects. The object tag makes the HTML code nonspecific but includes an attribute to specify which type of object it is. The Object tag does more than support ActiveX controls.

By using the Object tag, the browser can determine if it supports the object type (MIME type) before it downloads the object from the server. If it doesn't support the mime type, the HTML code between <OBJECT> and </OBJECT> can point to an alternative object type to download. As an example, there are a lot of sound file types. Some file types provide for richer sound quality but also require special applications on the client to play that type of sound file. In this case, the Object tag can specify the special application but provide a different, lower-quality sound file as the alternate type. The alternative should be some generic type widely supported on the Internet. If there is no suitable alternative object, HTML text can be added to let the user know that something is not being loaded and perhaps point them to a download location for the appropriate application, such as the advanced sound file. The following example illustrates this general use of the Object tag (don't worry about the syntax, that will be explained later). Microsoft Internet Explorer has limited support for non-ActiveX actions of the Object tag; the above mentioned intent of the Object tag is not fully supported in the Microsoft 3.0 browser. **Http://www.blooberry.com/html/intro.htm**. is a great resource for which information regarding which browser supports what tag, as well as what attributes are supported.

Listing 8.1 illustrates the general use of an Object tag. The object type and mime type in the listing are meant to be fake objects (I made them up). They have no corresponding object so the text and image should be displayed instead of the fake object. This listing shows you how to compensate for the browser's lack of ability to load the object. Every Object tag should also have an alternate display such as a link or text so that browsers that don't support objects can still go through your site. Do not expect this page to work in your browser; this code is meant to be an example.

**Listing 8.1   Alternative Text Can Be Displayed Instead of the Object**

```
<HTML>
<HEAD>
<TITLE>Object with Alternative Text</TITLE>
</HEAD>
<BODY>

<OBJECT
DATA = mydata.abc
TYPE = "Application/myapp">
<A HREF="http://www.download.com">Download</A> the necessary application
from here.
</OBJECT>
</BODY>
</HTML>
```

The Object tag has both a beginning and ending tag. The attributes placed in the opening tag identify object information such as the name of the object and the location to download the object. Since the object can have parameters, the <PARAM> tag is provided to support passing parameters to the object when it is loaded. For an ActiveX object, these parameters are the ActiveX control's properties. If the browser cannot load the object, it will display any HTML text or tags that are between the Object tags. If the Object cannot be loaded, then the Param tags are ignored. Any supported HTML tags can be placed in between the Object tags.

> **CAUTION**
>
> The ability to set an ActiveX property from the Param tag is not guaranteed unless the object was created with Visual Basic 5.0. If the control was created with Visual C++ or other high-level languages, the ability to set properties through the Param tag *must* be programmed by the developer via the PropertyBag or else the Data tag must be used. The data tag is described below in the Tag Attributes section.

## The HTML *<Object>* Tag Attributes

The Object tag's attributes are used to let the browser know how to display the object. Before the object is fully displayed, the ActiveX layer in the Microsoft Internet Explorer attempts to load the control based on these attributes. Table 8.1 lists all the attributes that apply to ActiveX controls (there are more attributes that are in the specification but are not related to ActiveX controls).

**Table 8.1   Object Tag Attributes**

| Attribute Name | Function |
|---|---|
| ALIGN | Position of the object |
| BORDER | Border of the object |
| CLASSID | Class identifier of the object |
| CODEBASE | ULR location of the object |
| DATA | Encoded initialization information (see caution below) |
| DECLARE | Object is declared but not loaded until it is referenced |
| HEIGHT | Height of the object |
| HSPACE | Horizontal gutter of the object |
| ID | Reference name of the object |
| NAME | Name of object when passed in a Form tag |
| TYPE | Mime type |

*continues*

**Table 8.1   Continued**

| Attribute Name | Function |
| --- | --- |
| VSPACE | Vertical gutter of the object |
| WIDTH | Width of the object |

Some of the attributes are used to load the control correctly, some are used to reference the object (such as in a VBScript), and some are used to visually display the control correctly. The first set of attributes focuses on the loading attributes, the second set focuses on referencing the attribute with code, and the third set of attributes focuses on the display of the control.

**Attributes that Load the ActiveX Control**   While some of the attributes are not critical to the object loading, there are a couple of attributes that have to be correctly set in order for the object to be loaded. The main attributes for an ActiveX object are the CLASSID (this should be familiar to you by now) and the CODEBASE. The classid is the unique identifier for this control, this is how the browser can find the control. The codebase is the location of where to download the control from. As with all attributes, the correct syntax is Attribute="value" where the attribute name is not case sensitive. CODEBASE will be treated the same as codebase.

The CLASSID attribute value should have the classid of the object, prefaced with the characters 'classid:'. The classid value can be found in the registry at HKEY_CLASSES_ROOT\\*XYZ*\\CLASSID where XYZ is the name of the control.

The registry on Windows NT 4.0 can be accessed via the **regedit.exe** application. It is used to navigate through the registry much like the Windows file system can be navigated with the Explorer.

When you get the regedit application, double-click the entry in the right side. This will bring up a dialog box. You can select that text (the classid), and copy it (control-c). You can then paste the number into your HTML page. Do *NOT* alter the number in any way, or your browser will not be able to find the control.

The preceding example, "ComCtl2.Animation.1," contains the version number. By looking at this name, you can figure out that the version number is 1.

Listing 8.2 illustrates how a Web page can use just the classid attribute. The Web page is entirely correct only if the control does not need any initialization data (such as properties), will not be referenced via VBScript, and is already on the machine. There are not a lot of controls that meet that criteria. Do not expect this page to load a control in your browser; this code is meant to be an example.

**Listing 8.2   A Web Page that Uses the Object Tag with the Classid Attribute**

```
<HTML>
<HEAD>
<TITLE>Basic ActiveX Control Page</TITLE>
```

```
</HEAD>
<BODY>

My interesting Web page.

<OBJECT CLASSID="CLSID:978C9E23-D4B0-11CE-BF2D-00AA003F40D0">
</OBJECT>

</BODY>
</HTML>
```

The CODEBASE attribute should be the URL location to download the control from. The URL should look like any Web address such as **http://www.mysite.org/controls/mycontrol.ocx**. As long as the control's extension is .OCX, you don't need to supply any more information. OCX should be the default extension if the control is built with Visual Basic 5. If you know that the control will already be on the client machine (such as a company intranet of only Windows machines), you don't need to use the codebase attribute.

Before the browser downloads the control, it will first check to see if the control currently exists on the system. If the control does exist, the browser checks to see if the control is the correct version (if one is specified). If the control does not exist on the client machine, the browser downloads the control and registers it. If the control is on the machine but is not the correct version, the browser downloads the control and registers it. If the control is the correct version, the browser is done with the codebase attribute.

The control's version is denoted in the codebase attribute by adding a '#Version=' then the version number. The version number's syntax is a four part number where each part is comma-delimited. In your Windows operating system, if you right-click an executable file (EXE), the version property page will have the version number such as 4.00.31.85. For the HTML page, the periods are replaced with commas. A valid codebase value with a version is http://www.mysite.com/mycontrols/mycontrol.ocx Version=4,00,31,85. The version is programmatically added to the control when it is built by the programmer. It is up to the programmer to make sure that different 'versions' of the same control have different version numbers. The higher the version number, the more recent it is. 4.00.31.85 is a newer version than 4.00.31.70.

A developer can easily choose any extension for the control he wants. If the extension is not OCX, then the download will have to be a *.cab (short for cabinet) file. The cab file is a compression technique to make the control smaller as it is shipped across the Internet. Other files that can go in the cab file are information files (*.inf) that tell the browser what to do with the control and any files that are in the cab file. There is a complete Cabinet Developer's SDK at **http://www.microsoft.com/workshop/prog/cab/**. Since this book assumes that controls are built with Visual Basic 5, I'll assume that controls used in this book have the extension of OCX. Visual Basic 5's Books Online has a section regarding CAB files.

> **CAUTION**
>
> Building a cab file can be a simple task or a complex task, depending on what you want to happen to the files included in the cab file. For example, if the control has an extension of .XYZ and isn't dependent on any other files, the only action necessary for the browser is to register to control. The browser automatically registers the control if the Extension is OCX. However, if the control is dependent on several other files (such as initialization files or other dynamic link libraries), the browser will need to be told where those files should be put and if any information needs to be added to the system registry.

Listing 8.3 illustrates a Web page that uses the classid and the codebase. The codebase can be an absolute reference to a Web page (the first object on the page) or it can be a relative reference from the location of the calling Web page (the second object on the page). Do not expect this page to load a control in your browser, this code is meant to be an example.

**Listing 8.3    A Web Page that Uses the Object Tag with the Classid Attribute and the Codebase Attribute**

```
<HTML>
<HEAD>
<TITLE>Basic ActiveX Control Page</TITLE>
</HEAD>
<BODY>

My interesting Web page.

<OBJECT
CLASSID="CLSID:978C9E23-D4B0-11CE-BF2D-00AA003F40D0"
CODEBASE="www.mysite.com/scripts/mycontrol.ocx">
</OBJECT>

<OBJECT
CLASSID="CLSID:978C9E23-D4B0-11CE-BF2D-00AA003F40D0"
CODEBASE="/../../scripts/mycontrol.ocx">
</OBJECT>

</BODY>
</HTML>
```

The DATA attribute is used to initialize the ActiveX control properties through 64-bit encoding. This data is encoded so the initialization of the ActiveX controls properties is unreadable. If you don't have to use the Data attribute, it is much easier to use the equivalent Param tags discussed later. Since the initiliation of properties is encoded, you will not be able to read the values of the properties. The encoding is meant for small but complex initialization. If an ActiveX control is poorly developed in a high-level language, all the initialization of the properties will be through 64-bit encoding. There is nothing wrong with this, but there are two drawbacks to using the data attribute. The first is that you have to know how to generate the 64-bit encoding. The second is that it is not easily read, so debugging will be difficult.

Listing 8.4 illustrates a sample Web page that uses the data attribute. Notice that the value of the attribute is prepended with information about the encoding and the MIME type. This particular control is the Calendar Control 8.0. Do not expect this page to load a control in your browser; this code is meant to be an example.

**Listing 8.4    Initializing an ActiveX Control's Properties Using the DATA Attribute in a Web Page**

```
<HTML>
<HEAD>
<TITLE>Basic ActiveX Control Page</TITLE>
</HEAD>
<BODY>

My interesting Web page.

<OBJECT ID="Calendar1" WIDTH=288 HEIGHT=192
  CLASSID="CLSID:8E27C92B-1264-101C-8A2F-040224009C02"
  DATA="DATA:application/x-oleobject;BASE64,K8knjmQSHBCKLwQCJ
ACcAgAACADEHQAA2BMAAM0HBAAXAA8AAIAAAAAAAACg
ABAAAIAAAKAAAQABAAIAAAABAAAAAQAAAAEAAAABAAAAAQAAAAEAAAAAAAA
AAAAAAAAAAAAAAAAAAAAAAAAAAAAAAAAAAAAAAAAAAAAAAAAAAAAAAAAAAAA
AAAAAAAAAAAAAAAAAAAAAAAAAAAAAAAAAAAAAAAAAAAAAAAAAAAAAAAAAAAA
AAAAAAAAAAAAAAAAAAAAAAAAAAAAAAAAAAAAAAAAAAAAAAAAAAAAAAAAAAAA
AAAAAAAAAAAAAAAAAAAAAAAAAAAAAAAAAAAAAAAAAAAAAAAAAAAAAAAAAAAA
AAAAAAAAAAAAAAAAAAAAAAAAAAAAAAAAAAAAAAAAAAAAAAAAAAAAAAAAAAAA
AAAAAAAAAAAAAAAAAAAAAAAAAAAAAAAAAAAAAAAAAAAAEAAAC8AkRCAQAFQXJp
YWwBAAAAkAFEQgEABUFyaWFFsAQAAALwCwNQBAAVBcmlhbA==">
</OBJECT>
</BODY>
</HTML>
```

**TIP**    If you have a hard time deciphering the encoding of the preceding listing, there are a couple of programs from Microsoft meant to make this type of work easy. Microsoft's ActiveX Control Pad (free on the Microsoft Web site) is an elementary application to add ActiveX controls to a Web page. Since it is free, the functionality is bare and the support from Microsoft is nonexistent. Microsoft's Visual InterDev (part of the Developer Suite) has an advanced version of the same functionality and dialogs of the ActiveX Control Pad. Once you select the object you want to add to the page, a property sheet comes up (just like in Visual Basic). You fill in the property sheet and design the visual properties of the object. When you insert the control into the page, the properties are set for you, either through the Data attribute or the Param tag (discussed in the following section).

If you use the DATA attribute and the data is just an URL (instead of encoding), you will need to use the TYPE attribute to let the browser know what type of data is being retrieved. If the browser doesn't support that MIME type, the data will not be downloaded and the object will not be initialized. Understand that using the data attribute as an URL is the hard way to work with the popular controls already on your Windows 95 or Windows NT machine (depending on the control—it may be impossible). The popular controls generally need the properties set through the data attribute encoded or set through the PARAM tag (discussed later). If you have created your own control, using the DATA attribute as an URL and the TYPE attribute to specify the MIME type may work for you.

Listing 8.5 illustrates how to use the DATA and TYPE attributes together. Do not expect this page to load a control in your browser; this code is meant to be an example. Comparing Listings 8.4 and 8.5, you can see that when the data is encoded, the datatype is already included. When the data is not encoded, the MIME type has to be specified via the TYPE attribute.

**Listing 8.5 Initializing an ActiveX Control by Using the DATA and TYPE Attributes Together**

```
<HTML>
<HEAD>
<TITLE>Declare Attribute</TITLE>
</HEAD>
<BODY>
    <OBJECT ID="MyControl"
    CLASSID="CLSID:0713E8A2-850A-131b-AXC0-4210302A8DA7"
    DATA="http://mysite/mydirectory/mydata.xyz"
TYPE="application/x-oleobject">
    </OBJECT>
</BODY>
</HTML>
```

The DECLARE attribute is used to let the browser know what object will be loaded, but not to load it until it is referenced. There are two situations where this is a cool feature. The first is to have a link point to an object that would not be able to be referenced from a single URL. The second is when one object is a parameter to another object. An example of this is the ever-popular tree control. The tree control is generally used along with a control of images. A tree element of type X will have an image that illustrates X and a tree element of Y will have an image that illustrates Y. In order to have the image control be a parameter of the tree control, the tree control will list the image control as a parameter with the PARAM tag (discussed later). The image control will then use the DECLARE attribute so that it is loaded only when the tree control needs it. Loading the control only when it is referenced is referred to as *late binding*.

Listing 8.6 illustrates how to use the DECLARE attribute. The first control is the tree control. The control has a property called ImageList where the second control needs to be referenced. The # sign in front of the reference to ImageList1 in the first control means that the referenced control is on the same page. The second control, the ImageList, needs to have the declare statement so that it is loaded only when the tree control is initialized. If you run this page as written, it will not run. This code is for discussion purposes only. Using the tree control and imagelist control actually require a lot more code to function but are perfect examples for the DECLARE attribute. Both of these controls use the DATA attribute to initialize the control. I've reduced the value of the DATA attribute so that the code listing is easier to read (and the DATA attribute is hard to read).

## Listing 8.6   Declaring an ActiveX Control that Will be Initialized by Another Control on the Same Web Page

```
<HTML>
<HEAD>
<TITLE>Declare Attribute</TITLE>
</HEAD>
<BODY>

    <OBJECT ID="TreeView1"
     CLASSID="CLSID:0713E8A2-850A-101b-AFC0-4210102A8DA7"
     DATA="DATA:application/x-oleobject;BASE64...">
      <PARAM NAME="ImageList" VALUE="#ImageList1"
VALUETYPE="OBJECT">
    </OBJECT>

    <OBJECT ID="ImageList1" DECLARE
     CLASSID="CLSID:58DA8D8F-9D6A-101b-AFC0-4210102A8DA7"
     DATA="DATA:application/x-oleobject;BASE64...">
    </OBJECT>
</BODY>
</HTML>
```

**Attributes that Reference the ActiveX Control**   Only two attributes are used to reference that ActiveX control: NAME and ID. The NAME attribute should be familiar to you. Any information passed in a form uses the NAME attribute. The NAME attribute is used on the Web server when the page is returned to reference the data sent back. This is no different for the ActiveX control. If you use the control inside a FORM where some information is being sent back to the server, the object tag will have to use the NAME attribute. The name can be any string value you want, such as "MyControl" or "TreeControl" or just "CNTR." Listing 8.7 illustrates how to include the NAME attribute on the Web page. The NAME attribute has no affect on any of the other attributes. It is used by the browser only to pass values back to the Web server.

## Listing 8.7   By Using the NAME Attribute, the ActiveX's Properties Can Be Passed in a FORM

```
<HTML>
<HEAD>
<TITLE>The Name Attribute</TITLE>
</HEAD>
<BODY>

<FORM METHOD="GET" ACTION="nextpage.htm">
    <OBJECT
     CLASSID="CLSID:978C9E23-D4B0-11CE-BF2D-00AA003F40D0"
     NAME="MyControl">
    </OBJECT>
```

*continues*

---

**Listing 8.7   Continued**

```
</FORM>
</BODY>
</HTML>
```

---

Remember that forms use the name/value pair to pass information back to the server. The NAME attribute and the VALUE attribute have to be set. The preceding example is valid according to the HTML specification, but probably will not be used in this manner for Internet Explorer 3.x. The problem is that the VALUE attribute is not listed in the object tag and the browser can't assume what it is. In order to pass back a value to the server in a form from an ActiveX object, you will probably want to set the name and value in VBScript and then include that information in an input tag of the form tag. The value could be any number of things: a property, a result of a method call, or some value as a result of a user event. This functionality may change in the 4.0 version of Microsoft's Internet Explorer.

The other reference attribute is the ID attribute. If you plan on managing the control in script, the ID is mandatory. The only way you can reference the control in script is from the ID. The ID is a string that you choose and can be just about anything. It is a good coding practice to name the ID something that reflects what the control does. Any reference to the control's methods, properties, and events in script will have to be prefixed with the ID. This is exactly the same as the name of the control in a true Visual Basic application. Listing 8.8 illustrates how you would reference a control from VBScript. Don't concentrate on the syntax of the script; this is only meant to be an example. A more detailed discussion of VBScript and ActiveX follows later in this chapter. Notice that Procedure1 changes the background color of the label to green. The object name is Label1 and the property is BackColor.

---

**Listing 8.8   By Using the ID Attribute, the ActiveX Control Can Be Manipulated in VBScript or Java Script**

```
<HTML>
<HEAD>
<TITLE>The ID Attribute</TITLE>

<SCRIPT LANGUAGE="VBScript">
<!--
Sub Procedure1()
     Label1.BackColor = "GREEN"
end sub
-->
</SCRIPT>

</HEAD>
<BODY>
    <OBJECT ID="Label1" WIDTH=132 HEIGHT=28
     CLASSID="CLSID:978C9E23-D4B0-11CE-BF2D-00AA003F40D0">
        <PARAM NAME="Caption" VALUE="My Cool Label Control">
        <PARAM NAME="Size" VALUE="3493;741">
        <PARAM NAME="BorderStyle" VALUE="1">
```

```
        <PARAM NAME="FontCharSet" VALUE="0">
        <PARAM NAME="FontPitchAndFamily" VALUE="2">
    </OBJECT>
  </BODY>
</HTML>
```

**Attributes that Control the Visual Display of the ActiveX Control**   Several attributes affect how the control will display on the page. They are ALIGN, BORDER, HEIGHT, HSPACE, VSPACE, and WIDTH. These attributes should be familiar to use but this section will focus on how the attributes relate to ActiveX controls. The ALIGN attribute focuses on the positioning of the control in relation to the objects around it. The values for align are: left, texttop, middle, textmiddle, baseline, textbottom, center, and right. The BORDER attribute specifies how large a border you want around the object. The HEIGHT and WIDTH specify how large the object should be. The HSPACE and VSPACE specify how much space should be in between this control and everything else.

# Working with the *<PARAM>* Tag

You have two choices of how to set the parameters of the ActiveX control. The first is through the DATA attribute of the OBJECT tag. The second is through the PARAM tag. The param tag is much easier to use because it follows the HTML standard name/value pair model. The data is not encoded so it is easy to see what has been passed to the control. The PARAM tag is enclosed within the OBJECT's beginning and ending tags.

The PARAM tag has two obvious attributes of NAME and VALUE. NAME is the name of the property of the ActiveX control and VALUE is what the property is to be initialized to. It also has two more attributes: VALUETYPE and TYPE. The VALUETYPE is used in Listing 8.6 to describe what type of information is contained in the VALUE attribute. The value can be DATA (not encoded), OBJECT, meaning an object's name (such as listing 8.6), or REF, meaning a Web address reference. The TYPE attribute indicates the MIME type of the data. The TYPE attribute would be used in conjunction with the VALUETYPE attribute being equal to REF. Because the parameter VALUEDATA is a Web site, the browser will have to know what type of data is being retrieved at that Web site. Listing 8.9 illustrates a couple of different controls that use the PARAM tag. This listing is meant to be an example and may not load in your browser.

## Listing 8.9   Using the PARAM Tag

```
<HTML>
<HEAD>
<TITLE>The ID Attribute</TITLE>



</HEAD>
<BODY>
    <OBJECT ID="Label1" WIDTH=132 HEIGHT=28
```

*continues*

**Listing 8.9 Continued**

```
    CLASSID="CLSID:978C9E23-D4B0-11CE-BF2D-00AA003F40D0">
        <PARAM NAME="Caption" VALUE="My Cool Label Control">
        <PARAM NAME="Size" VALUE="3493;741">
        <PARAM NAME="BorderStyle" VALUE="1">
        <PARAM NAME="FontCharSet" VALUE="0">
        <PARAM NAME="FontPitchAndFamily" VALUE="2">
    </OBJECT>


    <OBJECT ID="Marquee1" WIDTH=148 HEIGHT=40
     CLASSID="CLSID:1A4DA620-6217-11CF-BE62-0080C72EDD2D"
     CODEBASE="text.htm">
        <PARAM NAME="_ExtentX" VALUE="3916">
        <PARAM NAME="_ExtentY" VALUE="1058">
    </OBJECT>
</BODY>
</HTML>
```

There is no reason that the DATA attribute (encoded data) and the PARAM tag cannot be used together. However, it doesn't happen very often. Most controls use either the DATA attribute or the PARAM tag.

# Writing Web Pages with Microsoft Visual Interdev

Writing Web pages that have ActiveX Controls can be simple if the control is simple. The controls that have great functionality are usually more complex. Microsoft has developed an environment to make writing these pages easier. This tool is called Visual Interdev. It is sold separately or as part of the Visual Developer suite. To illustrate how easy it is to write a Web page with Visual Interdev, I'll write a Web page that uses a tab page control.

**N O T E** The first control used in this section is called *Calendar Control 8.0.* The OCX file for this control is *mscal.ocx* . The second control used is called *Microsoft Forms 2.0 Textbox.* The filename is *fm20.dll.* ■

The first thing to do is start up Visual Interdev and insert the control. Figure 8.1 shows the dialog box in which to add a new HTML page. This is reached from the File|New menu item, and by selecting the Files tab. You have a lot of different things that Visual InterDev will create for you. This will create a basic HTML file for you, as well as make a note of where you should start including your own HTML or ActiveX.

When you want to add an ActiveX control, use the Insert|Into HTML|ActiveX Control menu. This will display a window of all the ActiveX controls registered on the system. If you have developed a control but it is not displayed in this dialog box, make sure it is registered. Figure 8.2 illustrates the dialog box of all the controls on this system. The Calendar control is highlighted. Notice that behind this dialog box is the HTML file that Visual InterDev has written for you.

**FIG. 8.1**

Creating a new HTML page is the first thing you do after starting Visual Interdev.

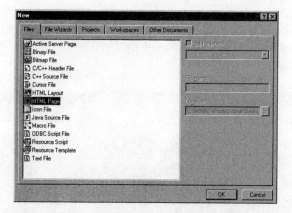

---

 **TIP** If your control is not registered, you can register it in Visual InterDev from the Tools | Register Control menu item. Or, you can go to a command prompt and type **regsvr32 x** where **x** is the path and file name of the control. If you just type in **regsvr32**, a dialog box will display all the options for using the regsvr32 application.

---

**FIG. 8.2**

The next step is to select the ActiveX control.

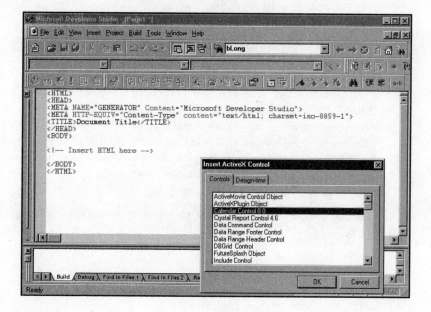

Figure 8.3 illustrates what happens once you choose the control and click OK. The HTML page is still open but is displayed behind the dialog box shown in this figure. This is where you design the control. You can set the properties displayed in the Properties dialog box or you can resize the object.

**FIG. 8.3**

You need to design the physical and programmable properties of the ActiveX control next.

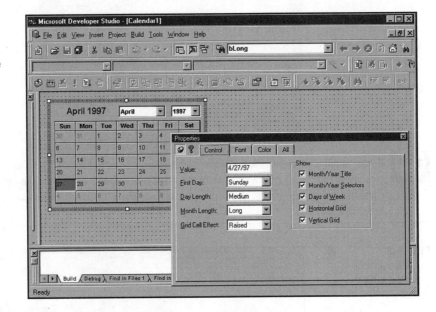

If you take the default properties and don't resize the object, the HTML page created is in Listing 8.10. Notice that Visual InterDev adds Meta tag information. The calendar control object tag was completely filled in by Visual InterDev. The default property of this control has no codebase value, so in order for this control to download, that attribute would need to be added. Any control you choose will not have the codebase value added. You can either add the text to the HTML page yourself or have Visual InterDev do it.

---

**Listing 8.10   An Example of Using the Calendar Control, the DATA Attribute Is Encoded**

```
<HTML>
<HEAD>
<META NAME="GENERATOR" Content="Microsoft Developer Studio">
<META HTTP-EQUIV="Content-Type" content="text/html; charset=iso-8859-1">
<TITLE>Document Title</TITLE>
</HEAD>
<BODY>

<OBJECT ID="Calendar1" WIDTH=288 HEIGHT=192 HSPACE=20 VSPACE=20 ALIGN="CENTER"
    CLASSID="CLSID:8E27C92B-1264-101C-8A2F-040224009C02"
    DATA="DATA:application/x-
oleobject;BASE64,K8knjmQSHBCKLwQCJACcAgAACADEHQAA2BMAAM0HBAASAA8AAIAAAAAAACg
```

```
ABAAAIAAAKAAAQABAAIAAAABAAAAAQAAAAEAAAABAAAAAQAAAAEAAAAAAAA
AAAAAAAAAAAAAAAAAAAAAAAAAAAAAAAAAAAAAAAAAAAAAAAAAAAAAAAAAAAA
AAAAAAAAAAAAAAAAAAAAAAAAAAAAAAAAAAAAAAAAAAAAAAAAAAAAAAAAAAAA
AAAAAAAAAAAAAAAAAAAAAAAAAAAAAAAAAAAAAAAAAAAAAAAAAAAAAAAAAAAA
AAAAAAAAAAAAAAAAAAAAAAAAAAAAAAAAAAAAAAAAAAAAAAAAAAAAAAAAAAAA
AAAAAAAAAAAAAAAAAAAAAAAAAAAAAAAAAAAAAAAAAAAAAAAAAAAAAAAAAAAA
AAAAAAAAAAAAAAAAAAAAAAAAAAAAAAAAAAAAAAAAAAEAAAC8AkRCAQAFQXJp
YWwBAAAAkAFEQgEABUFyaWFFsAQAAAALwCwNQBAAVBcmlhbA==
">
```

```
  </OBJECT>
<BR>
    <OBJECT ID="TextBox1" WIDTH=196 HEIGHT=112 ALIGN="CENTER" HSPACE=20
VSPACE=20
      CLASSID="CLSID:8BD21D10-EC42-11CE-9E0D-00AA006002F3">
        <PARAM NAME="VariousPropertyBits" VALUE="2894088219">
        <PARAM NAME="Size" VALUE="5186;2963">
        <PARAM NAME="FontCharSet" VALUE="0">
        <PARAM NAME="FontPitchAndFamily" VALUE="2">
    </OBJECT>
</BODY>
</HTML>
```

It's always best to design what the Web page will look like and and what it will do before doing it, so here is the design. The Web page will display both a text box (ActiveX control) and a calendar (ActiveX control). As a user maneuvers through the calendar, any special information about that day will be displayed in the textbox. At this point, I have added the textbox control and now some script needs to be written to make things happen.

Figure 8.4 illustrates what the page looks like in a browser. There has been no additional text added to the page so that you can see what the two controls look like without having to figure out what actually goes along with the control. The current day and month are chosen. Any month and year can be selected from a drop-down box list. The textbox is empty (because nothing has been added to it).

**N O T E**    Remember that an ActiveX control has methods, properties, and events. A property is a value of the object such as color or text. An event is a procedure that is triggered when a certain user interaction happens such as clicking an object. A method can be several things. A method can set or get a property value. A method can perform some function (such as arithmetic), or a method can fire off an event. ■

The textbox information will be changing based on user input so the script must be associated with events of the control. In order to add these events, the Visual InterDev script wizard (View|Script Wizard menu item) should be used. Figure 8.5 is the Script Wizard dialog box. The events are on the left side (divided between the two controls and the window). The properties and methods are on the right side. The icon for methods is a square with an exclamation point in it. The icon for properties is a square with lines (denoting the property sheet).

**FIG. 8.4**

Manipulating the calendar control and text box from a Web page.

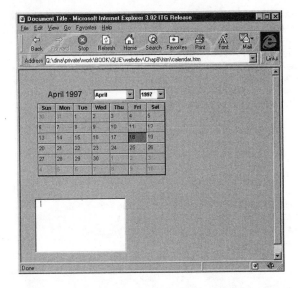

**FIG. 8.5**

A close look at the Visual InterDev Script Wizard.

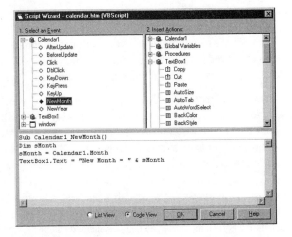

In order to set the text in the textbox, the NewMonth event is used. The NewMonth event is fired off anytime the current month is changed. With this control, the NewMonth event is fired off in two ways. The first is changing the month in the drop-down list box. The second is to click a greyed-out day number (the greyed out number indicates that the day is not in the current month). In order to set the textbox, the textbox control name has to be referenced. The code in this figure (the entire HTML page) appears in Listing 8.11. Only the DATA attribute has been shortened, although it has not changed from Listing 8.10. Notice that the Script Wizard has added the required <SCRIPT> tag, as well as the code I typed in to the event window regarding the NewMonth event. Visual InterDev is not necessary to write this Web page, but it does make programming ActiveX Web pages easier. The type of script language has to be set in the SCRIPT tag. The two choices are VBScript and Java.

### Listing 8.11 Using the NewMonth Event of the Calendar Control

```
<HTML>
<HEAD>
<META NAME="GENERATOR" Content="Microsoft Developer Studio">
<META HTTP-EQUIV="Content-Type" content="text/html; charset=iso-8859-1">
<TITLE>Document Title</TITLE>
</HEAD>
<BODY>
    <SCRIPT LANGUAGE="VBScript">
<!--
Sub Calendar1_NewMonth()
Dim sMonth
sMonth = Calendar1.Month
TextBox1.Text = "New Month = " & sMonth
end sub
-->
    </SCRIPT>
    <OBJECT ID="Calendar1" WIDTH=288 HEIGHT=192 HSPACE=20 VSPACE=20
➥ALIGN="CENTER"
     CLASSID="CLSID:8E27C92B-1264-101C-8A2F-040224009C02"
     DATA="DATA:application/x-oleobject;BASE64,...
">
    </OBJECT>
<BR>
    <OBJECT ID="TextBox1" WIDTH=196 HEIGHT=112 ALIGN="CENTER" HSPACE=20
➥VSPACE=20
     CLASSID="CLSID:8BD21D10-EC42-11CE-9E0D-00AA006002F3">
        <PARAM NAME="VariousPropertyBits" VALUE="2894088219">
        <PARAM NAME="Size" VALUE="5186;2963">
        <PARAM NAME="FontCharSet" VALUE="0">
        <PARAM NAME="FontPitchAndFamily" VALUE="2">
    </OBJECT>
</BODY>
</HTML>
```

**TIP**  If you are not using Visual InterDev or Microsoft ActiveX Control Pad, you MUST have some way of discovering methods, properties, and events. Some controls have documentation, but some don't.

**CAUTION**

In Listing 8.11 the script code (but not the script tags) are enclosed in HTML comments "<!--" and "-->." If you are writing this code in a different editor than Visual InterDev, you still must include these comments. There are several older browsers that do not support scripting. While the browser will ignore the <SCRIPT> tag, it will display the script code as text (because it thinks that is what it is). Microsoft's IE browser will treat any VBScript inside the <SCRIPT> tag as script and ignore the fact that it is HTML commented. This lets the page work on different browsers.

When you write a procedure for events, the procedure name must be the control ID (ID attribute) followed by an underscore and then the event name. In Listing 8.11, the Script for the new prodecure is `Calendar1_NewMonth()`, where `Calendar1` is from the ID attribute of the control and `NewMonth` is the event name. Notice that no parameters are passed to this procedure. Because the event is triggered by the system, no parameters will be passed. With this code, the text box will display `New Month = 5` if the month is May. Since the control store months are numbers, it is up to the programmer to switch from the numeric representation to the character representation.

Now to add a bit more work to the control. The Web page should be designed so that if a new month is chosen, any corresponding information should be added. If a particular day is clicked, any pertinent information should be added. In order to make sure that the text box information has both the month information and the day information, a couple of global variables will be added. *DayInfo* will be storage for the current day's information. *MonthInfo* will be storage for the current month's information. TextInfo will be storage for the combination of DayInfo, MonthInfo and anything else added to the text box. This can be done through the Script Wizard by using the right side; select Global Variables and right-click. A menu of choices will be displayed of New Global Variable or New Procedure. Choose New Global Variable and type in the name and click OK. The only addition to the Web page is made in the script section. Listing 8.12 is the new script section. The only added text is the "Dim variablename." Dim is the VB way of defining variables; it is short for dimension.

### Listing 8.12  Adding Global Variables to a Web Page in the VBScript Section

```
<SCRIPT LANGUAGE="VBScript">
<!--
dim MonthInfo
dim DayInfo

Sub Calendar1_NewMonth()
Dim sMonth
sMonth = Calendar1.Month
TextBox1.Text = "New Month = " & sMonth
end sub
-->
</SCRIPT>
```

**N O T E**   Notice that Listing 8.12 has dim and DIM, two different cases. The global variable dims were written  by Visual InterDev's Script Wizard. The DIM in `Calendar1_NewMonth()` I wrote outside of the script wizard. VBScript doesn't care what the case is of the keywords. VBScript is case-insensitive just like Visual Basic.  ▪

**T I P**   When I first wrote the script for this control, some of the events were not being fired when I expected them to. In order to debug this, I used the ActiveX control test container to watch the events as they were fired. Figure 8.6 illustrates what the messages look like when the calendar control events are fired.

**FIG. 8.6**

Using the ActiveX control test container to look at the events as they are fired off.

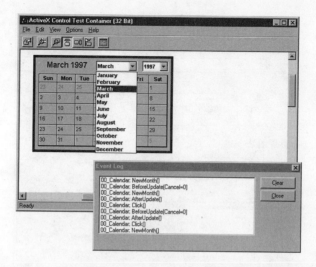

Listing 8.13 is the Web page with the code to update the textbox. It doesn't matter which procedure is first. Figure 8.7 illustrates what the Web page will look like. There is not a lot of code here, but the user can interact with the calendar control and the test control can be updated.

**Listing 8.13  Updating the Textbox Based on Events of the ActiveX Calendar Control**

```vbscript
<SCRIPT LANGUAGE="VBScript">
<!--
dim YearInfo
dim MonthInfo

Sub Calendar1_NewYear()
iYear = Calendar1.Year
YearInfo = iYear
MonthInfo = Calendar1.Month
TextBox1.Text = YearInfo  & MonthInfo
end sub

Sub Calendar1_NewMonth()
iMonth = Calendar1.Month
select case (iMonth)
case 1
    MonthInfo = " January is a cold month."
case 2
    MonthInfo = " Februrary is a snowy month"
case 3
    MonthInfo = " March is a green month"
end select
YearInfo = Calendar1.Year
TextBox1.Text = YearInfo  & MonthInfo
end sub
-->
    </SCRIPT>
```

**FIG. 8.7**
The Calendar Control and the Textbox Control interacting.

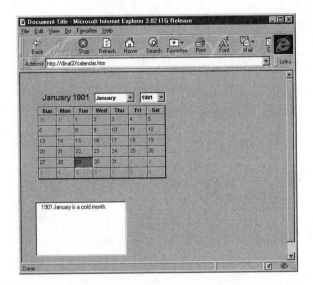

# Examining Different Types of ActiveX Controls

There are several types of controls. This last example in Listing 8.13 used a control that "sat" on the page (contained inside the browser window). There are controls that can "hover" over the browser such as the common control dialog (File Open). There are controls not visible to the user at all. You should look for controls that either add to the functionality of the page or save the user from having to do "extra" work. Adding functionality and making the user do extra work will affect the number of visitors that return to your page.

## Another Example—System Information

In this example, the Web page will have an invisible ActiveX control that reads the system information of the user's machine and fills in a form. The user can then submit the form back to the Web server. If you want to inventory a company's machines but don't want to walk to each machine, this is a good way to do it.

Using the *Microsoft SysInfo Control, Version 5.0*, with a file name of *SYSINFO.OCX*, I'll need the control to read the system information of the user's machine as soon as the Web page is loaded. In order to do that, I'll use the window_onLoad event. The SysInfo control doesn't have any events or methods, just properties of system information. As soon as the system information is loaded, I want it to fill in three text boxes in a form so that the user doesn't have to do any work but press the SUBMIT button. While this particular form is showing the user what is being passed back to the Web server, this was a design decision about the Web page. The INPUT tags could have been of type HIDDEN and the user would never have known that the information was being passed back.

Listing 8.14 is the entire contents of the Web page, and Figure 8.8 is how the page will load in the browser. In order to load the textboxes of the form when the page is first loaded, the `window_onLoad` procedure has to have the name of the textbox. Since the textbox is in an IN-PUT tag and the INPUT tag is in a form, the name is *FORM.ELEMENT.VALUE*. The INPUT tag is directly set by the SysInfo control's properties. That is all there is to it.

### Listing 8.14  Use the System Info ActiveX Control on a Web Page

```
<HTML>
<HEAD>
<META NAME="GENERATOR" Content="Microsoft Developer Studio">
<META HTTP-EQUIV="Content-Type" content="text/html; charset=iso-8859-1">
<TITLE>Document Title</TITLE>
    <SCRIPT LANGUAGE="VBScript">
<!--
Sub window_onLoad()
    MySysInfoForm.InputSysBuild.value = SysInfo1.OSBuild
    MySysInfoForm.InputSysPlatform.value = SysInfo1.OSPlatform
    MySysInfoForm.InputSysVersion.value = SysInfo1.OSVersion
end sub
-->
    </SCRIPT>
</HEAD>
<BODY>
Thank you for visiting my page. Here is your system information.
    <OBJECT ID="SysInfo1" WIDTH=39 HEIGHT=39
    CLASSID="CLSID:6FBA474B-43AC-11CE-9A0E-00AA0062BB4C">
        <PARAM NAME="_ExtentX" VALUE="1005">
        <PARAM NAME="_ExtentY" VALUE="1005">
        <PARAM NAME="_Version" VALUE="327680">
    </OBJECT>
    <FORM ACTION="sysinfo.asp" METHOD="GET" NAME="MySysInfoForm">
        <INPUT TYPE=TEXT NAME="InputSysBuild">
Build Number<BR>
        <INPUT TYPE=TEXT NAME="InputSysPlatform">
Platform<BR>
        <INPUT TYPE=TEXT NAME="InputSysVersion">
        System Version<BR>
        <INPUT TYPE=SUBMIT NAME="SUBMIT">
    </FORM>
</BODY>
</HTML>
```

# Another Example—Dialog Information

The last example will use the common dialog control, which will "hover" over the browser window. In this example, the event will be fired from inside a button inside a form. No separate VBScript section will be necessary. The `onClick` event of the button will contain the code. The code must first display the dialog box, then set the textbox with the file name. Both happen within the `onClick` event.

**FIG. 8.8**

The SysInfo displayed on a Web page

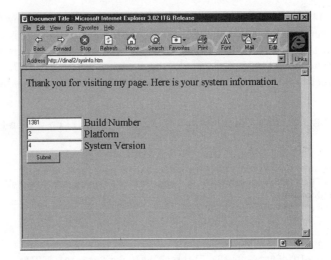

Listing 8.15 illustrates how easy it is to make this happen. The first thing the onClick event does is to pop up the dialog box to find the file, CommonDialog1.ShowOpen(). The next thing it does is assign the file chosen to the textbox in the form, FINDFILE.strFile.value. The objects in the form should have names. Figure 8.9 illustrates this Web page when the file is being chosen.

---

**Listing 8.15   Finding a File from a Web Page by Using the Common Dialog Control**

```
<HTML>
<HEAD>
<META NAME="GENERATOR" Content="Microsoft Developer Studio">
<META HTTP-EQUIV="Content-Type" content="text/html; charset=iso-8859-1">
<TITLE>Document Title</TITLE>
</HEAD>
<BODY>
Step 1) Please find the file you want to send to the server.
    <FORM NAME="FINDFILE">
        <INPUT LANGUAGE="VBScript" TYPE=BUTTON
          ONCLICK="call CommonDialog1.ShowOpen()
          FINDFILE.strFile.value = CommonDialog1.FileName"
         NAME="bFINDFILE" VALUE="Find File"><P><P>
        Step 2) You choose <INPUT TYPE=TEXT NAME="strFile">
    </FORM>
    <OBJECT ID="CommonDialog1" WIDTH=32 HEIGHT=32
     CLASSID="CLSID:F9043C85-F6F2-101A-A3C9-08002B2F49FB">
        <PARAM NAME="_ExtentX" VALUE="847">
        <PARAM NAME="_ExtentY" VALUE="847">
        <PARAM NAME="_Version" VALUE="327680">
        <PARAM NAME="DefaultExt" VALUE="*.*">
        <PARAM NAME="DialogTitle" VALUE="My Common Dialog Control">
        <PARAM NAME="InitDir" VALUE="c:\">
```

```
        </OBJECT>
      </BODY>
    </HTML>
```

**FIG. 8.9**
Finding the file by using
the Common Dialog
Control.

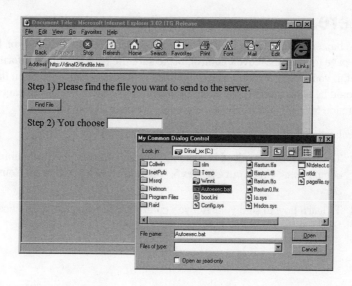

# Using ActiveX Controls

In this chapter, you've learned how to program a Web page with ActiveX controls. You may be under the impression that because you are not charged for the control when it is downloaded to your machine, that it is free. That is not correct. Please don't try to use any controls that have been downloaded to your machine from the Web except on the Web page they were downloaded with. They may be from reputable software manufacturers such as Microsoft, or they may be written by an individual. In either case, you cannot guarantee what the control will do, and the only "documentation" you have for that control is your discovery of it for properties, methods, and events. Any control downloaded from the Web should be treated with the same quality as a shareware product unless it is VeriSigned. VeriSign authentication means the code and company have been registered and can be held responsible for the behavior of their ActiveX component. If the control does not have a VeriSign authentication, you have no way of knowing who wrote it or to what extent it functions.

If you want to ensure a quality Web site and experience for your users, either purchase a control (there are several well-respected manufacturers) or make your own. A list of ActiveX control manufacturers can be found at **http://www.microsoft.com/gallery.asp**, known as the ActiveX Gallery. Do not think that because the control came from Microsoft, it will be of Microsoft quality. Microsoft has delegated the development of controls to third-party companies such as those listed in the ActiveX Gallery. The controls that come from Microsoft and are on the Gallery are meant to have low-functionality and there is generally no support for the controls.

Just because a control comes from the Web, doesn't make it free. ActiveX components are purchased and used the same way any other software is.

# From Here...

This chapter explored how to make a Web page with the Active X control. Before you design a Web page to have an ActiveX control, make sure the page is gaining information from the client. If you are performing a function that just as easily can be done on the Web server, then it should be done there. If you want to jump into writing ActiveX Web pages, first get the documentation for the controls and a good editor (such as Visual InterDev).

For related material on ActiveX, see the following chapters:

■ To learn what's involved in building ActiveX controls that communicate with server-side components, check out Chapter 5, "Making an ActiveX Control Communicate with a Server."

■ To learn how to sign your ActiveX controls with your digital certificate, see Chapter 6, "Making Your ActiveX Controls Web-Friendly."

# Using VBScript with Java Applets

This chapter introduces you to a completely different beast: the Java applet. It shows you how to use both Java applets you've created and those created by others. And it shows you how to integrate them with the rest of your Web page by using VBScript. ∎

**Learn about Java**

What Internet-development advantages Java offers over other languages.

**Identify the differences**

And similarities between Java applets and ActiveX controls.

**Build your own Web pages**

Find out what you need to do to add Java applets to your own Web pages.

**Writing Java applets**

Discover how to best write Java applets to be used from VBScript.

**Using Java applets**

Learn how to manipulate and use Java applets from VBScript just as you would ActiveX controls.

# Sorting out the Buzzwords

The computer industry has always been notorious for its buzzwords. Although every discipline has its own terminology, computer users seem to delight in speaking a language no one else can understand. Unfortunately, the Internet has thrust that language on the rest of us and, at the same time, added even more buzzwords to the mix.

Before going any further, let's clarify the words that seem to buzz around the topic at hand.

You are already familiar with Visual Basic and have probably been using it for awhile. You also know what VBScript is. But what is JavaScript?

JavaScript is a scripting language that you write alongside the HTML in your Web pages to do the same kinds of things you do with VBScript. Both have essentially the same capabilities and can be used to accomplish the same things. The only difference is in the languages themselves. You know that VBScript is a subset of Visual Basic and is very familiar if you are used to programming in Visual Basic. JavaScript, on the other hand, is loosely based on Java, which, in turn, is loosely based on C++. So if you come from a C++ or Java background, you will probably be more likely to prefer JavaScript.

You may have heard that JavaScript is a "simplified Java." It is not. It is a completely different language designed specifically for scripting tasks and is only loosely based on the Java language.

So that leaves Java itself. What is Java? Java is a brand new programming language created by Sun Microsystems. It was originally designed for consumer electronics and *smart home* applications. But when that didn't take off, Sun began looking for another home for Java. The Internet was the logical choice.

Java is a competitor of Visual Basic and C++. It allows you to create applications and compile and run them just as in those environments. It can be used to create server-side applications that communicate through CGI or one of the popular server APIs such as NSAPI and ISAPI.

But the big news about Java is that it also has the ability to create small applications, called applets, that can be used to enhance Web pages on the client side. These small applications work very much like ActiveX controls and can be manipulated by using VBScript to make your Web pages come alive.

In the next section you will see more detail on what Java is and why it is so cool. Then you'll see what an applet is and how to use applets with VBScript, just as you would an ActiveX control.

As you've seen in other chapters, Visual Basic is a very powerful language for building ActiveX controls and implementing server-side applications. Its intuitive environment allows you to create tools that get the job done quickly and easily.

Can you do everything you want to do with Visual Basic? Maybe, but think about these questions: Do you want to be able to use controls and applications written by others? Is the ability to run your applications on more than one platform important? If you answered yes to either of these questions then you definitely need to give Java a second look.

# Getting the Inside Story About Java

It's difficult to read anything computer-related these days without seeing a reference to Java. Some say it is the language of the future. Some say it will make all other languages obsolete. That's the hype anyway, but what's the truth?

Well, it turns out that Java is, in fact, a pretty amazing language. It's amazing because it's based on the revolutionary concept of *byte codes*.

## The Miracle of Byte Codes

After you write your application in Java, you compile it, just as you would if you were working with Visual Basic or C++. But instead of compiling the source code into machine code, it converts it instead to *byte codes*. Byte codes are a type of machine code, but they aren't the machine code native to the PC or the Mac or any other platform. They are the machine code for the Java Virtual Machine. The Java Virtual Machine is an imaginary computer that doesn't really exist. What good is machine code for a computer that doesn't exist? Well, the idea is that you can create a Java Virtual Machine (VM) in software that runs on a PC, another that runs on a Mac, and another for UNIX. These VMs can then each execute those byte codes produced by the Java compiler. The advantage is that these byte codes can run on any platform that has a Java VM running on it.

This special capability makes Java unique. Other languages have tried to make themselves multi-platform by keeping the source code the same across different machines. But this meant that the source had to be recompiled on each platform before it could run. Java has gone a step further. They have made their *machine code* multi-platform. So no additional compiling is necessary. As long as you are running the Java VM, you can run any compiled Java application out there. Since the Internet connects a huge variety of different machines running different operating systems, this level of portability is very important.

The downside, as you might expect, is that the Java VM doesn't execute Java byte codes as fast as your computer could run native machine code applications written specifically for it. So Java applications are bound to run slower than other applications. How much slower? It depends on how efficient the virtual machine is.

---

### Note: The Virtual Becomes Real

The Java Virtual Machine is an interesting concept. It is an abstract concept of a machine that doesn't really exist. Or does it? Chip manufacturers have now created chips that use Java byte codes as their native machine code. This was bound to happen. But the real question is, does it matter? One benefit of a real Java machine is that it would very likely run Java applications faster (all other things being equal) than Java Virtual Machines running on other platforms. Does this mean that we'll see a complete Java computer in the near future? Maybe. Perhaps it could form the heart of an inexpensive Web computer. Or perhaps it could be incorporated as a co-processor for PCs and other platforms. Then whenever Java code is to be executed, the co-processor will take over. Only time will tell if there's a place for a nonvirtual Java Virtual Machine.

---

# The Language

So what does Java code look like? Well, you might expect some revolutionary new language that looks like nothing you'd ever seen before. But if that's what you expect, you'll be disappointed. Java looks strikingly similar to good old C++. That's right, the same cryptic commands and curly brackets that sent you running to Visual Basic in the first place.

This, of course, is a good thing for the many C++ developers out there. The learning curve for them is relatively small. If you aren't a C++ person, though, the learning curve is a bit steeper.

So what's so revolutionary about a C++ clone? Well, Java really does make some important changes to the way C++ works. What is probably most significant is what it doesn't do. Java is a simple language and leaves out many of the difficult-to-understand, confusing, and bug-causing features of C++. Things like multiple-inheritance, pointers, structures, unions, and multi-dimensional arrays are all gone. This makes Java easier to learn, even for non-C++ folks.

But Java definitely is still very object-oriented. Java code is organized into classes which define a set of properties and methods that are manipulated at runtime. It supports multiple-level inheritance.

Another big advantage of Java over C++ is that you don't have to tediously care for and manage the memory you use. In C++ it's easy to allocate some memory and then lose track of your pointer to it. Once this happens, you can't use the memory anymore and you can't free it up either. In Java this sort of garbage collection and clean-up to free memory is handled for you automatically.

# Creating Java Applets

Java can be compiled and used to create stand-alone applications just like Visual Basic and C++. But Java can also be used to create Java applets. An applet, as the name implies, is a small application that can be downloaded when a browser pulls up your Web page. Once it is downloaded, the applet is executed and the results appear on your page. It might show up as an animation or a mortgage calculator or a game.

# Comparing Java Applets and ActiveX Controls

So what's the difference between a Java applet and an ActiveX control? Functionally, there isn't much of a difference. You can use both to enhance and activate your Web pages in a variety of ways. But there is a big difference in the way they are implemented.

First, Java Applets are always written in Java. ActiveX controls can be written in any language. Second, ActiveX controls are generally platform-specific to Windows. I say generally because you can write ActiveX controls in Java. But even when they are, it doesn't mean you can automatically use them wherever you use Java applets. That's because ActiveX controls are built on top of Microsoft's COM Architecture that is built into Windows. This architecture needs to be in place before the ActiveX control will work. Fortunately the COM Architecture has been ported to the Macintosh and to some flavors of UNIX. So everywhere you have the COM Architecture, you can port Java-written ActiveX controls.

Java Applets don't have any inherent dependence on architecture like ActiveX controls, but they do, sometimes, make use of platform-specific libraries. If you use a user-interface library for your Java Applet that was written exclusively for Windows, then you've negated the multi-platform benefit of Java. Although many libraries strive to be multi-platform, you still have to be careful what libraries you use.

So which is better? That depends on who you ask. Java proponents would emphasize the multi-platform benefits of the applet while ActiveX proponents would point to the higher level of integration that an ActiveX control provides and the proven history of the ActiveX (formerly OLE) architecture in Windows applications.

In the final analysis, though, you will probably want to be able to freely work with both ActiveX and Java Applets when you create your own Web pages. Fortunately, it isn't difficult.

# Dropping a Java Applet onto your Web Page

You are familiar with the <OBJECT> tag that is used to insert ActiveX controls into your HTML document. There is another tag for Java Applets: <APPLET>.

```
<APPLET CODEBASE="applets/java"
  CODE=CardGame.class
  WIDTH=150
  HEIGHT=220
  ALIGN=LEFT
  ALT="The Card Game"
  ID=game>
</APPLET>
```

**CODEBASE** identifies what subdirectory contains the Java Applets. **CODE** provides the actual file name of the Java Applet. This will always end in *.class*.

**WIDTH** and **HEIGHT** specify, in pixels, the area that the Java Applet will take up on the Web page. Remember, though, that a Java Applet *can* resize itself.

Only the properties **CODE, WIDTH** and **HEIGHT** are required. There are a number of other interesting properties available, though.

**ALIGN** determines how text will flow around the Java Applet on the HTML page. LEFT that the applet will appear to the left of the text. Other options are RIGHT, CENTER, TOP, MIDDLE and BOTTOM. These correspond exactly to the values for the ALIGN property of the <IMG> HTML tag.

**ALT**, as for other tags, provides alternative text, which is displayed in text-only Web browsers.

**ID** isn't required, but is important if you intend to access this applet from VBScript. This is the name you will use to access it.

**VSPACE** and **HSPACE** identify how much empty space should frame the applet vertically and horizontally. These work just like the corresponding <IMG> tag properties.

**DOWNLOAD** provides a number which is compared to the **DOWNLOAD** property on other objects and images on this page to determine the order in which they should be downloaded.

**NAME** provides another way of naming the applet. This name may be used by other applets on the page.

Between the <APPLET> tag and its end tag, there is often nothing at all. However, you can create Java Applets that accept parameters from the Web page. These parameters are then specified between the begin and end tags in this form:

```
<PARAM NAME="parametername" VALUE="value">
```

There can be any number of <PARAM> tags between the begin and end <APPLET> tag. The name of the parameter is specified by using the **NAME** property and the value you want to give the parameter is assigned to the **VALUE** property. Again, the Java Applet must be designed to accept parameters before you can pass them.

The </APPLET> ending tag is required.

# Accessing the Java Applet

You can access and manipulate Java Applets right from your VBScript code. In fact, you do it in almost exactly the same way you would access an ActiveX control:

```
<SCRIPT language = "VBScript">
<!--
Sub Document_OnLoad
document.game.DealCards
End Sub
-->
</SCRIPT>
```

The preceding code calls the function named DealCards in the Java applet inserted into the Web page in the last section. You must always prefix the name of the applet with document. You can refer to any public property or call any public function in the class.

# Creating Applets to Use from VBScript

You cannot simply insert an applet into your page and begin manipulating it from VBScript. The applet must be designed to allow you to take advantage of its capabilities.

There are several requirements. First, if you create the class in Java, you must inherit the class you create from the Applet class. If you wish to make properties and methods available from other classes, you must create wrapper properties and methods in the Applet-derived class and then delegate to the properties and methods of the other classes.

Second, you must make all those properties and methods you want access to in VBScript *public*. All public properties and methods of your Applet-derived class can be manipulated in VBScript.

Finally, the parameters that can be specified in the <APPLET> tag are not the same as the public variables which can be manipulated by VBScript. In order to make use of parameters you must use the getParameter() function.

# Creating a Sample Java Applet Scoreboard

I've created a simple Java applet and a VBScript HTML page to demonstrate how all this works.

## The Scoreboard Applet

The Java applet's name is scoreboard.java and it displays a number in big bold text. The idea is that you could create a game using VBScript and other Java or ActiveX controls and use this applet to display the current score.

Listing 9.1 is the source code for the scoreboard applet.

### Listing 9.1.   The *scoreboard.java* applet

```java
import java.applet.*;
import java.awt.*;

public class scoreboard extends Applet {

public int score=0;

public void updatescore() {
  repaint();
}

public void paint(Graphics g) {
  Font fnt = new Font("Helvetica", Font.BOLD, 24);
  g.setFont(fnt);
  g.drawString(String.valueOf(score), 20, 20);
  }
}
```

If you know Java, you'll easily understand how this works. If you don't, teaching you Java is well beyond the scope of this chapter. However, I will describe how this applet works and even if you've never seen Java code before, I'm sure you'll be able to follow along.

The first two lines are used to include some standard Java libraries. They give us the ability to create an applet and to use input/output commands.

The next line creates a new class called *scoreboard* that is inherited from the class named *Applet*. All applets are descendants of the Applet class or one of Applet's descendants. The rest of the listing fills in the details about this new scoreboard class. You know this because all the rest of the code is wrapped between the curly brackets ({ and }).

First, a public integer variable is created. It is named *score* and it is initialized to 0. This is the variable that will always hold the current score. Again, notice that it is public. That is what will make it available to you when you write your VBScript code.

Next, a public function is created called `updatescore`. The *void* indicates that it doesn't return a value and the empty parentheses afterwards indicate that it doesn't expect any arguments. All it does is call the `repaint()` function. This causes the applet to repaint itself and to execute any code in the paint function.

Finally, the last function is the `paint` function. This function is automatically called by the system whenever the applet is repainted. That happens when the applet is first loaded into the page and again anytime the `repaint()` function is called. It accepts one argument which identifies the graphic workspace on the applet where we will be printing the score.

The code in the `paint` function first creates a font object with bold Helvetica 24-point font. That object is then used with the `setFont()` function to make it the current font. Finally, the `drawString()` function is called. The number contained in the `score` variable is converted to a string and passed to the function to be printed. The `20, 20` indicate where on the applet the text will appear.

There are three key things to notice about this simple applet. First, it defines a class which is descended from the Applet class. VBScript can only access variables and functions from descendants of the Applet class.

The last two things you should notice are the public variable *score* and the public function `updatescore`. Because these are public, you'll be able to call them from VBScript.

# The VBScript Web Page

In order to put this applet to work, you need a Web page. Listing 9.2 shows my page.

---

**Listing 9.2.   The Web Page Demonstrating the Scoreboard Applet**

```
<HTML>
<HEAD>
<TITLE>Game</TITLE>
</HEAD>
<BODY>
<h1>Game</h1>
The Score Is:<p>
<APPLET CODE="scoreboard.class"
CODEBASE="e:\javaproj\game"
ID=sign
WIDTH = 70
HEIGHT = 30>
</APPLET>
<p>
<INPUT TYPE=button VALUE="Score + 10" NAME="BtnScoreTen">
```

```
<SCRIPT LANGUAGE="VBScript">
<!--
Sub BtnScoreTen_OnClick
  document.sign.score = document.sign.score + 10
  document.sign.updatescore
End Sub
-->
</SCRIPT>

</BODY>
</HTML>
```

Part
III

Ch
9

No, I haven't actually created a clever game to demonstrate this applet. I'll leave that to you. This is a pretty minimal page that just shows you how to drop the applet in and work with it.

Notice the <APPLET> tag. It identifies the name of the class using the CODE attribute and identifies where on my system that code could be found. An appropriate WIDTH and HEIGHT are specified. And, importantly, the applet is given an ID for VBScript to use when it references it. That's it!

After that, a simple form-style button is used to kick off the BtnScoreTen_OnClick VBScript subroutine. Whatever is in the applet's *score* variable is increased by 10. And, so that the user can see the change, the updatescore function is called. Notice that I specify the document and then the applet name to qualify the applet variable and function.

When you bring up the page, you see a box holding the number 0. Every time you click the button, the score is increased by 10. Nothing to it!

# Summary

Java applets provide yet another way for you to activate your Web pages. They have advantages and disadvantages when weighed against ActiveX controls, but fortunately, you don't have to choose either or. You can use both very easily and, from VBScript's perspective, almost seamlessly.

# From Here...

Later in the book, you'll find related chapters that will help you further understand the concepts presented in this chapter. Specifically, take a look at the following:

- Chapter 32, "Web-Enabling Visual Basic Applications," looks at the functionality provided by Microsoft's Internet extensions to the Win32 API, how this functionality has been encapsulated into the Internet ActiveX control provided with VB 5, and how this control can be used to build a Web spider that will check a Web site for broken links.

- Chapter 34, "Integrating Visual Basic with Java," takes you through integrating Java applets running in the Microsoft Java VM ActiveX Control with a VB application. It looks at how the Java VM control enables the VB programmer to interact with Java applets like ActiveX, calling methods built in Java.

# Active Documents

# ActiveX Documents: Serving Up VB in a Web Browser

Current Internet technology presents new and exciting application development opportunities. Client/server is becoming possible without the requirement of maintaining the code base on the client machines. With ActiveX Documents as a new tool in the arsenal of the Visual Basic developer, the creation of powerful thin client applications becomes a reality. When the client is enhanced or upgraded, the next use of the application can cause the latest client version to be downloaded. No longer will you have to trek from client system to client system, installing the latest version. When the user calls the application from a Web page, it will all be accomplished simply and easily.

In this chapter, you will explore the wonderful world of ActiveX Documents. You will examine their use to create a full-blown Visual Basic application that runs in the MS Internet 3.x Web browser. ■

## What is an ActiveX Document?

ActiveX Documents are not documents in the usual meaning of the word. They work more like applications. They must have a container in which to run, either Internet Explorer or MS Binder. They bear a strong resemblance to an ActiveX Control.

## The steps to design an ActiveX Document

There are choices to be made in creating an ActiveX Document, such as will it run in an EXE of DLL. Debugging and running an ActiveX Document requires some understanding of its structure.

## Using ActiveX Documents to build an application

Multiple ActiveX Documents can be assembled into an application. This requires communication between documents and an understanding of the structure of an ActiveX Document project. You may add Visual Basic Forms and menus to the project.

## ActiveX Document performance issues

A key issue is understanding the setup and distribution requirements. This may involve signing and security consideration. You will want to pay close attention to the size and downloading issues.

# Defining an ActiveX Document

Is an ActiveX Document a document or an application program? The answer in some respects is a confusing yes. When an ActiveX Document is compiled in Visual Basic, two components are created, the document with a .VBD extension and a server with either an .EXE or .DLL extension. This works much as Microsoft Word where Winword.exe uses the .DOC file to create a document that you can view. The ActiveX Document server creates the ActiveX Document that you will see.

As you are aware, a Word document can exist in another container such as Internet Explorer with Winword.exe acting as the server to supply the object that is displayed in the container.

## How is an ActiveX Document Application Different from Other Applications

The ActiveX Document application cannot run without a container. The process of placing an ActiveX Document in a container is called *siting*. This container must be either Internet Explorer 3.x or MS Binder. The container serves as the forms painter for the server program (which was created as part of the process of compiling the document), which then displays the document. If you are confused, don't worry. The essence of the issue is that when you call the document from the Internet Explorer, the server program starts and displays the ActiveX Document.

While this is somewhat confusing to explain, an illustration should remove the fog. The first step is to look at the Windows NT Task Manager. In Figure 10.1, you see that the only application running on the system is Microsoft Word.

**FIG. 10.1**

The Task Manager on Windows NT and Windows 95 is opened by using the Ctl+Alt+Del key combination.

Now Microsoft Internet Explorer will be opened and the ActiveX Document URL is entered in the Address text box. The ActiveX Document named WebDev11UDoc1.vbd is loaded into the browser as shown in Figure 10.2. If you didn't know differently, you would think that you were looking at an ActiveX control.

**FIG. 10.2**
The path shown in the Address text box is the location of the ActiveX Document.

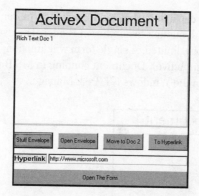

You have seen no evidence of the server program in the display of this ActiveX Document. If you look again at the Windows NT Task Manager as shown in Figure 10.3, you see that there are two additional applications running. The first of these is the Internet Explorer displaying the ActiveX Document. The second is the server program named WebDev11.

Part
IV

Ch
10

**FIG. 10.3**
The server program is started automatically based on Registry settings.

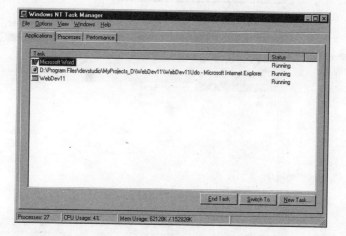

Now, you have seen the parts playing their role in the display of an ActiveX Document. As you will see later in this chapter, the server program will work for multiple ActiveX Documents in an application.

## Comparing Internet Explorer 3.0 and Binder Containers

MS Binder is the other container that the ActiveX Document can use. MS Binder is used to create a collection of documents such as Word .DOC files and Excel .XLS files that are related. The documents are in sections of the Binder.

To add an ActiveX Document to an MS Binder, Choose Start, Programs, Microsoft Binder. With Binder running, choose Section, Add from File. Navigate to the folder that contains the .VBD file, set Files of Type to All Files (*.*) and select the .VBD file to be added and click the Add button.

There are some differences in the capabilities between Internet Explorer and Binder as a container. You cannot move from one document to another in Binder. The usefulness of Binder as an application container is, therefore, limited. A single form will function, but it cannot call another form. Figure 10.4 shows an ActiveX Document running in MS Binder. In Figure 10.5, you see the running applications in the Windows NT Task Manager.

**FIG. 10.4**

MS Binder has each ActiveX Document in its own Section.

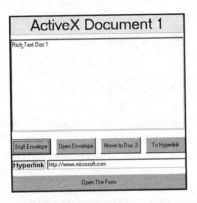

**FIG. 10.5**

The server program also starts automatically in MS Binder.

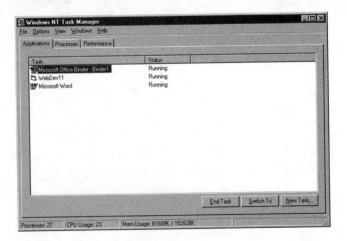

Since MS Binder has limited utility for running an application built of ActiveX Documents, no further attention will be given to Binder in this chapter.

## Comparing ActiveX Documents and ActiveX Controls

As you observed earlier, an ActiveX Document resembles an ActiveX Control when it is displayed in Internet Explorer. It is important to understand the similarities and the key difference between the document and the control. Most of the methods and terminology that you have learned in the creation of ActiveX controls applies to ActiveX Documents. The key difference is that the ActiveX Document will exist only in the Container. The ActiveX control can exist in a Form, a User control or an ActiveX Document.

# Examining ActiveX Document Events

There are key events that fire in the process of starting and displaying an ActiveX Document. Other key events are fired during the existence of the ActiveX Document. Finally, there are events that occur on the termination of the ActiveX Document. These events, discussed in the following sections, are useful in managing the ActiveX Document.

**Initialize Event**   When the Initialize Event occurs, the document has been created but has not yet been sited in the container.

**InitProperties Event**   The default values for the properties of the document are set. The document has not yet been sited in the container so the container properties are not yet available. This event may not occur if there have been properties saved in the Property Bag. (See Chapter 11, "Property Bags and Menus: Extending ActiveX Document Applications," for a further discussion of the Property Bag.)

**Show Event**   This event occurs whenever the user navigates to the document. The document is sited in the container where it is shown so that the container properties are now available. This is the first event that you can be certain will occur every time the document is displayed.

**EnterFocus Event**   This event always occurs just after the show event and also occurs each time the document receives focus.

**ExitFocus Event**   This event occurs when no object on the document or the document no longer has focus.

**Hide Event**   The hide event occurs when the user navigates off the document and also occurs just before the Terminate Event. This event can be used to destroy any global references before navigating to another document.

**Resize Event**   The Resize event occurs any time the container is resized.

**Scroll Event**   Scroll bars appear on the container when the container's Viewport is smaller than the ActiveX Document. The Scroll event occurs when the user clicks the container Scrollbars.

**Terminate Event**   Navigating off the document does not terminate or destroy the document. Internet Explorer keeps a four document cache. The document is destroyed when the user navigates to the fifth document. The Terminate event occurs just before the document is destroyed. The event can be used to clean up any global references.

**Other Events**   Two other events are worth study. These are the `ReadProperties` event and the `WriteProperties` event. These events are concerned with the saving of properties in the Property Bag and are covered in the next chapter. The Property Bag is a method of saving settings for an ActiveX Document from one use to the next.

# Designing an ActiveX Document

Creating an ActiveX Document with Visual Basic 5 is much like creating any other Visual Basic project. The first step is to open Visual Basic 5. Choose File, New Project. Form the dialog box that appears, select either the ActiveX Document .DLL or the ActiveX Document .EXE, depending on whether you want the server to be an in-process or out-process component. If you change your mind, the project can be changed from one to the other.

## Naming the Project

In the Project Explorer window, Select Project1(Project1). Open the Properties Window and give the project a name of your choice. In Figure 10.6, the name WebDev11Demo has been chosen.

**FIG. 10.6**

The name given will set the name of the .VBW (Workspace) file and the .VBP (Project) file.

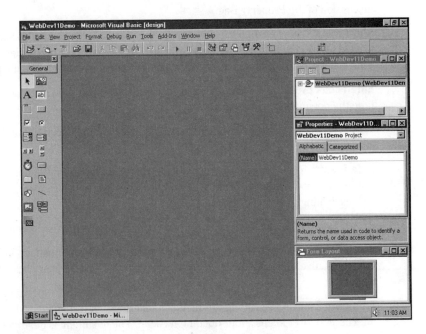

## Building the Document

You are now ready to start setting properties for the ActiveX Document. The document was created with a default name of UserDocument1. To change the name, select the UserDocument1, and change the Name property to MyUserDoc in the Properties window as shown in Figure 10.7

Now you will add some controls to the document. In Figure 10.8, you see that a Label control, a TextBox control, and a Command Button control have been added. Each of these has been left at the default values.

**FIG. 10.7**

The UserDocument will be named MyUserDoc.VBD.

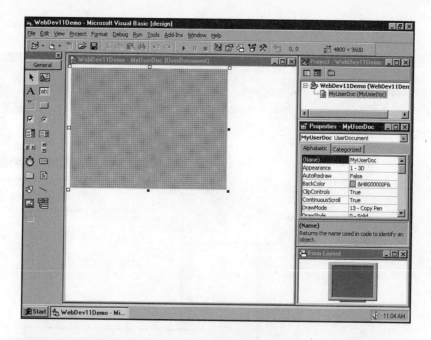

**FIG. 10.8**

The controls added are all standard ActiveX Controls, User-created controls, or third-party controls.

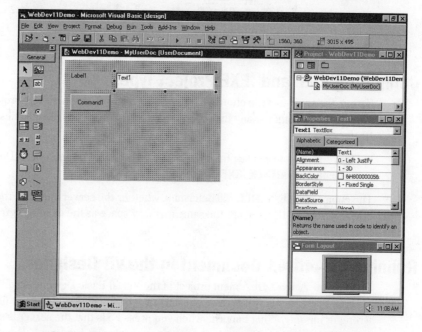

Now double-click the Command1 button to open a code window and add the following line of code:

```
Text1.Text = "The Button Has Been Clicked"
```

This is added to the `Click` event for the Command button control as shown in Figure 10.9.

**FIG. 10.9**

The phrase, "The Button Has Been Clicked," displays in the textbox when Command1 is clicked.

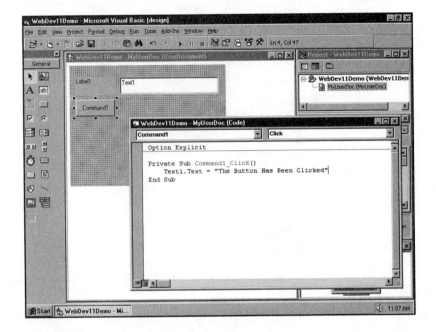

The project is now ready for a text drive. Choose File, Save Project.

## Comparing .DLL and .EXE Project Types

Earlier, the subject of the choice of .DLL or .EXE was mentioned. The project can be changed from one to the other at any time. Choose Project, *ProjectName* Properties as shown in Figure 10.10.

In Figure 10.11, you can see the Project Type selection. For an ActiveX Document, you must choose either an ActiveX .EXE or ActiveX .DLL.

The choice of .EXE or .DLL will determine whether the server runs In-Process or Out-Of-Process. In-Process .DLL's share the same memory space as the client program and usually run faster.

## Running an ActiveX Document in the VB Designer

Running the ActiveX Document project in the Visual Basic Designer is different than running other projects. When you press F5 to start the project, at first you may think that something is wrong or missing. What happens when you press F5 is that the server is started. You now must open the document in the container, in this case Internet Explorer.

Open Internet Explorer and enter the following in the Address box of the browser:

```
file://d:\program files\devstudio\vb\MyUserDoc.VBD
```

**FIG. 10.10**
Several project properties are available from this location.

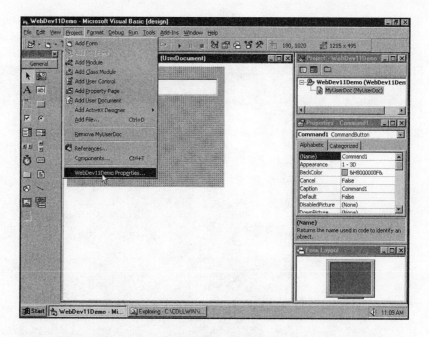

**FIG. 10.11**
This choice can be changed any time before the program is compiled.

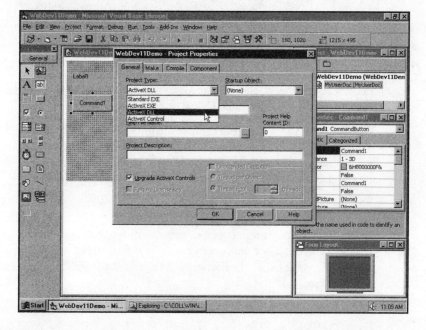

The path will vary based on where you have Visual Basic installed. When you started the Server, Visual Basic created a copy of the document in its root directory for testing purposes. This document will be deleted when the server is stopped from the Visual Basic Designer.

A permanent copy of the ActiveX Document is not created until the project is compiled. You will now see the ActiveX Document displayed in the browser container as shown in Figure 10.12.

**FIG. 10.12**

The browser background is set to match the background color of the ActiveX Document.

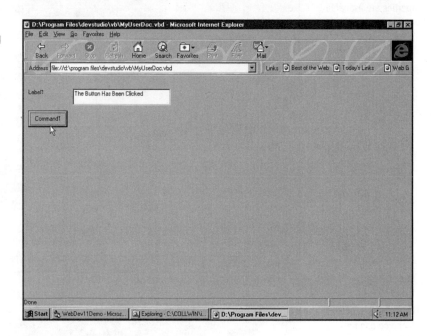

## Compiling the ActiveX Document

To compile the project, choose File, Make WebDev11Demo.Exe. If you have chosen to create a .DLL, Make WebDev11Demo.DLL will be displayed.

Two files are created when you compile the project. The first is the WebDev11Demo.exe or WebDev11Demo.dll and the second is the ActiveX Document, MyUserDoc.vbd. Both of these files are saved in the directory containing the project files. The .EXE or .DLL is registered on the system when it is compiled.

## Running the Compiled Project

Running a project after it has been compiled is different than running it from the Visual Basic designer. There is now a permanent copy of the ActiveX Document. Also the server does not need to be started before the document is requested through the browser. In the Address box of the browser, enter:

```
file://path\documentname.vbd
```

The ActiveX Document will open in the browser. If you check the Windows NT Task manager, you will see that the server program is running.

**N O T E**   Looking at the Task Manager only works if the server is an .EXE and runs in its own process. If it is a .DLL, it will be running in the client process and will not be listed in the Task Manager. ■

# Using ActiveX Documents to Build an Application

Building a slightly more complex ActiveX Document Application will demonstrate some of the features of the use of ActiveX Documents to build an application and show some basic techniques for communicating between ActiveX Documents and integrating ActiveX Documents into a Web-based application.

## Designing the Application

The application on the CD in the Chapter 10 directory is named WevDeb11. There is no known useful purpose for the application, except as a learning and demonstration tool. Please tear it apart, change it, and squeeze it for all that it has to give you.

The goals for the application are that it will show ActiveX Controls used on an ActiveX Document, communicate between ActiveX Documents through a global variable, link to a Web site, and use a form.

The controls and objects on the two ActiveX Documents are mirror images of each other. There is no point to be derived from this fact other than the ability to perform tasks from either document. The same form is called from each document and both documents and the form communicate with the global variable.

This all sounds like it should be a complex problem. It isn't. To put everything in perspective, creating the sample application required just over an hour, including testing and deciding what should be shown.

One final warning—the names of many of the controls have been left at the default value. This is not because this practice is advocated; in fact, it is not. It is sometimes useful to do this in a teaching environment.

## Communicating Between ActiveX Documents

Communicating between the ActiveX Documents is extremely simple and straightforward. All that needs to be done is to declare a global variable of the proper data type in a module, and the data repository is created. Listing 10.1 shows the declaration of the global variable Envelope as a data type string.

### Listing 10.1   mGlobal.bas—The Partial Contents of the Module

```
Option Explicit
'This global variable is the transport mechanism between
'the ActiveX documents
Global Envelope As String
```

Values are then passed into this variable and retrieved from this variable from the documents and the form.

## Looking Inside an ActiveX Document Project

There are several file types present in an ActiveX Document project. Table 10.1 lists the different types of files and their function.

### Table 10.1   File Types in an ActiveX Document Project

| Extension | Description |
|-----------|-------------|
| .BAS | Visual Basic Module |
| .DLL | Dynamic Link Library |
| .DOB | ActiveX Form File |
| .DOX | ActiveX Binary Form File |
| .EXE | Executable File |
| .FRM | Visual Basic Form File |
| .FRX | Visual Basic Binary Form File |
| .VBD | Visual Basic Document File |
| .VBP | Visual Basic Project File |
| .VBW | Visual Basic Workspace File |

## Adding a Form to the Project

Adding a form to an ActiveX Document project is very simple and straightforward. Choose Project, Add Form. A form is added with the default name of Form1. Change the name of the form to a name of your choice in the properties window and add the needed controls to the form. Since the form will never be the Start Up object in the project, code will need to be added to some event in one of the ActiveX Documents that will invoke the Show method on the form.

## Running the Sample Project

In the sample project directory on the CD, you will find both WebDev11.dll and WebDev.exe. Both versions of the server were compiled. The version on the CD, will, when the WebDev11UDoc1.vbd is loaded, start the WebDev11.exe server. Both are provided so that you can experiment with the project. The .EXE server is self-registering when it is run the first time. The .DLL version will need to be registered with the regsvr32.exe program.

If you encounter any problems, simply copy the project to your hard disk, open the project in VB 5, and recompile the project. Compiling will register the components.

The following "script" may help you discover some of the features in the sample project.

■ Enter the path to the WebDev11UDoc1.vbd on your hard drive in the Address box of your Internet Explorer browser.

■ When the document opens in the browser, you will see the ActiveX Document 1 label across the top of the page as shown in Figure 10.13.

**FIG. 10.13**
When the ActiveX Document is displayed in the browser, the server is running.

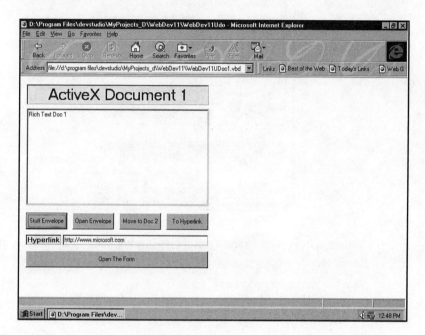

Part
**IV**

Ch
**10**

■ Enter some text in the large text box as shown in Figure 10.14, and click the Stuff Envelope Button. The contents that were in the text box are now in the global variable Envelope and the text box has a new message displayed confirming that the Envelope was stuffed. The code that accomplishes this is shown in Listing 10.2.

**Listing 10.2    Command1_Click()—The Contents of the Text Box are Placed in the Variable**

```
Private Sub Command1_Click()
    'Move the Contents of the RichTextBox in to the
    'global variable Envelope
    Envelope = RichTextBox1.Text
    RichTextBox1.Text = "Envelope is Stuffed"
End SubGlobal Envelope As String
```

■ Now click the Move to Doc 2 button. Document 2 is displayed in the browser. The code required to accomplish this is shown in Listing 10.3. Document 2 must be in the same directory as Document 1 for the code to work.

**FIG. 10.14**

The text box is a rich text box, which provides the ability to use formatting of the text.

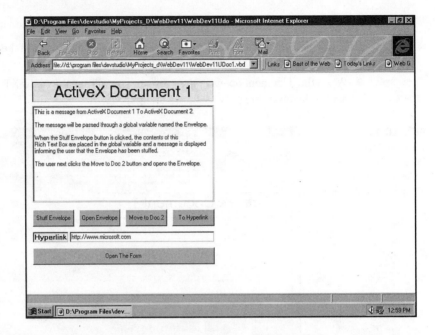

## Listing 10.3 Command3_Click()—Document 2 is Displayed in the Browser

```
Private Sub Command3_Click()
    Dim strPath As String      ' String to be parsed
    Dim strAbsPath As String   ' Result of parsing
    Dim intI As Integer        ' Character position counter

    ' Return the path of the current ActiveX document.
    strPath = Trim$(UserDocument.Parent.LocationName)

    ' Find the position of the last separator character.
    For intI = Len(strPath) To 1 Step -1
        If Mid$(strPath, intI, 1) = "/" Or _
            Mid$(strPath, intI, 1) = "\" Then Exit For
    Next intI

    ' Strip the name of the current .vbd file.
    strAbsPath = Left$(strPath, intI)

    ' Set the global variable to Me, allowing
    ' the WebDev11UDoc2 document to get any public
    ' properties, or call any public functions.

    Set gWebDev11UDoc1 = Me '

    ' Navigate to the second ActiveX document.
    UserDocument.Hyperlink.NavigateTo _
        strAbsPath & "WebDev11UDoc2.vbd"
End Sub
```

■ With Document 2 open, click the Open Envelope button, and you will see that the contents of the global variable are displayed in the text box, as shown in Figure 10.15.

**FIG. 10.15**

The formatting of the text has been preserved from the first text box.

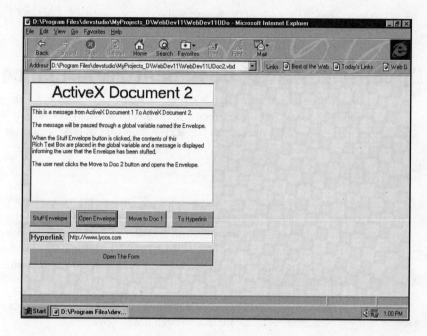

Part IV

Ch 10

■ Now click the Open The Form Button at the bottom of the document and the form will open as shown in Figure 10.16.

**FIG. 10.16**

The form is also able to communicate with the global variable.

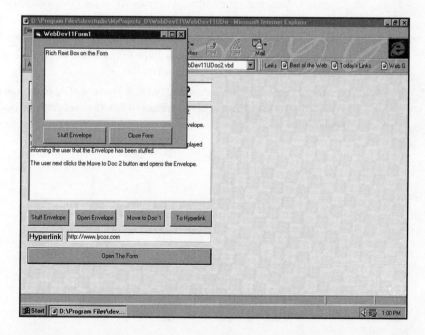

■ Finally, click the To Hyperlink button and you will move to the URL that has been entered in the Hyperlink text box.

A tour through the code of the project will convince you that the ActiveX Document technology is very straightforward and easy to use.

# Optimizing ActiveX Document Performance

The performance issues involved in the use of ActiveX Documents are the same as were discussed for ActiveX controls in Chapter 6, "Making Your ActiveX Controls Web-Friendly." The essence is to keep the documents and server small for fast download when that is necessary.

# From Here ...

This has been a brief overview of using ActiveX Documents to develop a Web-based application that uses the Internet Explorer as a thin client container for the application. The potential is here for powerful applications centrally administered and maintained with execution on the client. In the next two chapters, you will learn even more about this exciting technology. Not much has been heard yet about ActiveX Documents. You have an opportunity to be on the bow wave of this technology.

■ Chapter 2, "Up and Running: Browser-Based VB Programming," explores the array of technologies available for use through a Web browser.

■ Chapter 3, "Building ActiveX Controls with VB," examines your capability to build your own ActiveX controls with VB 5.

■ Chapter 6, "Making Your ActiveX Controls Web-Friendly," looks at the issues in making your ActiveX controls small and secure.

■ Chapter 11, "Property Bags and Menus: Extending ActiveX Document Applications," delves into the use of property bags in the initialization of the ActiveX Document and adding menus to the ActiveX Document.

■ Chapter 12, "Hyperlinks: Extending ActiveX Document Applications over Multiple Windows," reviews the use of hyperlinks to link to other ActiveX Document applications.

# Property Bags and Menus: Extending ActiveX Document Applications

In the previous chapter, you learned how to build a simple ActiveX document application and run it in the browser. In this chapter, you'll extend that knowledge and expose some of the more powerful features available to your ActiveX documents. ▪

**Extend the power of your ActiveX Documents with the new PropertyBag object**

The PropertyBag object enables your ActiveX documents to save data to a file with just a few lines of code.

**Use the PropertyBag object to save and restore "state" information from your ActiveX Document applications**

Think of the PropertyBag object as a literal "bag" where you save state information. Whenever the user returns to the document, you can take the information out of the PropertyBag, restoring the last state of the document.

**Create dynamic menus to change and enhance the functionality of Internet Explorer**

Since ActiveX document applications only run within the container application, you'll need to integrate your application with the container. This chapter has information about adding menus to Internet Explorer so that you can seamlessly bind the container and your application together.

# The PropertyBag Object

In this section, you learn the capabilities of the PropertyBag object, then you actually use the PropertyBag to *persist* data, that is, to save state information of instances of ActiveX documents.

What is the PropertyBag object? In short, it is simply an object that holds information about another object. You then use the PropertyBag to save and restore state information across instances of the calling object.

The purpose of the PropertyBag object is to persist, or hold information. It allows you to save information and restore it back to the object. Think of the PropertyBag as a literal "bag" where you keep objects—you place objects into the bag with the WriteProperty, and take them out with the ReadProperty. And you can put anything into the bag—data, variables, multimedia, or any type of object, and all its properties, too. Later in this chapter, you'll learn how to use the WriteProperty method to save information to the PropertyBag, then use the ReadProperty method to retrieve information by using the PropertyBag object. The values you save and restore with the PropertyBag object can be properties, methods, or even other objects!

## Building a PropertyBag Example

In the example from Chapter 10, you created a simple ActiveX document and demonstrated how to run it within the browser. Now you'll take the concepts you learned developing that application and add more sophisticated functionality to your ActiveX document applications.

You'll use a public television membership drive as the example. Rather than obscure the functionality you are going to learn with databases and data object connections, you'll create only the front end and use a single record. But as you progress, you'll see how the example can be the foundation for a real interface with databases (covered later).

First, you'll build a new base application, laying the groundwork for your examples for this chapter and the next. From the File menu, select New Project and choose the ActiveX Document .EXE icon.

Rename the project PropertyBagExample.

Click the UserDocument icon. Then, from the menu, select Project and click Add User Document. Rename it xdocParent.

Leave all the other properties of the document at their defaults. Now add two command buttons to your document. Set their properties as shown in Table 11.1 and Table 11.2:

### Table 11.1 Command Button1 Properties

| Property | Value |
| --- | --- |
| Name | cmdOpenChild |
| Caption | Open Child |

**Table 11.2   Command Button2 Properties**

| Property | Value |
|----------|-------|
| Name | cmdOpenAnotherChild |
| Caption | Open Another Child |

Don't worry about adding code to these buttons right away. You'll add code later, as you learn how to implement new functionality.

Since you'll be reusing parts of this form and some of its controls to design new forms later on, take some extra care in designing this form. Create the controls listed in Table 11.3 on your form:

**Table 11.3   Controls for xdocParent**

| Control Type | Name | Caption or Text |
|--------------|------|-----------------|
| Label | lblBanner | Public TV Pledge Drive |
| Label | lblNameFirst | First Name: |
| Label | lblNameLast | Last Name: |
| Label | lblMembershipLevel | Membership Level: |
| Label | lblIncentive | Incentive: |
| Label | lblPledgeAmount | Pledge Amount |
| Text Box | txtNameFirst | (none) |
| Text Box | txtNameLast | (none) |
| Text Box | txtPledgeAmount | (none) |
| Combo Box | cboMembershipLevel | (none) |
| Combo Box | cboIncentive | (none) |

Now size the form and arrange the controls so that your form looks like Figure 11.1, and save your work. You might want to dress up the form a bit by changing the font and color of the banner.

Now you are ready to put some content into your ActiveX document. Since this example is the front end for a public television membership drive, you'll need to have a list of suggested membership levels see Table 11.4 and their corresponding suggested pledge amounts. Ordinarily, you would retrieve these values from a database, but for this example, just put them directly into the Control List properties.

Part
IV

Ch
11

**FIG. 11.1**

Use a little extra care designing the Parent Document interface, since you'll be using it as a template for more ActiveX documents later on.

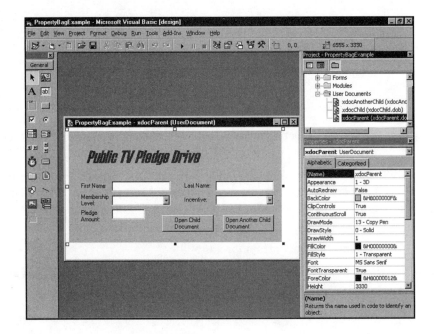

### Table 11.4    List Values for cboMembershipLevel

**List Value**

Individual

Contributor

Family

Supporter

Sponsor

Guarantor

Benefactor

It's standard practice during a pledge drive to offer various incentives to urge viewers to pledge contributions and a way for the station to express appreciation to the viewers. So now, fill the cboIncentive combo box with appropriate incentive gifts (see Table 11.5).

### Table 11.5    List Values for cboIncentive

**List Value**

Program Guide

Coffee Mug

**List Value**

---

Yanni CD

Mr. Bean Video

Coffee Table Book

Tote Bag

Limited Edition Print

---

Now you are ready to add some interactivity to the Membership Level combo box. Add the following code to set default values for txtPledgeAmount and cboIncentive, based on the user's selection in cboMembershipLevel.

```
Option Explicit
Dim msIncentiveIndividual, msIncentiveContributor, msIncentiveFamily As String
Dim msIncentiveSupporter, msIncentiveSponsor, msIncentiveGuarantor,
msIncentiveBenefactor As String

Dim mcSuggestedPledgeIndividual, mcSuggestedPledgeContributor,
➥mcSuggestedPledgeFamily As Currency
Dim mcSuggestedPledgeSupporter, mcSuggestedPledgeSponsor,
mcSuggestedPledgeGuarantor, mcSuggestedPledgeBenefactor As Currency


Private Sub InitializeVariables()

' Store the values of incentive gifts in document-level variables—

    msIncentiveIndividual = "Program Guide"
    msIncentiveContributor = "Coffee Mug"
    msIncentiveFamily = "Yanni CD"
    msIncentiveSupporter = "Mr.Bean Video"
    msIncentiveSponsor = "Coffee Table Book"
    msIncentiveGuarantor = "Tote Bag"
    msIncentiveBenefactor = "Limited Edition Print"

' Store suggested minimum pledge levels—

    mcSuggestedPledgeContributor = 60
    mcSuggestedPledgeFamily = 100
    mcSuggestedPledgeSupporter = 120
    mcSuggestedPledgeSponsor = 240
    mcSuggestedPledgeGuarantor = 600
    mcSuggestedPledgeBenefactor = 1000

End Sub

Private Sub cboMembershipLevel_Click()
' Define rules for default incentives and pledge amounts

Select Case cboMembershipLevel.Text
```

```
        Case "Individual"
            cboIncentive.Text = msIncentiveIndividual
            txtPledgeAmount.Text = mcSuggestedPledgeIndividual

        Case "Contributor"
            cboIncentive.Text = msIncentiveContributor
            txtPledgeAmount.Text = mcSuggestedPledgeContributor

        Case "Family"
            cboIncentive.Text = msIncentiveFamily
            txtPledgeAmount.Text = mcSuggestedPledgeFamily

        Case "Supporter"
            cboIncentive.Text = msIncentiveSupporter
            txtPledgeAmount.Text = mcSuggestedPledgeSupporter

        Case "Sponsor"
            cboIncentive.Text = msIncentiveSponsor
            txtPledgeAmount.Text = mcSuggestedPledgeSponsor

        Case "Guarantor"
            cboIncentive.Text = msIncentiveGuarantor
            txtPledgeAmount.Text = mcSuggestedPledgeGuarantor

        Case "Benefactor"
            cboIncentive.Text = msIncentiveBenefactor
            txtPledgeAmount.Text = mcSuggestedPledgeBenefactor

        Case Else
            cboIncentive.Text = msIncentiveIndividual
            txtPledgeAmount.Text = mcSuggestedPledgeIndividual


    End Select


End Sub


Private Sub UserDocument_Initialize()
' Save values in form-level variables.
' You can also retrieve these values from a database

    InitializeVariables

End Sub
```

So far this still resembles standard Visual Basic programming. In a few minutes, however, you'll be ready to expose the real power of ActiveX documents. Now is a good time to save your work, compile the ActiveX project as an .EXE file, and test it. Start Internet Explorer and point your browser to the xdocParent.vbd file (see Figure 11.2) in your project directory.

**FIG. 11.2**
The Parent ActiveX
Document running in
the browser container.

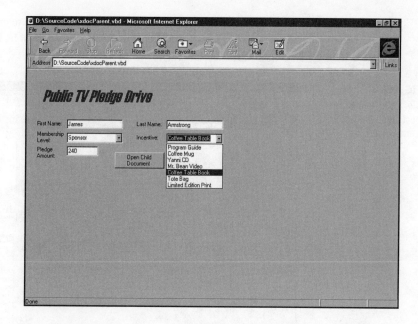

When you select a different membership level, the suggested contribution amount and incentive should change accordingly.

## Adding User Documents to the Example

So far, what you've created is very much like a standard Visual Basic application, except that it runs within the container application. Go back to Visual Basic and open the project. Add two more User Documents, naming them xdocChild and xdocAnotherChild.

**N O T E** Just because you named the ActiveX Documents xdocParent, xdocChild, and xdocAnotherChild, don't presume that Visual Basic 5 supports true inheritance between ActiveX documents. The example uses these names only for clarity, so you will be able to understand which document has been called by another document. While Visual Basic 5 comes still closer to supporting object-oriented methods like inheritance, it still doesn't fully support true object-orientation. ■

Copy the two control buttons from xdocParent and paste them into xdocChild and xdocAnotherChild. Copy the banner label from the parent document and paste it into the two new documents as well. This way you'll have homogeneous controls, and since you're not creating them from scratch, you can simply change their properties (see Figure 11.3).

**TIP** You'll find that copying and pasting common controls (as well as code) not only saves time, but aids in giving your applications a consistent look and feel and simplifies code maintenance.

On the xdocChild form, you'll only need to change the cmdOpenChild to cmdOpenParent and change its caption accordingly. Leave cmdOpenAnotherDocument as it is. Build the xdocAnotherChild, similarly.

**FIG. 11.3**

The "Child" ActiveX Documents are under construction.

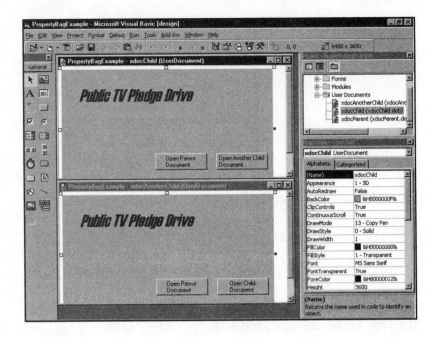

Now you have three ActiveX documents in your project, but there is no connection between them—in fact, if you ran the application now, there is no capability of invoking either of the new documents.

Start with the xdocParent, and add the following code to the control buttons:

```
Private Sub cmdOpenChild_Click()
' The NavigateTo method requires an explicit path unless
' the documents are in the same directory!

Hyperlink.NavigateTo "xdocChild.vbd"

End Sub
Private Sub cmdOpenAnotherChild_Click()

Hyperlink.NavigateTo "xdocAnotherChild.vbd"

End Sub
```

And add this code to xdocChild:

```
Private Sub cmdOpenParent_Click()

Hyperlink.NavigateTo "xdocParent.vbd"
```

```
End Sub

Private Sub cmdOpenAnotherChild_Click()

Hyperlink.NavigateTo "xdocAnotherChild.vbd"


End Sub
```

And finally, copy, paste, and modify the following code into xdocAnotherChild:

```
Private Sub cmdOpenParent_Click()
Hyperlink.NavigateTo "xdocParent.vbd"

End Sub

Private Sub cmdOpenChild_Click()

Hyperlink.NavigateTo "xdocChild.vbd"

End Sub
```

> **CAUTION**
>
> If you're keeping all of your ActiveX documents in the same directory as the .EXE file, it is not essential to type an explicit path. If the .VBD files can possibly be in different directories, however, you'll need to build the path dynamically.

Part
**IV**

Ch
**11**

You'll learn more about using the NavigateTo method in Chapter 12, "Hyperlinks: Extending ActiveX Document Applications Over Multiple Windows." For now, though, it's time to learn how to use the power of the PropertyBag.

# Adding the PropertyBag Object

Earlier in this chapter, you learned to think of the PropertyBag as a literal "bag" where you store other objects. In reality, the *bag* is a file. When you are using Internet Explorer as the container application, the file ends with the .VBD extension, when the container object is the Binder, the extension is .OBD. These files contain not only the object information written by the PropertyBag, but also information pointing to the appropriate .EXE or .DLL file. You save state information to the file using the WriteProperties event.

## Adding Persistence to the Example

Start by using the WriteProperties event to save the contents of one of the text boxes to the PropertyBag. Add this code to the UserDocument object of xdocParent:

```
Private Sub UserDocument_WriteProperties(PropBag As PropertyBag)
' Place the contents of txtNameFirst into the PropertyBag Object
' with the name sPropertyNameLast
```

```
PropBag.WriteProperty "sPropertyNameLast", txtNameLast.Text, "Empty"
```

```
End Sub
```

Note the last argument in the WriteProperty example. The "Empty" string is simply a default value used if nothing is placed in the sPropertyNameLast object. Although it is optional, using the default value this way can save cluttering up your data file with numerous default values.

Now place the reciprocal code in the ReadProperties event:

```
Private Sub UserDocument_ReadProperties(PropBag As PropertyBag)
' Read the contents of sPropertyNameLast into the
' txtNameFirst.Text object

txtNameLast.Text = PropBag.ReadProperty("sPropertyNameLast")

End Sub
```

## How the PropertyBag Works

Returning to the "bag" analogy, with the WriteProperty event you are storing the contents of txtLastName to the variable sPropertyNameLast. Then you place the variable into your PropertyBag. When you invoke the ReadProperty event, you take the variable out of the PropertyBag and place it into the text box.

Before you compile and test your application there is one more essential bit of code to add. Insert this code in the Change() event of txtLastName:

```
Private Sub txtNameLast_Change()
' If there are any changes to this control,
' The user is prompted to save changes

        PropertyChanged

End Sub
```

This code checks to see if the contents of the text box have changed. If they have changed, the PropertyChanged method sends a message to the container application (see Figure 11.4). Before navigating to another page, the user is asked if he wants to save the changes. If the user answers yes, the changes are deposited into the PropertyBag and the new state of the control is saved.

Compile your project and navigate to the .VDB page. When you point your browser to the xdocParentDoc.vbd file, Explorer loads the ActiveX document and the objects, if any, that you have stored to the PropertyBag. Enter some information into the controls, then click the Child Document button. You are prompted to save your changes. Now, from the Child Document, go back to the parent document. Your changes are still there—the data persists. You can even shut down Explorer and restart it—your changes are still there.

**FIG. 11.4**

The ActiveX document sends a message to the container application on the *PropertyChanged()* event.

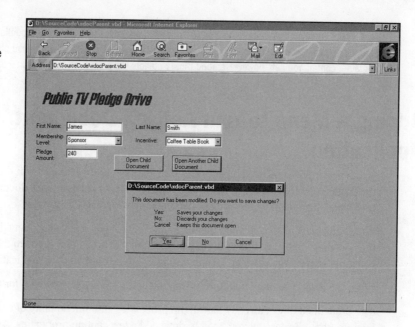

At this point, the only persistent information is in the Last Name textbox. To add persistence to everything else in your form, add the contents of the rest of the controls to the PropertyBag:

```
Private Sub UserDocument_WriteProperties(PropBag As PropertyBag)
' Place the contents of all the controls into the PropertyBag Object

PropBag.WriteProperty "sPropertyNameLast", txtNameLast.Text, "Empty"
PropBag.WriteProperty "sPropertyNameFirst", txtNameFirst.Text, "Empty"
PropBag.WriteProperty "cPledgeAmount", txtPledgeAmount.Text, "Empty"
PropBag.WriteProperty "sIncentive", cboIncentive.Text, "Empty"
PropBag.WriteProperty "sMembershipLevel", cboMembershipLevel.Text, "Empty"

End Sub

Private Sub UserDocument_ReadProperties(PropBag As PropertyBag)
' Read the contents of all the controls

txtNameLast.Text = PropBag.ReadProperty("sPropertyNameLast")
txtNameFirst.Text = PropBag.ReadProperty("sPropertyNameFirst")
txtPledgeAmount.Text = PropBag.ReadProperty("cPledgeAmount")
cboIncentive.Text = PropBag.ReadProperty("sIncentive")
cboMembershipLevel.Text = PropBag.ReadProperty("sMembershipLevel")

End Sub
```

If you want the user prompted to save changes after modifying any other fields, add the PropertyChanged event to that object's `Change()` event. Now when you navigate to another page or exit Explorer, all your data will be saved, then restored when you return to the page.

**N O T E** While ActiveX Documents can contain most controls, there are a few exceptions: You can't place an embedded object directly into an ActiveX document. Nor can you place an OLE container control. You can, however, embed binary objects like sound or video clips. ▨

# Adding a Menu to Your ActiveX Document Application

When a user accesses a Web page, that user may not know—or care—if the document she is viewing is an HTML page, contains ActiveX controls, or is an ActiveX document. So, it's considered good form to add an informational form to any ActiveX document.

Although you can't directly add menus to an ActiveX document, you can add custom menus to the container object. In this section, you learn how to add menu items to the Internet Explorer container object. You start by adding a simple "About" box to your application.

From the Project menu, click Add Form. Select the form template icon for the About Dialog.

The predefined object already has all the properties and functionality of a standard Windows SysInfo About Box, so all you need to do is add a few caption properties, shown in Table 11.6.

**Table 11.6    About Box Properties**

| Object | Caption |
| --- | --- |
| frmAbout | About PropertyBag Demo |
| lblTitle | PropertyBag Demo |
| lblVersion | Version 1.0 |
| lblDescription | ActiveX Document |
| lblDisclaimer | (Enter a copyright notice.) |

Now double-click the docParent to bring it to the front. From the Tools menu, select the Menu Editor.

Designing menus for ActiveX documents is functionally the same as designing menus for a regular Visual Basic application—with one key difference: The menus will be attached to the container application—in this case, Internet Explorer.

First refer to the container object's Help menu by typing **&Help** in the Caption box. This way, your ActiveX help form appears as a submenu to Internet Explorer's Help menu. Under Name, enter **mnuHelp**. So that your menu addition will appear as a submenu, select Right in the NegotiatePosition combo box.

Now add a menu item. Give it the caption About PropertyBag Demo and name it mnuAbout as shown in Figure 11.5.

**FIG. 11.5**

Extending the Container Object's Help Menu.

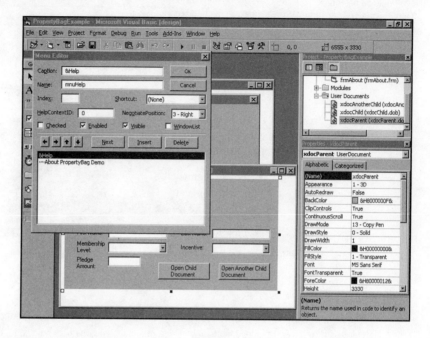

Now add the following code to attach the menu to the docParent:

```
Private Sub mnuAbout_Click
    frmAbout.Show vbModal
End Sub
```

**CAUTION**

When you use Internet Explorer as the container object, you must show all forms and dialog boxes as *modal*. The Microsoft Binder, on the other hand, will display modal or modeless forms. If you are not certain which container object will be used to view your ActiveX Document application, you can determine which container object the user has by using the App.NonModalAllowed property for conditional loading.

Now, after you recompile and run your project, you'll see your menu addition as illustrated in Figure 11.6.

While this example uses the Show method to display the Help form, you can also use menus to navigate between ActiveX documents. Rather than using the Show method to display an ActiveX document, remember that you must use the NavigateTo syntax, like this:

```
HyperLink.NavigateTo DocumentPathAndName
```

Part
IV

Ch

11

**FIG. 11.6**

Note how the NegotiateRight selection affects the menu extension.

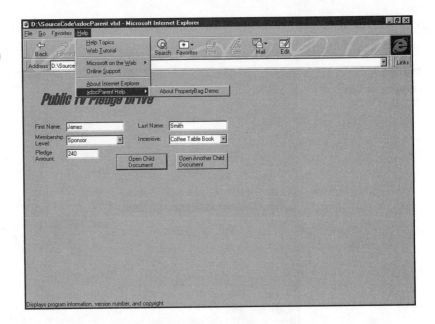

> **CAUTION**
>
> Microsoft Internet Explorer 3.0 will not display your menu modifications correctly if the user returns to a previously viewed ActiveX document containing a menu. Instead, the user will see that your menu title has moved to the left of the Help menu rather than beneath it. Fortunately, this behavior is only cosmetic and does not affect the functionality of your menus or Internet Explorer 3.0, but it will make your menu bar look odd when the user navigates back to the document.
>
> This bug will be fixed in Internet Explorer 4.0.

But you'll learn the methods of hyperlinks—and possible pitfalls to watch out for—in Chapter 12.

# From Here...

In this chapter, you learned how to use the new PropertyBag object to persist data from your ActiveX Documents. And you learned how to further customize your ActiveX Document applications by extending the container object with menus.

Chapter 10, "ActiveX Documents: Serving Up VB in a Web Browser," gives you the essential information you need to create ActiveX Documents. This section also covers issues of performance and security.

Chapter 12, "Hyperlinks: Extending ActiveX Documents over Multiple Windows," tells you how to make your ActiveX documents true Internet applications by adding hyperlinks. But, you'll learn more than how to add a simple hyperlink. You'll learn how to build dynamic paths between your documents, how to determine state information about the ActiveX documents, how to pass information across multiple windows, and methods for dealing with the unique "housekeeping" issues of ActiveX document applications.

Part

**IV**

Ch

**11**

# CHAPTER 12

# Hyperlinks: Extending ActiveX Document Applications over Multiple Windows

In the two previous chapters, you learned about creating ActiveX documents and how to save information with the new PropertyBag object. In this chapter, you'll extend that knowledge and learn how to add functionality and robustness to your ActiveX document applications.

Superficially, ActiveX documents look and act a lot like Visual Basic forms. But there are important differences in the ways ActiveX documents behave in their container application. You'll learn which events to use—and when to use them—to clean up browser cache memory after the user exits your document. ■

## Using hyperlinks to navigate among ActiveX document applications

You'll learn how to create hyperlinks to navigate among ActiveX documents, as well as Web pages and Microsoft Office documents.

## Passing information between ActiveX documents and applications

ActiveX documents don't have to exist in a vacuum—they can share information. This chapter demonstrates how to use public properties to read and write information between ActiveX documents and applications.

## Learn the fundamentals of creating "intelligent" ActiveX documents that determine their environment before they run

In a distributed, rapidly changing environment like the Internet or a corporate intranet, it's no longer sufficient to create an application for a single, inflexible environment. You'll get an overview of the concept of creating intelligent application objects for your ActiveX document applications, and you'll put this concept to use with a real-world example.

# Navigating Between ActiveX Documents

Navigating between ActiveX documents, whether documents in a single application, or among documents scattered about multiple Active X applications, all hinges on a single method: NavigateTo. But just because there is only one navigation method doesn't mean you are necessarily limited! You can, for instance, navigate to the following:

- A Web address

    Hyperlink.NavigateTo **http://www.microsoft.com**

- Another ActiveX Document

    Hyperlink.NavigateTo "xdocLookupCustomerAddress.vbd"

- A Microsoft Office Document (for example, a Word document, Excel spreadsheet, or Access database)

    Hyperlink.NavigateTo file://c:\MyDocuments\Presentations\SalesDemo.ppt

Each of these three methods of using NavigateTo comes with its own cautions and approaches, however. Let's look at each of them in more detail.

## Navigating to a Web Address

Navigating to a Web address is straightforward. If you want to NavigateTo a World Wide Web or FTP site, you can execute a single line of code and let Internet Explorer and its cache handle memory for you.

You can allow the user to enter an URL, or navigate directly to a hard-coded address. Considering the ephemeral nature of the World Wide Web, however, it is preferable not to hard-code a Web address. For example, you could have a button on your form with the following code in the OnClick event:

```
Hyperlink.NavigateTo "http://www.microsoft.com"
```

But it is considered better form, and far more maintainable to create a design with a text box that the user can modify, as shown in Figure 12.1

**FIG. 12.1**
Writing your application to navigate to a user-defined input is not only more flexible, but also more maintainable.

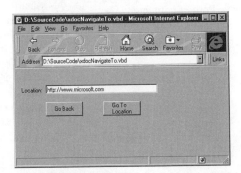

Place code like this in the "Go To Location" command button:

```
Private Sub cmdGotoLocation_Click()
' Navigate to the URL typed in the text box:
Dim sURL As String

    sURL = txtNavigateTo.Text
    Hyperlink.NavigateTo sURL

End Sub
```

Why not hard-code a Web address? One reason is that navigation protocols may change. In a few years, prefacing a Web address with "ftp://" and "http://" may seem as quaint as referring to a telephone number as "Liberty-6139" seems today. More immediately, Web addresses change frequently. While a large, well-established site is not likely to change its address, who knows what the URL of an address like **http://private.aol.com/users/home/ LorrainesLinguine.html** could be next month? What if Lorraine changes her Internet service provider? What if she registers a domain name? And what if she changes her specialty to veal Marsala?

## Navigating to a Microsoft Office Document

In the last chapter, you learned that an ActiveX document can't directly contain an embedded object, such as an Office document. What you *can* do, however, is use a hyperlink to *launch* another application within the browser. If you point the browser directly to the object, and the object starts it's own container object within the browser. For example, you can point directly to:

> Hyperlink.NavigateTo
> "file://c:\MyDocuments\Presentations\SalesDemo.ppt"

In this example, you aren't trying to embed the PowerPoint file in your ActiveX document. Instead, when you *hyperlink* directly to the file, and it starts *its* own container application within the browser. In this example, PowerPoint will run, then load the SalesDemo presentation inside Internet Explorer. You can hyperlink to any Office file, for example, a Word document, an Excel spreadsheet, an Access database, or a PowerPoint presentation. The Office document runs within Internet Explorer as shown in Figure 12.2.

## Navigating to Another ActiveX Document

In the previous chapter, you learned the basics of navigating to another ActiveX document. You simply point the browser to the address of the .VBD file:

```
Hyperlink.NavigateTo "C:\CustomerFiles\xdocLookupCustomerAddress.vbd"
```

In the real world, though, it's not always so simple. Navigating between ActiveX documents places extra responsibility on the developer. You have to monitor the location of .VBD files and the application files.

**Navigating in the Real World**   As applications become more and more distributed, the burden of dealing with unpredictable user environments falls on the developer. Several years ago, it

Part
**IV**

Ch
**12**

was a straightforward matter to write an application and hard-code the paths to all its sub-systems, secure in the knowledge that the runtime environment would not change. Whenever the runtime environment needed to change, there was time to plan and there were software maintenance resources in place to make the infrequent customizations.

**FIG. 12.2**

An Excel spreadsheet running in the browser container.

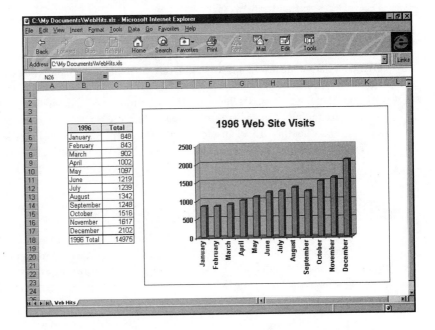

**N O T E**  The capability to hyperlink to any office file and have the Office application run within Internet Explorer is available with either Office 95 or Office 97. ■

Now, however, with applications designed to be distributed and run on local machines, the developer must not attempt to control the runtime environment, but to adapt his program dynamically to it. The program must be able to determine information about its environment.

When programming applications for the Internet and even intranets, you must first acknowledge that you relinquish a great deal of control. Distributed, event-driven applications must be written to adapt to this lack of control.

Years ago, programming was a much simpler endeavor. The developer often knew a great deal about the environment where the program would be used, and almost certainly knew the platform and the configuration. As desktop computer systems proliferated, however, programs had to get "smarter." The first reaction by software developers was to create flexible installations. Later the concept was developed that a program should be able to dynamically determine its environment. The concept of intelligent applications and intelligent objects moved from academic journals to the user's desktop.

Imagine, if you will, a program written for international distribution. If the developer had written the program in English, there would be no problem if the program were distributed only in, say, the United States, Western Canada, Great Britain, and India. But release this program in Montreal, Tokyo, or Barcelona, and it would require a complete rewrite. Instead, many programs are now written to dynamically determine information about their environments. An intelligent program checks its environment, determines if it is in, say, Saõ Paulo, and the on-screen labels and help files will default to Portuguese.

With Internet-enabled applications, you must anticipate similar problems in deployment. Your application must be able to determine something about its environment to run properly. As a developer, you no longer have the luxury of knowing exactly where and how your application will be installed or used.

For example, your ActiveX document application might be used on an intranet where the .EXE file resides on a shared directory, yet each user has copies of the .VBD files on his local hard drive.

But wait! What about the caution earlier, that .VBD files must be in the same directory as the .EXE file? That's not *quite* accurate—if they are not in the same directory, the application must point to the specific directory where the .VBD resides.

No, in the following example you don't have to worry about something as complex as the language of the user interface. What your ActiveX application needs to know first about its environment is something more prosaic: *where it is.*

As you learned in Chapter 10, "CGI Programming: The Original Web Programming Way," when you compile an ActiveX document application, all the files are created in the same directory. There is no need to define an explicit path if the .VBD files are in the same directory as the compiled .EXE file. But it would be naive to presume that every user who downloads your ActiveX application—no matter how rigid the *anticipated* environment—will use it in the way you prescribe.

Let's take a step back and take another look at the contents of a .VBD file. As described in the previous chapter, a .VBD file contains the information saved by the PropertyBag. But it also contains the name and location of the class that runs it. When you point the browser to the .VBD file, it launches the associated ActiveX document application .EXE or .DLL. Therefore, if you can keep track of the location of the .VBD files, the application file can be safely moved to another location.

### Determining the Dynamic Path: An Example

So, how do you keep track of where the user is in the application? Go back to the example in Chapter 10. Double-click the Module folder. From the menu, select Project, and select Add Module. Name the module basGetVbdPath. Now create the following public function:

```
Public Function GetVbdPath(sParentPath)
' Determine the current path by parsing the path
' of the calling object's location:

Dim iCounter As Integer

For iCounter = Len(sParentPath) To 1 Step -1
    If Mid$(sParentPath, iCounter, 1) = "/" Or Mid$(sParentPath, iCounter, 1) =
    ➡"\" Then Exit For
Next iCounter
```

```
' strip the name of the current vbdfile
GetVbdPath = Left$(sParentPath, iCounter)

End Function
```

What this code does is pretty basic. Rather than placing an explicit path after NavigateTo, you call the program, which determines the path and stores it in a string. Then you concatenate the path string with the name of the .VBD you wish to call like this:

```
Private Sub cmdOpenChild_Click()
' First call the function to determine the path,
' the build the proper NavigateTo syntax--

Dim sParentPath, sNewPath As String
sParentPath = Trim$(UserDocument.Parent.LocationName)

sNewPath = GetVbdPath(sParentPath)

UserDocument.Hyperlink.NavigateTo sNewPath & "xdocChild.vbd"

End Sub
```

Now you have built some "intelligence" into your ActiveX document application. Through this reusable function, you have created a method for the calling object to determine where to find the called .VBD file, regardless of the location of the application.

Before proceeding, be sure to modify all the code in each command button of the example application to look like the preceding example.

# Exchanging Information Between ActiveX Documents

In the previous chapter, you learned how to use the PropertyBag object to save state information about an ActiveX Document. But since each User Document has its own PropertyBag, how can you share information *between* ActiveX documents?

First, you'll need to create public properties for the User Document objects. Through the public property, other applications or ActiveX documents can read from or write properties to the object.

## Adding Public Properties to ActiveX Documents

Let's go back to the example and add functionality so you can understand how this works.

From the Project menu, click Add Module. In the Properties window, name the new code module basGlobalProperties. Double-click the module icon and add the following code in the Declarations section:

```
' Declare an object variable for the Parent Document
Public gParentDoc as xdocParent
```

Now you'll need to set the document reference, that is, you'll need to set the object to equal something, in this case, xdocParent. You can do this at a conditional event (like a command button click), or simply on the form initialize event:

```
Private Sub UserDocument_Initialize()
' Save values in form-level variables.
' You can also retrieve these values from a database

    InitializeVariables

' Set the global object reference to this document:

    Set gParentDoc = Me

End Sub
```

Note that the object is declared as public so that it can be referenced by other ActiveX documents and applications. Now return to xdocParent, first add a test box and name it txtNameLast. Now add a procedure to allow the object to read data and place it in the text box

```
Public Property Get sDocProp() As String
'   Note: If the editor defaults to "As Variant" in the
'   Declaration line, be sure to change it to "As String"

    sDocProp = txtNameLast.Text

End Property
```

And enter corresponding code for the Let property:

```
Public Property Let sDocProp(ByVal sNewValue As String)
'   Note: As before, remember to change the argument
'   from "As Variant" to "As String"

    txtNameLast.Text = sNewValue

End Property
```

This sort of code may look very similar to some of the methods you may have used with class modules in Visual Basic 4.0. In fact, the goal is the same. Setting these two properties exposes the sDocProp property as a public property. Now you can set the value of sDocProp from any ActiveX document through this exposed property.

You're ready to put this code into action. To proceed, copy txtLastName text box to the "child" documents, and add the following code to the Show event of the User Documents xdocChild and xdocAnotherChild:

```
Private Sub UserDocument_Show()
' Check to see if there is a value in gParentDoc
' If there is, assign its value(s) accordingly:

If Not gParentDoc Is Nothing Then
    txtNameLast.Text = gParentDoc.sDocProp
End If

End Sub
```

After you recompile and run the application, you can monitor the changes by watching the value of the Last Name text box in xdocChild and xdocAnotherChild. Figure 12.3 shows the new code in action.

Part
IV

Ch

12

**FIG. 12.3**

The contents of `txtLastName` are passed as a public property.

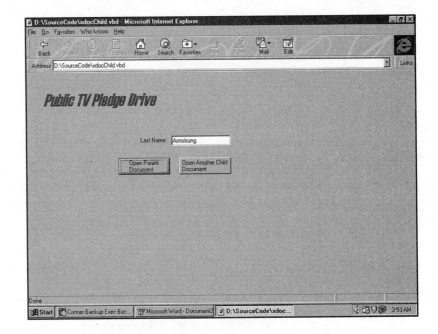

# The Life Cycle of an ActiveX Document

The only way to navigate among ActiveX documents is with a hyperlink, such as the NavigateTo method. Unlike the Show and Hide methods used in Visual Basic forms, however, navigating ActiveX documents by hyperlinks has somewhat different events.

Remember that although an ActiveX document may superficially appear to be similar to a form, it is actually very different. An ActiveX document has some of the familiar events of a Visual Basic form, such as Initialize and Show. It does not, however, have some key events that a form does, like Activate, Deactivate, Load, and Unload. In Visual Basic 4.0, you usually instanced objects on Form Load and destroyed objects on Form Unload.

Making the transition to ActiveX user documents requires some adjustment. Some of the significant events of the life cycle of an Active X document are listed in Table 12.1, in the order they occur.

**Table 12.1  Events in the Life of an ActiveX Document**

| Event | Description |
|---|---|
| Initialize | Always the first event to occur, the Initialize event fires every time you create an instance of the document. |
| Show | This event occurs when a user navigates to a document. It occurs immediately after the Initialize event. |

| Event | Description |
|-------|-------------|
| Hide | Occurs after the user navigates to another object (Web page, ActiveX document, and so on). |
| Terminate | This event occurs *immediately before* an ActiveX document is destroyed. This is the best place to clean up objects. |

Let's look at what goes on behind the scenes in the container object.

When a user points the browser to an ActiveX document, the ActiveX application first creates an instance of the document (the Initialize event). If you are going to be creating variables and objects for this document, now is the time to allocate memory for them. If you create two or more instances of a document, the event occurs for each instance created.

When the browser actually points to the document, the Show event occurs. This is the time to assign values to variables.

When the user navigates off the document, the Hide event occurs. The document is still in memory, however.

The Terminate event occurs immediately before the ActiveX document is destroyed from memory. This event automatically occurs as documents are removed from the cache.

## The Container Cache

Internet Explorer 3.0 can assist you with keeping memory leaks from crashing your ActiveX document applications. By design, IE 3.0 caches the last four documents in memory. This is separate from the disk cache—it is an automatic memory cache, illustrated graphically in Figure 12.4.

If the user returns to the previous documents by the following syntax, the cache is being accessed:

```
Hyperlink.GoBack
```

This is because the GoBack and GoForward methods access the history list—and the last four pages are stored in the memory cache—beyond that, they may or may not be stored in the disk cache.

But if the user executes

```
Hyperlink.NavigateTo "xdocActiveDocument"
```

a new instance of the object is created.

## Housekeeping with the Terminate Event

After objects have initialized, it is also the responsibility of the developer to make sure that they are destroyed properly. Memory leaks can be the most insidious bugs to identify. Users may complain of inexplicable crashes, and they may be equally inexplicable to the developer who tries to find their cause.

Part
IV

Ch
12

**FIG. 12.4**

Using the GoBack and GoForward methods navigates within the document cache. Internet Explorer 3.0 stores the last four documents in the cache.

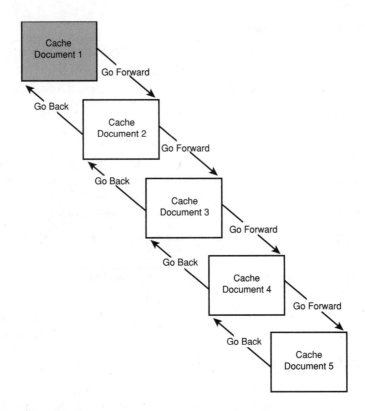

The ActiveX documents themselves are stored in a cache in the container object, but only to a level four deep, they are destroyed on loading a fifth object. This then, is an ideal time to set document-specific objects to Nothing. Remember that the Terminate event occurs immediately before the object is destroyed.

# Extending the Example

Return to the example and open xdocAnotherChild and rename the control buttons and their captions. Add navigation buttons on the left, as in Figure 12.5.

Change the command button and its code:

Now add the buttons cmdGoForward and cmdGoBack to the form and add this code to them:

```
Private Sub cmdOpen3rdChild_Click()

Dim sParentPath, sNewPath As String
sParentPath = Trim$(UserDocument.Parent.LocationName)

sNewPath = GetVbdPath(sParentPath)

UserDocument.Hyperlink.NavigateTo sNewPath & "xdoc3rdChild.vbd"
```

```
End Sub
Private Sub cmdOpenChild_Click()

Dim sParentPath, sNewPath As String
sParentPath = Trim$(UserDocument.Parent.LocationName)

sNewPath = GetVbdPath(sParentPath)

UserDocument.Hyperlink.NavigateTo sNewPath & "xdocChild.vbd"

End Sub
```

**FIG. 12.5**
Modify
xdocAnotherChild's
commands to include
modified command
buttons on the right
and the navigation
buttons on the left.

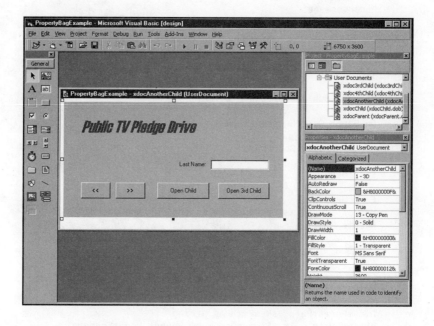

At this point, add another user document to your project and name it xdoc3rdChild. Construct it as in Figure 12.6 and add the following code:

```
Private Sub cmdOpen3rdChild_Click()

Dim sParentPath, sNewPath As String
sParentPath = Trim$(UserDocument.Parent.LocationName)

sNewPath = GetVbdPath(sParentPath)

UserDocument.Hyperlink.NavigateTo sNewPath & "xdoc3rdChild.vbd"

End Sub
Private Sub cmdOpenChild_Click()

Dim sParentPath, sNewPath As String
sParentPath = Trim$(UserDocument.Parent.LocationName)

sNewPath = GetVbdPath(sParentPath)
```

```
        UserDocument.Hyperlink.NavigateTo sNewPath & "xdocChild.vbd"

    End Sub

    Private Sub cmdGoBack_Click()

    On Error GoTo ErrorMessage

        Hyperlink.GoBack

    Exit Sub

    ErrorMessage:
    MsgBox "There is no document in the Cache!"
    Resume Next

    End Sub


    Private Sub cmdGoForward_Click()

    On Error GoTo ErrorMessage

        Hyperlink.GoForward

    Exit Sub

    ErrorMessage:
    MsgBox "There is no document in the Forward Cache!"
    Resume Next

    End Sub


    Private Sub cmdOpen4thChild_Click()

    Dim sParentPath, sNewPath As String
    sParentPath = Trim$(UserDocument.Parent.LocationName)

    sNewPath = GetVbdPath(sParentPath)

    UserDocument.Hyperlink.NavigateTo sNewPath & "xdoc4thChild.vbd"


    End Sub

    Private Sub cmdOpenAnotherChild_Click()

    Dim sParentPath, sNewPath As String
    sParentPath = Trim$(UserDocument.Parent.LocationName)

    sNewPath = GetVbdPath(sParentPath)

    UserDocument.Hyperlink.NavigateTo sNewPath & "xdocAnotherChild.vbd"


    End Sub
```

```
Private Sub UserDocument_Show()
' Check to see if there is a value in gParentDoc
' If there is, assign its value(s) accordingly:

If Not gParentDoc Is Nothing Then
    txtNameLast.Text = gParentDoc.sDocProp
End If

End Sub
```

Now you are almost done with the expanded example. Add another user document to your project and name it xdoc4thChild. Construct it as in Figure 12.6 and add the following code:

```
Private Sub cmdGoBack_Click()
On Error GoTo ErrorMessage

    Hyperlink.GoBack

Exit Sub

ErrorMessage:
MsgBox "There is no document in the Cache!"
Resume Next

End Sub


Private Sub cmdGoForward_Click()

On Error GoTo ErrorMessage

    Hyperlink.GoForward

Exit Sub

ErrorMessage:
MsgBox "There is no document in the Forward Cache!"
Resume Next
End Sub


Private Sub cmdOpen3rdChild_Click()

Dim sParentPath, sNewPath As String
sParentPath = Trim$(UserDocument.Parent.LocationName)

sNewPath = GetVbdPath(sParentPath)

UserDocument.Hyperlink.NavigateTo sNewPath & "xdoc3rdChild.vbd"


End Sub


Private Sub UserDocument_Initialize()
' Check to see if there is a value in gParentDoc
' If there is, assign its value(s) accordingly:
```

```
If Not gParentDoc Is Nothing Then
    txtNameLast.Text = gParentDoc.sDocProp
End If

End Sub
```

**FIG. 12.6**

The two additional User Documents being integrated into the project.

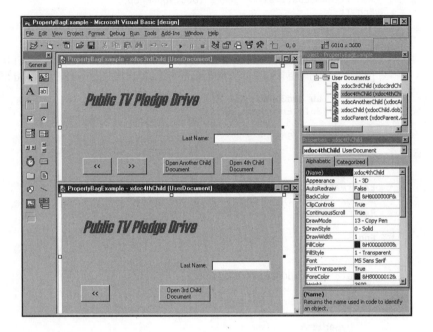

Remember the mention of "housekeeping" earlier? In xdocParent you created a global object which you use to pass properties between the ActiveX documents. Enter the following code into the Terminate event of xdocParent:

```
Private Sub UserDocument_Terminate()

    Set gParentDoc = Nothing

End Sub
```

Now when you run the application and navigate through the various pages, you'll notice that the last, or fifth, document does not fill the text box. That's because the first document (xdocParent) object no longer exists in the cache, as shown in Figure 12.7.

After the User Document has been terminated, the public properties you have been using no longer have any values to pass! What's the solution?

As you'll recall from Chapter 11, every User Document has its own PropertyBag and .VBD file. If your users will be moving from among a number of User Documents or HTML pages, you should save the state information of each page with the PropertyBag. Since you will not be able (and shouldn't try!) to control the user's workflow, you need to check for changes and save the state information to the PropertyBag of each user document in your application.

**FIG. 12.7**
Now when you invoke the fifth document, the first one is removed from the cache.

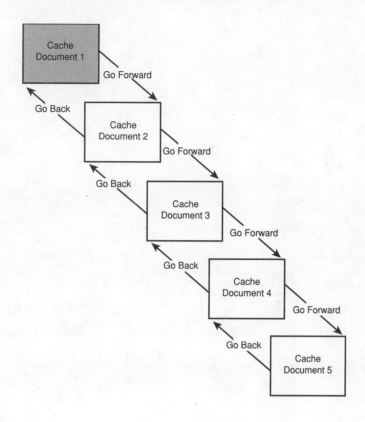

# From Here...

Chapter 10, "ActiveX Documents: Serving Up VB in a Web Browser," gives you an introduction to the basics of creating and running ActiveX document applications in their container applications.

Chapter 11, "Property Bags and Menus: Extending ActiveX Document Applications," shows you how to save state information of instances of your ActiveX documents. In this chapter, you'll also find information about adding menus to enhance your ActiveX document applications.

Part
IV

Ch
12

# Active Server Pages

# CHAPTER 13

# Active Server Pages and Server-Side Scripting

In the current realm of Internet and particularly World Wide Web development, one of the problems faced by developers has been the rapidly changing technology and standards. Add to this the growing expectations of the Web visitor, and the pressure for high-quality, interactive, state of the art Web pages is enormous. ■

**Active Server and Web browser dependence**

Active Server is a technology created by Microsoft that removes Web browser dependence in Web page development. Your content does not have to be created for the lowest common denominator of Web browsers. Active Server returns only standard HTML.

**Platforms supported by Active Server?**

At present, only Microsoft Internet Information Server supports Active Server technology.

**Scripting with Active Server**

At the present time, VBScript and JScript are supported by Active Server. There are plans by Microsoft to extend the scripting model to include other script languages such as PERL.

**Connecting to a database independent of the browser?**

Using Microsoft's Internet Database Connector, you can connect to any ODBC compliant database and have all of the processing performed by the server. The output is standard HTML.

**ActiveX controls as part of Active Server**

Active Server is compatible with ActiveX technology.

# Understanding Standards and Technology on the Internet

There are three primary areas where the rapid change of technology and standards are of particular concern to developers of Web content such as yourself:

- HTML standards as established by the W3 Consortium
- Web browsers as created by the various software developers
- Web servers as created by the various software developers

## HTML Versions

The W3 Consortium has assumed the responsibility for the creation and maintenance of standards for many areas of the World Wide Web, including HTML standards. If you are interested in more about the W3 Consortium, you can find all the information you need at **HTTP:// www.w3.org/pub/WWW**. The procedure for creating a new standard for HTML is largely consensual. The leading organizations in Web development such as the browser and server developers suggest new extensions to HTML which are then reviewed and subsequently accepted or rejected. When a new standard is created it is published. Draft documents that represent changes under consideration are also available.

## Browser Technology

The primary function of all Web browsers is the interpretation of HTML and the display of the resulting Web page. The current version of HTML is 3.2 and all current Web browsers support version 3.2—well sort of. It is important to remember that there are four types of browsers.

1. Text Only Browsers
2. Older Graphic Browsers
3. Netscape Navigator
4. Microsoft Internet Explorer

**Text-Only Browser**   An example of a text-only browser is LYNX, created at the University of Kansas. All of your creative efforts on a graphic display are lost on the LYNX user. Some Web pages offer a text-only version that shows what a LYNX user will see. Also, most browsers have settings that turn the graphic display off. One of the features that HTML provides is the ability to provide a text alternative to the graphic for text-only browsers. I have heard an unfortunate attitude expressed toward the users of LYNX and the other text-only browsers that is something like this, "I don't care about people on the Web who won't even get a graphic browser." Don't forget that there are users who are unable to see your glorious visual content. These are the vision impaired users. Computers are one of their very important and useful tools. (I will now get down from my soap box.) The number of users of text-only browsers is reported to be a small percentage of the total users of the World Wide Web. There is even a group that rates Web sites as to their LYNX friendliness.

**Older Graphic Browsers**   NCSA's Mosaic is an example of older browser technology. With the popularity of Netscape Navigator and Microsoft Internet Explorer, Mosaic hasn't kept pace with all of the latest developments. Mosaic does a reasonably good job with the HTML. Some of the newer features won't be handled properly. Features such as client side scripting, Java Applets, and Microsoft ActiveX Controls are not supported. The number of users of older Web browsers is reported to be small.

**Netscape Navigator**   Netscape Navigator is one of the major Web browsers in terms of percentage of users. Estimates are that the numbers is 60+ percent. However, Netscape's usage seems to be shrinking with the growth going to Microsoft. Generally, the newest version of Netscape Navigator will support all of the latest version of HTML (at present HTML 3.2). Netscape Navigator also supports client side JavaScript and Java Applets. It does not support VBScript or ActiveX controls. Because of the highly competitive nature of the race to dominate the Web in terms of Web browsers and Web servers, the features that are supported by Netscape are subject to change almost daily.

**Microsoft Internet Explorer**   The MS Internet Explorer is the most universal in the range of technology and features supported. This may be because Microsoft is trying to overcome the formidable lead of Netscape. Microsoft Internet Explorer is estimated at 30+ percent of the Internet browser users. Microsoft Internet Explorer usage seems to be growing at the expense of Netscape. MS Internet Explorer supports HTML 3.2, JavaScript, Java Applets, VBScript, and ActiveX Controls.

# Web Server Technology

There are a number of Web Servers available. Two of the most important are Netscape Enterprise Server and Microsoft Internet Information Server. Netscape Enterprise Server runs on both UNIX and Windows NT. Microsoft Internet Information Server runs on Microsoft Windows NT only.

There are a number of criteria upon which the selection of server software should be made and it is not this section's intent to provide an analysis of those. The key issues for this discussion are that Microsoft Internet Information Server supports Active Server and Netscape Enterprise Server does not. Because the selection of the server software is under the control of the publisher of Web material, this will not present a complicating factor except to note that Web content that is developed for MS IIS may not be transportable to other server platforms.

**N O T E**   In the world of software, every need is met with a solution. Chili!Soft is currently developing a product with the working name of ActiveDave. ActiveDave is soon to be renamed. ActiveDave's job is to enable the use of Active Server pages and objects with NT-based, non-Microsoft Web Servers. It is in beta release at the time of writing with a May 1997 release date predicted by Chili!Soft. It may bear watching. ■

Part
**V**

Ch
**13**

# Understanding Microsoft Active Server

Microsoft Internet Information Server 3.0 does not replace or change any of the functionality of Microsoft Internet Information Server 2.0. MS IIS 3.0 adds Active Server functionality to MS IIS 2.0. The Active Server can also be used with the MS Peer Web Server, which is available with MS Windows NT Workstation and the MS Personal Web Server for Windows 95. It is the same installation set of software in all cases and the functionality is identical.

Before MS IIS 3.0 can be installed, MS IIS 2.0, MS Peer Web Server, or Personal Web Server must be installed.

**N O T E** The installation of Active Server pages requires the installation of Microsoft Internet Explorer 3.01 for Windows 95 or Windows NT 4.0. The build required is 1215 or later. You can check the build of your version of Internet Explorer by opening Internet Explorer and choosing Help, About. MS IE 3.01 is usually supplied with the MS IIS 3.0 install set. In the event that it isn't supplied, it can be downloaded from the Microsoft Web site at **HTTP://www.microsoft.com**. ■

When MS Active Server Pages is installed, an icon is added to the MS IIS, Peer Web Server or Personal Web Server program Group titled Active Server Pages Roadmap. When you click this icon, documentation and samples of the use of Active Server are opened in your Internet Explorer browser, as shown in Figure 13.1.

**FIG. 13.1**

The frame on the left contains links to the documentation on Active Server. When a topic is chosen, it is displayed in the frame on the right.

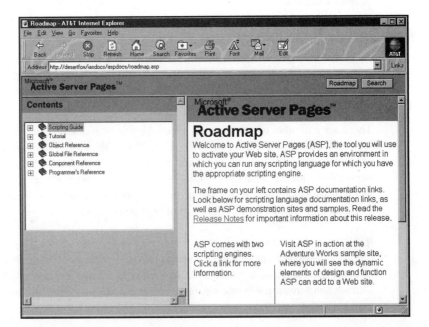

**N O T E** The TCP stack must be running for the Active Server functions to work. An easy method of starting the stack is to attach it to your Internet Service Provider just as if you were going to browse Web pages. If your Internet Explorer is set to automatically connect with your Internet Service Provider when you open it, the same will happen when you click the Active Server Pages Roadmap icon. Simply allow the connection to be made and the stack will be running.

If you receive an error informing you that the pages or site can't be found or that there is no program associated with the .ASP file extension, the probable cause is that the stack is not running. ■

## How Active Server Works

One of the limitations of client-side processing is that the Web browser must support the functionality that is called for in your Web page. If you attempt to use VBScript and the browser does not support VBScript, the script is simply ignored and may be displayed by the browser.

**T I P** If you don't want to have your client-side VBScript displayed in the event that the browser doesn't support VBScript, it can be placed inside comment tags. This is usually a good idea because VBScript looks confusing and ugly when displayed in a browser.

With Active Server Pages, all processing is performed on the server and only standard HTML is transferred to the client. The creation of a simple example will demonstrate what is happening.

1. The first step is to create a virtual directory in the Web site to house the example files. Open the administration of the Web site and create a directory named VB5_Demo. Set this directory as a virtual directory with the alias of VB5_Demo. Be sure to set the directory for Read and Execute.

2. Open Notepad and, in a new text file, enter the following HTML:

---

**Listing 13.1    VB5_Demo.ASP—The HTML for the Active Server Demonstration Page**

```
<%@ LANGUAGE="VBSCRIPT" %>

<HTML>
<HEAD>
<TITLE>VB5 Acitve Server Demo</TITLE>
</HEAD>
<BODY>
<% for i = 3 to 7 %>
<font size=<%=i%>>This Demonstrates an Active Server Page</font><BR>
<% next %>
</BODY>
</HTML>
```

---

Part

**V**

Ch

**13**

3. Open your Internet Explorer Browser and set the URL to **HTTP://ServerName/ VB5_Demo/VB5_Demo.ASP**. You will see the Web Page shown in Figure 13.2.

**FIG. 13.2**

The increasing size of the font results from the execution of the VBScript.

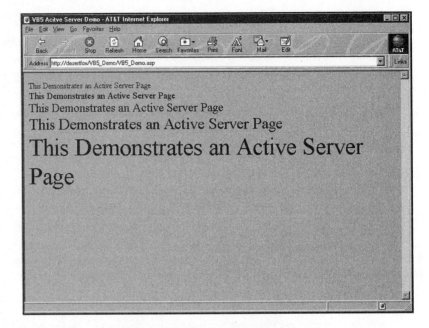

4. While the browser is open, choose <u>V</u>iew, Sour<u>c</u>e and the source file VB5_Demo.htm is displayed in Notepad as shown in Figure 13.3 and Listing 13.2 below.

**FIG. 13.3**

This shows the HTML version of the Active Server Page that was transferred to the browser.

**Listing 13.2   VB5_Demo.HTM—The HTML for the Active Server Demonstration Page When It Is Transferred to the Browser as VB5_Demo.HTM**

```
<HTML>
<HEAD>
<TITLE>VB5 Acitve Server Demo</TITLE>
</HEAD>
```

```
<BODY>

<font size=3>This Demonstrates an Active Server Page</font><BR>

<font size=4>This Demonstrates an Active Server Page</font><BR>

<font size=5>This Demonstrates an Active Server Page</font><BR>

<font size=6>This Demonstrates an Active Server Page</font><BR>

<font size=7>This Demonstrates an Active Server Page</font><BR>

</BODY>
</HTML>
```

 **TIP** Notice that the VBScript is enclosed in <% %> in an ASP page. This is necessary for the Active Server to recognize it as VBScript. It is different than the client script tag. This makes it possible to send VBScript from an Active Server page to a client page.

The HTML contents of the page requested and the page transferred are not the same. The page transferred contains no VBScript.

Now we will examine what has just happened in the interaction between the Web browser and the Web Server. The Web browser requested the document VB5_Demo.ASP from the Web server. The action expected of the Web server is to transfer the document. However, in this case, the Web server sees the .ASP extension on the document rather than .HTM. The Web server reads the document, interprets the VBScript and generates an HTML document that is transferred to the Web browser. The document transferred is named VB5_Demo.HTM. It is important to understand that the document VB5_Demo.HTM exists only on the browser, not on the server.

 **TIP** If the .ASP file does not execute, check in the Web server administration on the directory that contains the .ASP file. It must be set to Execute as well as Read. The failure does not provide an informative error message that will lead you to the conclusion that you have failed to set the execute permission. Just always double check in the event of problems.

# Looking at Client-Side Processing

A document named VB5_Demo.HTM has been created by the author and placed on the server. This document contains VBScript. The VBScript is for client-side processing. The HTML contents of the page are shown in Listing 13.3.

**Listing 13.3   VB5_Demo.HTM—The HTML for the Client-Side VBScript Demonstration Page**

```
<html>
<body>
<SCRIPT LANGUAGE = "VBScript">
for i = 1 to 5
document.write "<H1>This Demonstrates Client-side Processing</H1><BR>"
next
</SCRIPT>
</body>
</html>
```

In Figure 13.4, you see this page as it is displayed on the browser.

**FIG. 13.4**

The page displayed is not the same as the HTML and VBScript that was transferred by the server.

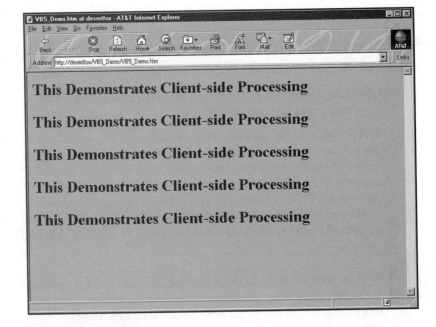

When you choose View, Source on the browser, you will see the file as it was transferred by the server displayed in Notepad (see Figure 13.5).

# Comparing Active Server to Client-Side Processing

The purpose of this detailed trip through the processing of VBScript on the server and then on the client is to demonstrate where the processing of the VBScript takes place. The only property of the Web page required to cause the server to process the VBScript is an .ASP extension.

**FIG. 13.5**

The page displayed by the browser is the result of processing the VBScript in the page transferred by the server.

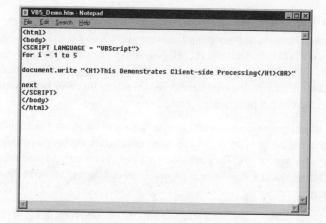

```
VB5_Demo.htm - Notepad
File  Edit  Search  Help
<html>
<body>
<SCRIPT LANGUAGE = "VBScript">
For i = 1 to 5

document.write "<H1>This Demonstrates Client-side Processing</H1><BR>"

next
</SCRIPT>
</body>
</html>
```

Web browsers will display the Web page shown in Figure 13.2 whether VBScript is supported by the browser or not. There is no VBScript transferred by the server to the browser.

The Web page shown in Figure 13.4 requires that the browser is VBScript enabled. At present, only Microsoft Internet Explorer will perform client-side VBScript processing. As the VB5_Demo.HTM page is written, a Web browser that cannot process VBScript will treat the entire page as HTML and display the VBScript rather than the results of the VBScript processing. The result is rather ugly.

 One big advantage of Active Server is that your code is secure. If you perform client-side processing, and a visitor to your page wants to see how you achieved the results, all that is necessary is to choose View, Source in most browsers. This means that each time your page is visited you have potentially given away your source code. This is not true with Active Server. All that the visitor has access to are the results of your processing on the server.

# Using VBScript

Looking at the VBScript in the two examples in the previous section of this chapter, you see that there are differences in VBScript when it is used in Active Server and client-side processing. Those differences will be examined later in the chapter. The differences do not affect the syntax, only the HTML surrounding the VBScript.

The first issue that needs to be examined is exactly what is VBScript. It is a member of the Visual Basic family. It is much like HTML in that it cannot stand alone because it is an interpreted language. It is always embedded in an HTML file and is composed of ASCII text statements. It never exists as a binary object. VBScript must by processed by an interpreter, in this case a Web browser that has an extension for the interpretation of VBScript. At present, Microsoft Internet Explorer is the only Web browser that has an extension for the interpretation of VBScript.

# Why Use a Scripting Language

The purpose of introducing scripting languages into Web pages is to overcome the inherent limitations of HTML. Essentially, HTML consists of formatting commands and links to inline objects and hyperlinks to other Web pages. HTML does not perform conditional logic (IF...THEN...ELSE). It does not handle variables. In other words, it cannot carry out the functions expected of a full programming language.

Scripting languages have an advantage over compiled languages in applications such as Web pages in that the script is processed by another program that is responsible for the interface with the system resources. They are also very easy to create and maintain. Changing a VBScript statement in a Web page is as simple as editing any text file. No compilation or link-editing is required.

VBScript is not the only scripting language in use on the World Wide Web today. JavaScript and JScript, which is Microsoft's implementation of JavaScript, are becoming widely used. Microsoft is creating a standard interface to scripting languages so it is expected that other scripting languages will be introduced to the Web.

# VBScript Language Elements

If you are familiar with Visual Basic in any of its versions, you will be right at home with VBScript. VBScript has all of the usual features and issues of a programming language.

**VBScript Data Types**   VBScript has only one data type, which is called Variant. Variant, as its name implies, can contain various types of data. The type of data that is stored in a variable is recorded in the variable as a subtype. If you have the number 100 stored in a variable of the Variant data type, when your code context treats it as a string, it behaves as a string. When you use it in a calculation it will behave as a number. VBScript will convert the data as necessary depending on the context.

The subtypes of the Variant data type are:

- **Empty**.   Variant is uninitialized. If the context uses it as a number, the value is zero. If the context uses it as a string it is a zero-length string ("").
- **Null**.   Variant contains no valid data. Nulls can be confusing. It does not mean blank. A null in a logical compare will not match any value.
- **Boolean**.   The value is true or false.
- **Byte**.   The value is an integer in the range of 0 to 255. This is not a signed value.
- **Integer**.   The value is a signed integer in the range of -32,768 to 32,767. Note that there is no unsigned integer.
- **Long**.   The value is a long integer in the range of -2,147,483,648 to 2,147,483,647.
- **Currency**.   -922,337,203,685,477.5808 to 922,337,203,685,477.5807 is the range of values.
- **Single**.   The values are a single-precision, floating point numbers in the range of -3.402823E38 to -1.401298E-45 for negative values to 1.401298E-45 to 3.402823E38 for positive values.

■ **Double.** The values are a double-precision, floating point number in the range of -1.79769313486232E308 to -4.94065645841247E-324 for negative values to 4.94065645841247E-324 to 1.79769313486232E308 for positive values.

■ **Date (Time).** The value is a number that represents a date and time between January 1, 100 to December 31, 9999.

■ **String.** Contains a variable length string that can be roughly 2 billion characters in length.

■ **Object.** Contains an object.

■ **Error.** Contains an error number.

The self-converting Variant type does not always work as expected. You will still encounter the occasional type mismatch error condition. There are some VBScript functions that allow you to examine the Variant subtype and to convert the subtype to eliminate the type mismatch problem. One of the consequences of the variant data type is that when a variable is declared, the type is not specified.

**VBScript Functions**    VBScript contains the functions that you are familiar with from Visual Basic. The full list of functions will not be covered here. There are some functions specifically for working with the Variant data type subtypes that deserve some mention. The first of these are two that are used to determine the subtype of a variable.

■ *VarType(varname)* returns a numeric value depending on the Variant subtype, for example 2 is an integer and 8 is a string.

■ *TypeName(varname)* returns a string that tells the Variant subtype, for example "byte" or "string."

There are several functions that test for specific Variant subtypes. Two examples include the following:

■ *IsArray(varname)* returns a true or false value depending on whether the variable is an array.

■ *IsNull(varname)* returns a true or false value depending on whether the variable value is null or not.

There are functions that will convert the Variant subtype, which will provide you with a fixed known subtype. Two examples are:

■ *CInt(experssion)* returns a value of the integer subtype.

■ *CStr(expression)* returns a value in the form of a string subtype.

The Visual Basic functions that you will not find in VBScript are Val() and Str(). You will need to use the CStr() or other Variant subtype conversion functions to accomplish the same result.

**VBScript Variables**    Declaring a variable in VBScript is very similar to Visual Basic. In Visual Basic, if you don't declare the type, the variable is a variant. In VBScript, you can't declare the type because all variables are of the type Variant. An example of a variable declaration is:

```
Dim MyVar
```

Multiple variables can be declared and separated by commas as in:

```
Dim MyVar, YourVar, OurVar
```

Give a variable an initial value:

```
MyVar = 10
```

The variable has also established the subtype of integer with the value of this assignment.

Variable naming restrictions are that the name must begin with an alphabetic character, cannot contain an embedded period, must not be longer than 255 characters, and must be unique within the scope of the variable.

Arrays may be created as:

```
Dim MyArray (10)
```

Multiple dimension arrays may be created as:

```
Dim MyArray (5, 10)
```

Arrays can be resized with the ReDim statement. If the values in the array are to be preserved during the resize the statement is as follows:

```
ReDim Preserve MyArray (30)
```

Variables in VBScript can have a scope and visibility of a single precedure or can have a script-wide scope and visibility. If the variable is declared in a procedure, its scope and visibility is limited to the procedure. If it is declared outside of a procedure, usually in the <HEAD> section of the HTML page, it will have script-wide scope and visibility.

**VBScript Constants**   A constant is data value that has a name. The value is substituted for the constant in a VBScript statement. The value of the constant never changes. An example of a constant is PI. PI has a value of 3.1416 and on and on. If you are writing a program that uses the value of PI in calculations, after you have declared the constant PI, you can use PI rather than typing out the number. This allows you to determine at the beginning that you will use PI with four decimal places uniformly throughout the program.

To declare a constant, the key word CONST is used. An example is:

```
CONST PI
```

After you declare the constant you need to initialize its value. For example:

```
PI = 3.1416
```

When you are declaring a string constant, the value is enclosed in quotation marks as:

```
Const MY_STRING
MY_STRING = "This is my string."
```

For date constants, the value is enclosed in the pound sign (#).

```
Const MY_BIRTHDATE
MY_BIRTHDATE = #5/15/1955#
```

**Control of Program Flow in VBScript**   There are two basic types of program flow control statements. These are conditional statements such as the If…Then…Else type of logic and the repetitive execution of code or Loops.

There is one type of program flow control statement that is present in Visual Basic that does not exist in VBScript. This is the GOTO statement. Whether the omission is intentional or an oversight is unknown. The primary issue that the lack of a GOTO statement presents to the programmer is the requirement to perform all error handling in line.

The conditional statements include the single line If…Then syntax:

```
If A = B Then Myfunction
```

and the multiple-line or block If…Then syntax as in:

```
If A = B Then
    Myfunction
Else
    Anotherfunction
End If
```

If statements can be nested just as in Visual Basic and the ElseIF usage is valid in VBScript.

The Select Case statement is also supported as in:

```
Select Case MyVariable
    Case Value1
        Function1
    Case Value2
        Function2
    Case Else
        FunctionElse
End Select
```

For repetitive processing, VBScript supports Do…Loop logic identical to the forms supported in Visual Basic. The Exit Do function is supported and the Do Until and Do While forms work. For example:

```
Sub MyDoLoopExample()
    Dim mycounter, someNumber
    mycounter = 0
    someNumber = 0
    Do Until someNumber = 100
        someNumber = someNumber + 1
        mycounter = mycounter + 1
        If someNumber > 10 Then Exit Do
    Loop
    MsgBox "The loop made " & counter & " repetitions."
End Sub
```

This loop should make 11 repetitions.

VBScript also supports the While…Wend and the For…Next statements.

**VBScript Operators**   VBScript has the full range of Visual Basic operators, including logical operators, comparison operators, concatenation operators, and arithmetic operators. When several operators are used in succession the Visual Basic rules of Operator Precedence are followed. The arithmetic operators are:

- $+$    Addition - $X = A + B$
- $-$    Subtraction - $X = A - B$
- $*$    Multiplication - $X = A * B$
- $/$    Division - $X = A/B$
- $\backslash$    Integer Division - $X = A\backslash B$ (X will be an integer)
- $\wedge$    Exponentiation - $X = A\wedge B$
- Mod    Modulus Arithmetic - $X = A$ Mod $B$

The comparison operators are used to compare values or objects. The result returned is True or False. The comparison is often used to determine as If $A = B$ Then…. The comparison operators available in VBScript are:

- $=$    Equality - $A = B$
- $>$    Greater than - $A > B$
- $<$    Less than - $A < B$
- $<>$    Not equal to - $A <> B$
- $>=$    Greater than or equal to - $A >= B$
- $<=$    Less than or equal to - $A <= B$
- Is    Tests to see if two objects are the same object. ObjectA Is ObjectB

Logical operators return a value of True or False. As an example, in a test that is selecting rows from a table based on testing the values found in column A and column B, you could use the logical statement "Select the row if Column A = 10 And Column B = 25." Using the And operator, both conditions must be true. A full explanation of the logical operators is beyond the purpose of this chapter. For a complete explanation, the VB 5.0 help files are excellent. The logical operators provided by VBScript are:

- And    Logical conjunction
- Not    Logical negation
- Or    Logical disjunction
- Xor    Logical exclusion
- Eqv    Logical equivalence
- Imp    Logical implication

There is one concatenation operator in VBScript, &. It is used to put two strings together. As an example, if you want to create a new string value that is made up of two other strings the statement would be:

```
StringVarNew = StringVar1 & StringVar2
```

If StringVar1 contained "ABC" and StringVar2 contained "DEF," then StringVarNew would contain "ABCDEF."

**VBScript Procedures**    VBScript uses two types of procedures, Sub and Function. The basic difference is that a function can return a value and a sub can't.

Both a Sub and a Function can take arguments. When you create a Sub, you use the form shown in Listing 13.4 below. It calculates your weight in kilograms based on your input in pounds.

**Listing 13.4    VBScript Sub Code Snippet—The VBScript to Create a Sub procedure**

```
Sub WeightConversion()
    WeightLbs = InputBox("Please enter your weight in pounds.", 1)
    WeightKg = WeightLbs / 2.2
    MsgBox "Your weight in Kilograms is " & WeightKg
End Sub
```

If you wanted to create a Function that would perform the weight conversion it would look like Listing 13.5,

**Listing 13.5    VBScript Function Code Snippet—The Function Receives the Weight in Pounds and Returns the Weight in Kilograms**

```
Function ConvertWeight(WeightLbs)
    ConvertedWeight = WeightLbs / 2.2
End Function
```

When this function is used the code is:

```
WeightKg = ConvertWeight(WeightLbs)
```

The Sub or Function can be placed anywhere in the HTML document. A suggested location is in the <HEAD> section of the document. When it is located here it does not affect the appearance of the document and does not have to be placed in comment tags to keep it from printing on a browser that is not VBScript capable.

**Coding Conventions**    Coding conventions are not mandatory and do not affect the code in any way. Coding conventions are aimed at improving the readability and maintainability of the code. Not everyone uses the same conventions. The key is to establish a set of conventions that you use and adhere to them. Code that you wrote two weeks ago can look like it was written by a stranger when you come back to it.

The most important coding convention is in the naming of objects, variables, constants, and procedures. If you can look at a name in VBScript such as sdblMySomething and tell that it is a variable that is a double precision floating point number that has script wide scope and visibility, then the naming convention is working for you. Looking at the variable name sdblMySomething, the first s tells that it has script-wide visibility and the dbl tells that it is a double precision floating point number.

Part

V

Ch

13

A suggestion for the naming of constants is to make them all upper case and separate parts with an underscore as in MY_CONSTANT.

Suggestions for the prefix of variables based on the data subtype include:

- bln    Boolean - blnMyBool
- byt    Byte - bytMyValue
- cur    Currency - curSomeMoney
- dtm    Date/Time - dtmBirthday
- dbl    Double - dblBigNumber
- err    Error - errMyError
- int    Integer - intMyNumber
- lng    Long - lngMyBigInteger
- obj    Object - objMyObject
- sng    Single - sngMyDecimalNumber
- str    String - strMyFirstName

Procedure names are best started with a verb. OpenMyFile conveys action, which is what a procedure does. The procedure named CheckValues follows the same convention.

Object names can be challenging since there are so many objects available in VBScript. A few examples will provide some guidance.

- ckb    CheckBox
- txt    Text Box
- cmd    Command Button

Commenting your code is vital. If you think that you have added too many comments, you are probably getting close to what you will want six months from now when you look at the code again. Some ideas for things that should be commented are:

- Comment variables when they are declared.
- Comment procedures. What is its purpose, what are the arguments, what is the return value, where is it used.
- Beginning of Script comments should lay out the purpose of the script and any assumptions that were made.

If you answer the questions of who, what, where, when, why, and how in your comments, you will be the exception and will have good comments.

Finally, use indenting and white space to setoff sections of code that go together. It will greatly improve readability.

Because most VBScripts are not long involved programs, there is a tendency to ignore comments and coding conventions. It will come back to haunt you; it always does me.

# Using Forms with VBScript

When working with Active Server, the goal is to maintain independence of the features supported by the Web browser. In order to create interactive Web pages, it is necessary to have the user input information from the client system. HTML forms are the method that you have available to collect information from the user at the client system. This does not require any features beyond HTML.

In order to understand the process that is at work here you will need to create two HTML pages. These pages should be saved in the VB5_Demo directory that you created earlier in the chapter.

The first HTML page will be named VB5_DemoForm.HTM. This will be the form that is used to gather the information from the user on the client system. The code for this file is shown in Listing 13.6.

**Listing 13.6 VB5_DemoForm.HTM—This Form Gathers the Information that is Used by the Active Server Page**

```
<HTML>
<HEAD>
<TITLE>VB5 Active Server Demonstration Request Form</TITLE>
</HEAD>
<BODY BGCOLOR = "#FFFFFF">
<H1>Demonstration Input Form</H1>
<H2>This Demonstration Will Calculate Your Approximate Age In Months</H2>
<PRE>
<FORM METHOD=POST ACTION="VB5_DemoForm.asp">
<P><B> Your First Name:      <INPUT TYPE="text" NAME="fNameVar" SIZE=40>
<P><B>  Your Last Name:      <INPUT TYPE="text" NAME="lNameVar" SIZE=40>
<P><B>          Your Age:    <INPUT TYPE="text" NAME="AgeVar"   SIZE=10>
</PRE>
<INPUT TYPE="Submit" VALUE="Do It"><INPUT TYPE="Reset" VALUE="Clear">
</BODY>
</HTML>
```

The second HTML page is the Active server page that will perform the processing based on the information provided by the input form. The code for this page is shown in Listing 13.7.

**Listing 13.7 VB5_DemoForm.ASP—This VBScript Active Server Page Creates the Response that is Returned to the Client System**

```
<%@ LANGUAGE="VBSCRIPT" %>
<HTML>
<HEAD>
<TITLE>VB5 Acitve Server Response Form Demonstration</TITLE>
</HEAD>
<BODY BGCOLOR = "#FFFFFF">
```

Part

V

Ch

13

*continues*

**Listing 13.7 Continued**

```
<H1>Demonstration Response Form</H1>

<%firstname = Request.Form("fNameVar")
   lastname  = Request.Form("lNameVar")
   ageyear =   Request.Form("AgeVar")
   agemo = ageyear * 12%>

<%Response.Write(firstname & " " & lastname)%>
Your Age In Months Is
<% Response.Write(CStr(agemo))%>

</BODY>
</HTML>
```

Before you examine the code to see what is happening, you should look at the pages with a browser. Open your Web browser and set the URL to **http://systemname/VB5_Demo/ VB5_DemoForm.HTM**. You will see the Web page shown in Figure 13.6 below.

**FIG. 13.6**

The data collection is performed by this HTML form, shown here with sample data entered.

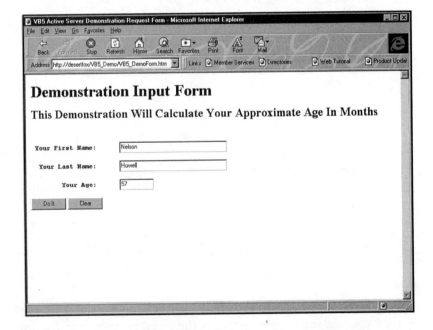

After entering your name and age as shown in Figure 13.6, click the command button labeled Do It. The data in the text boxes is submitted to the Active Server page and the response, seen in Figure 13.7, is returned to the client browser.

**FIG. 13.7**

The page returned was created by the Active Server page.

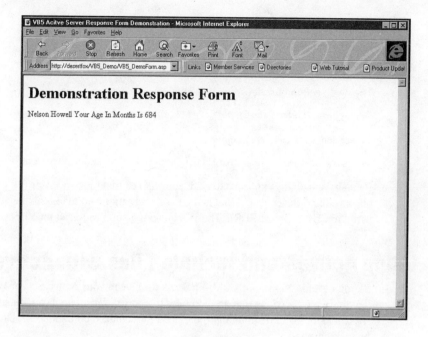

If the code for the two pages is examined, you will see that it is very simple code to create. There are three key sections in the VB5_DemoForm.HTM listing that deserve further examination. The first is the line of code:

```
<FORM METHOD=POST ACTION="VB5_DemoForm.asp">
```

This code states that the Form Method is to pass the information, and the file that it is to be passed to is VB5_DemoForm.ASP.

The next lines of code that are key are:

```
<P><B> Your First Name:      <INPUT TYPE="text" NAME="fNameVar" SIZE=40>
<P><B>  Your Last Name:      <INPUT TYPE="text" NAME="lNameVar" SIZE=40>
<P><B>          Your Age:    <INPUT TYPE="text" NAME="AgeVar"  SIZE=10>
```

These lines create the input test boxes that are used for the data entry.

Next is the command button that submits the data.

```
<INPUT TYPE="Submit" VALUE="Do It"><INPUT TYPE="Reset" VALUE="Clear">
```

The command button created is a "SUBMIT" button that has one purpose, it initiates the process of sending the request to the .ASP document.

When you examine the code in the Active Server Page, you again find three critical sections. The first moves the variables from the input form variables to the active server VBScript variables, as shown below:

```
<%firstname = Request.Form("fNameVar")
  lastname  = Request.Form("lNameVar")
  ageyear =   Request.Form("AgeVar")
```

The next line:

```
agemo = ageyear * 12%>
```

performs the calculation.

The next section of code:

```
<%Response.Write(firstname & " " & lastname)%>
Your Age In Months Is
<% Response.Write(CStr(agemo))%>
```

writes the data to the response HTML form that is passed to the client browser.

If you have had any exposure to CGI, you will see that the processes are very similar. There is one striking difference and that is the ease of creation and maintenance of the VBScript compared to CGI in C++ or PERL. There is no compilation required for VBScript.

# Using ActiveX and Include Files with Active Server

As you develop applications with VBScript for use on your Active Server Web site, you will find that there are functions that are common to many different applications and functions. There are two methods of responding to the need for standard components, using Include files and ActiveX objects.

## Using Server-Side Includes

If you have ever done development in C or C++, you can think of Server-Side Includes as being somewhat analogous to the #include directive. In the C language, the #include directive enables you to insert the contents of one file into another file at compile time. Development in C and C++ would be impossible if you could not #include files inline.

Server-Side Includes (SSI) perform a function similar to the #include directive. In its most basic form, SSI includes the contents of one file into an HTML stream before that file is sent to the client. The included file can be a text file, an .html file, an .asp file, a graphic file, or almost other file existing on the server.

**Imagine this scenario:** You have a Web site composed of hundreds of linked pages for your company. You want to provide a standard look and feel across all of your pages, so you can project a single image to any point on your site where a client may be browsing. On most Web pages there are standard headers and footers with links or graphics or some other unifying display that is consistent across the site. But, the information in these headers and footers changes throughout the month (or even day). If you had to go to each page and change the information within the .html or .asp file, you would need to hire a team of Internet savvy Kelly Temps just to keep you up-to-date. Or, you could use Server-Side Includes and only have to change one or two Include files. Any changes made to the included files would then ripple through your entire site the next time a page was requested.

**Scenario number two:** You have yet to reach this part of the chapter. You were so excited when you learned about procedures, you stopped at that point and spent the next week or so developing procedures. Now it is a week later and you have a number of generic, well-thought-out, tested procedures that you are going to use in your Web pages. A few years ago, before the wizards that we find in most development environments these days were even a thought, the best way to start a new program was to find an old one that did something similar and then use the highly efficient CPC system (copy, paste, code) to complete your task. Although Server-Side Includes are not analogous to code wizards, they will let you avoid the CPC syndrome when you want to include pre-existing procedures into your Active Server Pages applications.

Before we begin, you must be aware that we are going to be discussing two types of Server-Side Includes. The first is provided by Internet Information Server (IIS). The Includes that are provided by ASP when processing .asp files are currently limited to including external files. As you continue through this section, the IIS versus ASP nature of the discussion will be clearly marked.

A couple of steps are involved in using SSI to enhance the functionality of your Web applications. The first step is to decide what file(s) you want to include. The second step is to add the Server-Side Include statement into the target .stm or .asp file. An .stm file is the same as an .html file, but causes the file to be pre-processed by the SSINC.DLL (Server-Side Include dynamic link library) which actually handles the Include functions for those non .asp files.

Server-Side Includes are through the use of pre-processing directives. These directives have the following syntax:

```
<!-#<PREPROCESSING_DIRECTIVE>->
```

You will be examining a number of these directives, but first, you will move on to those that will be used most often in your development programming.

**N O T E**  The default extension for the files that will be processed for Server-Side Includes by IIS is .stm. To change the default extension, edit the registry entry for the Server-Side Includes extension. ■

**Including Files**  The following discussion on including files is applicable to both IIS and ASP. There are two ways that you can specify a Server-Side Include file to include within a target file. The only difference in the two methods is where the Server-Side Include file is in relation to the target file. The first is the virtual file include method:

```
<!-#INCLUDE VIRTUAL = "inclfile.txt"->
```

This will insert the file `inclfile.txt` into the HTML stream at the point that the Server-Side Include is found in the page. The file name is found in a directory, relative to the path for the base directory of the Internet Information Server (IIS). If you accepted the defaults when installing IIS, the base directory will be **\WINNT\SYSTEM32\INETSRV**, so the `inclfile.txt` will be located in that directory. You can also specify a path for a virtual include. The path will be in relation to the base directory of IIS as well. For example, to include the following file:

```
\WINNT\SYSTEM32\INETSRV\INCLUDES\HEADER.TXT
```

You would use the following include statement:

```
<!-#INCLUDE VIRTUAL="/INCLUDES/HEADER.TXT"->
```

Notice that the directory delimiters (slashes) are in the opposite direction to what most of you are familiar with (unless you have worked in the UNIX or AS400 environments lately). They are used in that fashion because the Server-Side Include specification was developed in the UNIX environment. Even though the standard uses the forward slash, the backward slash will work equally well for Server-Side Includes.

The second method to include a file is with the FILE include directive, which looks like this:

```
<!-#INCLUDE FILE = "inclfile.txt"->
```

Using the FILE include directive, the include file is located in relation to the location of the current target document. So, if you want to include a file in the same directory as the target file, leave off any directory path information. If you want to include a file that is under the target document—for example, a directory called scripts—then you would use the following statement:

```
<!-#INCLUDE FILE = "\scripts\inclfile.txt"->
```

You might be wondering why there are two methods of doing what appears to be the same thing. Well, the real reason that you are given these options is to increase the flexibility of your Web development. There are generally two classes of files that you want to include. The first class are application-specific files, like the custom header and footer that were mentioned previously under "Using Server-Side Includes." These might be in a sub-directory stored beneath the location of the corporate Web pages default directory. In the next case, you will want to include, in many applications, all of those functional and thoroughly tested procedures that you have already developed. The two file include methods give you the flexibility to easily process Server-Side Includes in both situations.

An included file can have another Include directive within it. This is useful when you want to include a number of common procedures found in multiple files. In the first Include file, you will include directives including the common procedures. Then, in the target file, you would only need to include the first file containing the other Include directives, instead of an Include reference for each and every common procedure file. Just be careful not to include a reference to a file within that file. This will create an endless include loop, NOT a good thing!

**File Information Includes**   In addition to including files into your document, you can also include a number of items (file size, last modification date) about a particular file into your HTML stream. The file information includes are not currently supported within the ASP environment. To include the size of a file, you would use the following directive:

```
<!-#FSIZE [VIRTUAL][FILE]="inclfile.txt"->
```

You can use either a virtual path or a relative path when using the FSIZE directive. The size of the file inclfile.txt, in kilobytes, will be included in the file. This is a particularly handy directive when specifying a file for download. You can include the filename and the file size, so your client will have an idea of how long a download might take. The number returned, using the FSIZE directive will be comma delimited in the thousands position. A 1 megabyte file will be returned as 1,024.

You can also obtain the date that a file was last modified to include in your HTML stream by using the FLASTMOD directive:

```
<!-#FLASTMOD [VIRTUAL][FILE]="inclfile.txt"->
```

This directive also can be used with files that are referenced using a virtual or a relative path. By default, the date that is returned by using the FLASTMOD directive is in the format Weekday MonthName DayNumber YearNumber. The format of this date, as well as the default size returned by FSIZE (kilobytes) can be changed by using the configuration directive option of SSI.

**Configuring Server-Side Includes**   There are a number of options that you can specify to override the default behavior of the data returned from an SSI call. The format used when setting a configuration option is:

```
<!-#CONFIG OPTION ="optionstring"->
```

The option string is relevant to the configuration option that you are setting. If you think about it, this is a powerful feature. You can change the format of the information returned from the include without having to provide any formatting for it in your scripts.

**Setting the Format of the FLASTMOD Directive**   As stated previously, by default, the FLASTMOD directive returns the last modified date of a file in the format Weekday MonthName DayNumber YearNumber (Tuesday, December 10, 1996). By using the CONFIG directive with the TIMEFMT option, you have the opportunity to specify the information returned by the FLASTMOD directive.

```
<!-#CONFIG TIMEFMT ="date/time format string"->
```

To specify a new date or time format, you create a format mask using the options specified in Table 13.1. The locale reference found in the table is referring to that on the server where the include is taking place.

**Table 13.1   Parameters for Specifying Date and Time Formats for the FLASTMOD Directive; Examples Based on a Date/Time of February 23, 1996 at 11:01:55 PM**

| Parameter | Description | Example |
| --- | --- | --- |
| %m | Month as a decimal number | 02 |
| %b | Abbreviated month name | Feb |
| %B | Full month name | February |
| %d | Day of the month | 23 |
| %j | Day of the year | 54 |
| %y | Year without century | 96 |
| %Y | Year with century | 1996 |

Part V Ch 13

*continues*

| **Table 13.1** | **Continued** | |
|---|---|---|
| **Parameter** | **Description** | **Example** |
| %w | Weekday as an integer | 5 (0 is Sunday) |
| %a | Abbreviated weekday name | Fri |
| %A | Weekday name | Friday |
| %U | Week of the year, Sunday first day | 8 |
| %W | Week of the year, Monday first day | 8 |
| %I | Hour in 12-hr format | 12 |
| %H | Hour in 24-hr format | 23 |
| %M | Minute as an integer | 01 |
| %S | Second as an integer | 55 |
| %P | AM/PM indicator for current locale | PM |
| %x | Date representation for current locale | 2/23/96 |
| %c | Date/time representation for current locale | 2/23/96 11:05:55pm |
| %X | Time representation for the current locale | 11:01:55PM |
| %z | Time zone abbreviation or blank | CST |
| %Z | Time zone, or blank if unknown | Central Standard Time |
| %% | Percent sign in mask | %M%%%S |

If you have ever used the Format function within Visual Basic or VBA, you will be very comfortable using the #Config formatting masks.

Here are a couple of examples of formatting a date and time, using different masks. For the purpose of these examples, assume that the last modified date/time on the file that you are going to use the #FLASTMOD directive on was February 6, 1991 at 11:05:09 PM.

```
<!-#CONFIG TIMEFMT ="%I:%M %P"->
```

formats the time as 11:05 PM. You can include seconds in the time as follows:

```
<!-#CONFIG TIMEFMT ="%I:%M:%S %P"->
```

To format the date as shown in the preceding paragraph, you would use the following date mask:

```
<!-#CONFIG TIMEFMT ="%B %dth, %Y"->
```

The configuration of the TIMEFMT remains in effect until the directive is called again within the page, or until a new page is loaded.

**Setting Default File Size Increments for the FSIZE Directive**  As mentioned in the section about the FSIZE directive, the default number returned is in kilobytes. If you want to specify the file size in bytes, generate the following directive:

```
<!-#CONFIG ABBREV ="bytes"->
```

This ensures that the file size returned to the HTML stream by the FSIZE directive will be in bytes, not in the default kilobytes. The number returned in bytes will be comma delimited in the thousands position as well.

**Setting SSI Error Messages**  When a Server-Side Include fails for any reason, by default, a detailed message is returned that contains information explaining why the include failed. In many cases, you do not want this information returned to the client. To prevent this from happening, set the ERRMSG configuration option.

```
<!-#CONFIG ERRMSG ="Server Encountered an SSI Error."->
```

Once this configuration option is set, the message set within the CONFIG directive will be the one returned to the client when an SSI error is encountered.

**The Echo Directive**  There are a number of "server" variables that are associated with any given request for the retrieval of a page. The Echo directive is not available in the ASP environment, but all of these server variables can be accessed within ASP by querying the Server object, discussed in Chapter 16, "Enhancing Interactivity with Cookies, Headers and the Server Object." Some of these variables are available to you for inclusion into the HTML stream that you return to your client, using SSI. The syntax of the Echo directive is:

```
<!-ECHO VAR ="VariableName"->
```

Depending on your requirements, you can use one or more or even all of the available variables. The most useful choices are shown in Table 13.2. For a complete list of all the variables available using the Echo directive, see your SSI documentation.

**Table 13.2** *ECHO* **Directive Server-Side Include Variables**

| Variable Name | Description |
|---|---|
| LAST_MODIFIED | The date the document was last modified |
| PATH_INFO | Additional information about the document path, returned with a virtual path name |
| PATH_TRANSLATED | PATH_INFO with the virtual path mapped to the directory path |
| QUERY_STRING | The information passed to the script following the ? in the URL |
| DATE_GMT | The current system date in Greenwich Mean Time |
| DATE_LOCAL | The current system date in the local time zone |

Part

V

Ch

13

*continues*

### Table 13.2  Continued

| Variable Name | Description |
| --- | --- |
| GATEWAY_INTERFACE | The current CGI revision level that is supported by the host server |
| HTTP_[header name] | All of the HTTP header information that will appear in a comma separated list |
| HTTP_ACCEPT | The MIME types that the browser can accept |
| HTTP_ACCEPT_LANGUAGE | The languages that the browser can accept |
| HTTP_USER_AGENT | The name of the browser software running on the client |
| HTTP_REFERER | The URL of the page that referred the client to the document on your site |
| HTTP_UA_PIXELS | The resolution of the client browser display |
| HTTP_UA_COLOR | The color palette of the browser display |
| HTTP_UA_OS | The operating system of the client browser |

An example of including some of the server-side variables follows:

```
<HTML><HEAD><TITLE>#ECHO VAR Samples </TITLE></HEAD><BODY>
<P>Here are some examples of using the echo function<BR></P>
The Local Date    :<!-#ECHO VAR="DATE_LOCAL"-><BR>
The Remote Host   : <!-#ECHO VAR="REMOTE_HOST"-><BR>
All HTTP Header Information: <!-#ECHO VAR="ALL_HTTP"->
</BODY></HTML>
```

The output from running this script will produce output like the following on the client:

```
Here are some examples of using the echo function
The Local Date  :Thursday December 26 1996
The Remote Host : 3.1.1.1
All HTTP Header Information: HTTP_ACCEPT:image/gif, image/x-xbitmap, image/jpeg,
image/pjpeg, */* HTTP_ACCEPT_LANGUAGE:en HTTP_CONNECTION:Keep-Alive
HTTP_HOST:selfanba HTTP_UA_PIXELS:1024x768 HTTP_UA_COLOR:color8
HTTP_UA_OS:Windows NT HTTP_UA_CPU:x86 HTTP_USER_AGENT:Mozilla/2.0 (compatible;
MSIE 3.01; Windows NT)
```

**Executing Commands Using Server-Side Includes**    The last directive that is currently supported only under IIS is the EXEC directive. Using this directive, you can execute a CGI script, a shell command, or an ISAPI application (all ISAPI apps are packaged as DLLs). After the command, app, and so forth has executed, the output is inserted into the HTML stream. If there is any HTTP header information in the returned data stream, only URL redirection information is recognized, and the message is replaced by the text This document has moved to 'new addr'.

The format of the EXEC directive follows the preprocessor directive format and looks like this:

```
<!-#EXEC [CGI][CMD][ISA] ="Command/App/Script/ToExecute"->
```

***The CGI Option***   Each of the options have slightly different meanings as they are implemented. The first, CGI, notifies the SSI processor that a CGI script (in its virtual path, if specified) is found in quotes after the equal sign. The CGI script can be formatted just as if you were calling it from your browser, with a ? and any parameters that need to be passed to the script delimited by +.

The capability to invoke CGI scripts inline, using SSI is a powerful tool. Remember when you read about the benefits of including files within your pages? These same benefits accrue to using CGI scripting inline. With a combination of these two methods, you can maximize code reuse while at the same time, minimize maintenance. A call to execute a CGI command in a cgi-bin subdirectory beneath the document directory looks like this:

```
<!-#EXEC CGI ="/cgibin/querytme.exe?1week+2days"->
```

This executes the `querytme.exe` CGI script, passing in `1week` and `2days` as parameters. The output of the script is inserted into the HTML stream immediately after the EXEC directive.

***A Commanding Option: CMD***   When the CMD option is specified on the directive line, the `CommandToExecute` is the shell program to run. You can specify command line parameters, using the CMD option as well. You can specify a full path for the command, or you can let the server walk the path (those directories included in the PATH environment variable) to find the file. If the file is not found, an error message is returned as the text of the call. In this example, we are going to call the command `cmdtest.exe` and pass it a few parameters:

```
<!-#EXEC CMD ="/utils/cmdtest.exe?10024"->
```

***Including an ISAPI Application***   When Microsoft released the ISAPI specification, it created an entirely new market for Internet development tools. With the ISAPI functions now residing within the Microsoft Foundation Classes, it is a quick and painless exercise to create Internet server applications using Visual C++ and IIS. This new API has also created another third-party boon for developers. What once would have been coded in CGI can now, in many cases, be purchased as an ISAPI application. These applications can be leveraged in the Active Server Pages environment as well. ISAPI applications are more efficient and perform better than CGI applications because they run in the same process space as IIS.

When you want to process an ISAPI application using SSI, you can also provide parameters, much like you did when using the CGI option. The syntax to call an ISAPI application named `isapitst.dll` with two parameters, an amount and a term, looks like this:

```
<!-#EXEC ISA ="/apps/isapitst?100.25+30">->
```

# Inserting ActiveX Controls

Standard functions can also be incorporated into ActiveX controls that are inserted into Active Server pages. One advantage is that the code is not as easily accessible for change. It is also possible to create more robust functions because error handling can be better addressed in ActiveX objects than in VBScript procedures.

In Chapter 3, "Building ActiveX Controls with VB," you examined, in depth, the requirements of creating an ActiveX Control. In this chapter, you will look at using an ActiveX Control in

Active Server scripting with VBScript. For the purposes of this illustration, the Browser Capabilities component that is provided and installed as part of Active Server will be used. This component uses the files Browscap.dll and Browscap.ini that are located in the Program Files\Websrv\System\Asp\Cmpnts\ directory, if you performed a standard install on Windows 95, or in the Winnt\System32\Inetsrv\Cmpnts\ directory, if you performed a standard install on Windows NT 4.0. It is registered with a ProgID of MSWC.BrowserType. The ProgID is used in Active Server to create the object in your VBScript.

```
<% Set MyBrowserCapObject = Server.CreateObject("MSWC.BrowserType") %>
```

This line of VBScript creates the object on the server. The full code listing is shown in Listing 13.8.

**Listing 13.8  VB5_Demo_ActiveX_Obj.ASP—This VBScript Active Server Uses an ActiveX Object to Collect the Information that Is Displayed on the Client Browser**

```
<%@ LANGUAGE="VBSCRIPT" %>

<HTML>
<HEAD>
<TITLE>VB5 Demonstration of ActiveX Object</TITLE>
</HEAD>
<BODY>
<H1>This is a Demonstration of an ActiveX Object:</H1>
<H2>This is a list of some of the characteristics of your Web browser.</H2>

<% Set MyBrowserCapObject = Server.CreateObject("MSWC.BrowserType") %>

<TABLE BORDER=1>
<TR><TD><B>Property</TD>     <TD><B>Value</TD>
<TR><TD>Browser Type</TD>     <TD><%= MyBrowserCapObject.browser %></TD>
<TR><TD>What Version</TD>     <TD><%= MyBrowserCapObject.Version %></TD>
<TR><TD>Major Version</TD>     <TD><%= MyBrowserCapObject.majorver %></TD>
<TR><TD>Minor Version</TD>     <TD><%= MyBrowserCapObject.minorver %></TD>
</TABLE>
</BODY>
</HTML>
```

The data that is displayed in the table is taken from property values of the ActiveX Object. Figure 13.8 shows the page displayed in the client browser.

When you choose View, Source in your browser, you see the HTML that was generated and sent to the client browser as shown in Figure 13.9.

**FIG. 13.8**
This page was created by using a combination of Active Server, ActiveX, and VBScript.

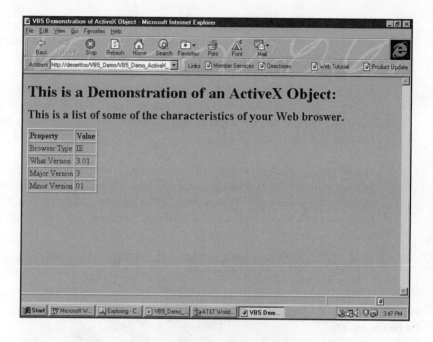

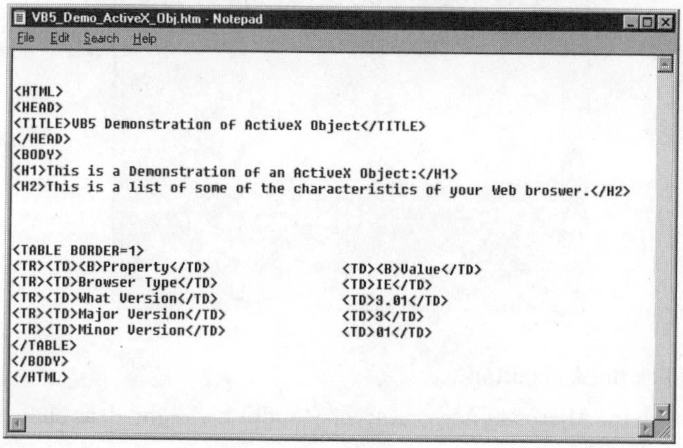

**FIG. 13.9**
The HTML generated is all standard HTML that is capable of being viewed by any Web browser.

Part
V
Ch
13

# Connecting to ODBC Databases

One of the most exciting features of Active Server is the database connectivity provided with the Active Data Object (ADO). It gives you the capability of connecting to any ODBC compliant database and creating fully capable database applications.

Open Database Connectivity (ODBC) is one of the tools provided by Microsoft that has opened database access dramatically. ODBC is a set of middleware that is positioned between the user interface software that displays data to a user and the database engine that stores the data.

When the user interface software wants data from the database, it sends a request in the form of a SQL (Structured Query Language) statement to ODBC, which then translates the SQL statement into the particular dialect of SQL used by the database engine.

**N O T E** If you are not familiar with SQL and ODBC, there are many excellent Que publications that will be of assistance. One of the advantages of ODBC is that it lessens the detailed knowledge required to work with a specific relational database management system. The key knowledge is of SQL. ■

The first step to working with ODBC is to create a DSN (Data Source Name). Before you do this, copy the sample database from the CD named VB5_DemoDB.MDB into the VB5_Demo directory that contains the Web pages that you have created in this chapter. This database happens to be a Microsoft Access 97 database. To create the ODBC DSN, follow the steps below:

- Choose Start, Settings, Control Panel and click the 32bit ODBC icon.
- Click the System DSN tab, as shown in Figure 13.10.

**FIG. 13.10**

The DSN for use with Active Server must be a System DSN.

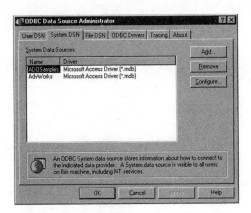

- Click the Add button.
- With the Microsoft Access Driver (*.mdb) highlighted, as shown in Figure 13.11, click the Finish button.
- Enter the Data Source Name VB5_Demo_DB in the appropriate text box and click the Select button, as shown in Figure 13.12.
- Locate the .mdb file and click OK. Then click OK as needed to close the ODBC Administrator and close the Control Panel.

You are now ready to create the Active Server page that will query the database and display the results. Create an HTML file named VB5_Demo_Select.ASP and save it in the VB5_Demo directory that was created earlier. The code that you need to enter into this file is shown in Listing 13.9.

**FIG. 13.11**

This shows the ODBC Version 3.0 Administrator.

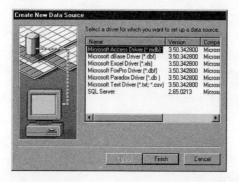

**FIG. 13.12**

The Select button opens a file dialog box that will let you locate the file VB5_DemoDB.mdb that you copied to your system.

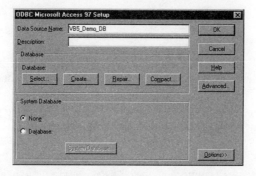

Part

V

Ch

13

---

**Listing 13.9    VB5_Demo_Select.ASP—This VBScript Active Server uses an Active Data Object to Access the Database**

```
<%@ LANGUAGE="VBSCRIPT" %>
<HTML>
<HEAD>
<TITLE>VB5 Demo Database Active Server Page</TITLE>
</HEAD>
<BODY>
<H1>Using an ActiveX Data Object (ADO)</H1>

<%
    Set MyConnection = Server.CreateObject("ADODB.Connection")
    MyConnection.Open "VB5_Demo_DB"
    Set MyRecordSet = MyConnection.Execute("SELECT * From NameList")
%>
<P>
<TABLE BORDER=1>
<TR>

<% For i = 0 to MyRecordSet.Fields.Count - 1 %>

<TD><B><%= MyRecordSet(i).Name %></B></TD>

<% Next %>
```

*continues*

**Listing 13.9   Continued**

```
</TR>
<% Do While Not MyRecordSet.EOF %>
  <TR>
  <% For i = 0 to MyRecordSet.Fields.Count - 1 %>
    <TD VALIGN=TOP><%= CStr(MyRecordSet(i)) %></TD>
  <% Next %>
  </TR>
<%
  MyRecordSet.MoveNext
  Loop
  MyRecordSet.Close
  MyConnection.Close
%>
</TABLE>
</BODY>
</HTML>
```

The first part of the listing to analyze is the creation of the database connection:

```
<%
    Set MyConnection = Server.CreateObject("ADODB.Connection")
    MyConnection.Open "VB5_Demo_DB"
    Set MyRecordSet = MyConnection.Execute("SELECT * From NameList")
%>
```

The first line of code creates a connection object "MyConnection" on the server. Next, the Open method of the connection is used to connect to the DSN "VB5_Demo_DB" that was created with the ODBC Administrator. Finally, the data from the database is retrieved in a record set named "MyRecordSet" using the Execute method on MyConnection with the SQL statement as the argument.

If you have ever worked with DBLib or the ODBC API, you will realize that a great amount has been accomplished in these three lines of code.

The next section of the code is concerned with cycling through the record set that was retrieved from the database and loading it into the table for transmission to the client browser for display. The results of the database access are seen in Figure 13.13.

**FIG. 13.13**

This database access was accomplished with only 34 lines of code.

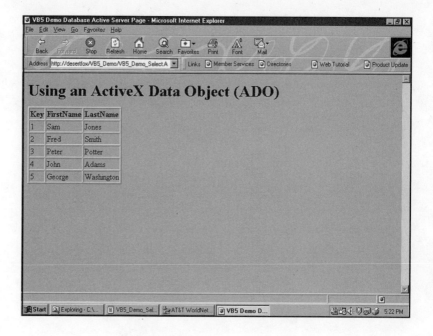

# From Here...

In this chapter, you have examined the concepts behind the programming options opened by the use of Microsoft Internet Information Server 3.0 Active Server. When all of the parts are combined, powerful, comprehensive applications can be created using Active Server, ActiveX and, VBScript. It is significant that this is all accomplished without reliance on capabilities in the client browser. Server-side programming is an excellent option when you are placing interactive content into Web pages, particularly when the Web browser is unknown. If your applications are developed on an intranet where the browsers are known, it may be appropriate to use client-side processing or a mixture of both. These decisions will be based on many factors. The following chapters may assist you in your choices.

- Chapter 3, "Building ActiveX Controls with VB," helps control construction.
- Chapter 7, "Using VBScript to Build HTML-Based VB Applications," provides an in-depth look at VBScript.

Part
**V**

Ch

# Managing States and Events with *Application* and *Session* Objects

**M**anaging users as they navigate through an application represents a common and easily handled challenge in the traditional client/server application development world. In the Web world, in contrast, Internet application developers find managing this challenge—in essence, maintaining a user's state—to be one of the greatest challenges to building a comprehensive Internet-based application. Because HTTP transactions between a browser and a Web server are independent, with no persistence or connection state being maintained, even tracking a user as she moves from one page request to another can be a difficult task.

To manage a user from her first page request, Active Server incorporated a model based on *Cookies* to generate a unique ID for users' browsers. On the first-page request, the session `OnStart` event fires. This event sets the scope of several properties for the life of this unique browser's session. At the same time, the event defines a `Timeout` property to manage the session length. The `Timeout` property measures inactivity from the Cookied browser. This chapter explores in detail the ability to track users, but goes way beyond that ability, in exploring the valuable set of functionality extended to programmers through the `Session` and `Application` Objects.

**The problem of tracking user sessions**

In most Web applications, tracking users and their activities from page to page requires a large portion of the overall programming effort.

**Setting up an application**

Active Server Pages uses directory structures and the global.asa file for managing applications.

**Understanding *Application* and *Session* Objects**

First, an overview of the `Application` and `Session` objects' scoping, events, and properties.

**Application Object, events and properties**

The Application Object provides a mechanism to track sessions and store variables and objects for application-wide use.

**Session Object, practical applications**

Use the `Session` Object to manage a user's flow from page to page, tracking user input, and caching information.

**N O T E**   *Cookies* are a feature of HTML 2.0 that enable an HTML author to write a variable or named piece of information to the client browser. If the browser supports HTML 2.0 or greater, this information is then saved as a file by the client browser program on the user's hard drive, and the browser automatically sends that information with any browser request to that domain. The Cookie has a duration property as well. For a detailed look at the implementation of Cookies on the Web, and how they work, see Chapter 20, "The OLEISAPI2 Interface and the Active Reference Object." To learn how to use Cookies in ASPs, read Chapter 16, "Enhancing Interactivity with *Cookies, Headers,* and the *Server* Object." ■

# Active Server Pages Solves the Problem of Managing User Sessions

In the typical Visual Basic client/server development environment, the Visual Basic program operates as the client, capturing any user input and responding to events such as a mouse movement. These user inputs, ranging from a mouse movement to the pressing of a keyboard button, leave the programmer with absolute control in managing the user's choices and experience. The Web world of development has some important distinctions that frame the entire development model.

Since Active Server Pages operates completely at the server, from VBScript execution to storing of variables, the normal Visual Basic model does not apply. The VBScript source code and the objects it invokes and references, come into play only when a user connects to the server by processing a form page or selecting an URL. In short, Active Server Pages is invoked only when a user moves from one page to another. At this point, when a browser requests a page, the HTTP request or transaction sends only the simple HTTP transaction, including the page requested along with form or URL fields and some general browser-related information such as Cookies.

**N O T E**   For a more detailed description, reference information on the HTTP transaction standard. ■

The simple HTTP record layout passed between the Web server and Web browser creates a challenge for managing an application;  one of the key challenges becomes tracking users as they move between pages. This includes maintaining, in an easily accessible way, some unique tracking ID, as well as any information that must be displayed or manipulated such as a shopping basket of selected products in an order processing system. Several standard workarounds have emerged for dealing with this challenge, and Active Server Pages builds on the best of these approaches.

## Tracking User Sessions: The Web Challenge

A key challenge of Web programming is tracking users from one page to the next and making information from their previous pages available on subsequent pages. This challenge can be met by using several basic approaches, but without Active Server Pages, the problem requires complex functions for generating unique IDs and difficult workarounds for keeping track of information, or, in other words, maintaining variables scoping during a user's working session.

The challenge of tracking a user's session requires generating a unique ID and then ensuring that on every subsequent page that ID and any added user information continues to be available. Two basic techniques available to Active Server Pages to accomplish this include the following:

- Using the Cookie feature of browsers
- Creating hidden fields/URL variables on a page

If you use the second technique, you must ensure that the hidden field or URL variable gets passed to all subsequent pages and is created as a new hidden field or URL variable on those pages. This is done to always keep the variable alive as a hidden form field or URL variable.

An enhanced approach to moving hidden fields around involves maintaining a variable's scope by using a database or text file on the server to store this information based on the unique ID. Constant retrieval every time a new page gets requested, and passing the unique ID from page to page as hidden fields and URL variables requires careful planning, because all possible page selections and flow must be carefully considered to ensure that unique IDs are not lost.

**Generating Unique IDs for Tracking Users**   The step of creating a unique ID and saving it as a variable requires more effort than you would expect at first glance. After generating and saving a unique ID, the ID must be carefully managed for it to be available to all subsequent pages during the user's session. Approaches to generating unique IDs generally result from some combination of date and time, user input, and IP addresses or, by using a database to generate a unique ID, such as a counter field in Microsoft Access. Unfortunately, all of these approaches require careful planning.

Take the approach of setting up a Microsoft Access table with a counter field and using the counter fields as the unique IDs for users entering the Web page. The first step becomes inserting a new record when the user first hits the page. However, since the insert of a new record will not return the counter field, a query must be done to retrieve that ID field. This is one example of the difficulties. You can't just request the last ordinal record because, of course, within a second or so of the insert command, a second user may have requested the same page and inserted a subsequent record. As a result, you must actually take some value such as date/time and insert that value as well so that you can retrieve the counter value. Even with this approach, you run the risk of having two transactions with the same date/time values, down to the second. To further complicate things, you must have the date/time field available as a form field in the HTML document to pass it as a parameter.

**Managing User IDs and Scoping with Cookie/Form/URL Variables**   Regardless of how you generate your unique ID, the immediate challenge that follows is keeping that ID alive or always in scope from one page to the next. Without the Active Server Pages Session Object, one approach involves ensuring that every HTML page passes the ID as either an URL variable or a Form field depending on whether the page request results from a hyperlink or Forms processing. This would take the form illustrated in Listing 14.1

Part

V

Ch

14

**N O T E** The empty string tests in Listing 14.1 determine if the variable exists because Active Server
script returns an empty string when you attempt to reference an HTML field that does not
exist. ■

**Listing 14.1   HIDDEN_VARIABLES.ASP—Scoping Hidden Variables from Page
to Page**

```
<%
'check if parameters are from a form or URL
'- - - - - - - - - - - - - - - - - - - - - - - - - - - - - - - - - - - - - - - -
IF NOT request.form("router") = "" then
    'Parameters are Form Based
    '- - - - - - - - - - - - - - - - - - - - - - - - -
    IF NOT request.form("userid") = "" then
        userid = request.form("userid")
    ELSE
        userid = 0 'New User
    END IF

    'Scope Router Variable for page processing
    '- - - - - - - - - - - - - - - - - - - - -
    router = request.form("router")


    '- - - - - - - - - - - - - - - - - - - - - - - - - - -
ELSEIF NOT Request.QueryString("router") = ""

    'Parameters are URL Based/Hyperlink
    '- - - - - - - - - - - - - - - - - - - - - - - - - -
    IF NOT request.QueryString("userid") = "" then
        userid = request.QueryString("userid")
    ELSE
        userid = 0 'New Users
    END IF

    'Scope Router Variable for page processing
    '- - - - - - - - - - - - - - - - - - - - - - - - - - -
    router = request.QueryString("router")


ELSE
        'Variables not correctly passed, an error has occurred
        'set error routing flag
        '- - - - - - - - - - - - - - - - - - - - - - - - - - - - - - - - - - -

        router = 0 'Error Routing for Lost Variables

'close IF, all variables set at this point
'- - - - - - - - - - - - - - - - - - - - -
END IF
%>
```

Cookies drives another approach to managing user IDs from page to page. In a Cookies-based model, no hidden information must be moved from page to page because the Cookie provides a variable that the server writes to the browser and the browser stores locally by domain name. As a result, whenever the browser requests a page from a site within the domain name, such as **http://www.melnick.com**, the browser will pass the Cookie variable along with the rest of the request to the Web server.

Listing 14.2 shows how a Cookie evaluation would simplify the process of scoping user IDs and routing variables as compared to managing the process from page to page. An issue here much more important than the complexity of the code comes from the problem that users may not necessarily move in a linear process through your Web pages. Users may bookmark and jump directly to a page or type an alternative URL directly into a browser, or click the Refresh button or the Back button. All of these maneuvers create uncertainty or more errors in the Listing 14.1 approach to managing users. Unlike the approach with hidden variables being kept alive, with Cookies, the variables are passed regardless of which page the user starts from. Your code loses its dependence on any order of page processing.

> **CAUTION**
>
> Cookies has received a lot of attention in recent months, and browsers, including Microsoft's IE 3.0, currently enable features to limit and potentially disable the use of Cookies.

> **CAUTION**
>
> In both Netscape 3.0 and IE 3.0, a flag can be set by the user that forces the browser to prompt the user every time a site attempts to write a Cookie. This prompt provides the user with the option of rejecting the Cookie. In addition, third-party programs are currently available to effectively disable Cookies as well. In practice, Cookies have become so prevalent that setting the prompt becomes quite annoying and as a result will probably not be actively used by any but the most vigilant and fearful users.

### Listing 14.2  COOKIES_VARIABLES.ASP—Cookies and User IDs

```
<%
'check if cookie variables are available
'------------------------------------------------
IF request.cookie("router") = "" then

    'Cookie Not Yet Set
    '----------------------------
    userid = 0 'New Account
    router = 0 'New Account
    '----------------------------
    'route to new account area and set cookie
    '----------------------------
ELSE
```

Part
**V**

Ch

**14**

*continues*

**Listing 14.2   Continued**

```
    userid = request.cookie("userid")
    router = request.cookie("router")

'close IF all variables set at this point
'-----------------------
END IF
%>
```

Without the use of Cookies, or when Cookie use only tracks the user ID and not other support-ing information, the process of passing the variables from page to page requires the use of both hidden fields and URL links that add variables into them. As shown in Listing 14.3, both Form and URL variables must be used, so the user can't move to another page without passing the variables you have assigned.

**Listing 14.3   FORMURL_FIELDS.ASP—Scoping Variables Through HTML**

```
<html><body>
<FORM ACTION="next.asp" METHOD="post">
<!----------------------------------------------->
<!--- hidden fields are added to URL link --->
<!--- so the link passes values          --->
<!----------------------------------------------->
<a href="profile_top.asp?userid=<%=userid%>&
➥router=<%=router%>">Next Page </a>
<a href="profile_display.asp?userid=<%=userid%>&
➥router=<%=router%>">Next Page </a>
<!----------------------------------------------->
<!--- hidden fields are stored for passing--->
<!--- in form submit action              --->
<!----------------------------------------------->
<INPUT NAME="router" VALUE="<%=router%>" TYPE=HIDDEN>
<INPUT NAME="userid" VALUE="<%=userid%>" TYPE=HIDDEN>
<CENTER>
<INPUT TYPE=SUBMIT VALUE="Continue" NAME="btn">
</CENTER>
</FORM>
</body></html>
```

The methods discussed previously provide a framework for how most of the CGI-based pro-grams currently operate with respect to variables, scoping, and user tracking. These tech-niques are based on a combination of HTML fields, Cookies, and unique ID generation. All these techniques become more stable and more insulated from the developer in the Active Server Pages Session and Application Objects.

# Active Server Pages to the Rescue

Active Server Pages provides an object model, which insulates the developer from all of the challenges relating to tracking users and generating unique IDs. The Session and

Application Objects not only provide support in generating unique IDs and maintaining the scope of variables, but also they implement the beginning of an event-driven model for developers. Active Server Pages defines an application as an execute permission-enabled directory served by an Internet Information Server (IIS). As a subset of the application, a session results when a browser requests a page from an application directory. The session involves one unique browser, so as other browsers request pages from the same application directory, they invoke additional sessions.

The first user to request a page from a directory that makes up an application invokes both an Application and a Session Object. As subsequent users request pages, they invoke additional Session Objects. The invoking of an Application Object kicks off the Application OnStart event, which executes scripts stored in the global.asa file. In addition, you can append variables and objects to the Application Object as new properties. When a developer's .ASP file adds a new Application property, the Web server memory space is used to store the variable for use by future .ASP files.

As a browser requests a page or file from the application directory, the Web server checks to see if that browser is involved in an active session. If it is not, the Web server returns the requested page to the browser and the Web server also writes a session ID value as a Cookie to the browser. By writing this Cookie, the Web server has provided a unique ID for tracking this user session or browser during the scope of the session. The Web server maintains this ID and also monitors the Timeout property set for this session. If the time-out expires, the Web server abandons all information associated with this session. In addition, at the same time that the Web server writes the Cookie, it processes the OnStart event, executing any scripts stored in the global.asa for the Session OnStart event. Similar to the Application Object, Session Objects can have additional properties appended, enabling the storing of variables and objects for use by .ASP files processed during that browser's session.

# Setting Up the Application

Developing an application primarily involves establishing a directory served by an Internet Information Server and has execute permissions. This directory location contains the source code for the application. The source code includes individual files that follow the naming convention name.asp. Web browsers will request these files similarly to the way files ending in .HTM or .HTML are requested. In addition to general ASP pages, each application can have a single file named global.asa, which stores scripts for the OnStart and OnEnd events for applications and sessions.

**CAUTION**

Though not explicitly restated here, to use Active Server Pages, the directory containing the described files must reside on a Windows NT Server with Internet Information Server (IIS) set up for your directory.

Part

V

Ch

# Internet Information Server (IIS) Directory Defines Application

Building an Active Server application requires a planned use of the hierarchical and logical directory trees created when configuring the Internet Information Server. In general, a single-served directory forms the application. All source files, including files ending in .ASA and .ASP will reside in a single-served directory. For more complex applications, a series of directories might be appropriate. In Table 14.1, the Root directory contains all pages associated with non-registered users. This area might use Session Objects to do extensive tracking on the pages visited to try to build profiles on nonregistered visitors. In the Root/Members directory, on the other hand, the purpose of the Session Object might be much more focused on the maintenance of logon status and member permissions. Finally, the Root/Secure/directory would maintain Session information on administrative privileges available and perhaps support the maintenance of a comprehensive audit trail.

**Table 14.1   Sample Directory Structure**

| Directory | Description |
|---|---|
| /Root/ | All visiting or nonlogged on users request pages |
| /Root/Members/ | Log-on page and all subsequent pages that require a logged-in user |
| /Root/Secure/ | Administrative area for site administrators to manage member accounts and system settings |

The key point to remember here is the scope of the Application and Session Objects. Within each of the different directories, the Application Objects and Session Objects are completely different, with different roles, different scopes, and no relationship between the objects in separate directories.

# Understanding the *global.asa* Role in an Application

The global.asa file provides the Application and Session Objects with the script, if any, to be invoked on the OnStart and OnEnd events for Application and Session Objects. Scripts for the OnStart and OnEnd events exist within the script tags with the RunAt property set to Server. These script tags can contain functions that can add properties to the Session and Application Objects for use by subsequent .ASP files within the scoped session or application.

The following provides a sample of how a global.asa file might be used. In the Application Object, the OnStart event adds properties to the Application Object to initialize a series of variables for maintaining information on how many members and visitors have come to the site since the application started. In contrast, the Session Object deals with a specific user starting a new session. The OnStart event for the Session Object increments application-wide information and initializes user-specific information. In addition, the Session Object OnStart event alters the default Timeout setting and sets the time-out to 30 minutes for this session, which means that after 30 minutes of no page requests the session will be abandoned. Finally, when the Timeout expires, and the Session Object OnEnd event is invoked, this event decrements application-wide tracking information.

**N O T E** The actual source code for the global.asa described can be found on the CD accompanying this book. ■

## Managing Source Code or .ASP and .ASA files

Source code must be contained in an .ASP or .ASA file. This requirement stems from the method the IIS uses to process Active Server Pages. When the Web server receives a request for a file, the IIS first checks the registered ISAPI filters. Active Server Pages rely on an ISAPI filter to catch .ASP files before returning anything to the Web browser. These files are then processed by the ISAPI filter, which strips out all <%%> tags, compiles VB Script, invokes any components called, while making Application and Session Objects available during the processing of all Active Server scripts. All of this occurs before the Web server returns the results to the Web browser.

**N O T E** ISAPI filters can be viewed by opening the Registry and looking under the IIS-related setting in the current control set. ■

 **TIP** .ASP and .ASA files are standard text files, which enables you to use any editor to manage your source code. Microsoft's Source Safe, originally designed for managing source code associated with C++ or VB project files, would be an effective tool for tracking version and checkout status on a multi-developer project, and Internet Studio could provide script development support as an .ASP file development tool.

Any type of file can exist in an Active Server Application directory including HTM/HTML, graphics images, video, sound, and .ASP/.ASA files. The important distinction here is that only .ASP/.ASA files invoke the filter that makes Session and Application Objects available during script processing.

The IIS also contains features such as Server-Side Include SSI, which you may use to further enhance your application management capabilities. This capability enables you to insert .ASP or other files into a requested .ASP file before the Web server invoking the ISAPI filter discussed earlier. These SSIs will be processed before script execution. The SSI features extend your ability to store files in different directories while still maintaining a single application directory for purposes of Application and Session Object scoping.

Part
V

Ch
14

> **CAUTION**
>
> Be careful using SSIs during development. The IIS keeps track of the last modification date/time of files, but the IIS caches frequently used files in memory. In other words, a direct page request causes the Web server to check if a cached file has been modified since its last execution. If it has been modified, the Web server recompiles the file. Unfortunately, Includes does not follow this checking process and as a result does not get recompiled. In these cases, the Web server must be restarted to flush cached .ASP files.

# Using *Application* and *Session* Objects

In leveraging `Application` and `Session` Objects for the development of your application, carefully consider what information and objects should be stored at the application and session level. A good example of the value of `Session` Objects is the storing of a user's logon status for security. However, with a misunderstanding of the `Session` Object's scoping, a major security hole could be created. The primary `Application` and `Session` Object methods, properties, and events include the following:

- `Abandon` Method      Session
- `Timeout` Property      Session
- `SessionID` Property      Session
- `OnStart` Event      Session/Application
- `OnEnd` Event      Session/Application

## Scope of *Application* and *Session* Objects

The most exciting features of the `Application` and `Session` Objects are their ability to scope the objects beyond a single page and scope the `Session` Object to a single user. Specifically, users invoke the `Application` Object when they request a page from an application directory for the first time since the Web server last started. This `Application` Object lives on from that moment until all sessions time-out or the Web server restarts. In contrast to invoking the `Application` Object, users invoke the `Session` Object when they request a page from a browser that is not currently involved in an active session. The `Session` Object, unlike the `Application` Object, will time-out based upon a 20-minute default, or a custom `Timeout` property, which you can set at runtime.

> **CAUTION**
>
> Avoid the temptation to store everything at the session level. Although at first the convenience of the `Session` Object can lead to caching everything about the user, remember that all this information must be maintained in the memory space of the IIS.

Once a user invokes a `Session` Object, all the `Session`'s properties and methods become available at runtime every time that same user requests an .ASP file. A user's session at the Web site now can be managed through the Session Object. As long as error trapping addresses the situation in which a user times-out, you now have complete control of a user's session and the ability to add properties to the Session Object. These properties can include anything from strings and status flags to database RecordSet Objects. The Session Object and its scope now create the first stable method for developers to manage a user's experience at a Web site, as a user moves from page to page or even from your site to another site and back to your site.

**N O T E** The Internet Information Server (IIS) manages the Session Object by writing a Cookie, or long integer, to the client browser. If IIS restarts, the Session abandons, or if the browser prevents Cookies, the Session Object will attempt to re-initialize on every page request. ■

The scope of the Session Object must be understood in the context of the Web. The IIS creates the Session Object by writing a long integer Cookie to the client browser and maintaining the long integer key and related properties such as the Timeout property and last hit date/time in the Web server's memory.

## The Beginning of an Event Model

The event model available in the Session and Application Objects represents a beginning to bringing event-driven programming to the Web, but stops short of providing what you may be hoping for. Because the Active Server Pages processes at the Web server and not the client, your source code cannot respond to the range of events that the client handles, such as mouse movements and keyboard presses. Instead, your code is invoked when the user processes a form or clicks a hyperlink. These events generate a request to the Web server, which invokes your source code.

The Application and Session Objects provide two events each —the OnStart event and the OnEnd event. The client invokes these events as follows:

- Application OnStart:   Invoked the first time users request an .ASP file from an application directory since the IIS last started or the application timed-out.
- Application OnEnd:   When all sessions time-out.
- Session OnStart:   Invoked by users when their browser requests an ASP page from the application directory either for the first time, or after a previous session with the client browser has been abandoned.
- Session OnEnd:   Invoked after a user's session time-out property value has exceeded the number of minutes allowed since the last page request, or the Abandon method has been invoked by your code.

When a user invokes an Application or Session event, you can execute functions on the Web server. All source code invoked by Session and Application events must be stored in the global.asa file within an application's directory. The format of this text file follows the model in Listing 14.4.

Part

**V**

Ch

**14**

**Listing 14.4    *GLOBAL.ASA*—Sample *Application/Session* Event Code**

```
<SCRIPT LANGUAGE=VBScript RUNAT=Server>
SUB Application_OnStart
END SUB
</SCRIPT>

<SCRIPT LANGUAGE=VBScript RUNAT=Server>
SUB Application_OnEnd
END SUB
</SCRIPT>

<SCRIPT LANGUAGE=VBScript RUNAT=Server>
SUB Session_OnStart
END SUB
</SCRIPT>

<SCRIPT LANGUAGE=VBScript RUNAT=Server>
SUB Session_OnEnd
END SUB
</SCRIPT>
```

The scope of variables used in the global.asa scripts does not extend to the page actually requested before the event. This means that to store a variable for use in the current requested page or subsequent pages, you must save the information to an Application or Session Object property. The properties of these objects provide the only means for allowing scripts in the .ASP file to use the information available in the scripts run during these events. As a result, these scripts become useful primarily for saving information directly to a database or file, or saving information to Application or Session Object properties for use during the scope of the application or session.

Taking some time to understand how to leverage these events provides big benefits in helping your program manage a range of issues from enhancing the user's Web experience to tracking site statistics. Don't make the mistake of overlooking the value of these events.

 **TIP** Session and Application events provide a key capability to manage user status control mechanisms such as logon security.

# Methods: Locking, Stopping, and Abandoning

Like events, the methods currently available seem quite limited compared to the event-driven development environments you may currently use in non-Web based programs. However, this represents a powerful beginning for the Web programmer. The only methods currently available to Session and Application Objects include Application Lock and Unlock methods and the Session Abandon method.

The Application Lock and Unlock methods allow you to change values to the properties shared across the application without fear of creating conflict with multiple users potentially changing the same property values concurrently. This Locking control will seem intuitive to database developers working in multi-user environments that share this same risk.

The Abandon method plays a valuable role for managing a session. Although during development and testing it can be useful for flushing a working session to begin again, it also has a role in the final application. For example, if a user requires the ability to log on and then perhaps log on again as a different user, the Abandon method could be used to allow the previously stored logon information to be cleanly dumped for a new logon.

These methods provide important functionality in using the Application and Session Objects, but for real functionality you must look to the properties provided and use the capability to add properties to the Application and Session Objects.

## Using Built-in Properties or Building Your Own

At first glance, the list of properties currently available appears quite unimpressive. But the real secret lies behind the built-in properties and the ability to add properties dynamically. Still the two built-in Session properties play an important role in all application development and should not be overlooked. The available properties include Session SessionID property and Session Timeout property.

The capability to add properties on-the-fly, provides the developer with an approach to maintaining persistence or state. By having a server-based Session Object to manage variables, a user's activities and input can be used during the entire session or visit to your Web application. The capability to build your own variables will be demonstrated later in this chapter and extensively in the case study provided in the appendixes of the book.

# The *Application* Object: How Much Can It Do?

The Application events and methods provide the infrastructure necessary to maintain application-wide information that can be leveraged for managing all users within an application. Uses range from tracking the number of users currently active to dynamically altering content provided to a particular user, based on the activity of other users at large. These features lay the foundation for building interactive communities and more. To understand the use of these events and methods, the following overviews the specific capabilities provided.

## Using the *Application OnStart* Event

The Application OnStart event can be likened to the initial load event of an application. This is not the loading of a single client, but rather the load event of the multi-user Web-based application. As a result, one use would be to initialize a series of variables that you need to frequently access in your application. The following example in Listing 14.5 opens a database and assigns a recordset of system error messages to the Application Object. As a result of loading this object, now *any page* processed can reference the recordset during execution and can utilize the recordset to loop through and display a particular error, based on a given situation.

Part
**V**

Ch
**14**

**Listing 14.5 SAMP_EVENTS.ASP—Sample *Application OnStart* Event**

```
<SCRIPT LANGUAGE=VBScript RUNAT=Server>
SUB Application_OnStart
REM Open ADO Connection to Database
  Set Conn = Server.CreateObject("ADODB.Connection")
  Conn.Open("DSNName")
  RS = Conn.Execute("SELECT * FROM TblSysMessages;")

REM Set Recordset to Application Object and Close ADO
  If rs.recordcount <> 0 then
    application.lock
    Set application.ObjErrMsg = RS
    application.unlock
  Else
    Rem Error Condition
  End If
  rs.close
  conn.close

END SUB
</SCRIPT>
```

**N O T E**   The loading of the database recordset involved the Server Object and the ADO database
Connection Object, which is discussed in more detail later in Part VII of this book. ■

# Using the *Application OnEnd* Event

The Application OnEnd event can be likened to the close of active forms or an application;
however, it provides more than that because it manages the environment for not just a single-
user system, but also for the multi-user Web-based environment. As a result, one use would be
to flush all temporary user accounts that may have been created during the course of the day.
This type of activity was previously available only by using time stamps and scheduled batch
programs, running as services in the background. Now, when all users time-out, a database
cleanup (or any other type of cleanup) can take place. The following example runs a SQL statement to purge all partially completed orders taken by a Web-based order processing system:

```
<SCRIPT LANGUAGE=VBScript RUNAT=Server>
SUB Application_OnEnd
REM Open ADO Connection to Database
  Set Conn = Server.CreateObject("ADODB.Connection")
  Conn.Open("DSNName")
  RS = Conn.Execute("Delete * FROM Orders where complete_status=0;")
  conn.close

END SUB
</SCRIPT>
```

## *Application* Locking Methods

Similar to database record and page locking, `Application` locking simply ensures that no other user has simultaneously attempted to update the `Application` Objects property. This locking feature applies only to the application, and not the `Session` Object, and should be used to avoid creating any conflict or lost data. The following section of code shows you a specific use of the `Session OnStart` event:

```
<SCRIPT LANGUAGE=VBScript RUNAT=Server>
SUB Session_OnStart
  application.lock
    application("counter") = application("counter") + 1
  application.unlock
END SUB
</SCRIPT>
```

## Scoping Application-Wide Variables

Adding properties to the `Application` Object provides one of the key values of the `Application` Object model. `Application` properties added this way are similar to global constants and variables in Visual Basic.

Practical uses of the `Application` properties include the ability to cache information frequently used to conserve resources. Current Web development environments require either database/file lookups or the passing of information from one page to the next in hidden fields. The first approach requires extensive resources as an application's load grows, and the latter approach becomes difficult as users hit the refresh and back buttons or bounce from page to page through direct typing of URLs.

With the `Application` Object, information can be saved to an `Application` Object property as the result of a single lookup. From then, any user can access that information. For example as a Web-based store opens its doors as a result of the first user request (`Application OnStart` Event), a store's opening greeting (including number of visitors, date/time, or current sale items) can be saved to an `Application` property as illustrated in the following code sample:

```
Application.lock
Application("dateinfo") = date
Application("timeinfo") = time
Application("visitors") = Application("visitors") + 1
Application.Unlock
```

As a result, all subsequent pages can display that information as part of a standard greeting as shown in the following code.

```
<HTML>
<BODY>
Welcome to our store, open for business since <%=Application("timeinfo")%> on
<%=Application("dateinfo")%> with <%Application("visitors")%> so far.
</BODY>
</HTML>
```

Part

**V**

Ch

**14**

More important than cached activity information, resources can be conserved by limiting the number of times components must be brought in and out of memory on the server. If you run a database-intensive site, as many users do, you may start your application by placing statements in every page to load DLLs into memory.

```
Set Conn = Server.CreateObject("ADODB.Connection")
Conn.Open("DSNName")
RS = Conn.Execute(SQL)
conn.close
```

This process not only loads the Connection Component DLL if it is not currently loaded, but also closes the object, allowing it be taken out of memory. For a frequently accessed site, it may make more sense to load the DLL when the application loads and leave it in memory for frequent use.

```
Set Conn = Server.CreateObject("ADODB.Connection")
Conn.Open("DSNName")
Application("conn") = Conn
```

By loading the Conn Object into the Application Conn property, it can now be referenced by all pages for use.

```
set db = Application("Conn")
  set rs = db.execute(sql)
```

**N O T E**   The preceding examples provide only a starting point for the range of uses the Application Object can play in the ASP application model you develop. Take the time to think through the activity and caching issues that relate to your application before implementing a model for your use of the Application Object. ▄

# The *Session* Object: Your Key to User Management

The Session Object, more than the Application Object, drives your Web-based environment. Look closely at how the deceptively small number of methods and events can completely streamline your method for managing a user's experience, as well as your system level tracking and control of that user. The Session Object, like the Application Object, enables new properties to be defined on-the-fly. And more importantly, the Session Object properties, like those of the Application Object, can be referenced on any page, anywhere, and any time during that active session.

## Understanding *Session* Events, Properties, and Methods

The SessionID provides, without a doubt, the prebuilt property to watch. This property provides the persistence in a user session you should be looking for, but the OnStart event, OnEnd event, and the Abandon method also play a valuable role in managing your application. The following sections document basic application of the prebuilt events and methods before a more practical discussion of how to put these to work.

***Session OnStart* Event**   The Session OnStart event can be likened to the initial load event of a form or application. It provides a mechanism to identify the first activity of new users and allows the initialization of whatever user information your application requires for managing the user session. At the OnStart event you may reference Application Object properties to track the new user in the context of your multi-user environment, but you will also want to bring into existence any user-specific information you need for managing that user's session. The event kicks off the script setup in the global.asa for the Session OnStart event in the following form.

```
<SCRIPT LANGUAGE=VBScript RUNAT=Server>
SUB Session_OnStart
  Rem Load User Specific Information
  Session("NewUserStatus") = 0

  Rem Load Application level info
  Application.lock
    Application("usercount") = Application("usercount") + 1
  Application.unlock
END SUB
</SCRIPT>
```

**N O T E**   Though you are learning about the use of the global.asa in detail, don't lose site of the fact that you don't need to create any event functions in the global.asa or even a global.asa file at all. ■

***Session OnEnd* Event**   The Session OnEnd event can be likened to the close of active forms or an application. However, this event does not require user action. In fact, most often the OnEnd event will be triggered by user inaction or time-outs. This event most often provides a mechanism for cleanup or closing of open resources. The system will lose all session information after this event, so any session information that you want to save must be saved during this event.

This event can be invoked by the user if he hits a page that executes the Abandon method. The Abandon method and the Timeout property provide the two mechanisms for terminating a session. An example of clean up that can be done at the end or termination of a session has been illustrated in the following sample of code.

> **CAUTION**
>
> A crash or stopping of the Web server also terminates events, because the Web server memory space is where all session and application information resides.

Part
**V**

Ch
**14**

```
<SCRIPT LANGUAGE=VBScript RUNAT=Server>
SUB Application_OnEnd
REM Clean up user activity information
  Set Conn = Server.CreateObject("ADODB.Connection")
  Conn.Open("DSNName")
  SQL = "Delete * FROM UserActivity where
➥sessionID = " & session.sessionid & ";"
  RS = Conn.Execute(SQL)
  conn.close
```

```
END SUB
</SCRIPT>
```

**Using the *SessionID* Property**    The Active Server creates the `SessionID` when a user first requests a page from an Active Server application. The `SessionID` gets written as a Cookie with a long integer value to the browser and provides the core mechanism the server uses to track session information stored in memory. You should not use the `SessionID` as a unique ID to track users across multiple sessions because the value's uniqueness is only guaranteed for the current application. This value gives your application the time it needs to generate an ID that can be used across multiple sessions and provides a unique ID for all sessions currently running. You can reference the `SessionID` on any page in the form

```
session.sessionID
```

This value provides a key mechanism for managing users as they move from page to page, and it relieves you from the responsibility of trying to track individual users during a multiple-page request session.

***Session Timeout* Property**    The server stores the `Session Timeout` property as a long integer that represents minutes and defaults to 20. The server takes full responsibility for tracking this 20-minute period. `Timeout` is tracked from the last date/time a page request is received by the browser. The `Timeout` property can be altered at runtime when you may set it in the `Session` `OnStart` event or any subsequent page. In determining how you will manage this property, you should consider the rate of hits by a single user during a session. For sites with long intervals between page requests, such as pages that require research, long review, or large amounts of input, you may want to increase the `Timeout` where more rapid sessions may require a shorter `Timeout`. Changing this property takes the form:

```
session.timeout = 30
```

> **CAUTION**
> Once the `Timeout` occurs, all session information is lost and the next page request will be treated as a new session.

***Session Abandon* Method**    The `Session Abandon` method provides a vehicle for you to force a session to terminate. Uses include the situation in which your user community takes the time to log off or in which you implement a discrete site exit page that invokes the `Abandon` method. This method takes the form:

```
Session.abandon
```

**TIP** During development, a page with the `Abandon` method provides a useful mechanism for restarting sessions. Often in development a lingering session can make testing difficult.

# Managing a User Session

The Session Object provides a rich environment for managing user sessions. The following sections show you a few examples of how you can put this object to work developing efficient applications. As described in the first part of this chapter, the challenge of managing a user session has historically required difficult, code-consuming techniques for generating unique IDs and then for keeping session-related information alive from page to page.

**Generating a Unique ID to Manage Users**   As illustrated in Listing 14.6, the SessionID property takes care of most of the first problem by generating a session ID to keep track of a user's session. However, during this process if you need to track users over a longer life than just one session, you still need to create an ID that guarantees uniqueness for your application. This process generally involves a database for storing this user and his related information. Once you design a database to store user information, you can rely on the wealth of features in databases to generate a guaranteed unique ID. A simple example of generating a unique user ID involves leveraging the counter field of a Microsoft Access database. The following code example in Listing 14.6 uses the current date and the SessionID to insert a record and then queries the table to retrieve the counter value once the record has been created. As a final step, the example sets the new counter value to a new session property for reference on subsequent pages.

> **N O T E**   Certain variable status designations such as the logonstatus variable have been subjectively assigned values for tracking that in no way reflect any preset or required approach to the tracking process. ■

**Listing 14.6   SESSIONTRACKING.TXT—Managing the Tracking of Users with *Session* Variables**

```
<%
  Set Conn = Session("conn")
Select Case session("logonstatus")

Case 1 ' Already Past finished this insert step
    msg = "<Center><h2><blink>Please Record your new Member ID:
➥" & session("memberid") & " </blink></h2></center>
➥<h3>Your Ideal Mate Profile has already been saved,
➥please complete the process and
➥relogon in edit mode to alter you profile </h3>"

Case 2 ' Proper Status for Insert of new account

    set rsInsert = Server.CreateObject("ADODB.Recordset")
    Conn.BeginTrans
    rsInsert.Open "Members", Conn, 3, 3

    ' --------------------------------------------
    'Insert Record Using AddNew Method of ADO
    ' --------------------------------------------
```

*continues*

**Listing 14.6   Continued**

```
rsInsert.AddNew
rsInsert("SignOnID")        = session.sessionid
rsInsert("AdmCreateDate")   = Date()
rsInsert.Update
Conn.CommitTrans
rsInsert.Close

' -----------------------------------------
'Look up generated record by referencing SessionID/Current Date
' -----------------------------------------
sql = "SELECT Members.SignOnID, Members.memberid, Members.AdmCreateDate FROM
➥Members WHERE (((Members.SignOnID)=" & session.sessionid & ") AND
➥((Members.AdmCreateDate)=Date())));"
Set RS = Conn.Execute(sql)
msg = "<h2><Center> Please Record your new Member ID:
➥" & rs("memberid") & " </center></h2>"

' -----------------------------------------
' Set Session Object with memberid value
' -----------------------------------------
memval = rs("memberid")
session("memberid") = memval
session("logonstatus") = 3
rs.close
End Select
%>
```

**N O T E**   Time and User IP address can be added to the record inserted into the database for
greater certainty of uniqueness.   ▨

**Using the *Session* Object for Caching User Information**   Once the user has a unique ID, the
next use of the *Session* Object focuses on the ability to cache user information you would have
previously stored in a database or text file for constant lookup and editing. The process of
querying a file or database every time users hit a page just to make basic information about
their sessions or accounts available reflects the status quo for current Internet applications.
This includes the lookup of a shopping basket for a user shopping in a web-based store or the
lookup of account information for personalizing a user page. While some developers attempt to
move that information from one form page processed to the next, this problem creates serious
challenges for application design.

A good example of a *Session* Object property would be storing a system message for display
on subsequent pages, as well as trapping basic name and last time online-type information. Like
the *Application* Object, properties can range in complexity from integers and string values, to
*RecordSet* Objects. The following example provides for storing personal information and redirection following a successful log on.

```
<%
' ------------------------------------------------------------
```

```
' Lookup User Info
'-------------------------------------------------
  sql = "SELECT members.admonlinedate, Members.MemberID, members.pass,
Members.FName,
➥Members.LName, Members.AdmExpDate, Members.AdmStatus FROM Members "
➥sql = sql & "WHERE (((Members.MemberID)=" & request.form("memberid") & "));"
  set db = session("conn")
  set rs = db.execute(sql)



'-----------------------------------------------------------
' Logon Fail
'-------------------------------------------------
If rs.eof Then 'No Record Found Bad ID
  rs.close
  session("msg") = "<h3><center>No Member ID equaling <em>" &
request.form("memberid") & "</em> exists</center></h3>"
response.redirect "fail.asp"

Else
'-----------------------------------------------------
' Success Logon Approved, Load Session and Status
'-----------------------------------------------
session("logonstatus") = 1
session("memberid") = rs("memberid")
session("AdmOnlineDate") = rs("AdmOnlineDate")
session("fname") = rs("fname") 'First Name

' Update User Database Record with Last Logon Date
sql = "UPDATE Members SET"
    sql = sql & " Members.AdmOnlineDate = #" & Date() & "#"
    sql = sql & " WHERE Members.MemberID=" & request.form("memberid") & ";"
    set rs2 = db.execute(sql)

rs.close
response.redirect "start.asp"

end if
%>
```

As shown in the previous code sample, the statement setting the logonstatus property equal
to a value creates the logonstatus property as a new Session property. No special statements
to dimension the property are required, and once this information gets loaded into the Session
Object, it can be referenced on any page requested by the browser that is sending the matching SessionID. The process for referencing the properties only requires a single statement of the
form:

```
session("propertyname")
```

# *Session* Objects for Security, Status, and Caching

For managing an application, the Session properties can play the role of tracking the user
status and security information. Because Session properties exist at the server without any
information passed to the browser except for the SessionID, session properties provide an

Part

V

Ch

14

effective method for managing logon and other statuses. An .ASP file with no purpose other
than the validation of a user's `logonstatus`, can be included by using the SSI feature of IIS.
This approach to user authentication provides an effective method for trapping users attempting to request a page they don't have authority to view. This method relies on the `Session`
properties alone and not on any Windows NT- based security controls as illustrated in the
following excerpt of code.

```
<%
Select Case session("logonstatus")

Case 0 'New Session No Status
      session("msg") = "<h3><center> You are currently not logged in or
➥your logon has timed out </center></h3> Please logon to continue your session,
➥sorry for any inconvenience</h4>"
      Response.Redirect "logon.asp"

Case 1 'Authenticated User Properly Logged On

Case 2 'New Member in Sign Up Process first page

Case 3 'New Member in Sign Up Process Record Created

End Select
%>
```

The process of actually validating a user after he or she enters a user account and password
further illustrates how to manage a site's security and user's status through the `Session`
Object. The following example in Listing 14.7 builds on the previous code, which simply adds
`Session` properties after a successful logon, and in this case evaluates all possible results of a
user's attempt to log on. The following example relies heavily on the `Response` Object's redirect
feature to route the user, based on the results of the logon validation.

### Listing 14.7   LOGONVALIDATE.TXT—Validating and Redirecting Users Requesting .asp Files

```
<Script Language=VBScript runat=server>
Function redirect()
   Session("msg") = session("msg") & " Please enter a valid Member ID
➥and Password, if you have forgotten your ID try our Search based on
➥First Name, Last Name and your password"
   Response.Redirect "logon.asp"
end function
</script>

<%
'---------------------------------
'_ -------------------------------
'Level 1 Basic Validation Testing
'-_ ------------------------------
'--------------------------------

'Test for Already Logged In
```

```
'------------------------------------
if session("logonstatus") = 1 then 'Already Validated
  session("msg") = "<h3><center>You are already logged in</center></h3>"
  Response.Redirect "start.asp"


'Test for Entry of Member ID before Running Search
'------------------------------------
elseif request.form("memberid")="" then ' NO Member ID Entered
  session("msg") = "<h3><center>No Proper Member ID Entered</center></h3>"
  Redirect 'Call Function to Exit Back to Logon Screen

'Run Search
'------------------------------
else 'Run Database Lookup
  sql = "SELECT members.admonlinedate, Members.MemberID, members.pass,
➥Members.FName, Members.LName, Members.AdmExpDate, Members.AdmStatus FROM
Members "
  sql = sql & "WHERE (((Members.MemberID)=" & request.form("memberid") & "));"
  set db = session("conn")
  set rs = db.execute(sql)
end if


'------------------------------
'------------------------------
'Level 2 Validation Testing
'------------------------------
'------------------------------
'Member ID Entered Now Run Search for Record
'------------------------------------------------
If rs.eof Then 'No Record Found Bad ID
  rs.close
  session("msg") = "<h3><center>No Member ID equaling <em>" &
➥request.form("memberid") & "</em> exists</center></h3>"
  Redirect 'Call Function to Exit Back to Logon Screen


'Customer Record Found Now Check Password
'------------------------------------------------
elseif not request.form("password") = rs("pass") then
  rs.close
  session("msg") = "<h3><center>Member ID OK
➥but Bad Password Entered</center></h3>"
  Redirect 'Call Function to Exit Back to Logon Screen

'Password OK now Check Expiration and Status
'------------------------------------------------
elseif not rs("admstatus") = 1 and rs("admexpdate") > date then
  rs.close
  session("msg") = "<h3><center>Not Active or Expired Account</center></h3>"
  Redirect 'Call Function to Exit Back to Logon Screen
```

Part

**V**

Ch

**14**

*continues*

**Listing 14.7 Continued**

```
'.....................................
'.....................................
' Level 3. Success Logon Approved, Load Session and Status
'.....................................
'.....................................
Else

   session("logonstatus") = 1
   session("memberid") = rs("memberid")
   session("AdmOnlineDate") = rs("AdmOnlineDate")
   session("fname") = rs("fname")


   ' Update users last online date
   sql = "UPDATE Members SET"
       sql = sql & " Members.AdmOnlineDate = #" & Date() & "#"
       sql = sql & " WHERE Members.MemberID=" & request.form("memberid") & ";"
       set rs2 = db.execute(sql)

   end if
   rs.close
   response.redirect "start.asp"
%>
```

▶ **See** "The Rest of the *Response* Object" for more information about the redirect feature, **p. 335**

The example in Listing 14.7 uses a script tag to create a callable function for redirecting the user in the event that they fail the logon process at any step. The user is forwarded to the start page with a logged-on status only in the event that she passes all checks including password, account number, currently active status, and valid expiration date.

# From Here...

The `Session` and `Application` Objects form the building blocks for good application design. By understanding the features that enable user and application management, you now move toward enabling the specific features of the Web-based application you intend to build. Based on an understanding of the VBScript syntax from earlier chapters, you now build upon the remaining Active Server objects including `Server`, `Request`, and `Response`, as well as exploring the specifics of components. These objects provide a complete understanding of the Active Server application development infrastructure, which is at your disposal.

From here, you will progress through the following chapters on the road to mastering the Active Server Page:

- Chapter 15, "Building a Foundation of Interactivity with *Request* and *Response* Objects," shows how you can use these objects to build interactive Web sites with a minimal amount of code.

- Chapter 16, "Enhancing Interactivity with *Cookies, Headers,* and the *Server Object,*" teaches you how you can use Cookies to track a specific user through your Web site by using the built-in Cookies functionality of ASPs.
- Chapter 17, "Constructing Your Own Server Components," helps you pull together all you've learned. With this knowledge you will be able to join the front lines of the revolution in n-tier client/server programming that is about to sweep through the computer world.

# CHAPTER 15

# Building a Foundation of Interactivity With *Request* and *Response* Objects

**Take a look at the old-fashioned way of adding interactivity to Web sites**

Before Active Server Pages, what did it take to deliver interactivity on the Web? Examine the classic case: the ubiquitous Guestbook implemented using the Common Gateway Interface and the Perl scripting language.

**Get a glimpse of the way it will be**

Examine the two Active Server objects designed to liberate Web developers from the timeconsuming and demanding requirements of CGI scripting.

**Create an ASP version of the Guestbook**

Use the Response and Request Objects to create a Guestbook in 33 lines of code (including comments).

The first new business asset the World Wide Web gave us, and the single most important thing about the Web that changes traditional business models, is interactivity.

There are many ways to make a Web site interactive. Forms are the most basic because they use static pages in an interactive, goal-directed manner. In other parts of this book, you learn about the other kinds of dynamic content that are not only possible now, but are actually easy to implement.

You will see that this capability can be tapped at two levels: First, *ActiveX controls* provide dynamic content on static pages; second, *Active Server Programs* provide dynamic content with dynamic pages. In other words, ActiveX controls provide objects to insert on a page, whereas Active Server Pages (ASP) provide objects to create pages on-the-fly. With all this power, the ASP developer can now reach the ultimate in interactivity: commercial transactions.

In this chapter you lay a foundation for the next generation of basic interactivity. Even at this fundamental level, we feel strongly that with such a quantum leap in productivity and ease of use, ASP development will spawn an equally abrupt leap in the amount of "interactive variety" on the Web. ■

# In the Beginning...

The beginning of interactivity on the Web is the Common Gateway Interface (CGI). In the UNIX world, CGI remains the predominant technology of interactivity. CGI is an open architecture; it can be implemented in almost innumerable ways. This open-mindedness comes with a price, however. CGI is difficult to write and maintain, especially for those unfamiliar with UNIX computing. It is processor-intensive: Each CGI call spawns another process for the server, increasing demands on processing resources. Database connectivity remains the most difficult and expensive aspect of CGI interactivity. All of these weaknesses are reasons that CGI has limited appeal to online business models.

Arguably the most popular means of implementing CGI is the Practical Extraction and Reporting Language (Perl). For all their shortcomings, these two technologies, CGI and Perl, are modern miracles. CGI worked with stateless servers, and Perl was a powerful language designed to work with text files. They were mutually reinforcing.

There was only one problem: Most Webmasters had little hope of exploiting this synergy, unless they hired a Perl programmer. We used to define a serious Webmaster as one who wasn't intimidated by the CGI/Perl alliance. To a serious Webmaster, interactivity was worth whatever cost it exacted, whether in cash to buy the Perl programs called scripts, or in the exertion necessary to learn a new programming language. This make or buy decision is really tough for most people who face the dilemma. The Web is a technology for all of us, not just the big corporations and the well-trained Information Technology staffs. How maddening it is to be within reach of the prize and yet frustrated by ignorance.

Imagine, for a moment, the number of people who have had a great Web idea but who couldn't implement it. There are at least a dozen things over the last year we would like to have hosted on our Web sites. Multiply this by millions. There is a pent-up supply of creativity behind this block to dynamic interactivity. Active Server Programs will set loose this creativity. Its "scripting for the rest of us," for all of us who have never learned the ins and outs of Perl programming. Just imagine what the Web is going to look like when all of those ideas are implemented. It's going to be marvelous.

---

### A Little Story

When one of the authors brought his first commercial Web site, **investing.com**, online in June of 1995, there was one *de rigueur* interactive feature he had to include—the Guestbook. The author's boss said, "I just want a form that has three lines and a button. How tough can *that* be?" Three days later after scouring the Internet, changing the source code to work on our site, uploading it to the UNIX server, changing the file permissions, testing, debugging, and testing again, he finally had a working Guestbook. Three days. That's one day for each line on the form. The button's a bonus.

Perhaps the single most frustrating thing about working with the Internet is having to be almost equal parts programmer and businessman. Most people don't have time to make them equal parts. The only option is to write as little code as possible and to suffer the consequences.

This quandary leads to one other important point about this section. In the past, one could not take interactivity for granted. At the processor level, for example, interactivity is a subtle and sophisticated series of events. Looking at the technical details that follow will help you understand what is happening, and it should help you appreciate the luxury of relying on ASP objects to attend to these details on your behalf.

Before you begin to see, in detail, what this liberation force of Active Server Programming will bring, take a look at a typical (and justly famous) guestbook written in Perl by Matt Wright, a very good Perl programmer; many of us owe him much for his ubiquitous gem. By the way, Matt's source code is seven pages long! We're not going to clog up this chapter by listing it all here, but we are going to abstract key code blocks from it. If you've never done this kind of programming before, consider yourself lucky.

On the CD

**N O T E** The entire CGI/Perl Guestbook is included on the CD. For our purposes, we are ignoring the e-mail component of the application as well as, in the CGI version, the feedback form.

The ASP Guestbook components (that you examine shortly) are also included in their entirety on the CD. The Access 97 database, which is used to store Guestbook entries, is also available. ∎

OK, so what does it take to make a Guestbook work using CGI, and why is it so difficult?

# CGI Input

The first step is to get information from the client to the server. The CGI/Perl technique parses the standard input from the POST method, used in the form found in guestbook.html. Standard input is UNIX-speak for the stream of data used by a program. This stream can be all of the characters entered from a keyboard up to and including the Enter keypress, or it can be the contents of a file that is redirected to a program.

The Guestbook gets its stream of data from the transmission received through the POST method, used by the form in addguest.html. Recall from earlier, that in the HTTP transaction between the client and the server, something like this stream of data is called the "request body" (a term used often throughout this book). In the case here, this stream is a collection of name/value pairs for each form variable on the Guestbook (for fields left blank, the name variable has no value— which is, itself, a value). Here's your first look at the CGI source code (it reads standard input into a memory buffer for the number of characters passed to the server from the client):

```
# Get the input
read(STDIN, $buffer, $ENV{'CONTENT_LENGTH'});
```

Next, in Listing 15.1, the program splits these name/value pairs and stores them in an array (another memory buffer that stores values in a row, rather like a stack of kitchen plates). It can tell the boundary between pairs because the & character is used to encode them.

---

**Listing 15.1    GUESTBOOK.PL—An Associative Array of Form Variables and Their Values**

```
# Split the name-value pairs
@pairs = split(/&/, $buffer);

foreach $pair (@pairs) {
    ($name, $value) = split(/=/, $pair);
```

---

Now, each row in the array called @pairs has a string that contains the data entered in the form. Each row might also contain other special characters if the form data itself contains spaces or non-alphanumeric characters like & or %. These non-alphanumeric characters are converted to their hexadecimal ASCII equivalents. A % sign is inserted before these hex numbers to identify them as encoded characters (if the form data itself included a % sign then that character must first be converted to *its* ASCII value of 25. So that this value is not misinterpreted as the numeric value 25, it too must be encoded as %25). Spaces are always encoded with the plus sign.

---

 **T I P**    If you ever find that you need to imitate the client (e.g., when you set the value of Cookies or you need to append a query string to an URL), rely on the Server Object's URLEncode method to do the dirty work for you.

---

So, when a Web client program makes a request of a Web server, the client passes everything from the type of client software making the request to the name/value pair of form variables filled in by the user on the client side of the transaction.

For example, when visitors to a Web site fill in the Guestbook form completely, they send the following variables to the Web server: realname, username, URL, city, state, country, and comments. Each variable has a value, and the pair is sent to the Web server in a form like this:

realname=Michael+Corning.

The entire string of variable/value pairs is encoded with the ampersand character like this:

realname=Michael+Corning&username=mpc%40investing%2Ecom...

**N O T E**    Note the hexadecimal value for @ and . are 40 and 2E respectively, and each is identified as an encoded character with the %. Actually, this is a rather clever scheme that is very efficient. I've heard it said that the best way to tell a true programmer is to look at her tax return. Real programmers file in hex. ■

---

### A Note from the Author

This highlights an important point as we move from the programmer's world to the business world: Because HTML is a formal specification, a generally accepted standard, all browsers are compelled to send form data to a Web server the same way. It follows that there need be only one program that's necessary to decode the environment variable in the server that contains that string of form data.

It does not follow, however, that there is only one way to produce this program. Programmers live to find new and more efficient ways to do things. It matters not how pedestrian the process is, even something as prosaic as a query string. That's not the point. It's a matter of aesthetics. It's a matter of quality.

It's this perfectionism that's so engrained in the programmer's work ethic that has made the Internet what it is today rather than some leftover notes on a white board at the Advanced Research Program Agency in the Department of Defense. To programmers, the Internet is never good enough.

So, back in Listing 15.1, because each name/value pair is separated by an equal sign, the script puts everything to the left of the = in the name field and to the right of the = in the value field. Presto! A decoded query string.

Next, in Listing 15.2, any special non-alphanumeric characters must be identified and converted back to their original values.

### Listing 15.2 GUESTBOOK.PL—Decode Non-alphanumeric Characters

```
# Un-Webify plus signs and %-encoding
    $value =~ tr/+/ /;
    $value =~ s/%([a-fA-F0-9][a-fA-F0-9])/pack("C", hex($1))/eg;
    $value =~ s/<!--(.|\n)*-->//g;

    if ($allow_html != 1) {
        $value =~ s/<([^>]|\n)*>//g;
    }

    $FORM{$name} = $value;
}
```

Keep in mind that all of this splitting and decoding of strings is going on behind the scenes during ASP processing. As you will see shortly, the QUERY_STRING is the same regardless of the technology driving the server. We will turn to a detailed discussion of the Request Object in the next section, but first take a look at what else is lurking in guestbook.pl.

## CGI Output

After the Perl script has figured out exactly what the Guestbook was saying, the program in Listing 15.3 opens the Guestbook's data file. Once open, the data file moves any contents currently in the file into another array (the Perl script is written so that new entries can be inserted or appended to existing data, according to the user's preference). The data file is then immediately closed with the close statement.

**N O T E**  It's interesting to note that at this level of programming, and when file I/O is limited to text format, you have to make many design choices that are moot when you use more abstract technology such as database tables. The ASP alternative in the section, "Guestbook Made Easy," later in this chapter, uses databases to store guestbook entries, and we leave sorting issues to the database engine; we don't have to worry about it when we first store the entries in a file.

Remember, we're showing you all this so that you appreciate how much work Active Server Pages is saving you. ∎

**Listing 15.3  GUESTBOOK.PL—Editing of the Guestbook Entries File**

```
# Begin the Editing of the Guestbook File
open (FILE,"$guestbookreal");
@LINES=<FILE>;
close(FILE);
$SIZE=@LINES;

# Open Link File to Output
open (GUEST,">$guestbookreal");
```

Listing 15.4, then, writes the form data to the Guestbook data file.

**Listing 15.4  GUESTBOOK.PL—Writing the Entries to the Guestbook Entries File**

```
for ($i=0;$i<=$SIZE;$i++) {
    $_=$LINES[$i];
    if (/<!--begin-->/) {
        if ($entry_order eq '1') {
            print GUEST "<!--begin-->\n";
        }
        $FORM{'comments'} =~ s/\cM\n/<br>\n/g;
        print GUEST "<b>$FORM{'comments'}</b><br>\n";
        if ($FORM{'url'}) {
            print GUEST "<a href=\"$FORM{'url'}\">$FORM{'realname'}</a>";
        }
        else {
            print GUEST "$FORM{'realname'}";
        }
        if ( $FORM{'username'} ){
            if ($linkmail eq '1') {
                print GUEST " \&lt;<a href=\"mailto:$FORM{'username'}\">";
                print GUEST "$FORM{'username'}</a>\&gt;";
            }
            else {
                print GUEST " &lt;$FORM{'username'}&gt;";
            }
        }
    print GUEST "<br>\n";
        if ( $FORM{'city'} ){
```

```perl
        print GUEST "$FORM{'city'},";
    }

    if ( $FORM{'state'} ){
        print GUEST " $FORM{'state'}";
    }
    if ( $FORM{'country'} ){
        print GUEST " $FORM{'country'}";
    }
    if ($separator eq '1') {
        print GUEST " - $date\n<hr>\n";
    }
    else {
        print GUEST " - $date<p>\n\n";
    }
    if ($entry_order eq '0') {
        print GUEST "<!--begin-->\n";
    }
    }
    else {
        print GUEST $_;
    }
}
close (GUEST);
```

## Examples of How Much Easier ASP Is than CGI

Did you notice all of the embedded HTML code. Again, with Perl and CGI using text file data storage, you have to do everything at the beginning. That is, you store everything you will later need to display the contents of the data file. In one respect, you are not only storing data entered from the form, you are storing the *programming* necessary to display it later.

Again, with ASP, you don't have to be so meticulous. You can also be more flexible. For example, you might change your mind and not want to display comments entered in the Guestbook in bold type. With ASP, you change the tag once. With the data file, you have to change it many times and only in certain places (for example, around the comments but not around the name [if the name were also meant to be in bold type]).

Things are looking pretty good, aren't they? With ASP technology you are going to be seeing a lot more interactivity and variety because more people will understand Active Server Pages than who currently understand CGI, don't you think?

Ninety-two lines of code! As we said previously, the other five pages of the guestbook.pl script are dedicated to sending an e-mail message to the person who just submitted an entry into the Guestbook and to displaying the contents of the entry for confirmation.

Whew!

**N O T E**    Care must be taken when designing interactive systems, even something as simple as a guestbook. The problem arises when there is a mistake in data entry. Haven't you ever filled

*continues*

*continued*

in a guestbook and submitted it to later regret it? You look at your entry and find an embarrassing misspelling, you accidentally entered the form twice.

Interactivity that is data-based is much more forgiving. Exploit that power and make the interactive experience more pleasant and less threatening for the visitor. In the short run, such thoughtfulness is a competitive advantage. ■

# Interactive Liberation

In this section, we are going to introduce the basics of the `Request` and `Response` Server Objects. You will learn just enough about these remarkable assets to construct a simple guestbook, exactly like the one you just looked at. In Chapter 16, "Enhancing Interactivity with `Cookies`, `Headers`, and the `Server` Object," you will have fun with a really powerful feature of Active Server Pages: their ability to call themselves.

## The *Request* Object

In Chapter 14, "Managing States and Events with `Application` and `Session` Objects," you caught your first glimpse of the `Request` Object in action. There we saw how its `Cookies` collection was used to give the developer control over ASP sessions. In this section you explore a detailed discussion of this object. You will be going into some of the inner workings of HTTP. If that is material that you have been able to avoid up to this date, refer to the notes and sidebars we provide to fill the gaps in your understanding.

The `Request` Object is the first intrinsic server object you need to fully understand. It is the connection between the Web client program and the Web server. Across this connection flows information from the following sources: the HTTP `QueryString`, form data in the HTTP `Request` body, HTTP `Cookies`, and predetermined `ServerVariables`. Because the `Request` Object accesses these collections in that order, so will we.

Calls to this `Server` Object take the following generalized form:

```
Request[.Collection]("variable")
```

As you can see, it is not necessary to specify which collection you are referring to when using the `Request` Object. It will search for the variable in all collections until it finds the first one, and it searches in the order given previously. If it finds no occurrence of the variable in any collection, `Request` returns empty.

If you do specify a collection, however, you ensure two things:

- ■ **Optimized performance**: If you are passing large amounts of data, and the variable you want to reference is in the `ServerVariables` collection, you get it immediately instead of walking through all the collections looking for it.

- ■ **Minimized errors**: If you happen to use the same variable name in two different collections, the Active Server will stop when it finds the first occurrence of the variable.

If the variable you want is in another collection, there is an error. Avoid it by specifying the collection when you call the Request Object.

**The *QueryString* Collection**    The QueryString collection is the first one the Active Server searches. This is because query strings come from an HTTP GET method, and the GET method is the default request method in HTTP (makes sense because it's the original method appearing in HTTP/0.9 in 1991—the POST method didn't appear until HTTP/1.0 when HTML forms were introduced).

## ON THE WEB

For more information about the GET method, see the very readable and historic documents of the early development of Web and the HTTP protocol at

**http://www.w3.org/pub/WWW/Protocols/Classic.html**

Query strings are the text that follows a question mark in an URL (which, by the way, is the reason they are called "query [or "question"] strings"), and can be sent to a Web server two ways:

■ From form variables passed to the server using URL encoding with the GET method (not the POST method)

■ Manually, either by entering the query string directly behind the URL, or by programming the string to be appended to it (a form isn't necessary)

The first method is, by far, the most common way to create the query string. The second method is used by the Active Server when the client doesn't support (or has disabled) Cookies, and when you want to pass a parameter to an .asp file but don't want the trouble of a form. Session properties could also be used to pass parameters to an .asp file (see Chapter 11, "Property Bags and Menus: Extending ActiveX Document Applications"), but using the manual form of setting query strings takes less overhead (see note at the end of Chapter 11).

▶ **See** "URL Encoding" for more information about variables passed to the server using URL encoding, **p. 857**

**A Look Under the Hood of HTTP**    HTTP is a stateless protocol. This means that each request from a client requires a new connection to the server. In the strictest implementation of the protocol, this means that an HTML document with text and an image requires two separate transactions with the server: one to get the text and a second connection to retrieve the image.

If the browser is capable, an HTTP connection header can be sent to the server with the keyword "Keep-Alive" so that subsequent calls by the client to the server will use the same TCP network connection. Internet Explorer 3.0 supports this header and owes much of its improvement in performance to this HTTP enhancement.

In HTTP/1.0 there are three primary methods with which a Web client requests information from a Web server: GET, POST, and HEAD. We will focus here on the first two.

As we said, GET is the most often used request method used on the Web. Every hypertext link uses it implicitly. When an HTML form is used, however, the HTML author decides which method to use to implement the form element's ACTION. With forms there are issues the author needs to face in order to choose wisely. For the ASP developer, knowledge of the difference between these two methods ensures that the use of the Request Object will not yield unexpected results. For example, if you use a POST method in your form, don't expect to find the variable/value pairs appearing in the Request.QueryString collection. This collection is populated only when the form uses the GET method.

The difference lies in the fact that the GET method is basically the *read* request of HTTP, and the POST method is the *write* method. That's why the GET method is still the default request method because most of the time you want to merely read the contents of an HTML file somewhere.

Sometimes, however, you only want to read something special, so you include a query string along with your read request. Relying on an appended string is one of the major weaknesses of the GET method. The problem is that the URL and the query string go into an environment variable on the server. Each system administrator sets aside a fixed amount of memory for all environment variables. Many DOS programmers faced the same challenge as well. Because the environment space is limited, so is the size of the query string. There is no specific size to this limit, but there is always *some* size.

The POST method, on the other hand, does not use a query string to communicate with the server. This frees it from the limitations of the old GET method and enables much more complex form data to be sent to a Web server. With the POST method, content is sent to the server separately from the request to read an URL. For this reason, the server variables CONTENT-TYPE and CONTENT-LENGTH are used by the POST method (and not by the GET method).

Because the POST method is the *write* request of HTTP, we should not leave it before we note one important attribute of this method: It can write persistent data to the server. In other words, it can (theoretically at this writing) upload files. In November 1995, a Request For Comment was published by researchers at Xerox PARC. Their recommended changes to the HTML Document Type Definition (the formal specification of some aspect of HTML) were simple, and the results of implementing the changes profound. It is important to remember that the POST method can write data to the server, and the GET method can't.

Confused? Let's recap with Table 15.1.

### Table 15.1 Who's Who in the *Request* Object?

| Activity | GET | POST |
| --- | --- | --- |
| Appends query string to requested URL? | Y | N |
| Limited in amount of data passed to requested URL? | Y | N |
| Typically used outside of HTML forms? | Y | N |
| Sends form variables to the Request.QueryString collection? | Y | N |
| Uses the QUERY_STRING server variable? | Y | N |

| Activity | GET | POST |
|---|---|---|
| Sends data to requested URL in separate transaction with server? | N | Y |
| Uses CONTENT-TYPE and CONTENT-LENGTH server variables? | N | Y |
| Sends form parameters to the Request.Form collection? | N | Y |
| Can write data to the server? | N | Y |

Every time you use a search engine you send a GET request to a server with a query string attached. For example, when you enter the following URL in your Web client

```
http://guide-p.infoseek.com/Titles?col=WW&sv=IS&_
➥lk=noframes&qt=HTTP+GET
```

you are telling the InfoSeek search engine to find all files in its database that have the words HTTP and GET. Everything after the ? is the query string and would appear in the QueryString collection of the Request Object. Note, this URL is one long string with no spaces (they've been URL encoded and will be converted back to spaces on the server).

**N O T E**   There are actually four variables being passed to the server, though we are interested in the variables used to query the InfoSeek database. Note, too, that the qt variable has two values: HTTP and GET. As we will see in a moment, the Request Server Object creates something like a 3-D spreadsheet when it parses an HTTP query string like this, creating a collection of variables and their values and a separate collection for variables that have more than one value. ■

Now that you have a better understanding of the differences and similarities of GET and POST methods, return to a focused discussion of the QueryString collection.

The full specification of this method includes the way you access variables with multiple values:

```
Request[.Collection]("variable")[(index)¦.Count]
```

The brackets indicate optional details. You must always specify the variable in the Request collections to be retrieved, and you can optionally specify the collection name or information about any data sets that might be coming in from the client.

 **TIP**   If, for some reason, your application needs to see the URL-encoded query string being sent from the client, you can access this string by calling the Request.QueryString object without any parameters at all. The result is the single string of characters received by the Web server and stored in its Request.ServerVariables collection.

What is a data set? It is a collection of data with a common parent, and the parent, in turn, is a member of the QueryString collection. An example will make this clear.

Suppose there is a form that is filled out by a financial planner. Financial planners can have many different designations, and they may want to be identified with all of them. So they fill out a membership application form giving their names and addresses. At the bottom of the form is a multi-select list box. If one particularly ambitious planner wants to add yet another acronym to his name, he must select all those designations that currently define his competence.

As a result, the filled-out form is sent to the membership program on the Web server with all the usual personal identification fields along with this special field named `"designations"` that contains the following values: CFP, CPA, and CFA.

The `Request.QueryString` collection would have an item for each of the form variables, including one for `"designations"`. The `"designations"` item would have a collection of its own (sometimes referred to as a data set) and would return the value 3 with the call:

```
Request.QueryString("designations").Count
```

You could enumerate this data set two ways: First, by simply executing the command

```
Request.QueryString("designations")
```

you would see this result: CFP, CPA, and CFA (note it is a single comma-delimited string).

Alternatively, you can walk through the data set with the following code block:

```
<% For I = 1 to Request.QueryString("designations").Count %>
   <BR><% =Request.QueryString("designations")(i) %><BR>
<% Next %>
```

The result is three separate text strings, one for each designation in the collection.

**The Form Collection**   As we said in the previous section, the POST method in HTTP/1.0 was designed to enable large amounts of data to be passed between client and server. In contrast, the GET method is limited to a fixed number of characters that it can append to the URL (limited by operating environment constraints on the server). This data is processed by the server as if it were STDIN data (such as data entered from a keyboard or redirected from a file). The data passed to the server with the POST method is usually formatted the same way as the GET method (by URLEncoding), but it can also be formatted in a special way when necessary.

There is one other subtle difference in terminology between GET and POST. With the GET method, elements of the query string are referred to as *variables*, and with the POST method they are *parameters*. This distinction serves to reinforce the simplicity of GET and the open-ended sophistication of POST.

Fortunately for ASP developers, the way we handle Form and QueryString collections is virtually identical. The most important things to remember about these two collections and the methods that populate them are:

- Choose the method best suited for your purposes (GET for simple requests, POST for complex or data-intensive ones).

- Look for the results in the correct ServerVariables collection (GET uses the QUERY_STRING variable, POST uses the HTTP request body to convey its information and uses the ServerVariables CONTENT_LENGTH and CONTENT_TYPE to specify attributes of the incoming data stream.

■ In your .asp code, explicitly specify the collection you want the `Request` Object to interrogate (given your understanding of the above nuances).

# The *Response* Object

The `Response` Object is responsible for managing the interaction of the server with the client. The methods of this object include:

■ `AddHeader`

■ `AppendToLog`

■ `BinaryWrite`

■ `Clear`

■ `End`

■ `Flush`

■ `Redirect`

■ `Write`

All but the `Write` method are advanced features of this powerful `Response` Object. In this section, you will learn the two ways this function is performed in .asp files, and you will see examples of when one method is more convenient than the other. We will also make some stylistic suggestions aimed at making your .asp files easier to read and to debug.

As with our preliminary discussion of the `Request` Object, we introduce enough of these tools of the ASP trade to construct a simple Guestbook. In Chapter 16, "Enhancing Interactivity with `Cookies`, `Headers`, and the `Server` Object," we will cover the salient features of the remaining collections, methods, and properties of the `Response` and `Request` Objects.

**The *Write* Method**    The most fundamental process of ASP development is writing to the HTML output stream destined for the client. Everything else that .asp files may (or may not) do ultimately ends up at the `Write` method.

`Response.Write` has a simple syntax. It needs only a quoted text string or a function that returns a string.

**T I P**    You can put parentheses around the string or function, but you can save a keystroke if you skip the parentheses and insert a space between `Response.Write` and its parameter.

There are two ways of instructing the Active Server to output characters: explicitly with the `Response.Write` syntax, and implicitly with the .asp code delimiters. That is, anything appearing *outside* the <% (to mark the beginning of Active Server Pages source code) and %> (to mark its end) tags is implicitly written by the Active Server to the HTML file returned to the client.

**CAUTION**

Do not nest <%...%> tags. That is, once you use <% in your source code, don't use it again until you have first used the closing source code delimiter, %>. This is a trap that is particularly easy to fall into when you are using the special case of the <%...%> delimiters, such as when you are writing the value of a variable or method to the output stream.

Specifically, whenever you need to output a value, surround the expression with the <%= ...%> tags. But remember to first close off any open script with the %> tag. If you look closely at the following example (that would fail if you tried this at home), you will see that you are nesting tags.

```
<%
If True Then
      <%= varResult%>
Else
      Call MyProgram
End If
%>
```

In the extreme, you could write all your .asp files using `Response.Write` to send all HTML commands to the client. All the other characters in your .asp file, then, would be .asp source code, and every line would be wrapped in the <%...%> marker. Alternatively, all the HTML source code in your .asp file could be written as if it were merely an HTML file, and you would cordon off the ASP commands with judicious use of the <%...%> delimiters.

Good programmers are far too lazy to use this method, but Listing 15.5 works:

**Listing 15.5    A Method for People Who Like to Type <% and %**

```
<%Response.Write("<!-- Created with HomeSite v2.0 Final Beta  -->")%>
<%Response.Write("<!DOCTYPE HTML PUBLIC " & CHR(34) _
& "-//W3C//DTD HTML 3.2//EN"& CHR(34) & ">")%>
<%Response.Write("<HTML>")%>
<%Response.Write("<HEAD>")%>
<%Response.Write("<TITLE>Registration Results</TITLE>")%>
<%Response.Write("</HEAD>")%>
<%Response.Write("<BODY>")%>
<%Response.Write("<FONT SIZE=+3>Thanks for writing! </FONT><P>")%>
<%Set objConn = Server.CreateObject("ADODB.Connection")%>
<%objConn.Open("guestbook")%>
<%Set objRst = Server.CreateObject("ADODB.Recordset")%>
<%Set objRst.ActiveConnection=objConn%>
<%objRst.LockType = 3%>
<%objRst.Source = "tblGuestbook"%>
<%objRst.CursorType = 3%>
<%objRst.Open%>
```

Choosing which syntax to use should be guided by the rules of syntax in the English language and the rules of good government: less is better. Use punctuation only when it is absolutely necessary or when it improves clarity; write the fewest laws possible to ensure order and civility. In ASP development use the fewest delimiters possible.

There are two reasons for this: laziness and program maintenance. Clearly, `<%...%>` has fewer (though awkward) keystrokes, so it serves the laziness inherent in all good programmers; and fewer odd characters makes for more lucid logic (unnecessary delimiters are distracting to the human eye and virtually transparent to the server's eye). Lucid logic is easier to maintain (thereby further serving the programmer's natural laziness—do I belabor the point?).

There is one other reason for choosing implicit `Write` over the explicit, but we will have to wait a moment to see why.

Listing 15.6 is easier to type and easier to read:

### Listing 15.6    GUESTBOOK.ASP—Opening the Guestbook Database

```
<!--#INCLUDE VIRTUAL="/ASPSAMP/SAMPLES/ADOVBS.INC"
<!-- This document was created with HomeSite v2.0 Final Beta  -->
<!DOCTYPE HTML PUBLIC "-//W3C//DTD HTML 3.2//EN">

<HTML>
<HEAD>
        <TITLE>Registration Results</TITLE>
</HEAD>

<BODY>
<FONT SIZE="+3">Thank you for registering!</FONT><P>
<%
Set objConn = Server.CreateObject("ADODB.Connection")
objConn.Open("guestbook")
Set objRst = Server.CreateObject("ADODB.Recordset")
Set objRst.ActiveConnection=objConn
objRst.LockType = adLockOptimistic
objRst.Source = "tblGuestbook"
objRst.CursorType = adOpenKeyset
objRst.Open
%>
```

**TIP** As with URLEncoding, there is one special case when `Response.Write` will get confused: when the character string `%>` appears in the method's parameter. This happens, for example, when you use `Response.Write` to define an HTML TABLE WIDTH as a percentage of the screen. If you absolutely must use `Response.Write` in these circumstances, use the following modification: `%\>`

There is also another time when `Response.Write` can be a hassle: when you have embedded quotes in the string. As a matter of fact, this is a perennial programming problem. My favorite solution is to insert `CHR(34)` wherever an embedded quote appears.

**N O T E** A small .asp file, respfix.asp, is included on this book's CD to demonstrate each of these workarounds. By the way, the source code makes use of the PLAINTEXT tag to render .asp syntax directly, without processing the .asp command first. There is also a note about errors (that cannot be trapped) if you don't implement the workarounds properly. ■

**T I P** Because VBScript functions and subroutines can only be created using the `<SCRIPT>`...`</SCRIPT>` tags and not the `<%...%>` tags, if you need to return HTML from a VBScript procedure, `Response.Write` is exactly what you need because you can't use `<%=...%>`.

If most of your .asp file is .asp source code (for example, it has lots of ADO programming in it as the following Guestbook does), then you will use `Response.Write` only when you need to include HTML source code and it is not convenient to insert the end of .asp source tag, `%>`. This is awkward to describe, but easy to see, so take a careful look at the ASP version of the Guestbook that follows. Note: There isn't a single use of `Response.Write` in it.

**N O T E** It's worth emphasizing a subtle point here that will be frustrating to you later if you overlook it now. You separate script from HTML with either the `<%...%>` .asp source code tags or the `<SCRIPT>`...`</SCRIPT>` VBScript tags. Use the latter when you are creating named script functions, and when you do, use the `Response.Write` method to send HTML back to the client. Pay close attention to the demos and templates scattered throughout this book, and you will quickly make this second nature, part of your growing ASP programming sensibility. ∎

# Guestbook Made Easy

Now that you understand the basic operation and tradeoffs for using the `Request` Object and its `QueryString` and `Form` collections, take a look at how ASP can radically reduce the work required to deliver even the most basic kind of interactivity on the Web.

## Standard HTML

Using ActiveX and exploiting the power of ADO (which we will dive into with gusto in Part IV, "Active Documents"), our Active Server Program uses 33 lines of code instead of 92, and it gives us the feedback form to boot! And we don't know about you, but we can actually read the Active Server Program.

The first part of the .asp file, given in Listing 15.7, is simple HTML.

**N O T E** What is important to note here is that the following HTML code is part of the program that processes the form data but that this first block does something the Perl script did not: It provides the feedback form displayed after the client posts their entry. ∎

### Listing 15.7 GUESTBOOK.ASP—The Header of the Guestbook Feedback Form

```
<!--#INCLUDE VIRTUAL="/ASPSAMP/SAMPLES/ADOVBS.INC"
<!-- This document was created with HomeSite v2.0 -->
<!DOCTYPE HTML PUBLIC "-//W3C//DTD HTML 3.2//EN">

<HTML>
<HEAD>
```

```
        <TITLE>Registration Results</TITLE>
</HEAD>

<BODY>
<FONT SIZE="+3">Thank you for registering!</FONT><P>
```

### A Quick Review

For those readers who are new to HTML, here's a brief detour into the header of an .html file (only in this case it's an .asp file that will produce HTML output).

The first line is a Server-Side Include directive. This tells the Active Server to insert everything in the adovbs.inc file, viz., all VBScript constants, into the guestbook.asp file while it interprets the VBScript.

The second line is required to meet the specs on HTML/3.2, and it is inserted automatically by my ASP editor, HomeSite.

The HTML and BODY tags are closed with </HTML> and </BODY> tags at the end of the .asp file (see Listing 15.10). They tell the Web client that everything in between needs to be treated as HTML output. Within the HEAD section, nothing is printed to the Web client's display window. The text within the TITLE tags is printed in the border of the Web client's main window. The FONT tag increases the default font by three sizes.

## ASP Code

At this point we start writing .asp code. In the first block, Listing 15.8, we are making a connection with a database and a table. We need access to the table that permits us to append a new record and edit the contents of that record with the values passed to guestbook.asp from guestbook.html. We instruct the Active Server to open this table with a keyset cursor, using optimistic record locking, and we instruct it to complete the update of Guestbook entries with Listing 15.9.

> **N O T E**  Note how we have organized the .asp code in Listing 15.8 so that we only need one set of <%...%> tags. ∎

### Listing 15.8  GUESTBOOK.ASP—Opening the Connection to a Database and a Table Within that Opened Database

```
<%
Set objConn = Server.CreateObject("ADODB.Connection")
objConn.Open("guestbook")
Set objRst = Server.CreateObject("ADODB.Recordset")
Set objRst.ActiveConnection=objConn
objRst.LockType = adLockOptimistic
objRst.Source = "tblGuestbook"
objRst.CursorType = adOpenKeyset
' Alternatively you could move the values from the previous four
' lines of code onto the next line as properties of the Open method.
objRst.Open
```

**N O T E** Note the form variables have already been decoded using the Request Object. We don't need all the low level source code provided by the Perl script. See Listing 15.1 and Listing 15.2. ■

---

**Listing 15.9 GUESTBOOK.ASP—Adding a New Entry**

```
objRst.AddNew
objRst("realname") = Request.Form("realname")
objRst("username") = Request.Form("username")
objRst("url")      = Request.Form("url")
objRst("city")     = Request.Form("city")
objRst("state")    = Request.Form("state")
objRst("country")  = Request.Form("country")
objRst("comments") = Request.Form("comments")
objRst.Update
%>
```

---

**N O T E** If you're accustomed to doing database programming in Microsoft Access or Visual Basic, · then you will find programming in ADO very easy. The only real difference between Listing 15.9 and Access or Visual Basic is the use of the Response Object and its Write method. ■

Note the ending %> tag. If you think about these tags as if they were, themselves, programming logic (for example, similar to the If...Then...Else construct), then you can see that to forget the %> would be like forgetting the End If in a regular code block. You're certainly welcome to surround all ASP commands with <%...%>, but why bother?

# Back to HTML

Having updated the underlying table with the new Guestbook entry, we continue writing the HTML file to the client (see Listing 15.10). If we add another dozen lines to this program, we can also redisplay the contents of the form and include a button that permits reentry. Alternatively, we could rename the guestbook.htm file into guestbook.asp and have it call itself changing the original "Submit" button to an "Update" button. We'll show you how to do this in Chapter 16, "Enhancing Interactivity with Cookies, Headers, and the Server Object."

---

**Listing 15.10 GUESTBOOK.ASP—Finishing Touches**

```
<HR>
<A HREF="guestbook.html">Return to Guestbook</A>
</BODY>
</HTML>
```

---

That's all there is to it. Remember our story at the beginning of this chapter? Well, if ASP was around back then, we would have been able to say to our boss, "Sure, boss; that's a slam dunk. We'll have a Guestbook for you before lunch."

## More Power to You

We have just skimmed over the power and features of the Request and Response Server Objects, just enough to be able to construct a simple Guestbook. There's much more available to the Active Server Program developer, however.

As you continue reading this book, please keep in mind one very important idea somewhere near the front of your mind: Active Server Programming is going to enable those of us who are not professional programmers to do things not even they have been able to do before. We are going to see an explosion of creativity the depth and breadth of which will surprise everyone. Everyone but you. You're leading the way.

# From Here...

In this chapter, we have built a new programming foundation for interactivity. You have seen what it used to take to get a simple Guestbook implemented on our Web sites, and you have tried your hand at doing it the ASP way. It really is amazing how much work we can get done with two ASP objects like Request and Response, isn't it?

We turn our attention next to a discussion of the rest of the features of the Request and Response Objects, and we will introduce the Server Object.

- Chapter 16, "Enhancing Interactivity with *Cookies*, *Headers*, and the *Server* Object," gets you into the nitty-gritty details of Cookies, especially the Cookies collection of the Response Object.

- In that same chapter, you will come to understand the nature of HTTP headers and you will see how many of the Response Object's methods are designed to help you exploit these sophisticated and subtle aspects of HTML programming.

- We then introduce the Server Object and its very useful methods that can take a lot of the drudgery out of ASP development.

- Finally, the chapter also looks at a very cool feature of Active Server Pages: their ability to call themselves. In order to work this magic you need to have mastered the Request Object, and you need to brush up on your Session Object, too.

# Enhancing Interactivity with *Cookies*, *Headers*, and the *Server* Object

**T**his chapter brings you up to a level in your capability to create pages that interact with the reader of your Web site. You will learn how to make your .ASP code more efficient and easier to manage; you will complete your survey of the Request and Response Objects; and you will get your first detailed look at the Server Object. All of this should help you bring more life and vitality to your work on the Web. ■

### ASP files that talk to themselves

A fascinating feature of Active Server Pages is their ability to call themselves. Learn how to exploit this novel feature in this section.

### The *Request* Object

This section completes your introduction to the Request Object. Learn all about cookies and the ServerVariables Collection.

### More on *Response* Objects

Cookies are found in both the Response and Request Objects. Learn the difference and how to use each.

### The *Server* Object at your service

The *Server* Object completes this chapter. Learn how it can take over the most laborious and tedious tasks in your Internet development.

# The Good Stuff

In Chapter 15, "Building a Foundation of Interactivity with Request and Response Objects," you learned how form data moves between client and server. This is the Web's most basic kind of interactivity. In that chapter, you had one guestbook.asp file, and you called it once to update your Guestbook's data file. This chapter covers error trapping, and provides a fuller treatment of client feedback.

▶ **See** "CGI Input" for more information about form data, **p. 313**

In this chapter, then, you enhance your basic Guestbook application with those two additional features. To accomplish this goal you need only remember what you already know about the Request Object and you will learn how to get a form to call itself. Previously, you had separate guestbook.html and guestbook.asp files. In this chapter, however, you only have one guestbook.asp file. As you will see, this *reflexive* feature of the Active Server Pages (ASP) may be its most useful feature (with the exception of ADO, which is treated in depth in Chapter 25, "Introducing ActiveX Data Objects").

## Using Its Own Output—Program Recursion

Recursion is a simple programming technique. You need it when a program must reuse its own output. The biggest problem with the technique is that it consumes memory at an alarming rate, and when recursion goes awry it will cause something called a *stack overflow*. As a result, it is not commonly used.

By the way, you can visualize stack overflow if you've ever worked in a restaurant: Dinner plates are stored in spring-loaded cylinders. As you add plates, the stack gets higher, and as you take plates away, each plate in the stack moves up. If you stack plates too high, they can overflow onto the ground and make a mess. Now memory is silent as light, but it, too, can get in a muddle if you try to push too many calls to the same program into a limited amount of memory. Each call to a recursive program is a plate.

When an .ASP file calls itself, however, the program contained in that file is not using recursion; it only looks as if it is. It's safe, and it will be one of the most immediately important features of ASP development. The key to the technique is the astute use of the Request.Form method.

There are a couple of design objectives the ASP developer needs to keep in mind:

- Default values for form variables must cooperate with the contents of the Request.Form collection
- Overhead should be minimized by caching session resources like connections and recordsets

**N O T E** The advanced Guestbook program, guestbookpro.asp, is included on the CD. It uses the same Guestbook database as its less sophisticated cousin. ■

In this section you look at how .ASP files work when they call themselves. In the next section, you include the code that you need to minimize overhead.

**The ASP Program Model**    The reason Active Server Pages has so little trouble calling itself is ironic: ASP programs run on a stateless server. That's right—the one thing that makes database programming challenging makes reflexive programming easy. When you think about it, it's easy to understand: When an .ASP (or HTML) file requests the attention of the server, it is served and then forgotten. Subsequent HTTP requests for the same file are totally unaffected by anything requested before. Form variables get passed exactly the same way with .ASP files as with HTML files. In a sense, every instance of an .ASP file is different from every other; the only thing they share is a name. Except for the referrer data (which contains the name of the file making the request) that's passed in the HTTP request, the request is an HTTP request, not the request of your specific Active Server Pages.

Part
V

Ch
16

The point of all this is that your focus is on the HTTP request, not the file making the request. Think of each call made by an .ASP file as one being made to a different file. In each case, the called .ASP file has access to the `Request.Form` collection sent in the HTTP request transaction.

**Setting Default Values**    When an .ASP file loads, the form fields it contains can have one of three values: a default (for example, you could hardwire a value in its `VALUE` property), the value in some named parameter of the `Request.Form` collection, and, finally, a null value.

For .ASP files that call themselves, the simplest technique is to put the `Request.Form` command in the `VALUE` property of the form field. For example, your Advanced Guestbook can use the code block in Listing 16.1 as a prototype for all the other fields:

**Listing 16.1    GUESTBOOKPRO.ASP—Use Default Unless a Previous Value Was Entered**

```
<%
varRealName = Request.Form("realname")
If IsEmpty(varRealName) Then
        varRealName = "Katy Corning"
End If
%>
```

The entry in the `<FORM>` block of the ASP program would look like this:

```
<INPUT TYPE="TEXT" NAME="realname" SIZE=70 VALUE="<%=varRealName%>">
```

From these examples you can see that the `VALUE` property is set with a variable, and the variable is initialized with `NULL` when the form is first called (or the Refresh button is pushed). If the variable is empty, initialize it with the field's default value.

However, on subsequent calls, the guestbookpro.asp file sees some value (perhaps the original default value, perhaps some value entered by the user) in the `Request.Form` collection's *realname* parameter. In this case, the variable used to set the VALUE property of the field gets the value in the Form collection. It's actually deceptively simple, once you get the hang of it.

Take a closer look at form fields that don't have VALUE properties.

On the Advanced Guestbook, you have a check box that the users select if they want to be notified of announcements on the Web site. To set the check box's default value, you have to see if it was *on* in the previous instance of the Guestbook form.

```
<%
If Request.Form("chkNotifyMe")="on" Then
        varCHECKED = "CHECKED"
End If
%>
```

**TIP**  The comparison is case sensitive. One thing you can do to control case sensitivity is force the left side of the expression to a case of choice, usually uppercase, using the UCase() function, and then compare the result to the test value (in uppercase if that's your case of choice).

From your example, it would look like this:

```
If UCase(Request.Form("chkNotifyMe"))="ON" Then
```

Actually, this is a good habit to use, regardless. That way you never have to wonder if something is case sensitive or not, or whether case sensitivity in an application changes as programs upgrade.

# Caching Tasks

If your .ASP file that calls itself uses ActiveX Data Objects (ADO), then you also have to attend to caching tasks. In this case, the stateless nature of HTTP is not a blessing as it was in "The ASP Program Model" section, but it's not quite a curse either. You just have to be careful that, if your .ASP file has gone to the trouble of making a connection to an ADO data provider, you don't make it do that again each time the .ASP file is called. This concern extends to any recordsets that might also be opened during previous calls to your .ASP file.

As noted in Chapter 14, "Managing States and Events with Application and Session Objects," you can create Session Objects identified with individual parties by using your Web application. Each user has a unique system-generated ID attached to every place she goes in your application. In the same way, ADO Connection and RecordSet Objects can be identified uniquely.

In your Advanced Guestbook you test for the existence of these objects in the manner of Listing 16.2:

> **Listing 16.2  QUESTBOOKPRO.ASP—Testing for Objects**

```
<%If IsObject(Session("SessionConnection")) Then
    ' Reuse the ADO Objects
    Set objConn = Session("SessionConnection")
    Set objRst  = Session("SessionRecordSet")%>
```

```
    <FONT COLOR="Green">
    Using the Cached Session Connection and RecordSet
    </FONT><P>

<% Else

    ' This is the first time this user has called the file.
    ' Create the ADO Objects necessary to update the Guestbook.
    Set objConn = Server.CreateObject("ADODB.Connection")
    objConn.Open("Guestbook")
    ' Initialize the Session property with the Connection Object
    Session("SessionConnection") = objConn

    Set objRst = Server.CreateObject("ADODB.Recordset")
    ' Initialize the Session property with the RecordSet Object
    Session("SessionRecordSet") = objRst %>

    <FONT COLOR="Yellow">
    Opening the Connection and RecordSet
    </FONT><P>

<% End If %>
```

Part

V

Ch

16

Take a good look at the Advanced Guestbook application at the Web site. I think you'll be amazed at how much work is being done with one program.

You have now completed your survey of basic Web interactivity by using Active Server Pages instead of CGI. Now it's time to look at the next level of interactivity that this new technology enables. In the rest of this chapter, you will see that you cannot only enable a richer interactive environment for the user and the Web site, but also enhance the interactivity between the client program and the server. You will reach this higher level of interactivity between client and server because you will do so on their turf: HTTP transactions using Request and Response headers.

# The Rest of the *Request* Object

You have covered the simplest and most often used methods and collections of the Request and Response Objects. You now complete your survey of the fundamentals of interactivity by exploring the nooks and crannies of Cookies, server variables, buffers, headers, and other arcane features.

## How to Get a Header in Life

On the Web, there are always three entities communicating with each other: Web server, Web client, and the user. Clearly, the language, images, and perhaps sound displayed on the screen or sent through the computer's sound card are how both the server and client software communicate with the user.

*continues*

*continued*

But how do the server and client communicate with each other?

With headers. Headers come in all shapes and sizes. Well, actually they come in four varieties: General, Request, Response, and Entity. These collections of data tell the server vital information such as the media type of the returned entity. Remember, HTML can be almost any kind of information, from text, images, and sound to binary files, and BLOBS. For all of the transporting infrastructure to work properly, knowledge of what is being transported is vital.

Most of the material in this section refers in one way or another to message headers.

---

**N O T E**   The definitive word on HTTP/1.0 is found at **http://www.ics.uci.edu/pub/ietf/http/ rfc1945.html#Product**. Section 4.2 describes all the details of message headers. A careful reading of this document is almost prerequisite to the serious use of most of the following features of the Response Object. ▪

# The Cookies Collection

Cookies are an odd name given to an important task in programming stateless environments like the Web. If you're interested in all the technical details of this technique, direct your browser to an Internet draft titled "HTTP State Management Mechanism," which is the official word on Cookies. It can be read at **http://portal.research.bell-labs.com/~dmk/cookie-2.31-2.33.txt**.

**Cookies: A Basic Recipe**   You first looked at Cookies in Chapter 14, "Managing States and Events with `Application` and `Session` Objects." There, you learned about its use by the Active Server as a way to identify individual users and to do what's known as *manage state*. In that context the Active Server did all the work. In this chapter, you look at reading and writing Cookies yourself. Most readers probably have not used Cookies yet. Until I found the Cookies Collection, I hadn't either; I had no idea how. You will see that reading and writing them really couldn't be easier. In fact, of all the header-oriented methods in ASP development, working with Cookies is the most direct and will probably be the most popular.

As you might guess, in the context of the `Request` Object, Cookies are read. In the section titled "The Rest of the `Response` Object," you will learn how to write them.

To properly understand the function of Cookies takes some concentration. It's not difficult to understand, just backward. Here's what I mean: Cookies are unusual in HTML because they are data written to the local client storage media. Except, perhaps, ActiveX controls and Java applets, nothing else in HTML writes to disk. But the real function of Cookies is to *request data*. That is, Cookies are used by clients to make specific requests of a particular server (defined as the domain and/or the path to an HTML document or an ASP application).

Cookies get confusing because we tend to think of them in the context of writing, not reading. Writing by the server is a necessary evil because Web clients usually never write data themselves; they must rely on the server to do that.

So, Cookies are used to request things. Here's an excellent example of what I mean: When Microsoft first hosted the version of their Web site that could be configured to individual client preferences, they used Cookies. Once the preferences were selected and stored on client computers, subsequent requests for the MSN home page looked just like previous ones. The Cookies enabled the client to make a special request of the MSN Web server to deliver a custom document. See? Cookies are important because of what they do *after* they are created.

So, what's in a Cookie? A name? Yes. But what if two different servers need the same name? As other sites enabled the client to customize the interface to the server, this became more likely. The solution is stored in Cookie *attributes*. The two most important attributes are *domain* and *path*. One or both of these data points serve to uniquely match the Cookie with its server. When the server wrote the Cookie, it could have included a path back to itself. Say your ASP application is found at **your_company.com/data/web**. Suppose further that you have another ASP application at **your_company.com/data/web/tutorial**. If both applications have a Cookie named *last_visited* and if the client sends both *last_visited* cookies to the server, Request.Cookies(*last_visited*) will return the value of the cookie stored at **your_company.com/data/web/tutorial**.

**Fancy Cookies**   Cookies can also have *dictionaries*. It's true.  Dictionary objects can be anything that stores a term and a value, like its namesake stores a term and a definition. When it comes to Cookies, think of the dictionary as a dictionary of synonyms. Look at an example:

Say you need to store a Cookie called `client`. This cookie can have two key names: `last_name` and `first_name`. You access each with the following syntax:

```
Request.Cookies("client")("first_name")
```

```
Request.Cookies("client")("last_name")
```

A `Request.Cookies` call without specifying a key will return an URLEncoded string of the name/value pairs for all entries in the Cookies dictionary. For example:

```
strQuery = Request.Cookies
```

would assign the variable strQuery the string value of

```
LAST%5FNAME=Mansfield%2DCorning&FIRST%5FNAME=Katy
```

**N O T E**   There's a demo program on the CD, cookies_walk.asp, that shows writing and reading Cookies with data you enter. ■

**Working With *Request.Cookies***   Unlike its twin, `Response.Cookies`, `Request.Cookies` can appear anywhere in the HTML BODY section. As you will see in the next section, `Response.Cookies` is an HTTP header transaction. This means it must be completed before the entity body in the HTTP transaction is begun. Remember, headers are the means by which client and server communicate; the entity body is the part of HTTP that the client and server use to communicate with human users.

As previously noted, the syntax is simple:

```
Request.Cookies("cookie-name")¦("key-name")
```

If you request an undefined Cookie or key, the `Request` Object returns a null value.

Because Cookies is a collection, you can move through the collection with Listing 16.3. Note that this works without further modification with any Cookies Collection.

**Listing 16.3   COOKIES_WALK.ASP—Walking Through a Cookies Collection**

```
<H1>It's a Cookies Walk</H1>
<HR>
<UL>
<%
For Each cookie In Request.Cookies %>
        <LI>Cookie: <B><% = cookie %></B> = <% = Request.Cookies(cookie) %>
        <UL>
        <% For Each key in Request.Cookies(cookie) %>
        <LI>Key: <B><% = key %></B> is <% = Request.Cookies(cookie)(key) %>
        <% Next%>
        </UL>
<%Next%>
</UL>
```

# The *ServerVariables* Collection

This collection tells you everything the server knows about the client and itself. There are three groups of data in this collection, which includes the following:

- HTTP Request
- Server Environment
- Everything else

As with all collections, you can use the `For Each...Next` control structure to enumerate the collection.

> **N O T E**   A two-file demo is included on the CD, demo_servervar.htm and demo_servervar.asp, to show how selecting the two Request Methods, `GET` and `POST`, affects the `ServerVariables` Collection.
>
> The Cookies demo mentioned previously also calls the demo_servervar.asp file and shows the effect on the `HTTP_COOKIE` variable in the `ServerVariables` Collection. ■

The HTTP Request group of variables describes important parts of the HTTP request transaction with the server. Things like `REQUEST_METHOD`, `CONTENT_LENGTH`, and `CONTENT_TYPE` are included here. Other important data points are the `REMOTE_ADDR` and the `REMOTE_HOST` variables. These two data points give you some idea of the IP address of the requesting client, and this is often used in programs that send e-mail via Web forms. The addresses returned (when they are, and that doesn't happen with all Web clients) are not always reliable or useful. Online services have the same host, but often use a unique identifier in the address for individual users. However, this same user will have a different IP address the next time he logs on to the service. Other times no address resolution is provided by the client software, usually because the user is coming from behind a firewall (a computer that protects a trusted network from unwelcome intrusions by outside computers).

The Server group of data points reports facts about the server, such as SCRIPT_NAME and SERVER_NAME; these facts might be important in an intranet setting where there are as many HTTP servers as there are clients (for example, every Windows 95 machine is running the "Personal Web Server" application). Another important fact is SERVER_SOFTWARE; this would be important if all servers on an intranet were not running the same version of IIS (for example, IIS 2.0 does not have all the power and speed of IIS 3.0, because the ActiveX Server Engine is an add-on to the former and an integral part of the NT operating system in the latter).

The final group of server variables have the form HTTP_<header_name>. Some of the most useful variables are contained here. You'll find the Cookies Collection here, as well as the HTTP_REFERRER variable. This variable tells you the URL used to engage the current HTTP request transaction (unless the URL was entered manually), so you can see from whence your visitors have come. Another interesting fact is the HTTP_USER_AGENT; this variable tells you what kind of client software is being used at the other end (which can be helpful when you want to present HTML code that is optimized for any given client).

# The Rest of the *Response* Object

Now return to your old friend, the Response Object. You have already covered the most frequently used method for this object, the Response.Write method. The rest of this object contains properties and methods almost exclusively for the management of HTTP headers.

Begin with your favorite topic, Cookies.

## *Response.Cookies* Collection

Think of writing Cookies in the same way you would write a Registry entry in Windows 95 or an .INI file entry in Windows 3.1. Actually, in .ASP development, writing Cookies is much easier than it ever was in Windows. There are no special API functions to write (and maintain when you upgrade Windows). Just read and write, and let the server do the work. This is the way programming was always meant to be, isn't it?

> **N O T E**  The NAME field is the only required field for Cookies, and its value is URL-encoded. When you get to the Server Object later in this chapter, you learn how to use this method to do the dirty work of encoding Cookies values. ∎

> **CAUTION**
> Always put your Response.Cookies calls before the <HEAD> section of your .ASP files. These are header transactions (as are most of the rest of the Response Object's methods) and will fail if the server has already written the header of the HTTP response transaction to the client.

If you spy on the Cookie collection by using the `Request.ServerVariables("HTTP_COOKIES")` variable, you see that this collection can get full quickly. One of the reasons for this is that each Cookie is *attached* to SessionIDs (which have their own Cookie in this collection, "`ASPSESSIONID`"). Fortunately, the server takes care of the details. If you set a "`LAST_VISITED`" cookie to the current time, all you have to do is `Request.Cookies("LAST_VISITED")` and you have its value, regardless of what else lurks down there in the Cookie jar.

As you learned in the discussion of the `Request.Cookies` method, Cookies can have *dictionaries* (sometimes called *data sets*). These are like fields in a database record, and they're called *keys* (what keys have to do with Cookies is anybody's guess). The syntax is simple:

```
Response.Cookies("NAME")("FIRST")="Michael"
Response.Cookies("NAME")("LAST")="Corning"
```

When a Cookie has keys, it also reports TRUE when the HasKeys attribute is tested. The other attributes are Domain, Path, Expires, and Secure. Domain and Path provide information that uniquely identify Cookies with the same name as when they were created by interacting with different Web servers. For example, many servers will write a Cookie called *last_visit* and the Domain and Path attributes permit each server to identify its own Cookie and not confuse it with the Cookie left by another server. The Expires attribute tells the server when it can safely ignore the Cookies' value, and the Secure attribute tells the server that the Cookie can only be used in a secure transaction.

**N O T E**   Cookie attributes can only be set, not read directly. This is because they are useful only to the server. ▪

# Response Properties

The properties of the `Response` Object control how the HTML output stream is to be processed. Properties such as ContentType, Expires, and Status all have counterparts in HEAD tags that you may have used before, but we think you will find using Response properties to be simpler.

**The *Buffer* Property**   This property is important if you use the other properties and methods of the Response Object extensively. It is important because it permits you to relax the constraint that you must finish manipulating the HTTP headers *before* you start sending the body of the HTML transaction to the client.

Remember, the HTTP headers are used between the client and the server and are invisible to the output of the HTTP transaction; in other words, none of the header data appears on the client program's screen. Usually, the client and server are intolerant of any interference on the part of the human readable component of the transaction unless the Buffer Property is set true.

When true, none of the output data is sent to the client until all the .ASP scripts are complete, or until the Response.Flush or Response.End methods are called.

**N O T E** The cookies.asp file on the CD uses `Response.Buffers=True` to permit the
`Request.QueryString` ("yesno") variable to be displayed before the BODY section
begins further down in the script. The cookies2.asp file on the CD uses conventional programming style
to effect the same result.

**The *ContentType* Property**  This property is used to instruct the client how to display the
HTTP Response Body sent by the server. For .ASP files, setting this to "text/plain" will render
the actual HTML source code instead of interpreting it. If you look on the bottom of the /lab/
cookies.asp screen you will see an option, "View Source Code." If you select this, you send a
query string to the .ASP file that instructs it to set the `Response.ContentType` property to
"text/plain." You can see the same result if you select the other option, "`ServerVariable`
Collection," and choose View Source from your client program.

**N O T E** Notice that there are no <HTML><HEAD><BODY> tags used in demo_server.asp. If those
tags are present, they override the `ContentType` property.

**The *Expires* Property**  This property tells the browser how many minutes it has to live from
the last time it updated. The default value is 0, meaning that every time the page is visited, it is
refreshed. The twin cookies.asp files are an interesting test of this property. Take a closer look.

The /lab/test/cookies.asp file calls the lab/cookies.asp file. Note carefully: The cookies.asp file
in the child directory calls its counterpart in the parent /lab/ directory. The first time this
parent Cookie is called, its LAST_VISITED Cookie is set to the current time. From that page, you
select the "Set Test Cookie" option and the child Cookie page fires updating its LAST_VISITED
Cookie to the current time. *Note this time before you return to the parent Cookie.* Now, when you
immediately select the "Set Lab Cookie" link, you will note that the LAST VISITED Cookie's
value *did not change*. Why?

Because the page was cached. If you look at the top of the parent Cookie page you will see that
it tells you nothing new will appear on that page for at least one minute. For that minute, the
Web client retrieves the cached copy instead of refreshing the link.

OK, so switch back and forth, now, between these two pages. Note the time on both pages. As
long as there is a difference of less than 60 seconds between the two pages, the parent Cookie
will not be refreshed. But as soon as the child Cookie page has a time one minute or more later
than the parent Cookie page, it will refresh with a new time.

Clearly, you need to pull the demo files from the CD and conduct this experiment for yourself.

**The *ExpiresAbsolute* Property**  The only difference between the ExpiresAbsolute and the
Expires properties is that the former includes a date and time. Use the pound sign (#) to delimit this value. For example:

```
<% Response.ExpiresAbsolute=#December 21, 1997 1:00:00 AM# %>
```

The time is converted to Greenwich Mean Time before the Expires HTTP header is sent.
GMT is the time that all servers use to stay synchronized.

If you leave the time blank, midnight on the date given is assumed. If the date is blank, the time on the date the script is run is assumed.

**The *Status* Property** The Status property forces the server to send whatever response value you give it. The most visible example would be to put the following line of code at the top of your .ASP file:

```
<% Response.Status="401 Unauthorized"
```

The result of a call to an .ASP file with this line in it would be a username/password dialog to request authorized access to the page.

# *Response* Methods

The methods of the Response Object covered as follows help you do odd jobs around the Web site. You probably won't have much occasion to use these methods, but you need to be aware of what they can do, should the need arise.

**The *AddHeader* Method** This method is not for the fainthearted. If you looked at the demo_servervar.asp program, you noticed that the end of the collection contained a whole bunch of ServerVariables that started with the "HTTP_" prefix. These headers are generally accepted data points that some or all client programs can consistently interpret.

Some of the most commonly used headers are HTTP_REFERRER, HTTP_USER_AGENT, and, of course, HTTP_COOKIE. When a client program sees these headers from the server in response to a request it made, it knows what the server is trying to "say" to it. This is what was meant earlier about the "other" interactivity going on over the Web; that is, the interactivity not between user and machine, but between Web client and Web server.

One of the header fields exchanged in this category is the WWW-Authenticate header. This header *exists* in the HTTP specification but can be *customized* to meet the specific requirements of authentication required by any given server. It is possible that some challenge-response processes would require more than one WWW-Authentication header. The AddHeader method was created to cover this contingency.

**The *AppendToLog* Method** This method adds a string of no more than 80 characters to the IIS log file. You must have IIS configured to log server transactions. You can confirm (or enable) logging by running the Internet Information Services Manager and selecting the Logging tab from the services window you select (for example, WWW service). This dialog box will also tell you where the log file is located.

> **CAUTION**
>
> Because the IIS log file is comma delimited, you cannot append a string with embedded comments. You may find it necessary to URLEncode the string first, but you will have to decode the string later if you need to refer to it.

One example of using this method is appending the HTTP_USER_AGENT to the transaction. This way you can find out which browsers are going to certain pages on your Web site.

**The *BinaryWrite* Method**    Binary files are not text files. They are usually required by custom applications running on the client's computer. This method enables the ActiveX Server Engine to send this kind of file to the client. This method can be used in a way similar to the way Server Components are used (see the next section, "Server Components," for a detailed discussion). That is, you can create a component that creates objects, and then you can instantiate objects in your .ASP file as follows:

```
Set objImage = CreateObject(ImageComposer)
imgPortland = objImage.PhotoShoot
Response.BinaryWrite imgPortland
```

**The *Clear* Method**    The Clear method is used in conjunction with the Buffer method mentioned previously. This method, along with the End and Flush methods coming up next, is useful when there is a lot of .ASP processing necessary before a final result is ready to send to the client. This will make for some very creative and resourceful .ASP code.

For its part, the Clear method erases the content of the response body. Remember, that's the part of the HTTP transaction that the client displays on the screen; it is not the same thing as the information contained in the response header. If the .ASP code finds an error in processing or data, or if it needs to start processing over for any other reason, the Clear method gives it a clean "sheet of music."

The syntax is simple:

```
Response.Clear
```

**The *End* Method**    The End method stops .ASP processing in its tracks. It functions like the Stop command in Visual Basic. When the ActiveX Server Engine sees this method, it flushes the buffer (which assumes, of course, that the Response.Buffer = True method was executed in the first line of the .ASP file). Any contents in the buffer (including the response body, if any) are sent to the client. To send nothing, use the Response.Clear method first. As with its cousins, the syntax for this method is direct:

```
Response.End
```

**The *Flush* Method**    This method will send the buffer to the client without stopping the processing. It, too, only operates without error if the Response.Buffer method has been set to true.

```
Response.Flush
```

**The *Redirect* Method**    This method is most commonly used when you want to send clients to another URL instead of sending them an HTML stream. This is commonly needed when a Web site is substantially altered or moved. When someone returns to your site from one of their Shortcuts, Bookmarks, or Favorites entries, the Redirect method can be waiting for them in the now defunct HTML page. When a client requests this page before it can stream the entity body of the document back, the server sees that the URL contains a Redirect header and consequently changes the location of the requested URL. This is done without the users knowing it, though they will see that the URL in the Location box is different than what they entered.

**N O T E**    This is also a useful method when you want certain clients to see HTML optimized for them. You can do the same thing by using client-side scripting, but this alternative suffers the single weakness of all other client-side scripting strategies: not all clients script. ■

**N O T E**    To avoid this kind of confusion, it may be better to have an explicit message in the body of the outdated HTML page that tells the client that the URL is different and to update their Shortcut, Bookmark, or Favorites entry. ■

# The *Server* Object

The `Server` Object can be a real workhorse and time saver. Its primary mission is like all programming utilities that have come before it: do the same old thing, and do it well and quickly. In one (limited) respect, utilities have been the precursor to objects. They have always been reusable code that did a clearly defined *administrative* task. Batch updates, directory maintenance, you name it; if it qualified as drudgery work, a programmer sat down and composed a utility program to do it. On the desktop, macros have generally served this function with distinction.

In the new world, we have come full circle: The utility is now an object (not a fully polymorphic, inheritance-capable object) with its own property and methods. It may not have an impeccable object-oriented pedigree, but it will quickly earn the affection of all Webmasters who can now delegate such routine tasks as rotating ads to it.

To start off correctly, remember that the intrinsic methods of the `Server` Object have two general roles:

- To do things humans find difficult, such as encode URL and HTML strings, and keep track of the physical and logical representation of file paths
- To create objects that can do almost anything else

## Server Property: *ScriptTimeout*

This is the only property for the `Server` Object. It is designed to give the ASP developer some control over the contingency of script processing time. Note I said *script* processing. If a server script calls a server component then the `ScriptTimeout` property will not control that component (the developer of the component is responsible for that). So, if there is a chance that something might take an inordinate amount of time (this is the Internet, after all, and we all know it is not the fastest thing alive) to complete, you can take steps to avoid being deadlocked as a result.

This property is read/writeable. To read the value of this property, use the following expression:

```
<% =Server.ScriptTimeout %>
```

If you need to set the property, for example, to three minutes, do it like this:

```
<% Server.ScriptTimeout = 180 %>
```

The default value of this property is 90 seconds.

Part

**V**

Ch

**16**

# Managing HTML

HTML was meant to be read by a machine, not by people. In the spirit of maximum productivity that drives nearly all Microsoft product development and usability testing, the Active Server provides some great little text manipulation utilities.

***CreateObject*** Five Server Components ship with the Active Server: `AdRotator`, Browser Capabilities, Content Linking, `TextStream`, and the Database Access Component. (This last component exposes interfaces to three more objects, the `Connection`, `Command`, and `RecordSet` objects.) The `Server.CreateObject` method is how to create instances of all these components. To be more precise: each of these components produces an object. Remember, an object contains both data (properties) and programs (methods). Once created, these component objects act on things they were designed to do. For example, the `TextStream` component produces an object that acts on text files. Most of what you do with text files—opening and closing, reading, and writing—qualifies as utilities, something done the same way over and over again.

Because you tackle these utilities in alphabetic order, the first one you examine is the `HTMLEncode` method.

***HTMLEncode*** `Server.HTMLEncode` is closely related to `Response.Write` and, in special cases, to the implicit write method (for example, text appearing outside .ASP code tags). All of these methods write to the outgoing HTML data stream. To sort all this out, first see what the `Server.HTMLEncode` method needs for input and what it does with that input after processing.

Simply put, `Server.HTMLEncode` wants to see exactly what you do. If you want to see the actual HTML source code on your client's window, you give that string of characters to `Server.HTMLEncode`. It's pretty smart. It knows which characters in the input string will cause confusion to the rendering engine in the client, so it replaces these problematical characters with something the client will properly render.

The most obvious culprit is the angle brackets; they're the characters that tell the client rendering engine that the following text is HTML source and that it should interpret the text as commands.

**N O T E** Take a look at the HTML_tips_traps.asp file on the CD for examples and comparisons of these issues and methods. ■

ASP development adds another problem, for the <> characters can confuse the server too, and the server will be confused before the client will be. In fact, it's possible that the ActiveX Server

Engine will make your original problem even more confusing for the client. Confused? Try this again, only differently:

On both the client-side and the server-side, the < and > tells the software that everything in between those characters is source code, not text. But when you actually want to print the angle bracket (say you want to display an actual HTML tag on the screen), how do you tell the software to print it instead of interpret it? That depends on which software you're worried about. Any text surrounded by angle brackets is interpreted. On the server, any text surrounded by <% and %> is interpreted.

---

**CAUTION**

When trying to output HTMLEncoded text, mistakes can be hard to interpret because of the mess it can make of the resulting HTML data stream. Other times context plays a role so that the same nonalphanumeric characters can have different effects.

In the latter category, my favorite is sending %> to the HTML data stream. Sometimes, the Active Server chokes when it hits what it thinks is the end of .ASP code without first having encountered <%, the beginning tag for ASP code. Yet if you refresh the errant .ASP file, it seems no longer to be confused.

The safest approach is to experiment with the various techniques, find the one that gives the most consistent results, and stick with it. For example, you have already seen that sending %> can be trouble. Mitigating the potential threat by using Server.HTMLEncode is a good idea, but remember to include the escape character. The syntax is

```
<%=Server.HTMLEncode("%\>")%>
```

---

**N O T E**    Server.HTMLEncode needs the = before it in order to send the encoded stream to the client. This is because the output of Server.HTMLEncode can be used in ways other than writing to the client (for example, its output can be the input to Response.Write).

Response.Write does not need the equal sign (output to the client is implicit; it's the only thing it knows how to do), but the equal sign won't get in its way either. You may find it easier to always remember to put the = before methods whose output goes to the client (including Response.Write) than it is to remember which one doesn't need it.

On the other hand, if others are going to see your source code, you might want to write it properly. Otherwise, it's like leaving too much space between your tie and your belt; to those who care about such minutiae, the appearance can be embarrassing. ▪

---

Generally speaking, using the Server.HTMLEncode method is safer than the Response.Write method. The reason: Server.HTMLEncode always replaces the angle brackets with their *entity names*. Entity names are the special character strings that begin with the & and end with the semicolon. Examples include &gt;, which always yields the ">" character; &lt;, which yields the "<";  , which is a non-breaking space. Response.Write sends the literal character to the output stream, so it might backfire on you (but at least it will only be the client that gets confused).

**N O T E**   A text file on the CD lists the most common entity names. But you shouldn't need to bother; `Server.HTMLEncode` makes the list almost obsolete (except for the one entity name `Server.HTMLEncode` can't capture, the perennial ` `). ■

**T I P**   When troubleshooting this kind of code, you can sometimes squeeze a little more troubleshooting data out of your Web client by looking at the HTML source code. The ActiveX Server Engine writes to the data stream up to the point of error, and sometimes it prints more data than is reported by the error alert.

**MapPath**   The `MapPath` method is necessary because of one thing: the definition of an .ASP application; namely, all files stored in and under a virtual directory.

**N O T E**   If you come from a Novell network environment, you are already familiar with logical drives (indeed, in the old Dark ages Of Software (DOS) days we had operating system commands like `SUBST` that also mapped directories to drive letters). ■

IIS also uses this kind of technique to shorten the identity of a collection of files. This works great under HTTP with its object-centric orientation. The virtual directory is part of the URL for the Web site. But what happens when you need to do something to a file in that virtual directory, and you are not going to access it through a Web server?

For example, previously you learned about the Content Linking Component. This component needs access to a text file and will access it through the server's file system.

To access the file properly, the Content Linking Component must know where the file is. If the file is stored somewhere in the virtual directory, you can find it by using the `MapPath` method relative to the virtual directory. If the file is somewhere else, you need to take your bearings from the `ServerVariables` Collection's `PATH_INFO` variable. Here's how you do each thing:

Say that your application is called /web (that's its virtual directory) and that it is physically located in the c:/data/web directory. Recall that when you set up the virtual directory in the Internet Information Services Manager application, you specified this physical directory then. The `PATH_INFO` variable in the `ServerVariables` Collection keeps a record of this physical path. Therefore, when you invoke the `Server.MapPath` method using the `Request.ServerVariables("PATH_INFO")` syntax, you return the following string:

```
c:\data\web
```

If, in fact, the file you need to access is inside the virtual directory, you can specify its location relative to that directory. Here, the presence or absence of an initial slash character (forward or backward are recognized) controls whether or not the mapped path starts at the root of the virtual directory or relative to the current one.

If the parameter passed to the `MapPath` method begins with a slash, then `MapPath` begins at the top of the virtual directory. If no slash precedes the path passed to `MapPath`, then the result of the method is the fully qualified path to the file from the current directory.

**N O T E** This is one of those topics that is so hard to describe, yet easy to demonstrate. We have included another of our famous demo applets on the CD to show you, not only what we've been talking about, but also how you might use it in your own applications. ■

**URLEncode**    You have already broached the topic of URLEncoding; you encountered it in the context of the QueryString passed in a GET request to the server. In this chapter, you have made your own query strings when you wanted to call an .ASP file in a particular way (see the demo_cookies and demo_servervars .asp files for examples). You also noted that Cookies are URLEncoded (although you won't need to encode Cookie values since the Response.Cookies method does that for you).

The most common use for this method may just be in passing variable strings between .ASP pages. To render a string according to the rules of URL encoding, simply send the string to the Response.URLEncode method like this:

```
<% http://lab/test.asp?Server.URLEncode("Katy Mansfield-Corning") %>
```

and you will send the correct string to the test.asp file that looks like this:

```
Katy+Mansfield%2DCorning
```

## Managing Data With *CreateObject* (ADODB...)

The use of the Server.CreateObject method is noted at the end of this chapter for the sake of consistency. Note the Server Component identifier used in the section heading. The "ADO" part of it stands for ActiveX Data Objects. The developers had to add the "DB" when they released Beta 2 because the underlying Server Component had been substantially improved. If you look in the Registry, you will see an entry in there identified by "ADODB." The ellipsis is there because there are three objects intrinsic to the ADODB component.

Before you leave this topic note two things:

■ Whenever you invoke this method in an .ASP file, you must always use the Server.CreateObject syntax.

■ Remember that you also can use ADO in programming environments other than .ASP (Visual Basic, for example).

Outside of .ASP, the CreateObject is handled as it usually is in that environment. Again, with VB, the syntax is simply CreateObject.

# From Here...

With this chapter, you leave the Server Objects for the moment. Later in the book, you will need everything you've learned so far. The following chapter concludes Part V with a discussion of a very important part of .ASP development—Server Components.

Server Components permit something crucial to all modern programming development environments—extensibility. What the "Integrated Development Environment (IDE)" did for developers using Visual C++, Visual J++, Visual Basic 5.0, and the Visual InterDev, server components will do for users of applications written by Active Server Pages developers.

Perhaps put a better way, the advent of Server Components makes it possible to extend the functionality of the Active Server without interrupting what it already does so well. If the IDE was a boon to professional programmers, then Server Components will have the same impact on power users and Webmasters who do not hold themselves to a professional programming standard. It's an IDE for the rest of us.

- Chapter 15, "Building a Foundation of Interactivity with *Request* and *Response* Objects," shows how you can use these objects to build interactive Web sites with a minimal amount of code.

- Chapter 17, "Constructing Your Own Server Components," shows you how to create your own components, including design-time components that help you create Active Server Pages.

- Chapter 25, "Introducing ActiveX Data Objects," explains this exciting new technology for including data access in Web pages.

# Constructing Your Own Server Components

**Programming with class**

Exposing the methods within your classes provides the functionality of your server component.

**Understanding the OLE server**

Learn how an OLE server will become your server component.

**Creating the component**

Get a step-by-step guide to server component construction in Visual Basic.

**O**ftentimes you'll want to use server-side functions that just cannot be accomplished through the use of a scripting language, either alone or in combination with the components that ship with Active Server Pages. When you hit this particular wall, you have a few options. You can check the market and try to find prebuilt components that satisfy your requirements. You can contract with a third party to build a component for you. Or you can build your own component.

When you create your own server components, you have the benefit of using a component built by someone who really understands your business. As you encapsulate line-of-business functions within your components, you can use them on your server and in your client applications or even give them to your clients for use on their systems (for a nominal fee, of course). This chapter focuses on creating server components by using the Visual Basic programming language. If you already are familiar with VB, this will be a snap. If you are coming to VB a little later in the game, this chapter will provide you with the skills to begin creating components right away. ■

# Why Use Visual Basic for Component Creation?

There are a number of reasons why Visual Basic is an ideal tool for creating many of the server components that you will use. VB has grabbed the hearts and minds of millions of developers out here in the real world. As you already have learned, VBScript is a subset of Visual Basic. Everything you've learned about VBScript is immediately applicable to development in the VB environment, with a number of useful features not found in its younger sibling.

You will find (or already have found) hundreds of custom controls, such as ActiveX Components, that currently are available for use with Visual Basic. More controls seem to be available each day. The rub is that most of these components require an interface to use them in your development. VB provides a perfect way to wrap the functionality of these third-party components for use in your Active Server Pages development. In addition to the custom controls available in Visual Basic, you also have access to the Win32 API. You can access any number of functions on the system that are impossible to get to using scripting alone. You also can use almost any DLL (dynamic-link library) to add additional functionality to the components that you create.

As stated previously, millions of developers have used Visual Basic for a number of years because of its ease of use and flexibility and the speed with which they can develop applications. If you were to hire a new Active Server Pages developer, it is likely that he or she would have VB skills. If not, those skills are just a class or two away.

Another advantage of developing your server components in VB is that there are so many resources available to help you. There are forums on CompuServe, and AOL. The Microsoft Web site provides a wealth of information about VB (a knowledge base, news groups), as well as links to other valuable sites. There are hundreds of quality sites out there dedicated to Visual Basic.

Of course, another benefit of developing your components in Visual Basic is that there are so many excellent sources of information available to help you in your own neighborhood. There are hundreds of texts at your local bookstore with *even more* information about creating objects in VB than you'll find in this one chapter alone.

# Finding A Touch of Class

Component creation is a process of building objects that you will instantiate in your Active Server Pages scripts. To create objects in Visual Basic, you need to define a blueprint to expose the functions within your object to other applications, in this case ASP. You will use classes to provide this blueprint, or definition and interface, for your objects.

Creating class modules in Visual Basic is the method through which you can develop reusable components. Public procedures within classes are the method through which you can expose functionality from within your class to other objects within your application and to other applications within the system. By creating your functionality within the class framework, you are able to harness the incredible power and ease of use in Visual Basic for your component needs.

# Introducing Classes

As you begin to develop components, consider some of the following details of class development. A *class* is the description, or blueprint of the object that will be created when the class is instantiated. You can follow some basic guidelines from general object-oriented development to ensure that your class will be a good component candidate.

The idea of *data-hiding* or encapsulation, is a fundamental principle of object-oriented development. What this means in practice is that access to the data variables within your class should be performed only through member functions of the class. Effectively, you will be hiding the class data from the client program. This ensures that the client application will not unwittingly corrupt the Private object data. This also lets you change the Private members of your class under the covers—without changing the Public interface.

Think of your component in terms of properties and methods. The *properties* are a set of definitions that control attributes of your component. *Methods* are the actions that the component will take on your behalf. Look to the components that ship with Active Server Pages and Visual Basic to see how the properties and methods work together to provide the components' functionality.

Always strive for limiting the functionality of a component to a basic set. Don't try to put the entire business in a single component. Try to view component creation as an exercise in creating building blocks. If the blocks are too big, you lose flexibility in the design; if they are too small, it will take forever to build the structure.

# Understanding Object Lifetime: Class Creation and Destruction

When the client application instantiates your object (class), there is an opportunity to perform one-time initialization actions for your class. You do this in the Class_Initialize event of the class object. This is a handy place to initialize Private data members and perform any initial error checking, as well as any other functions that need to occur before any of the class methods (functions and/or subroutines) are invoked.

There is also an opportunity to perform actions immediately before the object is destroyed. This processing is performed in the Class_Terminate event of the class. You can destroy any memory that was allocated during the life of the class or perform any other required cleanup.

# Instantiating an Object

Once you have defined and coded the class, you can create an instance of the class in Visual Basic by initializing an object variable to that class type:

```
Dim TestClass as New ClassName
```

You also can instantiate a class object by using the CreateObject method within your script:

```
Dim TestClass
Set TestClass = Server.CreateObject("Component.ClassName")
```

The variable `TestClass` now has a reference to the newly created object. Now you can invoke any of the methods of the newly created object by using the method name with the newly created object reference:

```
Avalue = TestClass.MethodName(Parm1, Parm2... ParmN)
```

When you are finished with the object, set the object variable to `Nothing` to ensure that all memory associated with the object will be released.

```
Set TestClass = Nothing
```

## Understanding Class Methods

When you learn about the methods of a class, you are learning about the set of `Public` functions and subroutines that reside within the class. Methods are just a convenient way to talk about the procedures available to the user of a component. This is also an easy way to think of these functions, like the methods available to any of the other *objects* within Visual Basic: the form methods, the button methods, and all of the other intrinsic objects in VB that expose their functionality (methods) to you as a developer.

Any subroutine or function that you create in your class module will be visible to the client program if it is declared as `Public`.

```
Public Function CalculatePayment(LoanAmount, Term, InterestRate)
```

When you use the `Public` identifier in front of the function declaration, the `CalculatePayment` function is *visible* to any client that instantiates the class or to any variable that is assigned a reference to it. `Private` functions within a class are used to provide functions and services that the `Public` functions can use to fulfill client requests.

## Using Property Procedures

In Visual Basic development, as well as HTML development, user interface objects have properties that you set to determine the look and actions of these elements. For example, to access the background color of a text box in the VB environment, you would access its `BackColor` property:

```
text1.BackColor = &H00FFFF00&
```

The use of properties is a simple and intuitive way to access the attributes of an object. You can provide the same functionality to access the properties of your components. This will be a familiar syntax to VB and Active Server Pages developers and will let you use the `<object>.<method>` notation with any component that you create. Using property procedures also will let you immediately validate the value of the property being set. If invalid data is passed in or a value out of range is provided, the component can respond immediately, instead of waiting for some point downstream in your code to notify the calling program of the error.

Once you have determined what properties you want to provide for your class, you will set aside `Private` variables to hold these properties. You then need to provide the framework for accessing and updating these class properties.

**The *Let* Procedure**    The `Let` procedure enables your class users to set the value of a class property under the class's control. Take a quick look at a `Let` property procedure:

```
Public Property Let HostName(aHost)
   If Not Len(aHost) Then
      Err.Raise vbObjectError + CTRANSACT_ERR_HOSTLEN, "CTransact.Host", _
               "Set Host Name: Host Length Invalid"
   Else
      m_sHost = aHost
   End If
End Property
```

You certainly could declare the `Private` class variable `m_sHost` (declared as a string) as a `Public` variable and then let the user set the host name directly. If you did that, you wouldn't have the opportunity to ensure that the host name was valid. Within the `Let` procedure in the preceding code, in addition to testing for a zero length string, you could also try to ping the host to ensure that it was a valid address or perform additional validations on the passed-in value. When using the `Let` procedure, you can provide the calling application with immediate feedback as to the status of the component property being set.

In addition to allowing for data validation when the property is set, you also can update other associated variables within your class. If there is another property, say the port to connect to, that is based upon the host that is entered, you can set the port property when the host name is set. This again cannot be performed if you just declared the `m_sHost` variable as `Public`. Using the `Let` procedure can ensure that you don't get any component breaker values in the `Private` variables of your class. If, for example, a user were to put a `NULL` value into a variable, it could easily generate a runtime error in another method that references that variable. The rule continues to be better safe than sorry.

**The *Get* Procedure**    The majority of your coding will set property values of the objects created within the script. Most of you could go the better part of a day without ever requesting the value of an object's property, but there are times when you need to check a property and determine its value. A good example would be the `.text` property of an entry field.

To provide the getting of a property within your class, you create a `Property Get` procedure. Using the preceding example, you would provide the `HostName` property procedure to your calling application with the following procedure:

```
Public Property Get HostName() As Variant
   HostName = m_sHost
End Property
```

# *Public* Procedures in Your Classes

The `Let` and `Get` procedures are wonderful for creating properties within your class. Eventually though, you need your class to perform some function in order to become useful. To expose functionality to an external application from within your class, you declare a function or subroutine `Public`. This enables the application that created an instance of your class to access the procedure.

Any procedure that is not directly used by the client application should be declared `Private`. This ensures that the client does not inadvertently call a function or subroutine that it should not. `Private` functions are used to perform internal activities for the component. As you will see in the component example, "Creating Your Server Component," the `Public` interface usually is the smallest part of the class code. The component interface is intentionally kept small and simple. If the implementation of the method changes (the `Private` functions), there is no need to change the external (`Public`) function declaration.

## Handling Errors Within Your Classes

There are two ways you can handle errors within your classes. The first requires you to provide all methods as functions and return a completion code for all `Public` procedures. This requires a well-defined set of return codes and requires the client program to check for errors inline after each call to the component returns.

A better way to handle error conditions within your class is to use the VB error-handling framework. If an error occurs within a class module, you will use the `Raise` method of the `Err` object to pass notification of the error to the calling program. The error percolates through the procedure levels to a place where an error handler has been registered within the calling program.

You notify the client application of an error by calling the `Raise` method of the `Err` object. The syntax for raising an error is shown here:

```
Err.Raise(Number, Source, Description, HelpFile, HelpContext)
```

The only required parameter is the `Number`. When you are creating server components, you usually should include the `Source` and the `Description` parameters as well. Say that you are trying to open a local file in a method in your new class. The file cannot be opened because the program cannot find the file on the disk. A runtime error that the component invoked in your code looks something like this:

```
Err.Raise vbObjectError + 55, "CFileMgr.ReadFile," "Cannot find file specified"
```

The constant `vbObjectError` is a base number to add to your component specific error number. This is the constant that is used when raising runtime errors within an OLE server.

# OLE Servers—Exposing Your Class

Up to now, a number of pages in this chapter have been spent discussing the class module and how it provides the blueprint for your Active Server Pages when your component is invoked. This is well and good, but components live by more than class alone. You need to wrap the class in a suitable way so that you actually can create an instance of it. To do this, you create the class within an OLE server.

There are two types of OLE servers that you can create with Visual Basic. OLE servers can run either *out-of-process* or *in-process*. The distinction is basically evident in the server names. An out-of-process server executes in a separate process from the client application that creates an instance of the server (component). An in-process server is packaged as a dynamic-link library and, when instantiated, shares the same process space with the application.

An in-process server has a number of inherent strengths that ensure that it is the type you will build when creating your server components. First, because the server will be running in the same process space as the calling application, the component will be faster, because there is no need to pass data across process boundaries. Second, because the server is packaged as a DLL, if it is already loaded in memory when a new instance is created, there is virtually no load time for the new object.

There are, however, a number of restrictions to keep in mind when creating in-process servers as components in Visual Basic:

- The servers are available only as 32-bit code.

  You must create the components by using Visual Basic Professional or Enterprise Edition, version 4.0 or above. No 16-bit code support is provided.

- One `Public` class member is required.

  Because the visible functionality of your object is defined by the `Public` classes within your DLL, at least one class must be `Public`.

- No user interface allowed.

  Any user interface that you would embed into your class will not be visible to the browser requesting information from an Active Server Pages script and potentially could lock the server process requesting the service.

- No static or global variables.

  If you package multiple classes in your component, avoid the use of globals or statics in any shared modules. These will only complicate your coding and can lead to incorrect or corrupted memory across multiple instances of any given object.

# Creating Your Server Component

It's time to begin creating your Active Server Pages component. It's useful to take a moment and discuss what it is, exactly, that your component will do for you. Many of you are working in heterogeneous environments, interacting with PCs, minis, mainframes, and, yes, even UNIX boxes. The component that you are going to build will provide access to a number of transactions living on a multiple host system.

Here's the scenario: Say that for a number of years, your hypothetical company has been processing TCP/IP requests from external vendors to authorize credit card transactions. You have a well-defined transaction header structure that is used to send a transaction through the system. You want to provide the same authorization transactions from your Web servers.

There are a number of commercial packages out there (even Microsoft's own Internet Control Pack) that provide generic TCP/IP communications. The problem with most of these packages is that they are set up to provide an event when a transaction (or any data, for that matter) is received back from a previous request. By design, they are *asynchronous,* meaning that the receipt of the response from the transaction occurs some time later. The program or thread execution will not *block* waiting on a response from the server. This is ideal for interactive client/server applications where you are doing other things while waiting for a response (or multiple responses). Due to the stateless nature of connections on the Internet, there is no facility to continue to process the script and then respond to this "transaction complete" event later.

So what you are going to build is a TCP/IP transaction class that lets you call a method that sends a transaction to your host system and waits for a response before returning from the procedure call. All formatting of the transaction takes place within the class, as well as all of the communications details. The only things that the script must provide are a host name and port to connect to, an account to validate, and an amount to authorize. We're sure you can think of a number of situations in which you would want to leverage TCP/IP transactions from your servers. This component can easily be modified to accept different header and transaction types. Out-of-the-box, it should give you a good sense of the steps involved in building your own server components.

## First Steps

The first thing you need to do is ensure that you have a copy of the 32-bit version of Visual Basic, either the Professional or Enterprise Edition. Then open up a new project to begin creation of your transaction component.

It's that easy! Now you are ready to begin.

## Slimming Down the Server

When you start a new project in Visual Basic, there are a number of custom controls and object references that get added to your project for free, or they seem so at the time. In fact, they are not free at all. If you open the file AUTO32LD.vbp (found in the directory where the VB32.exe lives on your system) in Notepad, you see the default objects that are loaded each time you request a new project. To permanently change these defaults, you can edit this file to remove the object references.

Any component or reference that you do not use but do retain in your project when it is built, tags along for the ride, even though it never is invoked. This adds overhead to your application and swells the number of disks required to distribute your new component.

So now you will remove all the custom controls that you can from your newly created default project to reduce this overhead:

1. Select Tools, Custom Controls, or press Ctrl+T.
2. Select Tools, References.
3. Once Form1 is selected, select File, Remove File from the main menu. This removes the form from the project.

The first step brings up a dialog box with all the controls available for your use, shown in Figure 17.1, as well as those currently active in your project. Those that are active will have the check box checked. Remove all the currently selected objects by removing the check in any checked box. Then click the OK button to save your changes.

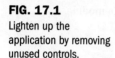

**FIG. 17.1**
Lighten up the application by removing unused controls.

The second step brings up a dialog box with all the references available for your use, in addition to those currently in use for the project. If you are not going to be performing any database functions by using the Jet database engine, remove the reference to the DAO library. This cuts your distribution down by over a meg. If there are any other references that you will not need, remove them as well by unchecking the checked boxes.

There are no user interface attributes in your server component, so remove the default form that loaded in your new project. To remove Form1, as outlined in step three, select the form from the project window. If the project window is not visible, press Ctrl+R to show it.

## Main Street: The *Sub Main* Function

While all functionality that you will expose to your client application—in this case, an Active Server Pages script—is through the `Public` methods of a class, there still is component-level initialization that can take place when the component is created. Component-level initialization takes place in the `Sub Main` procedure of the component.

To add the `Sub Main` procedure to your new project, you need to add a code module. To do so, follow these steps:

1. Select Insert, Module from the main menu.
2. Press F4 to pull up the module properties.
3. Change the name `Module1` to `CTransact_Main`.
4. Move back to the newly named `CTransact_Main` code window.
5. Type in **Sub Main**, and then press Enter.

These steps add a new module to the project. The module defaults to `Module1` in the project window. You are creating a component that will provide transaction processing for your server, and this component will be called `CTransact`, so you will call the module with `Sub Main` in it `CTransact_Main`.

You now have created an empty Sub Main procedure in the CTransact_Main module:

```
Sub Main()

End Sub
```

Because you will perform no component-level initialization in your transaction component, you can leave the Sub Main procedure empty. Even though no explicit initialization takes place, you must have a Sub Main procedure defined in your component, or you will receive an error when you try to instantiate the component.

## The Project Dialog Box

Now is a good time to save your project. Before you do that, though, set up the project so that the compiler creates an OLE in-process server instead of a normal Windows executable program. The settings regarding the code generation are found on the Options dialog box. To get there, follow these steps:

1. Select Project, Properties from the main menu.
2. Select the General tab on the dialog box.
3. Select ActiveX DLL in the Project Type selection.

As shown in Figure 17.2, you will notice a number of user-definable options for the project. The first thing you need to do is specify the Project Name. The Project Name will be the name you will use when specifying an object to create within your Active Server Pages script.

1. Type the name **CTransact** in the Project Name field.
2. The last field that you will edit on the project is the Application Description entry field. This will be the text that you will see when you browse the objects and components currently available on a system. You want to provide a short and concise description of your component.
3. Type **TCP/IP Transaction Black Box** in the Application Description field.
4. Click the OK button to save the project changes that you just made.

**FIG. 17.2**
The Project tab defines your component naming.

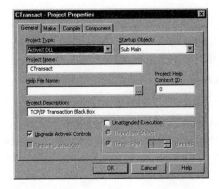

5. Select <u>F</u>ile, Sa<u>v</u>e Project from the main menu.

You will be prompted to save the `CTransact_Main.bas` module in the default directory. Accept the default directory or create a new directory from the Save As dialog box, and then save the module. When prompted for the project name to save, replace the Project1 name with `CTransact`.

Congratulations! You have just completed the first task in creating your component.

# Creating Your Transaction Class

Now the real work begins. Up to now you have been dealing with the administration of creating a server component, setting up the project, selecting project options, and creating a main procedure. Now you begin to develop the class data and methods that will perform the transactions that you have been working toward.

The first step is, of course, to create the class module. The class information will live in its own class code module, a file with a .CLS extension. To create the class module, select <u>I</u>nsert, <u>C</u>lass Module from the main menu.

Now you've added a new class module to your project. If the class module is not currently selected, select the module from the project window by double-clicking the name Class1 or by selecting Class1 and then clicking the View Code button of the project window. Remember that if your project window is not visible, you can pop it up using Ctrl+R.

In the next few steps, you will rename your class, set it to be `Public`, and select the instancing options. With the class code window active, press the F4 key to bring up the class properties window. It will look like the one shown in Figure 17.3.

1. Change the name Class1 to `Transaction`.
2. Set the `Public` property to True.
3. Set the `Instancing` property to Creatable MultiUse.

The first of the preceding steps, changing the name, is important, because the name of the class is referenced when you create an instance of your component. Just as you take care in naming your class methods, you need to make a good choice for the class name.

The `Public` property determines the visibility of the class outside your OLE server. If you were to leave the class private, no one could access any of the transaction functions that you will build into the class.

The last property of your class that you set was the `Instancing` property. This property determines how the OLE server is managed when it is instantiated by a client application. You selected the `Creatable Multi-Use` property, which enables the object, if already created, to be supplied by the existing object. If no object currently exists, one will be created. Contrast this to the `Creatable Single Use` option, where each `CreateObject` request causes a separate copy of the OLE server to be started. The Creatable Multi-Use option uses memory more efficiently and is the primary choice for externally created components like the one you are building.

**FIG. 17.3**
Editing class properties is just like changing any VB object's properties.

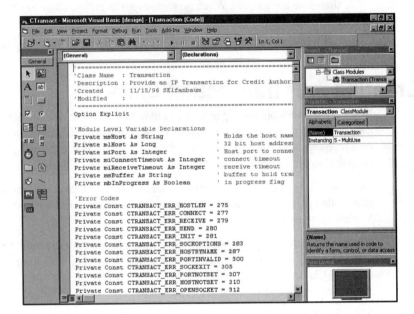

## The WinSock Methods

To perform TCP/IP transactions, you will be using the Windows Sockets library calls in this section. One of the nice things about Visual Basic is that you can declare just about any dynamic-link library and use it in the VB environment. To use these WinSock functions within your component, you need to declare them to Visual Basic. This is done with the declare statements shown in Listing 17.1, in the general code of the Transaction class.

---

**Listing 17.1   TRANSACTION.CLS—Declaring the WinSock Functions to Visual Basic**

```
'Winsock calls in VB format, for 32 bit, WSOCK32.DLL
Private Declare Function bind Lib "wsock32.dll" (ByVal s As Long, _
                              addr As sockaddr_type, _
                              ByVal namelen As Long) As Long
Private Declare Function inet_addr Lib "wsock32.dll" (ByVal s _
                              As String) As Long
Private Declare Function gethostbyname Lib "wsock32.dll" _
                              (ByVal hostname As String) As Long
```

---

There are a number of other Win32 API functions that you will be using in your class. You can find all the declarations for these functions in the TRANSACTION.CLS module, in the declarations section.

There is also a number of helper procedures within the class that handle the dirty work of the TCP/IP communications. Generally, the flow for the transactions follows this path:

1. Connect to the host.
2. Send the transaction to the host.
3. Receive a response.
4. Check the return code of the response.
5. Pass the response back to the calling application.

Each of the preceding steps has a `Private` procedure that handles one part of the communications chore. Listing 17.2 shows the code for the `fn_Connect` function, which connects to the host system. All the helper procedures do one activity and return a Boolean value if the activity is completed successfully.

### Listing 17.2 TRANSACTION.CLS—The *Connect* Function

```
Private Function fn_Connect(iSocket As Long, lAddress As Long, iPort As Integer)
As Boolean
    Dim sockaddr As sockaddr_type
    Dim rc As Integer

    sockaddr.sin_family = AF_INET
    sockaddr.sin_port = htons(iPort)
    sockaddr.sin_addr = lAddress
    sockaddr.sin_zero = " "

    rc = connect(iSocket, sockaddr, Len(sockaddr))
    If rc = SOCKET_ERROR Then
        Err.Raise vbObjectError + CTRANSACT_ERR_CONNECT,
                    "Transaction.fn_InitSockets", fn_GetLastSockError()
        Exit Function
    End If

    fn_Connect = True
End Function
```

If the connection fails, an error is raised, passing back the error code as well as the text describing the reason for the connection failure. The `fn_GetLastSockError` function returns the error text for the most recent socket error, utilizing a call to the Windows Sockets extension function `WSAGetLastError()`. For additional information about the WinSock 1.1 specification, check out the Microsoft Web site at **http://www.microsoft.com**.

# *Private* Class Variables

The first thing you need to do after setting up the declarations for WinSock and Win32 API functions is to create your `Private` class variables, as shown in Listing 17.3. They are dimensioned as `Private` so that your client does not have access to them, and cannot accidentally change one of their values at an inopportune time.

---

**Listing 17.3   TRANSACTION.CLS—Declaring Class Variables *Private***

```
'Module Level Variable Declarations
Private msHost As String           ' Holds the host name
Private mlHost As Long             ' 32 bit host address
Private miPort As Integer          ' Host port to connect to
Private miConnectTimeout As Integer   ' connect timeout
Private miReceiveTimeout As Integer   ' receive timeout
Private msBuffer As String         ' buffer to hold transmitted data
Private mbInProcess As Boolean     ' in process flag
```

---

It is great that you have all these `Private` variables to use in your class, but you also need to get some pertinent information from the component user so you can send your transaction on to the correct host. In the section "Using Property Procedures," we talked about property procedures that enable your users to set properties within your component. Two properties that must be set for you to perform your transaction are the `Host` and `Port` properties. These will provide you with the name of the host to send the transaction to, as well as the port to which the host will be listening. The property procedure for the `Host` property is shown in Listing 17.4.

---

**Listing 17.4   TRANSACTION.CLS—Property Procedures Enforce Data Hiding**

```
Public Property Let Host(aHost As String)
    If Len(aHost) = 0 Then
        Err.Raise CTRANSACT_ERR_HOSTLEN, "Transaction.Host", "Set Host Name: Host
➥Length Invalid"
        Exit Property
    End If
    mlHost = fn_GetHostByName(aHost)
    If mlHost = 0 Then
        Err.Raise CTRANSACT_ERR_HOSTBYNAME, "Transaction.Host",
➥fn_GetLastSockError()
        Exit Property
    End If

    msHost = aHost
End Property
```

---

Notice in the code in Listing 17.4 that you are handling errors by raising runtime errors that your component user will catch in his or her code. If the Host length sent in by the application is zero, you will raise an error. Also, if the host name cannot be resolved to a physical address (the `fn_GetHostByName` function provides the name resolution services), an error is also raised. If you were setting properties just by allowing your component user access to a `Public` variable `sHost`, you would have to check for a valid host name each time you performed a transaction. By handling this check through the use of a property procedure, you can raise the error if needed immediately when the property is set.

# The *Public Transact* Method

There is only one `Public` procedure in the `CTransact` class. This is the procedure that initiates the transaction and returns a completion code to the calling program. The function must be declared as `Public` so it will be visible from outside the component.

The first part of the method (or procedure) is the declaration. Parameters are passed to the method and a return code of type `Long` will be sent back when the transaction is completed.

```
Public Function Transact(transaction As Integer, Version As Integer, _
        inBuffer As String) As Long
```

There are a number of authorization transactions that can be processed by the back-end service. Also, to support new versions of transactions as time goes on, a version is passed in as a parameter as well. This is a handy way to enhance transactions while not having to change any of the clients currently using a previous version. The buffer that is passed in is the authorization string formatted by the Active Server Pages script.

The first part of the code, found in Listing 17.5, ensures that a valid `Host` property has been set as well as a value for the `Port` property.

**Listing 17.5   TRANSACTION.CLS—Verifying that Required Class Properties Have Been Set**

```
If miPort = 0 Then
    Err.Raise CTRANSACT_ERR_PORTNOTSET, "CTransact.Transact", _
            "Port must be set prior to invoking Transaction method"
    Exit Function
End If
If mlHost = 0 Then
    Err.Raise CTRANSACT_ERR_HOSTNOTSET, "CTransact.Transact", _
            "Port must be set prior to invoking Transaction method"
    Exit Function
End If
End If
```

You check for a valid host when the property is set, but you must also ensure that the property has been set before you begin the transaction. You could have added another `Private` variable as a flag, say `blnHostSet`, but it is just as easy to check the value of the `miPort` and `mlHost` variables. It also saves a bit of memory (the less module-level variables you use, the better).

The interaction with the host system is through a standard header that is defined by the type `TRAN_HDR`. All of the transactions are performed using this header, and the return code from the transaction will be put in the ReturnCode member of the TRAN_HDR type. Ideally, you would send the structure in the transaction. In the C or C++ programming languages, you would just cast the structure variable as a char * or a void * and be done with it. In Visual Basic, you need to send the transaction as a string. To do this, we ended up creating a little C DLL to perform the conversion from a string to a type and back again.

**N O T E**   On this book's CD, you'll find the source code for VBUTIL.DLL and the project files to re-create it by using Microsoft's Visual C++ product. ■

The next part of the code fills in the TRAN_HDR type, converts it to a structure, and prepares to send the transaction over the wire (see Listing 17.6).

**Listing 17.6   TRANSACTION.CLS—Using the VBUTIL *CopyStructToString* Function to Simplify the String Conversion**

```
hdr.PacketNumber = Format$(transaction, "00000000")
hdr.Version = Format$(Version, "0000")
hdr.ReturnCode = "9999"
hdr.OperatorNumber = ""
hdr.RecordLength = Len(hdr) + Len(inBuffer)

msg = Space$(Len(hdr))
rc = CopyStructToString(hdr, msg, Len(hdr))
```

Notice that you must pre-allocate the msg (which will host the string representation of the TRAN_HDR type) string by filling it with spaces equal to the size of the header into which you are going to copy it. If you forget to pre-allocate the msg string, you receive an error.

Now comes the heart of the communications functions. All the TCP/IP functions have been created for you as Private procedures in the class, and calling them within the Transact method is shown in Listing 17.7. As each function is called, the function returns codes that are checked after the call is made to ensure that you are still communicating with the host system.

**Listing 17.7   TRANSACTION.CLS—The Bulk of the Communication Is Transparent to the *Transact* Method**

```
socket = fn_OpenSocket()
    If socket = 0 Then
        Err.Raise CTRANSACT_ERR_OPENSOCKET, "CTransact.Transact",
➥fn_GetLastSockError()
        Exit Function
    End If

    If fn_Connect(socket, mlHost, miPort) Then
        If fn_SendData(socket, msg & inBuffer) Then
            msBuffer = fn_ReceiveData(socket, 60)
            If Len(msBuffer) Then
                rc = fn_CloseSocket(socket)
```

```
        rc = CopyStructToString(hdr, msBuffer, Len(hdr))
        retCode = hdr.ReturnCode
        ' remove rich header from data buffer
        msBuffer = Mid$(msBuffer, Len(hdr) + 1)
    Else
        Exit Function
    End If
  Else
    rc = fn_CloseSocket(socket)
    Err.Raise CTRANSACT_ERR_SEND, "CTransact.Transact",
➥fn_GetLastSockError()
    End If
  Else
    rc = fn_CloseSocket(socket)
  End If
```

There are a couple of return code type variables used in the Transact method. The first, retCode, holds the value of the returned code from the host transaction. This is a four-character string variable. The second, rc, is an integer that holds the transaction specific return code that is sent back to the calling program. Once you receive the return code (retCode) from the host, you interrogate it, as shown in Listing 17.8, to return the appropriate value to the calling application.

**Listing 17.8  TRANSACTION.CLS—Formatting the Return Code for Your Calling Application**

```
'Based upon the return code from the transaction, pass a value
  'to the calling app
  Select Case Left$(retCode, 2)
    Case "00"
      rc = TRANSACT_RC_SUCCESS
    Case "IL"
      rc = TRANSACT_RC_INVALID_ACCOUNT
    Case "IR"
      rc = TRANSACT_RC_INVALID_TRAN
    Case Else
      rc = TRANSACT_RC_SERVER_ERROR
  End Select

  Transact = rc
```

# Compiling the Component

The last step in building your transaction component is to generate the DLL. In the section "The Project Dialog Box," you set the project options to generate an OLE server. Now you just need to instruct the compiler to generate an OLE DLL:

1. Select File, Save Project from the main menu.
2. Select File, Make OLE DLL File.

That's it. You now have successfully built your first Active Server component. Of course, you can use this component with Visual Basic, Access, Excel, or any other application that supports OLE components. The new component was registered automatically for you on the system where it was initially created.

# Using Your New Server Component

Now that you have built the component, you need to create the form and Active Server Pages script to invoke that component. If you are going to use the component on a machine other than the one you created it on, you need to register the component on that machine.

## Registering Your New Object

When you create the OLE DLL file in the Visual Basic environment, the component is registered automatically on the machine where it is compiled. If you want to move the DLL and associated support files to another machine, you need to register the new control after you place it on the system. There are a couple of ways to do this. If you are going to distribute your component, you can create an installation program using the VB Setup Wizard or another third-party installation package. The control will be registered during the installation process.

You also can just move the files to the new machine and register the control using the REGSVR32.EXE program that ships with Visual Basic. You can find the registration application on the Visual Basic CD-ROM in the \TOOLS\PSS directory. Here's how to register the control by using the REGSVR32 program:

1. Move the component DLL, and any supporting files (VB40032.DLL for example) to the new machine.
2. Copy the REGSVR32.EXE file to a directory that is in the path on the target system (for example: \WINDOWS\SYSTEM).
3. Switch to the directory where you copied the DLL file.
4. Type **REGSVR32 COMPONENT.DLL**.
5. When the component has been registered, you receive a successfully registered dialog box. Click OK to dismiss the dialog box.

## Testing the Component

The easiest way to initially test your new component is to start another instance of Visual Basic, create a simple form, and create an instance of the component. Then you can set the properties and call the Transact method. This lets you fine-tune the component before you try to integrate it into your Active Server Pages scripts.

To test the component, start another instance of Visual Basic. Add a command button to the Form1 that's displayed at startup. Double-click the newly created command button to bring up the code window. Now type the following code found in Listing 17.9 into the code window to test your new component.

### Listing 17.9   form1.frm—Test Script for the New Component

```
Private Sub Command1_Click()
    Dim tran As New Transaction
    On Error GoTo COMMAND_ERR

    tran.Host = "localhost"
    tran.Port = 7511
    rc = tran.Transact(1000, 0, "TEST TRAN")
    MsgBox rc
Exit_Sub:
    Exit Sub

COMMAND_ERR:
    MsgBox "Error: " & Err.Number & " " & Err.Description
    Resume Exit_Sub
End Sub
```

The only action left to take before testing your component is to add a reference to it in your new project:

1.   Select Tools, References from the main menu.
2.   Scroll down the list and check TCP/IP Transaction Black Box.

While testing, it's helpful to force errors to ensure that error handling within the component is functioning correctly. For example, you can comment out the line `tran.Host = "localhost"`. This generates an error because, as you may remember from the `HostName` property procedure code found in the section "The Let Procedure," the host must be set prior to calling the `Transact` function.

The error will be raised in the component and caught in the calling application by this directive:

```
On Error GoTo COMMAND_ERR
```

In your Active Server Pages development, you will not be popping up message boxes on your server, but at a minimum, you surely will want to log any communication errors for further study and return an appropriate response to your client.

## Component Testing on the Net

To test the component on your server, you need to build a simple form that calls an Active Server script and passes the appropriate parameters to it (account number, authorization amount). Then you can create your transaction object, call the `Transact` method, and return the results to your client.

**N O T E**   The HTML form code and the Active Server Pages script to process the authorization request can be found on this book's CD. (The assumption is that you might not want to read through another bare-bones HTML forms lecture at this juncture.)  All of the Visual Basic code for the component, as well as the CTRANSACT.DLL, are on the site. We also included the source code and DLL for the VBUTIL.DLL functions. ■

# From Here...

With this chapter on building your own components, you've finished the section on working with Active Server Pages objects and components. You've walked through the steps to generate your own components in Visual Basic. You now have all the tools and knowledge to create an infinite variety of applications for your Internet/intranet site by using custom components.

Here's what to look forward to in coming chapters:

- Chapter 25, "Introducing ActiveX Data Objects," covers the data access objects that ship with Active Server Pages. They provide an intuitive method of accessing external data from your ASP applications."

- Chapter 26, "Integrating the Advanced Data Connector into Web Database Applications," looks at the technology that ActiveX Data Objects uses to provide caching of data records on the client, and how this technology can be used with other Web technologies.

# Server-Side Programming

# CHAPTER 18

# The WinCGI Interface and Visual Basic

**D**atabase access is at the heart of nearly every worthwhile application. HTML does not support the idea of databases or calls to a database API. The primary way that Web programmers have added database functionality to their applications is by using the Common Gateway Interface (CGI).

CGI is not a piece of software, but rather an interface definition that allows an HTML application to invoke a program on the server and pass it data. Depending on the implementation of the client application, the server application may send data back to the browser for display to the user. Web search engines such as Yahoo! and AltaVista are good examples of this kind of database interactivity.

If you read Appendix A, "Standard CGI, WinCGI, and Visual Basic," you'll see that CGI technology does not lend itself to Visual Basic programming because of VB's lack of an easy way to read from stdin and write to stdout. Because of this, Bob Denny, one of the creators of WebSite, a Windows-based Web server, created Windows CGI, called WinCGI. WinCGI uses .INI files to pass data to and from the Web server. As a result, integrating Visual Basic into a Web server environment becomes not only practical, but straightforward.

**Learning Windows Common Gateway Interface Architecture**

Learn how WinCGI addresses many of the difficulties that Visual Basic programmers face when using CGI.

**Installing the WebSite Server**

Learn how to painlessly install the software you need.

**Testing the Server**

Learn how to verify that the server started and that you can view HTML from both local and remote computers.

**Managing the Server**

Learn how to properly care and feed the WebSite server.

**Understanding Windows CGI Internals**

Learn how the browser, the Web server software, and the server application work together.

**Creating a Windows CGI Application**

In just a few easy steps, create a simple example that works.

**Debugging Windows CGI Applications**

Create an application that accepts form input, processes it, and returns the results in HTML form.

In this chapter, you learn how to create applications in Visual Basic that make use of the WinCGI technology. You learn how to install and manage the WebSite server. You also learn how to create an HTML file that instructs the Internet server software to start the WinCGI application and pass the results back to the browser. ■

# Windows Common Gateway Interface Overview

The Windows Common Gateway Interface has become the most popular implementation of CGI for Visual Basic programmers. The reason for this is that WinCGI creates a support environment that addresses many of the difficulties that Visual Basic programmers face when using standard CGI. It is sold as part of the WebSite Internet server.

Web server software is oriented toward finding files on a server and passing them back to the client or browser. It is not designed to perform other tasks such as  sending automatic e-mail, reading a database, or updating a database. In order to accomplish these tasks, the designers of this popular Internet server created a product called the Windows CGI.

**N O T E**   Originally, WinCGI was a shareware product that ran under Windows 3.1. A 32-bit version of WinCGI has been written and is sold with WebSite version 1.1. WebSite 1.1 is a quality product that has the advantage of running under Windows 95, as well as under Windows NT 4.0.

You can obtain an evaluation copy of WebSite 1.1 by accessing the O'Reilly and Associates Web site at www.ora.com. If you are a non-profit organization, you may be able to deploy your server for free. ■

Two other ways are available to create a Web server that can use WinCGI. Netscape's FastTrack and Enterprise Web servers support WinCGI. In addition, there is a way of adding WinCGI support to Microsoft Internet Explorer 3.0. In the ActiveX SDK from Microsoft is an ISAPI programming example that implements WinCGI as an ISAPI DLL. The example  requires adding a Registry database entry and a little code modification to make it more usable, but if you are brave and have a little free time, then you might venture.

> **CAUTION**
>
> Microsoft's IIS Web server does not support WinCGI as a native interface, but only through the ISAPI extension provided in the ISAPI programming examples from the original ActiveX SDK. You will not be able to use any of the examples from this chapter with an IIS Web server without installing and configuring the ISAPI WinCGI extension.

All CGI programs suffer from performance problems when deployed on a Web site that has a lot of traffic. WinCGI is no exception. Part of the scalability problem comes from the architecture. According to the CGI specification, CGI starts a separate process for each request made and initiates the server application within that process. This approach consumes more resources than having one task create a separate thread for each request.

WinCGI adds to this overhead by using files to transfer data to and from the server application. The result is a very convenient programming environment that doesn't scale as well as some other approaches. The ISAPI DLL version described in the preceding paragraph could perform better than the other approaches because DLLs can be shared by multiple programs at the same time, reducing the overhead to a degree.

To do real programming by using Windows CGI, we have to install a server that supports this flavor of CGI. In the next sections, you learn how to install and manage the O'Reilly WebSite server. Then you will be ready to learn about the details of Windows CGI.

# Installing the WebSite Server

Before you can install WebSite server, you must obtain a copy of it. There are two easy ways to do this. The first way is to go to the O'Reilly and Associates Web site at www.ora.com and download an evaluation copy of the software. There are some strict licensing terms with this approach but the price is right. These terms shouldn't get in the way of someone who is teaching themselves about Web programming, but read them carefully before deploying a production system. You may have to purchase a copy of the server software to do this, depending on the non-profit status of your organization.

The second method is to purchase the manual for the server in a bookstore. The manual is called, *Build Your Own WebSite*, and its ISBN number is 1-56592-232-8. Included with the book is a CD that contains a single-license version of the server software. This version is virtually identical to the downloaded version, but it contains more utilities, which are really useful. In addition, it gives you something other than a bunch of Web pages to read to get you started. If this is your first attempt at webmeistering, you will need the manual.

Unlike most servers, WebSite runs under Windows95, as well as Windows NT. This can be an advantage because Windows 95 is much less expensive than Windows NT Server.

The minimum hardware requirements are as follows:

- 80486 CPU (Pentium 90 recommended)
- 12M RAM for Windows 95; 24M recommended
- 16M  RAM for Windows NT; 32M recommended
- 10M free space for program files
- VGA Video display adapter
- Modem

As you can see from this list, the hardware requirements are the same or less than you probably own as a minimum, and even the recommended hardware is only slightly larger than that which is common among programmer's machines at the time of this writing. In practice, the minimum hardware stated above is probably adequate for teaching yourself how to do development, and the recommended hardware will become necessary as you begin to deploy your server on the Internet, or a company intranet.

It may seem strange to pay for a Web server when Microsoft is providing Internet Information Server as part of the NT Server operating system. If you don't want to upgrade to NT Server, or if you require the built-in Windows CGI support, WebSite may be a better solution for you.

Installing the server software is painless if your machine is already set up for TCP/IP. TCP/IP is required for the server to function properly even if you are running stand alone with no plans to deploy your hardware on the net.

Should you install WebSite as an application or as an operating system service? The answer is that it depends on how you want to use it. Operating system services start up when the operating system boots up. This means that the computer can function as a Web server even when no one is logged on. It will restart automatically whenever the system has to be rebooted (such as after a power failure).

If you decide to use WebSite as an application, then you will have to start it manually, or put it in your startup group. This is actually a feature for a developer who only wants to run the server when doing actual programming and testing. You don't have to become familiar with the intricacies of system service management if you are not already up to speed on this topic. Starting off by using WebSite as an application is recommended, and you can change it to a service later if you decide to do so.

Software installation is also painless. You simply insert the CD in the drive and run the Setup.exe program on the disk. A garden variety setup procedure then appears and holds your hand while you answer a few questions. At this point, you are ready to test the server.

# Testing the WebSite Server

The next step in the installation process is the testing of the server. This testing verifies that:

- The server started up
- You can view an HTML file from the local computer
- You can view an HTML file from a remote computer
- You can run the server self-test

The first step is to start the server. You do this by choosing the WebSite Server icon from the WebSite 1.1 programs, as shown in Figure 18.1.

This should start the WebSite software. You can see if the server is loaded by looking in the Tray portion of the Task bar, as shown in Figure 18.2.

**FIG. 18.1**

Start the Web server software by choosing WebSite Server from Programs and then WebSite 1.1.

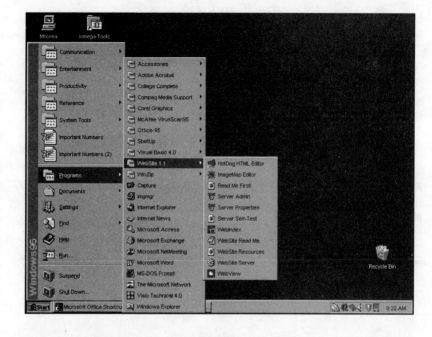

**FIG. 18.2**

The WebSite icon is visible in the taskbar tray whenever the server is running.

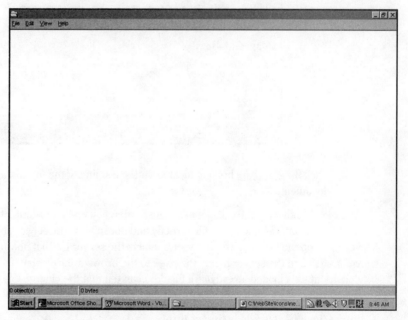

# Local Access to the Server

With the server running, you are ready to load a document. To do this, follow these steps:

1. Be sure that your TCP/IP connection is open. Check your operating system documentation to do this. If you are already operating over a network or a Web service provider, assume that it is working and proceed.

2. Start your browser.

3. Choose Open from the File menu and choose the following file. Be sure to use the installation path that you chose if you did not choose the default:

   **C:/WebSite/wsdocs/index.html**

Upon pressing Enter, the following page appears as shown in Figure 18.3.

**FIG. 18.3**

The WebSite welcome page allows you to test the server to see if it can handle local access to the server.

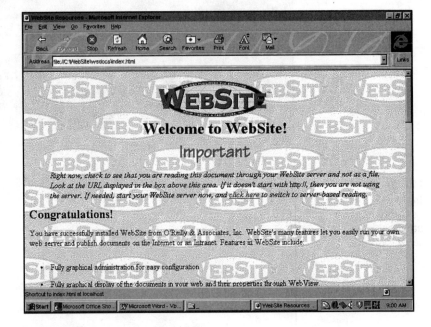

4. Click the *click here* hotspot located on the last line of the first paragraph in the index.html document.

The reason you click the hotspot is because when you open a document by using the file menu, the browser interacts with the file directly and doesn't use the server at all. However, whenever you click on the hot spot, the browser contacts the server for that link (in this case, your own computer) and the server hands the page to the browser for display. The link is to the same document as is loaded already as a file. You can tell that the change has taken place because the address of the page shown is now:

**http://localhost/wsdocs/index.html**

instead of the earlier

**file://c:/WebSite/wsdocs/index.html**

If all of these steps work correctly, then your server is running and able to locate local files for a local server.

## Remote Access to the Server

The next test is to see if the WebSite Server can be accessed from a browser on another machine. To do so, follow this procedure:

1. Make sure that the server is up and running.

2. Start a browser on another machine.

3. Key in the following URL in the Address textbox:

   **http://server.IP.address/wsdocs/index.html**

   Note: Server.IP.address is the IP address of your server such as 123.234.45.55.

4. Now you should see the following page on the browser as shown in Figure 18.4.

**FIG. 18.4**
The WebSite welcome page allows you to test the server to see if it can handle remote access also.

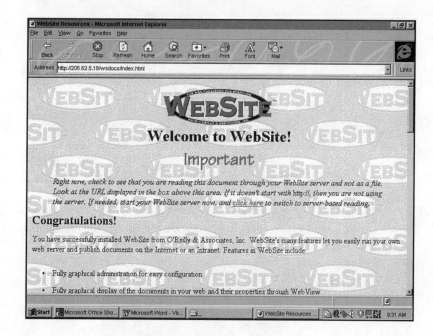

Part
VI
Ch
18

There is no need to press the *click here* link if you are accessing the document from a remote client. In this case, if the server were not running, then you would see no Web page in your browser, but an error message would likely appear instead.

By the same procedure, you can access your server by using its domain name, if it has been registered with DNS. You would simply type in the name of the domain instead of the IP address. The result would be identical.

# Managing the WebSite Server

Now that you have determined that the server is working properly, you will want to understand something about its care and feeding. The primary method for administering WebSite is through the Control Menu. You access this menu by right-clicking the server icon, which is normally in the Taskbar Tray. Figure 18.5 shows what this looks like.

**FIG. 18.5**

The WebSite Control Menu allows you to manage the server through a user interface.

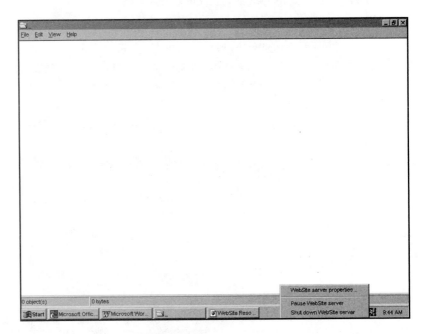

Two of the choices in this menu are self-describing. It is clear what Shut down WebSite server and Pause WebSite server will do when selected. The top selection, WebSite server properties is where you control the behavior of the WebSite server, and thereby your entire Web site. Figure 18.6 shows the WebSite Server Properties sheet.

**FIG. 18.6**

The WebSite Properties sheet provides a user interface for controlling the settings that control the behavior of the server.

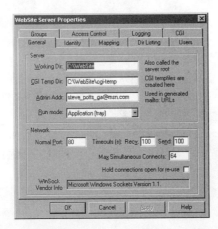

Some of the more important properties areas follows:

- Working Directory—The server root.
- Administrator Address—The e-mail address of the Web master for this site.
- Run Mode—Where you change from running WebSite as an application to running it as an operating system service and vice versa.
- Timeouts—May have to be increased to 180 if you are on a modem line.
- Maximum Simultaneous Connects—May have to be lowered so that at least a few users get decent response times. It is better to refuse additional connections than to have a server that is annoyingly slow.

## Activating the Administrator Account

An Administrator account is a requirement to perform many of the maintenance functions for the server. Upon installation, WebSite has an account called Admin, but it is dormant. In order to use it you need to perform the following steps:

1. Choose the Users tab from the Website Server Properties. Figure 18.7 shows this page.

**FIG. 18.7**
The Users Properties sheet provides a user interface for adding users, assigning passwords, and putting users into groups.

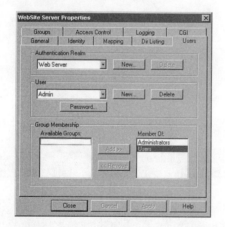

2. In the User Listbox, select the Admin user.
3. Click the Password Button and assign a password for the Admin user. You must do this to activate the Admin account. If you hate passwords and don't fear a security breach, then use admin as the password also. Beware, however, for this very reason the first password that hackers try is always "admin."
4. Add the Admin user to both the Administrators and the Users groups.
5. Press Close and wait for the beep before continuing. If the server is not running you will not get the beep.

# Using WebView to Manage your Site

If you are planning a new Web site, it is likely that your site will contain dozens or even hundreds of documents that contain links to each other and to other sites around the world. A good site is one that doesn't have all sorts of broken links and error messages to frustrate users. If your site is paid for out of advertising budgets, then a sorry Web site will lower sales because the surfers will conclude that you are a sloppy company with sloppy workmanship.

Fortunately, WebSite comes with a utility called WebView to help you get your applications properly installed and linked. This utility is shown in Figure 18.8.

**FIG. 18.8**

The WebView utility provides a user interface for managing the Web applications on your site.

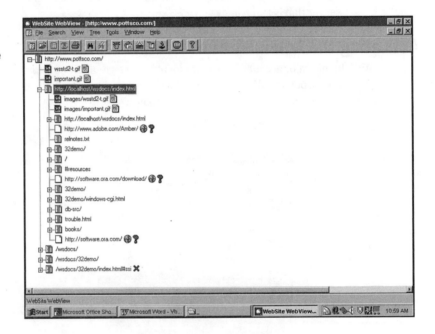

WebView is shown because it can be a great help to the Web site manager whenever you can't get your Windows CGI programs to work. The first thing to notice in Figure 18.8 is that WebView uses the same interface the Windows 95 Explorer uses complete with "+" and "-" boxes. This works just like Windows 95 in that it expands or contracts the file tree as you click these controls.

The second interesting feature is the use of special icons to help you read the tree quickly. Notice the "x" icon on the last line of the tree. This indicates a broken link; this target doesn't exist.

Another useful icon is the "?." This icon indicates that the link refers to a server that can't be verified at the present time. This display is used when you are working while disconnected from the Internet, such as when you take your laptop on an airplane.

The yellow document icon designates an HTML page. If it has no icons at the end of the reference, then that document is sound.

Finally, images are shown by a different icon that has a figure in it. These icons don't add functionality, but they make WebSite easier to use than an equivalent text status would allow.

# Logging

One of the most powerful administration tools available for managing a Web site is logging. Logs collect information about the activities that take place on your site for your use in managing, debugging, measuring usage, and diagnosing problems. WebSite provides three logs:

- The access log—Records each request and the server's response to it.
- The server log—Records each time the server is restarted. It also logs each time the configuration changes.
- The error log—Records errors like failed user authentication.

A utility called QuickStat can be used to create a summary of the information in the access log. It reports on all of the requests to your Web site and how they were handled. Figure 18.9 shows the QuickStats screen.

**FIG. 18.9**
The WebView utility provides a tool called QuickStats to give you a summary of the activity on your Web site.

The first section tells you the total number of request and hosts that made those requests. It also tells the number of days in the sample, up to seven days. The bottom section gives more information about those requests such as erroneous requests, CGI requests, and statistics such as average requests per day. This could be used to determine advertising rates if you can verify that these requests were legitimate customers and not just webcrawlers or your own testing traffic.

Three different formats are used for access logs:

- Windows format—The largest in size, but is the easiest to import into Visual Basic.
- Combined NCSA/CERN format—Delimits its log entries by using quotation marks.
- Common or older NCSA/CERN format—The most widely used and is therefore more recognizable to Web masters who manage multiple server software packages.

If you have no experience with any type, then choose the Windows format. If you have experience, then you will most likely choose the one that you are the most familiar with.

Logging is controlled by using a page in the server properties tab set. Figure 18.10 shows this page.

**FIG. 18.10**

The Logging Sheet in the Server Control Properties controls the behavior of the logging inside the server.

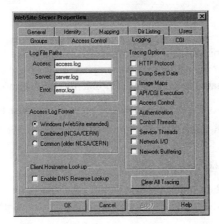

The first section on the log page tells the name of the logs and where they are located. By default, the logs are stored on the local machine in the \WebSite\logs subdirectory. You may move the logs to new directories or even to new machines if you wish.

**CAUTION**

The server cannot operate without logs. If you move the log files to another machine, then the server will shut down if that other server is unavailable.

Another feature on the Logging Properties page is called Enabling Client Hostname Lookup. Incoming requests always contain the IP address of the requesting browser. By enabling client hostname lookup you can log the domain name of the requesting browser, if it has one, instead of just the address. Of course, in order to do this, the server has to make a request to the DNS for every incoming request that can cause performance problems. Inside a company intranet however, this feature might prove very useful if you are trying to figure out who the company snoops are.

WebSite has 11 different server-tracing options to select from. These are used to find errors. When no tracing options are selected, the server log records a date/time stamp for each server startup and configuration change like this:

```
=================================
Sat Jan 11 07:21:23 1997
Server Startup: WebSite/1.1
=================================
```

```
=================================
Sat Jan 11 11:27:20 1997
Server Configuration Updated
=================================
```

In the case where you are having a problem, the trace options can give you a lot of good information. The following recommendations should be followed:

- Minimize the size of the HTML document being requested. This makes the log file smaller.

- Reduce the number of simultaneous connections to one.

- Request an object directly (such as a GIF file) instead of the entire HTML document.

You select the tracing options by clicking the check boxes. The purpose of each of these is as follows:

- HTTP Protocol—Records the incoming header data for each request from a browser and the server's response to the request.

- Dump Sent Data—Records what the browser sees when the server responds. These dumps are useful for debugging, but they are huge, so use them sparingly.

- Image Maps—Records the information that the server sends back when a client requests a location on a clickable image map.

- API/CGI Execution—Records the server's activity when a browser requests an URL containing a CGI program. CGI tracing is particularly useful for debugging you CGI programs. When this tracing is enabled, the server log receives a number of entries. In addition, any temporary files are saved instead of being deleted as they normally are. This allows you to inspect the INI files that the server creates in order to pass to your Visual Basic Program.

- Access Control—Records the server's decisions concerning access restrictions. This is useful when a requester reports trouble accessing your server.

- Authentication—Records all attempts at authentication. It shows which succeeded and which failed. It also shows why they failed.

- Control Threads, Service Threads, Network I/O, Network Buffering—These options are used by technical support when you call for technical support.

Click the CGI/API Execution check box at this time to be ready for the examples later in this chapter.

All of the log files are simple ASCII (text) files. This means that they can be viewed by using the Windows 95 Notepad applet. Figure 18.11 shows the server log being viewed in this way.

Part
VI

Ch
18

**FIG. 18.11**

All of the logs can be read by using the Notepad applet that comes standard with Windows 95 and Windows NT 4.X.

# Understanding How Windows CGI Works

The Common Gateway Interface specification identifies how communication must take place between the three parties to the transactions: the browser, the Web server software, and the server application being run. Figure 18.12 shows the relationships between these three:

**FIG. 18.12**

The Internet Server software acts as a middleman between the browser and the server application.

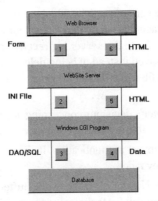

Windows CGI programs may perform any task that can be done on the server, but database update and query is the most common. The order of processing for Windows CGI transactions is as follows:

1. A user loads an HTML file that contains a form into his browser.

2. The browser displays it and gives the user several data entry controls like text boxes, list boxes, check boxes, and so forth, to which to respond.

3. The user fills in the appropriate data and then clicks the Submit button.

4. The data and the name of the program to be run are sent to the Web server that sends the user the original HTML file.

5. The server prepares the data for program consumption by placing all of the CGI parameters into an INI file.

6. The server then calls the program specified in the HTML file.

7. The Windows CGI program reads the INI file.

8. The Windows CGI program uses the Data Access Object (DAO) to access the database.

9. The DBMS responds to the DAO request and passes data back to the Windows CGI program.

10. The Windows CGI program processes the data and prepares a response to the user in HTML format.

11. The program then passes the HTML back to the server software.

12. The WebSite server transmits the HTML back to the browser.

13. The browser displays the file.

As an example, see what would happen if a Web surfer looked up the word "Tahiti" in a Windows CGI written search engine. The following sequence of events would take place:

1. The user types in the URL of the search service or clicks a hyperlink that takes her to that server.

2. The server hears the request and sends an HTML file to be used to refine the search criteria. Figure 18.13 shows a typical search screen.

Part VI
Ch
18

**FIG. 18.13**
The search program sends a data gathering screen like this one.

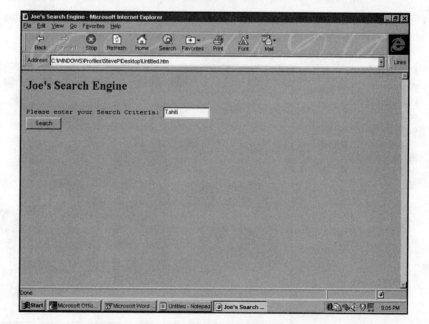

3. The user fills in "Tahiti" as the keyword for the search.

4. The user clicks the SUBMIT button, which has "Search" written on it.

5. The clicking of the SUBMIT button instructs the browser to package up the data and send it to the Web server.

6. The Web server gets the request and reads it. It starts a process on the server and writes the information to an .INI file.

7. It invokes the searching program, which can be written in any language that runs on the server. For the sake of this example, the language will be Visual Basic 5.0.

8. The Visual Basic search program reads from the .INI file and gets the word "Tahiti" as input.

9. The search program creates a SQL statement like the following:

```
SELECT URL, Description FROM SITES_TABLE WHERE TOPIC="TAHITI"
```

10. Visual Basic opens the database and executes the query.

11. The result of the query is passed back by the database engine to the search program.

12. The VB search program dynamically creates HTML statements and embeds the data from the DBMS in the middle of it.

13. The search program writes the HTML statements by using a routine called Send(). This routine sends the HTML back to the Web server.

14. The server software accepts the output and sends it to the browser.

15. The browser treats the response as just another HTML file and displays it on screen. Figure 18.14 shows how this is done.

**FIG. 18.14**
Windows CGI processes CGI requests in a unique manner. It converts the header into named variables within the server and the raw data is loaded into an .INI file.

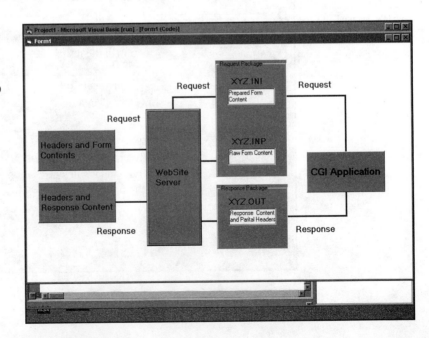

The preceding example was pretty clear except for one place where magic took over—when the browser sent the data to the server. How did the server know where to look for the program? The following sections will explain how this happened.

# The Structure of an URL

The browser had loaded the search page from a server and thereby knew the address of the server where the CGI program was stored. It knew that by reading the URL that got sent to the browser.

A complete URL consists of six parts:

- The protocol—which is normally http:
- The hostname—like www.pottsco.com, or it can be a dotted quad IP address like 227.27.65.3.
- The port number—This is nearly always omitted because of the universal acceptance of port 80 for HTTP.
- The path—/sales/reports/mar97.htm
- The parameters—like bytes=0-100, 300-500. This is relatively new to the standard and not often used.
- Argument String—like ?search=Tahiti&Month=12. This string is used as the input to standard CGI programs that use GET instead of POST. GET is not often used with Windows CGI because the definition of GET is that it only retrieves data but doesn't change it. Because most CGI applications do change data, the POST command is normally used for Windows CGI.

When a browser is given an URL to find by an HTML document, it uses the first three arguments to locate the correct server. The combination of the protocol, IP address, and port number are all that are necessary to find the server. Once the server is located, the browser sends the rest of the URL to the server over the net. The browser doesn't send the first part of the URL to the server because the server already knows its identity. It only needs the path, parameters, and argument to determine what to do.

When a correctly formed Windows CGI request is received by the WebSite server, it will not have either parameters or arguments, but only the name of a program. The server will know from the name that this is a Windows CGI program and it will look in the win-cgi directory for that program. It creates the .INI file and starts the program. It does other tasks while waiting for the Windows CGI program to finish.

## Creating a Simple Windows CGI Example

Before we continue our discussion of how CGI works, let's stop long enough to get a very simple example to work. To do this, open Visual Basic and create a new project called Testing123.VBP. Include the Windows CGI module called CGI32.BAS. This module contains the framework for connecting Visual Basic to the WebSite server and can be found in the C:\WebSite\cgi-src\ directory.

Next, remove all of the custom controls that you won't be using. Keep only the ones that you don't get an error message for when you try to remove them. Do the same with all of the references to OLE objects.

Now that you have as small a project as possible, create a new module and call it TESTING123.BAS. Save it in a new directory called C:\WebSite\cgi-src\Testing123\. You can store it anywhere, but keeping all of your CGI projects in directories under the cgi-src directory will keep you from hunting for them. Now you are ready to add code. The CGI32.BAS program contains the main() subroutine and the design of Windows CGI states that you add all of your code as a subroutine called CGI_Main(). Key in the following code, as shown in Listing 18.1.

**Listing 18.1   Your Code Is Placed in These Two Subroutines**

```
' This Routine sends dymanic HTML to the client
Sub CGI_Main()
Send("Content-type: text/html")
Send(" ")
Send("<HTML><HEAD><TITLE>Testing123!</TITLE></HEAD>")
Send("<BODY><H1>Testing123?</H1>")
Send("Testing123 from Visual Basic!")
Send("<P>It is now " & Now)
Send("</BODY></HTML>")
End Sub
Next, key in the following subroutine:
Sub Inter_Main()
'Notify the user that this is a CGI program
MsgBox "Please run this code using a browser"
End Sub
```

Create the executable by choosing Make Testing123.exe from the File Menu. Tell the dialog box that you want to save the file in the C:\Website\cgi-win\ subdirectory.

Next, start your favorite browser after making sure that the WebSite server is up and running. Then type the following in the address box:

**http://localhost/cgi-win/Testing123.exe**

The result will be displayed in your browser as shown in Figure 18.15.

If you try to run the application interactively, the following message box appears as shown in Figure 18.16.

This example gave you a good look at a simple running Windows CGI program. Let's look at some of the files that were created by the server while the program was running.

**FIG. 18.15**

The WebSite server runs the Windows CGI program and displays the results in the browser.

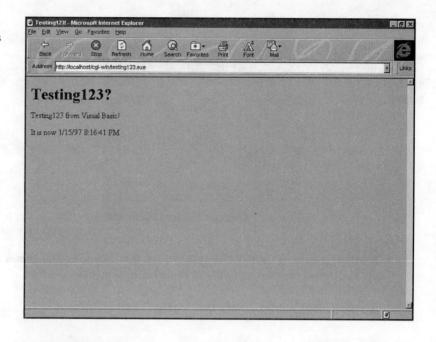

**FIG. 18.16**

The Windows CGI program runs interactively but only displays a warning message that the program is meant to be run from a browser through the Web server.

As you recall, when we discussed tracing earlier in this chapter, you were instructed to turn the CGI/API tracing on so that the files that were created during the running of a CGI program would not be erased after the processing is over. To find out where these files are located, click the WebSite icon in the taskbar tray and look at the General page as shown in Figure 18.17.

In this figure, the CGI Temp Directory is C:\WebSite\cgi-temp, which is the default location. Verify the directory in your own system and look in it for the files.

The first file that is created is the input file. This file contains the raw form content that the server receives from the HTML file that invoked the CGI program. Because this example didn't have any form data, this file will be created but it is empty. It is called 9WS.OUT on my system. Because these are temporary files, WebSite 1.1 doesn't give them any fancy name; the name is always xWS.OUT, where x is some integer assigned by the system.

**FIG. 18.17**
The CGI Temp Directory is where all temporary files are created during the execution of a CGI program.

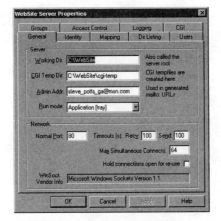

> **N O T E** The naming convention used here is unique to WebSite and will be different for each Web server that supports the WinCGI interface, such as Netscape's FastTrack Web server. ■

The next file of interest, Listing 18.2, is called 9ws.ini.

**Listing 18.2 The INI File Contains Client Information**

```
[CGI]
Request Protocol=HTTP/1.0
Request Method=GET
Request Keep-Alive=No
Document Root=C:\WEBSITE\HTDOCS\
Executable Path=/cgi-win/testing123.exe
Server Software=WebSite/1.1f1
Server Name=localhost
Server Port=80
Server Admin=steve_potts_ga@msn.com
CGI Version=CGI/1.3 (Win)
Remote Address=127.0.0.1
User Agent=Mozilla/2.0 (compatible; MSIE 3.01; Windows 95)

[System]
GMT Offset=-18000
Debug Mode=Yes
Output File=C:\WebSite\cgi-temp\9ws.out

[Accept]
image/gif=Yes
image/x-xbitmap=Yes
image/jpeg=Yes
image/pjpeg=Yes
*/*=Yes
```

```
[Extra Headers]
Accept-Language=en
UA-pixels=800x600
UA-color=color8
UA-OS=Windows 95
UA-CPU=x86
Host=localhost
```

This file contains a number of instructions for the CGI program. It tells the CGI program where to put the output, the name of the executable CGI program to be started, the versions of software that are running, configuration setting, the e-mail address of the Webmaster for this site, and a lot of other useful information. This information is loaded into your program as global variables by the framework as you will see later in this chapter.

One part of this .INI file that is interesting is the Server Name listing. This is the name of the hardware that the WebSite server is running on. In this case, it is listed as "localhost." This is because we ran the program by typing the following

**http://localhost/cgi-win/Testing123.exe**

in the browser address textbox. This tells the browser to submit the request to the server running on this machine. This is a very useful thing to do because it allows you to develop your applications and test them by using only one machine.

The final file is the output file. The name of this file is 9WS.OUT. It is shown here:

```
Content-type: text/html

<HTML><HEAD><TITLE>Testing123!</TITLE></HEAD>
<BODY><H1>Testing123?</H1>
Testing123 from Visual Basic!
<P>It is now 1/17/97 4:03:32 PM
</BODY></HTML>
```

This code should look familiar. It is the result of all of the Send() statements that you put into your code. This file will be passed back to the browser that caused this program to be run. If the request was successful, the file will contain data to be displayed. If it was unsuccessful, it will contain an error message.

Now that you have seen an example work, you are ready to learn the cast members of this play. This is the topic of the following sections.

# Understanding the Windows CGI Framework for Visual Basic

The first thing that we did after we created the project was to add the CGI32.BAS module to the project. This module constitutes the framework for Windows CGI and provides a number of subroutines that work in conjunction with the WebSite server to create the magic connectivity that allows Windows CGI to work with Visual Basic. The framework module does the following:

■ Defines the `Main()` subroutine for your CGI program.

■ Defines a set of CGI variables.

■ Defines a number of functions that simplify both input/output and error handling.

■ Creates the global exception handler that catches runtime errors and ensures that the client browser gets an error message when your program fails.

## The *Main()* Routine

Because the Windows CGI programs have no user interface, your Visual Basic program has no need for any forms. Visual Basic expects that an applications entry point is either a form load or a subroutine named `Main()`. The `Main()` is defined in the CGI32.BAS module, so don't create another one. This subroutine opens the .INI file created by the WebSite server and converts it into a set of global variables available for your program's use. It also creates the `On Error` subroutine that ensures that your program will still provide some response, even if it fails.

## CGI_Main()

After the `Main()` routine gets done with its setup processing, it makes a call to a subroutine called `CGI_Main()` that you create and that must exist. This is, in essence, equivalent to the `Sub Main()` in normal Visual Basic programs. This is where you place your code that processes the input and creates the output. In the preceding example, you keyed in several `Send()` subroutine calls. After `Main()` got done executing, it called `CGI_Main()`, which called the `Send()` routines.

## Inter_Main()

The `Inter_Main()` subroutine exists just in case someone tries to run your executable to see what it is. Instead of dying a horrible death, it very gently tells the user the message of your choice and terminates in an orderly fashion. This subroutine must exist also.

## CGI Variables

When a browser makes a CGI request of a server, it communicates quite a bit of information in addition to the URL of the program to be run. Table 18.1 summarizes this information.

**Table 18.1   Windows CGI Global Variables for Visual Basic**

| Variable Name | Contents |
| --- | --- |
| `CGI_ServerSoftware` | The name and version of the server software like WebSite 1.1 |
| `CGI_ServerAdmin` | The e-mail address of the Webmaster for that server |
| `CGI_Version` | The compliance version of the CGI server |

| Variable Name | Contents |
|---|---|
| CGI_GMTOffset | The number of seconds from GMT |
| CGI_RequestProtocol | The name and revision of the HTTP protocol of the request |
| CGI_Referer | The URL that referred to the CGI program |
| CGI_From | The e-mail of the user |
| CGI_RemoteHost | The hostname of the client machine running the browser |
| CGI_RemoteAddr | The IP address of the RemoteHost |
| CGI_AcceptTypes | The CGI accept types |
| CGI_NumAcceptTypes | The number of CGI accept types |
| CGI_ExecutablePath | The path of the CGI program being executed |
| CGI_LogicalPath | The extra path information |
| CGI_PhysicalPath | The physical path (translated logical path) |
| CGI_RequestMethod | The method passed from the client (GET or POST) |
| CGI_ServerPort | The port number in the request |
| CGI_ServerName | The server's hostname |
| CGI_QueryString | The encoded portion of a GET request |
| CGI_ContentFile | The full pathname of the file containing attached data |
| CGI_ContentType | The MIME content type of requests |
| CGI_ContentLength | The length of the attached data in bytes |
| CGI_FormTuples | The name=value pairs |
| CGI_NumFormTuples | The number of name=value pairs |
| CGI_HugeTuples | The large name=value pairs |
| CGI_NumHugeTuples | The number of HugeTuples |
| CGI_AuthUser | The username of the authorized user |
| CGI_AuthPass | The password of the authorized user |
| CGI_AuthType | The authorization method |
| CGI_AuthRealm | The realm of the authorized user |
| CGI_ExtraHeaders | The extra headers from the browser |
| CGI_NumExtraHeaders | The number of extra headers |
| CGI_OutputFile | The full pathname of the file that will contain the response |
| CGI_DebugMode | The CGI Tracing flag from the server |

Part
**VI**

Ch

**18**

In the event that you need to respond to a GET request, the encoded string will appear in the CGI_QueryString global variable. See Chapter 19, "ISAPI, OLEISAPI, and Visual Basic," for information on how to parse this string.

Let's look at an example where an application uses some of these variables:

1. Create a new project called GlobalCheck.VBP and add the CGI32.BAS file to it.

2. Create a CGI_Main and Inter_Main that look like Listing 18.3.

**Listing 18.3   The *CGI_Main()* Subroutine Can Contain References to the Global Variables**

```
Sub CGI_Main()
    Send ("Content-type: text/html")
    Send (" ")
    Send ("<HTML><HEAD><TITLE>GlobalCheck!</TITLE></HEAD>")
    Send ("<BODY><H1>GlobalCheck?</H1>")
    Send ("GlobalCheck from Visual Basic!")
    Send ("<P>The Server Name is " & CGI_ServerName)
    Send ("</BODY></HTML>")
End Sub

' This routine only executes if the user tries to run the application manually
Sub Inter_Main()
    MsgBox "This is a CGI Program"
End Sub
```

3. Open your favorite browser and type the following:

**http://localhost/cgi-win/GlobalCheck.exe**

The output should look like Figure 18.18.

All of the preceding global variables may be used in your programs just like any other variables. They are especially valuable when the version of the client's browser is important when you formulate your response.

## Utility Functions

As you saw, there are several utility functions that are important to the execution of your Windows CGI program. The following is a summary of the Windows CGI Utility routines:

■ The Send() subroutine is used to write output to the .OUT file. This file is sent to the calling browser as soon as the CGI program completes. A typical Send() call is like the following:

```
Send ("<P>The Server Name is " & CGI_ServerName)
```

■ The ErrorHandler() subroutine is called when a runtime error occurs. The OnError statement is armed in the Main() function so you don't have to worry about this. This doesn't mean that you can't set up local error handlers, but they must call the global error handler when they finish processing.

```
On Error GoTo OnPostError
.

.

.
OnPostError:

' Error handling

If Err >= CGI_ERR_START Then Error Err 'If it is a framework error
Send("<H2>There was a problem:</H2>")
Select Case sSelector
Case "DEL"
    Send("Name doesn't exist")
Case "INS"
    Send("Session is full")
Case Else
    Send("Internal Error: Invalid input")
End Select
```

This is an example of using a local error handler to handle incorrect input from a program. The programmer calls his own error handler. When the error occurs, this local error handler is called. The program first checks to see if the error is in the range of error codes that is generated by the framework. If it is in this range, the `ErrorHandler()` function is triggered. If not, then the error is handled here. Handling the error means generating some HTML statements that describe the problem and ending the program.

Part
VI

Ch

18

**FIG. 18.18**
The global variables contain information about the system that can be used by your Visual Basic program to make decisions or as output.

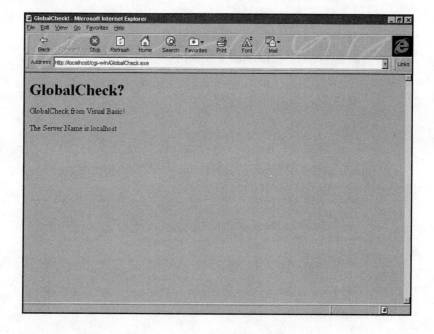

The `FieldPresent()` function tests for the presence of a named form field. If a check box in an HTML form is left unchecked by the user, then the browser will not send any mention of it to the CGI program. The absence of this field means that it was not checked by the user. If the program attempts to read the data from the .INI file, using `GetSmallField()`, Windows will trigger an ugly error. To head this off, have your programs check for the presence of a checkbox field. If this function returns TRUE, then the user checked the check box, but if it returns FALSE, then the user didn't check it.

The `GetSmallField()` function is defined in the framework to retrieve values from the .INI file by name. If a form passes data to the CGI program, it is placed in the .INI file by the WebSite server before invoking the CGI program. The .INI file in Listing 18.4 was generated while the pizza32 example that ships with WebSite 1.1 was running.

**Listing 18.4   The INI File Is Generated by the Server Based on the Input from the Client-Sap**

```
[CGI]
Request Protocol=HTTP/1.0
Request Method=POST
Request Keep-Alive=No
Document Root=C:\WEBSITE\HTDOCS\
Executable Path=/cgi-win/pizza32.exe
Server Software=WebSite/1.1f1
Server Name=localhost
Server Port=80
Server Admin=steve_potts_ga@msn.com
CGI Version=CGI/1.3 (Win)
Remote Address=127.0.0.1
Referer=http://localhost/cgi-win/pizza32.exe
User Agent=Mozilla/2.0 (compatible; MSIE 3.01; Windows 95)
Content Type=application/x-www-form-urlencoded
Content Length=134

[System]
GMT Offset=-18000
Debug Mode=Yes
Output File=C:\WebSite\cgi-temp\bws.out
Content File=C:\WEBSITE\CGI-TEMP\BWS.INP

[Form Literal]
name=Ralph Blackwelder
address=123 4th St.
phone=123-4567
city=Altadena (free)
topping=pepperoni
topping_1=sausage
topping_2=anchovies

[Accept]
image/gif=Yes
image/x-xbitmap=Yes
image/jpeg=Yes
```

```
image/pjpeg=Yes
*/*=Yes

[Extra Headers]
Accept-Language=en
UA-pixels=800x600
UA-color=color8
UA-OS=Windows 95
UA-CPU=x86
Host=localhost
Pragma=No-Cache
```

The [Form Literal] section contains the fields, name, address, phone, city, topping, topping_1, and topping_2. In order to process this data in your Visual Basic program, you have to get these values into VB variables. The following code does this:

```
Dim buffer as String
buffer =  GetSmallField("ClassName")
```

These functions allow you to interact with the WebSite server through the CGI32.BAS framework in a fashion that is much easier than the standard CGI allows.

# Debugging Windows CGI Applications

At this point, you should have a good grasp of the processing that takes place behind the scenes in a Windows CGI program. Next, let's create an application that accepts form input, processes it, and returns the results in HTML form.

Normally, Visual Basic programmers like to work within the VB environment to develop applications. We normally develop client server applications by using a local Jet Engine database and run the entire application on one machine. After that works, we migrate the database to the server machine and the front end to the client machine.

To set up a similar methodology for Windows CGI programming, do the following:

1. Create an .INI file that contains the information you need in your CGI program.
2. Write your Visual Basic code to process this data. Debug it in the environment until you get it to work.
3. Use the Jet Engine database to process the data until you get it to work.
4. Change the database to the production database and verify that this works.
5. Write an HTML file that calls it as a hyperlink (HREF) and run it locally by using the WebSite server on the development box.
6. Create a real HTML file with a FORM that calls the CGI program running on the development box.
7. Go to a remote client and enter the URL of the calling HTML file. Verify that this works.

Let's create an example by using this methodology. First, using NotePad applet that comes with Windows NT and Windows 95, create a file that looks like Listing 18.5.

**Listing 18.5 The INI File Contains the Data from the Client**

```
[CGI]
Request Protocol=HTTP/1.0
Request Method=POST
Request Keep-Alive=No
Document Root=C:\WEBSITE\HTDOCS\
Executable Path=/cgi-win/maillist.exe
Server Software=WebSite/1.1f1
Server Name=localhost
Server Port=80
Server Admin=steve_potts_ga@msn.com
CGI Version=CGI/1.3 (Win)
Remote Address=127.0.0.1
Referer=http://localhost/cgi-win/maillist.exe
User Agent=Mozilla/2.0 (compatible; MSIE 3.01; Windows 95)
Content Type=application/x-www-form-urlencoded
Content Length=134

[System]
GMT Offset=-18000
Debug Mode=Yes
Output File=C:\WebSite\cgi-temp\mail1.out
Content File=C:\WEBSITE\CGI-TEMP\mail1.INP

[Form Literal]
name=John Hendrickson
address=123 4th St.
phone=123-4567
city=Atlanta

[Accept]
image/gif=Yes
image/x-xbitmap=Yes
image/jpeg=Yes
image/pjpeg=Yes
*/*=Yes

[Extra Headers]
Accept-Language=en
UA-pixels=800x600
UA-color=color8
UA-OS=Windows 95
UA-CPU=x86
Host=localhost
Pragma=No-Cache
```

Alternately, you can look in the cgi-temp directory for any file that is named ?ws.ini where ? can be any number. These ini files have been created by running WebSite applications. You can rename and edit one of these files instead of typing in one.

Store this file in the temporary directory, which is normally C:\WebSite\cgi-temp. Name it MAILLIST.INI.

Create a directory called C:\WebSite\cgi-src\MailList. Start Visual Basic and create a new executable project called MailList. Store this project in the MailList directory. Delete the form and add the CGI32.BAS module to the project as is our custom.

Add a new module called MailList.BAS and in it create the `CGI_Main()` routine with the code shown in Listing 18.6.

### Listing 18.6   This Listing Shows How the *GetSmallField()* Subroutine Is Used to Get Data

```
Sub CGI_Main()

    'Declare local variables

    Dim strName As String
    Dim strAddress As String
    Dim strPhone As String
    Dim strCity As String

    'Load INI data into local variables

    strName = GetSmallField("name")
    strAddress = GetSmallField("address")
    strPhone = GetSmallField("phone")
    strCity = GetSmallField("city")

    'Verify that it worked

    MsgBox " The name is " & strName

End Sub

Sub Inter_Main()
    MsgBox "This is a CGI Program.  Use a browser to run it"
End Sub
```

Next, give the project a command-line argument by choosing Project Properties from the Project menu. When the Project Properties window displays, choose the Make property sheet and enter the full path name of the INI file as shown in Figure 18.19.

Next, step through the program just like you would any other Visual Basic program until you see the MessageBox appear as shown in Figure 18.20.

**FIG. 18.19**

The behavior of the Windows CGI program can be simulated by placing the name of the .INI file in the Command-Line Argument's textbox in the Project Properties window.

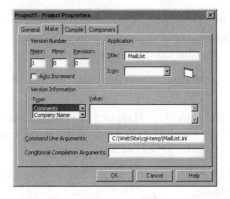

**FIG. 18.20**

The behavior of the program can be simulated by using Command-Line Arguments for the .INI file and MessageBoxes to verify the correct values.

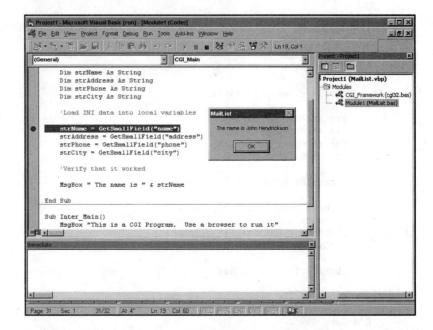

Now that we are sure the program is working correctly, we can replace the MessageBox with Send() calls. Change the CGI_Main() code by changing it to the code in Listing 18.7:

**Listing 18.7   This Code Shows How to Use the *Send()* Commands to Create a Response File**

```
Sub CGI_Main()

    'Declare local variables

    Dim strName As String
```

```
        Dim strAddress As String
        Dim strPhone As String
        Dim strCity As String

        'Load INI data into local variables

        strName = GetSmallField("name")
        strAddress = GetSmallField("address")
        strPhone = GetSmallField("phone")
        strCity = GetSmallField("city")

        Send ("Content-type: text/html")
        Send (" ")
        Send ("<HTML><HEAD><TITLE>MailList</TITLE></HEAD>")
        Send ("<BODY><H1>MailList</H1>")
        Send ("<P>The Name is " & strName)
        Send ("<P>The Address is " & strAddress)
        Send ("<P>The Phone is " & strPhone)
        Send ("<P>The City is " & strCity)
        Send ("</BODY></HTML>")

    End Sub

    Sub Inter_Main()
        MsgBox "This is a CGI Program.  Use a browser to run it"
    End Sub
```

If you run this code from within the Visual Basic Environment, you will see that a file called mail1.out is created. This file name was used because you specified on this line of the .INI file that the output was to be placed in this file.

```
Output File=C:\WebSite\cgi-temp\mail1.out
```

The contents of the mail1.out file looks like you would expect them to. They are displayed as follows:

```
Content-type: text/html

<HTML><HEAD><TITLE>MailList</TITLE></HEAD>
<BODY><H1>MailList</H1>
<P>The Name is John Hendrickson
<P>The Address is 123 4th St.
<P>The Phone is 123-4567
<P>The City is Atlanta
</BODY></HTML>
```

If you access this file from a browser, it will look like Figure 18.21.

As you can see, this file displays correctly except for the display of the Content-type text/html line, which is normally removed by the WebSite server from the body and placed in the HTTP statement when being sent to a server.

**FIG. 18.21**

The behavior of the program can be simulated by using Command-Line Arguments for the .INI file and MessageBoxes to verify the correct values.

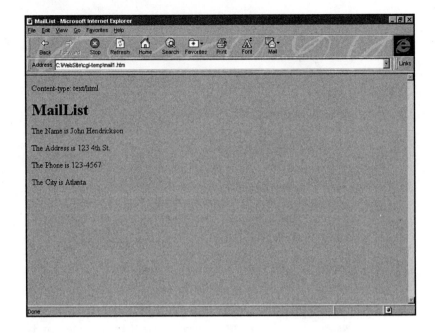

# From Here...

In this chapter, you learned about the WebSite Server software and how to install and manage the installation. You learned how to create Visual Basic Applications that can be run in this environment. You saw what goes on behind the scenes to make it all work correctly. Finally, you learned how to debug WebSite applications by using the Visual Basic Development that we are all accustomed to. In Chapter 22, "Using Data Access Objects with the WinCGI Interface," you will learn how to add database processing to your application.

To round out your knowledge of using Visual Basic for developing client/server applications, you should also review the material in the following chapters of this book:

■ To learn how to use Visual Basic with Microsoft's Internet Information Server, see Chapter 19, "ISAPI, OLEISAPI, and Visual Basic."

■ For information on how to use Windows CGI to create database applications see Chapter 22, "Using Data Access Objects with the WinCGI Interface."

■ For information on standard CGI, see Appendix A, "Standard CGI, WinCGI, and Visual Basic."

# ISAPI, OLEISAPI, and Visual Basic

**O**nce Microsoft made the decision to get into the Web server market, they decided to do it in a very Microsoft way. This involved making two decisions about their Web server:

**The advantages offered by SAPI programming over CGI programming**

SAPI programming offers many performance advantages over CGI programming. We'll look at what these performance advantages are, and how to take advantage of them.

**Some of the disadvantages and considerations to be taken into account before jumping into SAPI programming**

SAPI programming isn't as easy as CGI programming, and has the potential of crashing an entire server. You'll learn how this is possible, and how to prevent this potential problem.

**The Microsoft ISAPI interface, how it works, and how it is similar and different from the CGI interface**

Every Web server that provides a SAPI interface is unique. We'll take a close look at Microsoft's Internet Server Application Programming Interface (ISAPI) and how it works.

- Their Web server would be tightly integrated into NT Server and the rest of their BackOffice line. This includes tying their Web server into the native NT monitoring system, and allowing server logging into SQL Server, their BackOffice database server.

- Building in an Application Programming Interface (API), so that the Web server could be extended through the use of Microsoft's various programming tools.

Once Microsoft had developed its Web Server API (known as the Internet Server API or ISAPI), they began touting the benefits of it everywhere there was anyone to listen. Microsoft said it was so superior to CGI programming that everyone should switch over to ISAPI programming. Well, they were right and wrong about ISAPI programming being superior to CGI programming, but we'll get to that later.

Microsoft wasn't the only Web server vendor to develop the idea of adding an API to their Web server. Netscape and O'Reilly were hard at work developing their own Server API's (SAPI) for their respective Web servers at the same time that Microsoft was developing theirs. And now, just about every commercial-grade Web server has some sort of SAPI available for extending the server functionality, for more or less the same reasons that Microsoft gave.

Fortunately, Microsoft didn't stop with developing only their ISAPI interface; they built an OLEISAPI interface on top of it. OLEISAPI enables Visual Basic developers to build ISAPI applications; the actual ISAPI interface is designed more for C/C++ developers. Microsoft's whole reasoning for adding the ISAPI interface was to make Web server application programming easier, and enablingVisual Basic to write for this interface was very important to them. ▪

**N O T E**   SAPI, or Server Application Programming Interface, is a term being used in this chapter to refer to the general concept of Web server interfaces. SAPI is not used to refer to any specific vendor's Web server API. Microsoft's SAPI is known as ISAPI. Netscape's SAPI is known as NSAPI. There is also WSAPI (O'Reilly's WebSite), ASAPI (Apache), and numerous others. These are all SAPIs that are designed for use with a specific Web server. ▪

# Advantages of SAPI over CGI Programming

Two basic arguments are used to tout the advantages of SAPI programming over CGI programming: speed and overhead.

## Why CGI Applications are so Slow

For each CGI call made by a browser client, the server must run a separate process. This process runs in its own memory space, and cannot take advantage of any resources previously opened by the Web server. This means that when a CGI application accesses a database, it has to reopen and close that database each time it runs, no matter how many times the database has been accessed before by the Web server, either directly or via the same or other CGI applications. This takes time, and the more often the CGI application is called, the more time it takes.

Another source of overhead is in the startup and shutdown of each CGI application as the application is loaded into memory by the operating system, and then unloaded when the application is finished. Starting up an application takes time. And the bigger the application, the more time it takes to startup and shutdown. For some large CGI applications, this can greatly slow the application down. Compound this problem with running many large CGI applications at the same time, and it can really slow down a Web server. If the Web site is really busy, it may even run into limitations on the maximum number of active processes that can be running simultaneously on the machine, and CGI requests may have to sit and wait for other CGI applications to end before they can be run.

## Why SAPI Applications are Fast

SAPI applications, in contrast, are actually extensions to the server application. On Windows-based Web servers, the SAPI applications are built as DLLs that are called directly from the Web server. This makes the SAPI applications part of the Web server application.

By making SAPI applications part of the Web server process, the overhead associated with starting up and shutting down a separate application is eliminated. Once the DLL is loaded the first time, it is kept in memory as part of the server process.

Because the SAPI DLLs are not unloaded until the Web server is shut down, that allows the SAPI application to keep open any resources that will be needed on a frequent basis. For example, a database connection may be kept open constantly, instead of having to open and close the connection with each request. Yes, the first request to the SAPI application will still encounter a lot of the overhead involved with loading the DLL and opening the database connection, but none of the following requests will have to deal with any of that overhead.

> **CAUTION**
>
> Depending on the Web server, once a SAPI DLL is loaded, it will not necessarily remain loaded until the Web server is shut down. Some Web servers may keep track of how often a particular SAPI DLL is called, so that DLLs that have not been called within a certain period of time can be unloaded automatically. Because of this, it is important that SAPI DLLs be written to properly clean up after themselves when being unloaded.

# Disadvantages in SAPI Programming

Despite what you may hear from your favorite Web server vendor about the benefits of using its SAPI for your Web application programming, SAPIs are not without problems and shortcomings. These shortcomings need to be taken into consideration when planning any SAPI programming.

## SAPI Applications are not Portable

With one notable exception, each Web server SAPI is implemented and supported by that particular Web server vendor. This means that a SAPI application that you might write to run on a Netscape Web server cannot run on a Microsoft Web server, and vice versa. The sole exception to this rule is Microsoft's ISAPI interface, which has been implemented by O'Reilly in their WebSite Web servers, in addition to their own proprietary WSAPI interface. This means that any ISAPI applications that you develop to run on Microsoft's Web server, can also be run on an O'Reilly Web server. However, when you begin developing applications for O'Reilly's WSAPI interface, your applications will only run on O'Reilly Web servers.

## An Unstable SAPI can Crash the Web Server

Because SAPI applications are running as part of the Web server process, a buggy SAPI DLL can cause severe problems for the Web server by corrupting memory, resources, or even crashing the Web server process. The various Web server vendors are putting a lot of resources into trying to solve this problem, and are putting in place error trapping around the calls to the SAPI DLLs, but it will be awhile before this problem goes away. Because of this potential, just about every Web server vendor, including Microsoft, recommends developing your SAPI application as a CGI application first. Once the application is stable as a CGI application, then consider converting it to a SAPI application.

## SAPIs are Language Dependent

Most SAPIs are designed for using C/C++ as the primary programming language for building applications that use the SAPI. There are one or two other languages that may be used to build SAPI applications, but most other languages are off limits. There are one or two SAPIs designed for using languages other than C/C++ as the SAPI application programming language, but these are more likely to be designed for using Java than Visual Basic. To use a language like Visual Basic to build SAPI applications, you have to have some form of SAPI extension designed for adapting a particular SAPI for use with Visual Basic. Microsoft's OLEISAPI interface is an example of one of these adapters that we'll look at later in this chapter.

## SAPIs are Usually Multi-threaded

SAPIs are implemented with the same threading model that the Web server on which they are built uses. This means that SAPI applications built to run on most Web servers have to be implemented as thread-safe DLLs. This means that any add-ons that adapt the SAPI for a nonthreaded programming language has to take steps to eliminate the threads when calling the SAPI application. It also makes for design demands in the implementation of SAPI applications in languages that do support threads, so that the separate threads don't stomp all over each other's data.

---

### Threads

A *thread* is a single-execution path within an application. Just about all Visual Basic applications have been single-threaded applications up until now, with only a single path of execution. A multi-threaded application is performing several different things at one time. A good example of a multi-threaded application is Microsoft Word 95 where, as you are typing your document, Word is checking your spelling in the background, and marking the misspelled words as you continue typing. Visual

Basic 5 enables you to make nonvisual applications that fall under certain conditions, multi-threaded, in a very Visual Basic way. We'll explore the implementation of threads in Visual Basic 5 in Chapter 23, "Using Remote Data Objects with the OLEISAPI2 Interface."

**N O T E** An effort is under way right now to establish a new, open, interface, called *FastCGI*, for use with Web server application programming. FastCGI keeps the CGI application running as a separate process so that it can't harm the Web server application, but keeps it running at all times, eliminating the primary reasons for CGI applications being slow. FastCGI opens a connection to the CGI application from the Web server, sends the necessary information to the CGI application, and waits for the CGI application to send back the results. The current benchmarks of FastCGI are comparable to SAPI performance, and FastCGI applications could be created by using any programming language. It remains to be seen how widely FastCGI will be adopted and how many major Web server vendors will add it to their Web server programming options. ■

# The ISAPI Interface

Microsoft's Internet Server Application Programming Interface (ISAPI) is designed to appear similar to the CGI interface, where some of the server variables are passed to the ISAPI application outright. However, most of the important information that the application will need, still remains to be retrieved and parsed (unlike the WinCGI interface where the submitted data was already parsed into variables).

**N O T E** The ISAPI interface being discussed here is only available on Microsoft's IIS Web server. The only other Web server vendor that implements the ISAPI interface is O'Reilly, who provides programmers with both their own, and Microsoft's ISAPI interface. ■

## The ISAPI Structure

When an ISAPI DLL is called, Microsoft's Internet Information Server passes a structure to the DLL that contains key information. This structure contains some key fields that hold information vital for the proper functioning of the ISAPI application. It also contains several fields that contain values of key CGI server variables. The rest of the fields are used for passing information back to the Web server. The fields in this structure can be found in Table 19.1.

**Table 19.1   The Fields in the ISAPI Structure, Which Are Passed to the DLL Extension**

| Field | Type | In/Out | Description |
|---|---|---|---|
| cbSize | Integer | In | Tells the DLL how large this structure is. |
| dwVersion | Integer | In | The version of the ISAPI interface being used. |

*continues*

Part
**VI**

Ch

**19**

**Table 19.1    Continued**

| Field | Type | In/Out | Description |
|---|---|---|---|
| ConnID | Handle | In | The handle of the browser connection. This variable is passed with each of the ISAPI Server functions to tell the server which client connection is being serviced by the DLL. |
| dwHttpStatusCode | Integer | Out | The HTTP response code that should be returned with the resulting data, to tell the client whether or not the request was successful. |
| lpszLogData | String | Out | This string is filled in by the DLL with any information that needs to be placed in the server log. |
| lpszMethod | String | In | The method used to call the DLL, either GET or POST. This is the same as the REQUEST_METHOD CGI variable. |
| lpszQueryString | String | In | The query string sent by the client to the server. If the client used the GET command, this field will contain the parameters that were sent by the client. This is the same as the QUERY_STRING CGI variable. |
| lpszPathInfo | String | In | Contains the path to the DLL as sent by the client. This is the same as the PATH_INFO CGI variable. |
| lpszPathTranslated | String | | This string contains the absolute path to the DLL as found on the server, including drive letters. This is the same as the PATH_TRANSLATED CGI variable. |
| cbTotalBytes | Integer | In | The total length of the parameters sent by the client. This is the same as the CONTENT_LENGTH CGI variable. |
| cbAvailable | Integer | In | The number of bytes of the parameters loaded into the next field, lpbData. |
| lpbData | String | In | This has a portion, if not all, of the data that was sent by the client. |
| lpszContentType | String | In | The content type of the data sent by the client. This will usually contain "text/html" as the content type. |

Now, if you've examined this table carefully, and you have just read the preceding chapter on the WinCGI interface, as well as Appendix A, "Standard CGI, WinCGI, and Visual Basic," you're probably thinking "That's it? Where are all of the other server variables? And what if not all of the data sent by the client is contained in the lpbData field?" Well, that's what a couple of the ISAPI server functions are used for.

## The ISAPI Server Functions

Four server functions are provided with the ISAPI interface. The first three of these functions are self-explanatory, but the fourth requires a little explanation. These four functions can be found in Table 19.2.

**Table 19.2   The Four ISAPI Server Functions**

| Name | Description |
|------|-------------|
| GetServerVariable | Gets each of the server variables provided in the CGI interface. The server variables can only be retrieved one at a time by using this function. |
| ReadClient | Gets all of the data sent by the client that is not already loaded into the lpbData field in the ISAPI structure. |
| WriteClient | Writes all that is to be returned to the client. This function is the equivalent of writing to standard out (stdout) in the CGI interface and writing to the output file in the WinCGI interface. |
| ServerSupportFunction | Performs a variety of miscellaneous functions such as redirecting the client to another URL, sends another URL to the client instead of the one requested, and sends and formats the complete HTTP response header. |

Part
VI
Ch
19

## Required ISAPI DLL Functions

Along with the four ISAPI server functions, are two functions required in the ISAPI extension DLL. These functions always use the same names, and the Web server keeps them straight by what the DLL name is that was called by the client.

The first function, *GetExtensionVersion*, is called when the DLL is first loaded, upon the Web server receiving its first request for the DLL. It does nothing more than tell the Web server which version of the ISAPI interface the DLL was written for. It returns the ISAPI version number and a text string that describes the DLL extension that was called. The assumption is that, even if Microsoft alters the ISAPI interface in the future, IIS will still support the previous versions of the interface. This function is how IIS will know which ISAPI version it needs to use with this particular DLL.

The second function, *HttpExtensionProc*, is the one called to perform all of the application functionality. The ISAPI structure is passed into this function as the only argument, and then the DLL has control of all application processing. If the ISAPI interface changes in the future, it will be this function, the ISAPI structure, and the server functions that are likely to change. The *GetExtensionVersion* function will never change.

# The OLEISAPI Interface

Once Microsoft had their ISAPI interface in place, they realized that they needed to provide an easier interface for use with Visual Basic. What they came up with is an ISAPI extension for IIS that implements a second SAPI interface called OLEISAPI. It is through this second SAPI interface that Visual Basic is really able to take advantage of the ISAPI interface, through VB's ActiveX (OLE) server capabilities.

> **N O T E**   The OLEISAPI interface is not limited to use only with Visual Basic. It can easily be used with any programming language or tool that is capable of creating OLE or ActiveX server applications or DLLs. ■

## The OLEISAPI Method Call

The OLEISAPI interface is both much more simple than the straight ISAPI interface, and much more limited. The OLEISAPI calls the Visual Basic application through any method in any class desired. These class methods have to be declared as *public*, and they have to take exactly two string parameters, the first of which holds the variables sent from the client, and the second through which Visual Basic returns the HTML document, or other resulting object, back to the client through the server. This method should look like the following:

```
Public Sub MyMethod(astrRequest as String, astrResponse as String)
```

where MyMethod is the name of the method, `astrRequest` is the string of variables that were sent from the client browser, and `astrResponse` is the HTML document that this method is returning to the client. There is nothing in the response variable when this method is called, the results of this method are placed in this variable before the method ends.

> **N O T E**   Notice that the OLEISAPI interface passes only the parameters that were sent from the client. An OLEISAPI application does not have access to any of the server variables, such as the TCP/IP address of the client, the user name of the client (if the user was authenticated), or any of the other server variables that you might want to use in a Web application. ■

## Dealing with Variables

When the OLEISAPI method is called, it is passed the string of variables just as the string was sent to the server from the client. This means that the string of variables is in pairs of key/ value, separated by an ampersand. This string will look something like the following:

```
Key1=Value1&Key2=Value2&Key3=Value+Number+3...
```

You will need to parse and convert this string into the key/value pairs before you can begin working with them. Each pair is delimited by an ampersand (&), and the key is separated from its corresponding value by an equal sign (=). Once you have the pairs parsed out, and split the key from the value, you will need to convert the plus signs (+) to spaces, and when you find a percent sign (%), it will need to be removed and the following two characters converted into a hex value which should then be converted into its ASCII character equivalent (any special characters in the actual keys or values are converted into their hex values in order to keep them separate from their special use versions). The step where the plus signs are converted into spaces can happen at any time in this process, but the conversion of the hex values, and the removal of the percent signs that mark the hex values, has to be the last step in this processing of the variable string. If the hex values are converted any sooner, any other special character processing could be triggered by a character that is really a member of the actual value and shouldn't be processed.

Let's step through an example of this variable processing. Let's say that we receive the following string of variables from the client browser:

```
Name=Davis&Company=B.+R.+Blackmarr+%26+Associates
```

If we go through and convert each of the plus signs to spaces, we now have this string:

```
Name=Davis&Company=B. R. Blackmarr %26 Associates
```

Now let's parse it into separate key/value pairs, giving us the following two key/value pairs:

```
Name=Davis
Company=B. R. Blackmarr %26 Associates
```

We separate the keys from the values, and we have our two pairs:

```
Pair 1 Key: Name
Pair 1 Value: Davis
Pair 2 Key: Company
Pair 2 Value: B. R. Blackmarr %26 Associates
```

And finally, we scan for any percent signs, remove them and treat the following two characters as a hex number which we convert into it's ASCII equivalent, and we have the following results:

```
Pair 1 Key: Name
Pair 1 Value: Davis
Pair 2 Key: Company
Pair 2 Value: B. R. Blackmarr & Associates
```

In this example, we converted the plus signs into spaces in the first step. We could just as easily have performed that function as the second or third step, but we definitely had to keep the step for converting the hex values into characters as the final step.

## Calling an OLEISAPI Application

When an OLEISAPI method is called from an HTML document, either as the target of a form, or as a regular link, the OLEISAPI DLL has to be called in the URL, with the ActiveX server name, class, and method added as additional information to be passed to the DLL. This requires using a form of passing information to an application as part of an URL where the EXE or DLL looks like another directory in the path to the target object. Let's look at an example of what this would look like. If your OLEISAPI DLL were located in the "scripts" directory, and your ActiveX server were called "MyServe" and contained the class "MyClass," which had a method called "MyMethod," which required no variables to be passed, it could be included in an HTML document as a link in the following form:

```
<A HREF="/scripts/oleisapi.dll/MyServe.MyClass.MyMethod">
```

If this method required a variable to be passed called "foo," the anchor would look like this:

```
<A HREF="/scripts/oleisapi.dll/MyServe.MyClass.MyMethod?foo=bar">
```

If this method were to be the target for an HTML form, the opening tag for the form could look like this:

```
<FORM ACTION="/scripts/oleisapi.dll/MyServe.MyClass.MyMethod"
METHOD="POST">
```

### CAUTION

If you are using the POST method to call an OLEISAPI method, you need to construct your HTML form so that at least one key/value pair will be sent with the form, even if the value portion of the pair is empty. Otherwise the OLEISAPI DLL will return an error message, without calling the method specified in the action URL for the form. You can see this for yourself by playing with the first and second examples in this chapter, using the POST method form without checking any of the check boxes on the form.

### CAUTION

The OLEISAPI interface is very limited in how much data it is capable of passing to the ActiveX server method. Depending on the version of the DLL you have, the limit could be as small as 4K of data, or as large as 32K. If you find that you need more than is being passed through to your Visual Basic ActiveX server DLL, you might want to pull the source code out of the ActiveX SDK and tweak it a little to provide the amount of data that you require.

# Preparing an NT Server for OLEISAPI Programming

Before you can call any OLEISAPI applications on an IIS Web server, there are a few preparations that will have to be made. The first of these preparations is to place the OLEISAPI DLL into an executable directory. This is usually the scripts directory, or any subdirectory under the scripts directory. Depending on how your IIS server is configured, you might be able to place the OLEISAPI DLL in another directory on the server, but the directory has to be reachable via an URL by the client browser.

In order for the IIS server to be able to create ActiveX objects, and thus call your OLEISAPI application, you will need to configure your NT server to allow IIS to create ActiveX objects. By default, only Administrator and System have the Access and Launch permissions necessary to create ActiveX objects, and IIS does not run as either of these. IIS tries to create ActiveX objects by using the permissions of IUSR_MACHINENAME (where MACHINENAME is substituted with the machine name), and this account needs to be granted Access and Launch permissions before this can happen. This can be set up by following these steps:

1. Log into your NT server as administrator.

2. Choose Run from the Start menu.

3. Enter **DCOMCNFG.EXE**, with the path to your winnt/system32 directory, and select OK.

4. Select the *Default Security* tab.

5. Click the *Edit Default* button in the *Default Access Permissions* box on the *Distributed COM Configuration Properties* dialog box, as seen in Figure 19.1.

6. In the *Registry Value Permissions* dialog box, click the *Add* button.

7. In the *Add Users and Groups* dialog box, click the *Show Users* button.

8. Select the IUSR_<Your machine name> entry in the list of users and groups, then click the *Add* button, as seen in Figure 19.2 (the machine in Figure 19.2 is named BULLFROG, so the IUSR_BULLFROG entry is selected). You can leave the Type of Access as "Allow Access" (which should be the default).

9. Click *OK* on the *Add Users and Groups* dialog box, and again on the *Registry Value Permissions* dialog.

10. Click the *Edit Default* button in the *Default Launch Permissions* box on the *Distributed COM Configuration Properties* sheet, and repeat steps 6 through 9.

11. Click the OK button on the *Distributed COM Configuration Properties* sheet. Your system should now be ready to run OLEISAPI applications.

**Part**
**VI**

**Ch**
**19**

**FIG. 19.1**
The DCOM Configuration Properties *sheet*, where you configure Access and Launch permissions for Users and Groups on NT.

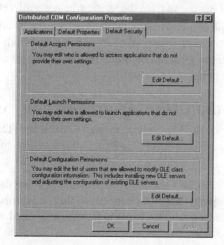

**FIG. 19.2**

Adding
`IUSR_BULLFROG` to the
list of users with Access
permission on DCOM
objects.

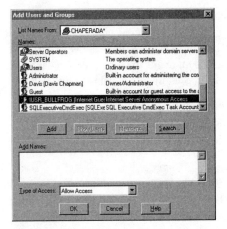

# Building a Simple OLEISAPI Application

Before we begin building an OLEISAPI application, let's determine what the application needs to do. What we'll do is take our OLEISAPI application through three basic stages. In each stage we'll expand on the functionality we built in the previous stage, ending with something we can take with us for use in future OLEISAPI applications. In these stages, we will focus on the processing of the parameters that are passed from the client browser to our application. We can outline these stages as follows:

1. In the first stage, we will simply return the string of parameters passed in the form that they were passed, in an HTML document.

2. In the second stage, we will build a class that parses the string of parameters into their individual key/value pairs. We will use this class to build an HTML document that lists the key/value pairs that were sent from the client, which we will return to the client.

3. In the third stage, we will complete our parameter processing by adding the capability to correctly convert any special characters that are in the data, which were passed as hex values. We will format these values in the same HTML document as in step 2, returning to the client a list of the parameters passed.

## Sending Simple Data to the OLEISAPI Application

Before we begin building our OLEISAPI application, we will need an HTML form to use for sending data to our application. We will place this form in the root directory of our IIS Web server.

To illustrate the differences in the GET and POST methods of sending data to our OLEISAPI application, we will build a simple HTML document containing two forms, the first using the GET method, and the second using the POST method. Otherwise, the two forms on our HTML document will be basically identical.

In order to keep our value submission simple, we will limit our input fields to check boxes. With HTML check boxes, the name/value pair is sent only if the check box is checked. If no check boxes are checked, no data is sent to the server. This will provide an excellent medium to experiment and see how sending no data affects the OLEISAPI application with both the GET and POST methods (as mentioned earlier, the POST method is likely to return an OLEISAPI error without calling the OLEISAPI application if it is called with no data). We will be using the HTML document in Listing 19.1 for our first two stages, and then change to allow more flexible input for sending to our third stage version. You can see what this HTML document looks like in Figure 19.3.

---

**Listing 19.1  EX1.HTM—The HTML Form Used for the First OLEISAPI Example**

```
<HTML>
<head>
<TITLE>OLEISAPI Programming Example 1</TITLE>
</head>
<body bgcolor=#C0C0C0>
<H1>OLEISAPI Programming Example 1</H1>
<p>
<I>FormDump</I> - Form Decoder and Dumper
<HR>
<H3>This is a GET operation</H3>
<FORM action="/scripts/oleisapi.dll/isapiex1.Isapi1.DoGet"
method=get>
<p>
<INPUT TYPE="CHECKBOX" NAME="check1"
VALUE="SystemInfo">System Information
<p>
<INPUT TYPE="CHECKBOX" NAME="check2"
VALUE="MemoryStatus">Memory Status
<p>
<INPUT TYPE="CHECKBOX" NAME="check3"
VALUE="ProcessInfo">Process Information
<p>
<INPUT type="submit" value="Do Query">
</FORM>
<hr>
<H3>This is a POST operation</H3>
<FORM action="/scripts/oleisapi.dll/isapiex1.Isapi1.DoPost"
method=post>
<p>
<INPUT TYPE="CHECKBOX" NAME="check1"
VALUE="SystemInfo">System Information
<p>
<INPUT TYPE="CHECKBOX" NAME="check2"
VALUE="MemoryStatus">Memory Status
<p>
<INPUT TYPE="CHECKBOX" NAME="check3"
VALUE="ProcessInfo">Process Information
<p>
<INPUT type="submit" value="Do Query">
</FORM>
</body>
</HTML>
```

Part
**VI**

Ch
**19**

**FIG. 19.3**

The HTML Document we will be using through the first two stages of our application development.

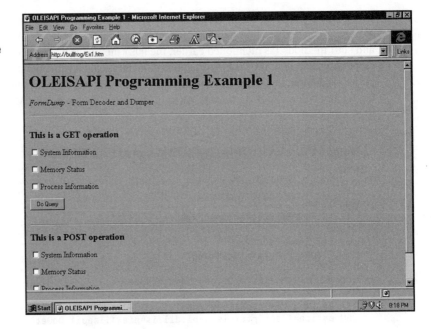

## Declaring the Class OLEISAPI Methods

To begin our application development effort, we will need to begin a new Visual Basic project. We will be making an ActiveX DLL in this project, and we will name the project *isapiex1*. Once the project has been initialized, open up the project properties (*isapi1 Properties* on the *Project* menu) and select the *Unattended Execution* option. This option allows our DLL to run as a thread-safe DLL (we will get more into Visual Basic threaded execution in Chapter 23, "Using Remote Data Objects with the OLEISAPI2 Interface").

For testing and debugging purposes, you might want to create a second project, which is a standard EXE. In this project, you will place a call to the methods which are called by the OLEISAPI DLL, passing the parameter strings that would be passed from the browser client. An example of this using a formless application is the following:

```
Sub Main()
    Dim oleisapi As New Isapi1
    Dim strResponse As String
    Dim strRequest As String

    strRequest = "check2=MachineName"
    With oleisapi
        .DoGet strRequest, strResponse
    End With
End Sub
```

You can place any string of parameters into the strRequest variable, and then step through the entire application processing, checking all variables and watching all processing.

When you create this second project, the classes will be changed to *Private* instancing, so you will have to remember to change them back to *Multiuse* once you reopen the ActiveX DLL project.

For this application, we will be performing the same processing regardless of whether the GET or POST method is called, so what we'll do is declare two methods, one to be called using the GET method, and the other using the POST method, and from these we'll call a common function which will perform all of our processing. We'll call our two methods, *DoGet* for use with the GET method, and *DoPost* for use with the POST method. We'll place these two functions into a class called *Isapi1*, which we'll declare as *Multiuse* instancing. We'll place in it the two methods, *DoGet* and *DoPost*, as seen in Listing 19.2.

> **Listing 19.2   ISAPI1.CLS—The *DoGet* and *DoPost* Methods that Will Be Called from the Web Browser**

```
Public Sub DoGet(astrRequest As String, astrResponse As String)
    astrResponse = ProcParams(astrRequest, "GET")
End Sub
Public Sub DoPost(astrRequest As String, astrResponse As String)
    astrResponse = ProcParams(astrRequest, "POST")
End Sub
```

# Returning the Variable String Passed from the Client

For this first step, we can build a very simple ProcParams function. All that we really need to do is build an HTML document that returns the method used by the client, and presents the string of variables sent from the client. We do have to include the Content-type line for the HTTP message header to be returned with our document. Once we are done building the HTML document, we return it to the calling routine, which will place it into the results parameter of the called method. Our initial implementation of ProcParams can be found in Listing 19.3, and the resulting HTML document can be seen in Figure 19.4.

> **Listing 19.3   ISAPI1.CLS—The *ProcParams* Function Which Builds the Response HTML Document Using the Values Passed from the Client**

```
Private Function ProcParams(astrRequest As String, _
                            astrMethod As String) As String
    Dim strHTML As String

    'Begin building the return HTML document with the
    'content-type header line
    strHTML = "Content-type: text/html" & vbCrLf & vbCrLf
    'Build the HTML document
    strHTML = strHTML & "<HTML><HEAD><TITLE>"
    strHTML = strHTML & "OLEISAPI Programming Example"
    strHTML = strHTML & "</TITLE></HEAD><BODY BGCOLOR=#C0C0C0>"
    strHTML = strHTML & _
```

*continues*

**Listing 19.3  Continued**

```
                    "<H1>OLEISAPI Programming Example</H1><HR><P>"
        strHTML = strHTML & _
                    "The method used to submit this was <STRONG>"
        'Tell the user what method was used to call this application
        strHTML = strHTML & astrMethod & "</STRONG></P><P>"
        'Tell the user how many parameters were passed
        strHTML = strHTML & _
                    "The values submitted are as follows:</P><P>"
        'Show the parameters that were passed
        strHTML = strHTML & astrRequest
        'Close the HTML document
        strHTML = strHTML & "</P></BODY></HTML>"
        'Return the HTML document to the calling routine
        ProcParams = strHTML
    End Function
```

**FIG. 19.4**

The resulting HTML document from our stage 1 OLEISAPI application.

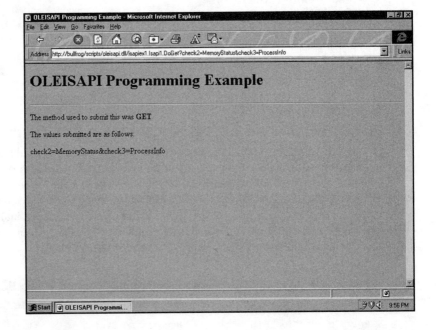

 **TIP** If you need to recompile your OLEISAPI DLL after you have called it from your IIS Web server, you will need to shut down the Web service. Part of the performance benefit of OLEISAPI DLL applications, is that the Web server holds them in memory, even when they are not being actively used. Because of this, you will not be able to recompile your project until the old version is unloaded from memory. The only way to get the IIS Web server to unload your DLL is to shut down the IIS server. Once you have brought the server down, you can start it right back up again, and until your DLL is called again, it will not be loaded into memory, allowing you to recompile your project.

**TIP** If you have Visual Basic installed on the same machine as your IIS Web server, Visual Basic will register your ActiveX DLL when it is compiled. If you move your DLL, or compiled it on a different machine than your IIS server, you will need to run the REGSVR32.EXE application from a DOS prompt, specifying your DLL name on the command line as the only argument. This will register your DLL, and once your DLL is registered, it will be found when it is called, regardless of where on the system it might be located (as long as it was registered in that location).

## Preparing for Processing the Parameters Passed by the Client

For our next stage, we will create a second project, basically identical to the first, only we'll name this one *isapiex2*. We'll copy in our Isapi1 class and rename it Isapi2. We'll alter the URLs in our HTML form that calls our application, and we're ready to get started on this version.

What we're focusing on in this stage is parsing up our parameters that are passed from the client browser. We know that these values will be coming in key/value pairs, so why don't we define a *ParamValues* type that consists of one key and one value like in Listing 19.4.

### Listing 19.4   GENERAL.BAS—The ParamValues Type Declaration

```
'This type structure will be used for holding all of
'the values that are passed by the HTML form. These
'values are all passed in the form of "<Key>=<Value>"
'so we will store them as a key and value pair.
Type ParamValues
    Key As String
    Value As String
End Type
```

We know that we are likely to be receiving any number of key/value pairs in the string of parameters passed from the browser. We will need to have some place to hold these pairs in an easy-to-access form, but it'll be easier to reuse if we encapsulate all of the parameter processing and holding into a new class that we'll call *Parameters*. We can declare this class as either Multiuse or Private, because we'll only declare a local instance of this class within the ProcParams function.

We know that we will need some form of array to hold the pairs of parameters that we receive, and we'll probably want to keep track of how many pairs we have. We can accommodate these needs by declaring the array and counter in Listing 19.5 in our new Parameters class.

### Listing 19.5   PARAMTRS.CLS—The Variable Declarations for the Parameters Class

```
'This array of the ParamValues type structure will
'be used to hold the parsed-up parameters that are
'passed to this class.
Private cpvParameterValues() As ParamValues
```

Part **VI**

Ch **19**

*continues*

**Listing 19.5   Continued**

```
'This variable will be used to hold the number of
'parameters that were passed from the HTML form
'and are being held in the array of ParamValues
'Key/Value pairs
Private ciNumParameters As Integer
```

# Parsing the String of Parameters

For this class to be useful, it'll need to have a complete understanding of the formatting in which variables are passed from Web browsers. It'll need one primary starting point through which is passed the string of parameters that needs to be parsed and loaded into the array of *ParamValues*. We can name this function *ParseParameters* and declare it as a Public function, as it will need to be called from the class that has received the string of parameters in the first place. For this function to be really useful, it could return as a result value the number of key/value pairs it found in the string.

Before we get into the coding of this function, let's think through the steps that this function will need to take in parsing up the string of parameters.

1. Check the length of the string to make sure that there are parameters to be parsed. If there are none, return 0 as the number of parameter pairs found.

2. Replace all of the plus signs with spaces.

3. Find the first ampersand in the string.

4. Split the string on the ampersand, holding onto the right portion for future parsing, and placing the left portion into a string to be parsed into the key and value portions.

5. Find the equal sign in the string. If there is no equal sign, then there is something wrong with the string that we assumed to be a key/value pair.

6. Increment the counter to designate that another pair has been found.

7. Resize the array of ParamValues, increasing it by one, making sure to preserve anything already loaded into it.

8. Split the string on the equal sign, placing the left portion into the key position of the new ParamValues array slot, and placing the right portion of the string into the value position.

9. Find the next ampersand, then repeat steps 4 through 8.

10. If there are no more ampersands, perform steps 5 through 8 on the remaining string.

11. Return the number of key/value pairs that were found in the string.

Sounds straight ahead enough, so look at an implementation of this in Listing 19.6.

**Listing 19.6    PARAMTRS.CLS—The *ParseParameters* Method, Which Is Passed the String of Key/Value Pairs to Be Parsed**

```
Public Function ParseParameters(astrParams As String) As Integer
    Dim strCurParam As String
    Dim strRemainParams As String
    Dim lCurPos As Long

    'Initialize the number of pairs found to zero
    ciNumParameters = 0
    'Was there any parameters passed?
    If Len(astrParams) > 0 Then
        'Yes, scan the string and replace all
        'plus signs with spaces
        strRemainParams = ReplaceChars(astrParams, "+", " ")
        'Find the first ampersand, which is used to delimit
        'between key/value pairs
        lCurPos = InStr(1, strRemainParams, "&", vbTextCompare)
        'Loop as long as ampersands continue to be found
        Do While (lCurPos > 0)
            'Copy everything to the left of the ampersand into
            'the holding variable for the current parameter
            strCurParam = Left(strRemainParams, (lCurPos - 1))
            'Truncate everything up to the ampersand off of the
            'remaining string of parameters
            strRemainParams = Mid(strRemainParams, (lCurPos + 1))
            'Find the equal sign, separating the "Key" from
            'the "Value"
            lCurPos = InStr(1, strCurParam, "=", vbTextCompare)
            'Was an equal character found?
            If lCurPos > 0 Then
                'Increment the number of parameters found
                ciNumParameters = ciNumParameters + 1
                'Increase the size of the array into which the
                'parameters are being placed, preserving the
                'pairs that have already been copied in
                ReDim Preserve cpvParameterValues(ciNumParameters)
                'Copy the Key into the array
                cpvParameterValues(ciNumParameters).Key = _
                        Left(strCurParam, (lCurPos - 1))
                'Is there a value portion for this parameter?
                If lCurPos < Len(strCurParam) Then
                    'Yes, copy the value into the array
                    cpvParameterValues(ciNumParameters).Value = _
                            Mid(strCurParam, (lCurPos + 1))
                End If
            End If
            'Look for the next ampersand delimiting the next
            'pairs of parameters
            lCurPos = InStr(1, strRemainParams, "&", vbTextCompare)
```

*continues*

**Listing 19.6   Continued**

```
      Loop
      'There are no more ampersands, the remaining parameter
      'pair is in the holding variable from which all other
      'parameter pairs have been parsed out. Find the equal
      'sign separating the key from the value
      lCurPos = InStr(1, strRemainParams, "=", vbTextCompare)
      'Is there an equal character?
      If lCurPos > 0 Then
          'Increment the number of parameters found
          ciNumParameters = ciNumParameters + 1
          'Increase the size of the array into which the
          'parameters are being placed, preserving the
          'pairs that have already been copied in
          ReDim Preserve cpvParameterValues(ciNumParameters)
          'Copy the Key into the array
          cpvParameterValues(ciNumParameters).Key = _
                          Left(strRemainParams, (lCurPos - 1))
          'Is there a value portion for this parameter?
          If lCurPos < Len(strRemainParams) Then
              'Yes, copy the value into the array
              cpvParameterValues(ciNumParameters).Value = _
                          Mid(strRemainParams, (lCurPos + 1))
          End If
      End If
  End If
  'Return the number of parameter pairs that were found
  ParseParameters = ciNumParameters
End Function
```

# Replacing Substitute Characters

Now, let's be honest, there was one step in that last function that we kind of skipped over, not listing the steps actually involved, and reducing it to a one-line function. We did this because we did make it into a single-function call. This was the step where we "replace all of the plus signs with spaces." All we did was call a function named ReplaceChars, passing the string of parameters, a plus sign as the character to look for, and a space as the character to substitute for the plus signs.

We could eliminate the second and last arguments to this function by writing it so that it would know to look for plus signs, and that they should be replaced with spaces, but that would limit the usability of this function to this one instance. If we write our ReplaceChars function to expect to be passed the character to be replaced, as well as the character to replace the first character, it could be useful in many more circumstances. We'll place this function into the Parameters class, although it might be more appropriate to place it into a generic module of functions that can be called from anywhere, and can be reused in subsequent applications.

In our ReplaceChars function, which can been found in Listing 19.7, we take a slightly inefficient approach, because it was easier to write and get bug-free than a more efficient approach might have been. Our version follows these steps:

1. We start scanning for the character to be replaced at the first character in the string.

2. If we find the character that needs to be replaced, we split the string at that point, building a new string with the entire string to the left of the character that was found, the replacement character, and the entire string to the right of the character to be replaced.

3. We repeat steps 1 and 2 until there are no more characters to be replaced.

As we gradually replace all of the occurrences of the character that needs replacing, we continuously rescan the portion of the string that we have already replaced all occurrences on the character that needs replacing. If we really wanted to be efficient, we would only scan that portion of the string that we have not already scanned. Unfortunately, achieving this efficiency would sacrifice the simplicity of the approach that we did take, and the strings that we are scanning in this application will not be long enough to warrant a more efficient approach.

**Listing 19.7  PARAMTRS.CLS—The *ReplaceChars* Function, Which Is Called to Replace All Occurrences of a Particular Character with Another Character**

```
Private Function ReplaceChars(astrOrigString As String, _
                              astrCharToRepl As String, _
                              astrNewChar As String) As String
    Dim strNewStr As String
    Dim strCopyStr As String
    Dim lCharPos As Long

    'Copy the original string into a holding variable
    strCopyStr = astrOrigString
    'Copy the original string into the target variable,
    'just in case there are no occurrences of the character
    'that is to be replaced
    strNewStr = strCopyStr
    'Find the first occurrence of the character that needs
    'to be replaced
    lCharPos = InStr(1, strCopyStr, astrCharToRepl, vbTextCompare)
    'Loop while this character continues to be found in the string
    Do While (lCharPos > 0)
        'Substitute the replacement character for the character
        'needing to be replaced
        strNewStr = Left(strCopyStr, (lCharPos - 1)) & _
                    astrNewChar & Mid(strCopyStr, (lCharPos + 1))
        'Copy the new string back into the holding variable
        strCopyStr = strNewStr
        'Scan the string for the next occurrence of the character
        'that needs to be replaced
        lCharPos = InStr(1, strCopyStr, astrCharToRepl, _
                                            vbTextCompare)
    Loop
    'Return the resulting string to the calling routine
    ReplaceChars = strNewStr
End Function
```

Part

**VI**

Ch

**19**

# Retrieving the Name for a Key

Once we have our array loaded with key/value pairs, we will need to be able to retrieve specific values from the array. One of the most simple would be to request the key and value by the parameter number. This would allow us to loop through the keys to determine if a certain key/value pair was sent, or if there were multiple values submitted with the same key (the keys within an HTML form are not required to be unique). To provide for this need, we'll add a public function to retrieve the name of a specific key, with the key specified by it's parameter number. All we need to do is check to make sure that the parameter key number requested is a valid array position, then we can return the key string in that position, as seen in Listing 19.8.

**Listing 19.8   PARAMTRS.CLS—The *GetKeyNameByNum* Function, Which Returns the Name of the Key Specified If It Exists**

```
Public Function GetKeyNameByNum(aiParamNum As Integer) As String
    'Check the parameter number passed, make sure that
    'there are at least that many parameters available
    If aiParamNum <= ciNumParameters Then
        'The number is for a valid parameter, return the
        'parameter key name
        GetKeyNameByNum = cpvParameterValues(aiParamNum).Key
    Else
        'The number requested is greater than the number
        'of parameters passed by the HTML form, return
        'an empty string
        GetKeyNameByNum = ""
    End If
End Function
```

# Retrieving the Value for a Parameter

We can do the same thing that we did for retrieving the key name, to also retrieve the parameter value. We need to perform the exact same check, and we'll end up with the function in Listing 19.9.

**Listing 19.9   PARAMTRS.CLS—The *GetKeyValueByNum* Function, Which Returns the Value of the Key Specified If It Exists**

```
Public Function GetKeyValueByNum(aiParamNum As Integer) As String
    'Check the parameter number passed, make sure that
    'there are at least that many parameters available
    If aiParamNum <= ciNumParameters Then
        'The number is for a valid parameter, return the
        'parameter value
        GetKeyValueByNum = cpvParameterValues(aiParamNum).Value
```

```
        Else
            'The number requested is greater than the number
            'of parameters passed by the HTML form, return
            'an empty string
            GetKeyValueByNum = ""
        End If
End Function
```

## Retrieving the Value for a Particular Key

For those times when we want to get the value of a specific key, and we know that the name of
the key is unique, we will want to provide a function for retrieving the value by specifying the
key name. In this function, we'll want to get a little more involved than in the previous two
functions.

1. First, we want to make sure that we have parameters to search through. If we don't have
   any, return an empty string.

2. If we do have some parameters to search through, we'll want to begin with the first array
   position, and loop through each position until either we run out of positions, or we find a
   matching key.

3. We compare the key in the array position we are currently checking to the key that we
   are looking for.

4. If the key matches, return the value for this position.

5. If the key does not match, and we are not at the end of the array, move to the next array
   position and repeat steps 3 through 5.

6. If we made it through the entire array without finding a matching key, return an empty
   string.

The function that performs this can be seen in Listing 19.10.

Part
**VI**

Ch

**19**

**Listing 19.10  PARAMTRS.CLS—The *GetKeyValue* Function, Which
Returns the Value of the Key Specified. This Function Requires that the
Key Name Be Passed**

```
Public Function GetKeyValue(astrKeyName As String) As String
    Dim iCurKey As Integer: iCurKey = 1
    Dim bDone As Boolean: bDone = False

    'Are there any parameters to search for the requested key?
    If ciNumParameters < 1 Then
        'No, return an empty string
        GetKeyValue = ""
```

*continues*

**Listing 19.10 Continued**

```
    Else
        'Yes, loop until either the matching key value has been
        'found, or all parameters have been checked
        Do While (iCurKey <= ciNumParameters) And Not bDone
            'Does the current key match the requested key?
            If astrKeyName = cpvParameterValues(iCurKey).Key Then
                'Yes, set the flag to indicate that the requested
                'parameter has been found
                bDone = True
                'Return the parameter value
                GetKeyValue = cpvParameterValues(iCurKey).Value
            Else
                'No, increment the parameter counter to the
                'next key/value pair
                iCurKey = iCurKey + 1
            End If
        Loop
        'Did we find the matching key?
        If Not bDone Then
            'No, return an empty string
            GetKeyValue = ""
        End If
    End If
End Function
```

This completes our current implementation of the Parameters class. We will be extending it a little further once we get to our stage 3 implementation.

# Listing the Values Passed for the Client to See

Now that we have a means of parsing and retrieving the string of parameters that we receive, let's update our *ProcParams* function to take advantage of our new functionality. We will make two basic alterations to our previous version.

1. First, we'll create a local instance of the *Parameters* class, and call the `ParseParameters` function, passing the string of parameters that we received from the client.

2. Second, instead of just showing the string of parameters that was received, we'll tell the user how many key/value pairs were received, and build a table showing the key/value pairs to the user. We'll retrieve the key name and value of each parameter pair by specifying the parameter number which is also the row in the table that we are assembling.

Our updated version of *ProcParams* can be found in Listing 19.11, and the resulting HTML document can be seen in Figure 19.5.

**Listing 19.11   ISAPI2.CLS—The Updated *ProcParams* Function, Which Specifies How Many Variables Were Passed and What Their Values Are**

```
Private Function ProcParams(astrRequest As String, _
                            astrMethod As String) As String
    'Create a local instance of the Parameters class
    Dim pcParams As New Parameters
    Dim iNumParams As Integer
    Dim iCurParam As Integer
    Dim strHTML As String
    'Pass the parameters sent from the HTML form
    'to the local instance of the Parameters class
    iNumParams = pcParams.ParseParameters(astrRequest)
    'Begin building the return HTML document with the
    'content-type header line
    strHTML = "Content-type: text/html" & vbCrLf & vbCrLf
    'Build the HTML document
    strHTML = strHTML & "<HTML><HEAD><TITLE>"
    strHTML = strHTML & "OLEISAPI Programming Example"
    strHTML = strHTML & "</TITLE></HEAD><BODY BGCOLOR=#C0C0C0>"
    strHTML = strHTML & _
                "<H1>OLEISAPI Programming Example</H1><HR><P>"
    strHTML = strHTML & _
                "The method used to submit this was <STRONG>"
    'Tell the user what method was used to call this application
    strHTML = strHTML & astrMethod & "</STRONG></P><P>"
    'Tell the user how many parameters were passed
    strHTML = strHTML & "There were <STRONG>" & CStr(iNumParams)
    strHTML = strHTML & _
                "</STRONG> values submitted as follows:</P>"
    'Build a table of the parameters that were passed
    strHTML = strHTML & _
        "<TABLE BORDER=2><TR><TH>Key</TH><TH>Value</TH></TR>"
    'Were there any parameters passed?
    If iNumParams > 0 Then
        'Loop through each of the parameters
        For iCurParam = 1 To iNumParams
            'Place the parameter key into the table
            strHTML = strHTML & "<TR><TD>" & _
                        pcParams.GetKeyNameByNum(iCurParam)
            'Place the parameter value into the table
            strHTML = strHTML & "</TD><TD>" & _
                        pcParams.GetKeyValueByNum(iCurParam)
            strHTML = strHTML & "</TD></TR>"
            'Loop to the next parameter
        Next
    End If
    'Close the HTML table and document
    strHTML = strHTML & "</TABLE></BODY></HTML>"
    'Return the HTML document to the calling routine
    ProcParams = strHTML
End Function
```

Part
VI

Ch

19

**FIG. 19.5**

The resulting HTML document from our second stage version of our OLEISAPI example.

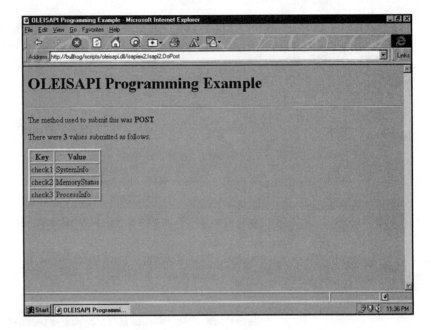

## Dealing with Special Characters in the Data

In our final stage, we will be adding functionality to deal with special characters that are part of the data being sent to our OLEISAPI application. Before we get into coding out application, we will need to change the HTML form that we are using to submit our data. We need to have input fields where we can type in any text we want to see transmitted so that we can check for correct processing of these special characters. We'll use the HTML form in Listing 19.12 for this stage. This HTML form can be seen in Figure 19.6.

**Listing 19.12   EX3.HTM—The HTML Form Used for the Third Example, Illustrating the Decoding of Hex Values**

```
<html><head><title>OLEISAPI Programming Example 3</title></head>
<body bgcolor=#C0C0C0>
<h1>OLEISAPI Programming Example 3</h1>
<p>More Variety in what is being sent to the OLEISAPI
application.</p>
<hr><p>
<a HREF="/scripts/oleisapi.dll/isapiex3.Isapi3.DoGet?arg1=foo">
This link</a> simply invokes the OLEISAPI directly via a URL.
<hr><p>
<form action="/scripts/oleisapi.dll/isapiex3.Isapi3.DoPost"
method="POST">
<input type="submit" value="Click here"> to see this
form use the <strong>POST
</strong>
technique to invoke an object method called DoPost.
```

```
<p><table align=center border=0>
<tr><td align=right valign=top><font size=4>Value 1</td>
<td align=left><input name="Val1"></td>
<tr><td align=right valign=top><font size=4>Value 2</td>
<td align=left><input name="Val2"></td>
<tr><td align=right valign=top><font size=4>Free form text</td>
<!— Note that the next input field, which is type "textarea" —>
<!— may not display correctly in all browsers —>
<td align=left><input name="TextVal" type="textarea" size="20,5"
maxlength="250"></td></table></form>
<p><hr>
<form action="/scripts/oleisapi.dll/isapiex3.Isapi3.DoGet"
method="GET">
<input type="submit" value="Click here"> to see this
form use the <strong>GET
</strong>
technique to invoke a different method on the same object
called DoGet.
<p><table align=center border=0>
<tr><td align=right valign=top><font size=4>Value 1</td>
<td align=left><input name="Val1"></td>
<tr><td align=right valign=top><font size=4>Value 2</td>
<td align=left><input name="Val2"></td>
<tr><td align=right valign=top><font size=4>Free form text</td>
<!— Note that the next input field, which is type "textarea" —>
<!— may not display correctly in all browsers —>
<td align=left><input name="TextVal" type="textarea" size="20,5"
maxlength="250"></td></table></form>
<p><hr>
</body>
</html>
```

**FIG. 19.6**

The HTML form that we
will use for testing the
third stage or our
OLEISAPI application.

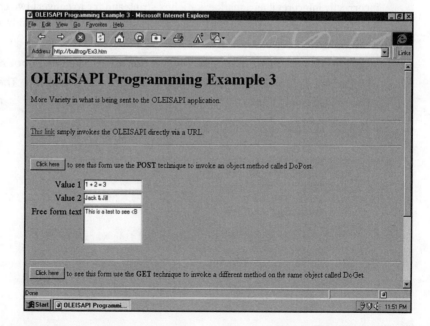

Part
VI

Ch

19

# Decoding Hex Character Values

All that we really need to do in order to add the capability to handle special characters, is to add the capability to decode the hex values that might be embedded within the string of parameters. In order to do this, we will need to build a function that understands the way that these hex values are placed into the parameter string. We'll add this function to our Parameters class that we started in the second stage of this application. The hex conversion function will need to perform the following steps:

1.  Initialize a target string as an empty string.

2.  Search for the first percent sign.

3.  If a percent sign was found, parse off everything in the string to the left of the percent sign, and add it to the target string.

4.  Remove the percent sign, and copy the two following characters into a holding variable.

5.  Convert the two characters into the actual hex value that they represent.

6.  Convert the hex value into the ASCII character that it represents and add it to the target string.

7.  Scan the remaining string for any more percent signs.

8.  Repeat steps 3 through 7 until all percent signs have been found.

9.  Add the remaining string to the target string, and return the target string to the calling routine.

Note that in this function, we take care not to rescan the portion of the string that we have already scanned. We have to do this because one of these hex values could be a percent sign that belongs as part of the data. If we stumbled across one of these percent signs, we would incorrectly interpret it as a marker for a hex string and try to convert two characters that are not really a hex value. We can see the implementation of this function in Listing 19.13.

> **Listing 19.13  PARAMTRS.CLS—The *ConvertHexValues* Function Which Finds Hex Values in the Parameters and Converts Them into Their ASCII Character Equivalents**

```
Private Function ConvertHexValues(astrOrigString As String) _
                          As String
    'Initialize the target string as an empty string
    Dim strNewStr As String: strNewStr = ""
    Dim strCopyStr As String
    Dim lCharPos As Long
    Dim strHexStr As String
    Dim lHexValue As Integer

    'Copy the original string into a holding variable
    strCopyStr = astrOrigString
    'Scan the string for the first percent sign
    lCharPos = InStr(1, astrOrigString, "%", vbTextCompare)
    'Loop as long as percent signs are found
```

```
    Do While (lCharPos > 0)
        'Add whatever was in front of the percent sign
        'onto the target string
        strNewStr = strNewStr & Left(strCopyStr, (lCharPos - 1))
        'Increment the position marker on place
        lCharPos = lCharPos + 1
        'Copy the two characters that make up the hex
        'value into a holding variable
        strHexStr = Mid(strCopyStr, lCharPos, 2)
        'Truncate everything through the hex value
        'off of the front of the holding copy of the
        'original string
        strCopyStr = Mid(strCopyStr, (lCharPos + 2))
        'Convert the hex value into it's ASCII character
        'and add it to the end of the target string
        strNewStr = strNewStr & Chr(Val("&H" & strHexStr))
        'Scan for the next percent sign in the remaining
        'string
        lCharPos = InStr(1, strCopyStr, "%", vbTextCompare)
    Loop
    'Add what's left of the original string onto the
    'end of the target string
    strNewStr = strNewStr & strCopyStr
    'Return the resulting string to the calling routine
    ConvertHexValues = strNewStr
End Function
```

# Completing the Parameter Parsing Picture

Our final step in building the third stage of our application is to plug our hex conversion function into our `ParseParameters` function. Since the hex conversion has to be the last step in processing the string of parameters, it makes sense to call our hex conversion function as each individual key and value are being loaded into their slots in our array of ParamValues, as in Listing 19.14.

**Listing 19.14    PARAMTRS.CLS—The Updated *ParseParameters* Function, Which Now Converts Any Hex Values in the Parameters as They are Being Placed into the Holding Array**

```
Public Function ParseParameters(astrParams As String) As Integer
    Dim strCurParam As String
    Dim strRemainParams As String
    Dim lCurPos As Long

    'Initialize the number of pairs found to zero
    ciNumParameters = 0
    'Was there any parameters passed?
    If Len(astrParams) > 0 Then
        'Yes, scan the string and replace all plus signs with spaces
        strRemainParams = ReplaceChars(astrParams, "+", " ")
```

*continues*

**Listing 19.14   Continued**

```
'Find the first ampersand, which is used to delimit between
'key/value pairs
lCurPos = InStr(1, strRemainParams, "&", vbTextCompare)
'Loop as long as ampersands continue to be found
Do While (lCurPos > 0)
    'Copy everything to the left of the ampersand into
    'the holding variable for the current parameter
    strCurParam = Left(strRemainParams, (lCurPos - 1))
    'Truncate everything up to the ampersand off of the
    'remaining string of parameters
    strRemainParams = Mid(strRemainParams, (lCurPos + 1))
    'Find the equal sign, separating the "Key" from
    'the "Value"
    lCurPos = InStr(1, strCurParam, "=", vbTextCompare)
    'Was an equal character found?
    If lCurPos > 0 Then
        'Increment the number of parameters found
        ciNumParameters = ciNumParameters + 1
        'Increase the size of the array into which the
        'parameters are being placed, preserving the
        'pairs that have already been copied in
        ReDim Preserve cpvParameterValues(ciNumParameters)
        'Copy the Key into the array, converting any
        'hex values in it back into the ASCII characters
        'they represent
        cpvParameterValues(ciNumParameters).Key = _
                ConvertHexValues(Left(strCurParam, _
                                    (lCurPos - 1)))
        'Is there a value portion for this parameter?
        If lCurPos < Len(strCurParam) Then
            'Yes, copy the value into the array, converting
            'any hex values in it back into the ASCII
            'characters they represent
            cpvParameterValues(ciNumParameters).Value = _
                ConvertHexValues(Mid(strCurParam, _
                                    (lCurPos + 1)))
        End If
    End If
    'Look for the next ampersand delimiting the next
    'pairs of parameters
    lCurPos = InStr(1, strRemainParams, "&", vbTextCompare)
Loop
'There are no more ampersands, the remaining parameter
'pair is in the holding variable from which all other
'parameter pairs have been parsed out. Find the equal
'sign separating the key from the value
lCurPos = InStr(1, strRemainParams, "=", vbTextCompare)
'Is there an equal character?
If lCurPos > 0 Then
    'Increment the number of parameters found
    ciNumParameters = ciNumParameters + 1
    'Increase the size of the array into which the
    'parameters are being placed, preserving the
```

```
                'pairs that have already been copied in
                ReDim Preserve cpvParameterValues(ciNumParameters)
                'Copy the Key into the array, converting any
                'hex values in it back into the ASCII characters
                'they represent
                cpvParameterValues(ciNumParameters).Key = _
                            ConvertHexValues(Left(strRemainParams, _
                                            (lCurPos - 1)))
                'Is there a value portion for this parameter?
                If lCurPos < Len(strRemainParams) Then
                    'Yes, copy the value into the array, converting
                    'any hex values in it back into the ASCII
                    'characters they represent
                    cpvParameterValues(ciNumParameters).Value = _
                            ConvertHexValues(Mid(strRemainParams, _
                                            (lCurPos + 1)))
                End If
            End If
        End If
        'Return the number of parameter pairs that were found
        ParseParameters = ciNumParameters
    End Function
```

And the results of our working application can be seen in Figure 19.7. In this figure, the values seen in the table were submitted by using the GET method. This method sends the parameter string as part of the URL, so you can see how each of the special characters were encoded as hex values.

**FIG. 19.7**
The resulting HTML Document from our completed OLEISAPI application. Note the special characters encoded as hex values in the URL.

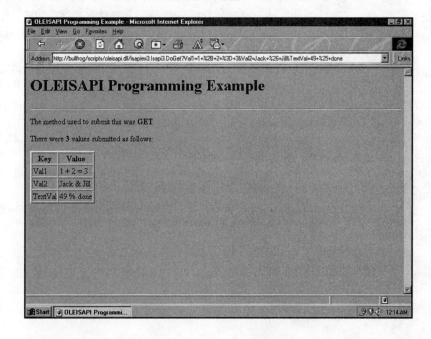

# From Here...

In this chapter we took a look at Web server SAPIs as an alternative to CGI programming. We learned that the primary drawbacks to CGI applications is the overhead associated with starting up a new application with each call, and having to reopen any needed resources with each run of the application. We also looked at some of the benefits offered by Web server SAPIs, as well as some of the drawbacks.

At this point, we turned our attention toward Microsoft's Internet Information Server ISAPI interface, and how it works. Once we had developed a reasonable understanding of the OLEISAPI interface, we dove into the usage of the interface in an application by building a simple ActiveX DLL, taking advantage of this opportunity to build some functionality that we are likely to want to use in future OLEISAPI applications.

So where do we go from here? Most Web applications are not a simple matter of parsing up some parameters that were sent from a Web browser. Most Web applications also interact with some resource located on the Web server, or accessible from the Web server, such as a database. Much of the advantage that is gained in building ISAPI applications is in the ability to maintain the connection to the resource that is required by the application, but this also entails other issues that need to be discussed. We shall take a look at some of the issues that arise when holding open a resource like a database connection in Chapter 23, "Using Remote Data Objects with the OLEISAPI2 Interface." From here you might want to check out the following chapters:

- To learn about how VBScript can be used on the server instead of building applications, read Chapter 13, "Active Server Pages and Server-Side Scripting."

- If you want to learn about the WinCGI interface available on some (not all) Web servers, read Chapter 18, "The WinCGI Interface and Visual Basic."

- To learn about the new OLEISAPI2 interface, and how it provides Visual Basic with a faster and more complete interface, check out Chapter 20, "The OLEISAPI2 Interface and the Active Reference Object."

- To see how Netscape decided to implement their SAPI, and what that means to the Visual Basic programmer who wants to use it, check out Chapter 21, "Providing an OLEISAPI-Like Interface for Other Web Servers."

- To learn about using a database in an OLEISAPI2 application, read Chapter 23, "Using Remote Data Objects with the OLEISAPI2 Interface."

- If you want to see how the standard CGI interface works, see Appendix A, "Standard CGI, WinCGI, and Visual Basic."

# CHAPTER 20

# The OLEISAPI2 Interface and the Active Reference Object

In the last chapter, you learned how to use the OLEISAPI interface with Visual Basic to build ISAPI applications on top of Microsoft's IIS Web server. The only problem is that the OLEISAPI interface is quite limited in its capabilities. What if you wanted to use some of the more advanced capabilities of today's newer Web browsers, but still wanted to be able to provide a version that could be used by older Web browsers? You would need to know what browser your application user was running, and which version it is to be able to determine what your options might be.

When you were building WinCGI applications, this was not a problem, because you had complete access to this information in the INI file generated by the Web server. All you had to do was check the value of the CGI_UserAgent variable, or retrieve the User_Agent value from the CGI section of the configuration file. While you were at it, there were many more variables that were available to you, from the Web server software in use, to the server name, to the TCP/IP address of the user. This is all useful information that can be taken advantage of in numerous Web applications, if you only have access to it.

## The new OLEISAPI2 interface

This new interface can be used with Microsoft's Internet Information Server to build Server-based applications with more functionality than with the original OLEISAPI interface.

## The Internet Message Format

All HTTP messages, with the exception of those coming from very old Web clients and servers, use what is known as the Internet Message Format to pass not just the objects being requested, but also a large amount of other information about the browser and the server, as well as about the objects being requested.

## Using cookies to maintain state for a Web client

One of the most prominent solutions for the problem of application "state" is the use of client-side cookies. You'll look at how cookies work and how you can use the OLEISAPI2 interface to set and retrieve cookies.

## Determine what Web browser your users are using to access your Web site

Among the headers that are passed to a Web server from a Web browser is the identity of the Web browser being used.

Luckily, Microsoft recognized that by not allowing access to any of this information in the OLEISAPI interface, they were limiting the type and scope of the applications that could be built by using it. As a result, Microsoft began working on a new ISAPI interface for use with languages like Visual Basic. This new interface is called OLEISAPI2. Despite the similarity of names, this OLEISAPI2 interface bears little resemblance to the original OLEISAPI interface. Instead of shutting you off from the HTTP message header information, it provides you with full access to them, and much more. In order to understand all of the information you can get from the browser-submitted request, and what you can set to be returned to the client, you need to have a basic understanding of how messages are passed between Web browsers and Web servers. ■

# The Internet Message Format

The Internet Message Format is a standardized format for documents exchanged between Internet applications. This format is used by Internet mail, Usenet Newsgroups, and HyperText Transfer Protocol (HTTP). Because of this, all server-side applications need to format all of their output in the Internet message format, or else the Web browser will not understand or interpret the resulting output correctly.

The Internet Message Format is divided into two sections, the header and the body. The header contains a number of lines containing information about the message. Each of these lines contains a field name, and a field value, separated by a colon. These fields can contain the protocol being used, the object type of the message body, the size of the object that makes up the message body, the date of the object, and so on. This header section is separated from the message body by an empty line. A typical HTML page formatted in the Internet Message Format can be seen in Listing 20.1.

---

**Listing 20.1   HTTPRETN.TXT—A Typical HTML Page in the Internet Message Format as Sent to a Web Browser**

```
HTTP/1.0 200 OK
Date: Monday, 16-Dec-96 16:56:32 GMT
Server: Microsoft-Internet-Information-Server/3.0
Content-type: text/html
Last-modified: Thursday, 12-Dec-96 14:42:45 GMT

<HTML><HEAD>
<TITLE>A Typical HTML Document</TITLE>
</HEAD><BODY>
<H1><CENTER>A Typical HTML Document</CENTER></H1>
<HR>
<P>This is a typical HTML Document, as transferred to a Web
browser, formatted as an Internet Message.</P>
</BODY></HTML>
```

---

A few things to notice in Listing 20.1. The first line does not follow the header formatting rules, but instead contains the protocol and version being used (HTTP/1.0), followed by a space, then a status code (usually 200, which means the response is being returned with no problems encountered), a space and then the word "OK" to signify that everything is all right. This first line could contain a different status code other than 200. A Table of the possible status codes and their interpretations can be found in Table 20.1

**Table 20.1  The List of HTTP Status Codes**

| Code | Meaning | Explanation |
|------|---------|-------------|
| 200 | OK | Request was serviced without any problems. |
| 201 | Created | Used with HTTP extension commands to create files on the server. |
| 202 | Accepted | Used with HTTP extension commands to send files to the server. |
| 204 | No content | The document is an empty file. |
| 301 | Moved permanently | This is usually accompanied with a new URL for the Web browser to automatically take you to the new location. |
| 302 | Moved temporarily | This is usually accompanied with a new URL for the Web browser to automatically take you to the new location. |
| 304 | Not modified | Used with HTTP extension commands to update files on the server. |
| 400 | Bad request | The server could not understand the request. |
| 401 | Unauthorized | The URL requested is restricted access and the user is not authorized to access it. |
| 403 | Forbidden | The client sent a forbidden or illegal command. |
| 404 | Not found | The requested URL was not found on the server. |
| 500 | Internal server error | This is the status code that any bugs in your server applications need to return to the client. |
| 501 | Not implemented | A command was sent by the client that is not implemented in the server. |
| 502 | Bad gateway | This response is generated by a gateway or proxy server when it receives a bad response from the Web site server, or another gateway or proxy server. |
| 503 | Service unavailable | The Web server is unavailable for taking requests. |

Part

**VI**

Ch

**20**

**N O T E** The list of status codes provided here will soon be very incomplete. This list of status codes is from the HTTP 1.0 specification (RFC 1945). For a complete listing of the possible status codes that will be in use once support for the HTTP 1.1 specification becomes common, see RFC 2068. ▨

Other lines to note in the header section in Listing 20.1 is the line specifying the content-type. This tells the Web client what the object being sent is and what to do with it. This example specifies that the file being sent is an HTML text file. This could just as easily specify that the file is a GIF or JPEG image, an AU audio file, an MPEG video file, or any other type of file that might be received from a Web server.

The last line in the header specifies the date and time that the HTML file was last modified. Usually, what Web browsers will often do, is request to be sent just the header of an URL, so that it can check this last modification to determine if a file has been updated since a cached version was downloaded. If a Web page has not been modified since last visited, the browser will often display the cached version, increasing response time by not downloading unnecessary files and images.

 **T I P** If your server-side application doesn't seem to be sending anything to the client browser, and you know that there was a form sent, check to be sure that you are sending an empty line between the header and body sections of the file to be returned to the client.

# The OLEISAPI2 Interface

With the OLEISAPI2 interface, Microsoft decided to take a different approach than they had with the original OLEISAPI interface. It's still available from Microsoft's Web site as a programming example for use with Visual C++. But this time it's not an ISAPI programming example, it's an ATL (Active Template Library) 1.1 programming example, to demonstrate the type of applications that can be built with the new ATL 1.1 for use with Microsoft's Visual C++.

So what's different about the approach taken with the OLEISAPI2 interface? This time, all interaction between the OLEISAPI2 interface and the Visual Basic application is through an ActiveX (OLE) Automation Object. This object is the only parameter that is passed to the Visual Basic methods, and the Visual Basic routines call methods and access properties of this object to extract all of the information about the request, and to send the results back to the client.

**N O T E** The Active Request Object you discussed here is not the same as the Request object discussed in the section on Active Server Pages a few chapters earlier. While these request objects may have some qualities in common, they are really very different objects and are used with very different technologies. ▨

**N O T E**  Because the OLEISAPI2 interface uses a mutlithreaded Automation object, it can only be used on Windows NT 4.0, with IIS 2.0 or higher. Earlier versions of Microsoft's OLE Automation did not use OLE threading, and may cause problems when using the OLEISAPI2 interface. ■

## The Active Request Object

The Active Request object is the key to the OLEISAPI2 interface. As the only parameter passed to the Visual Basic methods specified in the URL (just like in the original OLEISAPI interface, only with the new DLL name), it makes the entire ISAPI interface available to the Visual Basic application that is called (with a few very minor omissions). Most of the elements in the ISAPI structure that you looked at in the previous chapter are available as properties of the Request object, as can be seen in Table 20.2.

**Table 20.2  The Active Request Object Properties**

| Property | Data Type | Read/Write | Description |
|---|---|---|---|
| Method | String | Read only | This property contains the method used to submit the query to the Web server. Normally, this value would be "GET" or "POST." |
| QueryString | String | Read only | This property contains the string of key/value pairs that was submitted to the server if the "GET" method was used to submit the data (or if the data was encoded as part of the URL in the HTML page). |
| PathInfo | String | Read only | This property contains the URI (Uniform Resource Indicator) that was requested by the client. This contains the OLEISAPI2 DLL and the Visual Basic class and method that were called. An example of this might be "/scripts/oleisapi2.dll/myclass.mymethod." |
| PathTranslated | String | Read only | This property contains the actual physical path of the object requested by the client. An example of this might be "C:\Inetsrc\scripts\oleisapi2.dll\ |

Part
VI

Ch
20

*continues*

**Table 20.2    Continued**

| Property | Data Type | Read/Write | Description |
|---|---|---|---|
| | | | myclass.mymethod." |
| UploadType | String | Read only | This property indicates the MIME type of the data that was uploaded to the server by the client. |
| UploadComplete | Boolean | Read only | This property tells the Visual Basic application whether all of the submitted data has been retrieved from the Request object. |
| TotalUploadLength | Long | Read only | This property gives you the total length of the data that was submitted by the client. |
| LogRecord | String | Read/Write | This property contains a short string that will be written to the server's log record for this HTTP request. The length of this string will be truncated, so don't write any more than you really need to into this log. |
| ResponseStatus | String | Read/Write | This property contains the response status code and message that will be returned to the client. This will hold a default value of "200 OK," but can be set to any of the available and valid HTTP response codes (as listed in Table 20.1). |
| ResponseType | String | Read/Write | This property will be used to tell the client browser the MIME type of the data being returned by the server. The browser will use this value to know how to display the object that is created by the Visual Basic application. This will be defaulted to "text/html." |

Along with the properties listed in Table 20.2, the Request object also has a few methods, which map almost directly onto the ISAPI interface methods. These methods are listed in Table 20.3.

**Table 20.3   The Active Request Object Methods**

| Method | Description |
|--------|-------------|
| GetServerVariable | This method takes a single string as a parameter, and returns a string containing the server variable requested. This can be used to get any of the server variables that are specified in the ISAPI documentation, or can be used to retrieve any specific header submitted by the client. |
| AppendHeader | This method takes a single string as a parameter. The parameter should be a complete header string, complete with the name and value, to be returned to the client along with the response. |
| GetFirstUploadChunk | This method takes one variant as a parameter. The first portion of the data submitted by the client (assuming the POST method was used) will be returned in the variant that was passed to this method. If the data submitted by the client is not very much, the entire query string may be retrieved with this method, if not you will need to use the next method to retrieve the rest of the query string. This method should only be called once, any additional calls to this method will produce an error. |
| GetNextUploadChunk | This method is to be used after using the previous method to retrieve the initial portion of the submitted data. This method requires two parameters, the first is the length of the data to be returned, and the second is the variant variable into which the data string should be placed. This method should only be called after the GetFirstUploadChunk has been called, otherwise it will produce an error. |
| WriteResponse | This method takes a single variant as a parameter. This method returns the contents of the single parameter to the client. This method has to be called at least once, because the message headers are not returned to the client until this method is called for the first time. |

Through this combination of properties and methods, the Request object allows the Visual Basic application to access anything it may need or want from the client or server, and can return any data type and response to the client that the application may call for. The exposed methods in the Visual Basic application are reduced to a single parameter, which is the request object itself, like this:

```
Public Sub MyMethod(aReq as Request)
```

# Reading Submitted Data

One of the first things you probably need to do in your Visual Basic method is to get all of the data that was submitted by the client. This data may be in two different places, depending on which method was used to submit it, so the first thing you need to do is check the method, as follows:

```
Dim strMethod As String
strMethod = aReq.Method
```

If the GET method was used, the entire query string will be in the QueryString property of the Request object, and can be easily retrieved as follows:

```
Dim strReqParameters As String
strReqParameters = aReq.QueryString
```

Now if the POST method was used to submit the data (which is more likely, as there is a limit to the amount of data that can be submitted by using the GET method), things get a bit more interesting. First, check to see if there is anything to be retrieved by checking the UploadComplete property. Assuming that there is something, you need to retrieve the first portion of it by using the GetFirstUploadChunk method, and then convert it from Unicode to a standard Visual Basic string. Next, you need to recheck the UploadComplete property to see if there is any more to be retrieved. If there is, then you need to take the length of what you have already retrieved, and subtract that from the total length of the uploaded data, and use the GetNextUploadChunk method to retrieve the next portion. This next section needs to be converted into a standard string and added to the first section. If you are expecting a large amount of data, you might want to call the GetNextUploadChunk method several times, asking for chunks around the same size as the original section, instead of asking for all of the remaining data at once. This whole operation results in a section of code that looks something like this:

```
Dim strReqParameters As String
Dim vParams As Variant
Dim strUploadType As String
Dim iAmtRead As Integer

If Not aReq.UploadComplete Then
   aReq.GetFirstUploadChunk vParams
   strReqParameters = StrConv(vParams, vbUnicode)
   iAmtRead = Len(strReqParameters)
   Do While Not aReq.UploadComplete
      aReq.GetNextUploadChunk (aReq.TotalUploadLength - iAmtRead), vParams
         strReqParameters = strReqParameters & StrConv(vParams, vbUnicode)
         iAmtRead = Len(strReqParameters)
   Loop
End If
```

**N O T E** The reason that two methods have to be used to retrieve the data submitted by using the POST method is directly related to the ISAPI structure that is passed to ISAPI DLLs. In this structure, along with the QueryString and Method properties, is the first chunk of the data submitted by using the POST method. The DLL does not have to call any of the ISAPI functions to get this data, as it is supplied as one of the variables of the structure itself. This is the section that is retrieved by using the GetFirstUploadChunk method. If the submitted data is larger than the ISAPI interface can place in this variable, the rest of the data has to be retrieved by using the ISAPI `ReadClient` function, which is what the `GetNextUploadChunk` method does. If the original ISAPI interface were designed such that all of the submitted data would be in the ISAPI structure, or that you had to use the `ReadClient` function to retrieve all of the submitted data, then there would be only one method for retrieving this data. ∎

At this point, you should have your query string as it was submitted by the client. You still need to parse it up and convert all of the special characters, but at this point, you can pass it off to the `Parameters` class object you built in the previous chapter and let it do all of the work.

# Reading Request Headers

If you need to get the values of any of the server variables, or any of the HTTP headers that were submitted by the client, you have to use the `GetServerVariable` method. This method is really easy-to-use, and returns a string that you can capture and use in whatever ways you desire. For instance, if you wanted to get the TCP/IP address of the client, you would use the following:

```
Dim strAddr as String
strAddr = aReq.GetServerVariable("REMOTE_ADDR")
```

You can also use this same method to retrieve any of the headers from the request that was submitted by the client, although this does require knowing what the headers are that the client will have submitted, but this can be determined by requesting all of the HTTP headers by using the ALL_HTTP variable name (but then you'll need to build a routine for parsing through all of the headers that you receive). For instance, if you wanted to find out what Web browser the client is using, you could do the following:

```
Dim strBrowser as String
strBrowser = aReq.GetServerVariable("HTTP_USER_AGENT")
```

A list of the server variables that you could retrieve can be found in Table 20.4.

**Table 20.4   ISAPI Server Variables that Can Be Retrieved Using the *GetServerVariable* Method**

| Variable | Description |
| --- | --- |
| AUTH_TYPE | This is the authentication method used to authenticate the user (if access is restricted on the Web server). If this is empty, then no authentication is being used. |
| CONTENT_LENGTH | This is the length of the data that was submitted by the client. This should be the same as the `TotalUploadLength` property of the Request object. |
| CONTENT_TYPE | This is the MIME type of the data that was submitted. This should be the same as the `UploadType` property of the Request object. |

*continues*

**Table 20.4   Continued**

| Variable | Description |
| --- | --- |
| GATEWAY_INTERFACE | This is the version of the CGI interface that is implemented by the Web server. |
| PATH_INFO | This is the requested method as submitted by the client. This should be the same as the `PathInfo` property of the Request object. |
| PATH_TRANSLATED | This is the actual path of the requested method on the server. This should be the same as the `PathTranslated` property of the Request object. |
| QUERY_STRING | This is the query string that was submitted if the `GET` method was used. This should be the same as the `QueryString` property of the Request object. |
| REMOTE_ADDR | This is the TCP/IP address of the client. |
| REMOTE_HOST | This is the system name of the client, or gateway or firewall through which the request is being passed. |
| REMOTE_USER | This is the user name that was supplied by the client if authentication is being used. |
| REQUEST_METHOD | This is the method that was used to submit the request. This should be the same as the `Method` property of the `Request` object. |
| SCRIPT_NAME | This is the name of the script that is being run. |
| SERVER_NAME | This is the name of the server. |
| SERVER_PORT | This is the TCP/IP port that is being used by the server to receive requests. |
| SERVER_PROTOCOL | This is the protocol being used by the server. This should normally be HTTP/1.0. |
| SERVER_SOFTWARE | This is the name and version of the Web server software that is being used. |
| AUTH_PASS | This is the password used by the client for authentication. |
| ALL_HTTP | This is all of the HTTP headers that were submitted by the client, that do not fit into any of the preceding variables. Each of these headers will be separated by a line-feed (on separate lines). |
| HTTP_ACCEPT | This is a list of the MIME types that can be accepted by the client. This normally provides just the MIME types that the browser will natively display, but does not include any that the browser may use plug-ins or ActiveX controls to display. |

# Setting Response Headers

When you are ready to begin returning your results to the user, the first thing you need to do is determine what the status of your response should be. Did everything work correctly? Or, was there a problem with the user's input? Did something cause your application to have an error condition? All of these situations should effect what value should be returned in the status code. If everything went well, then you should return a status code of 200. If an error condition was encountered in your application, then your error handling routine should return a 500 status code, with some sort of message to tell the user what happened. All of the status codes listed in Table 20.1 can be returned to the user by setting the `ResponseStatus` property of the Request object, as in the following examples:

```
aReq.ResponseStatus = "200 OK"
aReq.ResponseStatus = "500 SQL Error, Column not found"
aReq.ResponseStatus = "401 Unauthorized to edit the requested records"
```

**N O T E** You should always include a brief textual description of the reason for the specific status code being returned. This description will be displayed in the window title bar of the user's browser. ▧

The other thing that you need to specify before returning anything to the user is the type of object that you are about to return. This type description has to be a valid MIME (Multipurpose Internet Mail Extensions) type, so that the browser will know how to display the object. Usually, you'll be setting this to "text/html," but there's always an occasion that you'll need to specify a different MIME type. You can set this value by using the `ResponseType` property of the Request object, as in the following code:

```
aReq.ResponseType = "text/html"
```

---

### Multipurpose Internet Mail Extensions (MIME)

The MIME specification was originally developed so that multiple file and object types could be embedded in e-mail messages that were being delivered across the Internet. Because of MIME's universal status as a standard, portions of its functionality have been adopted for use in other technologies. One of the key features of MIME is that file classification types, in which every file has a type specification that places it into a general category (for example, text, image, audio, video, application, and so on) and a specific type within the category (for example, text/html, video/mpeg, video/quicktime, image/gif, image/jpeg, and so on). These MIME file types are used by Web browsers to know how to display each object that it receives, or which plug-in or control to use to display the object.

---

Now that you've set the status code and response type, what's left to be set? Well, there's always a need for additional, specific-use headers that may be returned to the client. Sometimes these headers are purely for informational purposes, but sometimes they are used for important purposes, as you'll see a little later in the discussion of client-side cookies. You can set any header that you want or dream up by using the `AppendHeader` method of the Request. object. For instance, if you wanted to include a copyright header with your HTML page that you have built, you could include the following code when building your response:

```
aReq.AppendHeader "Copyright: 1997 Davis Chapman"
```

This would result in your HTTP message being returned to the client looking something like the following:

```
HTTP/1.0 200 OK
Date: Mon, 16-Apr-97 16:56:32 GMT
Server: Microsoft-Internet-Information-Server/3.0
Content-type: text/html
Last-modified: Thursday, 12-Dec-96 14:42:45 GMT
Copyright: 1997 Davis Chapman


<HTML><HEAD>
<TITLE>A Typical HTML Document</TITLE>
</HEAD><BODY>
<H1><CENTER>A Typical HTML Document</CENTER></H1>
<HR>
<P>This is a typical HTML Document, as transferred to a Web
browser, formatted as an Internet Message.</P>
</BODY></HTML>
```

**N O T E** You need to be sure that you set all of your headers, status codes, and response types before writing any of the resulting object to the Request object. The first call to the WriteResponse method flushes the headers and sends them to the client, along with the contents of the parameter to the WriteResponse method. Once the Web server has begun sending the HTTP message body to the client, it cannot go back and add any more headers to the message. ▪

## Sending the Response

Once you have set all of the headers that you need to, you are ready to begin sending the actual response to the user. This is done by using the WriteResponse method. Because the data being passed to the WriteResponse method is handled as a variant, you can pass any type of data that you need to, in the form that the data needs to be returned to the client. For instance, you could return a simple HTML document to the user with the following code:

```
aReq.WriteResponse "<html><body><h1>This is a simple response</h1>"
aReq.WriteResponse "<p>This is a simple response to the submitted query."
aReq.WriteResponse "</p></body></html>"
```

**N O T E** The WriteResponse method must be called at least once in every OLEISAPI2 application, even if there is nothing to be sent to the user. Calling this method causes the headers to be flushed and sent to the user, providing the user with the status code and message that should inform the user why there is nothing being returned. If the WriteResponse method is never called, the headers are never returned to the user, leaving the user with no legal HTTP response to his or her submission. ▪

## Debugging OLEISAPI2 Applications

Unfortunately, there is no simple and easy way to debug OLEISAPI2 applications. You have few options available to you for stepping through your code in a debugger:

1. Build your application as an OLEISAPI application, passing the potential query strings from the Main() subroutine. Once you've got your application debugged, convert it to an OLEISAPI2 application and examine each element carefully to make sure that you don't miss anything, and that you've converted it correctly.

2. Compile your ActiveX DLL as native code with all debugging flags turned on (as in Figure 20.1). Next recompile the OLEISAPI2 DLL by using Visual C++ with all debugging flags turned on. Copy the CGIWRAP.EXE application (from the ISAPI examples section of the ActiveX SDK) into the same directory and rename it OLEISAPI2.EXE. Build a DOS BAT file to set all of the environment variables as if you were calling a standard CGI application. In the last line of the BAT file, run Microsoft's CodeView Debugger (available with Visual C++). Load up the OLEISAPI2.EXE application, and then step through all three in the CodeView debugger. An example BAT file can be found on the CD that accompanies this book.

3. Build your own Request object in Visual Basic, populating its properties with the appropriate values, allowing you to step through your code from a Main() subroutine in the Visual Basic debugger.

**FIG. 20.1**
Turning on the debugging flags in the Visual Basic compile options.

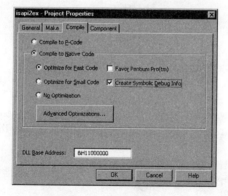

# Client-Side Cookies

One of the advantages of the OLEISAPI2 interface is that this interface makes it easy to set and receive client-side cookies. Cookies are a mechanism that was first developed by Netscape as a means of maintaining client-state information. Cookies are maintained by the browser and are returned to the Web server specified with each subsequent request. Cookies can contain any information that the Web programmer decides is important to maintain, and can be passed to any Web server specified in as narrow or wide a domain as desired.

> **N O T E**   Cookies have received a lot of unfavorable publicity, including how some Web advertising
> companies are using cookies to track your browsing, noting what sites you visit and which
> advertisements you see and respond to. There is a large number of people that view this practice as an
> invasion of privacy, and take steps to prevent cookies from being set on their browsers. Because of this
> practice, whenever you choose to use cookies, be sure that you take pains to program your application
> so that it will still work even if it does not receive cookies back from the users. ■

## Setting Cookies

You can tell a Web browser to set and maintain a cookie by including the Set-Cookie header in
the HTTP message being sent to the client. There are several options that may be included in
this header, with the actual cookie being the only required, and always first, of these options to
be included. For instance, if I wanted to set a cookie for a user identification number, and
wanted it to be returned to my server (bullfrog.chaperada.com) with every request, I could use
the following code:

```
aReq.AppendHeader "Set-Cookie: UID=123; path=/; domain=bullfrog.chaperada.com"
```

This would result in the following HTTP header being sent to the client browser:

```
HTTP/1.0 200 OK
Date: Mon, 16-Apr-97 16:56:32 GMT
Server: Microsoft-Internet-Information-Server/3.0
Content-type: text/html
Last-modified: Thursday, 12-Dec-96 14:42:45 GMT
Set-Cookie: UID=123; path=/; domain=bullfrog.chaperada.com

<HTML><HEAD>
<TITLE>A Typical HTML Document</TITLE>
</HEAD><BODY>
</BODY></HTML>
```

If your users have their browser set to warn them before accepting a cookie, they would see
the warning window in Figure 20.2 before their browser would display the HTML document.

**FIG. 20.2**

Microsoft Internet
Explorer warning the
user that the Web server
has requested that the
browser accept and
store a cookie on its
file system.

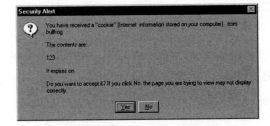

Along with the domain, path, and value of the cookie, there are other attributes that you can include in the Set-Cookie request. All of the cookie attributes are listed in Table 20.5.

**Table 20.5    Cookie Attributes that Can Be Set Using the Set-Cookie HTTP Header**

| Variable | Example | Description |
|---|---|---|
| cookie | UID=123 | This is the actual cookie that will be returned by the browser with subsequent requests to the Web server specified. This attribute has to be included with every Set-Cookie header, and has to be the first attribute following the header name. |
| expires | expires=Mon, 14-Apr-1997 00:01 GMT | This attribute tells the browser when this cookie should be thrown away, because it has expired. |
| domain | domain=www.abcdef.com | This attribute tells the browser what Web server or servers to send this cookie to. If the first part of the server name is left off (for example, .abcdef.com), the cookie will be sent to all Web servers in this domain, not just the one that set the cookie. |
| path | path=/ | This attribute specifies the area on the Web server that should be sent the cookie. If the path is /, then all requests to the Web server will be sent the cookie. If the path is /onedept, then only requests that are from this section of the Web server will be sent the cookie. No requests from the top-level directory, or any other second-level directories will be sent the cookie. |
| secure | secure | This attribute tells the browser that the cookie should only be sent to the Web server through a Secure Sockets Layer (SSL) connection, where all communications between the browser and server are encrypted. If this attribute is left out, then the cookie will be sent regardless of whether the connection is encrypted or not. |

Part

**VI**

Ch

**20**

# Receiving Cookies

Once a browser has accepted a cookie from your Web server, it will always send the cookie to the Web server or servers specified in the domain option of the Set-Cookie command, to all URLs from the specified page on down through the Web servers file system. As you can see in the Headers section on the display in Figure 20.3, the browser returned the contents of the cookie in the HTTP header HTTP_COOKIE. This means that you could retrieve the contents of this cookie with the following line of code:

```
Dim strCookie as String
strCookie = aReq.GetServerVariable("HTTP_COOKIE")
```

**FIG. 20.3**

An HTML document displaying all of the headers that were sent from the Web browser to the Web server, including the cookie that was accepted in Figure 20.2.

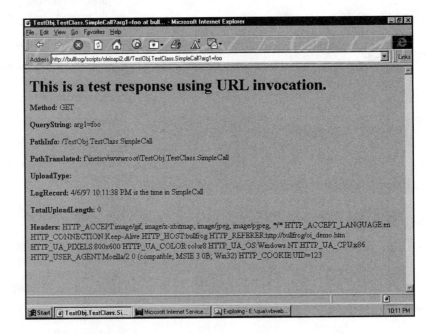

**N O T E**   The HTML document shown in Figure 20.3 was produced using the example Visual Basic project that is distributed with the OLEISAPI2 interface executables and source code. When you download the OLEISAPI2 interface from Microsoft's Web site, you will find the source code for this project included. ■

Once you have the value of the cookie (or cookies), you can parse it into key and value pairs so that it can be used for whatever processing you desire.

 **T I P**   Because the contents of cookies are passed "as is" over the Internet, it is good practice to use some form of encryption when using cookies to store user names, passwords, or user identification numbers. If you are setting these values in an unencrypted form, and the user is monitoring the cookies that are being set on his or her browser, they may not appreciate seeing their login name or id in an unencrypted form. It will likely cause the user to not trust your server or application, and potentially not visit your site again.

# Building an OLEISAPI2 Application

For your first OLEISAPI2 application, you are going to adapt the OLEISAPI application that you built in the previous chapter to use the OLEISAPI2 interface. While you're making this modification, you'll make the resulting HTML document not just return the submitted data, but also display a few server variables and request headers, such as the browser being used, the referring page, and the data encoding.

## Configuring the Project

Before you can begin adapting your project for using the OLEISAPI2 interface, you need to enable the Visual Basic development environment to know about and understand the Request object. You'll do this by including the OLEISAPI2 type library in your project references from the Project¦References menu entry, as in Figure 20.4. If you cannot find the OLEISAPI2 type library in the references dialog box (or you haven't included it in an application before), you will need to select the Browse button, and locate the OLEISAPI2 DLL on your system, as in Figure 20.5. This will add the OLEISAPI2 type library to the Visual Basic references dialog box, and enable you to use the OLEISAPI2 interface in your Visual Basic application.

**FIG. 20.4**
Enabling OLEISAPI2 support in the Visual Basic development environment.

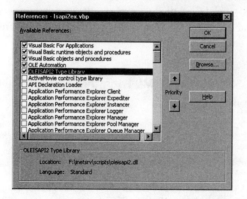

**N O T E** Including the OLEISAPI2 type library in your Visual Basic project does not just enable you to compile your application, but also adds the Request object into the Visual Basic Intellisense Word Complete functionality. ■

**FIG. 20.5**

Browsing your system to locate the OLEISAPI2 DLL so that OLEISAPI2 support may be enabled in the Visual Basic development environment.

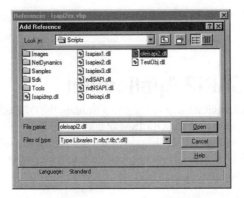

As with your previous application, you'll specify that your ActiveX DLL will be compiled as native code, and you'll mark it for unattended execution. You'll name your project "isapi2ex," and your primary class "IsapiClass."

# Preparing the HTML Form

Because this is an adaptation of the application you developed in the previous chapter, you'll take the HTML form that you used in that final version of your application and adapt it for your purposes in this application. As you can see from Listing 20.2, the primary changes to your HTML form are the URLs for your Visual Basic application. First, the DLL name has been changed from oleisapi.dll to oleisapi2.dll. Second, you have updated the object and class names to reflect your new Visual Basic project. Otherwise, as you can see in Figure 20.6, your HTML form looks basically the same.

---

**Listing 20.2   OI2EX.HTM—The HTML Form that You Will Be Using to Call Your OLEISAPI2 Application**

```
<html><head><title>OLEISAPI2 Programming Example</title></head>
<body bgcolor=#C0C0C0>
<h1>OLEISAPI2 Programming Example</h1>
<p>More Variety in what is being sent to the OLEISAPI2 application.</p>
<hr><p>
<a HREF="/scripts/oleisapi2.dll/isapi2ex.IsapiClass.DoGet?arg1=foo">
This link</a> simply invokes the OLEISAPI2 directly via a URL.
<hr><p>
<form action="/scripts/oleisapi2.dll/isapi2ex.IsapiClass.DoPost"
method="POST">
<input type="submit" value="Click here"> to see this
form use the <strong>POST
</strong>
technique to invoke an object method called DoPost.
<p><Table align=center border=0>
<tr><td align=right valign=top><font size=4>Value 1</td><td align=left>
<input name="Val1"></td>
<tr><td align=right valign=top><font size=4>Value 2</td><td align=left>
```

```html
<input name="Val2"></td>
<tr><td align=right valign=top><font size=4>Some text</td><td align=left>
<input name="Val3"></td></Table></form>
<p><hr>
<form action="/scripts/oleisapi2.dll/isapi2ex.IsapiClass.DoGet"
method="GET">
<input type="submit" value="Click here"> to see this
form use the <strong>GET
</strong>
technique to invoke a different method on the same object called DoGet.
<p><Table align=center border=0>
<tr><td align=right valign=top><font size=4>Value 1</td><td align=left>
<input name="Val1"></td>
<tr><td align=right valign=top><font size=4>Value 2</td><td align=left>
<input name="Val2"></td>
<tr><td align=right valign=top><font size=4>Some text</td><td align=left>
<input name="Val3"></td></Table></form>
<p><hr>
</body>
</html>
```

**FIG. 20.6**

The HTML form that you will be using to test your OLEISAPI2 application.

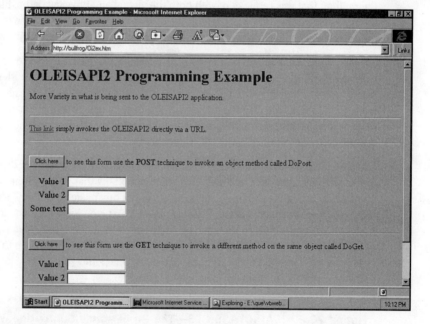

## Building Your OLEISAPI2 Application

Just like in the previous chapter, all of the work will be performed by the ProcParams subroutine. The first thing that you'll need to change is the parameters that you are passing to this subroutine. Now, the only parameter that you need to pass into this subroutine is the Request object.

Part
VI

Ch
20

Once you are in the subroutine, you'll need to determine the method used to submit the data to your application, and use the appropriate code to extract the query string from the request object. You'll use the exact same code to get the query string that you saw earlier in this chapter when you were discussing how to get the query string, just enclosed in an IF..THEN..ELSE statement to control which method you use. Once you have the query string, you'll pass it to the Parameters class that you built in the previous chapter, and things begin looking just like they did in the previous version of this application.

Once you have your parameters loaded into your Parameter class, you'll start building your HTML document that you're going to return. Notice that you don't need to start your HTML document with the header type line. If you remember from your discussion earlier in this chapter, you'll take care of that just before you return the document to the user, by setting the ResponseType property of the Request object.

Before you begin building the table containing the data that was sent, you are going to display for the user, some of the information that you have available about the request. The first thing you list is the query string that was submitted (assuming that the GET method was used, if the POST method was used this string will be empty). You follow this with the path information for the method that was requested, with both the virtual and physical paths. Finally, you'll display the type of encoding that was used on the data that was submitted. If the GET method was used, this string will be blank, otherwise it should contain "application/x-www-form-urlencoded."

The last thing that you will be adding before the table of parameters are a few headers that were sent with the request by the user. First, you'll display the browser identification and version. Next, you'll display the host name. Third, you'll display the Web page that the user came from. Finally, you'll display the list of MIME types that the browser can accept. Once you've displayed all of this information, you'll build the table of parameters that you built in the previous chapter, and complete your HTML document.

Once you're ready to send your HTML document back to the user, you diverge from your previous application once again. At this point, you know that your routine has been successful, and will likely continue to be so, so you can confidently place a "200 OK" status code into the ResponseStatus property of the Request object. Next, you know that you are returning a "text/html" MIME type object to the user, so you'll specify this type as the ResponseType property of the Request object. Finally, you'll write the entire HTML document to the user using the WriteResponse method of the Request object. At this point, you've done all that you need to do, and you've got the subroutine specified in Listing 20.3.

**Listing 20.3   ISAPICLASS.CLS—The ProcParams Subroutine, Which Processes the Submitted Request and Builds the Output HTML Document**

```
Private Sub ProcParams(aReq As Request)
    'Create a local instance of the parameters class
    Dim pcParams As New Parameters
    Dim iNumParams As Integer
    Dim iCurParam As Integer
    Dim strHTML As String
```

```
    Dim strMethod As String
    Dim strReqParameters As String
    Dim vParams As Variant
    Dim strUploadType As String
    Dim iAmtRead As Integer

    'What method was used?
    strMethod = aReq.Method
    If strMethod = "GET" Then
        'If the GET method was used, all of your variables
        'should be in the QueryString property of the
        'Request object
        strReqParameters = aReq.QueryString
    Else
        'If the POST method was used, you have to retrieve
        'all of your parameters, and then convert them to
        'strings
        If Not aReq.UploadComplete Then
            aReq.GetFirstUploadChunk vParams
            strReqParameters = StrConv(vParams, vbUnicode)
            iAmtRead = Len(strReqParameters)
            Do While Not aReq.UploadComplete
                aReq.GetNextUploadChunk (aReq.TotalUploadLength - _
                         iAmtRead), vParams
                strReqParameters = strReqParameters & _
                         StrConv(vParams, vbUnicode)
                iAmtRead = Len(strReqParameters)
            Loop
        End If
    End If
    'Pass the parameters sent from the HTML form
    'to the local instance of the Parameters class
    iNumParams = pcParams.ParseParameters(strReqParameters)
    'Build the HTML document
    strHTML = strHTML & "<HTML><HEAD><TITLE>"
    strHTML = strHTML & "OLEISAPI2 Programming Example"
    strHTML = strHTML & "</TITLE></HEAD><BODY BGCOLOR=#C0C0C0>"
    strHTML = strHTML & "<H1>OLEISAPI2 Programming Example</H1><HR><P>"
    strHTML = strHTML & "The method used to submit this was <STRONG>"
    'Tell the user what method was used to call this application
    strHTML = strHTML & strMethod & "</STRONG></P><P>"
    'Tell the user what some of the request parameters were
    strHTML = strHTML & "QueryString: <STRONG>" & aReq.QueryString & _
                        "</STRONG><BR>"
    strHTML = strHTML & "PathInfo: <STRONG>" & aReq.PathInfo & _
                        "</STRONG><BR>"
    strHTML = strHTML & "PathTranslated: <STRONG>" & _
            aReq.PathTranslated & "</STRONG><BR>"
    strHTML = strHTML & "UploadType: <STRONG>" & aReq.UploadType & _
                        "</STRONG><BR>"
    strHTML = strHTML & "Browser Type: <STRONG>" & _
            aReq.GetServerVariable("HTTP_USER_AGENT") & "</STRONG><BR>"
    strHTML = strHTML & "Host: <STRONG>" & _
            aReq.GetServerVariable("HTTP_HOST") & "</STRONG><BR>"
    strHTML = strHTML & "Referred By: <STRONG>" & _
```

*continues*

**Listing 20.3   Continued**

```
                aReq.GetServerVariable("HTTP_REFERER") & "</STRONG><BR>"
        strHTML = strHTML & "Browser Can Accept: <STRONG>" & _
                aReq.GetServerVariable("HTTP_ACCEPT") & "</STRONG></P><P>"
    'Tell the user how many parameters were passed
    strHTML = strHTML & "There were <STRONG>" & CStr(iNumParams)
    strHTML = strHTML & "</STRONG> values submitted as follows:</P>"
    'Build a Table of the parameters that were passed
    strHTML = strHTML & "<TABLE BORDER=2><TR><TH>Key</TH>"_
                    & "<TH>Value</TH></TR>"
    'Were there any parameters passed?
    If iNumParams > 0 Then
        'Loop through each of the parameters
        For iCurParam = 1 To iNumParams
            'Place the parameter key into the Table
            strHTML = strHTML & "<TR><TD>" & _
                        pcParams.GetKeyNameByNum(iCurParam)
            'Place the parameter value into the Table
            strHTML = strHTML & "</TD><TD>" & _
                        pcParams.GetKeyValueByNum(iCurParam)
            strHTML = strHTML & "</TD></TR>"
            'Loop to the next parameter
        Next
    End If
    'Close the HTML Table and document
    strHTML = strHTML & "</TABLE></BODY></HTML>"
    'Set the result code
    aReq.ResponseStatus = "200 OK"
    'Set the content-type header line
    aReq.ResponseType = "text/html"
    'Return the HTML document to the calling routine
    aReq.WriteResponse strHTML
End Sub
```

# Adapting the Published Methods

The final change that you will need to make to your application is in your published methods. Because all of your functionality is really in the ProcParams subroutine, the DoGet and DoPost methods have little to do other than pass the Request object on to the ProcParams subroutine. Since the method is now extracted from the Request object, the DoGet and DoPost methods can't even be used to provide that little piece of information. As a result, they are reduced to the methods seen in Listing 20.4. You could just as easily have made the ProcParams subroutine Public, and eliminated the DoGet and DoPost methods altogether.

**Listing 20.4   ISAPICLASS.CLS—The Published Methods for Your Visual Basic Class**

```
Public Sub DoGet(aReq As Request)
    ProcParams aReq
End Sub
```

```
Public Sub DoPost(aReq As Request)
    ProcParams aReq
End Sub
```

You are now finished with your application. All you need to do at this point is compile it as an ActiveX DLL, copy it to your server, and register it using REGSRV32.EXE (unless you are compiling it on your server, in which case Visual Basic registered it for us). The resulting HTML document that is produced by your application can be seen in Figure 20.7.

**FIG. 20.7**
The resulting HTML document that was created by your OLEISAPI2 application.

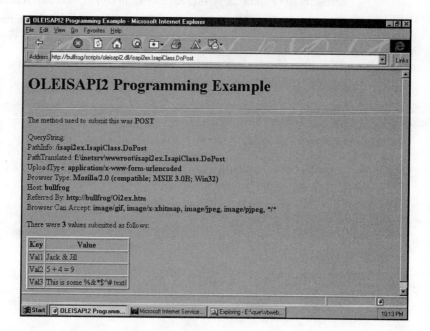

# From Here...

In this chapter, you looked at the new OLEISAPI2 interface, and how it makes the full ISAPI interface accessible from within a Visual Basic ActiveX DLL. Using this interface, you learned how you can take advantage of it to set and read client-side cookies, providing us with another means of tracking a specific user as they travel through your Web site. Finally, you used this knowledge to build a simple application that used the OLEISAPI2 interface.

From here you might want to do a little further exploration of the OLEISAPI2 interface, by checking out all of the headers that you can pull from the inbound HTTP message. Do some experimenting with cookies, setting and reading them, to learn how you can use them to maintain data that you would otherwise have to include as hidden fields on the HTML forms that you are sending to your users. Along with all of this, you might also want to check out the following chapters:

- To compare the ways of using client-side cookies with the OLEISAPI2 interface and in Active Server Pages, read Chapter 16, "Enhancing Interactivity with *Cookies, Headers,* and the *Server* Object."

- To see how you could build your own OLEISAPI-like interface for use with Netscape's Web servers, check out Chapter 21, "Providing an OLEISAPI-Like Interface for Other Web Servers."

- To learn how the OLEISAPI2 interface eliminates the bottleneck of single threaded access, read Chapter 23, "Using Remote Data Object with the OLEISAPI2 Interface."

- To see how you could use Microsoft's Transaction Server to build multitier applications on the Web, read Chapter 28, "Microsoft Transaction Server and Visual Basic."

# CHAPTER 21

# Providing an OLEISAPI-Like Interface for Other Web Servers

In the previous two chapters, you learned how easy it is to build ISAPI applications with Visual Basic by using the OLEISAPI and OLEISAPI2 interfaces. But, what if you have to work with another Web server, such as Netscape, Apache, Luckman, Oracle, or any of the other Web servers available for Windows NT? Well, if the other Web server happens to be O'Reilly's WebSite Web server, you're in luck because it supports the ISAPI interface, as well as their own WSAPI interface. This enables you to take the OLEISAPI DLLs and use them with the WebSite server in a way similar to the way you would use them with the IIS Web server.

---

**The ins and outs of the Netscape server application programming interface**

You'll look at how Netscape has opened their servers up for extensive customization and modification by exposing the internal workings and structures of their line of servers.

---

**The internal workings of ActiveX classes and the IDispatch interface**

You'll learn how Visual Basic creates ActiveX objects and DLLs that can be used with other programming languages via the IDispatch interface.

---

**How to build an OLENSAPI interface for Netscape Web servers**

By combining an understanding of the NSAPI interface with the IDispatch interface, you'll see how you can build a OLEISAPI-like interface for use with Netscape Web servers, and how you can take this knowledge to build OLEISAPI-like interfaces for just about any Web server that runs on Win32 platforms.

As far as the other Web servers are concerned, you have two choices:

1. Resign yourself to using the CGI or WinCGI interface.
2. Pull out a C++ compiler and build your own OLEISAPI-like interface.

If you choose the first option, you know that you will be taking on all of the associated overhead and performance limitations involved with building CGI applications. However, if you choose the second option, you provide yourself with the option of not just implementing a version of the OLEISAPI interface for a different Web server, but of extending the OLEISAPI interface by passing more information to the ActiveX DLL than is provided by the OLEISAPI interface. You also have the option of adapting the request object from the OLEISAPI2 interface to work with another Web server.

You can extend the OLEISAPI interface to include passing any or all of the Server, Request, and Client variables that are part of the CGI and WinCGI interfaces. This will enable you to build Visual Basic Web applications that include server-side state and security information, track a user's movements through your Web site, and build customized HTML documents based on what you know about the capabilities of the user's Web browser.

> **CAUTION**
> This chapter includes extensive examples built using the C programming language. If you aren't comfortable with the C or C++ programming languages, you might want to consider skipping a good deal of this chapter, if not the entire chapter.

> **N O T E**   The adapter that we will be building in this chapter is modeled on the original OLEISAPI interface, and does not use the Request object around which the OLEISAPI2 interface is built. By taking the principles of this chapter and applying them to the OLEISAPI2 interface, you could build an OLEISAPI2-type interface with a Request-like object for use with any of the other Web servers available for use on Windows NT. ■

> **CAUTION**
> The OLENSAPI DLL that we build in this chapter has not been thoroughly tested for using in a production system. Please do not use it in a production situation without thorough testing and debugging.

# The NSAPI Interface

When Netscape designed their Server API (NSAPI, or Netscape Server Application Programming Interface), they identified the basic steps through which each browser request must go. This included not only servicing the actual request, but also logging the request, validating the user, confirming that the requested resource exists in the location specified by the request, and more. Netscape also made the determination that these same steps were followed for not just their Web servers, but each of their entire family of servers. With this in mind, they designed a very open yet robust API that could easily be used internally to extend or adapt the functionality of each of these steps.

Actually, Netscape originally designed their servers using a very open modular approach. When they decided to make their server API available for use by outside programmers, it was only a matter of publishing and documenting the internal structures that were being used to implement, enhance, and extend their server functionality. This enables programmers to make direct replacements of entire sections of Netscape server processing through the NSAPI interface.

# The Request Processing Steps

Netscape servers follow a series of steps that every request follows:

1. AuthTrans. The server performs any user transaction authorization processing. This step categorizes the user into a specific user group identified by the user authorization database, based on any user identification information provided by the client. This step does not deny access to any resources, just identifies what group(s) the user may belong to.

2. NameTrans. The server takes the logical resource name and path that was received from the client and translates it to a physical resource name and path on the server. This step may even redirect the browser to another server.

3. PathCheck. The server determines whether the requested resource exists on the server, and what groups have access to the resource. This step makes the determination whether to allow or deny access to the requested resource. This step also makes certain path translations, such as converting the tilde character ("~") to the home directory of the user name that follows it (a standard function of most UNIX servers).

4. ObjectType. The server determines the MIME object type of the requested resource. This object type may be (and often is) modified in the Service step that follows.

5. Service.This is the step that we have seen with all of our server-side processing up to this point. This is the step in which the server builds all of the headers to be returned to the client, and sends the headers and the requested object back to the client. This is the step in which the server would call any CGI or WinCGI applications, and where we will be focused on our NSAPI programming efforts.

6. AddLog. The server logs any available information about the request.

**N O T E** Don't get the wrong idea about Netscape Web servers being more customizable than Microsoft's IIS Web server. Microsoft's ISAPI specification does provide the capability of customizing all of the same steps that Netscape's NSAPI specification does. The difference is that Microsoft's ISAPI specification uses a different interface than the one we examined in the previous chapters to customize the preceeding steps, so it actually consists of two separate interfaces. Netscape, however, uses the same interface for all of the steps. This means that Microsoft Web server extension programmers have to learn two separate interfaces in order to build all types of Web server extensions, while Netscape Web server extension programmers only have one interface to learn. ■

When the Netscape server starts up, it loads all of the functions that are configured to service each of the preceding steps, including any NSAPI extensions, and builds a table of these functions and the conditions that determine when to call one routine to service one of these steps, and when to call a different routine to service the same step, as seen in Figure 21.1.

**FIG. 21.1**

The function table is used by Netscape servers to determine which functions to call to service each step of a request.

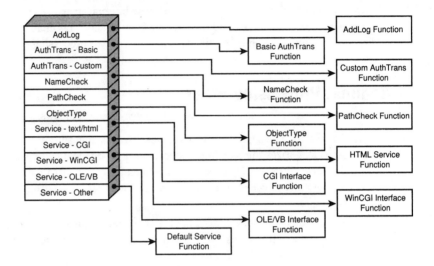

Because the table contains the NSAPI extensions for processing specific steps in the previous sequence, as well as the native functions for processing these steps, NSAPI extensions are used as a direct replacement for the step that they are designed to replace. There is no overhead because a particular step is being serviced by both a native Netscape set of functionality, and a NSAPI extension. If the NSAPI extension is servicing the step, the native Netscape functionality is completely bypassed. Because NSAPI extensions are hooked into the Netscape server at such a core level, these extensions become an integral part of the server itself, and not an add-on extension about which the server knows nothing until the extension is called, as with the Microsoft ISAPI interface.

## Netscape Configuration Files

So how do Netscape servers know how to build this function table? It is built from a couple of configuration files that control the entire process. There are actually three configuration files, but only two control the building of the processing function table; the third controls other startup configuration variables. These configuration files are listed in Table 21.1.

**Table 21.1   Netscape Web Server Configuration Files**

| Configuration File | Description |
| --- | --- |
| magnus.conf | Server startup configuration information. |

| Configuration File | Description |
|---|---|
| obj.conf | Server transaction configuration information. The processing table is built from the information in this configuration file. |
| mime.types | File extensions for mime-type identification and mapping. |

**NOTE** The name of the first configuration file, "magnus" was originally the code name given to the original Netscape Netsite Web server while it was under development. The name has stuck with the Netscape line of servers as an internal name for the server and an internal mime-type family.

These configuration files can be found in the Config subdirectory under the "httpd-<server name>" directory in the Netscape server install directory. On my system, which is named "bullfrog," this places the configuration files in the directory

```
F:\Netscape\Server\httpd-bullfrog\Config
```

**The obj.conf File** The obj.conf file informs the Netscape server which DLLs to load, which functions within the DLLs to map, and when to call each of those functions. There are multiple sections in the obj.conf file, each controlling different aspects of the server processing. A typical obj.conf with a Session extension can be seen in Listing 21.1.

**Listing 21.1  OBJ.CONF—A Typical Netscape obj.conf Configuration File, Containing a Single NSAPI Extension for Servicing Specific Service Calls**

```
# Use only forward slashes in pathnames—backslashes can cause
# problems. See the documentation for more information.

Init fn=flex-init access="F:/Netscape/Server/httpd-bullfrog/logs/access"
                ➥format.access="%Ses->client.ip% - %Req->vars.auth-user%
                ➥[%SYSDATE%] \"%Req->reqpb.clf-request%\"
                ➥%Req->srvhdrs.clf-status% %Req->srvhdrs.content-length%"
Init fn=load-types mime-types=mime.types
Init fn=load-modules \
                shlib="F:/Msdev42/projects/olensapi/Release/olensapi.dll"
                ➥funcs=olensapi-form

<Object name=default>
NameTrans fn=pfx2dir from=/ns-icons dir="F:/Netscape/Server/ns-icons"
NameTrans fn=pfx2dir from=/mc-icons dir="F:/Netscape/Server/ns-icons"
NameTrans fn=document-root root="F:/Netscape/Server/docs"
PathCheck fn=nt-uri-clean
PathCheck fn=find-pathinfo
PathCheck fn=find-index index-names="index.html,home.html"
ObjectType fn=type-by-extension
ObjectType fn=force-type type=text/plain
Service method=(GET¦POST) type=magnus-internal/olevb fn=olensapi-form
Service method=(GET¦HEAD) type=magnus-internal/imagemap fn=imagemap
```

*continues*

Part
VI

Ch
21

**Listing 21.1 Continued**

```
Service method=(GET¦HEAD) type=magnus-internal/directory fn=index-common
Service method=(GET¦HEAD) type=*~magnus-internal/* fn=send-file
AddLog fn=flex-log name="access"
</Object>

<Object name=cgi>
ObjectType fn=force-type type=magnus-internal/cgi
Service fn=send-cgi
</Object>
```

**Server Initialization** The first two lines of this configuration file are a comment to any-body that is modifying this file. The reason that forward slashes are used for all directory paths is because Netscape Web servers were originally created to run on UNIX systems, and still retain a lot of characteristics of this platform as Netscape tries to maintain as much of a common code-base for all platforms on which their Web servers run.

**N O T E** The pound sign ("#") is used in the first column of a line to mark the line as a comment in the Netscape configuration files. This is a standard that can be found in most UNIX files, whether a configuration file or executable script files. ■

The section following this initial comment is the server initialization section. The lines in this section all begin with the section keyword "Init." There are several flags used in the entries in the initialization section that we will see in other sections. There are also some flags that are only used in the initialization section. These flags are listed in Table 21.2. These flags are al-ways used in the following form:

```
<flag>=<value>
```

where the flag informs the server what the value is to be used for.

**Table 21.2 The Flags Used in the Netscape obj.conf Configuration File**

| Flag | Description |
| --- | --- |
| fn | Tells the server what function to execute. |
| shlib | Provides the absolute path and name of a DLL to be loaded that contains NSAPI extension functions. |
| funcs | Lists the function names to be mapped from the DLL specified by the shlib flag. The value for this flag can contain multiple function names, but they must be enclosed within double-quotes and separated by commas. |
| type | Informs the server which MIME types are to cause the server to use this function for performing the processing for the step specified at the first of the line. |

| Flag | Description |
| --- | --- |
| method | Specifies which client methods (for example, GET, POST, HEAD) should cause the server to use this function to perform the processing for the step specified at the first of the line. |

In the initialization section, the function load-modules is called to tell the server to load a specific DLL, and to map the specified functions within that DLL. Once a particular DLL has been loaded, another line in the initialization section can call one of the functions that was mapped from the DLL for performing any initialization functionality needed by the DLL. The flags for a custom NSAPI function can be extended, and are passed to the function specified as additional server variables available for use by the function. Looking at the last line in the initialization section,

```
Init fn=load-modules \
            shlib="F:/Msdev42/projects/olensapi/Release/olensapi.dll"
          ➥funcs=olensapi-form
```

we can see that it is telling the server to execute the "load-modules" function, which will load an external NSAPI extension into the server. The DLL to be loaded is specified by the "shlib" flag, and the one function, "olensapi-form," will be linked into the processing function table.

**N O T E**   In the magnus.conf and obj.conf configuration files, a dash is normally used instead of the underscore character in function names. These are converted into underscores by the Netscape server when it is interpreting the configuration files. ▪

**N O T E**   Because the configuration files tell the Netscape servers what functions to call in the NSAPI DLLs, these functions can be named anything the programmer desires. This is in direct contrast to Microsoft's ISAPI interface, where two specific function names were used in each ISAPI DLL. ▪

If the NSAPI DLL specified in the last line of the initialization section had its own initialization function that had to be called, the last two lines of the initialization section would have looked something like the following:

```
Init fn=load-modules \
            shlib="F:/Msdev42/projects/olensapi/Release/olensapi.dll"
          ➥funcs="olensapi-init,olensapi-form"
Init fn=olensapi-init db=olensapidb userid=davis
```

In this example, the OLENSAPI DLL had two functions that the Netscape server needs to map, olensapi_init and olensapi_form. The server initialization then calls the olensapi_init function, making two additional server variables available to this initialization function, presumably specifying the database to open and user ID to use to log into the database.

***Request Processing***   The next two sections of the obj.conf configuration file cover request processing. The second of these two sections covers CGI processing, and the first of these two sections covers default processing. In the default processing section, the request processing steps are grouped in the order that they are executed. This server is not using any user authentication so, as a result, there are no AuthTrans entries.

There are three NameTrans entries, calling the functions specified for each request, mapping the specified logical directories to the specific directory location on the server file system. Notice that these functions are called in order, the first two mapping two specific logical directories to a specific directory on the server, and the last mapping any unmapped logical directories in relation to the "root" document directory on the server.

Following the NameTrans entries, are three PathCheck entries. The first of these cleans the URI specified by the client for Windows NT specific entries. The second function locates the specified resource on the file system. The third and final PathCheck function checks to see if the URI specified only specifies a directory in the file system. If the URI specifies a directory, this last function determines the default HTML document to be returned to the client.

The next two entries are ObjectType processing functions. The first of these two functions maps the requested resource to a MIME type based on the resource name extension. These file type mappings are specified in the mime.types configuration file, which we will examine shortly. If a corresponding MIME type is not found, the second ObjectType function forces the MIME type mapping to "`text/plain`."

The next four processing entries control the Service processing step. The first three of these specify which functions to call for each of three specific MIME types, all of which are in the magnus-internal MIME family. This MIME family is resource types that exist internally to the Netscape Web server, and are not returned to the client. Let's examine the first of these three entries:

```
Service method=(GET¦POST) type=magnus-internal/olevb fn=olensapi-form
```

First, the method flag specifies which client methods this function will service (`GET` and `POST` only). The type flag tells us that the MIME type to be passed to this function is "`magnus-internal/olevb`." Finally, when a `magnus-internal/olevb` resource is requested using either the `GET` or `POST` commands by a user, the server will call the `olensapi_form` function, which we loaded during the server initialization section.

The fourth Service entry line is called for MIME type "*~magnus-internal/*." This tells the server that for any MIME resource type that is not in the "magnus-internal" MIME family, it should call the "send_file" function.

The final entry in the default processing section is the AddLog entry. This tells the server that, once this step has been reached, to call the flex_log function, which logs the request to the server transaction log.

**The mime.types File**   The mime.types configuration file is used to map file extensions to MIME types. A section of this file can be found in Listing 21.2.

**Listing 21.2   MIME.TYPES—A Section From the mime.types Netscape Server Configuration File, Which Is Used to Map File Name Extensions to MIME Types for Use in Request Processing**

```
type=text/html                    exts=htm,html
type=text/plain                   exts=txt
type=text/richtext                exts=rtx
type=text/tab-separated-values exts=tsv
type=text/x-setext                exts=etx

type=video/mpeg                   exts=mpeg,mpg,mpe
type=video/quicktime              exts=qt,mov
type=video/x-msvideo              exts=avi
type=video/x-sgi-movie            exts=movie

enc=x-gzip                        exts=gz
enc=x-compress                    exts=z
enc=x-uuencode                    exts=uu,uue

type=magnus-internal/imagemap     exts=map
type=magnus-internal/parsed-html exts=shtml
type=magnus-internal/cgi          exts=cgi,exe,bat
type=magnus-internal/olevb        exts=vb
```

For the most part, these MIME types do not affect request processing, but are passed along to the client, so that the browser can determine how to display the resource that it is being sent. However, the last four lines of this excerpt are of particular interest to us, as these are the entries that tell the server that the requested resource is an internal MIME type, and will require handing the *Service* processing to a specific function designed to process each of the specific resource types. In the last of these entries, you can see that resources requested with the name extension ".vb" are mapped as the "magnus-internal/olevb" MIME type, which, as we saw in our examination of the obj.conf configuration file, should cause the Netscape server to call the olensapi_form function to perform the Service step processing.

# Netscape Server and Request Environment Variables

When the Netscape server calls a NSAPI function, it makes the various server and request variables that are a part of the CGI and WinCGI specifications available to the NSAPI function in what is called a pblock, which stands for Parameter Block. These pblock structures are basically a linked list of name/value pairs, very much like what we created to hold our data values in our OLEISAPI examples. These server and request variables are indexed, using a hashing algorithm, to make access to the values of these variables fast.

Although the structure of these pblocks is fairly simple, and is specified in the NSAPI documentation, direct access to the values held in these structures is discouraged. Instead, Netscape has specified a series of functions that are to be used to access their variables. This is done because Netscape reserves the right to alter the way pblocks are built, and that would effectively break every NSAPI extension that directly accesses pblock values. Netscape does

Part
VI

Ch
21

promise that the pblock access functions will continue to work correctly, regardless of how the internal structure of pblocks might change. These functions can be found in Table 21.3.

**Table 21.3   Netscape NSAPI Functions Used to Access, Set, and Modify pblock Values**

| Function Name | Description |
|---|---|
| pblock_findval | Returns the value of the specified key, if found in the specified pblock. |
| pblock_nvinsert | Adds a key/value pair to a pblock. |
| pblock_remove | Removes the specified key/value pair from a pblock. |
| pblock_pblock2str | Converts the specified pblock into a string of key=value pairs, like is passed from the client browser. |
| pblock_str2pblock | Converts a string of key=value pairs into a pblock. |

# NSAPI Function Definition

Regardless of what you name your NSAPI function, and which processing step it executes in, it will always need to be defined with the same prototype. This function prototype is as follows:

```
int funcname (pblock *pb, Session *sn, Request *rq);
```

The parameters for this function are defined in Table 21.4.

**Table 21.4   The NSAPI Function Parameters**

| Parameter | Type | Description |
|---|---|---|
| pb | pblock | Any parameters specified to be passed to this function in the obj.conf configuration file. |
| sn | Session | Session-Wide variables, including the client name, type, address, and so on. |
| rq | Request | Request-specific variables. These are variables that specify the method used, the length of the request data, the URI that was requested, and so on. |

The *Session* structure that is passed to this function contains the information listed in Table 21.5.

## Table 21.5 The NSAPI Session Structure

| Variable | Type | Description |
|---|---|---|
| client | pblock | The IP and DNS addresses of the client. |
| cds | SYS_NETFD | The socket descriptor for the current connection with the client. This is used for sending information to the client. |
| clauth | pointer | Pointer to client authentication information. |
| inbuf | netbuf* | Pointer to the open input buffer being received from the client. |

There is additional information held in the Session structure, but this is all that is of primary concern to us at this time. The Request structure contains a little more information that we need to be concerned with, and can be seen in Table 21.6.

## Table 21.6 The NSAPI Request Structure

| Variable | Type | Description |
|---|---|---|
| vars | pblock | Server working variables. |
| regpb | pblock | Parameters that are related to the request, such as the method used, the URI requested, the protocol used, and so on. |
| headers | pblock | The headers that were sent by the client browser, including the browser type, the browser's capabilities, and so on. |
| srvhdrs | pblock | The headers that will be sent back to the client with the resulting object. |

Like the Session structure, this is not the entire Request structure, but only the variables that we need to be concerned with for building NSAPI extensions.

The last thing that we need to be concerned with is what is to be returned from a NSAPI function. There are a series of return codes that may be returned, and each has a different effect on how the server continues to process the current request. These return codes, along with their descriptions, can be found in Table 21.7.

## Table 21.7 NSAPI Function Result Codes

| Result Code | Value | Description |
|---|---|---|
| REQ_PROCEED | 0 | Function was successful; if the server is in the AuthTrans, NameTrans, or Service processing steps, the server should skip all additional functions in the |

*continues*

**Table 21.7 Continued**

| Result Code | Value | Description |
| --- | --- | --- |
| | | current step and continue with the next processing step (for example, if the server is in the NameTrans step, it would skip any other NameTrans functions and start on the PathCheck step). |
| REQ_NOACTION | -2 | Function did nothing; the server should continue with the next function in the same processing step, if there is any additional functions in the current step. |
| REQ_ABORTED | -1 | An error occurred, and the server should send a message to the client to inform the user of the error. |
| REQ_EXIT | -3 | The connection to the client should be closed. |

Most of the time, when building NSAPI extensions, you will return either the REQ_PROCEED or REQ_ABORTED result codes. If your NSAPI extension is performing user authorization or path resolution, you might also be returning the REQ_NOACTION result code, to let the server know when your function did nothing.

## Netscape Server Functions

Since we are primarily concerned with building NSAPI extensions to handle the Service request processing step, we'll examine only those functions that are of particular use to us in this step.

> **N O T E** If you are interested in digging deeper into how to build NSAPI extensions to perform the Service, as well as the other steps, the complete NSAPI documentation is available from the Netscape Web site, at **http://home.netscape.com/**. ▪

We've already briefly listed the NSAPI functions for manipulating, altering, and reading the pblocks. These functions are essential for pulling information from the server for what would normally be environment variables in the standard CGI interface. These functions are also key for setting values in the message header. This is the HTTP message header that is to be returned to the client with the results of whatever processing we perform in the Service step.

**Reading Data from the Client**   If the client used the GET command to request a resource from the server, there is nothing for the NSAPI extension to read from the client, as the entire query string can be found in the URI that was sent by the client. As a result, the entire query string can be found in the regpb pblock in the Request structure that was originally passed into your NSAPI function, and can be retrieved using the following function:

```
szTmpStr = pblock_findval("query", rq->reqpb);
```

This function returns a pointer to the query string, which can then be copied into another string for manipulating, using standard string manipulation functions.

It is only when the client uses the POST command that the query string is sent separately from the message headers. This is when you need to use some special NSAPI server functions to read the data that the client sent. You have two basic ways of reading the client data: as an entire block, or one character at a time.

In order to read an entire block of data received from the client, you would use the net_read function, which requires several parameters be supplied to it. These parameters are listed in Table 21.8.

**Table 21.8   Required Parameters for NSAPI Function net_read**

| Parameter | Type | Description |
| --- | --- | --- |
| sd | SYS_NETFD | This is a platform-independent socket descriptor that is used to identify the open connection to the client. |
| buf | char* | This is a character pointer to the buffer into which the data received from the client is to be placed. |
| sz | int | This is the size of the buffer to which the previous parameter pointed. |
| timeout | int | This is the number of seconds to wait before abandoning the attempt to read data from the client. |

The net_read function returns the number of bytes that was read from the client, which could easily be less than the size of the buffer into which the data was placed. If we were to use this function to read data from the client, we would code it like the following:

```
iNumRead = net_read(sn->csd, pszBuffer, iBufferSize, 30);
```

where pszBuffer pointed to a data buffer that was the size specified in iBufferSize. After calling this function, we would check the value in iNumRead to see how much was actually read into pszBuffer.

We could also read in the data from the client one character at a time using the netbuf_getc function, which takes an open netbuf as its only parameter, and returns the next character to be read from that input buffer, very much like the fgetc() file input function in the C programming language. If we use this function to read in the data, we would need to retrieve the content length from the request headers, and then loop until all characters had been retrieved. The code to do this might look something like the following:

```
request_header("content-length", &szCLStr, sn, rq);
// Convert the Content Length string to an integer
iCLen = atoi(szCLStr);
// Loop until all characters have been read from the network buffer
for (i = 0; i < iCLen; i++)
    szBuffer[i] = netbuf_getc(sn->inbuf);
```

In this snippet of code, we retrieved the content length from the client headers using the request_header function (which allows you to search all pblocks in both the Session and

Request structures for a particular key, and then copies the value of that key into the string buffer passed into the function). We converted the content length value into an integer, and then looped for that number of times, reading one character at a time from the network input buffer and copying it into a character array (that presumably will hold the entire number of characters).

The request_header function used in this code snippet allows you to make a single function call to find and make a copy of a particular header that was either received from the client, or will be sent to the client. This is normally at least two function calls using the pblock functions, the first to get a pointer to the particular pblock value, and a second to copy the value into another string. This assumes that you know which pblock in either the Session or Request structures contains the header that you want. The request_header function allows you to not know which pblock structure is holding the desired header, but will find it for you, regardless of its location within those two structures.

**Sending Data to the Client**   Sending data back to the client is much simpler, as there is only one function that you really need to be concerned with. This is the net_write function. The net_write function takes three parameters: the socket descriptor that identifies the network connection to the client, a pointer to a buffer containing the data to be sent, and the amount of data to be sent to the client. The net_write function returns the number of bytes that were sent to the client. By comparing the return value to the amount of data that was to be sent, you can determine whether the function was completely successful. In code, the net_write function would probably look something like the following example:

```
iNumWritten = net_write(sn->csd, pszBuffer, strlen(pszBuffer));
```

where `pszBuffer` points to a buffer with character data to be sent to the client.

**Sending the Headers to the Client**   Before you begin sending data back to the client, there are two NSAPI functions that have to be called. These are protocol_status, which specifies the HTTP status code to return to the client, and protocol_start_response, which sends the HTTP status and server headers to the client to let the client know that the response is on its way.

The protocol_status function requires four parameters, the first two being the Session and Request structures that were passed to your NSAPI function. The third parameter is the HTTP response code to be returned, and the fourth is a string pointer containing a description of the reason behind the HTTP response code. The string pointer in the fourth parameter can be NULL, if there is no reason description to be returned.

The protocol_start_response function takes only the Session and Request structures as its only parameters. This function causes the server to send the HTTP response line and all of the message headers that the server has prepared to send to the client. This is followed by the NSAPI extension calling the net_write function to send the resulting object or HTML document to the client. All three of these functions might be used together in the following way:

```
protocol_status(sn, rq, PROTOCOL_OK, NULL);
protocol_start_response(sn, rq);
// Write the HTML document to the client
net_write(sn->csd, pszResults, strlen(pszResults));
```

This would probably be followed by returning the REQ_PROCEED result code to the server as the NSAPI function exits (and releasing any memory that was allocated within the function, of course).

# Calling VB ActiveX Methods From C

When you are calling a Visual Basic method in an ActiveX DLL from another programming language such as C, you place yourself right in the midst of ActiveX programming. This is where programming languages like Visual Basic definitely provide the programmer with an easier time by hiding all of the detail work involved with ActiveX programming.

In order to call a Visual Basic method, perform the following steps:

1. Look up the CLSID (Class ID) from the registry database using the class name.
2. Load the ActiveX DLL into the process space and acquire a pointer to the IUnknown interface.
3. Query the IUnknown interface to get a pointer to the IDispatch interface.
4. Query the IDispatch interface to get the method ID of the method being called.
5. Call the IDispatch Invoke method to call the Visual Basic method.

If this looks like a complicated set of steps to go through, it is. Unfortunately, to build an OLEISAPI-like interface for the Netscape NSAPI interface, or for the server API of any other Web server, this is what you have to understand in order to build the interface that will allow you to use Visual Basic to do your SAPI programming. Once you are able to do the Visual Basic programming, you can forget all of this internal ActiveX detail.

## Normal and Unicode Character Strings

The first thing to know about ActiveX programming is that all of the ActiveX API calls require Unicode character strings instead of normal character strings. Before calling any ActiveX API calls that require a string as a function parameter, you have to convert any normal strings to Unicode strings. This is done using the MultiByteToWideChar function, which is a standard Win32 API function.

Likewise, in order to convert text strings that are returned from ActiveX API functions, the strings need to be converted back from Unicode to standard character strings. As you can probably guess, this conversion back is done using the WideCharToMultiByte Win32 API function.

## Looking Up the CLSID

Before an ActiveX object can be loaded and pointers to interfaces retrieved, you have to know the Class ID, or CLSID, of the ActiveX Class being called. The Class ID is a globally unique, 16-byte identifier that is used to identify not just the ActiveX DLL that is being called, but the class within the DLL that is being requested. You have to know this CLSID before you can work with the DLL, and in order to know what this CLSID is, you have to look it up in the registry database. You can look up the CLSID for any ActiveX Class using the CLSIDFromProgID ActiveX API call. This API function takes two parameters, the first being the Unicode Visual Basic ActiveX project and class name, and the second being a pointer to a variable of type CLSID. Combine this with the Unicode conversion functions, and your code to look up a CLSID for a Visual Basic class named "nsapiex.MyClass" would look like the following code snippet:

```
CLSID clsid;
OLECHAR *lpszOleChar;

// Allocate memory for the Unicode string
lpszOleChar = malloc(sizeof(WCHAR) * strlen("nsapiex.MyClass"));
// Convert the class name from ASCII to Unicode
MultiByteToWideChar(CP_ACP, MB_ERR_INVALID_CHARS, "nsapiex.MyClass",
 strlen("nsapiex.MyClass"), lpszOleChar, strlen("nsapiex.MyClass"));
// Look up the ActiveX Class ID
CLSIDFromProgID(lpszOleChar, &clsid);
```

This code (plus some error checking, of course) would leave you with the class ID for the "nsapiex.MyClass," which you can then use to load into the application process space and begin getting pointers to its interfaces.

## Getting a Pointer to the IDispatch Interface

When you first create an instance of an ActiveX class, you acquire a pointer to the *IUnknown* interface. This is an ActiveX interface that is required in every ActiveX object, regardless of what the object does. The IUnknown interface has three methods that can be called, the first of which is the QueryInterface method, which can be used to get a pointer to any other ActiveX interface that is implemented in the object.

An instance of the ActiveX class can be created using the *CoCreateInstance* ActiveX API call. This function requires the CLSID that we retrieved from the registry using the CLSIDFromProgID function. We could continue our previous code snippet and create an instance of our Visual Basic ActiveX DLL class with the following code:

```
IUnknown *punkObj = NULL;

CoCreateInstance(clsid, NULL, CLSCTX_SERVER, IID_IUnknown,
                                    (LPVOID *) &punkObj);
```

Once we have our pointer to the IUnknown interface, we can call the IUnknown::QueryInterface method to acquire a pointer to the *IDispatch* interface, which will enable us to call methods in our Visual Basic ActiveX DLL. The QueryInterface method requires two parameters, the first being an interface identifier, and the second being a pointer to an interface pointer for the requested interface. We can continue our code snippet with the following code to acquire a pointer to the IDispatch interface:

```
IDispatch *pdispObj = NULL;
HRESULT hr;

hr = punkObj->QueryInterface(IID_IDispatch, (void**)&pdispObj);
```

We should check the return value that is being held in the hr variable, to make certain that our request was successful. If we are successful, we now have a pointer to the IDispatch interface in the pdispObj variable.

## Looking Up the Dispatch Method ID

The IDispatch interface was originally designed with Visual Basic in mind. Most ActiveX interfaces have a series of methods that can be called to the interface through a pointer. The problem is that the methods have to be known at the time that the program is compiled. This doesn't work with the Visual Basic model, where there are multiple ActiveX controls that may be added to a Visual Basic project at any time. The Visual Basic programmer needs to be able to call the various methods contained within the ActiveX controls, or within other ActiveX server applications like Word and Excel, without having to know which methods are contained within which ActiveX interfaces. To solve this problem, the ActiveX architects at Microsoft came up with the IDispatch interface.

The IDispatch interface is an integral part of ActiveX Automation functionality. The IDispatch interface contains a table with the names of and pointers to every callable method within the ActiveX class. This provides a means for applications and programming languages to call methods in ActiveX applications and DLLs without having to know ahead of time what interface to use in order to call the method. By calling the IDispatch::Invoke method, passing the identifier for the method you want to run, the specified method in the ActiveX class will be executed, as in Figure 21.2. This is often referred to as the dispinterface.

**FIG. 21.2**
The IDispatch ActiveX interface Invoke method looks up the requested method in its Vector Table, and executes the requested method.

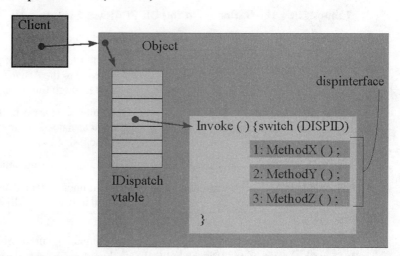

IDispatch::Invoke(DISPID)

**Part**
**VI**

**Ch**
**21**

Before you can call the IDispatch::Invoke method, you have to know the method ID of the method you want to call. You can get the method ID of the method you want to call using the IDispatch::GetIDsOfNames method. Our previous code snippets can be extended to look up the ID of the DoPost method in the Visual Basic ActiveX DLL using the following code snippet:

```
OLECHAR wzMethod[PARAMLEN];
DISPID dispidMethod;
OLECHAR *pwzName;

// Convert the method name to Unicode.
MultiByteToWideChar(CP_ACP, 0, "DoPost", -1, wzMethod, PARAMLEN);
// Find method name
pwzName = wzMethod;
hr = pdispObj->GetIDsOfNames(IID_NULL, &pwzName, 1,
                             LOCALE_USER_DEFAULT, &dispidMethod);
```

This will leave us with the method ID for the DoPost Visual Basic method in the dispidMethod variable. We now have the IDispatch::Invoke method ID that we need to call our Visual Basic method.

# Calling the Visual Basic Method

Before we can call the Invoke method and execute our Visual Basic method, we have to prepare the parameters that are going to be passed to our method. These parameters that are strings have to be converted into Unicode strings, and then the parameters are all loaded into an array of VARIANTARGs, each of which consists of a flag that indicates the data type of the argument and a UNION of datatypes, so that any variable may be placed in the VARIANTARG. The parameters are loaded into this array in reverse order, so that the last parameter that the Visual Basic method will be expecting is placed in position 0, the next to last parameter is placed in position 1, and so on. This array of parameters is placed into a structure called DISPPARMS, which contains the variables listed in Table 21.9.

**Table 21.9   The Variables in the DISPPARMS Structure**

| Variable | Type | Description |
|---|---|---|
| rgvarg | VARIANTARG* | A pointer to the array of parameters that are to be passed to the ActiveX method that is being called through the IDispatch::Invoke method. |
| rgdispidNamedArgs | DISPID* | A pointer to an array of IDispatch IDs that are passed as named arguments (which we will not be discussing here). |
| cArgs | unsigned int | The number of arguments being passed. |
| cNamedArgs | unsigned int | The number of named arguments being passed in the rgdispidNamedArgs variable. |

We can now use the method ID and our structure containing our variables to call our Visual Basic method through the IDispatch::Invoke method. If we have two parameters that we want to pass to our method, with a third parameter that we want to return that contains the output of our Visual Basic method, we could extend our previous code snippets with the following excerpt:

```
DISPPARAMS dispparms;
VARIANTARG varg[3];
OLECHAR wzParam1[PARAMLEN];
OLECHAR wzParam2[PARAMLEN];
BSTR bstrParam1 = NULL;
BSTR bstrParam2 = NULL;
BSTR bstrRetval = NULL;

// Convert parameters to Unicode
MultiByteToWideChar(CP_ACP, 0, pszParam1, strlen(pszParam1),
                                      wzParam1, PARAMLEN);
MultiByteToWideChar(CP_ACP, 0, pszParam2, strlen(pszParam2),
                                      wzParam2, PARAMLEN);
// Allocate and copy strings into BSTRs
bstrParam1 = SysAllocString(wzParam1);
bstrParam2 = SysAllocString(wzParam2);
bstrRetval = SysAllocString(L"");
// Setup parameters
dispparms.rgvarg = varg;
dispparms.rgdispidNamedArgs = NULL;
dispparms.cArgs = 3;
dispparms.cNamedArgs = 0;
// Push in reverse order
varg[0].vt = VT_BSTR | VT_BYREF;
varg[0].pbstrVal = &bstrRetval;
varg[1].vt = VT_BSTR | VT_BYREF;
varg[1].pbstrVal = &bstrParam2;
varg[2].vt = VT_BSTR | VT_BYREF;
varg[2].pbstrVal = &bstrParam1;
hr = pdispObj->Invoke(dispidMethod, IID_NULL, LOCALE_USER_DEFAULT,
                DISPATCH_METHOD, &dispparms, NULL, &excep, NULL);
```

We can now take the contents of varg[0].pbstrVal and convert them from Unicode back to a normal string, and we've got the results of our Visual Basic method. Compare all of the steps we have had to go through to call one Visual Basic ActiveX DLL method, to the amount of code required to do the same with Visual Basic:

```
Dim Obj As Object

Set Obj = CreateObject("nsapi.MyClass")
Obj.DoPost(pszParam1, pszParam2, pszResult)
```

You begin to see just how much the Visual Basic programming language is doing behind the scenes when you are doing any ActiveX programming.

# Building an OLENSAPI Interface

Modeling our OLENSAPI interface after the OLEISAPI interface, we'll make a couple of assumptions about how we need our interface to work. First, even though a number of ActiveX server classes are not thread safe, we won't use a critical section around our calls to load and execute our Visual Basic ActiveX DLL. With VB5, we can now create thread safe ActiveX DLLs. (This will make our interface unusable with previous versions of VB). Second, because the

Netscape NSAPI interface was designed around the standard C programming language, for portability reasons, we'll build our OLENSAPI interface using standard C, instead of C++. This means that we will have to make a few adaptations in our ActiveX API calls, as they were originally designed for use with C++.

**N O T E**  We could have built our interface using C++ by editing all of the Netscape header files, placing

```
#ifdef __cplusplus
extern "C"{
#endif
```

at the beginning of each file, and

```
#ifdef __cplusplus
}
#endif
```

at the end of each file. ▓

Outlining the steps that our OLENSAPI interface needs to perform, we have the following sequence of steps:

1. Initialize the ActiveX environment.
2. Determine which method was used to call the OLENSAPI interface, GET or POST.
3. Check the content length to determine how much data we should have received from the client.
4. Retrieve the query string from either the query header (if using the GET command), or the input buffer (if using the POST command).
5. Parse the requested URI into the Visual Basic Class name and Method name.
6. Grab the desired request and session variables to pass to the Visual Basic ActiveX DLL, and format them as a query string.
7. Look up the CLSID for the requested Visual Basic class.
8. Create an instance of the requested Visual Basic class.
9. Acquire a pointer to the IDispatch interface.
10. Look up the method ID of the desired Visual Basic method.
11. Convert the parameter string to Unicode and package the parameter strings for passing to the Visual Basic method.
12. Invoke the requested Visual Basic method.
13. Convert the resulting HTML document back from Unicode to normal character strings.
14. Set the response code to designate that the request was successful, and send the headers and resulting HTML document.
15. Release the ActiveX interface pointers and clean up any allocated memory.

16. If an error occurred during the call to the Visual Basic method, format and send an error message as an HTML document.

We will take a departure from the OLENSAPI model in that we will pass our Visual Basic routine an additional parameter string containing some session and request variables that we can make use of in our Visual Basic application. Otherwise, this will be following very much in the footsteps of the OLEISAPI interface, except that the NSAPI interface will be on the front end instead of the ISAPI interface.

# OLENSAPI Defines, Includes, and Variables

Before we jump into the C code to implement our OLENSAPI interface, we have to make sure that we have defined the appropriate constants and included all of the definition files that we will be needing. The first NSAPI include file that we have to specify is the "netsite.h" include file, which requires us to make two defines before including this header file. This header file defines the server and platform specific information, so before we include this file we have to define our platform (XP_WIN32), and our server (MCC_HTTPD), we will have all of the correct files included.

> **NOTE** The Netscape NSAPI interface is available on all of Netscape's servers, not just their Web servers. This is why we have to specify that we are building this NSAPI extension for their Web server (HTTP), instead of their Proxy, Catalog, or other servers in their SuiteSpot lineup. ■

The "netsite.h" header file includes all necessary Windows include files, so you will not have to worry about including these yourself. The rest of the NSAPI includes are very much standard for all NSAPI extensions, and include the pblock structures that will be passed to our NSAPI function. The other include files are the standard C header files that are required for any specific programming needs that we run into when writing our code.

The only global variable that we will need to define is the flag that we will be using to indicate that the ActiveX environment has been initialized. We end up with the declaration section of our OLENSAPI interface that is in Listing 21.3.

---

**Listing 21.3   OLENSAPI.C—The Constant Definitions and Includes Needed to Build a NSAPI Extension**

```
//-----------------------------------------------------------------
// The following two defines are used by the NSAPI header files
// to determine the operating system platform and the server
// for which this NSAPI extension is intended to be used.
//-----------------------------------------------------------------
#define XP_WIN32
#define MCC_HTTPD
//-----------------------------------------------------------------
// This header file performs all of the platform specific
// includes of the standard include files
//-----------------------------------------------------------------
```

Part

**VI**

Ch

**21**

*continues*

---

**Listing 21.3  Continued**

```
#include "netsite.h"
//----------------------------------------------------------------
// The following three are standard headers for SAFs.  They're
// used to get the data structures and prototypes needed to
// declare and use SAFs.
//----------------------------------------------------------------
#include "base\pblock.h"
#include "base\session.h"
#include "frame\req.h"

#include "frame\protocol.h"  // protocol_start_response
#include "frame\log.h"       // log_error

#include <stdio.h>
#include <string.h>
#include <ctype.h>
//----------------------------------------------------------------
// These two defines are used to control the length of the buffer
// used to pass the variables to the VB ActiveX DLL and the size
// of the HTML document that can be passed back.
//----------------------------------------------------------------
#define PARAMLEN 1024
#define BUFLEN 4096

// TLS is used to store OLE initialization flag
static DWORD gdwTLSIndex = (DWORD)-1;
```

# The Primary NSAPI Function

Because we can name our NSAPI function anything we want, we'll call it "olensapi_form" to reflect the purpose for which we are implementing it. As can be seen in Listing 21.4, the first thing that we do is check to see if we need to initialize the OLE or ActiveX environment. Once we have made sure that the OLE environment has been initialized, check to see which method was used to call our interface.

**Listing 21.4  OLENSAPI.C—The olensapi_form Function that Is Called By the Netscape Server to Process the Visual Basic Request**

```
NSAPI_PUBLIC int olensapi_form(pblock *apPb, Session *apSn,
                                              Request *apRq)
{
    char *szMethod;      // ptr to method string in pblock
    char *szCLStr;       // ptr to Content-length string in pblock
    char *szType;        // ptr to Content-type string in pblock
    char *szTmpStr;      // ptr to query string in pblock
    char *szQStr;        // actual query string to work on
    int iCLen;           // content length
    int iPostLen;        // number of chars read from net_buf
    char *szRequestURL;  // URL Requested
```

```c
char *szPath;        // URL Path
char *szClass;       // Class Requested
char *szVBMethod;    // Method Requested (not the same as the
                     // method used
char *szTemp;        // A temporary character string pointer
char *szSStr;        // A string to hold server variables to
                     // be passed to the ActiveX DLL
char *szIp;          // A pointer to the client IP address
char *szAgent;       // A pointer to the client browser info
char *szReferer;     // A pointer to the URL that referred
                     // the client

// Has OLE/ActiveX been initialized yet?
if (!TlsGetValue(gdwTLSIndex))
{
    // No, so let's initialize it
    OleInitialize(NULL);
    TlsSetValue(gdwTLSIndex, (void*)TRUE);
}

// Allocate memory for the string of Server variables
szSStr = malloc(sizeof(char) * (PARAMLEN));
//-----------------------------------------------------------
// If the method is GET, we can get the name=value pairs
// from the query string, but if it's POST, then we need to
// read in all the input from the network and stuff it into
// a string. If it's neither, we complain vigorously and exit.
//-----------------------------------------------------------
szMethod = pblock_findval("method", apRq->reqpb);

// Is the method POST?
if (strcmp(szMethod, "POST") == 0)
{
    // If there's no content-length, it's a bogus request
    if (request_header("content-length", &szCLStr, apSn,
                                apRq) == REQ_ABORTED)
    {
        protocol_status(apSn, apRq, PROTOCOL_FORBIDDEN,
                            "No content-length.");
        log_error(LOG_WARN, "formproc", apSn, apRq,
                            "No content-length.");
        return REQ_ABORTED;
    }

    // Convert the Content Length string to an integer
    iCLen = atoi(szCLStr);

    // If the content-type isn't right, it's a bogus request
    request_header("content-type", &szType, apSn, apRq);

    if (strcmp(szType, "application/x-www-form-urlencoded")
                                                != 0)
```

*Part*

**VI**

Ch

**21**

*continues*

**Listing 21.4  Continued**

```
        {
            protocol_status(apSn, apRq, PROTOCOL_FORBIDDEN,
                                    "Content wrong type.");
            log_error(LOG_WARN, "formproc", apSn, apRq,
                                    "Content wrong type.");
            return REQ_ABORTED;
        }

        // If the content length is 0 or negative, it's
        // a bogus request
        if (iCLen < 1)
        {
            protocol_status(apSn, apRq, PROTOCOL_FORBIDDEN,
                                    "Content length <=0.");
            log_error(LOG_WARN, "formproc", apSn, apRq,
                                    "Content length <=0.");
            return REQ_ABORTED;
        }

        // Allocate space to put the query string after we
        // read it in
        szQStr = malloc(sizeof(char) * (iCLen + 1));
        // Retrieve the POSTed query string using the
        // PostToQStr function
        iPostLen = PostToQStr(apSn->inbuf, szQStr, iCLen);

        //-------------------------------------------------------
        // If the amount of data we read in != content-length,
        // then we will consider the request bogus, although in
        // theory we could keep going with the actual length
        //-------------------------------------------------------
        if (iPostLen != iCLen)
        {
            protocol_status(apSn, apRq, PROTOCOL_FORBIDDEN,
                                    "Bad content length.");
            log_error(LOG_WARN, "formproc", apSn, apRq,
                                    "Bad content length.");
            free(szQStr);
            return REQ_ABORTED;
        }
    }
    // Is the method GET?
    else if (strcmp(szMethod, "GET") == 0)
    {

        //-------------------------------------------------------
        // Make a copy of the query string to work on, since we're
        // going to be chopping it up most mercilessly
        //-------------------------------------------------------
        if (pblock_find("query", apRq->reqpb))
        {
            szTmpStr = pblock_findval("query", apRq->reqpb);
            iCLen = strlen(szTmpStr);
            szQStr = malloc(sizeof(char *) * (iCLen + 1));
            strcpy(szQStr, szTmpStr);
```

```
        }
        else
        {
            // if there's no query string, nothing we can do
            protocol_status(apSn, apRq, PROTOCOL_BAD_REQUEST, NULL);
            log_error(LOG_WARN, "formproc", apSn, apRq,
                                    "No query string.");
            return REQ_ABORTED;
        }
    }
    // Is the method unknown?
    else
    {
        protocol_status(apSn, apRq, PROTOCOL_FORBIDDEN,
                                    "Invalid method.");
        log_error(LOG_WARN, "formproc", apSn, apRq,
                                    "Invalid method.");
        return REQ_ABORTED;
    }

    // Retrieve the requested URI
    szRequestURL = pblock_findval("uri", apRq->reqpb);
    //----------------------------------------------------------
    // If we didn't find a URI, we can let this vall through to
    // the error handling routine to return an error message to
    // the user.
    //----------------------------------------------------------
    if (!szRequestURL)
    {
        szRequestURL = malloc(sizeof(char) * 20);
        sprintf(szRequestURL, "No method");
    }

    // Copy the URI into a string that we can manipulate
    szPath = malloc(sizeof(char *) * strlen(szRequestURL));
    strcpy(szPath, szRequestURL);
    // If the first character is a slash, position the szClass
    // pointer to start with the Object name in the next position
    if ('/' == *szPath)
    {
        szClass = szPath + 1;
    }
    else
    {
        szClass = szPath;
    }
    // Find the first period, which demarks the VB Class
    // being called
    szVBMethod = strchr(szPath, '.');
    if (szVBMethod)
    {
        // ProgIDs can have zero or one periods in them,
        // so we want to find the third period that marks
        // the method being called
        szTemp = strchr(szVBMethod + 1, '.');
```

*continues*

Part

**VI**

Ch

**21**

**Listing 21.4  Continued**

```
        // Separate ProgID from the method name
        if (szTemp)
        {
            *szTemp = '\0';
            szVBMethod = szTemp + 1;
        }
        else
        {
            *szVBMethod = '\0';
            szVBMethod++;
        }
        // Find the third period that marks the "vb"
        // extension, and chop it off of the string
        szTemp = strchr(szVBMethod, '.');
        if (szTemp)
        {
            *szTemp = '\0';
        }
    }

    // Grab pointers to the Server variables we want to pass
    // to the VB ActiveX DLL
    szIp = pblock_findval("ip", apSn->client);
    szAgent = pblock_findval("user-agent", apRq->headers);
    szReferer = pblock_findval("referer", apRq->headers);

    // Format the server variables into a query string
    sprintf(szSStr, "method=%s&ip=%s&agent=%s&referer=%s",
                szMethod, szIp, szAgent, szReferer);
    // Call the ActiveX object method specified
    if (!CallObject(szSStr, szQStr, apSn, apRq, szClass,
                                szVBMethod, iCLen))
    {
        // An error condition was returned, so send the user an
        // error message
        ErrorResponse(szQStr, apSn, apRq, szClass, szVBMethod,
                                            iCLen);
    }

    // Release all allocated memory
    free(szPath);
    free(szQStr);
    free(szSStr);
    // Return a PROCEED status code
    return REQ_PROCEED;
}
```

If the POST method has been used to call our OLENSAPI interface, we check to see how much data has been sent to us by the client browser. If the browser did not send us anything, or if the content type is not "application/x-www-form-urlencoded," then we have received a bad POST request. If this is the case, we'll return an error condition, log the error, and let the server take care of the rest. If we do have a positive content length, we'll retrieve the content from the network input buffer using the `PostToQStr` function, which we'll look at shortly. If the amount of data retrieved from the network input buffer is not the same as the content length specified in the message header, we know we have a corrupted request, so we should return an error condition and log the error.

If the GET method has been used, copy the "query" message header into our query string variable. We don't care if the query string is empty because an empty query string is still a valid GET message.

If the method used was neither GET nor POST, return an error condition and log the error, as it was an invalid request that we shouldn't have received in this NSAPI extension. A good addition to this OLENSAPI interface would be to include processing for the HEAD command, where the headers are returned without the HTML document that the Visual Basic ActiveX DLL would normally be generating.

Once we have the query string, we need to know which ActiveX class is being called, and which method within the ActiveX Class we are supposed to invoke. To get this information we find the URI header that we received from the client, remove any leading slashes from the URI, and then parse it into ActiveX Class name and method name, removing the ".vb" extension from the method name.

The last bit of information we need before we call our ActiveX class is the session and request headers that we want to include in the information being passed to the Visual Basic method. In this case, we are going to be passing the method used to call this module, the TCP/IP address of the client, the browser being used by the client, and the HTML page that generated this request. We'll get pointers to each of these values in the session and request pblocks, and then create a string with this information formatted as a query string. We could have grabbed all of the available session and request variables, but in the interest of brevity, and only wanting to pass the session and request variables that we will be needing, we will only be sending a small subset of the session and request headers to the Visual Basic method.

We now have all that we want to send to our Visual Basic method, as we'll call the `CallObject` function that will perform all of the ActiveX magic that we looked at earlier. If an error occurs in this function, we'll call the `ErrorResponse` function, which will send the user an error message with the key information about the request included. Once we have completed these requests, we'll release all memory that we have allocated in this function and return a REQ_PROCEED response code, telling the server to skip all of the other Service functions.

## Reading in the Posted Data

Our function that reads the data submitted with the POST command is fairly simple. As can be seen in Listing 21.5, the `PostToQStr` function enters a loop, in which it reads one character from the network input buffer, adding the characters to a character string, until all characters have been read. Once all characters have been read, a NULL character is added to the end of the string, and the number of characters read is returned to the calling routine.

**Listing 21.5 OLENSAPI.C—The *PostToQStr* Function that Reads in Posted Data and Copies It into a Query String to Pass to the Visual Basic ActiveX DLL**

```
int PostToQStr(netbuf *apBuf, char *aszQStr, int aiCLen)
{
    int i;                      // index into szQStr
    int iChar = !IO_EOF;        // char read in from netbuf

    i = 0;

    //----------------------------------------------------------
    // Loop through reading a character and writing it to szQStr,
    // until either len characters have been read, there's no
    // more input, or there's an IO error.
    //----------------------------------------------------------
    while (aiCLen && iChar != IO_EOF)
    {
        // Get the next character from the input buffer
        iChar = netbuf_getc(apBuf);

        // Check for error in reading
        if(iChar == IO_ERROR)
        {
            break;
        }
        // Add the character to the string
        aszQStr[i++] = iChar;
        // Decrement the number of characters we still need to read
        aiCLen--;
    }
    // Terminate the query string with a NULL character
    aszQStr[i] = '\0';
    // Return the number of characters read
    return(i);
}
```

# Calling the Visual Basic ActiveX DLL

As can be seen in Listing 21.6, the CallObject function is where things get real interesting. This is where the ActiveX functionality with the IDispatch interface that we looked at earlier, is implemented. There is one subtle difference; however, because we are using standard C for building our OLENSAPI interface. Standard C is used because the Netscape interface is designed with standard C in mind, and therefore some of our ActiveX calls take some unusual twists and turns. We'll point out the differences in how we had to alter the code snippets that we looked at earlier in order to get them to work with standard C as we go through the code.

**Listing 21.6 OLENSAPI.C—The *CallObject* Function, Which Converts and Loads the Parameters and Calls the ActiveX DLL**

```
BOOL CallObject(char *apszSStr, char *apszQStr, Session *apSn,
                        Request *apRq, char *apszProgid,
                        char *apszVBMethod, int acbAvail)
```

```
{
    BOOL bSuccess = FALSE;
    BOOL bInCritSec = FALSE;
    HRESULT hr;
    CLSID clsid;
    // We will need pointers to both the ActiveX interfaces,
    // and their VTables, as this is ANSI C, not C++
    IDispatch *pdispObj = NULL;
    IDispatchVtbl *plpDispVTbl = NULL;
    IUnknown *punkObj = NULL;
    IUnknownVtbl *plpUnkVtbl = NULL;
    OLECHAR wzMethod[PARAMLEN];
    OLECHAR wzParams[PARAMLEN];
    OLECHAR wzSrvParams[PARAMLEN];
    BSTR bstrSrvParams = NULL;
    BSTR bstrParams = NULL;
    BSTR bstrRetval = NULL;
    CHAR *pszResults = NULL;
    DWORD dwBufLen = 0;

    OLECHAR *pwzName;
    DISPID dispidMethod;
    DISPPARAMS dispparms;
    VARIANTARG varg[2];
    EXCEPINFO excep;

    // Initialize everything up front so cleanup is safe
    memset(&dispparms, 0, sizeof(DISPPARAMS));
    memset(&varg, 0, sizeof(VARIANTARG) * 3);
    memset(&excep, 0, sizeof(EXCEPINFO));
    memset(wzParams, 0, PARAMLEN);
    memset(wzSrvParams, 0, PARAMLEN);

    VariantInit(&varg[0]);
    VariantInit(&varg[1]);
    VariantInit(&varg[2]);

    // Convert Class name to clsid
    hr = GetClsidFromProgIdA(&clsid, apszProgid,
                             lstrlen(apszProgid) + 1);
    if (FAILED(hr)) goto Err;

    //-------------------------------------------------------------
    // Instantiate object - This is slightly different from
    // the normal CoCreateInstance that most C++ programmers
    // are probably used to, as the implicit pointers in C++
    // are not there in standard ANSI C, thus we have to pass
    // the address for a couple of the objects
    //-------------------------------------------------------------
    CoCreateInstance(&clsid, NULL, CLSCTX_SERVER, &IID_IUnknown,
                                   (LPVOID *) &punkObj);
    if (!punkObj) goto Err;
    // We got the IUnknown interface, now we need to get a
    // pointer to it's VTable
    plpUnkVtbl = punkObj->lpVtbl;
```

Part

**VI**

Ch

**21**

*continues*

**Listing 21.6 Continued**

```c
// Now we'll ask the IUknown interface for a pointer to the
// IDispatch interface
hr = plpUnkVtbl->QueryInterface(punkObj, &IID_IDispatch,
                                            (void**)&pdispObj);
if (FAILED(hr) || !pdispObj) goto Err;
// We're done with the IUnknown interface, so we can free up
// these pointers and release this interface
plpUnkVtbl->Release(punkObj);
plpUnkVtbl = NULL;
punkObj = NULL;

// Convert the method name and args to Wide character.
if (0 == MultiByteToWideChar(CP_ACP, 0, apszVBMethod, -1,
                                      wzMethod, PARAMLEN) )
{
  goto Err;
}

if (strlen(apszQStr) != 0)
{
    if (0 == MultiByteToWideChar(CP_ACP, 0, apszQStr, -1,
                                        wzParams, PARAMLEN) )
    {
        goto Err;
    }
}
else
{
    wzParams[0] = (WCHAR)0;
}
if (strlen(apszSStr) != 0)
{
    if (0 == MultiByteToWideChar(CP_ACP, 0, apszSStr, -1,
                                        wzSrvParams, PARAMLEN) )
    {
        goto Err;
    }
}
else
{
    wzSrvParams[0] = (WCHAR)0;
}
// Allocate and initialize the system strings that will be
// passed into the VB method.
bstrParams = SysAllocString(wzParams);
if (!bstrParams) goto Err;
bstrSrvParams = SysAllocString(wzSrvParams);
if (!bstrSrvParams) goto Err;
bstrRetval = SysAllocString(L"");
if (!bstrRetval) goto Err;

// Find method name
pwzName = wzMethod;
// Get a pointer to the IDispatch VTable
```

```
plpDispVTbl = pdispObj->lpVtbl;
// Get the Dispatch method ID
hr = plpDispVTbl->GetIDsOfNames(pdispObj, &IID_NULL,
            &pwzName, 1, LOCALE_USER_DEFAULT, &dispidMethod);
if (FAILED(hr)) goto Err;

// Setup parameters
dispparms.rgvarg = varg;
dispparms.rgdispidNamedArgs = NULL;
dispparms.cArgs = 3;
dispparms.cNamedArgs = 0;

// Push in reverse order
varg[0].vt = VT_BSTR | VT_BYREF;
varg[0].pbstrVal = &bstrRetval;
varg[1].vt = VT_BSTR | VT_BYREF;
varg[1].pbstrVal = &bstrParams;
varg[2].vt = VT_BSTR | VT_BYREF;
varg[2].pbstrVal = &bstrSrvParams;

// Now make the invocation.
hr = plpDispVTbl->Invoke(pdispObj, dispidMethod, &IID_NULL,
                    LOCALE_USER_DEFAULT, DISPATCH_METHOD,
                    &dispparms, NULL, &excep, NULL);
if (FAILED(hr)) goto Err;

// Assemble result
dwBufLen = wcslen(*(varg[0].pbstrVal));
if (dwBufLen > 0)
{
    // Convert the resulting HTML document from wide character
    // to ASCII
    pszResults = (char *)malloc(dwBufLen + 1);
    if (0 == WideCharToMultiByte(CP_ACP, 0, *(varg[0].pbstrVal),
                        -1, pszResults, BUFLEN, NULL, NULL))
    {
        goto Err;
    }
    // null terminate string
    *(pszResults + dwBufLen) = 0;
}

// Tell the Netscape server what MIME type we are getting
// ready to pass it
param_free(pblock_remove("content-type", apRq->srvhdrs));
pblock_nvinsert("content-type", "text/html", apRq->srvhdrs);

// These two lines send the headers to the client, and set
// everything up so successive net_write()s will work properly.
protocol_status(apSn, apRq, PROTOCOL_OK, NULL);
protocol_start_response(apSn, apRq);

// Write the HTML document to the client
net_write(apSn->csd, pszResults, strlen(pszResults));
bSuccess = TRUE;
```

Part

**VI**

Ch

**21**

*continues*

**Listing 21.6 Continued**

```
    // Always fall through to cleanup
Err:
    if (pdispObj)
    {
        // Release the IDispatch interface
        plpDispVTbl->Release(pdispObj);
    }
    VariantClear(&varg[1]);
    VariantClear(&varg[2]);
    if (NULL != pszResults)
    {
        // Release any memory being held
        free(pszResults);
    }
    // Return the success status
    return bSuccess;
}
```

We start our CallObject function by initializing all of our variables and structures that will be used in our ActiveX calls. Once we have made sure that we have no residual data in any of our variables, we'll call the GetClsidFromProgIdA function to look up the CLSID of the requested Visual Basic class in the registry database.

Next, we'll create an instance of our ActiveX class, grabbing a pointer to the class' IUnknown interface. Because we are building this in C, we have to pass the address of our CLSID and the interface specifier that we want. These addresses are implied in C++, but once we go back into standard C, we have to make the address explicit.

Once we have a pointer to the IUnknown interface, we have to diverge from standard ActiveX programming once again, as we cannot directly call the IUnknown interface's QueryInterface method, but have to get a pointer to the IUnknown interface's vtable, which contains pointers to all of the interface's methods. It is through the IUnknown vtable that we can call the QueryInterface method to get a pointer to the IDispatch interface. Notice that the QueryInterface takes a pointer to the IUnknown interface as an additional argument. This argument is implicit in C++, but has to be explicit in standard C.

Once we have our pointer to the IDispatch interface, we can release our pointer to the IUnknown interface, as we no longer need access to this interface. Next, we convert all of our method names and parameter strings to Unicode (also known as Wide character strings), and allocate the system memory for these strings to be passed into the ActiveX method.

The next thing we will do is look up the method ID of the Visual Basic method we are going to be calling. Like the IUnknown interface, we cannot directly access the IDispatch interface methods, but have to get a pointer to the interface's vtable and use it to get to the interface methods.

Once we have the method ID, we'll package our parameters to be passed to the Visual Basic method, and call the Invoke method to run our Visual Basic application.

If we have anything in the result parameter, we'll convert it back to a normal string. We'll replace the server "content-type" header with the value "text/html," so the browser receiving the resulting document will know how to display it. Next, we'll set the result status to "OK," send the headers, and then send the resulting HTML document to the client.

In cleaning up, we'll release our pointer to the IDispatch interface, release any memory we allocated in this function, and return the success status.

## Looking Up the CLSID of the Visual Basic DLL

In the previous function, we called another function, GetClsidFromProgIdA, to perform the CLSID look-up. This is another function that we have to build to perform this look-up, which can be seen in Listing 21.7. If we examine this function, we'll see that it is almost the same as we outlined in our code snippets earlier when we were looking at what was involved in looking up the CLSID for an ActiveX class in the registry. In order to make this routine a bit more robust, we have added error checking, but otherwise it is almost exactly like our code snippet that performed our CLSID look-up.

**Listing 21.7  OLENSAPI.C—The *GetClsidFromProgIdA* Function Which Looks Up the ActiveX CLSID for the Visual Basic Class**

```
HRESULT GetClsidFromProgIdA(LPCLSID apclsid, char* apszName,
                                          long acbName)
{
    HRESULT hr;

    //------------------------------------------------------------
    // The class name has to be converted from ASCII to wide char
    // before using it to look up the entry in the registry.
    //------------------------------------------------------------
    // Allocate a wide char string for the Class Id name.
    OLECHAR *lpWideCharProgId;
    lpWideCharProgId = malloc(sizeof(WCHAR)*acbName);
    // Make sure the memory allocation was successful
    if (!lpWideCharProgId)
    {
        // We couldn't allocate the memory, return an OUT OF
        // MEMORY error
        hr = ResultFromScode(E_OUTOFMEMORY);
        goto LError;
    }

    // Convert the Class Id name to wide chars.
    if (0 == MultiByteToWideChar(CP_ACP, MB_ERR_INVALID_CHARS,
                  apszName, -1, lpWideCharProgId, acbName) )
    {
        // If an error occurred, find out what it was and return
        // the error code
```

Part

**VI**

Ch

**21**

*continues*

---

**Listing 21.7   Continued**

```
        hr = (HResultFromLastError());
        goto LError;
    }

    // Now get the class Id from the Class name.
    hr = CLSIDFromProgID(lpWideCharProgId, apclsid);

LError:
    // Check to make sure that the memory for the wide char
    // class name was allocated before we release it
    if (lpWideCharProgId)
    {
        // Release the memory used for the wide class name
        free(lpWideCharProgId);
    }
    // Return the result code
    return(hr);
}
```

---

# Error Handling and Response

In Listing 21.7, if an error occurs while converting the string to Unicode, we call a function named HResultFromLastError. As can be seen in Listing 21.8, this function gets the last error code from the operating system, and converts it into an HRESULT value, which is returned to the calling routine.

**Listing 21.8   OLENSAPI.C—The *HResultFromLastError* Function that Returns Result Error Codes from System Errors**

```
HRESULT HResultFromLastError()
{
    DWORD dwLastError = GetLastError();
    return HRESULT_FROM_WIN32(dwLastError);
}
```

Our more important error routine is the one that is called by our NSAPI function if an error occurs during our CallObject function. This error routine, named ErrorResponse, builds and returns an HTML document to the client, informing the user that an error occurred. This function provides the user with important debugging information such as the ActiveX class name, Visual Basic method, HTTP method, and the query string that was sent to the server by the client. We can build the ErrorResponse function like the version in Listing 21.9.

**Listing 21.9   OLENSAPI.C—The *ErrorResponse* Function Which Sends the User an Error Message**

```
void ErrorResponse(char *apszQStr, Session *apSn, Request *apRq,
                char *apszProgid, char *apszVBMethod, int acbAvail)
```

```
{
    char pszBuf[BUFLEN];

    // Tell the Netscape server what MIME type we are getting
    // ready to pass it
    param_free(pblock_remove("content-type", apRq->srvhdrs));
    pblock_nvinsert("content-type", "text/html", apRq->srvhdrs);

    // These two lines send the headers to the client, and set
    // everything up so successive net_write()s will work properly.
    protocol_status(apSn, apRq, PROTOCOL_OK, NULL);
    protocol_start_response(apSn, apRq);

    // Build the HTML error message document
    _snprintf(pszBuf, BUFLEN, "<body><h1>"
        "OLENSAPI call failed</h1><p><b>Progid is:</b> %s\n<p><b>Method "
        "is:</b> %s\n<p><b>GET parameters are:</b> %s\n<p><b>POST "
        "parameters are:</b> %.*s</b></body>",
        ((NULL != apszProgid) ? apszProgid : ""),
        ((NULL != apszVBMethod) ? apszVBMethod : ""),
        ((NULL != apszQStr) ? apszQStr : ""),
        (acbAvail > 0 ? acbAvail : 1),
        (acbAvail > 0 ? apszQStr : ""));

    // Send the HTML document to the client
    net_write(apSn->csd, pszBuf, strlen(pszBuf));
}
```

## OLENSAPI Initialization

The last function that we need to build for our OLENSAPI DLL is the DllMain function, which is called when the DLL is first loaded by an application, as each thread attaches and detaches, and when the DLL is unloaded by an application. In this function, we'll initialize our flag that we use to let us know whether we need to initialize our ActiveX environment. Our resulting function can be seen in Listing 21.10.

### Listing 21.10   OLENSAPI.C—The DllMain DLL Entry Point Function, Where DLL Initialization is Performed

```
BOOL WINAPI DllMain(HMODULE hMod, DWORD fReason, LPVOID pvRes)
{
    switch (fReason)
    {
    case DLL_PROCESS_ATTACH:
        // The DLL is first being loaded, allocate the TLS Index flag
        gdwTLSIndex = TlsAlloc();
        if (-1 == gdwTLSIndex)
            return FALSE;
        break;
```

Part

**VI**

Ch

**21**

*continues*

**Listing 21.10   Continued**

```
    case DLL_THREAD_ATTACH:
      // set this flag to true once ole has been initialized
      TlsSetValue(gdwTLSIndex, FALSE);
      break;

    case DLL_PROCESS_DETACH:
      // clean up global resources
      if (-1 != gdwTLSIndex)
        TlsFree(gdwTLSIndex);
      break;

    case DLL_THREAD_DETACH:
      break;
  }
  return TRUE;
}
```

## Compiling and Linking the OLENSAPI DLL

Before we can compile our OLENSAPI DLL, one last file needs to be created. This file is called OLENSAPI.DEF, and it contains the information in Listing 21.11. This file tells the linker to export the olensapi_form function, so that it can be called by the Netscape Server. We need to select the compile options to tell our compiler to build a standard Win32 DLL. We also need to link in an additional file, Libhttpd.lib, which comes with the Netscape server, and has the required stubs for the NSAPI functions that we have had to call from our DLL.

**Listing 21.11   OLENSAPI.DEF—The OLENSAPI Definition File, Which Instructs the Linker Which Functions Are to Be Exported**

```
LIBRARY OLENSAPI

DESCRIPTION 'NSAPI to OLE Gateway'

EXPORTS
    olensapi_form
```

## Configuring Netscape to Use the OLENSAPI DLL

Once we have compiled and linked our OLENSAPI DLL, we still have to configure our Netscape Web server to load and call our NSAPI extension. There are three additions that we have to make in the Netscape configuration files, which we looked at much earlier in this chapter. The first change we will be making is in the mime.types file. We'll load this file into Notepad, and scroll to the bottom of the file, where we'll add the following line in the section of magnus-internal MIME types:

```
type=magnus-internal/olevb      exts=vb
```

This will identify any URI's with the ".vb" extension as the MIME type of "magnus-internal/ olevb," which we will be using to cause the server to call our OLENSAPI DLL to handle the Service processing step.

The next file in which we will need to make changes is the obj.conf file. We'll load this file into Notepad, and add the following line just after the second Init line near the top of the file:

```
Init fn=load-modules
➡               shlib="C:/Msdev/projects/olensapi/Release/olensapi.dll"
➡               funcs=olensapi-form
```

You will need to change the value of the *shlib* flag to reflect the location of the OLENSAPI DLL on your system. This entry will tell the Netscape server to load this DLL and map the olensapi_form function into the request processing table.

In the midst of the next section in this same file, after the last ObjectType line and before the first Service line, add the following line:

```
Service method=(GET¦POST) type=magnus-internal/olevb fn=olensapi-form
```

This will tell the Netscape server to call the olensapi_form function for the Service step on any URI's that are the magnus-internal/olevb MIME type, which we specified earlier to be anything with the file extension ".vb." This should call our OLENSAPI function only if the command used was either the GET or POST command and should not call our DLL if the HEAD command is used.

Close and save both of these Netscape configuration files, and if your Netscape server is running, shut it down completely, and then start it back up again. If you are in the server administration application, you may need to click the button to apply the configuration changes.

**N O T E**  The Netscape documentation is very explicit in its instructions: The server should be shut down and then started back up. The documentation states very clearly that you cannot just select the restart option to reinitialize the server, as this will not cause the server to read in the new configuration files. ▪

**N O T E**  According to the Netscape documentation, there has to be a file with the name of the URI in the location on the server specified by the URI. This file can be empty, but the PathCheck step will fail if the file is not there. This DLL was tested on the Netscape FastTrack 2.0 server on both Windows NT 4.0 and Windows 95. Neither encountered any problems with this file not being present, despite what the Netscape documentation states. If you are using this DLL with an earlier version of a Netscape server, you might have problems if the file is not in the location specified, so you might want to place an empty file into the location specified by all of the URI's in your Web application that will really call this DLL. ▪

# Building a Simple NSAPI Application

Because we built our OLENSAPI interface to work very similarly to the OLEISAPI interface, we can make some minor modifications to one of our OLEISAPI applications to test our OLENSAPI interface. We'll start with the final version of our Visual Basic ActiveX DLL from Chapter 19, "ISAPI, OLESAPI, and Visual Basic," and make some minor modifications so that it'll work with our new interface.

## Extending the ProcParams Function

We'll make the majority of our changes in the ProcParams function. First, we'll add a second instance of the Parameters class to handle the session and request parameters that we are passing from our OLENSAPI interface. We'll add the additional parameter string to the function definition, and then pass the parameter string to the second Parameters class instance in the first line of code.

Once we are into building our HTML document to be returned to the user, and before we build the table with the parameters sent by the user, we'll build a table showing the session and request header values that we received from the OLENSAPI interface. The rest of this function is similar to the way we left it in Chapter 19, as can be seen in Listing 21.12.

### Listing 21.12   NSAPI1.CLS—The ProcParams Function in the Nsapi1 Visual Basic ActiveX DLL, Which Builds the HTML Document Listing the Parameters Sent from the HTML Form

```
Private Function ProcParams(astrSrvParams As String, _
            astrRequest As String, astrMethod As String) As String
    'Create a local instance of the Parameters class
    Dim pcParams As New Parameters
    Dim pcSrvParams As New Parameters
    Dim iNumSrvParams As Integer
    Dim iNumParams As Integer
    Dim iCurParam As Integer
    Dim strHTML As String

    'Pass the Server parameters sent from the HTML form
    'to the local instance of the Parameters class
    iNumSrvParams = pcSrvParams.ParseParameters(astrSrvParams)
    'Pass the parameters sent from the HTML form
    'to the local instance of the Parameters class
    iNumParams = pcParams.ParseParameters(astrRequest)
    'Build the HTML document
    strHTML = "<HTML><HEAD><TITLE>"
    strHTML = strHTML & "OLENSAPI Programming Example"
    strHTML = strHTML & "</TITLE></HEAD><BODY BGCOLOR=#C0C0C0>"
    strHTML = strHTML & "<H1>OLENSAPI Programming Example</H1><HR><P>"
    strHTML = strHTML & "The method used to submit this was <STRONG>"
    'Tell the user what method was used to call this application
    strHTML = strHTML & astrMethod & "</STRONG></P><P>"
```

```
'Tell the user how many server parameters were passed
strHTML = strHTML & "There were <STRONG>" & CStr(iNumSrvParams)
strHTML = strHTML & _
        "</STRONG> Server variables submitted as follows:</P>"
'Build a table of the parameters that were passed
strHTML = strHTML & _
        "<TABLE BORDER=2><TR><TH>Key</TH><TH>Value</TH></TR>"
'Were there any parameters passed?
If iNumSrvParams > 0 Then
    'Loop through each of the parameters
    For iCurParam = 1 To iNumSrvParams
        'Place the parameter key into the table
        strHTML = strHTML & "<TR><TD>" & _
                    pcSrvParams.GetKeyNameByNum(iCurParam)
        'Place the parameter value into the table
        strHTML = strHTML & "</TD><TD>" & _
                    pcSrvParams.GetKeyValueByNum(iCurParam)
        strHTML = strHTML & "</TD></TR>"
        'Loop to the next parameter
    Next
End If
'Close the table
strHTML = strHTML & "</TABLE><BR>"
'Tell the user how many parameters were passed
strHTML = strHTML & "There were <STRONG>" & CStr(iNumParams)
strHTML = strHTML & "</STRONG> values submitted as follows:</P>"
'Build a table of the parameters that were passed
strHTML = strHTML & _
        "<TABLE BORDER=2><TR><TH>Key</TH><TH>Value</TH></TR>"
'Were there any parameters passed?
If iNumParams > 0 Then
    'Loop through each of the parameters
    For iCurParam = 1 To iNumParams
        'Place the parameter key into the table
        strHTML = strHTML & "<TR><TD>" & _
                    pcParams.GetKeyNameByNum(iCurParam)
        'Place the parameter value into the table
        strHTML = strHTML & "</TD><TD>" & _
                    pcParams.GetKeyValueByNum(iCurParam)
        strHTML = strHTML & "</TD></TR>"
        'Loop to the next parameter
    Next
End If
'Close the HTML table and document
strHTML = strHTML & "</TABLE></BODY></HTML>"
'Return the HTML document to the calling routine
ProcParams = strHTML
End Function
```

## Adapting the *DoGet* and *DoPost* Methods

Of course, because we added an additional parameter string to be passed into our method by the OLENSAPI interface, we'll have to add the additional parameter string to both our DoGet and DoPut methods, as seen in Listing 21.13.

Part

VI

Ch

21

**Listing 21.13   NSAPI1.CLS—The Modified *DoGet* and *DoPost* Methods to Work with the OLENSAPI Interface**

```
Public Sub DoGet(astrSrvParams As String, astrRequest As String, astrResponse As
➥String)
    astrResponse = ProcParams(astrSrvParams, astrRequest, "GET")
End Sub

Public Sub DoPost(astrSrvParams As String, astrRequest As String, astrResponse
➥As String)
    astrResponse = ProcParams(astrSrvParams, astrRequest, "POST")
End Sub
```

**CAUTION**

It is important that in the Visual Basic project properties you select the "Unattended Execution" option before building the ActiveX DLL. On the test runs in which I did not have this option set, the Visual Basic method would lock up on the second call since bringing the Netscape server up. With the Unattended Execution option selected, I encountered no problems.

# Adapting the HTML Document to Call the OLENSAPI Application

Like our Visual Basic example for testing our OLENSAPI interface, we'll take the final HTML form from Chapter 12, "Hyperlinks: Extending ActiveX Document Applications over Multiple Windows," as our base HTML form for our OLENSAPI example. We'll need to change the URLs in the form to call our OLENSAPI version of the Visual Basic application. This means taking the URLs in our previous HTML form that were:

```
/scripts/oleisapi.dll/isapiex3.Isapi3.DoGet
```

and changing them to:

```
/nsapiex1.Nsapi1.DoGet.vb
```

Likewise, we'll take our previous URLs that read like this:

```
/scripts/oleisapi.dll/isapiex3.Isapi3.DoPost
```

and alter them to read:

```
/nsapiex1.Nsapi1.DoPost.vb
```

We wind up with the HTML form in Listing 21.14. When we click the first link, we receive the HTML response document seen in Figure 21.3.

## Listing 21.14   EXNSAPI.HTM—The HTML Form Used to Call Our Visual Basic ActiveX DLL

```
<html><head><title>OLENSAPI Programming Example</title></head>
<body bgcolor=#C0C0C0>
<h1>OLENSAPI Programming Example</h1>
<hr><p>
<a HREF="/nsapiex1.Nsapi1.DoGet.vb?arg1=foo">
This link</a> simply invokes the OLENSAPI directly via a URL.
<hr><p>
<form action="/nsapiex1.Nsapi1.DoPost.vb" method="POST">
<input type="submit" value="Click here"> to see this
form use the <strong>POST
</strong>
technique to invoke an object method called DoPost.
<p><table align=center border=0>
<tr><td align=right valign=top><font size=4>Value 1</td>
<td align=left><input name="Val1"></td>
<tr><td align=right valign=top><font size=4>Value 2</td>
<td align=left><input name="Val2"></td>
<!-- Note that the next input field, which is type "textarea" -->
<!-- may not display correctly in all browsers -->
<tr><td align=right valign=top><font size=4>Free form text</td>
<td align=left><input name="TextVal" type="textarea" size="20,5"
maxlength="250"></td></table></form>
<p><hr>
<form action="/nsapiex1.Nsapi1.DoGet.vb" method="GET">
<input type="submit" value="Click here"> to see this
form use the <strong>GET
</strong>
technique to invoke a different method on the same
object called DoGet.
<p><table align=center border=0>
<tr><td align=right valign=top><font size=4>Value 1</td>
<td align=left><input name="Val1"></td>
<tr><td align=right valign=top><font size=4>Value 2</td>
<td align=left><input name="Val2"></td>
<!-- Note that the next input field, which is type "textarea" -->
<!-- may not display correctly in all browsers -->
<tr><td align=right valign=top><font size=4>Free form text</td>
<td align=left><input name="TextVal" type="textarea" size="20,5"
maxlength="250"></td></table></form>
<p><hr>
</body>
</html>
```

**FIG. 21.3**
The resulting HTML
document created by
our OLENSAPI interface
and our modified Visual
Basic ActiveX DLL.

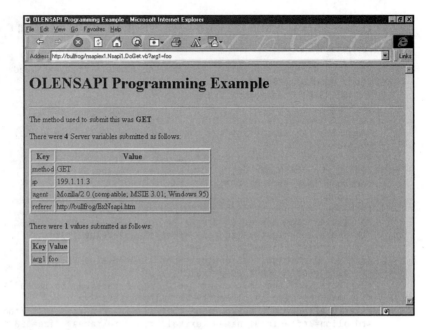

# From Here...

In this chapter, we took an in-depth look at the NSAPI interface, Netscape's equivalent to
Microsoft's ISAPI interface. We also took an in-depth look at what is involved in calling a Visual
Basic method in an ActiveX DLL from another programming language. We used this understanding to see how we could build an OLEISAPI-like interface for Netscape Web servers. We
then extended our OLENSAPI interface to provide our Visual Basic ActiveX DLL methods with
additional information not available from the OLEISAPI interface.

From here, you can take this understanding and make further modifications to the OLENSAPI
interface to provide your Visual Basic applications with additional information from the Session
and Request headers including authentication information and server software information.
You can also take this knowledge and apply it to other Web servers that run on the Windows
NT platform, such as the Alibaba or Web Commander Web servers, building OLEISAPI-like
interfaces for their server APIs.

You might also check out the following chapters for additional subjects that you might be interested in learning. Some of these chapters will supplement what you have learned in this chapter, while some will show you how other technologies can use Visual Basic to perform the
same function using a different approach.

■ To learn about using VBScript on the server to build dynamic HTML documents, read
Chapter 13, "Active Server Pages and Server-Side Scripting."

■ To see how the OLEISAPI2 interface uses a Request object to provide much of the additional functionality we've enabled in our OLENSAPI interface, check out Chapter 20, "The OLEISAPI2 Interface and the Active Reference Object."

■ To learn about database programming with a Server API, look at Chapter 23, "Using Remote Data Objects with the OLEISAPI2 Interface."

■ To see how Web applications can be built using Microsoft's new Visual InterDev, see Chapter 27, "Building Web Database Applications by Using Visual InterDev."

# Web Database Access

# CHAPTER 22

# Using Data Access Objects with the WinCGI Interface

It seems like the Internet is on everyone's mind (and word processor) these days. Every bookstore has shelves devoted to it, and even ordinary computer magazines have article after article about it. Up to this point, the Internet qualifies as one of the best ways to have fun on your computer. In the near future, however, it will also become the best way to create computer systems.

Many users and some programmers have not yet drawn the prime conclusion—the Internet is not fundamentally different than your Local Area Network. This statement doesn't marginalize the Net; it exposes it to the correct paradigm. Think of the Internet as your Local Area Network(LAN), then consider the fact that everyone in the world can be on this LAN for a very few dollars per month (in the USA at least).

To date, many proponents of the Internet have used it to publish company brochures, show libraries of photographs, and sell a few products like books and software. The next wave of applications will be unique to the Internet because they will be visually indistinguishable from applications that you run on your Local Area Network today.

**Creating a Minimal Database Application**

Add the Data Access Object to use an Access database to generate dynamic Web pages.

**Creating a Database Query Application**

Allow the user to select a specific record from the database for viewing and editing.

**Creating a Database Update Application**

Submit information from an HTML form to update a database record.

**Creating a Database Add Application**

Use the WinCGI interface to insert new records into a database table.

**Creating databased forms in an application**

See how to connect HTML forms to a database to provide users with an interactive, database Web application.

**Learn about database access from your Internet service provider**

See how to add database access to your site and create dynamic pages that can use SQL-formatted queries to update or retrieve database information.

In this chapter, we will look at the Windows CGI technology as an application development platform. In Chapter 18, "The WinCGI Interface and Visual Basic," you learned how to get Windows CGI loaded on your machine and tested. You then learned how to write and debug some very simple applications using this technology. In this chapter, we will build several applications of increasing complexity that will give you a head start in developing your own applications. ■

# The Minimal Database Application

The hardest task in any new technology is getting that first application to run. This application is very simple, but teaches all of the structure of a working Windows CGI application. It contains the following elements:

- A Windows CGI program that accepts the data from the file, opens a database, queries the database, and creates the HTML output.
- An HTML file that contains the form.
- An HTML file that contains a hypertext link to the Form file.

This application simply asks the user to enter in the two character abbreviation for a state. It then looks up the full name of the state in a database and returns the answer.

The database consists of only one table, the State Table (see Figure 22.1). This table contains only two fields: StateCode and StateName.

**FIG. 22.1**

A simple database is created to be used in the Minimal Database Application.

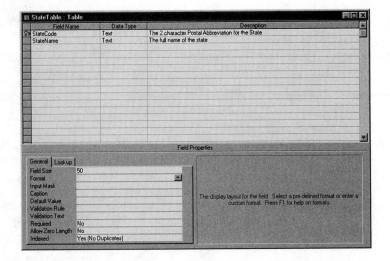

# Creating and Running the Application

Follow this procedure to create the application:

1. Create the Visual Basic project that will contain this application. To do this, create a project called Minimal.vbp.

2. Make sure that you include the following file:

   `C:\WebSite\cgi-src\CGI32.BAS`

   As we saw in Chapter 15, "Building a Foundation of Interactivity with `Request` and `Response` Objects," this file contains global variables and routines that create the Windows CGI framework within Visual Basic.

3. Next, choose References from the Project menu and check the DAO 3.5 box as shown in Figure 22.2. Without this reference checked, Data Access Objects like databases and recordsets won't be recognized by Visual Basic.

**FIG. 22.2**
A reference to the Data Access Object (DAO 3.5) in the References window is necessary for applications that use the database objects.

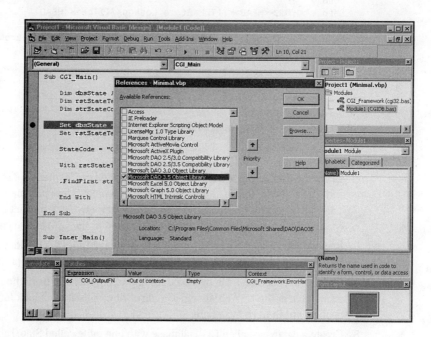

4. The next step is to include the code in Listing 22.1 in the project in a separate module.

## Listing 22.1 Accessing Database Information in a CGI Program

```
Sub CGI_Main()

    Dim dbsState As Database
    Dim rstStateTable As Recordset
    Dim strStateCode As String
```

*continues*

**Listing 22.1 Continued**

```
    Dim strStateName As String

    Set dbsState = OpenDatabase("C:\VB\CGIDatabase.MDB")
    Set rstStateTable = dbsState.OpenRecordset("StateTable", dbOpenSnapshot)

    strStateCode = "GA"

    strSearch = "StateCode = '" & strStateCode & "'"

    With rstStateTable
        .FindFirst strSearch
        strStateName = rstStateTable("StateName")
    End With

    Send ("Content-type: text/html")
    Send (" ")
    Send ("<HTML><HEAD><TITLE>State Lookup</TITLE></HEAD>")
    Send ("<BODY><H1>State Lookup</H1>")
    Send ("The StateCode" & strStateCode & "is for" & strStateName)
    Send ("</BODY></HTML>")

End Sub


Sub Inter_Main()
MsgBox "This is a CGI Application"
End Sub
```

5. Using the debugging techniques that you learned in Chapter 18, "The WinCGI Interface and Visual Basic," place a valid .INI file as a command line parameter for the project. This will allow you to debug the application interactively. It doesn't matter what project created the file for now. They are usually stored in the C:\WebSite\cgi-temp\ directory.

6. Remove the Form from the project and save it as Minimal.VBP. Remove all other references and ActiveX controls that you are not using from the project.

7. Create the executable file by choosing Make Minimal.exe from the File menu. Store the executable in the C:\WebSite\cgi-win\ directory. WebSite will look for Windows CGI applications in here by default.

8. Create a database called CGIDatabase with one table called StateTable.

9. Add two columns: StateCode and StateName.

10. Add about 10 states to the table along with their Postal Codes.

11. Open your favorite browser and type in the following URL:

    **http://localhost/cgi-win/Minimal.exe**

12. Observe that the running application looks like Figure 22.3.

Notice that the name of the state did not appear anywhere in the code. It was obtained by doing a database lookup.

**FIG. 22.3**

The application opens the database and retrieves the StateName that corresponds to the StateCode of "GA," which is hardcoded. The application is called directly without using an HTML file containing a Form.

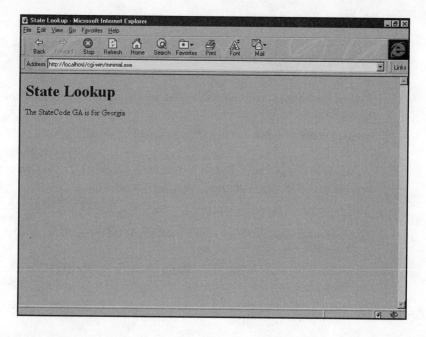

## Understanding the Code

The code for this example is surprisingly simple. The first step is to create the CGI_Main routine that the Windows CGI Framework (CGI32.BAS) will call after it sets up the environment. The next step is to declare the database variables as shown here:

```
Sub CGI_Main()

    Dim dbsState As Database
    Dim rstStateTable As Recordset
    Dim strStateCode As String
    Dim strStateName As String
```

Next, we have to open the database and the table as a recordset. I have opened the recordset as a snapshot because this database is single user and static. The commands to accomplish this are shown here:

```
Set dbsState = OpenDatabase("C:\VB\CGIDatabase.MDB")
Set rstStateTable = dbsState.OpenRecordset("StateTable", dbOpenSnapshot)
```

Then we create a string variable which contains the criteria needed for the search:

```
strStateCode = "GA"
```

The literal "GA" could have been placed in the strSearch directly, but we decided to place it in as a string variable.

```
strSearch = "StateCode = '" & strStateCode & "'"
```

Having done this, we are ready to do the search. We use the `FindFirst` method to move the recordset cursor to the record that contains the "GA" code.

```
With rstStateTable
.FindFirst strSearch
```

Finally, having the correct record located, we can retrieve the column that we want into the string variable called `strStateName`:

```
strStateName = rstStateTable("StateName")
End With
```

All that is left to do now is display the results in a browser. The following set of `Send()` routines create the HTML code with the correct tags for display:

```
Send ("Content-type: text/html")
Send (" ")
Send ("<HTML><HEAD><TITLE>State Lookup</TITLE></HEAD>")
Send ("<BODY><H1>State Lookup</H1>")
```

The connection between the Visual Basic variables and the HTML code is made in the following `Send()` call:

```
    Send ("The StateCode  " & strStateCode & "  is for  " & strStateName)
    Send ("</BODY></HTML>")

End Sub
```

As in all Windows CGI applications, there has to be a subroutine called `Inter_Main` that keeps the application from crashing if it is called from a command line.

```
Sub Inter_Main()
MsgBox "This is a CGI Application"
End Sub
```

This code mixes your existing knowledge of Visual Basic and the Data Access Object with your new knowledge of Windows CGI. At this point, we need to improve on this application by creating an HTML file that refers to this application using a hyperlink.

# Invoking the Program with a Hyperlink

The next logical step in the creation of our application is to make it callable from another HTML file via a hyperlink. This is important because we want to free our users from the details of having to type in a full URL every time that they want to run an application.

The most user-friendly procedure for running a program is to set up the browsers on the client machines in your intranet to point to the company home page on the intranet server. Next, a hyperlink points to an HTML file where data is normally entered by the user. This file contains a "Submit" button that sends the data that was entered to the Server. The server calls the CGI program and then passes the response file back to the user.

The code in Listing 22.2 demonstrates how to set up the hyperlink:

---

**Listing 22.2    A Hypertext Link Can Be Used to Connect an HTML File to a CGI Application**

```
<head>
<title>Link to Minimal.exe</title>
</head>

<center>
<H1>Link to the Minimal.exe CGI Database Example</H1>
</center>

<P>
<li>
Check out the <a href="/cgi-win/minimal.exe">Minimal Program</a>
for an online demonstration of datbase processing.
</ul>

<P>
Above all...
<center>
<h1>Have Fun!</h1>
</center>

</body>
</html>
```

---

**FIG. 22.4**

A Windows CGI program can be called by a hyperlink embedded within an HTML File.

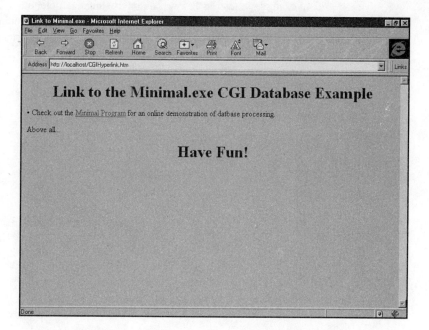

The HTML file contains a link which causes the CGI program to run and send the output to the client's browser.

## Understanding the Code

The most important lines in the HTML code are shown below. The following lines of code direct the browser to display the text:

```
<P>
<li>
Check out the <a href="/cgi-win/minimal.exe">Minimal Program</a>
for an online demonstration of datbase processing.
</ul>
```

The most interesting part is where you see the "href=." This is telling the browser that the words "Minimal Program" are really a special area on the screen. If they are clicked, the browser is to go to the server that sent this page, look in the /cgi-win/ directory and execute the minimal.exe file if found. The server and the browser are written so that the server will wait for the Minimal.exe program to complete its processing and to pass back the results, if any, generated by the CGI program. In this case, the result was a lookup of the code "GA" with the word "Georgia."

## Creating the Form

The preceding example in Listing 22.2 was an interesting example, but it lacked the capability to gather data from the user and use it as the basis of performing the lookup in the database. The code in Listing 22.3 shows us an HTML page that doesn't merely call the CGI application; it gathers the data entered by the user and passes it along also.

**Listing 22.3   The *Form* Tag Indicates that the Data within the Form is Going to Be Passed to the Server for Processing**

```
<html>

<head>
<title>Link to LookupState.exe</title>
</head>

<center>
<H1>Link with a form to the LookupState.exe CGI Database Example</H1>
</center>

<FORM METHOD="POST" ACTION="/cgi-win/LookupState.exe">
<B>State Code: </B>
<INPUT TYPE="text" NAME="StateCode" SIZE="2">
<INPUT TYPE="Submit", VALUE="Look Up State">

</FORM>

</body>
</html>
```

This form is invisible when displayed in the browser. The Text control and the submit button are the only parts of the form that are displayed as shown in Figure 22.5.

**FIG. 22.5**
An HTML form captures user input and communicates it to the server.

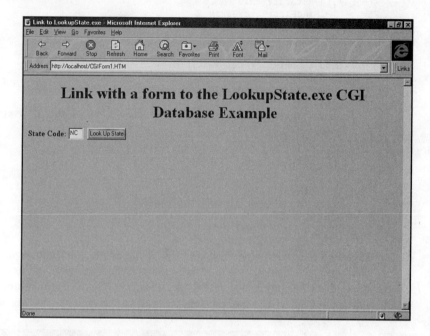

On the server side, the program that is referred to in the ACTION= statement is called using the same Windows CGI processing that we have discussed earlier in this chapter. The Visual Basic program that processes the request looks at the INI file that the server creates to find the data input by the user. Listing 22.4 shows this code.

**Listing 22.4   The *GetSmallField()* Subroutine Retrieves the Data that the User Entered in the Form and Stores It in a Local Variable**

```
Sub CGI_Main()

    Dim dbsState As Database
    Dim rstStateTable As Recordset
    Dim strStateCode As String
    Dim strStateName As String

    Set dbsState = OpenDatabase("C:\VB\CGIDatabase.MDB")
    Set rstStateTable = dbsState.OpenRecordset("StateTable", dbOpenSnapshot)

    strStateCode = GetSmallField("StateCode")

    strSearch = "StateCode = '" & strStateCode & "'"
```

*continues*

**Listing 22.4   Continued**

```
    With rstStateTable
       .FindFirst strSearch
       strStateName = rstStateTable("StateName")
    End With

    Send ("Content-type: text/html")
    Send (" ")
    Send ("<HTML><HEAD><TITLE>State Lookup</TITLE></HEAD>")
    Send ("<BODY><H1>State Lookup</H1>")
    Send ("The StateCode  " & strStateCode & "  is for  " & strStateName)
    Send ("</BODY></HTML>")

End Sub


Sub Inter_Main()
    MsgBox "This is a CGI Application"
End Sub
```

After the Visual Basic program completes its processing, the output is passed back to the Web site server which passes it to the browser on the client machine. At this point, the browser just knows that it has received an HTML file. It displays it to the user. The answer to the user's question is displayed on the screen in this way, as shown in Figure 22.6.

**FIG. 22.6**

A Windows CGI program can be called by a hyperlink embedded within an HTML File.

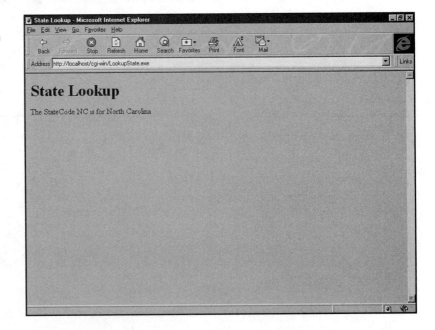

# Understanding the Code

The code in the HTML file is fairly simple to understand. The only section that is new to us is the following:

```
<FORM METHOD="POST" ACTION="/cgi-win/LookupState.exe">
<B>State Code: </B>
<INPUT TYPE="text" NAME="StateCode" SIZE="2">
<INPUT TYPE="Submit", VALUE="Look Up State">

</FORM>
```

The <FORM> and </FORM> tags delimit the form; it determines which data will be sent to the server. Any data gathered between the two tags will be sent to the Windows CGI application.

The <B> and </B> tags serve to provide a bold label. The two inputs do the work of the application. The "StateCode" text box provides the input area for the user data.

The Submit button tells the form that it is time to submit the request to the server. The browser looks to the <FORM> line for the ACTION= statement to learn what to do. In this example, the instruction is to run a program called LookupState.exe which is stored in the /cgi-win/ directory on the same physical machine that is running the server. The browser will now wait for the server to send output back to be displayed.

# Understanding the Processing

The WebSite Server created a file called bws.INI in the \cgi-temp\ directory. This file is used by the framework to process the request:

```
[CGI]
Request Protocol=HTTP/1.0
Request Method=POST
Request Keep-Alive=No
Document Root=C:\WebSite\htdocs\
Executable Path=/cgi-win/LookupState.exe
Server Software=WebSite/1.1f1
Server Name=www.pottsco.com
Server Port=80
Server Admin=steve_potts_ga@msn.com
CGI Version=CGI/1.3 (Win)
Remote Address=127.0.0.1
Referer=http://localhost/CGIForm1.HTM
User Agent=Mozilla/2.0 (compatible; MSIE 3.01; Windows NT)
Content Type=application/x-www-form-urlencoded
Content Length=12
[System]
GMT Offset=-18000
Debug Mode=Yes
Output File=C:\WebSite\cgi-temp\bws.out
Content File=C:\WebSite\cgi-temp\bws.inp
```

```
[Form Literal]
StateCode=NC
[Accept]
image/gif=Yes
image/x-xbitmap=Yes
image/jpeg=Yes
image/pjpeg=Yes
*/*=Yes
[Extra Headers]
Accept-Language=en
UA-pixels=800x600
UA-color=color16
UA-OS=Windows NT
UA-CPU=x86
Host=localhost
Pragma=No-Cache
```

An entire chapter could be devoted to the explanation of this file, but for the purposes of this discussion, a few interesting fields will be pointed out.

```
Request Method=POST
```

The fact that the form sent the request as a POST is communicated here. This means that the database may be updated by this request, and that the server will communicate the data by way of the INI file, instead of on the command line. All Windows CGI applications need to be accessed as POST.

```
Remote Address=127.0.0.1
```

This data tells what IP Address sent the request.

```
Output File=C:\WebSite\cgi-temp\bws.out
```

This instruction tells the Visual Basic program in which directory and file to place the output. The server stores this information and as soon as it is notified that the program has completed, it retrieves the data from this file and returns it to the browser.

```
[Form Literal]
StateCode=NC
```

The Form Literal section contains the actual data. The name of the field to the left of the parenthesis is used by the GetSmallfield() command to find the desired data. In this example, there is only one form variable being passed.

# Updating a Database

To this point, all of our examples have accessed data in a database. This section introduces data updating using the Windows CGI technology. This example will allow the user to input both a State Code and a State Name on the form. The application will then find the state with that code and modify the database with the data provided by the user. It assumes that the code for that state is already in the database and doesn't do anything to the database if it is not in there.

In this section, we will create an additional program that changes data in a database. The application on the front end is not much different than a query application. It consists of a form and some text controls like we saw earlier in this chapter. Listing 22.5 shows the HTML that we will use in this example.

**Listing 22.5   The Data to Update the Values in a Database are Entered into an HTML Form.  The *ACTION=* Parameter Tells the Browser and the WebSite Server which Program to Call**

```
<html>

<head>
<title>Link to UpdateState.exe</title>
</head>

<Body>

<center>
<H1>Link with a form to the UpdateState.exe CGI Database Example</H1>
</center>

<PRE>
<FORM METHOD="POST" ACTION="/cgi-win/UpdateState.exe">

<B>State Code: </B>
<INPUT TYPE="text" NAME="StateCode" SIZE="2">

<B>State Name: </B>
<INPUT TYPE="text" NAME="StateName" SIZE="20">

<HR>
<INPUT TYPE="Submit", VALUE="Update State">
</PRE>

</FORM>
</body>
</html>
```

The only difference between this example and a query example is the addition of the extra data input field. All of the code to do the actual updating resides on the server machine. Running this HTML file through a browser produces a screen that looks like Figure 22.7.

**FIG. 22.7**
Running the HTML file through a browser produces a screen that looks like this.

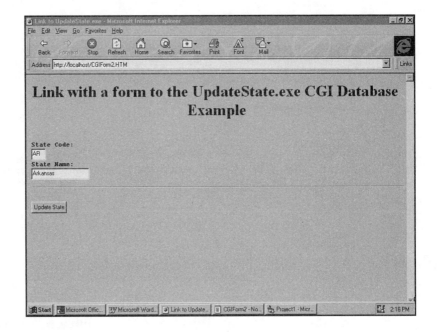

# Windows CGI Update Program

All that the HTML code will do is pass two data strings to the Visual Basic program. The Visual Basic program is responsible for updating the database. Listing 22.6 shows the Visual Basic code that processes this data. To prepare for this example, a row has been added with "AR" as the StateCode and a null string as the StateName as shown in Figure 22.8.

**FIG. 22.8**
A Windows CGI program can update a database using data entered by the user on his client browser.

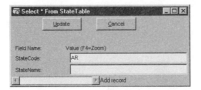

The code that performs the update is all Visual Basic code. Listing 22.6 shows the code that updates the record in the database.

> **Listing 22.6   This Code Finds the Correct Record, Updates the *StateName*
> Value, and Returns a Notification to the User that the Update Was Successful**

```
Sub CGI_Main()

    Dim dbsState As Database
    Dim rstStateTable As Recordset
```

```
        Dim strStateCode As String
        Dim strStateName As String

        Set dbsState = OpenDatabase("C:\VB\CGIDatabase.MDB")
        Set rstStateTable = dbsState.OpenRecordset("StateTable", dbOpenDynaset)

        strStateCode = GetSmallField("StateCode")
        strNewStateName = GetSmallField("StateName")
        strSearch = "StateCode = '" & strStateCode & "'"

        With rstStateTable

            .FindFirst strSearch
            .Edit
            rstStateTable("StateName") = strNewStateName
            .Update

        End With
        Send ("Content-type: text/html")
        Send (" ")
        Send ("<HTML><HEAD><TITLE>State Update</TITLE></HEAD>")
        Send ("<BODY><H1>State Update</H1>")
        Send ("The StateCode  " & strStateCode & "  was updated to read  " &
    strNewStateName)
        Send ("</BODY></HTML>")

    End Sub


    Sub Inter_Main()
        MsgBox "This is a CGI Application"
    End Sub
```

If an error occurs, the user is given some details that he probably doesn't understand and then the e-mail address of the web master is listed, as shown in Figure 22.9. The intent of this is to give you as much detail as possible whenever something goes wrong. The idea is that your user would e-mail you with details of what has gone wrong on the mainframe, or server, as you choose to call it. It looks like centralized support of applications is making a comeback.

This error is a Visual Basic error. It resulted because the first time this code ran, it was run against a Snapshot recordset, instead of a Dynaset type of recordset. Snapshots are, by definition, not updateable. After the code was changed to the correct type, the code ran properly and the screen in Figure 22.10 was displayed.

The fact that this HTML file was returned is a good sign, but it doesn't constitute proof that the update really occurred. To obtain this proof, you have to look at the data with a Database Management System and observe that the new value has been recorded correctly as shown in Figure 22.11.

Successfully completing the update proves that the Internet technologies can produce real applications that perform the same functions as today's client/server applications.

**FIG. 22.9**
If a Visual Basic error occurs, the Windows CGI framework will generate an error message and send it back to your users.

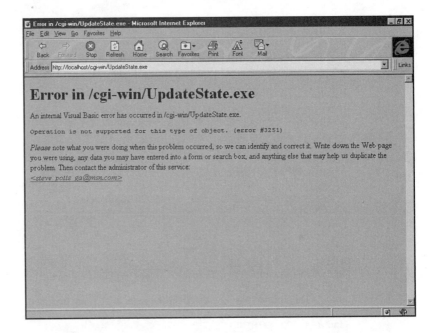

**FIG. 22.10**
The Visual Basic CGI program sends back a confirmation whenever the database is successfully updated.

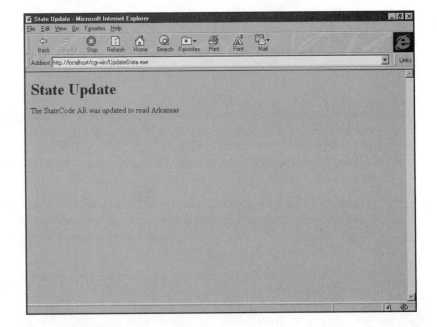

**FIG. 22.11**

Examining the data with
a Database Manage-
ment System proves
that the update was
successful.

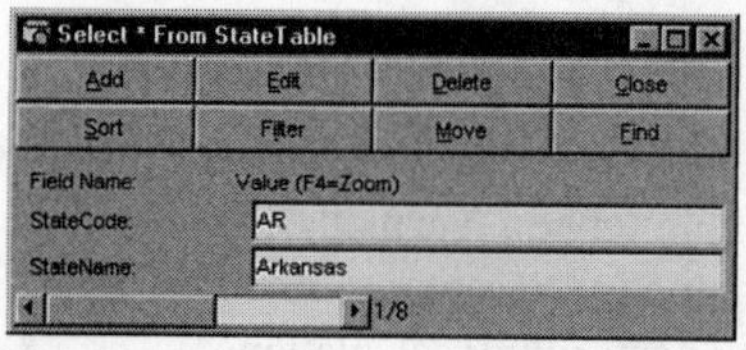

# Understanding the Code

Most of the code in this application is a repeat of things that we have explained earlier in the
chapter. There are a few places in the code that warrant an explanation.

```
Set dbsState = OpenDatabase("C:\VB\CGIDatabase.MDB")
Set rstStateTable = dbsState.OpenRecordset("StateTable", dbOpenDynaset)
```

Notice that the type of recordset being created has been changed from a Snapshot, which
cannot be updated, to a Dynaset, which can be. Failure to make this change resulted in
Error# 3251 being reported back to the server as you saw in Figure 22.9.

```
strStateCode = GetSmallField("StateCode")
strNewStateName = GetSmallField("StateName")
```

We retrieved a second field from the INI file which contains the data to be stored in the
StateName field of the StateTable in the database.

```
With rstStateTable

    .FindFirst strSearch
    .Edit
    rstStateTable("StateName") = strNewStateName
    .Update

End With
```

The .EDIT method tells the recordset to allow editing of the data. The .Update method alerts
the recordset that the updating is finished and that the record can be written to the database at
this time.

The With and End With are included as a coding convenience. Within these statements, the
objectname rstStateTable, is not needed.

```
Send ("Content-type: text/html")
Send (" ")
Send ("<HTML><HEAD><TITLE>State Update</TITLE></HEAD>")
Send ("<BODY><H1>State Update</H1>")
Send ("The StateCode  " & strStateCode & "  was updated to read  " &
➥strNewStateName)
Send ("</BODY></HTML>")
```

Finally, the confirmation that the data was updated correctly was sent back to the user. This is
critical because of the disquiet that users feel when the system accepts input without providing
feedback.

# Writing Programs with Multiple Forms

The primary difference between a Web page and a Web application is that an application can have multiple forms instead of a single screen. Normally, these forms do more than tell you about a company's products or somebody's vacation to Aruba. They do real work, like accessing databases, changing values, and performing calculations.

This example application is unique because it is composed of a number of forms, not just one. When the user completes work on one form, the browser sends the responses to the WebSite Server. The server calls the Windows CGI program. This program not only performs its query and update work, but it constructs the next form and sends it to the client browser.

## Understanding the Application

This application simulates the Web site for a magazine called *Visual Basic Guru*. This magazine wants to reach new readers and get them to subscribe online. They want to let the reader review the articles published recently and let them sign up for a subscription. If someone wants to pay with a credit card, then the application shows a screen allowing them to do so. If they want to be billed, then a different screen is used that allows them to set up an account.

An HTML file is loaded in the browser that contains a reference to the Windows CGI program. When the user clicks a button, the CGI program is started by the WebSite server.

It receives an initial query from the user, and passes back a menu. Depending on the user's menu choices, the application could create a set of HTML statements and send them to the user's browser. The user puts the data into the form and submits it.

Based on the values in the data, the Windows CGI program could send another set of HTML to the browser. This continues until all of the required interaction has occurred. The final HTML that is sent thanks the user for his or her input and finishes. Figure 22.12 shows this process graphically.

## Creating the Main Menu HTML File

We will start this example by creating an HTML file that can be loaded into the user's browser to start this application. This file is an ordinary HTML file that looks like Listing 22.7 below:

**Listing 22.7   An HTML File Can Contain More Than One Form. Each of These Forms Can Point to the Same Visual Basic Application or They Can Invoke a Different One**

```
<html>

<head>
<title>Guru Publications</title>
</head>
```

```
<body bgcolor="#FFFFFF" background="wstile.gif">
<center>

<H1>
Visual Basic Guru Magazine</H1>
</center>

<center>
<img src="important.gif" width=148 height=36 align=center>
</center>
```

Visual Basic Guru magazine is written with the super-gearhead in mind.  Our authors are
among the most arrogant mammals on the planet.  Their condescending style will both amaze
and intimidate you, and you paid to have it happen!  VBGuru is the perfect magazine to set on
your coffee table when your non-technical friends drop in for an herbal tea.  They will thumb
through the pages of this glossy mag and be totally awed by your intelligence.  You won't even
have to tell them that you can't understand the articles either.  Unlike other elitist magazines such as
Scientific Canadian and National Geologic, VBGuru has pictures that can't even be comprehended by
anyone other than the author himself.  Subscribe today!

```
<FORM METHOD="POST" ACTION="/cgi-win/Magazine.exe">
<PRE>
<INPUT TYPE="text" NAME="DoWhat" SIZE="1" VALUE="    Subscribe">
                                    <INPUT TYPE="Submit",
VALUE="Subscribe">
</PRE>
</FORM>


<FORM METHOD="POST" ACTION="/cgi-win/Magazine.exe">
<PRE>
<INPUT TYPE="text" NAME="DoWhat" SIZE="1" VALUE="    Query" HIDDEN = "True">
                                    <INPUT TYPE="Submit", VALUE="Examine
Ariticles">
</PRE>

</FORM>
<FORM METHOD="POST" ACTION="/cgi-win/Magazine.exe">
<PRE>
<INPUT TYPE="text" NAME="DoWhat" SIZE="1" VALUE="     Exit">
                                    <INPUT TYPE="Submit", VALUE="Exit">
</PRE>
</FORM>


</body>
</html>
```

**FIG. 22.12**

The screen definitions can be created by the program. When the program executes, it passes these statements back through the response file to the browser.

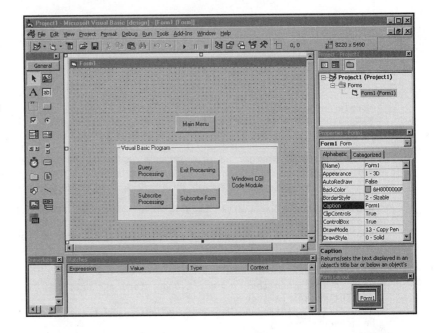

Running this code produces an ordinary looking page in the browser as shown in Figure 22.13.

**FIG. 22.13**

Using HTML statements, you can produce screens that look a lot like the VB Screens you have been producing in a client/server environment.

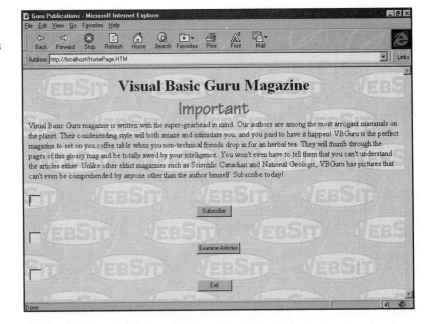

This form simulates a Visual Basic form with three buttons. Except for having to start the browser first and a few cosmetic differences, you can see how much this form looks like an ordinary Visual Basic form.

# Understanding the HTML Code

Most of the HTML code in Listing 22.7 is ordinary. The most unusual thing about this code is the use of three Submit buttons and three forms as shown here:

```
<FORM METHOD="POST" ACTION="/cgi-win/Magazine.exe">
<PRE>
<INPUT TYPE="text" NAME="DoWhat" SIZE="1" VALUE="    Subscribe">
                                    <INPUT TYPE="Submit",
➥VALUE="Subscribe">
</PRE>

</FORM>
<FORM METHOD="POST" ACTION="/cgi-win/Magazine.exe">
<PRE>
<INPUT TYPE="text" NAME="DoWhat" SIZE="1" VALUE="    Query" HIDDEN = "True">
                                    <INPUT TYPE="Submit", VALUE="Examine
➥Ariticles">
</PRE>

</FORM>
<FORM METHOD="POST" ACTION="/cgi-win/Magazine.exe">
<PRE>
<INPUT TYPE="text" NAME="DoWhat" SIZE="1" VALUE="    Exit">
                                    <INPUT TYPE="Submit", VALUE="Exit">
</PRE>
</FORM>
```

Notice that every one of these forms calls the same CGI program—Magazine.exe. Each form has a different value in the text control, which means that a different string is going to be sent to the WebSite server and on to Magazine.exe, based on which button was pushed. This allows us to simulate the calling of the Magazine.exe and pass it a parameter.

# Creating the Database

The next important step in the development of this application is database creation. The database will need three tables for now:

■ SubscriberTable—contains data about the subscriber.

■ CreditTable—contains credit card information about this subscriber.

■ AccountTable—contains account information for those clients who will be billed.

The database tables and the relationships between them are shown in Figure 22.14.

The manipulation of the data in these tables is the goal of this application. Several different forms will be sent to the user, but the system knows which form is returned and how to react.

**FIG. 22.14**

The three tables in the database hold the data that the users enter on the forms.

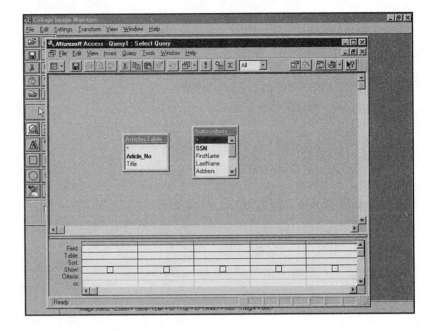

## Returning a Form

With the information from the user telling what button he clicked, the Magazine.exe is able to determine which form the user needs next. The code in Listing 22.8 shows the statements needed to create this HTML code.

**Listing 22.8   The Forms are Created By the Windows CGI Application. Values Passed from the Browser are Interpreted to Determine Which Form Should Be Called**

```
Sub CGI_Main()

    strCode = GetSmallField("DoWhat")

    Select Case strCode

    Case "Subscribe"
        Subscribe

    Case "Query"
        Query_Articles

    Case "Exit"
        Exit_App

    Case Else

    End Select
```

```
End Sub

Sub Inter_Main()
    MsgBox "This is a CGI Application"
End Sub

Sub Exit_App()
    Send ("Content-type: text/html")
    Send (" ")
    Send ("<HTML><HEAD><TITLE>Visual Basic Guru Magazine</TITLE></HEAD>")
    Send ("<BODY><H1>VB GURU Magazine says</H1>")
    Send ("<BODY><H1>    See You Later</H1>")
    Send ("</BODY></HTML>")

End Sub
```

This code uses the GetSmallField() function call to find out what form on the HTML page invoked the application, or, in other words, what button was clicked by the user. The result of this call is stored in the variable strCode. The Select Case statement causes the correct sub-routine to be called based on the value in strCode.

In this iteration, all of the subroutines except Exit_App() are commented out. When you run the application in a browser and click the Exit button, you see the screen shown in Figure 22.15.

**FIG. 22.15**
The Exit Screen tells the user that they are finished processing.

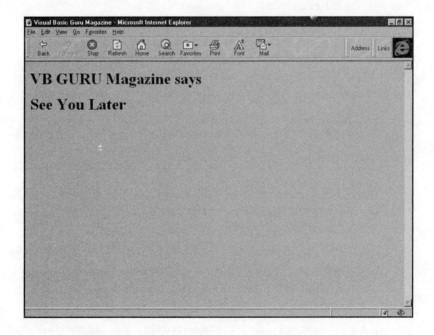

This screen is fairly simple. Later, you will see more complicated output. The next screen that we want to implement is the Query_Articles form. This form displays the titles of all of the articles in the database for the user to examine. The magazine hopes that this will entice him or her to buy.

The code to display these articles is shown in Listing 22.9.

---

**Listing 22.9   The Windows CGI Program Displays a List of Articles. The Articles are Stored in the Database in the *ArticlesTable***

```
Sub Query_Articles()

    Dim dbsMagazine As Database
    Dim rst As Recordset
    Dim strArticle As String

    Set dbsMagazine = OpenDatabase("C:\WebSite\cgi-src\Magazine\Magazine.MDB")
    Set rst = dbsMagazine.OpenRecordset("ArticlesTable", dbOpenSnapshot)

    With rst

    Send ("Content-type: text/html")
    Send (" ")
    Send ("<HTML><HEAD><TITLE>Visual Basic Guru Magazine</TITLE></HEAD>")
    Send ("<BODY><H1>VB GURU Magazine Recent Articles</H1>")
    Send ("<PRE>")

    Do Until rst.EOF
        strArticle = rst("Title")
        Send (strArticle)
        Send (" ")
        .MoveNext
    Loop

    End With

    Send ("</PRE>")
    Send ("</BODY></HTML>")

End Sub
```

---

This code has several interesting statements. The most interesting section contains the Do loop. The object of this subroutine is to create a listing of all of the titles in the AritclesTable. This requires that we follow this procedure:

1. Send some HTML to take care of the headers and the <HEAD> section of the HTML file.

2. Loop through the database and get the title for one article.

3. Create an HTML statement using the Send() subroutine.

4. Use the MoveNext method to get the next row.

5. When the end of file is reached, send the HTML statements needed to complete the response.

This will dynamically create the HTML needed to show the user the list of articles in the database. Figure 22.16 shows what the results look like.

**FIG. 22.16**

You can use the data in the database to build a dynamic HTML file for display by the browser.

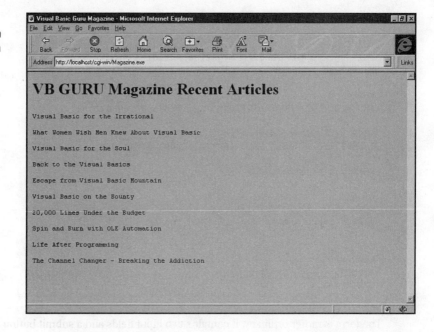

Notice how similar this screen looks to one that was created with static HTML. From the browser's point of view, HTML created on-the-fly by the Visual Basic application looks identical to HTML that is being retrieved from a file.

## Creating the Article Entry Screen

The end users of this system would have no need to add articles to this database. Each month, however, someone on the magazine's staff needs to enter the data into the system. An ordinary Visual Basic or Access application could be used, or in the spirit of the Internet, a Windows CGI application could be written. That way, the magazine could hire someone on the island of Bali to enter the data into the database as soon as the data is received.

This application can be very simple. It consists of a header, a form with two text boxes, and a submit button. The HTML code for this application is shown in Listing 22.10.

**Listing 22.10    A Simple Data Entry Screen Can Remove the Need for Physical Proximity to Maintain the Data in the Database**

```
<HTML>

<HEAD>
<TITLE>Update the VB Guru Magazine Articles</TITLE>
```

*continues*

**Listing 22.10    Continued**

```
</HEAD>

<BODY>

<CENTER>
<H1> Update the VB Guru Magazine Articles </H1>
</CENTER>

<PRE>
<FORM METHOD="POST" ACTION="/cgi-win/UpdateMagazine.exe">

<B>Article Code: </B>
<INPUT TYPE="text" NAME="ArticleCode" SIZE="8">

<B>Article Title: </B>
<INPUT TYPE="text" NAME="Title" SIZE="50">

<HR>
<INPUT TYPE="Submit", VALUE="Add the Article">
</PRE>

</FORM>
</BODY>
</HTML>
```

The form is rather ordinary. It contains two input fields and a submit button called "Add the Article." Figure 22.17 shows what this form looks like when it is running.

**FIG. 22.17**

A data entry screen can be written that runs over the Internet.

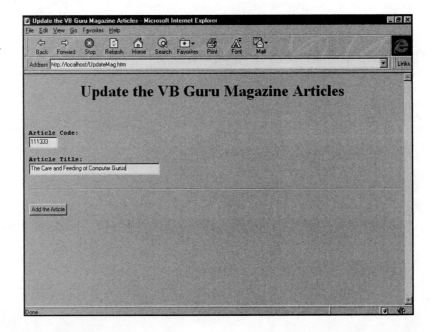

The interesting part of this application is in the Visual Basic code that actually updates the database. Listing 22.11 shows the `CGI_Main()` routine.

**Listing 22.11   The Code to Add a Row to the Article Table**

```
Sub CGI_Main()

    Dim dbs As Database
    Dim rst As Recordset
    Dim strArticle_No As String
    Dim strTitle As String

    Set dbs = OpenDatabase("C:\WebSite\cgi-src\Magazine\Magazine.MDB")
    Set rst = dbs.OpenRecordset("ArticlesTable", dbOpenDynaset)

    strArticle_No = GetSmallField("ArticleCode")
    strTitle = GetSmallField("Title")
    strSearch = "Article_No = '" & strArticle_No & "'"

    With rst

        .FindFirst strSearch
        If rst.NoMatch Then

            'add a row with this data in it

            rst.AddNew
            rst("Article_No") = strArticle_No
            rst("Title") = strTitle
            rst.Update
            rst.Close
            dbs.Close

            'Send a confirmation

            Send ("Content-type: text/html")
            Send (" ")
            Send ("<HTML><HEAD><TITLE>Magazine Update</TITLE></HEAD>")
            Send ("<BODY><H1>Magazine Update</H1>")
            Send ("The Magazine Code  " & strArticle_No & "  was added.")
            Send ("</BODY></HTML>")
        Else
            'Send a message to the user that this article is
            'already in the database

            Send ("Content-type: text/html")
            Send (" ")
            Send ("<HTML><HEAD><TITLE>Magazine Update</TITLE></HEAD>")
            Send ("<BODY><H1>Magazine Update</H1>")
            Send ("The Magazine Code  " & strArticle_No & " already exists")
            Send ("</BODY></HTML>")
        End If
```

*continues*

**Listing 22.11    Continued**

```
    End With

End Sub

Sub Inter_Main()
    MsgBox "This is a CGI Application"
End Sub
```

This program is a little different because it doesn't just update an existing record, it also adds a new record to the table.

## Understanding the Code

This code opens the database and the recordset in the ordinary fashion. It uses the GetSmallField() function calls to move the data from the INI file to the local variables. It then has to determine whether or not this record is already in the database. This code

```
.FindFirst strSearch
        If rst.NoMatch Then
```

determines this by doing a FindFirst search on that Aritcle_No. If it is not found, then the program will do the add processing. This processing requires several method calls to accomplish.

```
rst.AddNew
        rst("Article_No") = strArticle_No
        rst("Title") = strTitle
        rst.Update
        rst.Close
        dbs.Close
```

The Data Access Object (DAO) provides a method called AddNew which adds a blank row to the dynaset called rst. Then the two columns in this row are given the values of the strings that were read from the INI file. Finally, the Update method flushes the buffer and updates the table before closing both the recordset and the database.

Some HTML code is generated which outputs a message back to the user that the update was successful.

```
Send ("The Magazine Code  " & strArticle_No & "  was added.")
```

This Send() call is a good example of mixing Visual Basic variables in an HTML statement. The send code does the concatenation prior to handing the HTML back to the Web site Server.

If, however, the row was found, you don't want to add the row again. You could allow the database to discover the duplicate rows, but that would be a little sloppy. The error code back from the database management system would have to be interpreted anyway and HTML created to communicate with the user. The approach of checking for the existence of the row first is cleaner. Figure 22.19 shows the HTML file that is returned if the row already exists.

**FIG. 22.18**
A confirmation should be sent to the user that provides reassurance that the addition of the data to the database was successful.

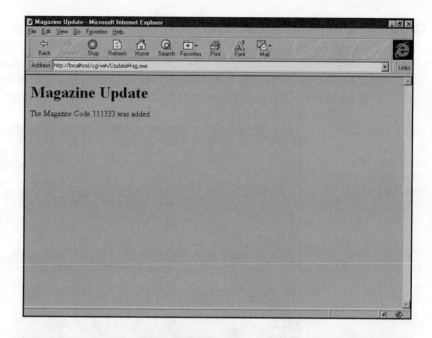

**FIG. 22.19**
It is important to communicate with the user in the event that the addition of the article is not successful. A different HTML message is the best way to do this.

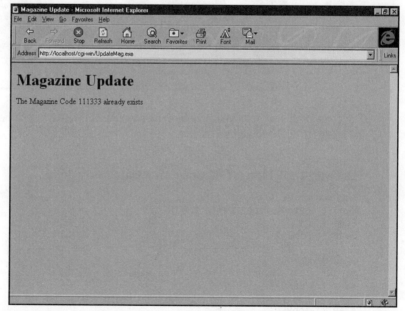

This simple transaction illustrates the power of Internet technology. A person anywhere on the planet can perform an update to this database without having any idea where it physically resides. Another person thousands of miles away can access the application from their computer seconds later and receive the newly updated version of the information.

## Creating the New Subscriber Screen

The final screen in this application is the Subscribe screen. This screen will appear whenever the VB Guru web site convinces a new customer that this is a magazine that they could enjoy. This screen's job is to gather the necessary information from the user and send it to the database for approval. Figure 22.20 shows what this screen looks like.

**FIG. 22.20**

The Subscribe screen lets the user enter the data needed to process her subscription.

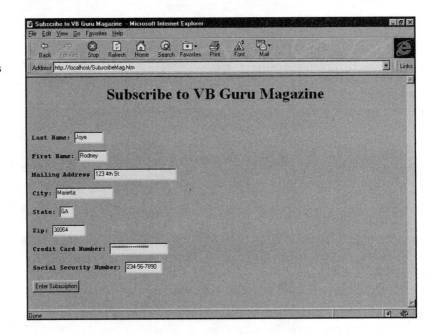

The code for this screen looks a lot like the screens that we have seen before. It is shown here in Listing 22.12.

**Listing 22.12   The HTML Code for a Data Entry Form**

```
Sub Subscribe()
Send ("Content-type: text/html")
Send (" ")
Send ("<HTML>")

Send ("<HEAD>")
Send ("<TITLE>Subscribe to VB Guru Magazine </TITLE>")
Send ("</HEAD>")

Send ("<BODY>")

Send ("<CENTER>")
Send ("<H1> Subscribe to VB Guru Magazine </H1>")
Send ("</CENTER>")
```

```
Send ("<PRE>")
Send ("<FORM METHOD=""POST"" ACTION=""/cgi-win/Magazine.exe"">")

Send ("<B>Last Name: </B><INPUT TYPE=""text"" NAME=""LastName"" SIZE=""8"">")

Send ("<B>First Name: </B><INPUT TYPE=""text"" NAME=""FirstName"" SIZE=""8"">")

Send ("<B>Mailing Address </B><INPUT TYPE=""text"" NAME=""Address""
SIZE=""30"">")

Send ("<B>City: </B><INPUT TYPE=""text"" NAME=""City"" SIZE=""20"">")

Send ("<B>State: </B><INPUT TYPE=""text"" NAME=""State"" SIZE=""2"">")

Send ("<B>Zip: </B><INPUT TYPE=""text"" NAME=""Zip"" SIZE=""10"">")

Send ("<B>Credit Card Number: </B><INPUT TYPE=""password""
NAME=""CreditCard_No"" SIZE=""20"">")

Send ("<B>Social Security Number: </B><INPUT TYPE=""text"" NAME=""SSN""
SIZE=""11"">")
Send ("<INPUT TYPE=""text"" NAME=""DoWhat"" SIZE=""1"" VALUE=""
AddSubscriber"">")

Send ("<INPUT TYPE=""Submit"", VALUE=""Enter Subscription"">")
Send ("</PRE>")

Send ("</FORM>")
Send ("</BODY>")
Send ("</HTML>")

End Sub
```

Although the HTML for this screen is ordinary, the fact that the HTML is generated by the Visual Basic program is new. Earlier, we saw how the Send() subroutine can communicate information back to the client browser. Here, the Send() routine is creating another screen for the user instead of the data. The user will use this new screen to request the data. This may seem a bit circular at first, but the fact that HTML is a completely interpreted language makes this possible.

Notice that the Password intrinsic control was used for the credit card control. This control behaves like the text control except that the users' keystrokes are not echoed back as they type. An * is placed for each character as it is typed.

**N O T E** Be aware that the HTML Password control only hides the contents of the field from the view of prying eyes. The contents of these fields are passed over the Internet in an unencrypted form. For this reason, a responsible Web site would also send the contents of a form containing a Password control containing sensitive information (like a credit card number) to a Web server running Secure Sockets Layer (SSL). Using SSL will send not just the contents of the Password control, but all of the form data to the Web server in an encrypted form. ■

Upon completion of the subscribers information, this application sends back a summary of what was sent as shown in Figure 22.21.

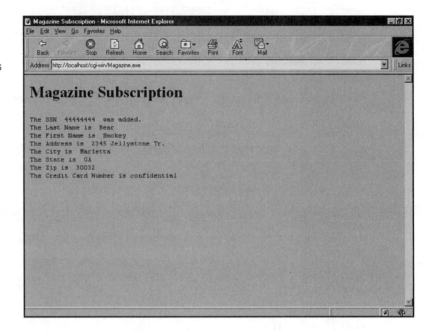

As you can see, all of the data that the user has provided appears on this screen for the user to verify. In a production system, the user would most likely be given a chance to review and change the responses prior to updating the database.

# Summary

In this chapter, you learned how to use the database updating features of Visual Basic and the HTML forms to create client/server applications that run over the Internet. The WebSite server made this possible by creating the INI file with the data passed in by the form and then channeling the feedback to the client browser. You learned how to query, update, and add rows to tables. In addition, you saw how to create HTML files on-the-fly using the Send() command.

# From Here...

In order to round out your knowledge on using Visual Basic for developing client/server applications, you should also review the material in the following chapters of this book:

- For information on how to use the Windows CGI interface with Visual Basic, see Chapter 18, "The WinCGI Interface and Visual Basic."

■ To see how you can use Remote Data Objects with SQL Server to provide database access through the OLEISAPI2 interface, see Chapter 23, "Using Remote Data Objects with the OLEISAPI2 Interface."

■ For information on standard CGI, see Appendix A, "Standard CGI, WinCGI, and Visual Basic."

# Using Remote Data Objects with the OLEISAPI2 Interface

**Multi-threaded programming**

Learn how multi-threaded programs work and how they affect accessing of global and shared variables and resources.

**Thread Synchronization Mechanisms**

Take a look at the various mechanisms that are available for synchronizing multiple threads, to keep them coexisting and cooperating successfully.

**Threads and Visual Basic**

Examine how threading is implemented in Visual Basic 5 and how it affects the design of your applications.

**Threading and the OLEISAPI Interfaces**

Examine how the multi-threading of the ISAPI interface is dealt with in the OLEISAPI extensions and what that means to your OLEISAPI ActiveX DLLs.

**Remote Data Objects**

Look at the Remote Data Objects that are available with the Enterprise Edition of Visual Basic, how they differ from Data Access Objects, and how they can be used in a server application.

In Chapters 16 and 17, you learned about the ISAPI interface for Microsoft's IIS Web server and the OLEISAPI extensions that make it easy to use Visual Basic to build ActiveX DLLs that can be called directly from a Web page. In this chapter, you look into another aspect of programming for the ISAPI interface, how it should allow you to hold open resources such as a database connection, and some of the considerations surrounding this aspect.

Most of the issues surrounding maintaining an open database connection have to do with the multi-threading aspect of building ISAPI extensions, and the fact that most resources like databases only allow a single thread to interact with any one database connection at a time. Most databases are multi-threaded internally, but each connection is single-threaded.

**N O T E** This chapter often uses the term OLEISAPI as an umbrella term that includes both the OLEISAPI and OLEISAPI2 interfaces. When specific features of either interface is being discussed, the specific name for that interface is used. ▪

# Multi-Threaded Programming

When Microsoft introduced Visual Basic back in the days of Windows 3.x, they had no choice to make VB a single-threaded programming language. All Windows 3.x applications were single-threaded, with only one path of execution at any one point in time. This was due to the fact that the version of multitasking that the Windows 3.x operating system did is known as cooperative multitasking. The key to cooperative multitasking is that each individual application makes the decision about when to give up the processor for another application to perform any processing that it might be waiting to perform. This made the Windows 3.x platform very susceptible to ill-behaved applications that would hold other applications prisoner while the application performed some long winding process, or even got itself stuck in some sort of loop.

With Windows NT and Windows 95, the nature of the operating system changed. No longer was the operating system performing cooperative multitasking, but it was now performing preemptive multitasking. In a preemptive multitasking operating system, the operating system decides when to take the processor away from the current application that has it and give the processor to another application that is waiting for it. It doesn't matter whether the application that has the processor is ready to give it up for use by another application; the processor is taken from it, without the application's permission. This is how the operating system enables multiple applications to perform computation-intensive tasks, and still have all of the applications making about the same amount of progress in each of their tasks. This capability of the operating system prevents the possibility of a single application holding other applications prisoner while it hogs the processor.

**N O T E** Because the Windows 95 operating system is really a mixture of 16-bit and 32-bit code, it is still possible for an ill-behaved 16-bit application to lock up the system, as a large amount of 16-bit code that remains a core part of the operating system. The 16-bit code on Windows 95 is still a cooperative multitasking environment, where only one application can be executing 16-bit code at a time. Since all of the USER functions thunk down to the 16-bit version, and a good portion of the GCI functions thunk down to the 16-bit version, it is still possible for a single 16-bit application to lock up the entire system.

On Windows NT, if all of the 16-bit applications are running in a shared memory space, an ill-behaved application can lock up all of the 16-bit applications, but it has no effect on any 32-bit applications. ▪

**Code Thunking**

Thunking is a mechanism where an application switches between running as a 32-bit executable, and running as a 16-bit executable. Because the structure of 16- and 32-bit machine code is different, the parameters and return values being passed between the 32- and 16-bit code has to be rearranged to be compatible with whichever of the two the application is switching to. Another thing that needs to be done in the thunk is to switch the processor between running in one mode to the other (32-bit mode and 16-bit mode). Thunking between the two modes is the method that Microsoft developed to switch between the two modes on their various operating systems.

# Performing Multiple Tasks at One Time

Along with the capability to allow multiple applications to run simultaneously comes the capability for a single application to be executing multiple threads of execution at any one point in time. A thread is to an application as an application is to the operating system. If an application has multiple threads running, it basically has multiple applications running within the whole application. This allows the application to get more things done simultaneously, as when Microsoft Word checks your spelling at the same time you are typing your document.

Because of the very nature of server applications, serving requests of multiple clients at any one time, they are almost always built as multi-threaded applications. When you build a DLL extension to a server application, it needs to be designed to be thread-safe. What this means is that there might be multiple threads calling the same, or different, functions in the same DLL at the same time. This affects how you can afford to design the DLL and how any variables are used within the functions that make up the DLL.

# Building Structures

Imagine that the OLEISAPI application you built in Chapter 20 was running two threads, each parsing its own set of parameters at the same time. Imagine also that the DLL was using a global array of ParamValue types to hold these key/value pairs. If the method of allocating and resizing the array consisted of checking the current size and adding one position onto the end of the array, you could easily find your two threads building an array populated something like the one in Figure 23.1, where array positions populated by the first thread were intermingled with those created by the second thread. This intermingling of the data could easily confuse each thread as the threads try to retrieve values from the array for each thread's processing needs, as each thread is just as likely to pull a value that actually belongs to the other thread. This would cause each thread to operate on wrong data and return to the user the wrong results.

If the application built these arrays as localized arrays, instead of global arrays, the threads would be able to keep access to each array limited to only the thread that was building the array. This would give you a picture more like that shown in Figure 23.2, where there is no intermingling of data from multiple threads. By taking this approach to using arrays and other memory structures, each thread can perform its processing, returning the results to the client confident that the results are correct, as the calculations were performed on uncorrupted data.

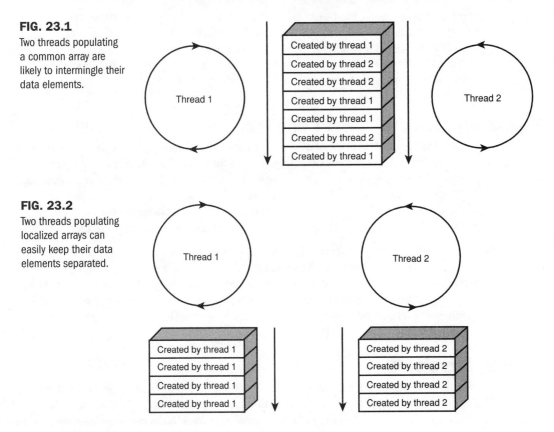

**FIG. 23.1**
Two threads populating a common array are likely to intermingle their data elements.

**FIG. 23.2**
Two threads populating localized arrays can easily keep their data elements separated.

## Managing Access to Shared Resources

Not all variables can be localized, and often there are resources that you want to share between all of the threads that are running in your applications. This creates an issue with multi-threaded applications. Suppose that you have three threads, all sharing a single counter which is being used to generate unique numbers. Because you don't know when control of the processor is going to be taken away from one thread and given to the next, you could find your application generating duplicate "unique" numbers, as shown in Figure 23.3.

As you can see, this doesn't work too well in a multi-threaded application. Because there is little that can be done to completely eliminate the need to share common resources between threads, and the complete elimination of sharing resources between threads would make every programmer's life much more difficult, there has to be a way to limit access to a common resource to only one thread at a time. In reality, there are four mechanisms for limiting access to common resources and synchronizing processing between threads, all of which work in different ways and are appropriate (or not) for use depending on the circumstances in which you need to use them. These four mechanisms are the following:

- Critical Sections
- Mutexes
- Semaphores
- Events

**FIG. 23.3**
Three threads sharing a single counter used to generate "unique" numbers can find that their "unique" numbers are not unique.

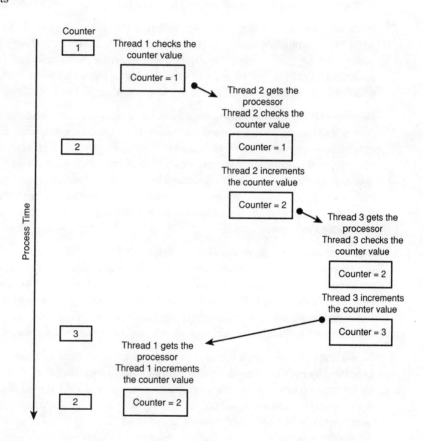

**Critical Sections**  A critical section is a mechanism that limits access to a certain resource to a single thread within an application. A thread attempts to enter the critical section before it needs to work with the specific shared resource and then exit the critical section after it is finished accessing the resource. If another thread tries to enter the critical section before the first thread exits the critical section, the second thread is blocked and does not take any processor time until the first thread exits the critical section, allowing the second to enter. Critical sections are used to mark sections of code which only one thread should be allowed to execute at a time. Critical sections don't prevent the processor from being taken away from that thread and given to another thread, they just prevent two or more threads from entering the same section of code.

If you use a critical section with your counter that you looked at in Figure 23.3, you could force each thread to enter a critical section before checking the current value of the counter. If each thread does not leave the critical section until after it has incremented and updated the counter, you can guarantee that, no matter how many threads you have executing and regardless of their execution order, truly unique numbers are being generated, as shown in Figure 23.4.

**Mutexes**    Mutexes, which stands for "mutually exclusive," work basically the same as critical sections, only mutexes are for use when the resource that is being shared is not just being used by the threads in a single application, but when the resource is being shared between multiple applications. By using a mutex, you can guarantee that no two threads running in any number of applications are accessing the same resource at the same time.

Because of the operating system-wide availability, mutexes carry a lot more overhead than critical sections do. Mutexes also have a lifetime that does not end when the application that created it shuts down. The mutex might still be being used by other applications that are still running, so the operating system has to keep track of which applications are using a mutex and, once there is no longer any need for the mutex to remain in existence, to destroy it. In contrast, critical sections have little overhead because they do not exist outside the application that created and is using them. After the application that created a critical section ends, the critical section is gone.

**Semaphores**    Semaphores work very differently from critical sections and mutexes. Semaphores are intended for use with resources that are not limited to a single thread at a time, but for a resource that should be limited to a fixed number of threads. A semaphore is a form of counter, and threads can increment or decrement it. The trick to semaphores is that a semaphore cannot go any lower than zero, therefore, if a semaphore is at zero, and a thread is trying to decrement it, that thread is blocked until another thread increments the semaphore.

To illustrate one way that a semaphore might be used, suppose you have a queue that is being populated by multiple threads, and one thread that is removing the items from the queue and performing processing on each item. If the queue is empty, the thread that removes items from it and processes them has nothing to do. This thread could go into an idle loop, checking the queue every so often to see if something has been placed into it. The problem with this is that the thread is taking up processing cycles doing absolutely nothing. These are processor cycles that could have been given to another thread that does have something to do. If a semaphore is used to control the queue, with each thread that places items into the queue incrementing the semaphore for each item placed in the queue, the thread that removes the items could decrement the semaphore just before removing each item from the queue. If the queue is empty, the semaphore is zero, and the thread removing items is blocked on the call to decrement the queue. This thread does not take any processor cycles until one of the other threads increments the semaphore to indicate that it has placed an item in the queue. The thread removing items is immediately unblocked, and it can remove the item that was just placed in the queue and begin processing it, as shown in Figure 23.5.

**FIG. 23.4**

Three threads using the same counter to generate unique numbers, with the counter protected by a critical section, can generate truly unique numbers.

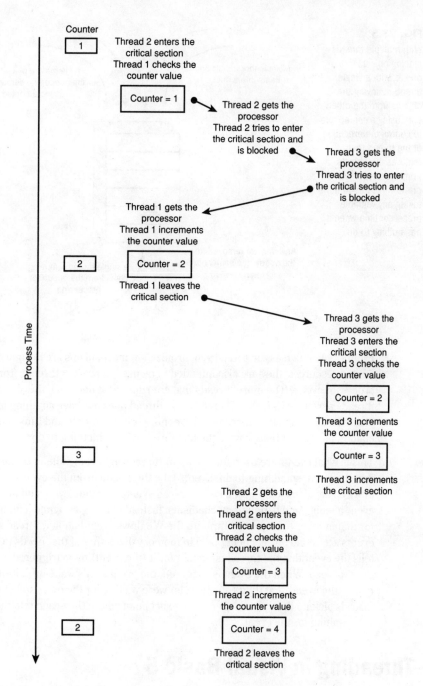

Counter

1

Thread 2 enters the critical section
Thread 1 checks the counter value

Counter = 1

Thread 2 gets the processor
Thread 2 tries to enter the critical section and is blocked

Thread 3 gets the processor
Thread 3 tries to enter the critical section and is blocked

Thread 1 gets the processor
Thread 1 increments the counter value

2

Counter = 2

Thread 1 leaves the critical section

Thread 3 gets the processor
Thread 3 enters the critical section
Thread 3 checks the counter value

Counter = 2

Thread 3 increments the counter value

3

Counter = 3

Thread 3 increments the critcal section

Thread 2 gets the processor
Thread 2 enters the critical section
Thread 2 checks the counter value

Counter = 3

Thread 2 increments the counter value

2

Counter = 4

Thread 2 leaves the critical section

Process Time

Part
VII

Ch
23

**FIG. 23.5**

With multiple threads placing objects into a queue, with a single thread removing the objects from the other end, using a semaphore to control the execution of the thread that removes the objects from the queue can prevent this thread from taking any valuable processor time when it has nothing to do.

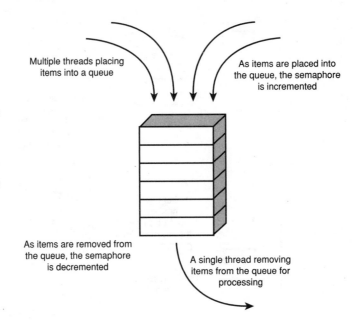

Multiple threads placing items into a queue

As items are placed into the queue, the semaphore is incremented

As items are removed from the queue, the semaphore is decremented

A single thread removing items from the queue for processing

**Events**   As much as the thread synchronization mechanisms are designed to control access to limited resources, they are also intended to be used to prevent threads from using unnecessary processor cycles. The more threads that are running at one time, the slower each of those threads performs its tasks. Therefore, if a thread does not have anything to do, block it and let it sit idle, allowing other threads to have more processor time and thus run faster until the conditions are met that provide the idle thread with something to do.

This is what events are used for—to allow threads to become idle until the conditions are such that they have something to do. Events take their name from the events that drive most Windows applications, only with a twist. Thread synchronization events do not use the normal event queuing and handling mechanisms. Instead of being assigned a number and then waiting for that number to be passed through the Windows event handler, thread synchronization events are actual objects being held in memory. Each thread that needs to wait for an event tells the event that the thread is waiting for it (the event) to be triggered and then the thread goes to sleep. When the event is triggered, the event sends wake-up calls to every thread that told it (the event) that they (the threads) were waiting for the event to be triggered. The threads pick up their processing at the exact point where they each told the event that they were waiting for the event.

# Threading in Visual Basic 5

As explained earlier, all Visual Basic applications before the release of VB 5 have been single-threaded applications. Most Visual Basic applications built using VB 5 will continue to be single-threaded applications. This is because the only Visual Basic applications that can be multi-threaded have to meet certain criteria—mainly that the Visual Basic application or DLL not require any user interaction. Threading in Visual Basic applications and DLLs is not quite your normal form of multi-threading; there are certain characteristics that set threads in Visual Basic apart from other programming languages that support threads.

## Serializing Requests

In ActiveX (OLE) DLLs created with Visual Basic 4 (and also ActiveX server applications), if two threads need to call methods in the same DLL, they have to take turns. The second thread has to wait until the first thread has finished its method call. This is called *serializing* requests. It doesn't matter if the two threads are calling the same method or different methods. The DLL can only accommodate a single thread at any one point in time.

If the threads or separate applications are calling to an out-of-process ActiveX server application—either on the same machine or another machine—the operating system takes care of making sure that the second call waits for the first to finish. If the two calls are coming from two threads to an ActiveX DLL, which is running as an in-process server, the application making the calls needs to make sure that the second thread waits until the first is finished.

The following are two issues with this serialization of requests:

- If the request being made by the first call takes a long time to complete, it creates a significant delay before the second call can be serviced.
- If the calls are being made to an in-process ActiveX server in a DLL, the programmer building the client application has to build in the thread synchronization to prevent two or more simultaneous calls to the same DLL.

Either way, if there were another option available that allowed multiple threads to make calls to the same DLL or out-of-process server such that they all could be serviced simultaneously, that option would be preferable.

## Apartment-Model Threading

With Visual Basic 5 comes the ability to build thread-safe ActiveX DLLs and out-of-process servers. There is one condition on any Visual Basic application before it can be multi-threaded—it has to need no user interaction. If the Visual Basic application has any user-interface, it is limited to being a regular old single-threaded Visual Basic application. If there is no user interaction involved, you can enable multi-threaded operation by selecting Unattended Execution on the project properties, as shown in Figure 23.6.

Part VII Ch 23

> **CAUTION**
>
> Selecting Unattended Execution suppresses all forms of user interaction, including message boxes and system error messages. These messages are redirected to either a message log or the system event log, if running on Windows NT.

**FIG. 23.6**

Setting Unattended Execution on a Visual Basic project, allows it to accommodate multiple threads of execution.

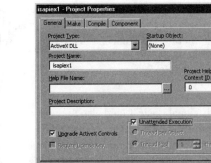

Microsoft simplified memory object management and thread synchronization when it made the decision to add threading capabilities to Visual Basic. Microsoft decided to implement something called apartment-model threading. With apartment-model threading, every thread is given its own individual copies of every memory object and variable that is used and accessed by the thread, as shown in Figure 23.7. In a sense, each thread is given its own apartment with everything the thread needs placed in the apartment, and the thread is forced to stay in its apartment. While this frees you, as the programmer, from having to worry about coordinating access to variables and resources between threads, it also limits what you can do. While it's not impossible, the apartment-model makes it very difficult to perform any cross-thread communication, and it involves an inordinately large amount of overhead, effectively discouraging any real cross-thread communications or resource sharing.

**FIG. 23.7**

Apartment-model threading with a Widget object class makes complete copies of the object for each thread.

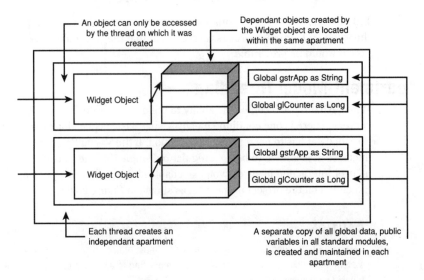

# Round-Robin Thread Pool

When using Visual Basic to create an out-of-process ActiveX server, you have more options to control how threads are created and used within your server application. You can select to have your application run with one of the following three thread assignment models:

- Only one thread of execution so that it runs just like any ActiveX server application you have built using earlier versions of Visual Basic. This mode also allows you to compile ActiveX servers built using earlier versions of Visual Basic without modification.

- A limited number of threads running in your application, with a round-robin assignment of thread to request. This can lead to an imbalance in the work load of individual threads, but controls the number of threads running on the machine.

- Each external request receives a separate thread, which provides you no way to control the total number of threads running on the machine on which the application is running, potentially degrading machine performance.

Of these three thread assignment models, the middle one is the one that really requires a detailed explanation. When you specify a number of threads to be allowed in an out-of-process ActiveX server application—as requests are received for objects from other applications—the ActiveX server application assigns the first request received to thread 1, the second to thread 2, the third to thread 3, and so on. After all of the threads have been assigned to server requests, the application starts with thread 1 again, starting around the active threads again, as shown in Figure 23.8.

**FIG. 23.8**
The round-robin thread assignment model, with five active threads servicing requests from four clients, pass each subsequent request to the next thread in the sequence.

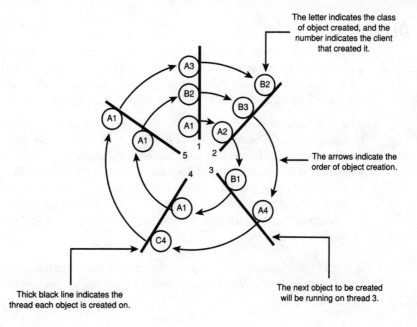

This could easily end up with one client application having several different threads servicing the application's various requests. It also means that any single thread in the Visual Basic ActiveX server application can have several different applications calling methods in the same thread. This requires you to take particular care when designing your out-of-process ActiveX server applications so that, if a particular thread has several different applications calling its various methods, any data received from any of these applications is not mixed with data from one of the other applications.

The other aspect of the round-robin method of assigning threads to requests is that it does not guarantee an even balance of requests to threads. If threads 1 and 2 are idle, and thread 2 is the last thread to be assigned to a request, thread 3 is the next thread assigned to a request, even though it might already be busy servicing three or four other requests.

# Threads and OLEISAPI

When you are building ActiveX DLLs using Visual Basic 5, you don't have all of the threading assignment options that you have with creating out-of-process ActiveX server applications. This is because DLLs are always executed as in-process ActiveX servers. As a result, when you select Unattended Execution on the project options for your OLEISAPI application, you find that the thread assignment options are all disabled (refer to Figure 23.6). You have the apartment-model with all of the global and dependent objects within each of your threads of execution, so you might want to be conservative on your use of global variables and objects, which would have to be created multiple times over.

## OLEISAPI

Because the OLEISAPI interface was originally designed for use with Visual Basic 4, it contains a critical section around the call to the method specified by the URL in the HTML form. This means that, at this point in time, you don't have to take any special steps in designing and building your OLEISAPI ActiveX DLL; but this might not always be the case.

As it is, because only one call to the OLEISAPI interface can be serviced at a time, this becomes a potential bottleneck. Yes, the OLEISAPI interface is much faster than the CGI interface, but the CGI interface could be running any number of the same single threaded application at one time, thus effectively servicing multiple requests simultaneously. With the OLEISAPI interface, you don't have that ability. Because each call to your OLEISAPI application is a potential bottleneck, holding up every other call to your OLEISAPI application, it is your responsibility to make sure that you build your application so that it will run as efficiently as possible.

**N O T E** For an excellent book on building efficient Visual Basic applications, check out *Visual Basic Optimization and Performance Tuning*, by Keith Brophy and Tim Koets, published by Sams Publishing.

Because the OLEISAPI interface prevents multiple calls to your DLL at one time, you don't need to place any thread synchronization objects around the access and usage of resources like databases. Because of the apartment-model of thread execution, it is debatable as to whether you need to use any of these mechanisms at all, as the database connection would be duplicated for each thread. Odds are that Microsoft's programmers have taken this into account, and with each additional thread, the database connection is not just copied, but creates another actual open connection to the database.

## OLEISAPI2

With the OLEISAPI2 interface, things have changed. The OLEISAPI2 interface no longer limits the calls to ActiveX DLLs with a critical section, but instead uses the critical section within the methods and properties of the Request object. This greatly increases the throughput of OLEISAPI2 applications, as none of the requests have to wait for other requests to complete before they can be called. The bottleneck of the original OLEISAPI interface is gone. This does mean that the OLEISAPI2 interface could potentially have problems with non-thread safe ActiveX DLLs, such as those that are not marked for Unattended Execution or those built with earlier versions of Visual Basic.

Does this mean that you, as a Visual Basic programmer, have to start using critical sections in your code to limit the access to a database connection, so that, if two or more requests are being serviced at the same time, there are no contingency problems with the shared database connection? Unfortunately, no. Because the Visual Basic ActiveX DLLs use the apartment-model of threading, the one database connection is really one connection for each active thread. If you have three requests being serviced at the same time, you have three database connections open at the same time.

Should the number of open database connections be a concern to you? Absolutely! If you are using a database with a limited number of connections available, you could easily run out of available connections on a busy Web site. Another concern should be that you are unable to eliminate the overhead of opening and closing the database connection. If you are using an enterprise database, this includes the overhead of logging into the database. Just because your Visual Basic methods are running in parallel does not mean that you no longer have to worry about writing optimized code. You still want your method to complete as quickly as possible and maintain an open database only while it is absolutely necessary.

# Remote Data Objects

Beginning with Visual Basic 4, Microsoft introduced Remote Data Objects (RDO) as an alternative to Data Access Objects (DAO). These new RDOs are included only with the Enterprise Edition of Visual Basic. What RDOs allow you to do is bypass the Microsoft Jet database engine and go directly to the ODBC datasource for SQL-based databases. In a sense, it's a lot like using pass-through mode on an entire database with DAOs, where the Jet engine is only providing a means of accessing the database but is not performing any database management.

RDOs are very similar to using DAOs in ODBCdirect mode, which was introduced with Visual Basic 5. The difference is that ODBCdirect mode uses RDOs to perform all of the database access. As a result, you have an additional layer of the DAOs on top of the RDOs, each adding its own layer of processing into the mix. However, there is nothing between RDOs and the ODBC interface to add overhead to your database access. The only way you can get any closer to the ODBC interface is to make ODBC API calls from Visual Basic, only you lose use of all built-in data controls available with the Visual Basic data access options.

You can gain many of the benefits of RDOs by using regular DAOs in ODBCdirect mode and still have the DAO object model to work with. However, the ODBCdirect mode is an in-between solution, you don't have full DAO functionality, and you don't have full RDO functionality. But if you're more comfortable with DAOs, or you need to go between multiple databases, some of which have to use the Jet engine, then you are probably better off using DAOs in ODBCdirect mode. On the other hand, if you are only going to be using SQL-based databases that have ODBC interfaces, you are better off in the long run to use RDOs.

# The RDO Object Model

The RDO object model is designed as a thin wrapper around the ODBC interface, providing a Visual Basic object model to the interface that can be used with all of the Visual Basic bound controls. In a lot of ways, the RDO object model is very similar to the DAO object model. The primary difference between the two is that the DAO object model was designed around ISAM (Indexed Sequential Access Method, also known as Flat-File) database access, while the RDO object model was designed for SQL (Structured Query Language) database access. This means that DAOs are well suited for working with databases like dBase, FoxPro, and Paradox, while RDOs are better suited for use with databases like SQL Server, Oracle, and Sybase.

The RDO object model consists of the following objects:

- rdoEngine— This is the base object, which is created automatically whenever RDOs are used in a Visual Basic application.
- rdoError—This object performs all of the RDO and ODBC error and message handling.
- rdoEnvironment—This object controls a logical set of connections and transactions. There can be multiple rdoEnvironment objects, but the first one is automatically created by the rdoEngine.
- rdoConnection—This object represents an open connection to a specific database.
- rdoTable—This object represents the stored definition of a database table.
- rdoResultset—This object represents the rows of data that result from a query run against the database.
- rdoColumn—This object represents a column of data.
- rdoQuery—This object represents a SQL query that can contain zero or more parameters.
- rdoParameter—This object represents a parameter associated with a rdoQuery object. This parameter can be an input parameter, output parameter, or both.

The relationships between these objects are shown in Figure 23.9.

**FIG. 23.9**
The RDO object model, showing the relationships between the objects, is very similar to the DAO object model.

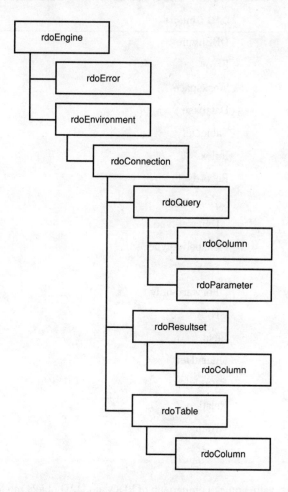

For the most part, RDOs can be used in much the same way that DAOs are used. The following are a few notable differences that must be taken into account:

- RDOs use the term *rows* instead of *records*, and *columns* instead of *fields*.
- RDOs do not allow you to use the Seek method to locate a record, because that is an ISAM search method where the DAOs have direct access to the database indexes.
- RDOs do not allow direct modification of the database schema, referential integrity, or security, because these are fully supported by the database administration tools. RDOs can use the native database Data-Definition Language (DDL) to perform these same tasks.

In Table 23.1, you can see the RDO objects and their corresponding DAO objects.

**Table 23.1    RDO Objects and Their Corresponding DAO Objects**

| RDO Objects | DAO Objects |
| --- | --- |
| rdoEngine | DBEngine |
| rdoError | Error |
| rdoEnvironment | Workspace |
| rdoConnection | Database |
| rdoTable | TableDef |
| N/A | Index |
| rdoResultset | Recordset |
| - N/A | - Table-type |
| - Keyset-type | - Dynaset-type |
| - Static-type | - Snapshot-type |
| - Dynamic-type | - N/A |
| - Forward-only | - Forward-only |
| - (cursorless) | - N/A |
| rdoColumn | Field |
| rdoQuery | QueryDef |
| rdoParameter | Parameter |
| N/A | Relation |
| N/A | Group |
| N/A | User |

This provides you with a quick comparison of RDO and DAO object models, and hopefully provides you with an understanding of how you can build on your existing understanding of DAOs to use RDOs to build database applications in Visual Basic.

# Enabling RDO Use in Visual Basic

Before you can actually begin using Remote Data Objects in your Visual Basic applications, you have to enable their usage in the Visual Basic development environment. You can do this by selecting Project|References. After the reference dialog box is open, scroll down until you find the Microsoft Remote Data Object 2.0 entry. Check the box to the left of this entry to include this reference in your project and then click OK, which is shown in Figure 23.10. You are now able to use RDOs in your Visual Basic application.

**FIG. 23.10**
Enabling the use of
Remote Data Objects
for a Visual Basic
project requires adding
Remote Data Objects in
the project references
dialog.

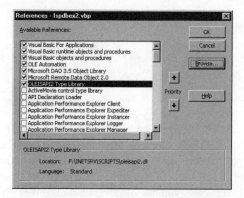

**N O T E** To learn how to include the OLEISAPI2 type library in your Visual Basic project, or where to get the OLEISAPI2 interface for use with your Web server, see Chapter 20, "The OLEISAPI2 Interface and the Active Reference Object."

# Building a Contact Database ISAPI Application

For your database OLEISAPI application, you'll build a simple contact management application with the capability to find, edit, and update contact information through a Web browser. While not a feature complete contact management system, it should provide enough functionality to illustrate what is involved in building a database Web application that uses the OLEISAPI interface.

Your database will have a single contact table. Although you should have additional classification and datebook tables, you'll keep it short and simple with only a single table. The database will also contain a single look-up table which holds state names and two-character abbreviations. Your database is a Microsoft SQL Server database and has two tables—one named Contact, which is structured as in Table 23.2, and one named States, which is structured as in Table 23.3.

**Table 23.2 The Contact Table Structure**

| Column Name | Data Type | Length |
| --- | --- | --- |
| ContactID | int identity | |
| FirstName | Text | 20 |
| LastName | Text | 20 |
| Address | Text | 40 |
| City | Text | 25 |
| State | Text | 2 |
| ZipCode | Text | 10 |
| Phone | Text | 15 |

**Table 23.3   The States Table Structure**

| Column Name | Data Type | Length |
|-------------|-----------|--------|
| StateCode   | Text      | 2      |
| StateDesc   | Text      | 20     |

After you have created the database, you need to define an ODBC data source for the database. Because this database is opened by the IIS Web server, and on NT ODBC configurations are normally defined for a particular user account, you need to make sure that the ODBC DSN is visible to the entire system. You have to define your data source as a system DSN and not a regular (personal) DSN. In this case, you name your data source WebSrvDB; and, in the SQL Server administrator, you create a new login for use by your application named WebVB, with a password of vbweb. You've limited this login to access your database, which is named WebSrv.

The application provides the user with the following functionality:

- The user can open a list of all of the contacts in the database.

- The user can select any one contact in the list and open that record for editing.

- After the user has edited a contact record, the record can be submitted to the server for saving in the database.

- The user has an ad hoc query capability, which returns as many records as match the selection criteria. If only one record matches the criteria, the record is returned to the user in a form so that the user can edit the record. If more than one record matches the selection criteria, they are returned in a list, allowing the user to select one for editing.

If this application were feature complete, you would also need to provide the user with a means of adding new records and deleting old records.

---

**Feature Complete**

An application is "feature complete" when it has all of the features and functions intended for the application to contain. This includes all of the normal functionality that users would normally expect to see in an application, along with all of the extra features that the application design team has decided to include. If some of these functions remain unimplemented, then the application is not feature complete. This is a term you hear being bandied about quite a bit when discussing pre-release versions of software. It is an important milestone when an application development team delivers the feature complete application to testing, as all of the remaining development work that remains is to fix all of the bugs that are found in the application by the test team.

---

# Defining a Starting Point from Which to Find a Contact Record

Before you begin programming your application, let's first build a Web page that acts as a starting point for your user. In Listing 23.1, you have an HTML document that provides a link that the user can click to get a listing of all contact records in the database. This link calls the ListContacts method in your OLEISAPI application that you will be building in this chapter. This document also provides a simple HTML form that can be used by the user to perform ad hoc querying on the contact table by entering partial values in the first name, last name, or city fields. This HTML document is shown in Figure 23.11.

---

**Listing 23.1   DBEX1.HTM   The HTML Form Used to Request a Contact Record to Edit**

```
<html><head>
<title>OLEISAPI Database Programming Example 1</title></head>
<body bgcolor=#C0C0C0>
<h1>OLEISAPI Database Programming Example 1</h1>
<hr><p>
<a HREF="/scripts/oleisapi2.dll/ispdbex.Isapidb.ListContacts">
Browse current contacts</a> to choose one for editing.
<hr><p>
<form action="/scripts/oleisapi2.dll/ispdbex.Isapidb.FindContact"
method="POST">
Enter search criteria to find a specific contact.
<p><table align=center border=0>
<tr><td align=right valign=top>First Name</td>
<td align=left><input name="FirstName"></td></tr>
<tr><td align=right valign=top>Last Name</td>
<td align=left><input name="LastName"></td></tr>
<tr><td align=right valign=top>City</td>
<td align=left><input name="City"></td></tr></table>
<input type="submit" value="Find"></form>
</body>
</html>
```

---

# Defining the Database to Be Used

Like the application in the previous chapter, you need to begin a new Visual Basic project, making an ActiveX DLL. You name your project ispdbex, and you start the project by creating a class named Isapidb. To complete the setup of your project, you add the general.bas file and also the Parameters class that you built in the previous chapter's examples.

You start your Isapidb class by adding a database variable in the declarations that you'll be using throughout your application. You also add two constants: the first being the ODBC configuration for your database, and the second being the URL for this class, which you use in building the HTML files that you'll be returning to the user. You place all of these in the declarations portion of the class, as shown in Listing 23.2.

**FIG. 23.11**

The HTML document that is the entry point to your contact database application provides the user with a simple data entry form.

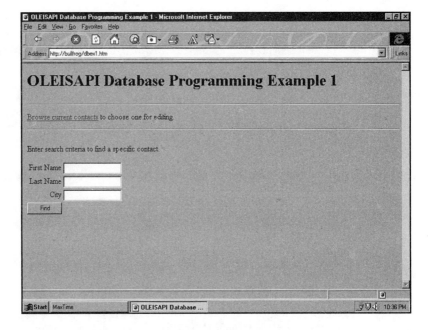

---

**Listing 23.2   ISAPIDB1.CLS   The *Isapidb1* Class Declarations for the Database Connection, Database Location, and the Constant for Where the OLEISAPI DLL Is Located**

```
Option Explicit

'Database variable and path
Private dbWebDB As New rdoConnection
Private Const DB_ENV = "UID=WebVB;PWD=vbweb;Database=WebSrv;DSN=WebSrvDB"
'The OLEISAPI and class path for insertion into HTML forms
Private Const OLEISAPI_PATH = "/scripts/oleisapi2.dll/ispdbex.Isapidb."
```

---

Normally, the DB_ENV and OLEISAPI_PATH are not declared as constants, but instead are variables that you want to populate from the registration database or a configuration file. This allows the site administrator to configure the Web server in whatever way he or she desires. For building and running this example, you need to alter the DB_ENV to reflect how you have built and configured the database on your system. The SQL scripts to create and populate the database can be found on the CD that accompanies this book.

---

Be sure to include the User ID (UID) and password (PWD) in the database environment information. If these are missing, your Visual Basic DLL causes a database login to pop up on the server screen when you are testing and debugging, and fails when in a production environment. Remember that this is a non-interactive Visual Basic routine, and it cannot get the User ID and password from any users when this is being run.

---

## Opening the Database

You open the database in the class initialization of the `Isapidb` class, as shown in Listing 23.3. I wish I could say that after the class is initialized, the instance should remain in memory, thus maintaining the database connection, but unfortunately, I can't. Every time a method in the class is called, the database is opened again, because although the DLL is kept in memory, the ActiveX class instances are destroyed the moment that control is returned to the OLEISAPI interface and the IIS Web server. It's still advantageous for you to open the database in this one location, instead of opening the database within each method that is exposed to external processes.

Part **VII**

Ch **23**

**Listing 23.3 ISAPIDB1.CLS Opening the Database Connection During the Class Initialization**

```
Private Sub Class_Initialize()
    'Open the database specified by the constant defined in the
    'class declaration section.
    With dbWebDB
        .Connect = DB_ENV
        .LoginTimeout = 5
        .CursorDriver = rdUseOdbc
        .EstablishConnection
    End With
End Sub
```

If you are going to be performing any significant processing before using any database access, you might not want to open the database connection in your class initialization. In this case, you want to build a common routine that can be called from any of your exposed methods in this class (or other classes within this project), which is called after you reach the point where you need the database access.

Because you are opening the database connection in the class initialization, it only makes sense that you close the connection in the class termination, as shown in Listing 23.4.

**Listing 23.4 ISAPIDB1.CLS Closing the Database Connection During the Class Termination**

```
Private Sub Class_Terminate()
    'Close the database connection, freeing the resources held open
    dbWebDB.Close
End Sub
```

## Informing the User of Any Errors

Before you get into the actual methods that are exposed and called by the OLEISAPI interface, let's do a little planning. You know that you need some means of informing the user of any errors that occur, so why don't you create a function to build an HTML document providing the user with the error messages and the SQL that caused the error? (In this example, you are only performing error checking on the database interaction, so each of the errors most likely have been caused by faulty SQL.)

You pass your error function the SQL that caused the error and a context appropriate message string to explain what the user was attempting to do when the error occurred. As you are building the HTML document, you loop through the errors returned by the database object, adding the messages from each error into the document, as shown in Listing 23.5.

**Listing 23.5   ISAPIDB1.CLS   The Function to Build an Error Message HTML Form and Return It to the Client**

```
Private Sub BuildErrorForm(aReq As Request, astrSQL As String, _
                                  astrErrMsg As String)
    Dim strHTML As String
    Dim errMsg As Error

    'Build the HTML document
    strHTML = strHTML & "<HTML><HEAD><TITLE>"
    strHTML = strHTML & "OLEISAPI Database Example"
    strHTML = strHTML & "</TITLE></HEAD><BODY BGCOLOR=#C0C0C0>"
    strHTML = strHTML & "<H1>OLEISAPI Database Example</H1><HR><P>"
    'Include the context error message
    strHTML = strHTML & astrErrMsg
    strHTML = strHTML & " The error messages are "
    strHTML = strHTML & "as follows:</P><P>"
    'Include the error numbers and description
    If DBEngine.Errors.Count > 0 Then
        For Each errMsg In DBEngine.Errors
            strHTML = strHTML & "Error Number : " & errMsg.Number
            strHTML = strHTML & "<BR>" & errMsg.Description & "</P><P>"
        Next errMsg
    End If
    'Include the SQL statement that caused the error to occur
    strHTML = strHTML & "The SQL that was attempted to run is as " _
                     & "follows:</P><P>"
    strHTML = strHTML & astrSQL & "</P><P>"
    strHTML = strHTML & "Please contact the application programmer about"
    strHTML = strHTML & " these errors to get them corrected.</P>"
    strHTML = strHTML & "</BODY></HTML>"

    'Set the result code
    aReq.ResponseStatus = "501 OK"
    'Set the content-type header line
    aReq.ResponseType = "text/html"
    'Return the HTML document to the calling routine
    aReq.WriteResponse strHTML
End Sub
```

## Letting the User Know that No Records Were Returned

Among the other HTML documents that you know you have to build is one informing the user that no records were found. This document is most likely to be returned as a result of the user performing an ad hoc query, but you can make it possible to call it as a result of any of our queries against the database. You are calling this function because there were no records returned by the database, so you don't need to pass the function any variables or objects to work with other than the Request object, as shown in Listing 23.6.

Part
VII
Ch
23

**Listing 23.6  ISAPIDB1.CLS  The Function that Builds the HTML Document Informing the User that No Records Were Found**

```
Private Sub BuildEmptyForm(aReq As Request)
    Dim strHTML As String

    'Begin building the return HTML document with the
    'content-type header line
    strHTML = "Content-type: text/html" & vbCrLf & vbCrLf
    'Build the HTML document
    strHTML = strHTML & "<HTML><HEAD><TITLE>"
    strHTML = strHTML & "OLEISAPI Database Example"
    strHTML = strHTML & "</TITLE></HEAD><BODY BGCOLOR=#C0C0C0>"
    strHTML = strHTML & "<H1>OLEISAPI Database Example</H1><HR><P>"
    strHTML = strHTML & _
        "There were no Contacts that matched the parameters entered."
    strHTML = strHTML & "</P></BODY></HTML>"
    'Set the result code
    aReq.ResponseStatus = "200 OK"
    'Set the content-type header line
    aReq.ResponseType = "text/html"
    'Return the HTML document to the calling routine
    aReq.WriteResponse strHTML
End Sub
```

## Returning a Contact Record for the User to Edit

Whenever the user makes a submission that results in only a single record being returned from the database, you want to return that record to the user in an HTML form so that the user can make edits to the record. You can do this by using the VALUE attribute of the HTML INPUT elements, providing the current value of each field in the record that was returned from the database, as shown in Listing 23.7.

By populating the HTML form using the VALUE attributes, you are also providing the user with a complete undo for all of the edits that might have been done. Any time the user clicks the RESET button on the HTML form, all of the INPUT fields are erased, and the string in the VALUE attribute is placed into the field, thus restoring the record to the state in which it was retrieved from the database.

**Listing 23.7 ISAPIDB1.CLS The Function that Takes a Resultset Containing a Single Contact Record and Builds an HTML Form that Allows the User to Edit the Data**

```
Private Sub BuildSingleForm(aReq As Request, adbrsWebRS As rdoResultset)
    Dim strHTML As String
    Dim strZipCode As String
    Dim strPhone As String

    'Build the HTML document
    strHTML = strHTML & "<HTML><HEAD><TITLE>"
    strHTML = strHTML & "OLEISAPI Database Example"
    strHTML = strHTML & "</TITLE></HEAD><BODY BGCOLOR=#C0C0C0>"
    strHTML = strHTML & "<H1>OLEISAPI Database Example</H1><HR><P>"
    strHTML = strHTML & "Here is the contact you selected for editing. "
    strHTML = strHTML & "Please make the desired changes and press the "
    strHTML = strHTML & "<STRONG>Update Contact</STRONG> button.</P><P>"
    'Build a table of the parameters that were passed
    With adbrsWebRS
        strHTML = strHTML & "<FORM ACTION=" & Chr(34) & OLEISAPI_PATH
        strHTML = strHTML & "UpdateContact" & Chr(34) & "METHOD=" & Chr(34)
        'Note the Contact ID being placed in a hidden field, so that it will
        'be returned with the form data.
        strHTML = strHTML & "POST" & Chr(34) & "><INPUT TYPE=" & Chr(34) _
                            & "HIDDEN"
        strHTML = strHTML & Chr(34) & " NAME=" & Chr(34) & "ContactID" _
                            & Chr(34)
        strHTML = strHTML & " VALUE=" & Chr(34) & .rdoColumns!ContactID _
                            & Chr(34) & ">"
        'The editing section will be "Preformatted" so that all fields
        'can be lined up
        strHTML = strHTML & "<PRE>" & vbCrLf
        strHTML = strHTML & "    First Name : <INPUT TYPE=" & Chr(34) _
                            & "TEXT" & Chr(34)
        strHTML = strHTML & " NAME=" & Chr(34) & "FirstName" & Chr(34) _
                            & " VALUE=" & Chr(34)
        strHTML = strHTML & .rdoColumns!FirstName & Chr(34) & " SIZE=20 " _
                            & "MAXLENGTH=20>" & vbCrLf
        strHTML = strHTML & "    Last Name : <INPUT TYPE=" & Chr(34) _
                            & "TEXT" & Chr(34)
        strHTML = strHTML & " NAME=" & Chr(34) & "LastName" & Chr(34) _
                            & " VALUE=" & Chr(34)
        strHTML = strHTML & .rdoColumns!LastName & Chr(34) & " SIZE=20 " _
                            & "MAXLENGTH=20>" & vbCrLf
        strHTML = strHTML & "      Address : <INPUT TYPE=" & Chr(34) _
                            & "TEXT" & Chr(34)
        strHTML = strHTML & " NAME=" & Chr(34) & "Address" & Chr(34) _
                            & " VALUE=" & Chr(34)
        strHTML = strHTML & .rdoColumns!Address & Chr(34) & " SIZE=40 " _
                            & "MAXLENGTH=40>" & vbCrLf
        strHTML = strHTML & "City, State, Zip : <INPUT TYPE=" & Chr(34) _
                            & "TEXT" & Chr(34)
        strHTML = strHTML & " NAME=" & Chr(34) & "City" & Chr(34) _
                            & " VALUE=" & Chr(34)
        strHTML = strHTML & .rdoColumns!City & Chr(34) & " SIZE=25 " _
```

```
                                   & "MAXLENGTH=25>, "
        strHTML = strHTML & "<INPUT TYPE=" & Chr(34) & "TEXT" & Chr(34)
        strHTML = strHTML & " NAME=" & Chr(34) & "State" & Chr(34) _
                                   & " VALUE=" & Chr(34)
        strHTML = strHTML & .rdoColumns!State & Chr(34) & " SIZE=2 " _
                                   & "MAXLENGTH=2> "
        strHTML = strHTML & "<INPUT TYPE=" & Chr(34) & "TEXT" & Chr(34)
        strHTML = strHTML & " NAME=" & Chr(34) & "ZipCode" & Chr(34) _
                                   & " VALUE=" & Chr(34)
        'We need to format the Zip Code before sending it to the user.
        'Before formatting, we need to right pad the zip code to bring
        'it to 9 characters in length.
        strZipCode = .rdoColumns!ZipCode
        If Len(strZipCode) < 9 Then
            strZipCode = strZipCode & String((9 - Len(strZipCode)), " ")
        End If
        strHTML = strHTML & Format(strZipCode, "&&&&&-&&&&") & Chr(34)
        strHTML = strHTML & " SIZE=10 MAXLENGTH=10>" & vbCrLf
        strHTML = strHTML & "            Phone : <INPUT TYPE=" & Chr(34) _
                                   & "TEXT" & Chr(34)
        strHTML = strHTML & " NAME=" & Chr(34) & "Phone" & Chr(34) _
                                   & " VALUE=" & Chr(34)
        'We need to format the Phone before sending it to the user.
        'Before formatting, we need to left pad the phone to bring
        'it to 10 characters in length.
        strPhone = .rdoColumns!Phone
        If Len(strPhone) < 10 Then
            strPhone = String((10 - Len(strPhone)), " ") & strPhone
        End If
        strHTML = strHTML & Format(strPhone, "(&&&) &&&-&&&&") & Chr(34)
        strHTML = strHTML & " SIZE=40 MAXLENGTH=40>" & vbCrLf
    End With
    'End the "Preformatting" of the form, and add the submission and
    'reset buttons.
    strHTML = strHTML & "</PRE><INPUT TYPE=SUBMIT VALUE=" & Chr(34) _
                                   & "Update Contact"
    strHTML = strHTML & Chr(34) & "><INPUT TYPE=RESET VALUE=" & Chr(34)
    strHTML = strHTML & "Reset Contact Information" & Chr(34) & ">"
    'Close the HTML Form and document
    strHTML = strHTML & "</FORM></BODY></HTML>"
    'Set the result code
    aReq.ResponseStatus = "200 OK"
    'Set the content-type header line
    aReq.ResponseType = "text/html"
    'Return the HTML document to the calling routine
    aReq.WriteResponse strHTML
End Sub
```

In the preceding listing, notice a couple of HTML tricks that you are performing. First, the ContactID field is being placed into an INPUT element that is type HIDDEN. This means that the ContactID field is returned with the rest of the data when the form is submitted back to the server, but the user never sees this field (unless he views the HTML source). This provides you with a way of returning the record key with the rest of the data, while protecting it from any edits.

Second, all of the editable fields in the HTML form were placed within a section marked as preformatted using the `<PRE>` HTML element. This allows you to line up all of the input fields, giving your form a crisp, professional software look with all of your prompts and text boxes lined up.

The third thing to notice is that you are formatting both the phone number and ZIP code fields before placing them into the HTML form. This allows you to keep these fields stored in the database in an unformatted state. You will also be doing this on the list HTML document, where you are presenting the user with a list of contact records to choose from. It also means that you have to be sure to remove the formatting from these fields when they are returned from this form before you update the database with the edited values.

# Returning a List of Contacts for the User to Choose From

The last of the stock functions builds the list of contact records. From this list, the user chooses a record to edit. This function is called when the database returns more than one record. You pass this function the resultset that is returned from the database and format the records into a table, as shown in Listing 23.8.

Key to making this HTML document work is that you place an anchor around the contact name in the table. Doing so provides the user with a link to take him directly to the edit HTML form you built in the preceding function, populated with the record selected from this table. You build the anchor tag using the `OLEISAPI_PATH` constant, the `GetContact` method name, and passing it the ContactID field as a parameter. Other than the Name column, the rest of the table is a straightforward HTML table with the values from each of the records as the column values.

---

**Listing 23.8   ISAPIDB1.CLS   The Function that Builds the HTML Document Containing a Table with All of the Contacts that Were Found**

```
Private Sub BuildMultipleForm(aReq As Request, _
                    adbrsWebRS As rdoResultset, alNumRecs As Long)
    Dim strHTML As String
    Dim strZipCode As String
    Dim strPhone As String

    'Build the HTML document
    strHTML = strHTML & "<HTML><HEAD><TITLE>"
    strHTML = strHTML & "OLEISAPI Database Example"
    strHTML = strHTML & "</TITLE></HEAD><BODY BGCOLOR=#C0C0C0>"
    strHTML = strHTML & "<H1>OLEISAPI Database Example</H1><HR><P>"
    strHTML = strHTML & "Here are the contacts available for your " _
                    & "selection. "
    strHTML = strHTML & "Please select the contact you wish to edit." _
                    & "</P><P>"
    'Tell the user how many parameters were passed
    strHTML = strHTML & "There were <STRONG>" & CStr(alNumRecs)
    strHTML = strHTML & "</STRONG> contacts found in the database.</P>"
    'Build a table of the parameters that were passed
```

```
          strHTML = strHTML & "<TABLE BORDER=2>"
          strHTML = strHTML & "<TR><TH>Name</TH><TH>Address</TH><TH>City</TH>"
          strHTML = strHTML & "<TH>State</TH><TH>Zip</TH><TH>Phone</TH></TR>"
          'Are there any records to place in the table?
          If alNumRecs > 0 Then
              'Loop through each of the records
              With adbrsWebRS
                  Do While Not .EOF
                      'Place the contact id into the table as a link,
                      'so that the user can select the contact record
                      'they want to edit.
                      strHTML = strHTML & "<TR><TD><A HREF=" & Chr(34)
                      strHTML = strHTML & OLEISAPI_PATH & "GetContact?ContactID="
                      strHTML = strHTML & .rdoColumns!ContactID & Chr(34)
                      strHTML = strHTML & ">" & .rdoColumns!FirstName & " " _
                                        & .rdoColumns!LastName & "</A>"
                      strHTML = strHTML & "</TD><TD>" & .rdoColumns!Address
                      strHTML = strHTML & "</TD><TD>" & .rdoColumns!City
                      strHTML = strHTML & "</TD><TD>" & .rdoColumns!State
                      'We need to format the Zip Code before sending it
                      'to the user. Before formatting, we need to right
                      'pad the zip code to bring it to 9 characters in
                      'length.
                      strZipCode = .rdoColumns!ZipCode
                      If Len(strZipCode) < 9 Then
                          strZipCode = strZipCode & String((9 - _
                                              Len(strZipCode)), " ")
                      End If
                      strHTML = strHTML & "</TD><TD>" & Format(strZipCode, _
                                              "&&&&&-&&&&")
                      'We need to format the Phone before sending it to
                      'the user. Before formatting, we need to left pad
                      'the phone to bring it to 10 characters in length.
                      strPhone = .rdoColumns!Phone
                      If Len(strPhone) < 10 Then
                          strPhone = String((10 - Len(strPhone)), " ") & strPhone
                      End If
                      strHTML = strHTML & "</TD><TD>" & Format(!Phone, _
                                              "(&&&) &&&-&&&&")
                      strHTML = strHTML & "</TD></TR>"
                      'Loop to the next record
                      .MoveNext
                  Loop
              End With
          End If
          'Close the HTML table and document
          strHTML = strHTML & "</TABLE></BODY></HTML>"
          'Set the result code
          aReq.ResponseStatus = "200 OK"
          'Set the content-type header line
          aReq.ResponseType = "text/html"
          'Return the HTML document to the calling routine
          aReq.WriteResponse strHTML
      End Sub
```

Part
VII

Ch

23

# Building a List of Contacts

If you look back at the list of functionality to provide in this application, the very first entry in the list is the ability to provide the user with a list of every contact record in the database. This is provided through the ListContacts method that is called from the anchor on the HTML document that you built as your starting point for the application. Your ListContacts method is fairly straightforward:

■ It opens the Contact table as a record set.

■ It checks to see how many records are in the set.

■ If there are no records in the record set, it calls the BuildEmptyForm function.

■ If there is one record in the record set, it calls the BuildSingleForm function, providing the user with the only records that were found in an HTML form so that it can be edited.

■ If there is more than one record in the record set (which is the most likely of these three), it calls the BuildMultipleForm function, providing the user with a list of contact records to choose from.

■ It returns the resulting HTML document to the client.

The ListContacts method is shown in Listing 23.9, and the resulting HTML document is shown in Figure 23.12.

> **Listing 23.9   ISAPIDB1.CLS   The Method that Returns All of the Contacts in the Database for the User to Choose One for Editing**

```
Public Sub ListContacts(aReq As Request)
    Dim dbrsWebRS As rdoResultset
    Dim lNumRecs As Long
    Dim strHTML As String
    Dim strSQL As String

    'Set up the error handling on the SQL statement
    On Error GoTo errorHTML
    strSQL = "Select * from Contact"
    'Open the record set using the SQL statement built earlier
    Set dbrsWebRS = dbWebDB.OpenResultset(strSQL, rdOpenStatic)
    'Determine how many records were retrieved
    If Not dbrsWebRS.EOF Then
        With dbrsWebRS
            .MoveLast
            lNumRecs =.RowCount
            .MoveFirst
        End With
    Else
        lNumRecs = 0
    End If
    'Was only one record retrieved?
    If lNumRecs = 1 Then
        'Build the single record edit HTML form
        BuildSingleForm aReq, dbrsWebRS
```

```
        Else
            'Were any records returned?
            If lNumRecs = 0 Then
                'Build the "No Records Returned" HTML document
                BuildEmptyForm aReq
            Else
                'There were multiple records returned, build
                'the multiple record HTML document for the
                'user to select the record to be edited
                BuildMultipleForm aReq, dbrsWebRS, lNumRecs
            End If
        End If
        'Close the ResultSet
        dbrsWebRS.Close
        'Exit the method before getting into the error handling
        'section
        Exit Sub
    errorHTML:
        'Call the Error HTML building routine, returning the HTML
        'form to the client
        BuildErrorForm aReq, "Contacts", _
            "Errors occurred while attempting to select the contact records."
    End Sub
```

**FIG. 23.12**

The listing of all contact records that was returned to the user. Notice that the name column has been formatted as links so that the user can select one and be returned that record in an HTML form ready to be edited.

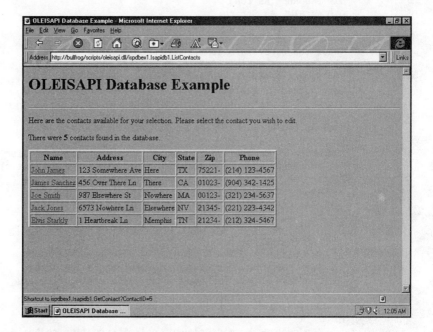

## Getting the Contact Requested by the User

When a contact record is selected from the list provided in the multiple record table, the ContactID for that record is submitted to the GetContact method. This method takes that

ContactID and builds a SQL select statement to retrieve the record that it identifies from the database. This method works basically the same as the ListContacts method, with the following two exceptions:

■ This method builds a SQL statement using a WHERE clause to be used in retrieving a specific record from the database, where the ListContacts selected the entire table.

■ This method can only call the BuildEmptyForm and BuildSingleForm functions, as there should be no circumstances in which this function should retrieve more than one record from the database.

These differences are shown in Listing 23.10, with the resulting record in an editable HTML form shown in Figure 23.13.

---

**Listing 23.10   ISAPIDB1.CLS   The Method Used to Retrieve a Specific Contact Record for Editing**

```
Public Sub GetContact(aReq As Request)
    Dim pcParams As New Parameters
    Dim dbrsWebRS As rdoResultset
    Dim iNumParams As Integer
    Dim lNumRecs As Long
    Dim strHTML As String
    Dim strSQL As String

    'Pass the parameters sent from the HTML form
    'to the local instance of the Parameters class
    iNumParams = RetrieveParameters(aReq, pcParams)
    'Build the SQL statement to retrieve the contact record
    strSQL = "SELECT * from Contact where ContactID = " _
                      & pcParams.GetKeyValue("ContactID")
    'Set up the error handling on the SQL statement
    On Error GoTo errorHTML
    'Open the record set using the SQL statement built earlier
    Set dbrsWebRS = dbWebDB.OpenResultset(strSQL, rdOpenStatic)
    'Determine how many records were retrieved
    If Not dbrsWebRS.EOF Then
        With dbrsWebRS
            .MoveLast
            lNumRecs = .RowCount
            .MoveFirst
        End With
        'We should have received only one record (or none)
        'so we can call the routine to build a single record
        'form at this point
        BuildSingleForm aReq, dbrsWebRS
    Else
        'No records were retrieved, call the routine to build
        'the "No records returned" HTML form
        lNumRecs = 0
        BuildEmptyForm aReq
    End If
    'Close the ResultSet
```

```
        dbrsWebRS.Close
        'Exit the method before getting into the error handling
        'section
        Exit Sub
    errorHTML:
        'Call the Error HTML building routine, returning the HTML
        'form to the client
        BuildErrorForm aReq, strSQL, _
            "Errors occurred while attempting to select the contact record."
    End Sub
```

**FIG. 23.13**

The contact record that was selected in the list is returned to the user in an HTML form for editing.

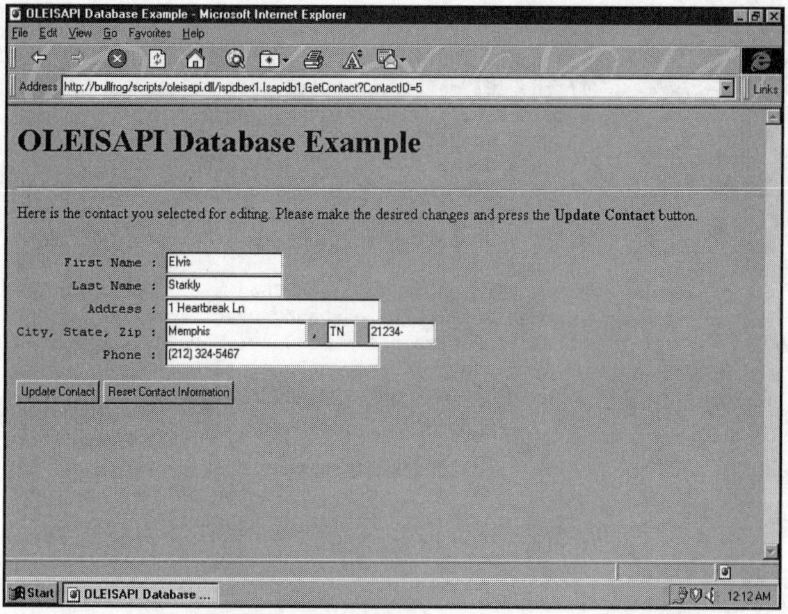

## Getting and Processing the Form Data

You might remember from Chapter 20 that there is a small amount of processing required by the OLEISAPI2 interface to extract the query string from the Request object. This is mainly because you have to look in two different places for the query string, depending on whether the GET or POST methods were used by the HTML form to submit the data.

This is a significant amount of code to repeat in every one of your exposed methods that can expect to receive any data to be submitted by the user. Instead, you can decide to encapsulate all of this processing in a single function, called RetrieveParameters. This function determines which method was used and retrieves the resulting query string. It then passes the query string to the Parameters class that was passed to it as a parameter and returns to the calling routine the number of fields that were extracted from the query string. This function is shown in Listing 23.11, and you can see how it is called on the first line of code in Listing 23.10.

**Listing 23.11  ISAPIDB1.CLS  The *RetrieveParameters* Function, Which Extracts the Query String from the Request Object and Passes It to the Parameters Class**

```
Private Function RetrieveParameters(aReq As Request, _
                            pcParams As Parameters) As Integer
    Dim strMethod As String
    Dim strReqParameters As String
    Dim vParams As Variant
    Dim iAmtRead As Integer

    'What method was used?
    strMethod = aReq.Method
    If strMethod = "GET" Then
        'If the GET method was used, all of our variables
        'should be in the QueryString property of the
        'Request object
        strReqParameters = aReq.QueryString
    Else
        'If the POST method was used, we have to retrieve
        'all of our parameters, and then convert them to
        'strings
        If Not aReq.UploadComplete Then
            aReq.GetFirstUploadChunk vParams
            strReqParameters = StrConv(vParams, vbUnicode)
            iAmtRead = Len(strReqParameters)
            Do While Not aReq.UploadComplete
                aReq.GetNextUploadChunk (aReq.TotalUploadLength - _
                                            iAmtRead), vParams
                strReqParameters = strReqParameters _
                                & StrConv(vParams, vbUnicode)
                iAmtRead = Len(strReqParameters)
            Loop
        End If
    End If
    'Pass the parameters sent from the HTML form
    'to the local instance of the Parameters class
    RetrieveParameters = pcParams.ParseParameters(strReqParameters)
End Function
```

# Placing the User's Edits into the Database

After the user has made his changes to the record and clicked the submit button, the UpdateContact method is called to save those changes in the database. This method does the following things:

- Creates a Parameter class instance and hands it the string of variables

- Builds a SQL UPDATE statement, pulling each of the variables from the Parameters object as it is needed

- Unformats the phone number and ZIP code variables before they are added to the SQL statement

- Executes the SQL statement

- If an error occurs, returns the standard error message HTML document to the user

- If no errors occur, returns a simple HTML document to the user, informing the user that changes that the user submitted have been saved in the database

The UpdateContact method is shown in Listing 23.12.

**Listing 23.12   ISAPIDB1.CLS   The Method Used to Submit Changes to a Contact Record for Updating in the Database**

```
Public Sub UpdateContact(aReq As Request)
    Dim pcParams As New Parameters
    Dim dbrsWebRS As rdoResultset
    Dim iNumParams As Integer
    Dim lNumRecs As Long
    Dim strHTML As String
    Dim strSQL As String

    'Pass the parameters sent from the HTML form
    'to the local instance of the Parameters class
    iNumParams = RetrieveParameters(aReq, pcParams)
    'Build the SQL update statement, extracting the values from the
    'parameter object as they are needed.
    strSQL = "Update Contact"
    strSQL = strSQL & " set FirstName = " & Chr(39) _
                    & pcParams.GetKeyValue("FirstName")
    strSQL = strSQL & Chr(39) & ", LastName = " & Chr(39)
    strSQL = strSQL & pcParams.GetKeyValue("LastName") & Chr(39)
    strSQL = strSQL & ", Address = " & Chr(39) _
                    & pcParams.GetKeyValue("Address")
    strSQL = strSQL & Chr(39) & ", City = " & Chr(39) _
                    & pcParams.GetKeyValue("City")
    strSQL = strSQL & Chr(39) & ", State = " & Chr(39)
    strSQL = strSQL & pcParams.GetKeyValue("State") & Chr(39)
    'The Zip Code and Phone number values need any formatting
    'to be removed before including them in the SQL statement
    strSQL = strSQL & ", ZipCode = " & Chr(39) _
                    & RemoveFormatting(pcParams.GetKeyValue("ZipCode"))
    strSQL = strSQL & Chr(39) & ", Phone = " & Chr(39)
    strSQL = strSQL & RemoveFormatting(pcParams.GetKeyValue("Phone")) _
                    & Chr(39)
    strSQL = strSQL & " where ContactID = " _
                    & pcParams.GetKeyValue("ContactID")
    'Set up the error handling on the SQL statement
    On Error GoTo errorHTML
    'Perform a direct execute of the update statement
    dbWebDB.Execute strSQL, rdExecDirect

    'Build the HTML document telling the user that the update
    'was successful
    strHTML = strHTML & "<HTML><HEAD><TITLE>"
```

Part

VII

Ch

23

*continues*

**Listing 23.12   Continued**

```
        strHTML = strHTML & "OLEISAPI Database Example"
        strHTML = strHTML & "</TITLE></HEAD><BODY BGCOLOR=#C0C0C0>"
        strHTML = strHTML & "<H1>OLEISAPI Database Example</H1><HR><P>"
        strHTML = strHTML & "The changes you submitted have been saved. "
        strHTML = strHTML & "</P></BODY></HTML>"

        'Set the result code
        aReq.ResponseStatus = "200 OK"
        'Set the content-type header line
        aReq.ResponseType = "text/html"
        'Return the HTML document to the calling routine
        aReq.WriteResponse strHTML
        'Exit the method before getting into the error handling
        'section
        Exit Sub
errorHTML:
        'Call the Error HTML building routine, returning the HTML
        'form to the client
        BuildErrorForm aReq, strSQL, _
            "Errors occurred while attempting to update the contact record."
End Sub
```

# Removing the Formatting from Formatted Fields

If you examine the preceding method closely, you see that it made a single function call to remove all of the formatting from the ZIP code and phone number variables. The RemoveFormatting function makes a series of calls to another function called RemoveCharacter, specifying the character to be removed, as shown in Listing 23.13. This allows the RemoveFormatting function to make one call to RemoveCharacter for each of the known formatting characters that might be found in either of these fields.

**Listing 23.13   ISAPIDB1.CLS   The Function Called to Remove All Formatting from Phone Numbers and ZIP Codes Before Saving Them in the Database**

```
Private Function RemoveFormatting(astrOrigStr As String) As String
    Dim strNewStr As String

    'Remove all opening parentheses
    strNewStr = RemoveCharacter(astrOrigStr, "(")
    'Remove all closing parentheses
    strNewStr = RemoveCharacter(strNewStr, ")")
    'Remove all dashes
    strNewStr = RemoveCharacter(strNewStr, "-")
    'Remove all spaces
    strNewStr = RemoveCharacter(strNewStr, " ")
    'Remove all forward slashes
    strNewStr = RemoveCharacter(strNewStr, "/")
    'Remove all backward slashes
```

```
        strNewStr = RemoveCharacter(strNewStr, "\")
        'Return the unformatted string
        RemoveFormatting = strNewStr
    End Function
```

Of these two functions, the RemoveCharacter function is the one that does all of the actual work. As can be seen in Listing 23.14, the RemoveCharacter function scans the string for any occurrences of the specified character. If one is found, it is removed, and the string is rescanned for any additional occurrences of the specified character. This function continues to loop until all occurrences of the specified character have been removed. This function places no other character into the place of the removed character, thus shortening the length of the string by as many occurrences were found.

Part
VII

Ch
23

**Listing 23.14   ISAPIDB1.CLS   The Function Called to Remove All Occurrences of a Specific Character from a String**

```
Private Function RemoveCharacter(astrOrigStr As String, _
                        astrCharToRemove As String) As String
    Dim strNewStr As String
    Dim lCharPos As Long

    'Copy the string into a holding variable
    strNewStr = astrOrigStr
    'Scan the string for the first occurrence of the specified
    'character
    lCharPos = InStr(1, strNewStr, astrCharToRemove, vbTextCompare)
    'Was the character found? If so, loop as long as it continues to
    'be found.
    Do While (lCharPos > 0)
        'Remove the character found from the string
        strNewStr = Left(strNewStr, (lCharPos - 1)) & Mid(strNewStr, _
                                    (lCharPos + 1))
        'Scan for another occurrence of the character in the string
        lCharPos = InStr(1, strNewStr, astrCharToRemove, _
                                        vbTextCompare)
    Loop
    'Return the resulting string to the calling routine
    RemoveCharacter = strNewStr
End Function
```

# Allowing the User to Perform Ad Hoc Queries

The final method specified in the list of functions that your application performs is the ability to do ad hoc queries. If you remember in your original HTML document, you built an HTML form that the user could use to perform searches on the first name, last name, and city. The information entered into this form is sent to the FindContact method, which is shown in Listing 23.15.

The key to making this form work for ad hoc queries is to allow the user to input any partial values into any combination of the fields in the form. When the form is submitted, the FindContact method goes through the data that was submitted and determines which fields had any values filled in. Those values have the wild card character appended to the end of the submitted string, and you build the SQL SELECT statement using the like qualifier. You don't want to include in the WHERE clause any of the values that were not submitted, so you want to use some sort of flag to keep track of whether the WHERE clause has been started, or whether you need to start it with each value that you find. This provides the user with the ability to enter as much or little of the contact name or city as is known, and returns a list of the matching contact records. If the search returns only one record, the user is returned that one record in the editable HTML form. Of course, there is a strong likelihood that the query entered by the user will result in no records being returned from the database, so this method is prepared to return an HTML form informing the user of that inevitability.

> **N O T E**  Because you are using Remote Data Objects instead of Data Access Objects, you have to use the SQL that is native to the database that you are using. Most enterprise and ANSI-standard SQL databases use the percent sign (%) as a wild card character, instead of the (*) character that the Jet engine uses. ∎

### Listing 23.15  ISAPIDB1.CLS    The Method Called to Perform Ad Hoc Queries Against the Contact Table

```
Public Sub FindContact(aReq As Request)
    Dim pcParams As New Parameters
    Dim dbrsWebRS As rdoResultset
    Dim iNumParams As Integer
    Dim lNumRecs As Long
    Dim strHTML As String
    Dim strSQL As String
    Dim strParmValue As String
    Dim bWhereStarted As Boolean: bWhereStarted = False

    'Pass the parameters sent from the HTML form
    'to the local instance of the Parameters class
    iNumParams = RetrieveParameters(aReq, pcParams)
    'Begin building the SQL query with the basic portion
    strSQL = "SELECT * from Contact "
    'Check to see if the FirstName was submitted as part
    'of the query parameters.
    strParmValue = pcParams.GetKeyValue("FirstName")
    If Len(Trim(strParmValue)) > 0 Then
        'We have a WHERE clause criteria, so set the
        'flag that indicates that the WHERE clause
        'has been begun.
        bWhereStarted = True
        strSQL = strSQL & "where FirstName like " & Chr(39)
        strSQL = strSQL & Trim(strParmValue) & "%" & Chr(39)
    End If
    'Check to see if the LastName was submitted as part
    'of the query parameters
```

```
strParmValue = pcParams.GetKeyValue("LastName")
If Len(Trim(strParmValue)) > 0 Then
    'Has the WHERE clause been started?
    If Not bWhereStarted Then
        'No, so start it and set the flag to indicate
        'that the WHERE clause has been started
        strSQL = strSQL & "where"
        bWhereStarted = True
    Else
        'The WHERE clause has been started, so insert
        'an "and" into the clause
        strSQL = strSQL & " and"
    End If
    'Add the last name onto the SQL WHERE clause
    strSQL = strSQL & " LastName like " & Chr(39)
    strSQL = strSQL & Trim(strParmValue) & "%" & Chr(39)
End If
'Check to see if the LastName was submitted as part
'of the query parameters
strParmValue = pcParams.GetKeyValue("City")
If Len(Trim(strParmValue)) > 0 Then
    'Has the WHERE clause been started?
    If Not bWhereStarted Then
        'No, so start it and set the flag to indicate
        'that the WHERE clause has been started
        strSQL = strSQL & "where"
        bWhereStarted = True
    Else
        'The WHERE clause has been started, so insert
        'an "and" into the clause
        strSQL = strSQL & " and"
    End If
    'Add the city onto the SQL WHERE clause
    strSQL = strSQL & " City like " & Chr(39)
    strSQL = strSQL & Trim(strParmValue) & "%" & Chr(39)
End If
'Set up the error handling on the SQL statement
On Error GoTo errorHTML
'Open the record set using the SQL statement built earlier
Set dbrsWebRS = dbWebDB.OpenResultset(strSQL, rdOpenStatic)
'Determine how many records were retrieved
If Not dbrsWebRS.EOF Then
    With dbrsWebRS
        .MoveLast
        lNumRecs = .RowCount
        .MoveFirst
    End With
Else
    lNumRecs = 0
End If
'Was only one record retrieved?
If lNumRecs = 1 Then
    'Build the single record edit HTML form
    BuildSingleForm aReq, dbrsWebRS
Else
    'Were any records returned?
```

Part
VII

Ch
23

*continues*

**Listing 23.15    Continued**

```
            If lNumRecs = 0 Then
                'Build the "No Records Returned" HTML document
                BuildEmptyForm aReq
            Else
                'There were multiple records returned, build
                'the multiple record HTML document for the
                'user to select the record to be edited
                BuildMultipleForm aReq, dbrsWebRS, lNumRecs
            End If
        End If
        'Close the ResultSet
        dbrsWebRS.Close
        'Exit the method before getting into the error handling
        'section
        Exit Sub
errorHTML:
        'Call the Error HTML building routine, returning the HTML
        'form to the client
        BuildErrorForm aReq, strSQL, _
            "Errors occurred while attempting to select the contact records."
End Sub
```

# Adding a State Look-Up

You now have a basic contact database application running on your Web site. But what if you want to use some look-up tables to provide for some of the code fields in your data? In this example, you only have one code field: your state field. Because there are a limited number of states and each has a specific two character official abbreviation, it makes sense to build a SELECT element for your users to select the appropriate state from. This allows you to provide users with the full name of the state, instead of them having to know what the various abbreviations stand for.

Because your HTML form that you are building for editing your contact records is currently only for editing existing records, you need to be able to specify which state record is selected when the form is first displayed. You can do this with the SELECTED attribute for the OPTION element. So, by passing in the appropriate state code to be initially selected, you can build your state select element with the function shown in Listing 23.16.

**Listing 23.16    ISAPIDB2.CLS    The *BuildStateSelect* Function, Which Builds an HTML *Select* Element, Populated from the States Table in the Database**

```
Private Function BuildStateSelect(astrStateCode As String) As String
    Dim dbrsWebRS As rdoResultset
    Dim lNumRecs As Long
    Dim strHTML As String
    Dim strSQL As String
    Dim strCurCode As String
    strSQL = "Select StateCode, StateDesc from States order by StateDesc"
    'Open the record set using the SQL statement built earlier
```

```
Set dbrsWebRS = dbWebDB.OpenResultset(strSQL, rdOpenStatic)
'Determine how many records were retrieved
If Not dbrsWebRS.EOF Then
    With dbrsWebRS
        .MoveLast
        lNumRecs = .RowCount
        .MoveFirst
    End With
Else
    lNumRecs = 0
End If
'Was only one record retrieved?
If lNumRecs = 1 Then
    'Build a TEXT edit with the state code
    strHTML = "<INPUT TYPE=" & Chr(34) & "TEXT" & Chr(34)
    strHTML = strHTML & " NAME=" & Chr(34) & "State" & Chr(34) _
                & " VALUE=" & Chr(34)
    strHTML = strHTML & astrStateCode & Chr(34) & " SIZE=2 " _
                & "MAXLENGTH=2> "
Else
    'Were any records returned?
    If lNumRecs = 0 Then
        'Build an empty TEXT edit field
        strHTML = "<INPUT TYPE=" & Chr(34) & "TEXT" & Chr(34)
        strHTML = strHTML & " NAME=" & Chr(34) & "State" & Chr(34) _
                    & " VALUE=" & Chr(34)
        strHTML = strHTML & Chr(34) & " SIZE=2 MAXLENGTH=2> "
    Else
        'Build a drop-down select element for selecting the
        'appropriate state
        strHTML = "<SELECT NAME=" & Chr(34) & "State" & Chr(34) & ">"
        With dbrsWebRS
            'Loop until all records have been included
            Do While Not .EOF
                'Grab the state code for our comparisons
                strCurCode = .rdoColumns!StateCode
                'Build the first part of the Option element
                strHTML = strHTML & "<OPTION VALUE=" & Chr(34) _
                            & strCurCode & Chr(34)
                'Does the current record match the State code
                'on the Contact record?
                If strCurCode = astrStateCode Then
                    'If so, then designate that it should be selected
                    strHTML = strHTML & " SELECTED"
                End If
                'Display the state name for the user to select by
                strHTML = strHTML & ">" & .rdoColumns!StateDesc _
                            & "</OPTION>"
                'Loop to the next record
                .MoveNext
            Loop
        End With
        'Close the select element
        strHTML = strHTML & "</SELECT>"
    End If
```

*continues*

**Listing 23.16 Continued**

```
      End If
      'Close the ResultSet
      dbrsWebRS.Close
      'Return the state element to be included in the form.
      BuildStateSelect = strHTML
   End Function
```

Obviously, if there are no records in the state table you cannot build a selection element, so you are providing the user with the same text element that you were originally using. Otherwise, this should build a selection element that you can include in the HTML form that you are building in your `BuildSingleForm` subroutine. You replace the original building of the state text element, which looked like this:

```
strHTML = strHTML & "<INPUT TYPE=" & Chr(34) & "TEXT" & Chr(34)
      strHTML = strHTML & " NAME=" & Chr(34) & "State" & Chr(34) _
                          & " VALUE=" & Chr(34)
      strHTML = strHTML & .rdoColumns!State & Chr(34) & " SIZE=2 " _
                          & "MAXLENGTH=2> "
```

with the following function call

```
strHTML = strHTML & BuildStateSelect(.rdoColumns!State)
```

Now you have a drop-down selection element for use by your application users. This is shown in Figure 23.14.

**FIG. 23.14**
Your new Contact edit HTML form is returned with a drop-down select element for the state field.

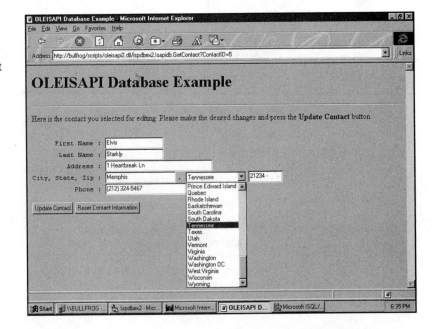

# From Here...

In this chapter, you have looked at how threaded applications work to perform multiple tasks at one time. You also looked at the various mechanisms used by these applications to control access to shared resources and synchronize execution of the threads. You then turned to threaded behavior in Visual Basic 5 and how that affects your programming decisions. Finally, you learned how all of this threaded functionality affects your OLEISAPI application and the considerations that you have to take into account, perhaps not at this point in time, but possibly in future versions of the OLEISAPI interface.

You then turned your attention to adding database functionality into your OLEISAPI applications, building a simple contact management database application that can be used over the Web. From here, you might want to enhance your application by building in the ability to add new contact records into and delete old records from the database. You might want to integrate this with the VBScripting and ActiveX controls, which you looked at in earlier chapters, to add the capabilities of dialing the phone to call the contact (assuming that the user's machine has both a network card and a modem attached). Maybe you could have the application populate a Word document with the information from the database, using VBScript to treat Word as an ActiveX server that can be manipulated within the IE 3 browser, just like any other ActiveX control. There are many directions in which you can take this example application and a number of technologies with which it could be integrated.

You might also want to check out the following other subjects:

- To learn about server-side scripting and how it can be used to overcome some of the limitations of OLEISAPI2 programming, see Chapter 13, "Active Server Pages and Server-Side Scripting."

- To learn how the OLEISAPI2 interface works and what functionality it provides for the Visual Basic programmer, check out Chapter 20, "The OLEISAPI2 Interface and the Active Reference Object."

- To see other new technologies for building database applications for the Web, check out Chapter 27, "Building Web Database Applications Using Visual InterDev."

- To learn about building distributed Web applications using Microsoft's Transaction Server, read Chapter 28, "Microsoft Transaction Server and Visual Basic."

# CHAPTER 24

# The Internet Database Connector: Providing Database Access on the Web

■ **Learn about database access from your Internet server**

See how to add database access to your site and create dynamic pages that can use SQL-formatted queries to update or retrieve database information.

■ **Learn about the Internet Database Connector**

Microsoft's IDC is a powerful tool to use in adding the new capabilities to your system and at the same time, it provides a secure environment in which your pages can be run.

**C**orporate database systems are built on making information widely available to qualified users. The information in these situations comes from many sources, ranging from discussion groups to proprietary systems. Probably the biggest repository of mass information is the database. If you've ever just browsed a database, without specifying meaningful criteria, you know what *mass* information means: There is often so much information represented that it makes the information less useful.

By making databases available on your Web server, you can help users make sense of this information and, at the same time, you'll be able to control access and presentation without the need for any special software to begin using the database effectively. In short, you have a new avenue to provide this access to the information that is probably already stored on your network. ■

**N O T E** This chapter focuses largely on the capabilities included with Microsoft's Internet Information Server. With IIS you can access any ODBC database for which you have a 32-bit ODBC driver, making the interface one of the most open on the market today. You can access everything from an Access database to a remote SQL Server from your Web pages. ▇

Database access with the Microsoft Internet Information Server is provided by giving you ODBC connectivity to the HTML pages that execute on the server when the user makes a request of the system. In this chapter, you'll see how to set up pages, what types of information you can provide, and how you can enhance the presentation of the information to make it the most meaningful to the people that request it.

> **CAUTION**
>
> Be aware that the database connector files are likely to contain and convey sensitive, and sometimes very confidential, information. For example, they may contain query information that calls out column names, table names, and database sources that map to your ODBC configurations on the server.
>
> In addition, when users click a link to a database connector file, they'll be able to see where you're keeping your scripts and other programs, as this information will show up in the URL that is displayed to them.
>
> It is extremely important that your programs, scripts, and supporting files reside in the scripts subdirectory structure and that you provide Execute-only privileges on that directory. Be sure you do not provide Read privileges. This opens your system to unneeded possibilities for trouble as people can browse and review the applications that are the core of your system.

# Introducing the Internet Database Connector

The Internet Information Server (IIS) provides access to the ODBC layer with the use of the Internet Database Connector (IDC). The IDC acts as a go-between for your system, providing the interaction between what is seen in the browser in terms of HTML, and how the information is queried at the database level. The overall access layer map is shown in Figure 24.1.

When users specify the IDC file in the URL from the browser, they are instructing the IIS system to use the IDC file and its statements to query the database and return the results. The IDC is specified in the URL, but the HTX file, or HTML Extension file, is what is actually returned to the user. The HTX file, still a standard HTML file, indicates how the resulting data is displayed, what lines constitute the detail lines of information, and more.

From Figure 24.1, you can see that the engine doing the database work with ODBC is HTTPODBC.DLL. This DLL, included when you install the IIS system, is an Internet Server

API (ISAPI) application that runs as an extension to the server software. This extension is database-aware and is able to use the two source files required to give the information back to the user.

**FIG 24.1**
The IDC provides for access to any ODBC data source.

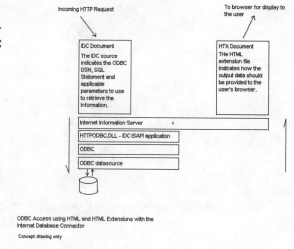

Incoming HTTP Request

To browser for display to the user

IDC Document
The IDC source indicates the ODBC DSN, SQL Statement and applicable parameters to use to retrieve the information.

HTX Document
THe HTML extension file indicates how the output data should be provided to the user's browser.

Internet Information Server

HTTPODBC.DLL - IDC ISAPI application

ODBC

ODBC datasource

ODBC Access using HTML and HTML Extensions with the Internet Database Connector

Concept drawing only

**TIP** If you did not install the ODBC component of IIS, you'll need to do so to use the IDC. This not only installs the ODBC portions of the environment, but it also configures the server to be aware of the IDC files you'll be using. If you do not install the ODBC components, when users click the IDC link on their Web page, they'll see a prompt to download the IDC file, rather than view the results of the query. See Figure 24.2 for an example of this prompt.

**FIG. 24.2**
If the server does not recognize the database connector, it will try to download the IDC page to the requesting user, rather than processing it and returning the results.

Unhandled File Type

Choose How to Handler

application/octet-stream - 146 bytes

Save As... | Configure Helper | Cancel

When you install IIS, the ODBC option must be selected. Although it may not indicate disk space requirements if you have already installed ODBC from other applications, it is still necessary to install ODBC to activate the IDC capabilities (see Figure 24.3).

Part
VII

Ch
24

**FIG. 24.3**

It's a good rule of thumb to select ODBC for all installations.

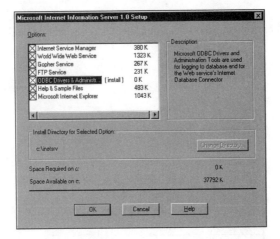

Listing 24.1 shows a sample IDC file, taken from the samples included with the server. The sample installs into the \SCRIPTS\SAMPLES folder on your system in the IIS directory structure.

---

**Listing 24.1   A Simple IDC Source File**

```
Data source: web sql
Username: sa
Template: sample.htx
SQLStatement:
+SELECT au_lname, ytd_sales from pubs.dbo.titleview
➥ where ytd_sales>5000
```

---

When this file is loaded by IIS, IIS examines the extension and determines what application should be used for the source file. For certain items, including the IDC extension, the server comes pre-installed, knowing what to do with the source when it's requested. One of the powerful capabilities and features of IIS is that it is able to use the same Windows-based extension resolution to determine what to do with a given request. Files with a GIF extension, for example, are known to be graphic images, and files with an IDC extension are database connector applets. You set up custom keys in the Registry. Associations are set up in the following subkey:

```
HKEY_LOCAL_MACHINE
        SYSTEM
                CurrentControlSet
                        Services
                                W3SVC
                                        Parameters
                                                ScriptMap
```

If you add a new entry, make it of the type REG_SZ and indicate the extension to associate with it. You need to include the period before the extension, such as .IDC, to correctly map the association. For the value, indicate the path and file name that executes when the specified extension is loaded. Remember: provide the path from the root and start the path with a backslash as this ensures, regardless of the current working directory, that IIS can locate the application.

If you are indicating parameters to the call, you can use a `%s` on the key value where you indicate the application to run. For example, suppose you have a DLL that you want to run any time a request is received to open a file with a .FUN extension. Your entry would be as follows:

```
.fun = c:\inetsrv\scripts\test\fundll.dll %s %s
```

When you use this option, the first time you use the `%s`, you receive the application to run that is passed to the URL. For example, if the FUNDLL is an application that processes a text file and searches it for a given value, you would expect the user to be passing in the name of the text file and the value to search for within it. When you provide the URL at the browser level, you first indicate the location of the file you want to run. A question mark is added by the browser, followed by any applicable parameters to the call.

For the examples here, the URL that is used is similar to the following:

```
http://holodeck3/scripts/search.fun?text+to+find
```

The resulting command line is the following:

```
c:\inetsrv\scripts\test\fundll.dll search.fun text+to+find
```

In the preceding line, each of the two items specified (the source file and search text) are passed as parameters.

**N O T E**  Since parameters are passed as a single string to your application, as in the preceding example with the `text+to+find` string, your application must be able to parse out the plus signs and rebuild the string, most likely in a buffer that can be used by your application to search the database or text file, as needed. ∎

The results-formatting file, or HTX file, is where things can get a little tricky. As you'll see throughout this chapter, the real power and capability of your system is exposed with the HTX file. Until the information is provided to the template, it's of no use to the requester as he will have not yet seen the information. You can have one of the best, most comprehensive databases around, but, if the presentation of the data is not what your audience needs, the information might as well be under lock and key.

Listing 24.2 shows a simple HTX template, provided in the samples with the IIS product, which displays the results of a query.

**Listing 24.2   HTX Source Files Provide Template Information for the Display of Results from Database Queries**

```
<HTML>
<HEAD><TITLE>Authors and YTD Sales</TITLE></HEAD>
<BODY BACKGROUND="/samples/images/backgrnd.gif">
<BODY BGCOLOR="FFFFFF">
<TABLE>
<TR>
<TD><IMG SRC="/samples/images/SPACE.gif" ALIGN="top" ALT=" "></TD>
<TD><A HREF="/samples/IMAGES/db_mh.map"><IMG SRC=
‡ "/SAMPLES/images/db_mh.gif" ismap BORDER=0 ALIGN="top" ALT=" ">
</A></TD>
</TR>
<tr>
<TD></TD>
<TD>
<hr>
<font size=2>
<CENTER>
<%if idc.sales eq ""%>
<H2>Authors with sales greater than <I>5000</I></H2>
<%else%>
<H2>Authors with sales greater than <I><%idc.sales%></I></H2>
<%endif%>
<P>
<TABLE BORDER>
<%begindetail%>
<%if CurrentRecord EQ 0 %>
<caption>Query results:</caption>
<TR>
<TH><B>Author</B></TH><TH><B>YTD Sales<BR>(in dollars)</B></TH>
</TR>
<%endif%>
<TR><TD><%au_lname%></TD><TD align="right">$<%ytd_sales%></TD></TR>
<%enddetail%>
<P>
</TABLE>
</center>
<P>
<%if CurrentRecord EQ 0 %>
<I><B>Sorry, no authors had YTD sales greater than </I>
‡ <%idc.sales%>.</B>
<P>
<%else%>
<HR>
<I>
The web page you see here was created by merging the results
of the SQL query with the template file SAMPLE.HTX.
<P>
The merge was done by the Microsoft Internet Database Connector and
➡the results were returned to this web browser by the Microsoft
➡Internet Information Server.
</I>
<%endif%>
```

```
</font>
</td>
</tr>
</table>
</BODY>
</HTML>
```

Right away, you will probably notice several different things with this file. First, it's a standard HTML document. There is no strange formatting, and many of the tags will be familiar if you have developed HTML before. Some of the real fun begins with the new capabilities offered by the HTX file. These new functions, above and beyond standard HTML, allow you to have the resulting Web page change depending on the information that is, or is not, returned from the query. For example, in the following section, you see the introduction of conditional testing examining for an empty set:

```
<%if idc.sales eq ""%>
      <H2>Authors with sales greater than <I>5000</I></H2>
<%else%>
      <H2>Authors with sales greater than <I><%idc.sales%></I></H2>
<%endif%>
```

There are several operators that are available when you design your pages. Throughout this chapter, you will learn more about how to use these new database-oriented features.

As mentioned earlier, the IDC source file indicates the ODBC data source that is used to access the database on your system. From the IDC file listing, you notice the "Data source" item. This item indicates that the "web sql" data source will be used. Before this sample will work on your system, you must have installed and configured the data source for that name.

In the next couple of sections, you'll learn how to set up the ODBC data sources for both SQL Server and Microsoft Access. You can use any 32-bit ODBC data source with your IIS application. Changes between setting up other data sources should be minimal, so you'll find that the IDC can work with nearly any database installation you may need to use.

# Building ODBC Data Sources for SQL Server Databases

One common problem with the database connector is improper set-up of the ODBC data source. This problem is not unique to the SQL Server; the problem exists across database sources. Therefore, it is very important to understand how to set up the driver for access by IIS.

You may recall that IIS is running as a service. This means that, while it's running, it's not logged in as you, the administrator. It is instead running in the background and logging in when needed. When it does, it is as either the anonymous user you've set up, or as the validated user that's been authenticated by the NT security subsystem. Since you want to give this service access to a database, and since you don't know whom the service will be logging in as, you need to set up the database source a bit differently than you may be accustomed to.

In recent releases of ODBC, Microsoft added a new option to the ODBC configurations. The System DSN (Data Source Name) is a way to set up a globally available data source. Since users that log on may be set up to have different access to your system and resources, you need to use the System DSN to make sure they have access to the right databases, regardless of where they log on, or who they log on as. Figure 24.4 shows the ODBC setup dialog box, started from the Control Panel.

 If you receive errors while trying to access an ODBC data source from your Web pages, one of the first things you should check is that the data source you are referencing is set up as a system data source. If, when you start the ODBC manager utility, the data source is listed in the initial dialog box, it's defined as a user-based data source, not a system DSN. Remove the user-based DSN and redefine it as a System DSN and you'll be able to see the database.

Remember, the only data sources that the Database Connector can use are the System-level data sources.

**FIG. 24.4**
ODBC setup for IIS requires that you select the System DSN to configure the driver.

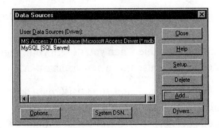

Once you select System DSN, you can use essentially the same options to set up the drivers. Note, too, that you can have more than one driver set up at the system level. This allows you to set up drivers for the different applications that you'll be running on the Web. Figure 24.5 shows the System Data Sources dialog box.

**FIG. 24.5**
You'll need to indicate the driver, database, and other information required to connect to your database engine.

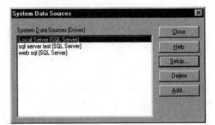

The Data Source Name you provide is what you'll be using in the IDC file as the data source, so be sure to make note of the database configuration names you set up.

**N O T E** In most cases, you'll want the configuration to be as specific as possible. If it's possible to indicate a default database or table (or both), be sure to do so. It takes some of the variables out of the Web page design that you create. By specifying as much information as possible, you help make sure that the information is accessible. Of course, this serves the dual role of providing some basic controls over what the end-users see when they visit your pages. Users are less likely to be wandering around your databases if they navigate to a default database, rather than the driver or IDC file indicating the table name. ■

# Building ODBC Database Sources for Microsoft Access Databases

Microsoft Access database data sources are established the same way as they are for SQL Server. You must set up each data source as a System DSN, making it available to the IDC as it logs into NT's security subsystem.

Of course, there are likely to be changes in the SQL Statement options you indicate in the IDC file. These differences relate to how Access interprets the SQL language elements. By and large, however, the statements should be nearly identical, especially in those cases where you issue SQL statements that are basically SELECT statements, rather than calling stored procedures.

When you create the DSN, you are prompted to select the database with which ODBC should connect. Be sure to provide this information because, even though you can indicate it in code, you can make the connection to the database far more bullet-proof with this option turned on. The system won't have to guess where to go to get the information.

# User Rights and Security Concerns

Using the IDC for database access is a wide open door to your database system. You should avoid allowing users system administrator level access to your databases because this provides a means for anyone to have administrative access to your system. Instead, consider using either of the following two options.

The first option, if you allow anonymous connections to your site, is to be sure the user you indicate as the anonymous user (usually IUS_<machine name>) has appropriate rights to the databases he or she needs.

The login process works by first validating the user who is using the anonymous login, if it is enabled. If enabled, and the user indicated as the anonymous user does not have sufficient rights, an error message is received by the user, indicating he or she may not have rights to the object(s) requested. If anonymous login is disabled, the IDC uses the current user's name and password to logon to the database. If this fails to gain access, the request is denied and the user is prevented from accessing the database requested.

In short, if you want anonymous users gaining access to your system, you need to create the user account that you want to access the information. Next, assign the user to the database and objects, allowing access to the systems needed.

The second option is to use NT's integrated security with SQL Server. Using this method, the currently logged-in user will be logged on to SQL Server and the same rights will be in force.

# Building Dynamic Web Pages

Once you have the database connection set up, you're ready to populate the database. One of the most popular ways of doing this is to create dynamic Web pages, those which build themselves on-the-fly to provide up-to-date information, are going to quickly become the mainstay of intranets and the Internet. This will occur because, with a dynamic Web page, you can always count on getting the latest and greatest information. With the IDC, you can create these dynamic Web pages and have them work against a database to retrieve the information you want to permit the user to review.

There are three components to this type of page:

- The initial source HTML document often containing form fields or other options
- The IDC file for making and carrying out the database commands and data acquisition
- The HTX file for presenting the information returned

**N O T E**  While it's not the intent of this book to teach all aspects of HTML, it's important to remember that the examples provided are just that—samples. You'll need to take these samples and adapt them to your organization's way of doing business on its intranet. In short, the HTML that may be required are the field, listbox, and check box options provided by HTML. Using these options, and the ODBC connectivity, you can allow the user to search the possibilities for making a meaningful interface for the user. ▪

When you create a form to prompt the user for information, you create fields and other controls much like you do when creating an application. You name the fields, and then pass the name and its value to the IDC to be used in your database query, if you desire. In the next sections, you will learn how to create these files and learn what makes them drive the output pages with the information from the database.

## Building Initial Forms to Prompt For Values

Generally speaking, you start the process of working with a database by presenting the users with a form that allows them to select the information they need. As is often the case, you have the ability to create forms that allow input that can be used to form the SQL Statements to be passed to the data source. In the cases where you're creating a form, there are two basic HTML tags that you use. These are the INPUT and FORM tags and they enable you to designate actions to take and information to accept on behalf of the user. Listing 24.3 shows a simple form that prompts for an author name to be searched for in the author's table.

### Listing 24.3   Simple HTML Form to Initiate a Database Query–(queform.htm)

```
<HTML>
<HEAD>
<TITLE>
Que Publishing's Very Simple Demonstration Form
</TITLE>
</HEAD>
<h1>Sample Form for Database Access</h1>
<FORM METHOD="POST" ACTION="/scripts/que/QueForm1.idc">
Enter Name to Find in the Pubs Database: <INPUT NAME="au_lname">
<p>
<INPUT TYPE="SUBMIT" VALUE="Run Query">
</FORM>
</BODY>
</HTML>
```

The key elements are the "POST" instructions and the text box presented to the user. The FORM tag indicates what should happen when the form is executed. In this case, the form sends information to the server, hence the POST method. The program or procedure that is run on the server, to work with the information sent in, is called out by the ACTION tag. In the example, the QUEFORM1.IDC is called and passed the parameters.

> **N O T E**   The letter case is not significant when you specify HTML tags. "INPUT" is the same as indicating "input" and does not cause any different results when it's processed by IIS. ■

It's not immediately apparent what the form parameters might be, but if you examine the one or more INPUT fields, you can see that they are named. The following syntax is the basic element required if you need to pass information back to the host in a forms-based environment:

```
<INPUT NAME="<variable name>">
```

The *<variable name>* is the name used to reference the value provided by the user. Much as a variable is defined in Visual Basic by Dimensioning it, you must define and declare the different variables and other controls that are used by your HTML. There are other tags that can be used with the INPUT NAME tag, including VALUE, which allows you to set the initial value of the item you're declaring. For example, the following line declares a new variable, MyName, and assigns an initial value of "Wynkoop" to it:

```
<INPUT NAME="MyName" VALUE="Wynkoop">
```

For the preceding example, the intention is to create a simple form that allows the user to type in a name, or portion of the name, that can be used to search the Authors table in the Pubs database. When the HTML is loaded, as shown previously, the result is that shown in Figure 24.6.

**FIG. 24.6**
Allowing the user to indicate values to pass to the database engine adds polished, functional benefits to your application.

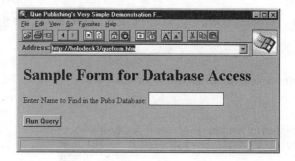

As you can see, the text box size is automatically determined for you as a default. There are Maxlength and Size tags that you can place in the INPUT NAME directive if you need to increase the size of the text box. Also notice that if you press Enter while using this form, the form is automatically submitted to the server, just as if you press the Submit button. Since there is only a single button on this form, the browser interprets this as a type of "there is only one thing for me to do, so I'll just do it automatically" situation.

The result of Listing 24.3 is that the browser opens a new URL on the server with the specification:

**http://holodeck3/scripts/que/QueForm1.idc?au_lname=<name>**

N O T E  You'll notice that the URL shown indicates a single computer name rather than an Internet domain name. This reflects the fact that it's running in an intranet environment. If you are running on the Internet for this access, the HOLODECK3 entry is replaced with the server you're accessing. ■

N O T E  If you watch your Web browser, it may only indicate that it's loading the URL that is included up to the "?" in these examples. The protocol is still passing the parameters to the host; they are simply not shown during the transfer by some browsers. ■

The <name> is the name you indicate in the text box prior to pressing Enter, or clicking the submit button. The next step is to run the query against the database engine and see what results are returned.

## Building Server Query Source Files

The query source files reside in files in your SCRIPTS area and have a file name extension of IDC by convention. When the URL is accessed, the server will run the indicated IDC file. As mentioned earlier in this chapter, the IDC file contains the SQL statements and directives necessary to carry out the commands, as needed. For this example, Listing 24.4 shows the source for querying the database.

**CAUTION**

To reiterate the previous Note about security, be sure you place your IDC files in directories that have been set up with Execute, but not Read, privileges. This is important because users can see column names, table names, SQL login names and passwords, and so on, if they can review your source files. This is all information that you want to ensure remains private.

---

**Listing 24.4   The IDC File that Is Called by QUEForm.HTM–(queform1.idc)**

```
Datasource: web sql
Username: sa
Template: queform1.htx
SQLStatement:
+SELECT au_lname, phone, address, city, state, zip
+ from authors
+ where au_lname like '%au_lname%%'
```

Part
VII

Ch
24

The output from this specific file is really nothing. The user never sees this file or output from it directly. This seems a bit strange, but the entire intent of the IDC is to define and perform the query against the data source indicated. Once the information is retrieved, the IDC calls the Template indicated and passes in the results to be returned as a Web page.

**N O T E**   In the example in Listing 24.4, notice that the where clause specifies like and that there is an extra percent sign in the comparison field. This is standard SQL syntax that allows you to search for wildcarded strings. You specify the part you know and the IDC appends an extra % character at the end. Since the percent sign is the wildcard for SQL Server, you can return all items that start with "B" for example.

Though your understanding of SQL need not be extensive, you will find it easier to work with the database if you have access to backup reference materials on SQL. You may want to consider Que's *Special Edition Using SQL Server* as a comprehensive guide to SQL and the management of an SQL Server. ■

Some basics about this source file are important to understand prior to working through it, to explain how it works. First, to reference a variable, you place it between percentages, as is the case with '%au_lname%' in the preceding listing. Note that the single quotes are required as the field is a text-based type.

You can reference variables anywhere in the script. This means, even for the items that are seemingly hard-coded, you can allow the user to specify them and then call them dynamically from the IDC file.

Second, in cases where your line length is shorter than your actual line, you can call out the item you want to work on, begin specifying the values, and continue indicating the expanding values as long as you place the + in the first column of the file. (The plus sign acts as a line-continuation character for these source files.)

The Data source indicated in the IDC relates to the ODBC data source you establish with the ODBC manager in Control Panel. Remember, the data source you use with the IDC must be a system DSN. If it's not, the call to the database will fail.

The Username, and optionally the Password, override any settings you may have established in ODBC, and they override the current user name, as well as it relates to the execution of the query. Other parameters that may be of interest or use in your integration of the IDC file into your installation are shown in Table 24.1.

### Table 24.1　IDC Optional Parameters

| | |
| --- | --- |
| Expires | If you submit a query over and over again, you may find that you're retrieving a cached copy of the information, rather than an updated database query. This can be especially problematic when developing applications, as you'll be continually testing the system, re-submitting queries, and so on. By setting the Expires tag, established in seconds, to a value that represents a timeframe that should pass before the query is retried, you avoid this problem. In other words, how long will it be before the information should be considered "stale" or in need of being refreshed for viewing. |
| MaxRecords | If you are connected over a slower speed connection, there are few things more frustrating than receiving a huge data file, then realizing that you only need certain bits of its information. For example, you may have a need to return only the first 100 rows of a table, as they will provide the most current, meaningful data to your sales effort. By limiting the MaxRecords, you can indicate this in the IDC file, limiting traffic and database interaction with the new option. |

You can call SQL Server's stored procedures from an IDC file if you want to specify it in the SQL Statement portion of the file. To do so, use the following syntax:

```
EXEC MySP_Name Param1[, Param2...]
```

Include the name of your stored procedure in place of MySP_Name.

In the stored procedure, be sure you're returning results sets, even if they represent only a status value indicating success or failure on the operation. Remember, as with other ODBC data sources, the stored procedure is passed to the server and the client awaits the response. If your stored procedure does not return a value to the calling routine, you may give the user the impression that you caused the browser to become frozen.

From here, once you retrieve the values you want to display, you can move on to the Results-set source files. These files do the work of formatting and displaying information to the user, which will be explained next.

## Building Results Source Files

The Results files are where the fun begins when working with the data that comes back from the query. The HTML extension files, with file name extensions of HTX, are referenced in the Template entry in the IDC. These files dictate how the information is presented, what the user sees, whether items that are returned actually represent links to other items, and so on.

Listing 24.5 shows the sample HTX file for the example you've been reviewing throughout this chapter. You can see that it has a few extra, not-yet-standard items that make the display of information from the database possible.

**Listing 24.5   A Sample HTX File–(QueForm1.htx)**

```
<! Section 1>
<HTML>
<HEAD>
<TITLE>Authors Details</TITLE>
</HEAD>
<TABLE>
<tr>
<TD>
<hr>
<P>
<TABLE BORDER>
 <caption>Query results:</caption>
 <TR>
 <TH><B>Author</B></TH>
 <TH><B>Phone</B></TH>
 <TH><B>Address</B></TH>
 <TH><B>City</B></TH>
 <TH><B>State</B></TH>
 <TH><B>Zip</B></TH>
 </TR>

<! Section 2>
<%begindetail%>
 <TR>
 <TH><B><%au_lname%></B></TH>
 <TH><B><%phone%></B></TH>
 <TH><B><%address%></B></TH>
 <TH><B><%city%></B></TH>
 <TH><B><%state%></B></TH>
 <TH><B><%zip%></B></TH>
 </TR>
<%enddetail%>

<! Section 3>
<P>
</TABLE>
<%if CurrentRecord EQ 0%>
  <H2>Sorry, no authors match your search criteria (<%idc.au_lname%>).</H2>
<%else%>
```

*continues*

Part **VII**

Ch **24**

**Listing 24.5    Continued**

```
   <H2>Authors with names like "<I><%idc.au_lname%></I>"</H2>
<%endif%>
</center>
</td>
</tr>
</table>
</BODY>
</HTML>
```

When the URL is accessed, the server runs the indicated IDC file. As mentioned earlier in the "Building Server Query Source Files" section, the IDC file contains the SQL statements and directives necessary to carry out the commands as needed. For this example, Listing 24.4 shows the source for querying the database.

**N O T E**    The lines starting with <! are comments and are not interpreted by the HTML client. ■

In the sample HTML in Listing 24.5, notice the three sections called out. These sections are inserted only to make reading and explaining the HTML a bit easier. They aren't necessary for the functioning of the document.

In Section 1, the entire purpose is to set up the page. You need to establish fonts, set up background images, do any initial formatting, and so on. You also need to start any tables that you want to use. Since you initiate a table, add the rows to it, then turn off the table, tables represent an excellent way to present data that include an unknown number of rows. For example, as in Figure 24.7, though two rows are shown, there could just as easily have been 24. The other advantage of using tables to display your database information is that the table automatically resizes to the user's visible browser area. You don't need to worry about column widths and other formatting issues.

**FIG. 24.7**

If you use tables to display data to the user, you'll be in keeping with an already familiar metaphor for the presentation.

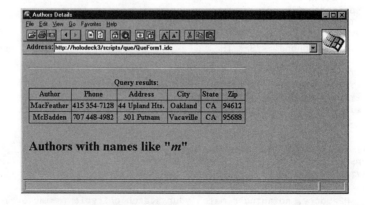

Section 2 is where you work with the detail lines that are returned as part of the data set. Notice this section is bracketed with `<%begindetail%>` and `<%enddetail%>` tags. Everything between these two tags repeats once for every row returned in the data set. In the preceding example, section 2 consists largely of building the table that displays the information that is returned. The following code excerpt provides an example of this loop:

```
<! Section 2>
<%begindetail%>
 <TR>
 <TH><B><%au_lname%></B></TH>
 <TH><B><%phone%></B></TH>
 <TH><B><%address%></B></TH>
 <TH><B><%city%></B></TH>
 <TH><B><%state%></B></TH>
 <TH><B><%zip%></B></TH>
 </TR>
<%enddetail%>
```

When you indicate the data to be included, you refer directly to the column names that are in the table or view that is referenced by the IDC file. Place a `<%` before, and `%>` after each column name. In English, the preceding code snippet is reserving a row to put new data into using the `<TR>` tag, placing the information into the row using the `<TH>` `</TH>` tags, and ending the row using the closing `</TR>` tag.

You can do comparisons in your file as well. For example, if you want to check to make sure that the `state` was returned as `AZ`, you could do so in one of two ways. Obviously, the preferred method is to change your `Where` clause in the IDC to reflect the fact that you want to filter out non-Arizona states.

Alternatively, you could indicate here that you want to test certain values. Consider the following code sample:

```
<! Section 2>
<%begindetail%>
<%if <%state%> eq "AZ"%>
<TR>
<TH><B><%au_lname%></B></TH>
<TH><B><%phone%></B></TH>
<TH><B><%address%></B></TH>
<TH><B><%city%></B></TH>
<TH><B><%state%></B></TH>
<TH><B><%zip%></B></TH>
</TR>
<%endif%>
<%enddetail%>
```

By using the `if` construct, you can test values and conditions in the data set. You can reference variables that come from the IDC file as well. To reference these, simply prepend `idc` to the variable name from the IDC file. So, if you want to reference the incoming variable from the original HTML form, you can do so by a statement similar to the following:

```
<%if <%idc.au_lname%> eq "Wynkoop">
    <TH><B>Building series...</B></TH>
<%endif%>
```

Part
**VII**

Ch
**24**

In this case, the query returns to the IDC and pulls the value for the `au_lname` variable, makes the comparison, and either executes or ignores the statements in the loop following the test. There are three different tests that you can perform. Each is described in Table 24.2.

**N O T E** You can also use `<%else%>` in your `If...else...endif` loop. ▬

| Table 24.2 | Comparison Operators for Use in HTX Files |
|---|---|
| EQ | Indicates an equivalent test, such as "Is item A equal to item B?" |
| GT | Tests for a condition in which one item is greater than the other. |
| LT | Tests for the condition in which one item is less than the other. |

In addition, there are two different data set related variables. `CurrentRecord` allows you to reference the number of times the Detail section executes. If, after the detail loop runs, you want to determine whether there are records in the data set, you can test this variable to see if it's 0. If it is, no information was returned, and you should display a meaningful message to that effect. The following code excerpt shows an example of testing this value.

```
<%if CurrentRecord EQ 0>
  <H2>Sorry, no authors match your search crit...
<%else%>
  <H2>Authors with names like "<I><%idc.au_lname%>...
<%endif%>
```

The other tag that corresponds directly to database-oriented actions is the `MaxRecords` option. `MaxRecords` relates to the `MaxRecords IDC` variable. Using this value, you can determine the total number of records that the IDC file allows. You use both `CurrentRecord` and `MaxRecords` in conjunction with `<%if%>` statements. They are implemented as controlling variables that help in your structuring of the logical flow of the HTX file. Just keep in mind that, after the processing of the detail section completes, if `CurrentRecord EQ 0`, there are no results returned from the call.

The final section of the HTX file is used largely to close different HTML tags that were used to set up the display of information on the resulting page. Remember, HTML expects most tags in pairs, so it's a good idea to close each item properly, as in the following:

```
<! Section 3>
<P>
</TABLE>
<%if CurrentRecord EQ 0%>
  <H2>Sorry, no authors match your search criteria (<%idc.au_lname%>).</H2>
<%else%>
  <H2>Authors with names like "<I><%idc.au_lname%></I>"</H2>
<%endif%>
</center>
</td>
</tr>
```

```
</table>
</BODY>
</HTML>
```

Notice, too, that the `CurrentRecord` variable is used to determine the message that is displayed to the user. There will be either a message indicating no matches, or one explaining that what was searched for is shown. You can also see, by referencing the `<%idc.au_lname%>` variable, that you can pull the user-specified value from the form.

The results of a successful search are shown in Figure 24.8.

**FIG. 24.8**

A successful match will show the hits on the PUBS database table, and will then show the message indicating what was searched for.

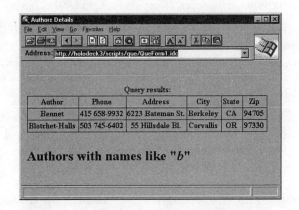

If the search of the database tables is not fruitful, the HTX displays a different message, indicating the failure of the process. Figure 24.9 shows this dialog box.

**FIG. 24.9**

If matches for information are not found, you should code a branch of logic to indicate the problem to the user.

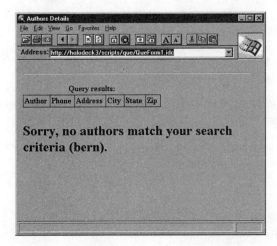

# Internet Database Connector: A Summary and Example

To recap how the IDC works overall, first, you code a form or other HTML document that calls the IDC file on the server. The IDC file is located in the protected /SCRIPTS directory and contains the information necessary to open the ODBC connection and submit a query to the database engine. As the results are returned, they are merged into another document, the HTX or HTML extension document. This HTX file includes the information needed to work with both the detail records and the header/footer information for the page.

The result to the user is the display of the requested information in an HTML document style. Of course, the resulting document, based on the HTX file, can include further links to queries or drill-down information, if needed. This technique allows a user to select high-level values and then narrow the scope, but increase the detail level provided, for the information as the user is able to narrow the parameters for the operation.

An excellent example of the drill-down technique is provided in Microsoft's samples located in the guestbook application. As you query the guestbook, you are returned high-level detail about the names found. The following is a look at the HTX file's Detail section to see what exactly is done to display the information from the database.

```
<%begindetail%>
Name: <a href="/scripts/samples/details.idc?FName=<%FirstName%>
➥ & LName=<%LastName%>"><b><%FirstName%> <%LastName%></b></a>
<p>
<%enddetail%>
```

So, for each name returned by the original query, the result shows the first and last names. This HTML sets up the names as links to their own details. The code indicates the A HREF tag and references the IDC that retrieves the detail information, DETAILS.IDC. As a result, when the users click this in their browser, they immediately execute the IDC file and retrieve the next level of detail. Figure 24.10 shows what this initial screen of details looks like when the items are first retrieved.

When you click a name to get the details, the IDC is called that retrieves the details from the Guests table on your system. If you take a look at the IDC, you see that it's quite simple, returning only a few columns of information based on the name selected from the previous query.

```
Datasource: Web SQL
Username: sa
Template: details.htx
SQLStatement:
+SELECT FirstName, LastName, Email, Homepage, Comment, WebUse
+FROM Guests
+WHERE FirstName = '%FName%' and LastName = '%LName%'
```

The final step is to show the information to the requester. The DETAILS.HTX template is called out in the IDC file, and it shows the detail information for the user, as requested. The detail section simply displays the user information that is provided. The HTX file makes heavy use of the <%if%> operator, and the comparison of the contents of a given field, to ensure that the only information provided to the user are those fields that are non-blank.

**FIG. 24.10**

The initial display of the Guestbook contents allows the user to select a name and drill down into the details for that name.

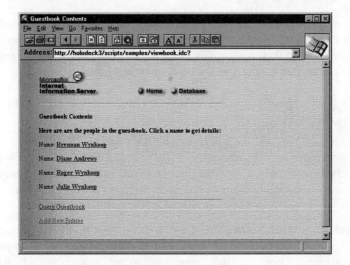

## Listing 24.6 The Detail Section from the DETAILS.HTX File

```
<%begindetail%>
<h2>Here are details for <%FirstName%> <%LastName%>:</h2>
<p>
<b><%FirstName%> <%LastName%></b><br>
<p>

<%if Email EQ " "%>
<%else%>
Email Address: <%Email%> <br>
<%endif%>
<%if Homepage EQ " "%>
<%else%>
Homepage: <%Homepage%>
<%endif%>
<p>
Primary Web Role: <%WebUse%>
<p>
<%if Comment EQ " "%>
<%else%>
Comments: <%Comment%>
<%endif%>
<p>
<%enddetail%>
```

Providing this type of increasing detail, based on a user's selection, is good for all parties concerned. It's good for your system because it can provide only the information needed to determine the direction to go to for the next level of detail. In addition, it's good for the users because it can mean less content to shuffle through to get to the information they really need. Since they will be determining what information is delved into, they'll be able to control how deep they want to go into a given item.

This technique is useful for supplying company information. You can provide overview type items at the highest level, on everything from marketing materials to personnel manuals. Letting people select their research path also alleviates you from the responsibility of second-guessing exactly what the user is expecting of the system.

# Reality Check

At the Integra Web site, the IDC is used for three different things. First, it's used to log the user's name and address information as they request download access to evaluation software. The user is prompted for the different contact elements, including name, address, and e-mail information. This information is saved to an SQL Server where the marketing team can pick it up, also over the Web, and review new sales leads.

Second, it's used to log purchases. Users are able to access the Web site, provide financial information (like credit card numbers and other information), and then purchase products directly from the Web site. Once completed, the transaction is saved to SQL Server to be passed along to the accounting department for billing purposes.

Lastly, database access is used to provide "Did you know" type of information on the site. The random banner that shows information about the company is generated by a mix of stored procedures and database-based information. The IDC file calls a stored procedure, which determines the next tidbit to show. Even the IDC file is automated in determining the HTX file to call when completed. By using parameters in the IDC file, a single IDC can be used to host the tidbits on any page created.

The IntelliCenter Reality Check site puts into play nearly all of the different techniques listed here, as they relate to the Microsoft Internet Information Server, including the ODBC logging. The review of the logs is a very frequent operation and is used to help drive course and online materials content from a marketing stance as well.

By putting content online, and announcing its availability both to internal student users and the customer community at large, IntelliCenter is able to see what types of materials interest people, and what other classes and activities might be of interest to customers.

In addition, as class students are assigned accounts on the IntelliCenter system, the usage statistics help drive the online research content. By looking after the content that is most requested on their system, it's possible to increase the online research materials to meet demand.

Database access is used, along with the IDC interface, to provide transcripts of the classes taken by a student, or a company's students, with access to the information guided by the individual that is signing in. A corporate leader from the company, as designated by the company, can review the different classes that have been taken by the company's employees.

At the same time, an employee can review their own records, and can gain access to online materials that relate to the classes taken to date.

# From Here...

As you can see, the IDC is a very powerful extension to the IIS environment. Chances are good that, after your initial installation of IIS to provide access to static HTML content, you'll quickly find that database-driven information is even more popular with the users you are serving.

More information is provided about these topics in the following areas:

- ▓ To see how the IDC can be extended with server side VBScript, see Chapter 13, "Active Server Pages and Server-Side Scripting."
- ▓ To learn how to cache data on the client and provide flexible scrolling through a set of database records, see Chapter 26, "Integrating the Advanced Data Connector into Web Database Applications."
- ▓ To see how a new type of ActiveX control, called Design-Time controls, can be used to build IDC and server-side scripts, see Chapter 27, "Building Web Database Applications by Using Visual InterDev."
- ▓ To learn how to integrate Microsoft's Transaction Server with IIS and IDC to build multi-tier Web applications, see Chapter 29, "Building Multi-Tier Applications."

Part
VII

Ch
24

# CHAPTER 25

# Introducing ActiveX Data Objects

Computing originally started on large machines with dumb terminals. With the advent of the personal computer and powerful workstations, much of the processing migrated to the desktop. The introduction of the Web server shifted the balance of power back to a centralized programming model. Today, Java and ActiveX controls have, yet again, enabled the desktop to reassert itself.

In this book, you have seen how the Active Server has enabled a more balanced level of power. That is, instead of these polarizing swings of focus from server to desktop and back again, the Active Server has shown its "diplomatic" side, enabling the ASP developer to decide the best combination of technologies that optimize processing load without sacrificing fault tolerance or scaleability.

As important as this egalitarian trait of ASP is, everything done so far in the book is trivial when compared to the innovations in ActiveX covered in this part of the text. These innovations are called ActiveX Data Objects (ADO).

The major theme of this chapter, then, is distributed, object-centric database management. Before getting into it, however, you should be aware of a few things. First, bandwidth is scarce on the Internet. Second, packet-switched networks are inherently latent (that is, they are

## Where did ActiveX Data Objects come from?

Review the historic roots of ActiveX Data Objects, and see how they extend existing systems like Open DataBase Connectivity.

## What's the underlying technology for ActiveX Data Objects, and how is it different from its predecessors?

Explore the exciting new software model that ActiveX Data Objects is based on. The prospects for this radically new approach to data management will take your breath away.

## The Objects and Components

You get your first good look at the basic building blocks of ActiveX Data Objects.

## An Object Model for ActiveX Data Objects

Introducing the methods, and properties of ActiveX Data Objects.

## Essential ActiveX Data Objects

See how the essential elements of an ActiveX Data Object program fit together and explore the interaction between object properties with a working .ASP file.

subject to delays). ActiveX Data Objects are so revolutionary that they (and you, as an ASP developer) are slightly ahead of their time.

The apparent impediments of bandwidth and latency may actually be a blessing. Most of your ADO learning curve will probably occur on intranets—where bandwidth is measured in tens, if not hundreds, of megabits and where latency is practically zero. By the time you break the bandwidth bottleneck with Asynchronous Transfer Mode (ATM) switches (or, better, when George Gilder's vision of the "fibersphere," the all-fiber network, becomes reality), ASP/ADO development will be second nature to you. With those caveats in mind, get ready to take a deeper look into this radical new resource: ADO. ■

# The Family Tree

Until Microsoft's acquisition of Fox Software in 1992, the database was conspicuously absent from Microsoft's desktop arsenal. Today, FoxPro (now matured into Visual FoxPro), Microsoft Access, and SQL Server round out a balanced database strategy. Each product is designed for a particular market. For example, Visual FoxPro uses an Indexed Sequential Access Method (ISAM) file format and is generally recognized as faster than Access but slower than SQL Server. As the other desktop application, Access uses a special file format accessed through the Jet Data Access Object (DAO) model. DAO gives the programmer direct access to the database structure, something not as easily done in Visual FoxPro. SQL Server, on the other hand, is a database server, not a desktop application. It is an industrial-strength application that is highly scaleable. All three products use ODBC to share data with each other.

There is one other thing that these three products have in common, setting them apart from ADO: Their ability to be deployed in a distributed network is defined by the Remote Data Object (RDO) specification found in Visual Basic's Enterprise Edition. Specifically, they work in *connected* networks. The Internet, on the other hand, is a *connectionless* network—a packet-switched network.

In fact, Web servers are even more problematic for programmers, especially database programmers, because they are "stateless" as well as connectionless. They're called *stateless* servers because once they serve a client request, they forget that the client ever was served. The server does not keep track of anything going on with the client application. Web servers have short memories.

In the desktop world, when two applications communicate, they do so for a given period of time. For example, when an Access database is linked to external files, it tests for the presence of those files as soon as it is opened. As long as the Access database remains running, any interruption in the connection (for example, say that a Novell file server goes down) triggers an event in Access, and a warning flashes in the Access application that the connection has been broken. In SQL Server, the server is aware of the presence of a client application as long as that application is engaged in a transaction with the database server. The length of time of such a transaction is not necessarily as short as it is with a Web server.

A Web server knows about a client application only long enough to deliver a file, but an Active Server is different. While it, too, disconnects from the client as soon as a file is returned, it remains connected as long as necessary to do two things: first, process the database and produce a recordset; second, enable the application to make subsequent calls and still have access to previously returned data.

# OLE DB

Before getting into the meat of ADO, take a closer look at the application program interface (API) on which ADO is built, OLE DB (OLE DB is Object Linking and Embedding applied to databases). ADO is the first Microsoft technology built on this exciting new initiative. If you thought that the Web spawned an avalanche of great software and business models on the Internet, just wait until developers hear about OLE DB! And, as an ADO programmer, you're leading the way!

First, it's best to set the context with a quick review of the interface, the Open Database Connectivity (ODBC) specification. ODBC is a desktop SQL-based specification whose API foundation is built on the C language. This means that it was designed for relational database systems, the kind with which you all are accustomed to working. ODBC is a real workhorse, enabling developers to build systems that integrate Jet databases, ISAM files in old FoxBase+ databases, and even SQL Server tables into one coherent user interface. ODBC is the lingua franca of all these relational dialects meaning it is the linguistic bridge connecting the disparate native languages of each database management system.

OLE DB, on the other hand, is a specification based on a C++ API, so it is object-oriented. OLE DB consists of *data consumers* and *data providers*. Consumers take data from OLE DB interfaces; providers expose OLE DB interfaces. ODBC now is a subset of OLE DB. Currently, Microsoft has developed an OLE DB data provider (code-named *Kagera*) that enables access to the old relational data. In fact, under some circumstances, OLE DB can access ODBC data faster than DAO or RDO. This is because DAO and RDO have to pass through the ODBC layer, and OLE DB connects directly to relational data sources. See Figure 25.1 for the subtle difference in the approach taken by ADO.

What's more, OLE DB can be used to extend the functionality of simple data providers. These more sophisticated and specialized objects are called *service providers*, and they can assemble everything needed by data consumers into a single table, regardless of data type (for example, ODBC, spreadsheets, e-mail messages, word processing documents, or file systems) or storage location (LAN, WAN, Internet, intranet). Service providers, therefore, are both consumers and providers. That is, a service provider could consume OLE DB interfaces and build a single table from that input; it then could expose OLE DB interfaces to a client application (such as an .ASP file using ADO) for constructing its HTML output.

**FIG. 25.1**
OLE DB simplifies the connection of your program to database information.

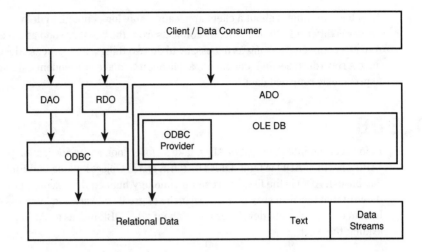

But OLE DB is, after all, a low-level specification. If you don't have time to learn a language lower down the food chain than Visual Basic, ActiveX is the answer. Specifically, ActiveX Data Objects use a language-neutral component technology to provide a high-level wrapper around the OLE DB API, which enables you to exploit all the power of OLE DB without resorting to low-level programming. On the one hand, this means that all Microsoft programming languages can use ADO to access data. On the other hand, ActiveX components (ADO is but one example) can themselves be built using any language that complies with the Component Object Model. All of these rather subtle relationships are depicted in Figure 25.2.

**FIG. 25.2**
ActiveX is a language-neutral wrapper, giving the component developer free choice of the best breed of development environments.

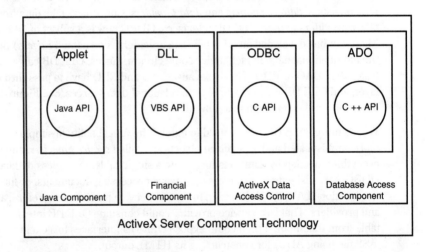

To recap: ADO works just like DAO and RDO, only more efficiently, especially in a stateless and connectionless environment like the Internet/intranet. ADO, an ActiveX component technology, is based on a C++ API called OLE DB (which betrays its family heritage from ODBC, written in C). Because ADO is a component technology, it is highly extensible, tying ADO to Microsoft's programming paradigm for the next millennium.

# Objects versus Components

The Active Server is a component of the Internet Information Server. Specifically, it is an Internet Server Application Programming Interfase (ISAPI) filter. This means that it is a Dynamic Link Library file that becomes part of IIS as soon as the operating system starts it running. This modular design of everything Microsoft publishes these days is a model for the way an ASP developer should write applications.

By exposing key ASP resources to the scripting engine running on the server (for example, VBScript, JavaScript, Perl, and others), the Active Server enables the ASP developer to extend the functionality of the Active Server itself.

Objects are the first internals available to the ASP developer. The functions exposed by objects are the most common functions required by Active Server Pages. Examples include creating instances of server components (which you will read about next), manipulating text strings with URL and HTML encoding, and many other advanced functions that you will read about in the rest of this part of the book.

Components have a similar function: to extend the functionality of the Active Server. However, they have one fundamental difference: They are .DLL files that run separately from the Active Server, but in the same address space as the server. Microsoft wrote these .DLL files, but you can create your own components in any language that produces code compliant with the Component Object Model (COM) specification. By creating .DLL files (and not .EXE files that execute in their own address space), you give your components maximum speed.

Active Server components (both those components intrinsic to ASP and those you create yourself) do not have a user interface. Indeed, if you forget this and design a server component with a msgbox or inputbox function, you will hang the server. This is because the program (namely, your errant server component) that is running is waiting for user input that never comes, because the user interface is invisible. In addition, server components need to support only three interfaces (IUnknown, IDispatch, and IClassFactory).

Finally, VBScript does not have a type library, so if you want to use variable types other than Variant, write a component. For example, if you want to extend the Active Server's mathematical power, you *do not* want to use the Variant data type; it will slow your mathematical processing to a crawl. Instead, create a program in Visual Basic, and compile it as an in-process .DLL file; register it with the operating system, and call it in your Active Server Pages.

# Down 'n Dirty

Remember, almost all new developments in computer programming today are innovative uses of objects. Whether you program in Visual Basic or in Active Server Scripting, you are object-centric. Get ready to relax your brain—you're going to need a lot of mental flexibility as the section proceeds.

To start, here's a simple example. Say that, using the TextStream Component, you treat a file as an object. That's not hard to imagine. One of the methods exposed by this Component is

Part
VII

Ch
25

`OpenTextFile`; again, fairly straightforward. But what happens in your brain when you think of data as an object? Treating a file as an object is simple—there's an object, a single object, and it's called a file. It's not a file that's part of a bigger file (unless you take the idea of a folder literally); it's just a file.

But data? A single data (okay, *datum*) is trivial, and ADO is far from trivial. You probably have to think of a data *source* in order to feel comfortable with the concept of data being an object. And what about queries and stored procedures? They result in recordsets that can range from zero rows to the total number of rows in the data source. One of the first things that you should do when you start working with the ADO is stop thinking of database tables literally. Instead, think of them as abstract objects with their own collections, properties, and methods.

Most Access developers already are familiar with a data object model, which is exactly what the Access Data Access Object (DAO) model is. These developers should recognize nearly all the terms used in ADO, other than the `Connection` Object. The name is different, but the functionality is familiar; ADO's `Connection` Object basically provides the same functionality as the `Workspace` Object in Access.

Familiarity, however, won't prepare even seasoned Access developers for some of the stumbling blocks that they'll confront in ADO. For example, if your programming career developed as ours did, you went from an ISAM world like FoxPro to the DAO world of Access, and the first thing you gave up was the record number. In Access (and ADO), the record number doesn't exist. Access introduced developers to the *bookmark*, instead. ADO follows this tradition, with its own twist: *pages*.

Absolute pages are navigated in ways allowed by the nature of the underlying recordset. That is, some recordsets can be navigated freely, up and down; others permit only row-wise, forward movement. You'll see examples of both in a moment. For now, be aware that there are subtle nuances lurking in ADO, and the Active Server developer may need to take great care in specifying how and from where recordsets are fetched. As you'll see shortly, the other new demand of ADO programming for those without SQL Server experience is having to understand new terms; for example, *cursor*. (If you don't know it now, that's okay; you will in a moment.)

# ADO and *Server* Objects

Using ADO, perhaps more than any other Server Component highlights the symbiosis between Server Objects and Components. The main reason for this interdependence is that, because Web applications are based on individual HTML pages, these applications can be problematical for the Active Server developer. The problem arises because, while on one hand, the application moves freely and easily between several forms or instances of the same form (as you will see demonstrated later), at the same time, a stable substrate of data underlies the dynamic interplay of user interface. The developer's challenge is to keep this data substrate available to any and all pages that need it.

There are two specific issues facing the ADO developer— performance and reference. Performance issues arise because you cannot spare the bandwidth to make repeated calls to server data stores for the same recordset (just because different pages need it). All pages should refer to the same fetched data.

Reference issues are similar to performance issues but different, because pages often will have to exchange data entered by the user; even more often, they will have to exchange data with each other (whether the data was fetched or entered). One or more pages needs to know what that data is and must be updated if that data is changed by another page in the application.

Figure 25.3 depicts these inter-relationships. A database contains information needed by an ASP application. The Active Server makes the call to fetch the data. If you use Session properties, discussed in the next section, you have to fetch this data only once; all the Active Server Pages will reference this copy of the data as necessary. If you do not use Session properties, then every time an .ASP file needs the data, it has to requery the data provider. Also note in the figure that data can "trickle down" from one page to several others. This data may affect and be affected by the data in the original database.

**FIG. 25.3**

The problem of ADO programming centers in repeated calls to a data provider for data.

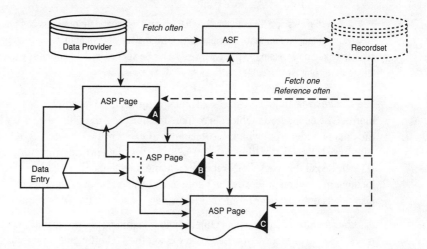

ASP has something for just this purpose, Session properties. Remember that VBScript is not yet able to reference a type library at design time and perform early binding. Therefore, all variables in VBScript are of type Variant. The performance issues that normally attend the exclusive use of variants usually are not issues in Active Server programming, because the client apps tend to remain thin. Intelligent design of server components enables the high-performance processing of variable data.

At any rate, Session properties can be created simply by setting them to a value. For example, a RecordSet Object can be created as a Session properties simply by stating the following:

```
Session("rstAuthors") = rstAuthors
```

# The ADO Object Model

As mentioned, of all the Server Components that ship with ASP, ADO is the most complex and the one with the most long-term effect on the future of programming. In this chapter, you focus on the highest level of the object model and look at some of the key properties and methods necessary to make ADO work at its most basic level. A key objective of this chapter is to stress that understanding the relationships between features of ADO is more important than an understanding of its parts.

## Exposed Objects

ADO exposes three primary objects to the developer: the Connection Object, the Command Object, and the RecordSet Object. For all practical purposes, the RecordSet Object is the most important; the Connection and Command Objects serve to enable the RecordSet Object's creation.

> **N O T E**   With version 1.0, everything in OLE DB exists so that data providers can present their data in tabular form (later versions of OLE DB may be able to output object-oriented data and semistructured data). From the perspective of Active Server Pages, the RecordSet Object is the key to the new level of interactivity that data-driven HTML enables. ■

**The *Connection* Object**   ADO's advantage comes from its ability to work in stateless environments. The Connection Object is responsible for recording the necessary information about the data provider from which the RecordSet Object will be created. ADO needs to inform the Windows NT server of the existence of an ODBC data provider by citing a Data Source Name (DSN). Recall that each DSN receives a name; the Connection Object refers to that name with its Open method and records the name in its ConnectionString property. The Open method also needs optional UserID and Password values, should the DSN require them.

Another feature of Connection Objects will be familiar to Access and SQL Server programmers. Like its predecessors, ADO can exploit the I/O efficiency of transactions by using the BeginTrans, CommitTrans, and/or RollbackTrans methods. These methods—at least, in Access—are part of the Workspace Object, and you can see how that object and the Connection Object exist for the same reason. Think of the Connection Object as the telephone and circuits that enable you to call your mother; they don't do the talking, but without them, there's no conversation.

If the Connection Object is like the telephone, then its Open method is like placing a call, and its Execute method is like opening your mouth. Actually, there are several ways to create a RecordSet Object. Essentially, you can do it with the Connection, Command or even the RecordSet Object itself. For the moment, we remain focused on the Connection Object. Listing 25.1 shows how you instantiate a Connection Object from the Database Access Component (identified by the ADO object id). You open this object by assiging it to the DSN named "Blotter".  And you create a new recordset by invoking the Execute method (in this instance you fetch all the records in a table named "tblBlotter").

### Listing 25.1   ADOBASIC.ASP— Using the *Connection* Object to Create a recordset

```
Set objConn=Server.CreateObject("ADODB.Connection")
objConn.Open("Blotter")
Set objRst=objConn.Execute "tblBlotter"
```

As mentioned, the Execute method takes a given SQL command and interrogates the DSN with it. Success yields a RecordSet Object that is created with the VBScript Set command. Using this approach creates an implicit RecordSet Object, by the way. This means that ADO has given you a minimalist RecordSet Object; more important, it generates the least powerful cursor. Specifically, the resulting cursor is the row-wise, scroll-forward, read-only variety. ADO, like good programmers, is profoundly lazy (the good kind of laziness, the kind that enables programmers to write great code).

**The *Command* Object**   The Command Object provides the second way to create a RecordSet Object. This object also creates a minimal cursor, but it was designed to exploit a key concept in database management: passed parameters. *Parameters* are variables stored inside queries and stored procedures. Think of queries, and especially stored procedures, as mini-programs compiled by the data provider. Like normal programs, these objects can accept data at runtime that affect how the object behaves. Queries designed like this are called *parameterized queries*. For example, if you want to list only certain records from a given table, you pass the name of the field and the value of interest to the parameterized query, and it filters out all other records from the resulting recordset.

Of course, you can always do this by stuffing variables into the SQL statement, but this can be very time consuming and frustrating, especially when you have to contend with embedded double and single quotes. Listing 25.2 demonstrates the simplest way to open a recordset with the Command Object.

Part VII
Ch
25

### Listing 25.2   ADOBASIC.ASP—Opening a Simple recordset with the *Command* Object

```
Set objCmd = Server.CreateObject(ADODB.Command)
objCmd.ActiveConnection ="intranet"
objCmd.CommandText="qryPhoneMessagesFor"
Set objRst = objCmd.Execute
```

As you can see, the structure of these commands is very similar to those used by the Connection Object. In order to execute a Command Object you need to tell it which connection to use and what SQL statement to use. There are many other ways to implement these basic requirements, but in all cases, the result is the same as that in Listing 25.2.

> **N O T E**   You have a choice when it comes to creating recordsets with the `Connection` Object and the `Command` Object: Refer to database objects such as queries, stored procedures, or table names; or use explicit SQL statements such as `"SELECT * FROM tblBlotter"`. Referring to objects can yield dramatic improvements in performance because they can exploit all the processing power of the data provider. However, using a SQL statement makes your code self-documenting; that is, you can tell exactly what your program is doing as it interacts with the data provider. In most cases, this advantage of self-documenting code is more than offset by the loss in performance; and besides, you can always explicitly document calls to database objects. ■

**The *RecordSet* Object**   When you use the `RecordSet` Object to *create* a recordset, you are using the `CreateObject` method of the Server Object to instantiate an explicit `RecordSet` Object. This means that you are responsible for specifying all the properties of the resulting recordset (unless you accept default values). Alternatively, you can create a recordset implicitly by using a `Connection` Object or the `Command` Object—but then you have no control over properties. If you need a dynamic cursor that is fully scrollable and permits batch updates, by using the `RecordSet` Object, that's exactly what you'll get.

> **N O T E**   Cursors and related constructs are important in ADO, because the ADO developer has complete control over details that can be overlooked safely when using DAO. You focus on cursors as follows, and at the end of this chapter you'll find a useful applet that demonstrates the interplay between cursors and concurrency and how both are controlled with `RecordSet` Object properties. ■

At this point, you have made the call, connected with the other end, and are ready to start talking. In the same way that a conversation is full of words, recordsets are full of data. To fill the recordset with data, then, you don't use an `Execute` method; you use the `Open` method. Like the `Execute` method, the `Open` method in a `Connection` Object context is different from the `Open` method with the `RecordSet` Object. With the `Connection` Object, the `Open` method opens a channel permitting data to flow; with the `RecordSet` Object, the `Open` method fills a recordset with data.

By now code like Listing 25.3 should be familiar. Regardless of the object and method you use to create a recordset of data, you always need to tell ADO where the database is stored and which table you need to manipulate. Again, the primary syntactical difference with the `RecordSet` Object is that it is populated with the `Open` method, not the `Execute` method.

**Listing 25.3    ADOBASIC.ASP—The Code Necessary to Create a *RecordSet* Object**

```
Set objRst = Server.CreateObject("ADODB.Recordset")
objRst.Source = "qryBlotterByDate"
objRst.ActiveConnection="Blotter"
objRst.Open
```

Each RecordSet Object contains a Fields collection of all the Field objects in the recordset. By manipulating the Fields collection, you change the structure of the underlying database table. That is, by referring to the Fields collection, you can construct SQL commands to update or otherwise modify the structure of the underlying tables at the data provider.

The real meat of the RecordSet Object, however, is in its methods and properties. To the extent that you do any serious database management by using an HTML user interface, your ADO programs probably will use all those methods at one time or another.

> **N O T E** Remember, the mission of ADO's underlying interface, OLE DB, is to be able to work with any data provider. Therefore, you would expect a rich set of methods and properties to accommodate all the different flavors, dialects, and technologies used to store data. OLE DB is designed to eventually embrace all formats from data streams to text files to object stores—an ambitious mission. ■

Properties may see less widespread use than methods (unless you find yourself immersed in such relational arcana as heterogeneous joins). Why? Because some ADO properties are not supported by some data providers. For example, not all data providers support bookmarks—Access does; FoxPro does not—nor do all Access cursors support bookmarks.

## Methods

The methods and properties in the following sections were selected from the entire ADO object model because they are used in the demo program in the "Database Programming" section at the end of this chapter. Nearly all the ADO code that you write will use them.

> **N O T E** At the end of this section is a table that summarizes the list of methods and properties for each object. ■

**Abandon**  The Abandon method applies to Active Server Session Objects. Sessions are created as soon as a user opens an .ASP file in a virtual directory of the Internet Information Server. This session stays open until one of two things happens. Either there is no activity from the user for 20 minutes (or the interval specified in the Timeout property of the Session Object), or an Abandon method is invoked.

If you need access to any connected database before the session expires (for example, to back up the database), you need to Abandon it first.

**CreateObject**  The CreateObject method applies to the Server Object. This method creates instances of server components (such as TextStream) and ADO objects (such as Connection and RecordSet). The similarity with this method to its namesake in Visual Basic is that the Server Object must be part of the call; namely, Server.CreateObject(), not merely CreateObject().

**Open**  The Open method applies to Connection and RecordSet Objects. With the Connection Object, the method opens a connection—a channel of communication—to a server; specifically, to a Data Source Name. When invoked by a `RecordSet` Object, this method opens a cursor in a table in the DSN. The cursor is a current row-pointer within the recordset created with the `Open` method.

**Requery**   The `Requery` method applies to the `RecordSet` Object created with the `Open` method. Its function is to re-fire the query that populated the recordset, fetching the current—perhaps updated—values from the underlying database table.

**Update**   The `Update` method also is used by the `RecordSet` Object. It moves the data in the copy buffer to the `RecordSet` Object. Until this event occurs, the underlying table can have one value and the `RecordSet` Object another; after the `Update` method, they have the same data—unless something interfered with the routine processing of updates. Examples include incompatible combinations of `CursorType` and `LockType` properties (such as keyset cursors with batch updating in Microsoft Access).

**N O T E**   One of the design goals of ADO was to make coding more efficient for programmers. One of the first thing ADO changes is the old `Edit` method. In ADO, if you want to change a field's value, you simply change it; you no longer need to explicitly invoke the `Edit` method first (it's implied). The `AddNew` method, however, is still required, for there is no other way for ADO to know your intentions. ■

# Properties

The properties in the following sections are listed in alphabetical order.

**ActiveConnection**   The `ActiveConnection` property tells ADO where the data is and how to access it. `ActiveConnection` functions like a telephone connection in that it enables communication but does not communicate directly. Some ADO connections are like station-to-station long distance. Others are more restricted, like a person-to-person call, limiting data access to only certain people with specific passwords.

**CursorType**   `CursorType` is an important property that applies to the `RecordSet` Object. It determines how hard the data provider has to work to make the records it stores available to your ADO program. The simplest cursor is a forward only, row-wise, read-only cursor. Other data providers can provide dynamic cursors that keep track of the status of underlying data.

**LockType**   The `LockType` property applies to `RecordSet` Objects and controls what results when the `RecordSet` Object executes its `Open` method. This property is important because it tells the data provider how to handle concurrency issues, should they arise.

**Name**   The `Name` property applies to the `Field` Object of the `RecordSet` Object.

**Source**   The `Source` property applies to `RecordSet` Objects. Usually, this is a text string of SQL commands to fetch data from the data provider. A shortcut is to use the name of the table alone; this is quicker than typing **SELECT * FROM tblBlotter**. Note, however, that if you want only a selected group of records or set of fields, you will have to use a SQL command, a query, or a SQL Server stored procedure.

# Essential ADO

In this final section of this overview of ADO, you will take a quick look at some database theory, and you will see the source code for the demo program, adobasic.asp, that you can find on the book's CD.

## Preliminaries

To help you come to terms with recordsets, we take a brief detour into the world of relational database management. The comments that follow are for those who have had little use for databases until now or those who have used database systems but didn't have a need to get into the theory of database management. More experienced readers can safely skip this section.

---

### I Thought a Cursor Was Needed Only for the Screen

You're familiar with a cursor. You're also aware of the feeling of panic and helplessness that comes when the cursor becomes invisible or freezes in its (mouse) tracks. Cursors tell you where you are and tell the computer what you want to do next.

In relational database management systems, and in SQL-based systems especially, cursors have a similar but deliberately invisible role to play.

Structured Query Language is called *set-based* and is fundamentally different from the *row-based* method used by business applications. It is small wonder that the spreadsheet was the first business application created for the personal computer. Virtually everything done in business can be best expressed in columns and rows.

There's more to life for SQL than business. SQL experiences the world with *sets*. Granted, the underlying tables of data that SQL uses may be stored in rows and columns—though not always—but the results of combining certain rows and columns results in a set. If you remember Venn diagrams from high school, you know that intersecting sets are the product of combining other sets. Those result sets were the areas where two or more circles overlapped or intersected.

Cursors originally were conceived to bridge the gap between these two worlds of sets and rows. They are a logical entity that *represents* the sets that SQL produces in a structure that business applications can manipulate. Without them, ADO wouldn't exist.

---

**Part**

**VII**

**Ch**

**25**

**Concurrency and Locking Issues**  An adage as old as the Internet says: *Information yearns to be free*. In the database business world, is a related truism: *Data needs to be changed*. The subject of this word play raises two serious problems for database developers.

On one hand, displayed data (especially when more than one row is being displayed) often needs to be up-to-date. This means that when someone adds or deletes a record, all other displays of data from that table need to reflect the change.

On the other hand, when the value of one or more fields of an existing record gets changed by more than one person and at the same time, there is a potential conflict, a collision of wills. The DBMS must be able to sense these collisions and manage them effectively.

Cursors play a part in both of these situations. More precisely, different cursor types play different roles in these different circumstances. Cursors have two primary flavors—static and dynamic. Static cursors, as their name suggests, can't see additions and deletions made by other users. For example, If a business application that works with only one record at a time is being built, it need not concern itself with the need to update the number of rows in a recordset. This is the kind of recordset that ADO creates by default. Other times, a dynamic cursor is needed.Dynamic cursors sense, on their own, when the number of rows or the content of fields changes.

**N O T E**   Not all data providers support dynamic cursors.

The ASP developer also needs to address the issue of concurrency and the related issue of locking. Locking techniques fall into two categories: optimistic and pessimistic. Optimistic locking is relatively easy for the DBMS to implement, for it assumes that collisions and conflicts will be rare and doesn't activate locks until just before updating, and only if a conflict exists. Pessimistic locking assumes the opposite, and locks on data are required before processing a record can even begin. Again, not all DBMSs support both, and when some do, they don't give you a choice between the two.

In one sense, these issues make coming to terms with relational databases a little easier. The choice isn't whether to use optimistic or pessimistic locking; it's whether to buy Microsoft Access (where locking is automatic and both types are supported) or to use an old version of FoxBase+ (where pessimistic locking must be done manually in code) as your DBMS. The point is, if your database engine doesn't support a relational feature, you have to design around that limitation or pick another engine. ▪

**Keys, Indexes, and Bookmarks**   Relational Database Management Systems always work more efficiently if they can uniquely identify individual records. They also work more efficiently if certain fields are indexed; that is, put in order, such as last names in alphabetical order. Tables need keys to do both these things. Indexes sort records based on the values of these key fields; if these values are unique, they serve double duty—they sort and uniquely identify records. In addition, if a SQL Server table has a key, it can have a keyset cursor. Access isn't as picky; a table of two fields and no indexes does not return an error when a dynaset (the closest thing to a keyset cursor that Access has) is created and updated.

In the demo program in the next section, you will see for yourself the effect on the underlying database table when you combine the CursorType and LockType properties with an Access database.

One more concept: bookmarks. Bookmarks are to cursors what cursors are to recordsets— they are placeholders. Some DBMSs (like FoxPro) keep track of record numbers. The Jet engine in Access and ADO do not. Instead, they rely on bookmarks to move the cursor to a previous location in a recordset. As you might guess, bookmarks are not supported by all cursors. Remember that  dynamic cursors get updated when records are added or deleted. As a result, bookmarks aren't supported (in part, because the row that they used to represent may be gone). Only static and keyset cursors (and dynasets in Access) support bookmarks.

So if you are working on recordsets with more than one record, and you need to be able to wander around this recordset as if it were a spreadsheet, you need to choose your cursor type carefully.

 **TIP**

SQL can get complex quickly; it was not designed to be read by humans. You can write your own SQL code by hand, if you want, but we don't recommend it. You should create SQL code in your application of choice. One favorite is Microsoft Access; its QBE grid is the most amazing piece of code that users have come across in years of programming. Perhaps SQL Server or something else works better for you. Regardless of the modeling method, when you have a SQL command that does what you need, cut the SQL code and paste it into your .asp file.

One of Visual InterDev's most important features is modeled after, and significantly extends, the QBE grid of Access.

## A Demonstration Program

The following demo program is discussed in three sections: initialization code, form processing, and database programming. This program has the great virtue of simplicity, and at this stage, clarity is more important for you than virtuosity.

**Initialization Code**    Listing 25.4 describes what the Chapter 24 demo program is for. It includes the standard HTML code for the beginning of HTML files.

**Listing 25.4    ADOBASIC.ASP—Describes the Function of the .asp File and Sets Up the First Part of an .html File**

```
'***********************************************************************
' Description:
'       An Active Server Program (ASP) file that demonstrates
'       many of the tips and techniques discussed in the book.
'       Most importantly, it illustrates the effect of the interaction
'       of two key recordset properties: CursorType and LockType.
'       It also demonstrates the reliance these properties have on the
'       underlying database management system (i.e., some DBMSs
'       do not support all CursorType or LockType values. In the context
'       of a cosmopolitan programming world like ADO, this is important
'        information.
' Arguments:
'       This program calls itself so when the txtCursorType and
'       txtLockType fields have value, they are passed back into the
'       program.
' Returns:
'       Nothing
' Modified:
'    Michael Corning 10/20/96. Final preparations for publication.
'***********************************************************************
<HTML>
<HEAD>
</HEAD>
```

*continues*

**Listing 25.4   Continued**

```
<BODY BGCOLOR="#EEEEEE" TEXT="#000000" LINK="#CC0000" ALINK="#FF3300"
[ic]➥VLINK="#330099">
<FONT FACE="Verdana" SIZE=2>
```

Next, some housekeeping chores. The two ways of indicating a comment in VBScript are
shown in Listing 25.5, as well as a test to see if you need to abandon an ADO session.

**Listing 25.5   ADOBASIC.ASP—The Two Ways to Comment VBScript Code**

```
' Note: using apostrophe for comments only works if they
' are inside the vbs tags (which you cannot use inside comments
' like this). Compare below using HTML comment.
REM You can also use the explicit REM statement instead of the
REM apostrophe.

REM When you're done, abandon the session so that you can
REM backup, move, or otherwise manipulate the underlying database
REM file. The session will abandon in 20 minutes, otherwise.
If Request("cmdQuit") ="Close" Then%>
        <FONT COLOR="Red">Closing connection</FONT><P>
        <%Session.Abandon
Else
        If IsObject(Session("SessionConnection")) Then
                Set objConn = Session("SessionConnection")
        %>
                <FONT COLOR="Green">Using the Cached Session connection</FONT><P>
        <% Else
                Set objConn = Server.CreateObject("ADO.Connection")
                objConn.Open("Blotter")
                Session("SessionConnection") = objConn
                ' Since we are experimenting with different Recordset
' Objects in this ASP file, we have moved the
' instantiation of it to the code block below that
' sets the recordsets
                ' properties for use by its Open method.
                ' Set objRst = Server.CreateObject("ADO.Recordset")%>
                <FONT COLOR="Yellow">Opening the Connection</FONT><P>
        <% End If

        ' Following two code blocks are necessary if you want to
' be able to use a default value
        ' AND be able to maintain your field entries between
' successive ASP file calls.
        If Request("txtCursorType") ="" Then
                intCursorType = 3
        Else
                intCursorType = Request("txtCursorType")
        End If
        If Request("txtLockType") ="" Then
                intLockType = 3
```

```
        Else
                intLockType = Request("txtLockType")
        End If
        %>
```

**Form Processing**    Listing 25.6 continues from the previous listing. It is simple, straightforward HTML form code. The only things that differ from standard HTML are in the beginning of this section: The form action calls the same file (namely, adoBasics.asp) that contains itself. This is similar to recursion but without the overhead or risk of running out of stack space. The second difference from orthodox HTML code is that values for form controls are variables (and, in Listing 25.5, are passed between calls to the adoBasics.asp file).

**Listing 25.6    ADOBASIC.ASP—How to Set Up a Form in an .asp File**

```
        <FORM ACTION="adoBasics.asp" METHOD="POST">
        <TABLE CELLPADDING=3 BORDER=1 CELLSPACING=0 WIDTH=600>
                <TR>
                        <TD COLSPAN=2>Cursor Type:
                        <!—
Remember to use HTML comment delimiters when you are commenting outside the vbs
delimiters.  Remember to put "=" before the Request object so that its value is
returned for the default value of the TEXT box.
—>
                        <INPUT TYPE="TEXT"
                                NAME="txtCursorType"
                                SIZE=3
                                VALUE="<% =intCursorType %>"></TD>

                        <TD COLSPAN=2>Lock Type:
                        <INPUT TYPE="TEXT"
                                NAME="txtLockType"
                                SIZE=3
                                VALUE="<%= intLockType %>">

                        <!—
These command buttons have a name,
so the subsequent calls to this ASP file
can tell when they've been pushed. Without a
name, a command button serves only to fire the
form.
—>
                        <INPUT TYPE="SUBMIT"
                                VALUE="Edit"
                                NAME="cmdEdit">

                        <INPUT TYPE="SUBMIT"
                                VALUE="Close"
                                NAME="cmdQuit"></TD>
                </TR>
```

*continues*

Part

**VII**

Ch

**25**

**Listing 25.6  Continued**

```
                <TR>
                        <TH><FONT SIZE="1">CursorType</TH><TH><FONT SIZE="1">
Description</TH>
                        <TH><FONT SIZE="1">LockType </FONT></TH><TH><FONT SIZE="1">
Description</FONT></TH>
                </TR>
                <TR>
                        <TD><FONT SIZE="1">0 </FONT></TD>
                        <TD><FONT SIZE="1">Keyset</FONT></TD>
                        <TD><FONT SIZE="1">-1 </FONT></TD>
                        <TD><FONT SIZE="1">Provider determines (usually read-only)
</FONT></TD>
                </TR>
                <TR>
                        <TD><FONT SIZE="1">1 </FONT></TD>
                        <TD><FONT SIZE="1">ForwardOnly</FONT></TD>
                        <TD><FONT SIZE="1">1 </FONT></TD>
                        <TD><FONT SIZE="1">Read-only</FONT></TD>
                </TR>
                <TR>
                        <TD><FONT SIZE="1">2 </FONT></TD>
                        <TD><FONT SIZE="1">Dynamic</FONT></TD>
                        <TD><FONT SIZE="1">2 </FONT></TD>
                        <TD><FONT SIZE="1">Row-by-row pessimistic locking
</FONT></TD>
                </TR>
                <TR>
                        <TD><FONT SIZE="1">3 </FONT></TD>
                        <TD><FONT SIZE="1">Static</FONT></TD>
                        <TD><FONT SIZE="1">3 </FONT></TD>
                        <TD><FONT SIZE="1">Row-by-row optimistic locking
</FONT></TD>
                </TR>
                <TR>
                        <TD><BR></TD>
                        <TD><BR></TD>
                        <TD><FONT SIZE="1">4 </FONT></TD>
                        <TD><FONT SIZE="1">Optimistic batch updates</FONT></TD>
                </TR>
        </TABLE>
        </FORM>
```

**Database Programming**   This final section, Listing 25.7,is the important stuff. A few things are worth emphasizing. First, in all ADO code there is no Edit method for the RecordSet Object. When you want to change a recordset field value, just change it. The Update method takes care of the rest of the overhead.

Second, the Requery method flushes out the data of local storage and attempts to permanently change the underlying database cursor. If everything worked as expected with the Update method, the Requery results in the new value.

Also note that we use a compiled query stored in the Access DSN. This provides any performance gains that might be invested in a cleverly designed Jet query. Finally, note the use of variables for setting the values of the key properties, CursorType and LockType. The user of the HTML form specifies these variables.

**Listing 25.7 ADOBASIC.ASP—Real Database Programming in an .asp File**

```
        <%
        If intLockType  < -1 Or intLockType > 4 Or intLockType = 0  Then
                Response.Write("Select a lock type value between -1 and 4 (but not
0)")
        ElseIf intCursorType  < 0 Or intCursorType  > 3 Then
                Response.Write("Select a cursor type value between 0 and 3")
        Else
                ' When ASP first called, Edit button has null value.
                If Request("cmdEdit") = "Edit" Then
                        Set objRst = Server.CreateObject("ADO.Recordset")
                        objRst.LockType = intLockType
' Pick up the entered type
                        objRst.Source = "qryBlotterByDate"
                        objRst.CursorType = intCursorType
                        Set objRst.ActiveConnection=objConn
                        objRst.Open%>
                        <TABLE CELLSPACING=0 BORDER=1 WIDTH=600>
                        <TR>
                                <TD><BR></TD><TH>Before</TH><TH>After</TH>
                        </TR>
                        <%For i=1 to objRst.Fields.Count-1%>
                        <TR>
                                <TD ><FONT SIZE="2">
                                        <%If objRst(i).Name="Rep" Then%>
                                                <B>Does Rep field value change?</B>
                                        <%else
                                                =objRst(i).Name
                                        End If%>
                                </FONT></TD>
                                <TD>
                                        <FONT SIZE="2"><%=objRst(i)%></FONT>
                                </TD>
                                <% If objRst(i).Name = "Rep" Then
' oldRep used below to see if the update
' succeeded
                                        oldRep = objRst("Rep")
                                        ' We're hard coding the field change here.
' Normally, the field data is edited
                                        ' with forms; but since there are no data
' bound HTML form controls, getting
                                        ' these new values into the recordset and
' the cursor at the data provider is
' not trivial.
                                        objRst("Rep") = objRst("Rep")+1
                                        objRst.Update
                                        ' Note: If you don't requery the recordset
```

*continues*

Part

**VII**

Ch

**25**

**Listing 25.7 Continued**

```
' after a failed update then the recordset
' value remains changed, but the underlying
' cursor is not.
                                objRst.Requery
                    End If %>
                    <TD>
                    <% If objRst(i).Name = "Rep" Then
                                ' See if the correct combination of
' CursorType and LockType properties
                                ' were selected for the Access database.
' If so, the new value will be on
                                ' the screen and in the cursor. SQL Server
' and other data providers may
                                ' respond differently than Access using the
' same property values.
                                ' Caveat developer.
                                If oldRep = objRst("Rep") Then%>
                                        <FONT SIZE="2"><%=objRst(i)%> <B>NO</
B></FONT>
                                <%Else%>
                                        <FONT SIZE="2"><%=objRst(i)%> <B>YES</
B></FONT>
                                <%End If
                    Else%>
                                <FONT SIZE="2"><%=objRst(i)%></FONT>
                    <%End If%>
                    </TD>
            </TR>
            <%next%>
            </TABLE>
        <%End If
    End if
End If%>

</FONT>
</BODY>
</HTML>
```

**For Your Part**   You should try the .ASP file for yourself. Experiment with it and keep track of the combinations of property values and outcomes. Remember that you are using an Access database and that other data providers might produce different results.

You also should make a working copy of this file on your own hard drive and experiment with other DSNs or tables in the referenced Access database. The program is fairly generic (except for the explicit field name, Rep), so relatively few changes will be necessary for you to use it with other Access tables, SQL Server, or other DBMSs.

# From Here...

This chapter introduced what may be the most important part of the Active Server: ActiveX Data Objects. ADO is the next generation of database technology from Microsoft. It retains all the power of the OBDC specification but extends this power to the Internet. Combined with DCOM to access data providers in widely dispersed locations, ADO will be even more powerful than RDO.

Also in this chapter, you explored some of ADO's most fundamental aspects and saw some of its most important points in a demonstration program. As exciting as this is, it still isn't "real database programming." You still haven't discussed what you can do with this new power.

For that, turn to the following:

- Chapter 26, "Integrating the Advanced Data Connector into Web Database Applications," looks at the technology that ActiveX Data Objects uses to provide caching of data records on the client, and how this technology can be used with other Web technologies.

- Chapter 27, "Building Web Database Applications by Using Visual InterDev," shows how you can use Microsoft's new Web application programming tool to build ASP database applications using ADOs.

Part
**VII**

Ch
**25**

# CHAPTER 26

# Integrating the Advanced Data Connector into Web Database Applications

**P**erhaps the most comprehensive tools available for developing Web-based applications with ODBC database are those included in the Advanced Data Connector, or ADC. The ADC is the development environment most like that of Visual Basic, giving you the ability to create data-bound controls contained within Web pages.

At this writing, there are two different versions available for the ADC software tools. Version 1.0, available on the Microsoft Web site at **http://www.microsoft.com/adc**, is compatible with version 3.*x* of the Internet Explorer. Version 1.1, also available on the Web site, is in beta and will likely be available soon.

Traditionally, the challenge facing the Web-based application developer is that of data handling at the client and server sides of the application. It was not possible to keep an active, open session on the server because of the inherent limitations built into the HTTP protocol. HTTP was designed to let you make a request, have the request fulfilled, then have no further communication until you make another request.

When Microsoft introduced the Internet Database Connector (IDC) technology, you gained the ability to query an ODBC data source. This is a good way to query a database independent of the browser. It's also a low-overhead approach to working with the database. Of course, the downside to this is how limited you are in terms of what you can do with the information because the results are static, and you're forced to manage the logic to perform any updates.

In the ideal world, you'd be able to manipulate the database as you do others, using the DAO. The DAO objects and methods give you full access to the database, tables, and queries or views. This is where the ADC comes in. The ADC gives you access to these types of methods.

The ADC gives you an interface to the remote data sources in ways similar to the traditional Visual Basic approach. Specifically, you have a control that is responsible for the connection to the server, and you can manipulate either that control, or others dependent on it, to retrieve and work with the database information. The ADC is based on the OLEDB specification for working with databases and business objects. You can find more about OLEDB at **http://www.microsoft.com/oledb**. ∎

# Understanding the Core ADC Components

The ADC includes several core components, shown in Table 26.1.

**Table 26.1   ADC Core Components**

| Component | Function |
|---|---|
| Virtual Table Manager (VTM) | You can think of the VTM as "faking out" the data objects, giving them a logical table to work with that represents the data returned from the server. |
| AdvancedDataControl object | This control, and the AdvancedDataSpace object, lets you set up forms that are bound to the database columns or fields. This is like the datacontrol in VB. |
| AdvancedDataSpace object | As with the AdvancedDataControl object, this control helps set up the environment to support the use of bound controls over the Internet. |
| AdvancedDataFactory object | The data factory is responsible for communicating over HTTP and working with the VTM to create the locally cached virtual tables, making them accessible to your application. This is the query and update interface to your database. |
| ADISAPI | ADISAPI (Advanced Data Internet Server API) is the API used by IIS to work with ODBC and the server-side datafactory objects. |
| Advanced TableGram Streaming Protocol (ADTG) | The ADTG is the Internet-shortcomings-aware protocol that is used to shuttle the information between the client and server systems. |

With all of these objects, you might wonder how this will impact the code you write for these Web-based applications. The good news is that the code is much like Visual Basic, and you will be able to leverage much of your education, testing, and experience to date with VB in your development of these applications. The bad news is that the HTML is getting longer, but you probably have expected that by now.

# Getting Started: Setting Up Your ODBC Datasource

In order to use the ADC, you have to set up a datasource on your IIS server. This datasource must be a system datasource, or the system won't be able to access it when the ADC process is running on the server.

One of the most common reasons for problems with the database connector is the setup of the ODBC data source. This is true across database sources not specific to SQL Server, so it's important to understand the details of setting up the driver for access by IIS.

Since IIS runs as a service, it's running in the background, logging in when needed as either the anonymous user you've set up or as the validated user that's been authenticated by the NT security subsystem. Because you want to give this service access to a database, and because you don't know what the service will be logging in as, you need to set up the database source a bit differently than you may be accustomed to.

Microsoft has an option in the ODBC configurations to support a System DSN. These special data sources give you a way to set up a globally available data source. Because users who log on may be set up to have different access to your system and resources, you need to use the System DSN to make sure they have access to the right databases, regardless of where they log in or who they log in as. Figure 26.1 shows the ODBC setup dialog box, started from the Control Panel. Note that there are several versions of the ODBC manager out there, so don't worry if yours doesn't look exactly as that shown in the figure; the functionality will be identical, as will the dialog box labels.

Part
VII

Ch
26

**TIP** If you find that you receive errors or have other difficulty trying to access an ODBC data source from your Web pages, one of the first things you should check is that the data source you're referencing is set up as a system data source.

When you start the ODBC manager utility, if the data source is listed in the initial dialog box, it's defined as a user-based data source, not a System DSN. Remove the user-based DSN and redefine it as a System DSN, and you'll be able to see the database.

Remember that the only data sources that the Database Connector can use are the System-level data sources.

After you select System DSN, you'll be able to use essentially the same options to set up the drivers. Note, too, that you can have more than one driver set up at the system level. This allows you to set up drivers for the different applications you'll be running on the Web. Figure 26.2 shows the Data Sources Setup dialog box for SQL Server.

**FIG. 26.1**

ODBC setup for IIS requires that you select the System DSN to configure the driver.

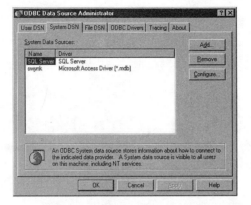

**FIG. 26.2**

Setting up a system-level ODBC driver configuration is much the same as establishing a new ODBC configuration. You'll need to indicate the driver, database, and other information required to connect to your database engine.

The Data Source Name you provide is what you'll be using in the ADC file as the DSN, so be sure to make note of the database configuration names you set up.

In most cases, you'll want the configuration to be as specific as possible. If it's possible to indicate a default database or table, be sure to do so. It will take some of the variables out of the Web page design you'll be doing. By specifying as much information as possible, you'll help ensure that the information is accessible.

## Setting Up Your Page to Use ADC

Your page uses an invisible data control to access the data source. This control is used as the source of the interface between the client page and the server objects providing the data. Once the ADC object has connected to the database, the fields that are bound to it are able to display the information needed.

You declare the object much as you do any other ActiveX control on your page. There are opening and closing OBJECT tags, indicating the class ID and parameters necessary for the object to initialize.

```
<OBJECT CLASSID="clsid:9381D8F2-0288-11d0-9501-00AA00B911A5"
    ID="SControl"
    CODEBASE="HTTP://<%=Request.ServerVariables("SERVER_NAME")%>/ADC/
    ➡msadc10.cab"
    WIDTH=1 HEIGHT=1>
    <PARAM NAME="Bindings" VALUE="Grid1;">
    <PARAM NAME="Connect" VALUE="DSN=SQL Server;QUEADC;UID=ADC;PWD=ADC;">
    <PARAM NAME="Server" VALUE="http://
    ➡<%=Request.ServerVariables("SERVER_NAME")%>">
</OBJECT>
```

 **TIP** When you code your page, be sure to update the CODEBASE parameter to point to a valid directory on your server. If you don't, the page won't be able to load the object as it won't be found. The "Server Name" reference allows the code to query to get the current server name and use it in the URL to find the CAB files associated with the ADC.

Be sure your `msadc10.cab` file is located at the directory location you indicate, and that, if you're using version 1.1 of the ADC, you update the CAB file name.

You must specify the Server parameter—this indicates where the ADC can find the server-side components of the connection, and where to look for other resources that may be required for the database work.

You'll notice that the width and height parameters are both 1 in this case. This is because the control is not a control that is seen when the page is "running." Instead, this control represents an invisible control that simply provides the links to the other controls on the form. If you're familiar with Visual Basic, the data control offered in that environment is much the same. It can be invisible, but you can still use it to control the information displayed in the form's fields.

The Bindings option tells the control what ActiveX controls on the page will be looking to the ADC control to provide database access. These controls are data-bound controls and range from text boxes to grids. Once again, if you're familiar with the Visual Basic environment, this equates to the grid controls, text boxes, and other controls able to be bound to the data control in that environment.

The Bindings option will allow you to call out nearly any number of items to bind to. The format of the parameter is

```
<PARAM NAME="Bindings" VALUE="MyGrid;txtLname.Text=Lname; txtFname.Text=Fname;">
```

The first option, MyGrid, references a grid loaded on the form. The last two options are referring to two different fields defined on the form, and placing the values of the Lname and Fname columns in those fields, respectively.

Using this approach, you can bind all of the columns from your data source to different fields on the page.

**Part**

**VII**

**Ch**

**26**

You can set many of these options in one of two different ways. First, you can call them out as PARAM values as shown previously, or you can use the ADC's object properties to set them. For example, to set the Server name, you can simply issue the statement

```
objADC.Server = "http://visionary"
```

and the parameter will be initialized to the proper server name.

## Connecting to the Database

You can connect to the database by using ADC in one of two ways. You can either call the connection string, or DSN, out in the PARAM block of the object, or you can dynamically call the connection method on the ADC object. In both cases, you'll need to indicate the DSN you'll use, the username, and the password.

For those times when you use the OBJECT tag/definition approach, you can use the following tag

```
<PARAM NAME="Connect" VALUE="DSN=SQL Server;UID=ADC;PWD=ADC;">
```

You'll recognize this same approach to DSNs from Access, Visual Basic for Applications, and Visual Basic. The DSN must, of course, match the system DSN you defined earlier, and the userID and password must be valid in the database.

When you set up the connection in this manner, it's a bit hard-coded, not easily controlled by your application. There will almost assuredly be times when you want to be able to more dynamically connect to the database. Such might be the case where you allow the user to select a connection destination of either Access or SQL Server.

In these cases, you can dynamically build the connection string, and you can call it at runtime. The syntax for this is:

```
objADC.Connect = "DSN=SQL Server;UID=ADC;PWD=ADC;"
```

The objADC object is an ADC object that you create and the Connect method is inherited by the object automatically when it's created.

Using this method, you can dynamically connect to the database when you need to, and you can control the database you end up connecting to by selecting an appropriate DSN for the string.

## Controlling the SQL Statement

The SQL Statement used to create the record set that you'll use on your form is set by a PARAM setting with the name of "SQL." The PARAM is defined to contain the SQL that will be sent to the server, parsed, and will return the values that you'll display—remember to update the fields you return so that column names will match those used to bind to the fields and controls on your form.

```
<PARAM NAME="SQL" VALUE="Select * from Authors">
```

# Understanding Key ADC Methods

You'll find yourself using several different ADC methods and properties time and time again. These methods are the basic tenants of moving around, updating, and controlling the user's movement through the database.

Table 26.1 shows these methods, along with a description and example code snippet showing the use of the option. Note that in all of these cases, the object objADC has previously been created and is referenced in the listing examples.

**Table 26.1   Key ADC Methods**

| Method | Description |
| --- | --- |
| SubmitChanges | After you've updated a record, its values remain in cache on your local system. To update the database, you must use the SubmitChanges method.<br>Syntax: objADC.SubmitChanges |
| CancelUpdate | As indicated under SubmitChanges, until you call the SubmitChanges method, updates that you've made to the information on the form is not sent to the database. If you want to prevent these changes from getting to the database (as is the case when the user presses Cancel on the form), you can use the CancelUpdate method.<br>Syntax: objADC.CancelUpdate |
| Refresh | Set the SQL Property of the object, then call the Refresh method, updating the fields bound to the control.<br>Syntax: objADC.SQL = "Select * from Authors", objADC.Refresh |
| MoveFirst | As with the DAO, MoveFirst will take you to the first record in the current dataset.<br>Syntax: objADC.MoveFirst |
| MoveNext | MoveNext takes you to the next record in the dataset. Remember, this is based on the order in the recordset, driven by the select statement you issued.<br>Syntax: objADC.MoveNext |
| MovePrev | The MovePrev method on the ADC object takes your record pointer to the previous record in the queue. It updates the bound controls with the next set of information from the database as necessary. You should also check the EOF property (e.g., objADC.EOF=TRUE) to see if you've hit the beginning of the set of data.<br>Syntax: objADC.MovePrev, If objADC.EOF then objADC.MoveFirst |
| MoveLast | As you might suspect, the MoveLast method will take you to the last record in the recordset. It's a good idea to use this as a recovery from an EOF=TRUE for MoveNext to ensure that you have a valid, current record. |

Part
VII

Ch
26

In the next section, you'll be able to see how these parameters, methods, and properties are used in an example application.

# Reviewing an Example HTML Page

In the following listing snippets, you can see an abbreviated listing from the sample application provided by Microsoft with the ADC documentation. It gives you a good look at building a form that not only uses these concepts, but also a grid from Sheridan that helps display the information from the server.

## Setting Up the Form

Standard form definition tags are used to set up the form. In these opening HTML statements, the input forms are implemented and named. They can be later referenced for database updates and queries as needed.

**N O T E** In the following listing, portions of the code that have been removed are represented in the code by a set of ellipses, " . . . "

```
...
<PRE> First Name      <INPUT NAME=SFirst SIZE=30> </PRE>
<PRE> Last Name       <INPUT NAME=SLast  SIZE=30> </PRE>
<PRE> Title           <INPUT NAME=STitle SIZE=30> </PRE>
<PRE> E-mail Alias    <INPUT NAME=SEmail SIZE=30> </PRE>

<INPUT TYPE=BUTTON NAME="Find"          VALUE="Find">
<INPUT TYPE=BUTTON NAME="Clear"      VALUE="Clear">
<INPUT TYPE=BUTTON NAME="Update"      VALUE="Update Profile">
<INPUT TYPE=BUTTON NAME="Cancel"      VALUE="Cancel Changes">
```

## Initiating the Grid Control

The next section, outlined by the <Object> tags, initiates the Sheridan grid control. Note that this control is assumed to be at the location specified on the server. The reference to Request.ServerVariables("SERVER_NAME") lets you find out the server name that is currently working with the Internet Explorer client.

The balance of the properties, for example AllowAddNew, are specific to the control and let you configure the control to suit your needs.

```
<OBJECT CLASSID="clsid:BC496AE0-9B4E-11CE-A6D5-0000C0BE9395"
    ID=Grid1

CODEBASE="HTTP://<%=Request.ServerVariables("SERVER_NAME")%>/MSADC/Samples/
➥Sheridan.cab"
    HEIGHT= 125
    Width = 495>
    <PARAM NAME="AllowAddNew"    VALUE="TRUE">
    <PARAM NAME="AllowDelete"    VALUE="TRUE">
    <PARAM NAME="AllowUpdate"    VALUE="TRUE">
```

```
        <PARAM NAME="BackColor"    VALUE="-2147483643">
        <PARAM NAME="BackColorOdd"  VALUE="-2147483643">
        <PARAM NAME="ForeColorEven" VALUE="0">
</OBJECT>
```

## Setting Up the *AdvancedDataControl* Object

Next, you must set up the AdvancedDataControl object so that it provides the connectivity to the backend database. This object is linked to the preceding grid control with the BINDINGS property. The properties for this object include the connect string that will be used to gain access to the remote database. As with the grid control, this object will be downloaded from the server, so you'll need to make sure you have it installed at the location indicated in the CODEBASE parameter.

**TIP** Note the ID property in particular as this is what you'll use to refer to the control later when you move around the virtual dataset.

This is one control measure that helps to make sure you're aware of all connections to your database and what their intent is. With this in mind, you'll want to make sure your ODBC configurations are as specific as possible. If you're providing SA-level access to data on your server, you're asking for problems as these approaches to working with the database become more prevalent.

```
...
<!-- Non-visual controls - AdvancedDataControl -->
<OBJECT CLASSID="clsid:9381D8F2-0288-11d0-9501-00AA00B911A5"
    ID="SControl"
    CODEBASE="HTTP://<%=Request.ServerVariables("SERVER_NAME")%>/MSADC/
    ➡msadc10.cab"
    WIDTH=1 HEIGHT=1>
    <PARAM NAME="BINDINGS" VALUE="Grid1;">
    <PARAM NAME="Connect" VALUE="DSN=ADCDEMO;UID=guest;PWD=guest;">
    <PARAM NAME="Server" VALUE="http://
    ➡<%=Request.ServerVariables("SERVER_NAME")%>">
</OBJECT>
```

## Completing the Application

Finally, now that the objects are initiated, you can work with the objects and the results set and perform the operations that you need to complete your application. The first SUBroutine, the LOAD routine, will run immediately on loading of the form. This routine populates the grid control with the initial results from the database. The .Refresh method is used to accomplish this, just as it is when the control is based in Visual Basic.

```
...
<!-- VBS scripting for composing queries, updating profiles, and retrieving
➡search results. -->

<SCRIPT LANGUAGE="VBScript">

Dim myQuery
```

Part
**VII**

Ch
**26**

```
SUB Load
     Grid1.CAPTION = "Arcadia Bay Corporate Phone Directory"
     'Initialize data grid with column names only.
     SControl.SQL = "Select FirstName, LastName, Title, Email, Building, Room,
     ➥Phone from Employee where 2 < 1 for browse"
     SControl.Refresh
END SUB
```

## Looking at the Results

If the user clicks the Find button, you can see a great example of how a query is issued against the database and how it is used to return the results of the query. The query is built in the variable myQuery. This string variable will contain the select statement that will be submitted against the grid control.

If you work down through this listing, you'll see that the query is built by using the .Value properties for the fields defined on the HTML form. These properties are inserted into the string if they are non-blank, then a percent-sign, "%" is appended, making the entry a wild card.

Finally, the .SQL property of the grid control is set to the value of the myQuery variable and the grid is refreshed to show the results of the query.

```
   ...
'Implement "Find" button - composes a dynamic SQL query to be processed by the
➥database and returns matching records to be bound to the SGrid object.

SUB Find_OnClick
     myQuery = "Select FirstName, LastName, Title, Email, Building, Room, Phone
     ➥from Employee"
     'Check QBE fields and compose a dynamic SQL query.
     IF (SFirst.Value <> "") THEN
          myQuery = myQuery + " where FirstName like '" + SFirst.Value + "%'"
     END IF
     IF (SLast.Value <> "") THEN
          myQuery = myQuery + " where LastName like '" + SLast.Value + "%'"
     END IF
     IF (STitle.Value <> "") THEN
          myQuery = myQuery + " where Title like '" + STitle.Value + "%'"
     END IF
     IF (SEmail.Value <> "") THEN
          myQuery = myQuery + " where Email like '" + SEmail.Value + "%'"
     END IF
     myQuery = myQuery + " for browse"  'Mark recordset for editing.
     'Set the new query and then refresh the SControl so that the new results are
displayed.
     SControl.SQL = myQuery
     SControl.Refresh

END SUB
```

If you're familiar with the DAO approach to database objects and methods, the navigation routines will look obvious to you. You'll notice the DAO-like statements in the next few subroutines.

Each performs as it does with the DAO, moving the logical record pointer around the dataset. The `SubmitChanges` method sends all updates to the server. When you call this method, the virtual tables are not updated, though they will likely reflect your changes as the control is bound to the data source.

**N O T E**  One thing to keep in mind as a difference between this and Visual Basic data-bound controls is that the information is not updated until you call the `SubmitChanges` method. To restore your dataset to its original state, use the `CancelUpdate` method. This will drop all changes you've made to the dataset. ■

```
'Submits edits made and pull a clean copy of the new data.
SUB Update_OnClick
        SControl.SubmitChanges
     SControl.Refresh
END SUB

'Cancel edits and restores original values.
SUB Cancel_OnClick
        SControl.CancelUpdate
END SUB
```

There's an interesting trend here that you've either noticed or will notice soon after you implement these types of pages on your Web site. There's a fair amount of code, ActiveX controls, and logic running behind this type of application. This is a far cry from the typically light-interaction-based systems that HTML is currently sporting on the Internet.

# Weighing the Benefits of ADC Technology

Be careful in your use of ADC technology. Only use the active connection and dataset pooling capabilities in those cases where another approach simply won't cut it. Though admonished by Microsoft as a dead technology, it's recommended that you consider the IDC approach first, if only for its smaller footprint at both the client and the server.

Since you can mix and match your approach to different portions of a given application, be sure you keep in mind that each page you design and develop should be considered alone relative to the best approach to the data management.

The ADC is the technologically and functionally superior model to use for developing applications. The downside is that it requires the use of Internet Explorer for the Visual Basic scripting, as of this writing, and it's heavy on the initial downloads of the various ActiveX controls. It may be better suited for intranet application development in cases where an application usage is casual.

In cases where you are building an application that will be used quite a lot, the initial download of the components is not much more than a typical installation of other software and may play out to be less of an issue in the design considerations.

**Part VII**

**Ch 26**

Finally, be sure to review the DAO model for details regarding different methods that are supported. Also, check the Microsoft site frequently, as more methods are added and additional controls become available. This is a technology that can bring some solid tools to the mainstream, frequently used Web-based application development arena.

# From Here...

The ADC technologies are a comprehensive solution to the need to have intelligent, database-oriented controls on your forms.  Using the ADC gives you the opportunity to develop much more functional forms when compared to some other Internet technologies, and the ADC will let you use the functionality offered by third-party utilities and add-ins.

From here, you'll want to pay special attention to the other chapters that cover alternative database access techniques, including the following:

Chapter 24, "The Internet Database Connector: Providing Database Access on the Web," shows how to build Web pages without any reliance on client-side functionality.

Chapter 25, "Introducing ActiveX Data Objects," shows how you can use DAO-like scripting to work against databases.

Chapter 27, "Building Web Database Applications by Using Visual InterDev," covers how you use InterDev to develop applications by using these different database access technologies.

# Building Web Database Applications by Using Visual InterDev

**S**o far, you have been exposed to many different concepts and skills associated with Web programming—network protocols, Internet architecture, client-side versus server-side programming issues, and, finally, different coding languages that give you the ability to develop Web applications. Almost all of these have been at the level of a technical programmer. This means you must have fairly good knowledge of HTML programming and development skills. ■

---

**Web-based application design**

Design, create, and manage Web-based applications using Visual InterDev.

**Page editing using FrontPage97**

Create, save, and modify pages while using the FrontPage97 editor for Visual InterDev.

**Using wizards to create Web pages**

Use the Visual InterDev wizards to creat Web pages and dataform pages.

**Accessing databases on the Web**

Build SQL queries and access database information from the Web application.

**Managing the Web site**

Manage a production Web application using Visual InterDev.

# Understanding Visual InterDev

Just as Visual Basic was the answer to creating Windows applications by using a GUI-style programmers interface, Microsoft has created a product that brings many of the Web programming tools together in a GUI programming tool. Visual InterDev is the newest addition to the Microsoft Visual family of tools. It gives Web application programmers the ability to create and maintain Web applications in an easy-to-use visual environment. Visual InterDev brings together several pieces of a Web puzzle and gives them to you in a coordinated, controllable development tool.

In addition, it comes with many wizards to allow quick creation of Web page functionality. Visual InterDev supports a team effort in application development and works with Visual SourceSafe for controlling changes made by multiple programmers. In addition, it works with Microsoft FrontPage so that non-programmers can work with the programming staff in the creation of Web pages. Finally, any OCX components that have ActiveX capabilities can be used within the Web application.

Other components that are included with Visual InterDev give you the ability to create images to be used on the Web pages and a tool to include music or sound. A more important tool is a Personal Web server that can be used as a stand-alone Web server for testing new Web applications. All of these tools give the Web programmer the ability to build state-of-the-art Internet and intranet applications.

In this chapter, you create a new Web application using Visual InterDev. This application makes use of the Biblio.mdb Access database that comes with Visual Basic. You see how easy it is to create a sophisticated multi-page Web site that allows the user to view, modify, and delete data in the database. Along the way, you are introduced to as many features of the product as possible.

# Designing a Web-Based Application

Creating a Web application can be seen as just another windows application. However, if you look closely at it, you see that it is not just another application. When designing a Windows application, it is usually a stand-alone program for a single computer; or it can be an application made to work in a network environment; or now, it can be a Web-based application to be used by anyone with access to the Internet. What should the application do and where should it be done? These are the questions that need answering.

For single computer use, the answers are easy. Everything is on one computer. No thought must be given to multiple database access and what programs are running where. In network applications, the database is usually on a file server or in a database server, and the programs might be running on the local computer or on an application server. This means that the database is in a central location for use by the application no matter where it is executing.

## Network versus Internet

When talking about network and Internet applications, the words might sound alike but they mean slightly different things. For instance, file servers in a network are PCs that act as the hard disk where database and other files are stored. These drives are connected to the user's PC using a standard drive letter. These drives are accessed like any standard hard drive. However, when using the Internet, all processing is done through a Web browser using HTML code.

In a Web application, any database files are accessed via the server name. Unless the user is connected to the Internet and is running the application, the database is not connected to the user's PC.

Where a standard application is made up of several windows forms that run on the user's PC, a Web application is made up of several Web pages that are linked together to form an application.

**N O T E**  All Web application page files are stored in script format. These *scripts* execute on the client or server when you view a Web page in a browser. ■

As you start creating your Web site and inserting new forms and pages, you might notice that many different types of files are added to your project directory. These files include the following:

- Wordpad or Notepad type text files (.TXT).
- Active Server Pages for interactive Web pages (.ASP).
- HTML pages for standard HTML-formatted Web pages (.HTM).
- HTML Layout files to create customized Web forms (.ALX).
- Image files to display pictures (.GIF or .BMP).
- Multimedia files to add sound and video to the Web application (.AVI, .WAV or .MID).

HTML files are created by using an HTML editor such as FrontPage, which is included with Visual InterDev. These can contain many embedded files, such as images, sounds, ActiveX Controls, and scripts. Currently Visual InterDev supports two scripting languages: Visual Basic Script and Microsoft JavaScript. Script code is embedded within the HTML code and is executed when the HTML page is downloaded to the client PC.

A Global.asa file contains the information that the server needs to start your application. There are four event procedures that are executed when the associated event occurs. Most times, Visual InterDev adds code to these events automatically, depending on what you have included in the pages.

Any Web application starts with a *virtual root*, which represents the directory that contains all the files included in your Web project. The virtual root contains the name of the Web server (called the *domain*) and the name of the Web project. This forms the first part of the URL address for the Web site you are creating. For example, to view a page named index.htm (see Figure 27.1), the address would be:

http://webserver/lbmsoftware/index.htm

**FIG. 27.1**

Home page from an existing Web application showing a Banner Title and links to other pages on the Web site.

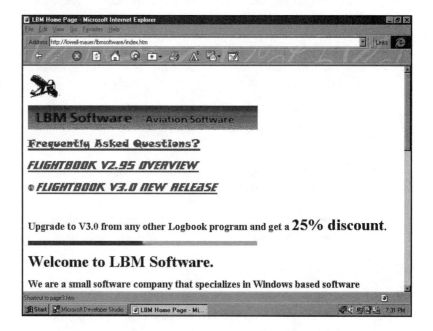

The home page is where users normally start when accessing a Web application. This page then links to other pages within the application and possibly outside of the application. To see how all folders and pages link, Visual InterDev lets you view any application's WWW Links (see Figure 27.2) on the Web, while you are connected.

Now that you have taken a brief look at what is included in a Web project, the first thing you really have to decide is what type of application you are creating for the Web. This is not as easy as it seems. Web applications can do anything from allowing the user to browse a list of some sort to purchasing products from your company, or even a mixture of many different functions. Web applications can be for internal company use (intranet applications), external customer usage (Internet applications), or a combination of both. Included with Visual InterDev are several sample Web applications that guide you through the creation of a Web project.

In this chapter, you create a Web application that allows the user to browse a list of book titles and then get information about the books (for example, author and publisher). In addition, the application will have the capability to add authors, and new books for any authors, in the database. Even though this will be a small application, it exposes you to many of the tools and techniques within Visual InterDev that you need to build larger, more complex Web applications.

**FIG. 27.2**
The WWW Links display of a Web application allows you to view all page relationships on one display.

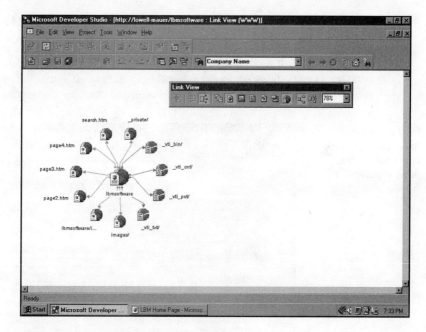

# Creating Your First Web Application

Before jumping feet first into creating a complete company-wide Web application, you should see how the environment works. Start by creating a Web project and then add a few simple pages and forms that will become the basis of the final application. This lets you get comfortable using the tools that are included with Visual InterDev.

First and foremost, Visual InterDev needs an active Web server to connect to in order to work. If you are connected to a development Web server, you can use that; but, if you are working with a single PC, be it Windows 95 or Windows NT, you can run Personal Web Server of Peer Web Services on their respective platforms. For the purposes of the book, Visual InterDev was used on a Windows 95 stand-alone PC using the Personal Web Server.

The hardest part of creating a Web application is deciding what it should *look* like. What style, color, and animation, if any, should be on the home page? These questions make it seem like Web developers are artists of some type. Well, they are. A measure of how good a Web site is, is by how many people visit it. The better it looks, the more people it attracts.

Your home page should say something about the company it represents and give the user the ability to move throughout the Web site to get to the information he needs. It must also be easy to follow and understand, in terms of input and where to move the mouse in order to navigate though the Web application.

A Visual InterDev application consists of a virtual root on a Web server and all of its files and subfolders. To create a new Web application, you are going to use the Web Project Wizard that

Part
VII

Ch

27

comes with Visual InterDev. The wizard connects to the Web server and then prompts you for the information it needs to create the application Web site.

Make sure the Web server is started or that you are connected to it and then start Visual InterDev. The first thing you notice when the program starts is that the help documentation is always available in the InfoView tab of the Project window (see Figure 27.3).

**FIG. 27.3**

The Visual InterDev main screen with all three areas displayed.

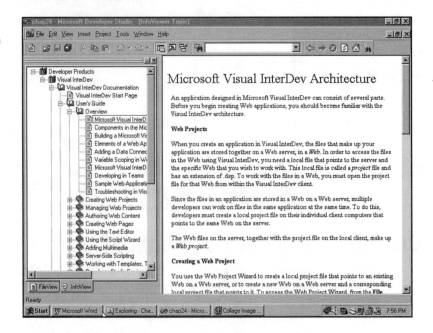

Let's stop and get familiar with the Visual InterDev development environment. The screen is divided into three areas: the Toolbars, the Project window and the Infoviewer (see Figure 27.3). The Infoviewer is used to edit the HTML source or preview what the page(s) look like when displayed by a Web browser.

The following steps will create a new Web application using one of the wizards that come with Visual InterDev.

1. To begin the wizard session, from the menu, select File, New or press Ctrl+N; then click the Projects tab. This displays the New dialog box (see Figure 27.4) where you see five wizards to choose from. Select the Web Project Wizard and choose a name for the project.

2. For this chapter, the project name is DemoWeb. Enter your project name and location for InterDev to save any files to. Click OK to continue.

3. This screen asks you to select the server to install this new project to. After you select the server, click Next.

**FIG. 27.4**
The Visual InterDev New File Dialog Box shows several options for creating a new Web page.

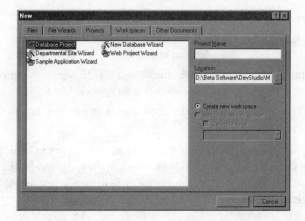

4. InterDev now contacts the server and gets a list of Web sites that are available on it. You can choose to add this project to an existing Web site or create a new one. Keep the default setting of a new Web and name it DemoWeb (see Figure 27.5). In addition, you can choose to have InterDev index your site to allow the user to perform full text searches if needed.

**FIG. 27.5**
Naming the new Web application that is being created.

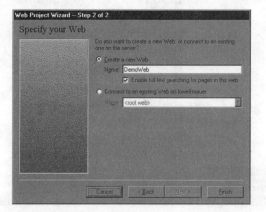

5. Click Finish to complete the creation process. Congratulations, you have a Web site at

    http://[server name]/DemoWeb

Look at your InterDev work area and you will see a new tab in the Project window. The FileView tab shows you the new Web site. Click the plus (+) sign to see the files that were automatically added to the project. These files are the following:

Part
VII

Ch
27

| File Name | Description |
|---|---|
| Global.asa | This file contains any code that needs to run when the Web application starts. |
| Search.htm | This file is the default HTML page that can search all the pages in Web application for specified text. |
| Images Folder | This folder contains any images that are used in the Web application. |

The first thing you need to add to your Web is the main form or the home page. Some applications call it the Default page. Add an HTML page and then, if you really like HTML coding, edit it using the InterDev HTML editor (see Figure 27.6) or, to add text and links to other Web pages without having to know HTML code, use the FrontPage97 editor.

**FIG. 27.6**

The default HTML source editor showing the HTML code from the Search page.

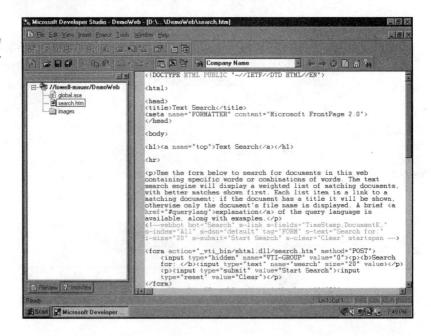

Every Web page you ever create begins with an HTML file. Any ActiveX control, Design-time ActiveX controls, HTML Layouts, or scripts you create are added to the HTML file as <OBJECT> or <SCRIPT> tags for that page.

To set the editor, select the search.htm page in the FileView window, then right-click it and choose Open With. This allows you to specify the default editor for any pages you need to modify (see Figure 27.7). Select Microsoft FrontPage Editor and then choose Close.

To create an HTML page as shown in Figure 27.8, follow these steps:

1. Choose File, New. From the Files tab, select the HTML Page (see Figure 27.9).

**FIG. 27.7**

Opening an HTML page for editing by selecting the editor of choice.

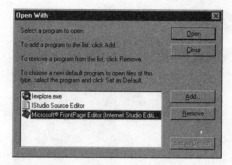

2. Click the <u>A</u>dd to Project check box to tell Visual InterDev that you want to add this page to an existing open project. If you have more than one Web project open, you can select the particular project that you want to add the page to from the drop-down list. Enter **default** as the File <u>N</u>ame of the page and click OK to finish creating the page.

**FIG. 27.8**

The Final Web page that will be created showing several Hyperlinks and an Image.

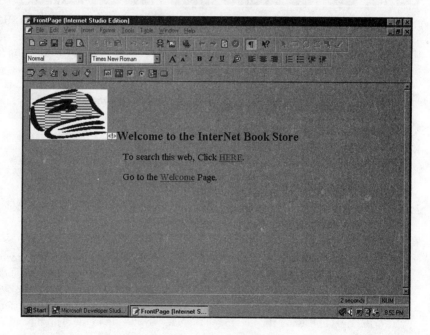

3. Using the FrontPage editor, you add the text shown and create a hyperlink to the search page. You also need to add a hyperlink on the search page to return to the home page named default.htm.

**TIP** When adding new pages and making changes to existing ones, it is always a good idea to save the changes.

Part
**VII**

Ch
**27**

**FIG. 27.9**
Choosing an HTML page
from the Files tab to
create.

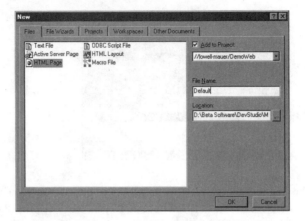

# Using the MS FrontPage97 HTML Editor

Visual InterDev comes with a modified version of the FrontPage 97 HTML editor. This lets developers create HTML pages using normal windows capabilities. This method does not require the developer to manually enter HTML tags. Edit the default.htm file by selecting it, right-clicking it, and choosing <u>O</u>pen. After opening a Web page with this editor you will be working within the FrontPage editor environment (see Figure 27.10). It is here where you can enter text, images, tables, hyperlinks, and so on—all without knowing HTML coding.

### TROUBLESHOOTING

**I have the source code for a Web page showing and I tried to open the FrontPage editor. Nothing happened. Why not?**

If you have a Web page open with one editor, Visual InterDev does not open it a second time with another editor. Close the source code editor and try FrontPage again.

The small symbol you see on the page (<!>) is a comment to show you where HTML code should be added. You can either ignore it or delete it from the page, as it does not affect any-thing. Now, using standard text editing features such as font size, style, centering, and bolding. Enter in the home page heading you want the users to see when they open this Web site. On the next line, enter the text to tell the user how to get to the search page. Center the text on both lines and then experiment with changing font sizes and colors. As you can see in Figure 27.8, the word HERE is a different color than the rest of the line. This means that a hyperlink is attached to that word and, by clicking it, the user goes to that Web page.

To create this hyperlink, select the word or words that you want the link attached to and then click the Create Hyperlink button on the toolbar to display the hyperlink properties form (see Figure 27.11). This is where you specify what Web page to jump to when these word(s) are clicked. To jump to a page within this Web application, just enter the URL as shown in Figure 27.11.

**FIG. 27.10**
The Initial Default Web page that is created has nothing on it to display.

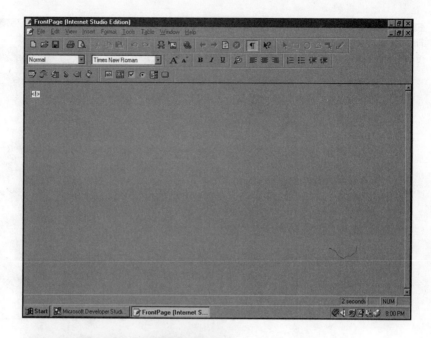

**FIG. 27.11**
Hyperlink Properties form showing Web page URL.

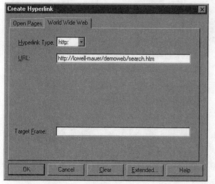

As you can see from the final default page, an image file has also been added to the page (see Figure 27.12). To add an image, follow these steps:

1. Place the cursor at the beginning of the first line.

2. Then choose Insert, Image to display the Image dialog box (see Figure 27.13).

3. To select an image file, click Browse and select any image you want to use. (I used book3.gif, which is included on the CD-ROM.) Click OK and the image is inserted into the Web page.

This livens up the page and makes it a little less boring. After you have made all of these additions to the default page, save the page and close it, but do not close the FrontPage editor. This makes it quicker to edit the next page. Now go back to Visual InterDev.

Part
VII

Ch
27

**FIG. 27.12**

Final Default Web page in the FrontPage editor.

**FIG. 27.13**

Selecting an image file to add to the Web page.

To change the search page so that is uses the home page you just created, follow these steps:

1. From the FileView tab in Visual InterDev, select the search page, right-click it, and choose Open to edit the page.

2. Scroll to the bottom of the page to find the words Back to Top.

3. Now add a new line below this one that says Return to HomePage and attach a hyperlink to this text that returns the user to the default page for this Web site.

4. To match the other link above it, change the font size and bold the text.

5. At any time you can preview the page to see what it looks like by choosing Preview in Browser from the File menu in either FrontPage or Visual InterDev. This shows you how the page looks and also lets you test the hyperlinks that you added.

# Getting the Most from Visual InterDev

Congratulations! You have created your first Web site. It might not be the biggest or the most sophisticated, but it works. Test it by right-clicking default.htm in the FileView window and selecting Browse With. This shows you the list of available browsers. Select Internet Explorer and click Open. Internet Explorer starts, contacts the server, and displays the page you created (see Figure 27.14). This is how a user sees the Web site that you created.

**FIG. 27.14**
DemoWeb in the Internet Explorer browser.

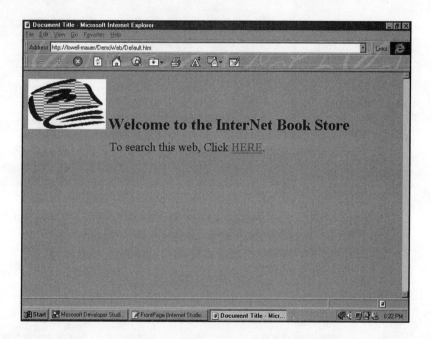

Click HERE to jump to the search page, scroll to the bottom, and click Return to Homepage to see how the links work. Now that you have a feel for what it's like to create a simple Web site, let's add some more complex pages and build an application that allows the user to interact with what he is looking at. Visual InterDev gives you some simple ways of controlling the Web site and adding pre-existing files to the Web application.

## Working Copies

While working within Visual InterDev, you might have noticed that some of the pages in the FileView are shown in color and some are *grayed* out (see Figure 27.15). When you open a file to edit, the file icon is then shown in color. This means that you have a working copy of that page on your hard drive; the *gray* icon indicates the file only exists on the Web server and no local copy is present.

**FIG. 27.15**
FileView showing working copy of the default.htm page.

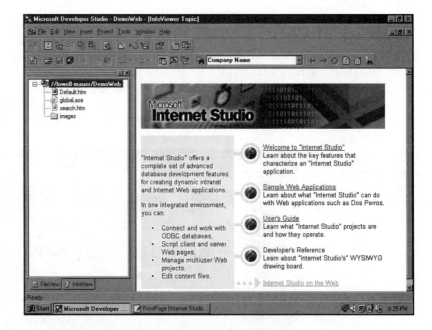

What all of this really means is that users can access your Web site even when you are updating pages in it. To get your changes put back onto the Web, you must *release* the working copy back to the Web. Right-click the page and then choose the Release Working Copy option. Double-clicking the grayed icon for that page opens the page for editing using whatever editor is set as the default.

## Adding Existing Web Files

If you have been doing Web development for any length of time, you might have existing Web page files that you want to include in this new Web application. With Visual InterDev it is very easy to import existing files to the project. Click the root level of the project, then click the Add Folder Contents or Add Files button on the toolbar. Locate the folder or files you want to add and select them. This automatically copies them into your Web project on the Web server.

**T I P** This is a quick way of adding any of the completed files for this Web application that are on the CD-ROM included with the book.

## Adding a Simple Active Server Page

Before jumping into a very complex active server page (like a database entry form), you are going to add a simple active page that allows you to get the feel for adding VBScript to the HTML form. Then you will test it. An Active Server Page has the extension of .asp for its file names. These pages are just HTML documents that contain embedded server-side scripting logic. This instructs the Web server to execute the script logic and remove it from the .asp page before sending it to the client browser. Visual InterDev comes with many controls and wizards that help you in the process of creating Active Server Pages.

However, to introduce you to the concept of the .asp, it is very helpful to build your first ActiveX Server Page by hand. To do this, choose File, New. From the Files tab, select the Active Server Page. Enter **Welcome** in the File Name text box. Finally, verify the location to save this file to—the location should be the same directory that holds the other files for this project. Click OK to add the new page to the project. The Active Server Page is now added to your project and the HTML code is displayed to you in the InterDev HTML editor. This source editor displays the HTML code in a color-coded listing. Any server-side script is shown is yellow (see Figure 27.16). If you look at the first line in the listing, you see that, by default, Visual InterDev generates client and server-side script as Visual Basic script. If you want, you can easily change this default to Microsoft's JavaScript by choosing Tools, Options and then going to the HTML tab.

**FIG. 27.16**

This is an example of an active Server Page source editor showing how different colors are used.

Part

**VII**

Ch

**27**

Using this editor, you are going to make some changes to the HTML code that is shown. First, replace the default HTML "Document Title" title tag with "Web Page Welcome".

Next, enter the following VBScript code immediately following the comment:

```
<!-- Insert HTML here -- >
```

Listing 27.1 displays a line of text four times in increasing size and changing color.

---

**Listing 27.1  ASPSIMP.TXT  Simple Active Server Page Script**

```
<%for i=3 to 6%>
<Font Size =<%=i%>
<%if i=3 then%>
<Font Color=red>
<%elseif i=4 then%>
<font Color=yellow>
<%elseif i=5 then%>
<font Color=brown>
<%else%>
<font Color=green>
<%end if%>
Welcome to the Web<BR>
<%next%>
```

---

Save this page and preview it by right-clicking anywhere in the source code and choosing the Preview <*page name*> option. You can see how the code was executed (see Figure 27.17).

**FIG. 27.17**

Final HTML page showing the Welcome text displayed four times.

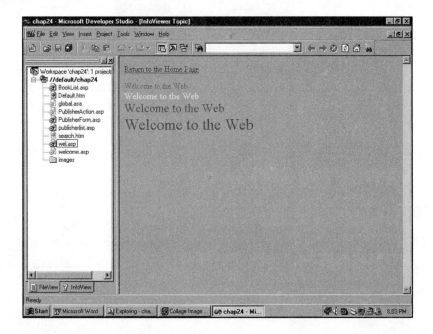

**N O T E**  After previewing the HTML page, if you make any changes to the scripting code or have added anything to the form, you must Refresh the page when previewing it again.  ■

Now you need to add a link to it from the default home page. Do this by opening the default page in the FrontPage editor and adding a line of text, with the link to this page associated with it (see Figure 27.18).

**FIG. 27.18**

This is the default home page with new hyperlink on it.

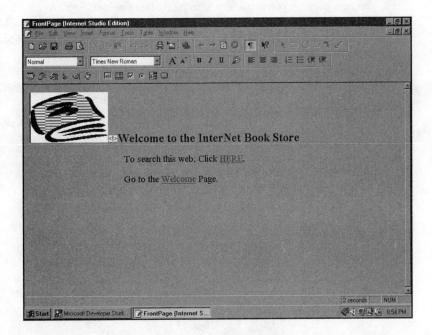

Finally, on the Welcome page, you need to add two more lines of code to give the user a way back to the home page. Using the default source editor, add the following HTML code just before the script code that is already there:

```
<Font Size=3>
<p><a href="default1.htm">Return to the Home Page</a></p>
```

As you can see, this is standard HTML code. You can also add this hyperlink by using the FrontPage editor (as shown earlier in the chapter). Preview the default page and test the new links that you have added.

# Getting the Most from a Database

Any number of sites that you have visited on the Internet should look a lot like this one. Most Web sites are for information only. This means that the pages are linked together via hyperlinks, and maybe the user can search the site looking for something in particular. What makes a Web application unique is that it allows users to interact with the data that is being displayed to them.

Part
**VII**

Ch
**27**

So, with this in mind, a database will be added to this Web site. It allows the user to browse a list of books and their authors, and lets the user update the information about the books using the FrontPage editor, you will create the book list page that contains a table to list the book titles and their respective authors.

Select File, New, choose HTML page from the Files tab, and name it **BookList**. Close the source editor and double-click the BookList.htm. This starts the FrontPage editor and displays the new page for you to modify. Start by putting the book3.gif on the top center of the page. Then, just below the picture, put the heading for this page, Internet Book List. On the third line, insert a hyperlink to allow the user to go back to the default home page. On the fourth line, you will insert a table (see Figure 27.19).

**FIG. 27.19**

The new HTML page displayed in the FrontPage editor.

Choose Table, Insert Table to display the Insert Table dialog box (see Figure 27.20). Then enter 2 Rows, 2 Columns, and a Border size of 2. In addition, in the Alignment box, select Center. For now, leave the other options alone. Click OK to add the table to the form.

Headings for the table are next. Click the upper-left cell of the table and enter the heading **Book Title**. In the next column, enter **Book Author**.

Now let's select both heading columns by moving the mouse pointer to the left-hand border of the upper-left cell. When the cursor changes to an arrow, click once to select the entire top row. Increase the font size by clicking the Increase Font Size button twice. Next, center and bold the headings.

**FIG. 27.20**
Insert Table dialog box.

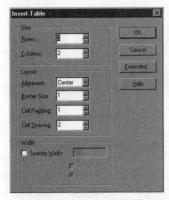

Select the second row and click the Center Text toolbar button to have all of the data text centered. The final result should look like Figure 27.21. Save the file, then exit from FrontPage to return to Visual InterDev.

**FIG. 27.21**
Finished empty Table form with Headings.

Now you have an empty page that displays very little. Before continuing, release the working copy of this page and rename it to BookList.asp. This makes the HTML page you created an Active Server Page and allows you to add ActiveX server objects to it from within Visual InterDev.

**N O T E**  Whenever you rename a file, Visual InterDev asks if you want any links that refer to this
page to be updated. Click Yes to continue. ■

To continue, you need to add a database connection to the project. Although Visual InterDev
works with MS SQL Server, you are using MS Access, which requires an ODBC connection to
connect to the database.

## Connecting to the Database

To create the ODBC connection, click the 32-bit ODBC icon in the Windows 95 Control Panel
to start the ODBC Data Source Administration (see Figure 27.22). Then, to add a new System
Data Source, go to the System DSN tab and choose Add. If Visual InterDev was installed correctly there should be an ODBC driver for Microsoft Access. Select the Access driver and click
Finish.

**FIG. 27.22**

The ODBC Data Source
Administration form.

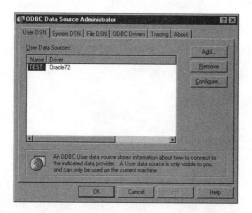

The ODBC Microsoft Access setup screen (see Figure 27.23) is then displayed. Enter
**BookStore** as the data source name and a description for this data source, then click Select to
choose the database to use. For this demo, the database is from Visual Basic and the name is
biblio.mdb. Click the OK button to finish the ODBC setup. Now, from Visual InterDev, the
ODBC data source BookStore can be accessed.

**N O T E**  Because this demo is on a stand-alone PC, the ODBC data source is on a physical drive. In
a network environment, the database could be anywhere. ■

To add a data connection to the project, right-click the root level of the project and click the
Add Data Connection button on the toolbar. Go to the Machine Data Source tab and choose the
data source that you just created (see Figure 27.29). Click OK to add the connection.

**FIG. 27.23**

ODBC Microsoft Access
97 Definition Setup
form.

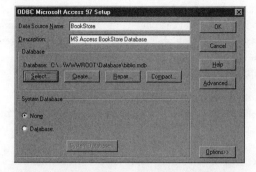

**FIG. 27.24**

New Data Connection—
Select Data Source
form.

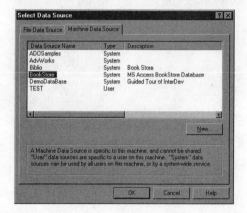

You are then shown the properties sheet for the connection (see Figure 27.25). Change the
Data Connection Name to BooksDB and close the properties sheet by clicking the button in
the upper-right corner of the form.

**FIG. 27.25**

Data Connection
Properties sheet.

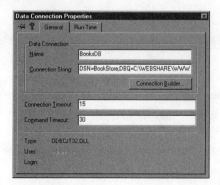

Part

**VII**

Ch

**27**

You might have noticed that the Global.asa file is now shown having a local copy, and a database icon is attached to it. The Global.asa page is the *Front Door* of your Web application. It lets the server set variables such as the database connection whenever a user enters your Web site for the first time. No matter which page the user goes to when first accessing your Web site, the Global.asa is executed once for that user.

When the database connection is established, a DataView tab is added to the project window. Click that tab and investigate the database you are using. At the top of the window, you see the name of the Web project. Expand the connection by clicking the plus (+) sign to the left of the DemoWeb project name. The database name is now shown. Expand the view again to include the table and view folders, then expand the tables folder to see the tables that are in the database. If you expand one of the tables, you see the columns in that table (see Figure 27.26).

**FIG. 27.26**
DataView window showing Database Tables and Columns.

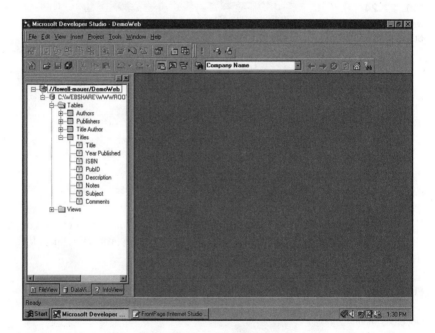

Finally, if you double-click any of the table names, you are shown the current record-set for that table (see Figure 27.27). It looks a lot like the datagrid in Microsoft Access. Additionally, if you are allowed to add, update, or delete records in the database, you can do it from this interface. Close the datagrid by choosing File, Close.

The database is now connected to your Web application, and you can add the objects that display the data to the user.

**FIG. 27.27**
Data Access Grid
showing current data
from table.

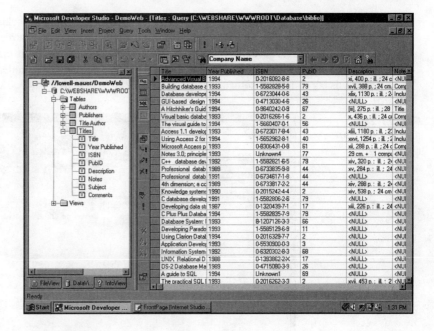

## Using the Query Designer

Visual InterDev comes with a very sophisticated database Query Designer, which gives you the ability to build and test the SQL statements used to access the database. Although you can use the Query Designer alone to build and test SQL statements, Visual InterDev comes with data-access controls that use the Query Designer to automatically generate server-side scripting code to execute the query on the Web server and send the results to the Web page on the client. These controls are a new type of ActiveX control called design-time ActiveX Controls. These controls can generate standard HTML and script logic that is viewable on any browser.

▶ For more information about Web Design-time ActiveX Controls, how they work, and how you can build your own, **see** Chapter 33, "Building Web Design-Time Controls," on **p. 805**

There are six design-time controls that are included with Visual InterDev, but other companies can build their own design-time controls to extend the functionality of Visual InterDev. The two controls that you will use in this Web application are the Data Range Header and the Data Range Footer. The first allows you to build a SQL query using the Query Designer and then automatically creates all of the server logic needed to retrieve records from the database. The second control is used with the Data Range Header to specify the end of the database formatted fields in the Active Server Page. You might be surprised to see how little code you have to enter yourself.

Part
**VII**

Ch

To add the Data Range Header, open the BookList.asp file by double-clicking it in the FileView window. This allows you to edit the HTML code. Scroll through the source code until you find the end of the first row definition in the table (see Figure 27.28). This is marked by the first closing </tr> tag in the source code. To add a new line to the source code, put the cursor right after this tag and press Return.

**FIG. 27.28**

BookList.asp HTML source code.

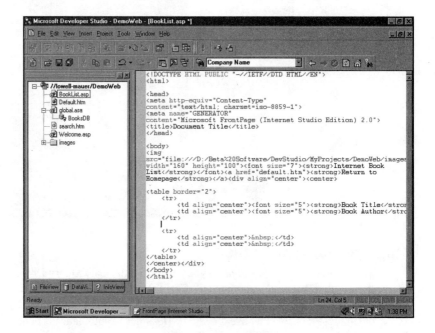

Choose Insert, Into HTML, ActiveX Control. A tab dialog box is displayed showing both standard ActiveX controls and design-time ActiveX controls that are registered on your PC. Click the Design-time tab to see the list of design-time controls. Add the Data Range Header Control by double-clicking it from the list. The property sheet for this control appears (see Figure 27.29) allowing you to set up the control for your Web page.

Change the ID to DataHeader, then select the BooksDB database connection from the Data Connection drop-down list. Then set the Bar Alignment to Centered. This centers the database paging buttons that are inserted at the bottom of the page. These paging buttons are what allow the user to page through the database records.

Click the Record Paging check box to allow the user to page through the results instead of showing the entire table at once. Then set the Range Type to 2 - Table. This indicates that the results will be displayed in an HTML table. Now click the Advanced tab and set the Cursor Type to 1 - Keyset. Leave the other options alone for now.

Finally, you need to add the SQL to specify what data to retrieve from the database. Click the SQL Builder button to go to the Query Designer, then close the Data Connections property sheet. You are now ready to create the query to access the database.

**FIG. 27.29**

Data Range Header
ActiveX property sheet.

If you have ever used Microsoft Access or Microsoft Query (which comes with Microsoft Office) then you already know how to use the Query Designer. Several different forms appear with the Query Designer (see Figure 27.30). Dock the floating Database Toolbar by dragging and dropping the left side of the query design window. To add a table to the Diagram window, simply drag and drop it in the window. This is where you can define *joins*, or relationships between tables.

At any time you can check your SQL by clicking the SQL- button or run the SQL by clicking the ! button. To add columns to the SQL statement, just click it or drag it into the Grid window. As you do this, you might notice that the SQL window shows you the SQL you are building as it changes. The last window at the bottom is the Results window that displays the SQL results when you execute the query.

Open the Views folder in the database and drag the All Titles view into the Diagram window. From the columns listed, select Title and Author by clicking them. You see them appear in both the Grid and SQL windows. Next, change the heading for the Titles column by entering **Book Title** in the Alias cell for that column. Finally, click the Sort Type cell and select Ascending to sort the books alphabetically. Run the SQL to see the results (see Figure 27.31).

Close the Query Designer by choosing File, Close. When prompted, choose Yes to update the DataHeader, then close the DataHeader control. This shows you the HTML code that was added to the page.

**TIP** You can edit any design-time control in a page by right-clicking anywhere in the source code that was generated by it and choosing the Edit Design-Time Control option from the pop-up menu.

Now let's add the HTML code that moves the data into the table. The Data Range Header loops through the SQL query-set and adds a new row to the table as needed. Take a closer look at the HTML source for BookList.asp. You might notice that a large amount of code (see Listing 27.2) has been added to the file.

Part

**VII**

Ch

**27**

**FIG. 27.30**
New Query Designer
Window.

Diagram Pane

Grid Pane

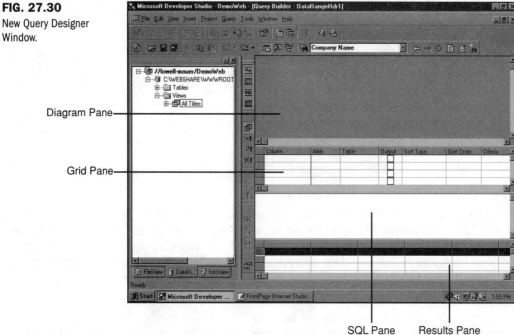

SQL Pane      Results Pane

**FIG. 27.31**
Finished database SQL
statement for the Book
List Table.

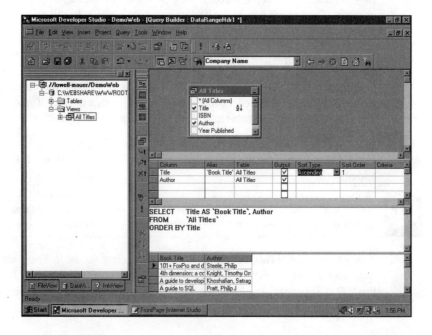

**Listing 27.2   BOOKLIST.ASP   Full HTML Code that Was Generated by the DataHeader and DataFooter Controls**

```
<!--METADATA TYPE="DesignerControl" startspan
    <OBJECT ID="DataHeader" WIDTH=151 HEIGHT=24
     CLASSID="CLSID:F602E721-A281-11CF-A5B7-0080C73AAC7E">
        <PARAM NAME="_Version" VALUE="65536">
        <PARAM NAME="_Version" VALUE="65536">
        <PARAM NAME="_ExtentX" VALUE="3986">
        <PARAM NAME="_ExtentY" VALUE="635">
        <PARAM NAME="_StockProps" VALUE="0">
        <PARAM NAME="DataConnection" VALUE="BooksDB">
        <PARAM NAME="CommandText" VALUE="SELECT Title AS 'Book Title', Author
FROM 'All Titles' ORDER BY Title">
        <PARAM NAME="CursorType" VALUE="1">
        <PARAM NAME="RangeType" VALUE="2">
        <PARAM NAME="BarAlignment" VALUE="2">
        <PARAM NAME="PageSize" VALUE="10">
    </OBJECT>
-->
    <% tEmptyRecordset = False
    fFirstPass = True
    tPageSize = 10
    tRangeType = "Table"

    fNoRecordset = False
    If IsObject(Session("DataHeader")) Then
        Set DataHeader = Session("DataHeader")
        If IsEmpty(Request("PagingRequest")) Then
            PagingMove = "Refresh"
        Else
            PagingMove = Trim(Request("PagingMove"))
            If Request("PagingRequest") <> "DataHeader" Then
                PagingMove = "Refresh"
            End If
        End If
    Else
        fNoRecordset = True
    End If

    tRecordsProcessed = 0
    tHeaderName = "DataHeader"
    tBarAlignment = "Center"

    If fNoRecordset Then
        Set cmdTemp = Server.CreateObject("ADODB.Command")
        Set DataHeader = Server.CreateObject("ADODB.Recordset")
        cmdTemp.CommandText = "SELECT Title AS `Book Title`, Author FROM `All
Titles` ORDER BY Title"
        cmdTemp.CommandType = 1
        Set cmdTemp.ActiveConnection = Session("BooksDB")
        DataHeader.Open cmdTemp, , 1, 1
        DataHeader.PageSize = tPageSize
```

*continues*

Part
VII

Ch
27

**Listing 27.2 Continued**

```
        If DataHeader.BOF or DataHeader.EOF Then
                tEmptyRecordset = True
                fHideNavBar = True
                Response.Write("No Records Available <br>")
        Else
                Set Session("DataHeader") = DataHeader
                Session("DataHeaderAbsolutePage") = 1
        End If
    Else
        If DataHeader.PageSize <> tPageSize Then
                tCurRec = ((Session("DataHeaderAbsolutePage") - 1) *
DataHeader.PageSize) + 1
                tNewPage = Int(tCurRec / tPageSize)
                If tCurRec Mod tPageSize <> 0 Then
                    tNewPage = tNewPage + 1
                End If
                If tNewPage = 0 Then tNewPage = 1
                DataHeader.PageSize = tPageSize
                Session("DataHeaderAbsolutePage") = tNewPage
        End If
        Select Case PagingMove
            Case "Requery"
                    DataHeader.Requery
            Case "<<"
                Session("DataHeaderAbsolutePage") = 1
            Case "<"
                If Session("DataHeaderAbsolutePage") > 1 Then
                    Session("DataHeaderAbsolutePage") =
Session("DataHeaderAbsolutePage") - 1
                End If
            Case ">"
                If Not DataHeader.EOF Then
                    Session("DataHeaderAbsolutePage") =
Session("DataHeaderAbsolutePage") + 1
                End If
            Case ">>"
                DataHeader.MoveLast
                Session("DataHeaderAbsolutePage") = DataHeader.PageCount
        End Select
        DataHeader.AbsolutePage = Session("DataHeaderAbsolutePage")
        If DataHeader.EOF Then
                Session("DataHeaderAbsolutePage") =
Session("DataHeaderAbsolutePage") - 1
                DataHeader.MovePrevious
        End If
    End If
    Do
        If tEmptyRecordset Then Exit Do
        If tRecordsProcessed = tPageSize Then Exit Do
        If Not fFirstPass Then
            DataHeader.MoveNext
        Else
            fFirstPass = False
```

```
        End If
        If DataHeader.EOF Then Exit Do
        tRecordsProcessed = tRecordsProcessed + 1 %>
<!--METADATA TYPE="DesignerControl" endspan-->
    <tr>
        <td align="center"><%=dataheader("Book Title")%></td>
        <td align="center"><%=dataheader("Author")%></td>
    </tr>

<!--METADATA TYPE="DesignerControl" startspan
    <OBJECT ID="DataFooter" WIDTH=151 HEIGHT=24
     CLASSID="CLSID:F602E722-A281-11CF-A5B7-0080C73AAC7E">
        <PARAM NAME="_Version" VALUE="65536">
        <PARAM NAME="_ExtentX" VALUE="3969">
        <PARAM NAME="_ExtentY" VALUE="635">
        <PARAM NAME="_StockProps" VALUE="0">
    </OBJECT>
-->
    <% Loop
    If tRangeType = "Table" Then Response.Write("</TABLE>")
    If tPageSize > 0 Then %>
        <HR>
        <% If Not fHideNavBar Then %>
            <TABLE WIDTH=100% >
            <TR>
                <TD WIDTH=100% >
                    <P ALIGN=<%= tBarAlignment%> >
                    <FORM ACTION="<%= Request.ServerVariables("PATH_INFO") &
stQueryString%>" METHOD="POST">
                        <INPUT TYPE="Submit" NAME="PagingMove" VALUE="  <<  ">
                        <INPUT TYPE="Submit" NAME="PagingMove" VALUE="  <    ">
                        <INPUT TYPE="Submit" NAME="PagingMove" VALUE="   >   ">
                        <INPUT TYPE="Submit" NAME="PagingMove" VALUE="  >>   ">
                        <% If Not fHideRequery Then %>
                            <INPUT TYPE="Submit" NAME="PagingMove" VALUE="
➥Requery ">
                        <% End If %>
                        <INPUT TYPE="Hidden" NAME="PagingRequest" VALUE="<%=
➥tHeaderName%>">
                    </FORM>
                    </P>
                </TD>
                <TD VALIGN=MIDDLE ALIGN=RIGHT>
                    <FONT SIZE=2>
                    <% If Not fHideNumber Then
                        If tPageSize > 1 Then
                            Response.Write("<NOBR>Page: " & Session(tHeaderName
& "AbsolutePage") & "</NOBR>")
                        Else
                            Response.Write("<NOBR>Record: " &
Session(tHeaderName & "AbsolutePage") & "</NOBR>")
                        End If
                    End If %>
```

Part

VII

Ch

27

*continues*

**Listing 27.2 Continued**

```
                         </FONT>
                     </TD>
                 </TR>
                 </TABLE>
         <% End If
         fHideNavBar = False
         fHideNumber = False
         stQueryString = ""
     End If %>
<!--METADATA TYPE="DesignerControl" endspan--></table>
</center></div>
```

This is the code that accesses that database and runs the query that you built. Imagine if you had to write this code yourself! To have the data displayed, find the section of code that displays the rows of the table, as follows:

```
<tr>
        <td align="center"> </td>
        <td align="center"> </td>
</tr>
```

Delete the existing source as shown in the preceding code and insert the following:

```
<tr>
        <td align="center"><%=dataheader("Book Title")%></td>
        <td align="center"><%=dataheader("Author")%></td>
</tr>
```

This displays the data for each row in the query.

 **TIP** The Data Range Header Control has a Copy Fields button on its property sheet that copies the column variables so you can paste into the source code.

The next step in the process to display the All Files view is to add the Data Range Footer Control. Find the `</table>` tag, which defines the end of the table definition. Put the cursor just before this tag. Choose Insert, Into HTML, ActiveX Control, and click the Design-time tab. Double-click the Data Range Footer Control to add it to the source code. Change the ID property to DataFooter, and close the control window. The code to end the data range loop is automatically generated. Save the finished page and close it.

The last thing you need to add to this page for it to become a part of the Web application is to link it with the home page. On the Default.htm home page, add a hyperlink to the BookList.asp page. Right-click it and select Preview BookList.asp to see the final results of all your hard work (see Figure 27.32).

This page displays the list of books and their authors a page at a time. By using the buttons at the bottom of the page, the user can control which page he wants to look at. This is important, especially if the query contains hundreds or thousands of rows; the user does not have to wait for the entire query to be returned to the PC before seeing the page.

**FIG. 27.32**
Final Book List Web
page.

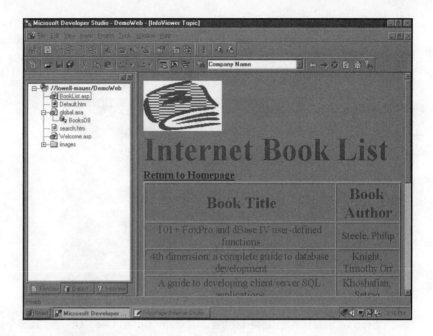

## Using the Data Form Wizard

So far, the Web application you have lets the user search the Web site, browse the book list from the database, and shows how text is displayed in different colors and fonts on the Welcome page. However, to have a Web application that is really complete, you need to allow the user to modify the data in the database. To do this, you want to build HTML forms to allow users to update, insert, and delete database records from a table or tables. All of these functions are performed through the user's Web browser. Using HTML, the code to perform this would have taken days to design, code, and test. But, with Visual InterDev, you can use the Data Form wizard to create the Web pages you need to access and update the database.

> **CAUTION**
>
> The Data Form wizard creates ActiveX Server Pages that execute only on servers that support the ActiveX controls.

You are going to use the Data Form wizard to create the first set of pages that you would need for a complete application. This first set allows users to work with the Publisher data table. They can add new publishers, delete, and modify existing information. You are now going to step through the Data Form Wizard to add these pages.

**Step 1: Start the Data Form Wizard** In Visual InterDev, choose File, New and the File Wizards tab to select the Data Form Wizard. Enter the File Name **Publisher** and click OK.

**Step 2: Specify a Title and a Database connection for the Page**   The dialog box in Figure 27.33 lets you set the Web page title and select the database connection. Enter **Publisher Information** for the title that will appear at the top of the Web page. Then open the Database Connection drop-down box and select the BooksDB database. Click <u>N</u>ext to continue.

**FIG. 27.33**

Set the Title and the database connection for the Web page.

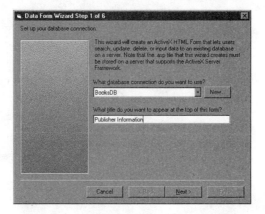

**Step 3: Select database tables and Columns to Use**   Choose Table as the database object to use and click <u>N</u>ext. You now get the list of tables that you can use in the query. Select the Publishers table from the <u>T</u>able/View drop-down list. When you select the table, all of the columns available in the table are listed (see Figure 27.34). Select what columns you want the users to see depending on what you want them to be able to do. For this demo, click the >> button. This moves all of the columns into the selected box. If you want to, you can change the order in which the columns are displayed on the form. Click <u>N</u>ext to continue.

**FIG. 27.34**

Selecting the table and the columns.

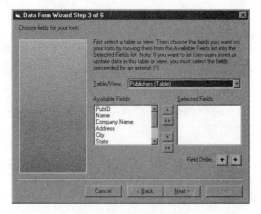

**Step 4: Choose the Database Access Options**   In this step, you can specify whether the user can edit the data or just browse (see Figure 27.35). If you allow the user to edit the data, then you can select Modify, Insert, Delete, and whether or not a feedback page is returned after an update to inform the user of the status of the database request.

**TIP** It is always a good idea to have a feedback page sent to users to confirm what they just did.

After you make your selections, click Next.

**FIG. 27.35**
Setting the database
access options.

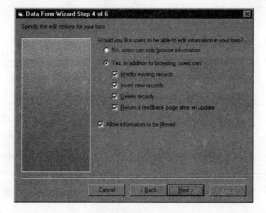

**Step 5: Set the Options for Displaying the data** You can display the data in a list, have the user choose a publisher to edit, and then go to the edit form. You can also specify how many rows to display in the list on one page (see Figure 27.36). After these options are set, click Next.

**FIG. 27.36**
Setting the Database
Form Display Options.

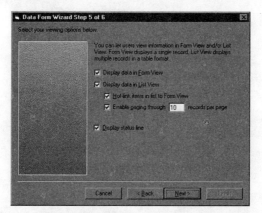

Part
**VII**

Ch

**27**

**Step 6: Select a Theme Style for the Pages** Choose a background theme from a list of available themes on your PC. This gives the data forms some color and style. As you select different themes, a sample is shown on the right of the dialog box. Click Next to finish the creation process.

The wizard automatically creates three new Active Server Pages that have all of the logic needed for the customized data forms. These forms are the following:

| File Name | Description |
| --- | --- |
| PublisherList.asp | This file contains the ActiveX controls to display the publisher table in a list format. |
| PublisherForm.asp | This file displays a single row of data that was selected on the publisherlist form. |
| PublisherAction.asp | This file contains all of the VB Script code that actually processes the database requests. |

The PublisherList form (see Figure 27.37) displays the publishers ID, Name, and Company. You might notice that it looks a little different than the list form that you created. This is because all of the other columns in the row were deleted from the list display code to keep this form easy to read.

**FIG. 27.37**
Finished Publisher List Form.

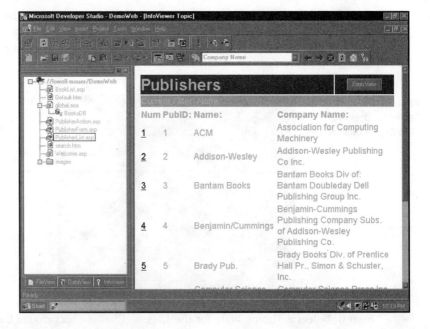

If you want to match my version of the form, you must delete the code that displays the titles as well as the data columns. If you click any of the row numbers that are displayed with the information, you are taken to the PublisherForm page, which displays the entire record for you to modify (see Figure 27.38), or you can click the Form View button at the top of the page to go directly to the Form page.

**FIG. 27.38**
Finished Publisher
Single Record Form.

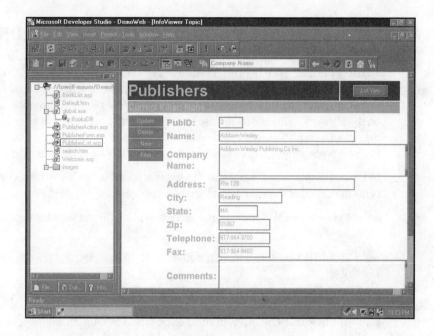

The different action buttons are displayed to the left of the data fields. The New button gives you an empty form to fill in and two buttons—one to finish the insert and the other to cancel the operation. The Delete button removes the record from the database and the Update button applies any changes that you have made to current data in the record. Whenever the user makes any changes to the database, he receives a response form to show him what he did and the status of the request. Finally, the Filter button lets the user enter any text to filter the data table by.

You have created a set of working data forms that allow the user to manipulate the database table. Now, once again, the final step in the process is to add the hyperlinks to the default form and data forms to allow the user to navigate between these new pages and the home page.

## Database Designer

One of the tools that comes with Visual InterDev is a Database Designer. This tool lets you create, edit, or delete database objects from a Microsoft SQL Server 6.5 database. This is done while you are connected to the database. The Database Designer supplies you with different forms that prompt you for the information needed to build the tables and views that are required for the Web application. Because the changes that you make to the database are not saved to the database until you save it, the tool allows you to experiment with changes to the database without actually affecting the existing design. Unfortunately, if you are using any other database, you cannot make use of this tool.

Part
**VII**

Ch
**27**

# Adding Client-Side Components to the Application

When starting a conversation about client-side components, the first question usually asked is, "What is the difference between client-side and server-side components?" The difference is where the processing occurs. Client-side components can be Java applets, ActiveX controls, Script Program Logic, or Web browser plug-ins. These pieces of program code are processed on the client PC. This allows the user to interact with the Web application locally. By having the user input information, you can then have that Web page pass the information on to another page for processing and then display the final information back to the user.

In the demo application, a calendar control was added to the Welcome.asp Web page and displays the date that the user selects. To add the calendar:

**Step 1: Open the Welcome.asp source** and place the cursor after the code that displays the welcome text.

**Step 2: Add a new line** and then right-click at this location and choose Insert Active<u>X</u> Control.

**Step 3: Scroll down the list of ActiveX Controls** and select Calendar Control.

**Step 4: Click this control and then click OK.** The Object Editor opens to allow you to modify the properties and size of the control (see Figure 27.39).

**FIG. 27.39**
ActiveX Calendar Control and properties page.

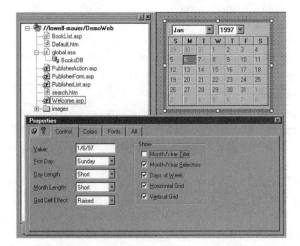

### A Note from the Author

The Calendar control that is used in this demo, is included with Microsoft Access 95. If you do not have this control, then substitute another control to use and modify what the demo is doing.

In the properties page, select the ALL tab and enter **MSACAL70.OCX** in the CodeBase property. This property indicates to the browser that if the control does not exist on the client PC to download and install it. Resize the calendar to whatever size you want and close both the properties page and the calendar form.

You see in the source for this page that Visual InterDev has automatically generated the necessary HTML code to display the calendar on the Web page. After the `</object>` tag, insert the following code:

```
<form method="post" name="form1">
<p><br>
<b><Font size=3>Date Selected:</font></b>
    <INPUT TYPE=text SIZE=20 NAME="Date">
</p>
```

This code puts the text Date Selected: on the page as well as a text box that displays the date selected from the calendar. You still need to insert code to have the date variable updated when the user changes the calendar date. The easiest way to do this is to use the Script Wizard. The wizard shows all of the objects currently embedded on the HTML/ASP page. To start the Script Wizard (see Figure 27.40), right-click anywhere on the source and choose Script Wizard from the pop-up menu.

**FIG. 27.40**

The Visual InterDev Script Wizard allows you to enter VBScript in the correct event routines.

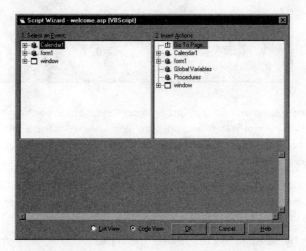

The Event pane lists the events that can be associated with the methods and properties of other objects in the Action pane. Click the Code View option button to display the code window. This is where you can enter custom script to execute when the user accesses the Web page. Open the events for the calendar control by clicking the plus (+) sign next to the control and select the AfterUpdate event by clicking it. This event is called every time the user selects a new date in the calendar. In the code window at the bottom of the form, enter the following code:

```
form1.date.value=calendar1.value
```

This code updates the Date variable to display the new date selected by the user. Click OK to close the wizard, and you see the changes that are made to the source for this page. Save the

Part
VII

Ch
27

Web page and preview it in the browser. The calendar and the date variable should be displayed (see Figure 27.41). Try selecting different dates and see what happens.

**FIG. 27.41**
Final Welcome page displaying the calendar control.

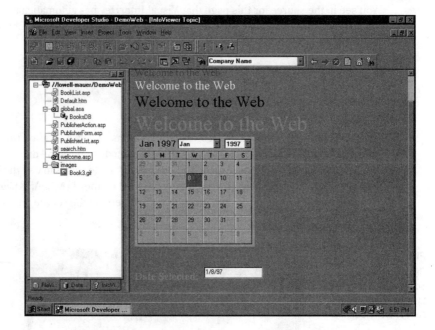

You might have noticed that the text box is empty the first time you view the page. To correct this, go back to the Script Wizard and open the Window events list. Select onLoad and enter the same line of code you entered for Calendar1.AfterUpdate. The default date is now displayed when the page is displayed.

Let's add some code and a command button to allow the user to enter a date and check to see if it is valid. If it is a valid date, change the Calendar display to match this new date. However, if it is invalid then display an error message to the user.

**Step 1: Start by putting the cursor after the HTML code** for the text box Date.

**Step 2: Then right-click** and choose Insert ActiveX Control from the pop-up menu.

**Step 3: In the list of ActiveX controls**, find and select the Forms 2.0 Command Button. Click the control and then click OK.

You see the command button and its related properties sheet (see Figure 27.42).

In the properties form, change the ID to ChgDate and the caption to Change Date. Close the control and then start the Script Wizard and look at the events for ChgDate. Select the Click event and then, in the code window, enter the following:

```
if isdate(form1.date.value) then
    calendar1.value = form1.date.value
```

```
else
    msgbox "Invalid date entered! Try Again.", 16, "Welcome Date Edit"
    call form1.Date.select()
end if
```

**FIG. 27.42**
Command button and
its properties form.

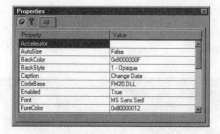

Save the form and then preview it to test the date entry code that you added (see Figure 27.43).
As you can see, the script wizard helps you through the process of adding Visual Basic Script.
ActiveX controls provide the means to interact with the Web application. You can have other
ActiveX Server Pages in the application that are called when the date changes to have data
updated or displayed to the user based on the date.

**FIG. 27.43**
Final Welcome page
with Command Button
control.

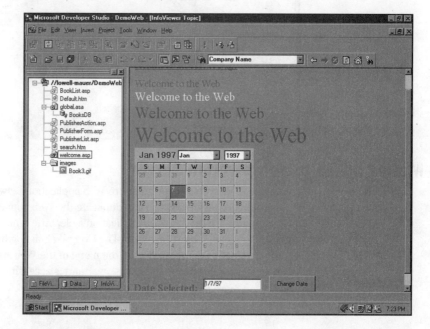

# Managing Your Web Site

Managing your Web site has to be one of the most difficult things in the world to do. The reason is that you never know when someone might be using the Web application. You can edit

any or all of the file content in local working files so it can be modified by using Visual InterDev or FrontPage97. However, master copies of the individual files in the project reside on the Web server. Visual InterDev updates the master copy with the changes from the working copy whenever you save the working copy during the editing process. You then release the working copy when it is no longer needed.

To see everything that links to your default home page, right-click it in the FileView window and select View Links (see Figure 27.44). You see all of the pages that the default page links to.

**FIG. 27.44**
Links view of the default home page.

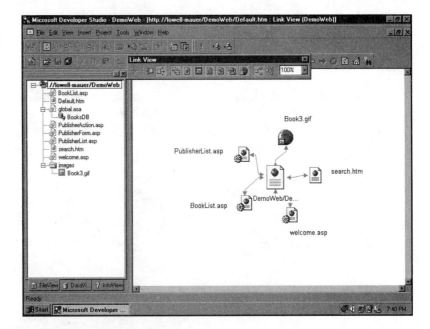

## Moving a Web to a Production Server

The Copy Web command allows you to copy an entire Web application between your development server and the production server, or you can duplicate the Web application on the same server under a different name. To move a Web application, select the Web application name in the FileView window and choose Tools, Copy Web. The Copy Web dialog box (see Figure 27.45) asks you for the destination server and what the name of the Web application will be on this server. The Web application is now on the new server and is accessible to the users.

**FIG. 27.45**

Copy Web form.

# Making Your Web Application Stand Out

The hardest thing for any programmer to do is to be an artist or a set designer. Web application design makes use of any artistic talents the developers might have. When you are on the Internet, look at the Web sites you visit. You see that there are many varieties of designs that are used for the application—backgrounds, images used for the hyperlinks, and so on. Visual InterDev comes with several tools that help make your Web application look and sound good. One of these tools is the Microsoft Image Composer.

## Image Composer

Microsoft Image Composer gives you the ability to create image compositions for displaying on-screen from Web sites. It allows you to use existing image formats or create new images. Figure 27.46 shows an example of an image in Image Composer that can be used in a Web site.

**FIG. 27.46**

Image Composer displaying a composite image containing many different GIF files.

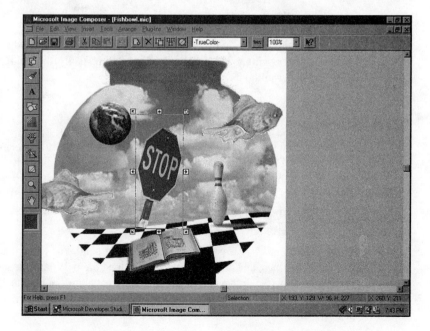

Part
**VII**

Ch
**27**

Compositions are made up of many smaller images called sprites. By using the FrontPage editor, you can add an image to any Web page and then define a hyperlink for that image. As an example, Figure 27.47 shows the Welcome.asp page with an image that returns to the default home page instead of text with a hyperlink embedded in it.

**FIG. 27.47**

The Welcome page with multiple images and their hyperlinks.

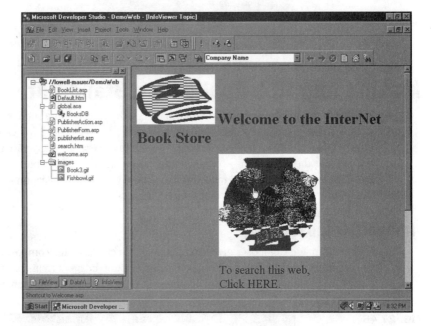

Each picture within this image (for example, globe, open book, fish, and so on) has its own hyperlink associated with it. This is done by drawing hotspots around the pictures and then assigning the hyperlink to it.

# From Here...

In this chapter, you learned how to make use of Visual InterDev to develop, test, and maintain a Web application. You were given a quick look at creating and using ActiveX Server Pages to process script on the server. In addition, database access was added with very little effort. Finally, you have seen how to add images to a Web page to enhance the look. It is impossible to provide in-depth coverage in one chapter, but hopefully you now have a basic knowledge of how to develop Web apps with Visual InterDev.

The Web application that was created is just a starting point. You can enhance and expand the pages you already have and add new ones as you need them. When you add any new pages to the application, it is very important to add the links that allow the user to "get" to these new pages and then return from them. For more information on Visual InterDev, visit the Microsoft Web site:

**http://www.microsoft.com/vinterdev**

Visual InterDev gives you the capabilities to create a Web application without being an HTML expert. It also allows you to add sophisticated, interactive forms to the application without having to build the forms personally. The following chapters give you more information on creating Web applications.

- To gain a better understanding of VBScript, read Chapter 7, "Using VBScript to Build HTML-Based VB Applications."
- To learn more about Active Server Pages, see Chapter 13, "Active Server Pages and Server-Side Scripting."
- To learn about site security and how using firewalls and proxy servers protect your site and affect your Web applications, see Chapter 31, "Internet Security and Web Applications."

# Distributed Processing

# CHAPTER 28

# Microsoft Transaction Server and Visual Basic

**T**here has been a lot of discussion in the client/server industry over the past few years about "second-generation" and "three-tier" architectures. These are applications infrastructures where the applications processing is not divided into the traditional two parts—the front-end user interface and the back-end database—but into at least three separate and distinct parts. There are several reasons given for why this application architecture is superior to the original client/server model, such as:

---

**Distributed transaction processing**

Distributed transaction processing involves spreading the logical and business rule processing over multiple computers. We'll go through how this works, and how it requires you to design your applications differently from traditional client/server applications.

---

**Microsoft's Transaction Server**

Microsoft recently released its own Transaction Server for use in building distributed transaction architectures. We'll dig into how Transaction Server works, and how it uses Microsoft's Distributed Common Object Model (DCOM) technology to provide a transparent platform for building distributed applications.

---

**Visual Basic and Transaction Server**

One of the key advantages offered by Microsoft's Transaction Server is the ability to build modules using Visual Basic (along with Microsoft's other development languages). We'll look at what is involved in building modules with Visual Basic that integrate with Transaction Server.

■ *Scalability.* The ability of an application architecture to scale up to hundreds of simultaneous users.

■ *Manageability.* The ease with which problems can be isolated, updates distributed, and configurations managed.

■ *Transparency.* The ability to switch server processing from one particular computer to another, as dictated by scheduled or unexpected system outages.

One of the key differences between traditional, or two-tier, client/server models and second generation, or three-tier (also known as *n*-tier, where *n* is any number greater than two), client/server architectures is in the use of what is known as *middleware.* Some of the most popular kinds of middleware are *Transaction Monitors* and *Object Request Brokers (ORB).* Microsoft's Transaction Server is a combination of these two technologies, providing you with a flexible and powerful Middleware component that can be used to build very large-scale distributed processing applications with minimal coding and configuration effort on your part.

**N O T E**   The typical three-tier architecture is composed of the following three tiers:

- The presentation tier, which consists primarily of the user-interface running on the desktop computer.

- The business-logic tier, which consists of shared application processing logic modules, running on one or more application servers. Each of these application servers is connected to multiple desktop computers.

- The data server tier, also known as the database server. There is usually one database server serving multiple application servers. If there are multiple database servers, they are normally spread out over a large geographical area with the common data replicated between them.  ■

In this chapter, we will take an in-depth look at Transaction Server, how it works, and how you can use it in building applications. We'll also look at what's involved to use Transaction Server with Visual Basic, and how you can design and code Visual Basic objects that can be integrated into Transaction Server to provide a large, distributed application. In the chapters immediately following this one, we'll look at how Transaction Server can be integrated into a Web site, to provide the ability to build an integrated enterprise-wide application system that stretches far beyond what most Web sites currently are capable of.  ■

# Understanding Distributed Transaction Processing

Imagine that your company has several independent database systems: one for maintaining the current inventory in the company warehouse, one for maintaining all items that have been requisitioned and should be arriving on the receiving dock, and a third database for maintaining customer orders and shipping information, like in Figure 28.1.

In this company, when an order came in, the order was entered into the order entry system, which produced a shipping order. This order was then taken to the warehouse, where each item in the order was removed and taken to the shipping dock to be packaged and sent to the customer. While at the warehouse, the employee filling the order finds that one or two items are out of stock. The employee then takes the order to the requisition department and has the missing items back ordered for later shipping.

At each of these points, the individual systems have to be updated, so that they are up-to-date. Even the Shipping Dock system has to be updated in order to produce an accurate shipping bill-of-lading, which correctly reflects the back-ordered items.

**FIG. 28.1**

A typical catalog company has systems to track current inventory, requisitioned or back-ordered items, and shipping orders.

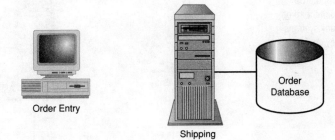

Order Entry

Shipping

Order Database

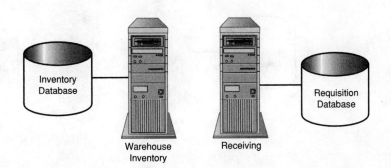

Inventory Database

Warehouse Inventory

Receiving

Requisition Database

This seems like a lot of wasted and duplicated effort. Wouldn't it make a lot more sense to connect all of these systems so that they could all exchange the necessary information to perform most of these tasks themselves? If we put a network in place and connected all of these systems to the network, as in Figure 28.2, the potential for these systems to exchange the appropriate information can be realized.

Unfortunately, anyone who has attempted to connect separate systems together in this way knows that once you have all of the systems on a network, the work is just beginning. Enabling all of these systems to work together is what middleware is all about.

Part

**VIII**

Ch

**28**

# Transaction Monitors

The original idea behind the client/server computing model was to split the application processing between two computers. This split was normally made where the database processing was all performed on the server, while all application processing was performed on the client, as in Figure 28.3. This model worked reasonably well, except for the fact that it was fairly easy to overload the client system with data, if the application allowed the database to return more data than the client computer could handle (remember that this was when the standard desktop computer was a 386 with 4M of RAM, and a 486 was a high-end workstation).

**FIG. 28.2**

A network could be used to connect all of the company systems so that they could exchange information with each other.

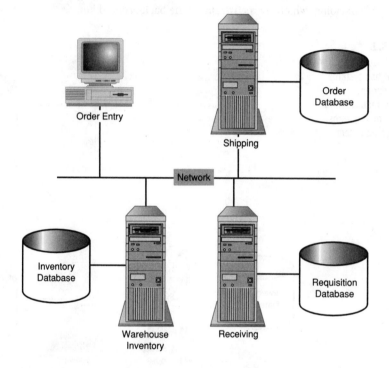

**FIG. 28.3**

The original idea behind client/server computing was to split the application processing between the client and the database server.

As the number of active users of these early client/server systems increased, the workload on the database would increase. A normal application would maintain an open connection to the database server for the entire time the application was running, as in Figure 28.4. This required the database server to have additional processing power in order to service all of those open connections, even if they were sitting idle. This also increased the cost associated with the database itself, as most traditional database license prices are based on the number of users that may be connected to the database simultaneously.

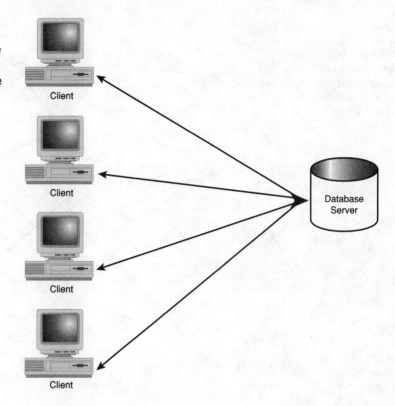

**FIG. 28.4**
As the number of users increase, the number of active connections that must be serviced by the database increases.

Client

Client

Client

Client

Database Server

As the number of databases that an application needs to interact with increases, the number of open connections that the application must maintain also increases. This adds to the processing load on the client computer, as well as the network management and configuration. The total number of connections that must be maintained can be calculated as the number of clients times the number of database servers to which the client connects, as can be seen in Figure 28.5.

This is a lot of configuration information that has to be maintained for each client computer. If one of the databases that an application uses has to be taken offline and the backup database brought online, the configuration of each and every client that connects to the database has to be updated to reflect the new database server (with care taken not to update the wrong database server information).

This is one of the primary problems that Transaction Monitors were designed to solve. A Transaction Monitor goes between the client systems and the database servers, as in Figure 28.6. Each of the clients maintain a single connection to the Transaction Monitor instead of the database servers. Likewise, the Transaction Monitor maintains connections to each of the database servers. This allows the Transaction Monitor to act as a traffic cop, passing each database query or update to the appropriate database, and to maintain only as many open database connections as are currently required, which allows the database servers to run more efficiently.

Part
VIII

Ch

28

**FIG. 28.5**
The total number of
open connections that
must be maintained can
be calculated as the
number of clients times
the number of servers.

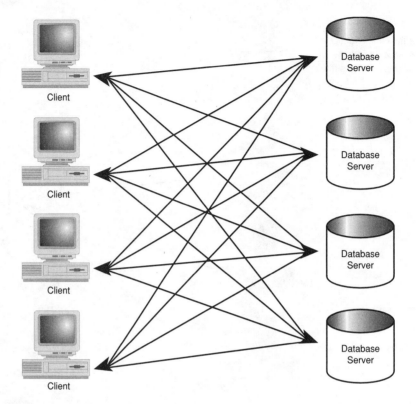

## Object Request Brokers

*Object Request Brokers* (*ORBs*) fall into a different category of middleware from Transaction
Monitors. ORBs provide location transparency to application modules and services. What
*location transparency* means is that when an application needs to interact with a server process,
the application does not need to know where that specific server process is located on the
network. The only process that the application knows the location of is the ORB client stub
located on the same machine as the application.

The ORB knows where all server processes are running, or on which machines the server
processes may be run. If a particular server process is not running when an application requests access to it, the ORB will start the server process on one of the machines for which the
process is configured to run. The client application does not know on which server the requested process is running, or if the server process is even running. The ORB keeps track of
all server processes for the client applications. The ORB may even perform load balancing
between two or more servers running the same process, so that each of the servers are servicing around the same number of requests.

Returning to our catalog sales company, it is reasonable to expect that the order entry system
would make use of various services that could be located on a series of servers on the company

network. One of these services could be a sales tax engine, which calculates the tax for each of the customer orders. It would make sense to keep this set of calculations on a server, as tax laws have a tendency to change. By keeping this processing module on the server, it would be a lot easier to update in this one location every time the tax laws changed, as opposed to having to update every order entry workstation in the company.

**FIG. 28.6**
A Transaction Monitor reduces the number of open connections to the number of clients plus the number of database servers.

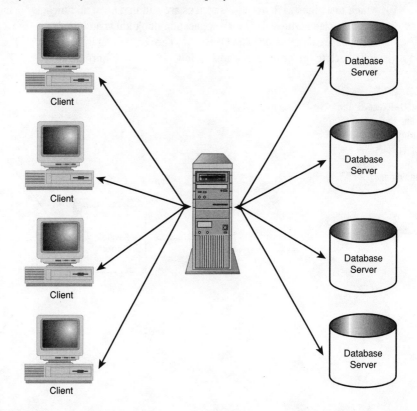

Another service that each of the order entry systems would be likely to take advantage of is a credit check application. By having all of the credit authorization requests go through a single server, it would be easy for that one server to maintain an open connection to the credit clearinghouse, as compared to outfitting each of the workstations with a modem and the software to call up the credit authority (not to mention all of the additional phone lines this would require).

A third service that each of the order entry systems would need to use might be the business rules engine. This would be the system that calculates shipping costs based on the quantity or weight of the ordered items, or that enforces minimum purchase rules. By keeping this module on one or two servers, you would once again be able to easily update the module as the powers-that-be within the company change the business rules that this module has to enforce.

Part
VIII

Ch
28

Considering that the functions provided by these server modules are critical to the core business of our catalog sales company, it's important to make sure that these modules are always available for the order entry systems. In order to make sure that these systems have high availability, they are probably loaded onto more than one system. If the order entry application made direct accesses to these services, then each copy of the application would have to know which machines each of these services are running on at all times. By using an ORB, the individual copies of the order entry application don't know and don't care what servers any of these services are running on. The ORB takes care of making the connections and passing the results back to the order entry application, as seen in Figure 28.7.

**FIG. 28.7**
The ORB relieves the client application from having to know which server computer each of the services are running on.

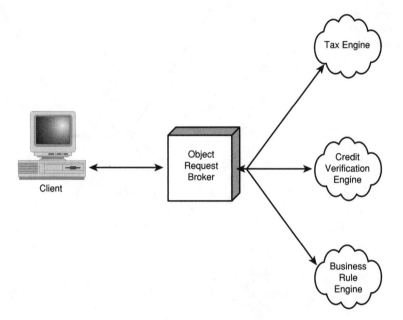

# Introducing Microsoft Transaction Server

Microsoft's Transaction Server is somewhat of a cross between a Transaction Monitor and an ORB, although it tends to lean more towards the ORB set of functionality. If you are running an application on a Windows NT system that has Transaction Server installed and you are using ODBC to access a database, Transaction Server transparently inserts itself between your application and the database to manage that connection (as well as all of the other open connections to the same database). Transaction Server also allows application functionality to be built as a series of ActiveX DLLs and be distributed across a network. We'll take a quick look at how Transaction Server provides this functionality.

## Managing Database Connections

When an application is using the ODBC interface to access a database, Transaction Server takes control of the database connection in order to provide a more consistent access, quicker connection, and transaction control. By placing itself between the application and the database, Transaction Server is able to open its own connection to the database, and to provide the application with a connection to Transaction Server instead of the database. This allows Transaction Server to limit the actual number of database connections to only as many as are necessary to service all of the application requests, as seen in Figure 28.8. This relieves the work of maintaining all of those connections from the database, allowing the database to perform better and be more responsive.

**FIG. 28.8**
By inserting itself between the applications and the database, Transaction Server is able to limit the number of active connections that the database has to service.

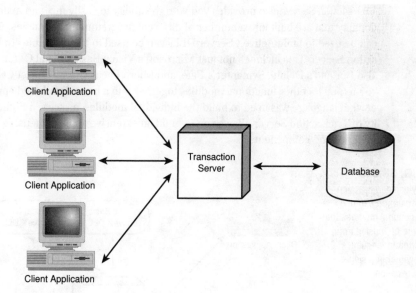

Client Application

Client Application

Client Application

Transaction Server

Database

When an application closes its connection to the database, Transaction Server maintains the open database connection so that the connection can be reused either by the application that closed the connection, or by another application (or client) that needs the same connection to the database. This allows application modules to be written in such a way that they only maintain open connections to a database for those periods of time that the application really needs to have the connection open. The performance penalty for closing and reopening a database connection is removed, making it more attractive to write applications that release the associated resources while they are not needed.

> **N O T E** By combining Transaction Server with OLEISAPI2 applications, the remaining bit of overhead that we want to eliminate by using a SAPI interface is removed by allowing the OLEISAPI2 application to disconnect each time that it is finished servicing a client call, and then reopening the database connection with each new call. ■

## Managing Distributed Objects

Transaction Server provides a facility for building distributed applications by allowing you to build functionality into a series of ActiveX server DLLs, and then distribute them across your

Part
VIII

Ch
28

network. Transaction Server keeps track of where each of these DLLs are located, and performs all of the communications between them and your application. This allows you to move your functionality modules to the most suited computer on your network, based on the processing load that each module will be requiring in order to service all of the requests from applications needing the services of the module. You can even double up and place the same module on multiple computers, and allow Transaction Server to load balance between the copies.

Transaction Server also provides you with the ability to easily mix and match modules of functionality that are built into a number of different programming languages. Any language that can be used to build ActiveX Server DLLs can be used to build modules to be used with Transaction Server. This includes not just Microsoft's Visual Basic, Visual C++, and Visual J++, but also Borland's Delphi, Symantec's Café, and Micro Focus' Visual Object COBOL. This enables you to pull together functional modules together into a large distributed application, regardless of what language was used to build the individual modules, as seen in Figure 28.9. This capability of Transaction Server allows you to build an extensive application using "best-of-breed" modules and components.

**FIG. 28.9**
By using Transaction Server, you can use functional modules that were built using many different languages together in a single application.

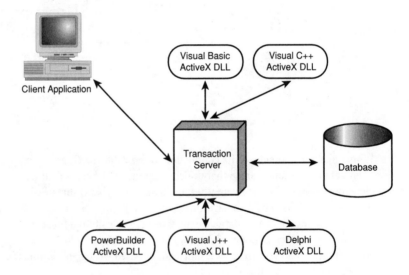

## Transaction Coordination

One of the many beneficial features of Transaction Server is the ability for it to provide coordinated transaction control through many objects and over multiple databases. Transaction Server accomplishes this by using the Microsoft *Distributed Transaction Coordinator* (*DTC*). The DTC was first released as part of SQL Server 6.5, and is included with Transaction Server. It provides a low-level infrastructure for distributed transactions, controlling and guaranteeing the outcome (either commit or rollback) across multiple databases and database connections. The DTC uses a two-phase commit protocol to ensure the outcome of these transactions.

**Two-Phase Commit**

A *two-phase commit* is where a data change (insert, update, or delete) to two or more databases absolutely has to be successful in all, or unsuccessful in all. If the situation dictates that the changes to the data cannot be committed in one of the databases without being committed in the others, then this is the situation where two-phase commit is necessary.

# Integrating Visual Basic Classes with Transaction Server

When building server objects for use with Transaction Server, there are a couple of basic details that have to be taken into consideration. These details affect the design of your objects and add a small amount of Transaction Server-specific code. We will be looking at each of these aspects as we build a simple Server object. We'll add onto this object with additional objects a little later.

## Initializing the Visual Basic Project

All server objects for use with Transaction Server have to be built as ActiveX DLLs, regardless of which programming language is used. Once you have started a new Visual Basic project with the target being an ActiveX DLL, you need to include a reference to the Microsoft Transaction Server Type library by choosing Project, References, as seen in Figure 28.10.

**FIG. 28.10**
You need to include a reference to the Transaction Server Type library when building a server object for use with Transaction Server.

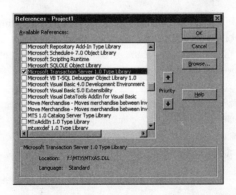

The object that we will be building is the warehouse inventory adjuster object for our catalog order company. For now, we'll be using just two database tables in a SQL Server database. These tables are the Products table, as seen in Table 28.1, and the Inventory table, which is in Table 28.2. We'll be adding additional tables as we expand the scope of this system later in this chapter and the following chapter. The SQL to create these tables and populate them with some initial data can be found on the CD.

Part
VIII

Ch
28

**Table 28.1    The Products Table**

| Column Name | Data Type | Size |
|---|---|---|
| Prd_ID | int | |
| Prd_Name | char | 8 |
| Prd_Desc | varchar | 40 |
| Prd_StandardStock | smallint | |

**N O T E**    The *int* and *smallint* data types in SQL Server are a fixed size, and thus do not require a column size to be specified. An *int* data type is defined as four bytes, and a *smallint* is defined as two bytes. The available number range that can be stored in each of these data types is completely dependent on what range of numbers can be represented by each of these storage allocations. ■

**Table 28.2    The Inventory Table**

| Column Name | Data Type | Size |
|---|---|---|
| Prd_ID | int | |
| Inv_Count | smallint | |

To wrap up our project initialization, we'll name our project InvMaint and give the project a description to remind ourselves what this module does at a later time. We'll also mark this module for unattended execution, so that it can run in a multi-threaded environment. We'll have a single class in this project, and we'll name it InvMnt.

**T I P**    It is a good idea to provide a project description for the modules that we are building in this and the following chapters. We will be building several DLLs and including references to DLLs that we have already built. By including a description, the project description will show up in the Project References dialog box. If we don't provide project descriptions, then only the project name will show up in the References dialog box.

# Stateless Objects

One of the keys to designing and building well performing components for use with Transaction Server is to design the objects and methods to be *stateless*. This means that there are no variables and conditions that are held within the object; all variables are received as parameters to the methods that are exposed, and all results are returned either as the result of the method or through method parameters that were passed by reference.

The primary reason for building stateless objects is because the same method may be called as part of several different applications. These calls may happen simultaneously or sequentially, but regardless, it is a high likelihood. Keep in mind that this is the same approach that you need to take when building thread-safe objects, as we saw in Chapter 23, "Using Remote Data Objects with the OLEISAPI2 Interface." It is possible to build stateful objects for use with Transaction Server, but these objects entail a lot more overhead and will not perform as well when the system is under load.

There are a few exceptions to the rule of building stateless objects. These exceptions consist primarily of information that the object will be using across all processes, such as the database connection information. In order to build our server object in a stateless manner, our declarations are limited to the database connect string, and the error number that we will be raising in the event of an error. This gives us the class declaration section found in Listing 28.1.

### Listing 28.1 INVMNT.CLS—The Declaration Section for Our Server Object Consists of Our Error Number and Our Database Connection Information

```
Option Explicit
'We always return the same error number
Private Const ERROR_NUMBER = vbObjectError + 0
'The database connect string
Private Const strConnect = "DSN=InvMntDB;UID=TxsVB;PWD=vbtxs;"
```

## Transaction Context

When an object is running with Transaction Server, it is running in the context of a transaction. There is a transaction attribute that controls how the objects interact with the current transaction within their context. This transaction attribute can have any one of four values, as seen in Table 28.3.

### Table 28.3  The Transaction Attribute Values

| Value | Description |
| --- | --- |
| Requires a transaction | Objects with this transaction attribute must execute within the scope of a transaction. If the object that called this object was executing within a transaction, then this object executes within the scope of the same transaction as the calling object. If the calling object is not executing within a transaction, then this object will start (and complete) a new transaction. |

*continues*

Part

VIII

Ch

28

**Table 28.3   Continued**

| Value | Description |
| --- | --- |
| Requires a new transaction | Objects with this transaction attribute will always begin (and complete) a new transaction, regardless of whether the calling object was running within a transaction or not. |
| Supports transactions | Objects with this transaction attribute will execute within the scope of the transaction of the calling object, if that object was executing within a transaction. If the calling object was not executing within a transaction, then this object will execute without a transaction. |
| Does not support transactions | Objects with this transaction attribute will always execute outside the scope of any transactions, regardless of the transaction state of the calling object. |

Using the transaction attribute on all objects running within Transaction Server, you can con-figure an extensive transaction model, separating objects into distinct transactions that are executed within the midst of other transactions.

For example, take the collection of objects in Figure 28.11. In this model, Object A calls Object B, which calls Object C. All three of these objects has their transaction attribute set to Requires a transaction. The transaction in which all three of these objects are executing will commit the changes made by these objects only if all three objects execute successfully. If any one of the three has an error, the entire transaction is rolled back.

**FIG. 28.11**

The transaction attribute enables you to define separate transactions within other transac-tions.

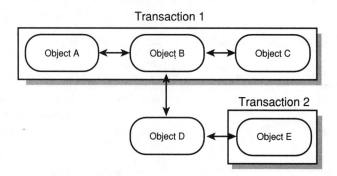

Notice that Object D is also called by Object B; only Object D has its transaction attribute set to Does not support transactions. This means that Object D will not affect the transaction within which Objects A, B, and C are executing. Object E, which is called by Object D, may have its transaction attribute set to either `Requires a transaction` or `Requires a new trans-action`. Because Object D does not support transactions, Object E will always start a new transaction, which is completely independent of the transaction of Objects A, B, and C. If Object E is set to `Requires a transaction`, and Object D was set to `Requires a new transaction`, then the transaction of A, B, and C would continue to be independent of the transaction of D and E.

In order to be able to tell Transaction Server whether or not an object was successful—or that it ran into problems—requires a few lines of code. The first task is to get a reference to the transaction context object, which is the transaction context within which the object is executing. This is done with the `GetObjectContext()` function, as in the following code:

```
Dim ctxObject As ObjectContext
Set ctxObject = GetObjectContext()
```

Once you have the transaction context, you can use the context object's two methods, `SetComplete` and `SetAbort`, to tell Transaction Server whether the object was successful or not. If your object executed without any problems, you would use the following call to tell Transaction Server that you are finished and that the transaction can be committed:

```
ctxObject.SetComplete
```

If your object ran into problems, you will want to use the `SetAbort` method to tell Transaction Server that the transaction should be rolled back, as follows:

```
ctxObject.SetAbort
```

**N O T E** The context object (`ctxObject`) does more than just control the transaction. It also controls the objects and the resources that those objects are consuming. When an object calls `SetComplete` or `SetAbort`, the object is informing Transaction Server that the object is finished processing and it can be deactivated, and all of the system resources being used by the object can be reallocated to other objects. If `SetComplete` or `SetAbort` are not called, Transaction Server does not know when it can release those resources for use by other objects. This eventually bogs down the system performance. ▪

We can take this understanding of how to use the context object to build our first object, which will maintain the current inventory of a particular product in the warehouse. We'll name our method `ChangeInv`, and we'll pass it a product identification number and the number of the product that we want to move. A positive number will add inventory to the warehouse, and a negative number will remove inventory from the warehouse. We'll also have this object tell us how many of the product remain in stock after our request, and (in the case of a negative number) how many will need to be back-ordered in order to fulfill our request. We can do this with the code in Listing 28.2.

Part
**VIII**

Ch

**28**

**Listing 28.2   INVMNT.CLS—The *ChangeInv* Method Adds and Removes Inventory from the Warehouse**

```
Public Function ChangeInv(aiPrdID As Long, aiChange As Integer, _
                          ByRef aiBackOrder As Integer, _
                   ByRef aiStockRemain As Integer) As Integer
    Dim ctxObject As ObjectContext
    Dim rdoConn As rdoConnection
    Dim strSQL As String
    Dim rdoRS As rdoResultset

    'Get our object context
    Set ctxObject = GetObjectContext()

    'Set up error handling
    On Error GoTo ErrorHandler

    'Obtain the RDO environment and connection
    Set rdoConn = rdoEngine.rdoEnvironments(0).OpenConnection("", _
                         rdDriverNoPrompt, False, strConnect)

    'Update the Inventory
    strSQL = "UPDATE Inventory SET Inv_Count = Inv_Count + " _
            + Str$(aiChange) + " WHERE Prd_ID = " + Str$(aiPrdID)
    rdoConn.Execute strSQL, rdExecDirect
    'Get resulting inventory which may have been further
    'updated via triggers
    strSQL = "SELECT Inv_Count FROM Inventory WHERE Prd_ID = " _
                                  + Str$(aiPrdID)
    Set rdoRS = rdoConn.OpenResultset(strSQL, rdOpenForwardOnly, _
                        rdConcurReadOnly, rdExecDirect)
    'Did we retrieve anything?
    If rdoRS.EOF <> True Then
        'Yes, get the current inventory count
        aiStockRemain = rdoRS.rdoColumns("Inv_Count")
        'Check if the inventory is overdrawn
        If aiChange < 0 And aiStockRemain < 0 Then
            'Set the number of items that are backordered
            aiBackOrder = 0 - aiStockRemain
            'Update the inventory count
            strSQL = "UPDATE Inventory SET Inv_Count = 0 WHERE Prd_ID = " _
                                  + Str$(aiPrdID)
            rdoConn.Execute strSQL, rdExecDirect
            aiStockRemain = 0
        Else
            'We are not overdrawn, so we don't need to back order anything
            aiBackOrder = 0
        End If
    Else
        'No, there is a problem as no product inventory record was found
        Err.Raise ERROR_NUMBER, "Could not find product inventory record."
    End If

    'Close the database connection
    rdoConn.Close
```

```
        'Tell Transaction Server that we have successfully completed our task
        ctxObject.SetComplete

        'Return a 0 to signal that we were successful
        ChangeInv = 0

    Exit Function
ErrorHandler:
        'Have we connected to the database yet?
        If Not rdoConn Is Nothing Then
            'If so, then close the connection
            rdoConn.Close
        End If

        'Tell Transaction Server that we had problems
        ctxObject.SetAbort
        'Indicate that an error occured
        ChangeInv = -1
End Function
```

## Registering Visual Basic DLLs with Transaction Server

Once you have built your Visual Basic project into an ActiveX DLL, you will need to register it with Transaction Server before it can be used. You do this through the Transaction Server Explorer. Once you have started up the Transaction Server Explorer, you will need to make sure that the DTC is running. You can tell if the DTC is running by looking at the color of the screen in the computer icon for your computer. When the DTC is running, the screen on the computer icon is green, and when the DTC is not running, the computer screen is black. If the DTC is not running, click the Computer icon for your computer, then choose Tools, MS DTC, Start.

**Creating Packages**    Before you can start registering components in Transaction Server, you must have a package into which you are going to install the components. *Packages* are logical groupings of objects that are generally used as a unit. As a general rule, you will want to create one package for every set of applications that will be making use of Transaction Server. You can create a package by following these steps:

1. Select the Packages Installed folder.
2. Choose File, New from the main menu.
3. On the first screen of the Package Wizard, choose Create an Empty Package, as seen in Figure 28.12.
4. Type in a name for the package, as shown in Figure 28.13. For our catalog sales company package, we'll call it **Inventory**. Then click the Next button.
5. If the objects in the package need to run under a specific login account, select the This User radio button, and provide the user name and password. Otherwise, leave the default radio button selected, as in Figure 28.14, which will run all of the objects in the

Part
**VIII**

Ch

**28**

package under the account of the users using the applications which use the objects in this package (this could affect the availability of resources for the process components, depending on how the access privileges are configured in the system security).

6. Click the Finish button to complete the process.

**FIG. 28.12**
For registering components that you have built, you will need to create an empty package into which the components will be installed.

**FIG. 28.13**
Provide the package with a name that reflects the functionality, or family of applications, that the components in the package will be providing.

**Installing Components**   Once you have a package, you can begin installing components into it. This is where you will be registering the ActiveX DLLs that you have and will be creating with Visual Basic. You can register your components by following these steps:

**N O T E**   In the following section, I use the terms "install" and "register" interchangeably. Installing components into Transaction Server and registering components with Transaction Server are two ways of referring to the same process. ▓

**FIG. 28.14**

If you need the components in the package to execute as a specific user login, for resource access purposes you will need to specify the user login and password.

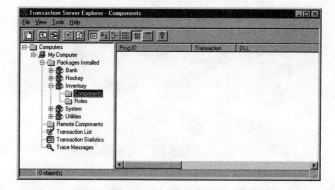

1. Select the Components folder in the package into which you want to install the components (in this case, it's the Inventory package that we just created), as seen in Figure 28.15.

**FIG. 28.15**

Select the Components folder in the package that you have created in order to install components into the package.

2. Click the Install New Component(s) button, as seen in Figure 28.16.
3. Click the Add Files button, and select the ActiveX DLL that you are wanting to register, as seen in Figure 28.17.
4. When you return to the Install Components dialog box, the upper list box should show the DLL that you are installing, and the lower list box should show all of the visible classes within the DLL, as in Figure 28.18.
5. Click the Finish button, and the components will be installed in Transaction Server, as seen in Figure 28.19.
6. Select the components you just installed, one at a time, and right-click the mouse. Select the Properties selection from the pop-up menu. On the component Properties Editor, select the Transaction tab, and select the transaction attribute desired for the currently selected component, as in Figure 28.20.

Part
VIII

Ch

28

**FIG. 28.16**
If you are installing components that you have built, you will need to select the Install New Component(s) option.

**FIG. 28.17**
You will need to select the DLL containing the components that you are installing.

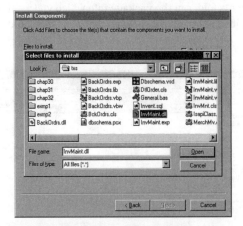

**FIG. 28.18**
The Install Components dialog box will display all of the components found in the specified DLL.

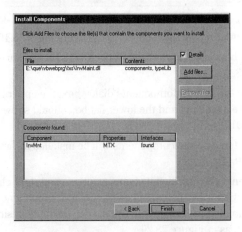

**FIG. 28.19**
Once you have installed the components, they will show up in the Transaction Server Explorer.

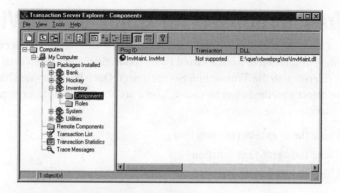

**FIG. 28.20**
You will need to open up the properties dialog for the installed component in order to specify the transaction attribute setting.

Whenever you recompile any ActiveX DLL built in Visual Basic, you will need to refresh the component information in Transaction Server. This can be easily done by deleting the component from the Transaction Server Explorer and reinstalling the component by following the same steps as were followed to install the component originally. Another way of refreshing the component information in Transaction Server is by choosing Tools, Refresh All Components.

---

### A Note from the Author

In working with Transaction Server 1.0, the Refresh All Components menu option would often scramble the component names in the package that I was working with. I would end up with what would look like two or three copies of the same component in the package, and some components would appear to be missing. I did not notice any problems when attempting to run the applications that used there components, but would most often end up deleting all of the components from the package and reinstalling them. Hopefully this behavior will be corrected in an upcoming service pack.

---

# Calling Transaction Server Objects from Visual Basic

Now that we have a component built and registered with Transaction Server, how do we call the method in this object from a Visual Basic application? First, the Visual Basic application has to get a reference to the Transaction Server object. Once the reference has been acquired, then the object's methods can be called. There are three ways that a reference to a Transaction Server objects can be acquired:

- Using the `CreateObject` function
- Using the `GetObject` function
- Using the New keyword

**N O T E** There is a fourth method for acquiring a reference to a Transaction Server object by another Transaction Server object, and that is through the use of the Context Object's `CreateInstance` method, which creates the object reference in the same transaction context of the current object (depending on the new object's transaction attribute). We'll see this method in use in the following chapters. ■

From a Visual Basic application, we can create our reference to our Inventory Maintenance object with the following code:

```
Dim obj As Object
Set obj = CreateObject("InvMaint.InvMnt")
```

**N O T E** The same Transaction Server object could have been created using the New keyword by using the following code:

```
Dim obj As New InvMaint.InvMnt
```

As a general rule, all Transaction Server components can be referenced in the same way as all other ActiveX server objects. Transaction Server works with the Operating System to make sure that when Transaction Server components are requested, they are created and called within Transaction Server. ■

From here, we can call the object methods by referencing them via the object we have just created, as so:

```
obj.ChangeInv(iiProductID, CLng(txtCount.Text), iBackOrder, iCurInventory)
```

So if we build a simple little applet using the Remote Data Control and the Data Bound Combo Box, we can call our object and see how Transaction Server works. The first thing we will need to do is to add the Remote Data Control and the Data Bound List Controls to our Tool Palette. We do this by choosing Project, Components, as seen in Figure 28.21.

With these two controls, we can build a simple form that provides a drop-down list box, containing the product descriptions from the Products table in the database. We accomplish this by binding the Remote Data Control to the ODBC configuration we have set up for our database, providing the user name and password that we have configured, and using the following SQL to populate the Remote Data Control:

```
SELECT * FROM Products
```

**FIG. 28.21**

You have to include the Data Bound List Controls and the Remote Data Control into your Visual Basic project before you can use them.

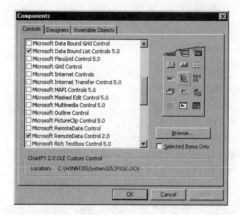

Next, we specify the Remote Data Control as the row source for the Data Bound Combo Box, and specify the Prd_Desc column as the `ListField`, `DataField`, and `BoundColumn`. We'll add a text box for the user to enter the number to add or remove from the inventory, and we have the form seen in Figure 28.22. The complete source code for this form can be found on the CD.

**FIG. 28.22**

We'll use a very simple form to call the method in the object we registered with Transaction Server.

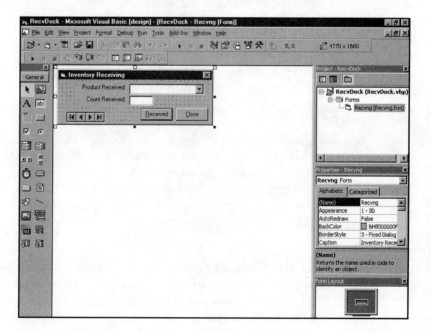

## Setting the Product ID

When the user selects a product, we need to have a variable into which to place the selected product ID, so we'll declare a variable in the form declarations using the code in Listing 28.3.

**Listing 28.3 RECVNG.FRM—The Declarations Section for Our Form, Declaring a Variable Which We Can Use for Holding the Selected Product ID**

```
Option Explicit
'We always return the same error number
Private Const ERROR_NUMBER = vbObjectError + 0
'The currently selected product ID
Dim iiProductID As Long
```

We'll set the product ID into this variable whenever the user selects a product from the list by navigating in the Remote Data Control to the currently selected row, and then getting the Prd_ID column from that row, as in Listing 28.4.

**Listing 28.4 RECVNG.FRM—When the User Selects a Product, We Need to Grab the Product ID from the Remote Data Control**

```
Private Sub dbcProduct_Click(Area As Integer)
    Dim varCurRecord As Variant

    'What is the currently selected item?
    varCurRecord = dbcProduct.SelectedItem
    'Move to the selected record in the result set
    MSRDC1.Resultset.Move 0, varCurRecord
    'Grab the product ID
    iiProductID = MSRDC1.Resultset!Prd_ID.Value
End Sub
```

**CAUTION**

The code that we are using to grab the selected product ID is dependent on the Remote Data Control being used for the ListField, DataField, and the BoundColumn. If we use the Remote Data Control for just the ListField, the dbcProduct_Click method will error out with an invalid bookmark error when you first click it to select a product. This is due to the fact that the control will start out with the selected item of 0, which the Remote Data Control will interpret as an invalid row. It will be after you have selected a row that the control will have a valid row number, but you will not be able to get to that point.

**N O T E** We could easily have waited until the user has clicked the Received button when calling the Transaction Server object to determine the selected item, but that would entail additional code in that specific method which we've been able to isolate by using the method that we have. This is not to say that this approach is better, because it's not, but it does isolate the functionality, allowing us to focus on the core functionality that we are implementing in each method. ■

# Calling the Transaction Server Object

When the user clicks the Received button, he can create a reference to the Transaction Server object that we have created by using the code snippets that we saw earlier, and can display for the user resulting in stock and back order amounts with the code in Listing 28.5.

**Listing 28.5    RECVNG.FRM—The Method Used to Create a Reference to Our Transaction Server Object, and Call the Method that We Created in the Object**

```
Private Sub cmdReceived_Click()
    Dim iBackOrder As Integer
    Dim iCurInventory As Integer
    Dim ProgID As String
    Dim obj As Object

    'Set up the error handling
    On Error GoTo ErrorHandler

    'Decide which component to use
    ProgID = "InvMaint.InvMnt"

    'Create the appropriate object
    Set obj = CreateObject(ProgID)
    'Were we able to create the object?
    If obj Is Nothing Then
        MsgBox "Create object " + ProgID + "failed."
        Exit Sub
    End If
    'Call the object method
    If obj.ChangeInv(iiProductID, CLng(txtCount.Text), iBackOrder, _
                             iCurInventory) = -1 Then
        Err.Raise ERROR_NUMBER
    End If

    'Release the object
    Set obj = Nothing

    'Display for the user what the current inventory is
    MsgBox "New Inventory received, current backorder count = " _
            + Str$(iBackOrder) + " and current inventory = " _
            + Str$(iCurInventory)
    Exit Sub

ErrorHandler:
    'Show the user the error message
    MsgBox "Error " + Str$(Err.Number) + " : " + Err.Description
    Exit Sub
End Sub
```

Part
**VIII**
Ch
**28**

Before we run our form, let's change the view in the Transaction Server Explorer to show the status of our object. We do this by selecting the Components folder in the package we have created. Next, choose View, Status. The right side of the Explorer will now show us the activity status of our object. If you run the form with the Transaction Server Explorer where it can be seen, you can watch as the object that we created earlier is instantiated and executed, as seen in Figure 28.23.

**FIG. 28.23**

When the form that we have created calls the object that we registered in Transaction Server, you can see as the object is created and run.

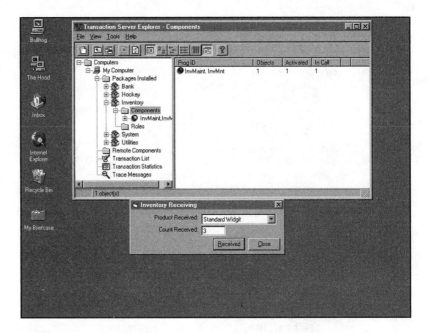

# From Here...

In this chapter, we learned about the different types of middleware, and how they enable client/server applications to be scaled for use by many more users than traditional client/server applications. We saw how Microsoft's Transaction Server is somewhat of a cross between a Transaction Monitor and an Object Request Broker, providing all of the functionality of the first, with a substantial amount of the functionality of the later. Later, we saw how we could build objects with Visual Basic that could be registered with Transaction Server for use by applications running on client systems. Finally, we saw how we could build a front-end application that uses the object that we built and loaded into Transaction Server.

In the following chapters, we will take our catalog order company example and expand the functionality by building the components that handle the back-order status and build the shipping orders, all running as independent components within the Transaction Server package that we started in this chapter. From here, you will want to check out the following chapters:

■ To see how we can extend the example we began in this chapter further by adding the automatic ordering of new inventory when we have exhausted the inventory in the warehouse, see Chapter 29, "Building Multi-Tier Applications."

- To learn how we can extend this system even further and provide an order entry system on the Web for our customers, read Chapter 30, "Building Distributed Web Applications."

- To learn about some of the security systems that we would want to put in place before opening up our integrated order entry system for all Web surfers, check out Chapter 31, "Internet Security and Web Applications."

# CHAPTER 29

# Building Multi-Tier Applications

The previous chapter took a look at Microsoft's Transaction Server, and how it can be used to build large distributed applications. This chapter builds on that knowledge by extending the catalog order company system from a simple warehouse inventory maintenance system, to an integrated system for automatically ordering additional items when products are depleted from the warehouse inventory.

We will also take a look at the shared memory capabilities of Transaction Server, and how it can be used to implement components that require persistent data that will be shared among all users of the components. We'll also take a quick look at how Transaction Server provides a framework for implementing role-based security in your applications, and how you can make your components role-aware. ■

## Instantiate and call Transaction Server components from other components

Building onto the example started in the previous chapter, several additional components will be built, some of which will make use of the methods of components already built.

## Shared information maintained by Transaction Server

Build a "next number" generator that uses the shared information functionality of Transaction Server to maintain the counter used to generate the unique numbers.

## Control transaction configuration over multiple components

Configure the transaction attributes of several components to have control over the transactions as necessary for the application.

## Configure and use role-based security

Take a look at how Transaction Server provides a framework for building in role-based security into an application, and how to take advantage of this in applications.

# Calling Components from Other Components

The previous chapter showed how to begin building a catalog order processing system by implementing a simple warehouse inventory maintenance system. This system consisted of an inventory maintenance module and a user interface where the user could specify the number of items to add or remove from the warehouse. This chapter begins by expanding on this system by adding another component that maintains the requisitions and back orders, and a third component that controls both of these modules by instructing each to modify their inventory or outstanding requisitions based on the number of items being received or shipped. Finally, adapt your front-end user interface to interact directly with this merchandise movement component, instead of the inventory maintenance component that was built in the previous chapter. The end result is a system that resembles the distributed system illustrated in Figure 29.1.

**FIG. 29.1**
Begin by adding to the inventory maintenance system to integrate in requisition maintenance and a higher level control of merchandise movement.

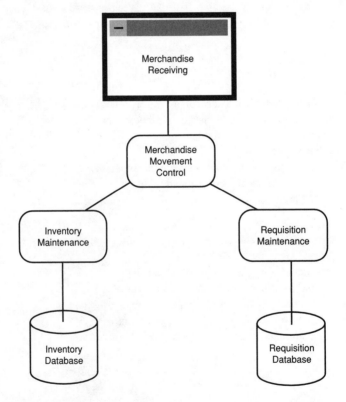

## Requisition Maintenance

Before beginning to build the requisition maintenance component, the requisition table should be added into the database. A completely separate database could be easily built to house this table, and according to our fictional corporate model, it is a separate system into which this table belongs. But for the purposes of this example here, just add it to the existing database.

The table will consist of only two columns (this is an extremely simplified system being built here, for purposes of illustration only) as can be seen in Table 29.1.

**Table 29.1    The Requisition Table**

| Column Name | Data Type |
| --- | --- |
| Prd_ID | int |
| Req_Count | smallint |

**N O T E**  The *int* and *smallint* data types in SQL Server are a fixed size, and thus do not require a column size to be specified. An int data type is defined as four bytes, and a smallint is defined as two bytes. The available number range that can be stored in each of these data types is completely dependent on what range of numbers can be represented by each of these storage allocations. ■

**Initializing the Back Order Project**  The Back Order component project will be almost an exact duplicate of the Inventory Maintenance module built in the previous chapter. A new ActiveX DLL project named BackOrdrs will need to be created, and a single class named BckOrdrs included. We'll also need to include the Remote Data Object and the Transaction Server Type library in the project references, as seen in Figure 29.2.

**FIG. 29.2**
Include the Remote
Data Object and
Transaction Server Type
library in the project
references.

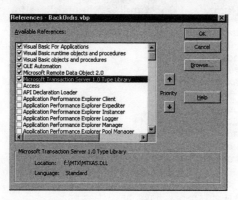

Next, use the same declarations section used in the Inventory Maintenance module, where the error number is declared (that will be raised in the event of an error), along with the database connection string, as seen in Listing 29.1.

---

**Listing 29.1   BCKORDRS.CLS—The Declaration Section of the Back Orders Maintenance Component Is the Same as the Declaration Section of the Inventory Maintenance Component**

```
Option Explicit

'We always return the same error number
Private Const ERROR_NUMBER = vbObjectError + 0
'The database connect string
Private Const strConnect = "DSN=InvMntDB;UID=TxsVB;PWD=vbtxs;"
```

---

**Getting the Number of Outstanding Back Orders**   The first method that should be added to our component is a simple method that returns the current number of outstanding requisitions that are in the database for a specific item. This method retrieves the Req_Count column from the Requisitions table for the product ID that is passed in as a parameter. If a row is returned, the value of the Req_Count column is returned. If no rows are returned, we will assume that there are no outstanding requisitions for the specified item, and will return a count of 0. If we encounter any problems, we'll return a negative count to indicate that an error occurred (this is possible because there should never be a negative number of outstanding requisitions). The code for this simple method can be seen in Listing 29.2.

---

**Listing 29.2   BCKORDRS.CLS—The *GetNumBackOrders* Method, Which Returns the Current Number of Outstanding Requisitions for the Specified Item**

```
Public Function GetNumBackOrders(aiPrdID As Long) As Integer
    Dim ctxObject As ObjectContext
    Dim rdoConn As rdoConnection
    Dim strSQL As String
    Dim rdoRS As rdoResultset

    'Get our object context
    Set ctxObject = GetObjectContext()
'Set up error handling
    On Error GoTo ErrorHandler
'Obtain the RDO environment and connection
    Set rdoConn = rdoEngine.rdoEnvironments(0).OpenConnection("", _
                    rdDriverNoPrompt, False, strConnect)
'Get resulting balance which may have been further
    'updated via triggers
    strSQL = "SELECT Req_Count FROM Requisition WHERE Prd_ID = " + _
                    Str$(aiPrdID)
    Set rdoRS = rdoConn.OpenResultset(strSQL, rdOpenForwardOnly, _
                    rdConcurReadOnly, rdExecDirect)
    'Did we receive any records from the database?
    If rdoRS.EOF <> True Then
        'Yes, get the number of current back orders
        GetNumBackOrders = rdoRS.rdoColumns("Req_Count")
    Else
        'No, there must not be any current back orders
        'for this product
```

```
        GetNumBackOrders = 0
    End If
'Close the database connection
    rdoConn.Close
'Tell Transaction Server that we have successfully
    'completed our task
    ctxObject.SetComplete
Exit Function
ErrorHandler:
    'Have we connected to the database yet?
    If Not rdoConn Is Nothing Then
        'If so, then close the connection
        rdoConn.Close
    End If
'Tell Transaction Server that we had problems
    ctxObject.SetAbort
    'Indicate that an error occurred
    GetNumBackOrders = -1
End Function
```

**Changing the Number of Back Orders**   Next, add a second method to change the number of outstanding requisitions for a specific item. Call this method ChangeNumBackOrders, and it'll work similarly to the ChangeInv method in our Inventory Maintenance component. This method will update the number of outstanding requisitions for a specified item, and then retrieve the updated number of ordered items. If there are no rows returned in the count retrieval, we'll assume that this is the initial ordering for this item, and we'll insert a new requisition record into the database. We'll return the total number of currently outstanding requisitions for the specified item through a third parameter that we'll pass to the method. This allows us to use the method return value for returning the success/failure flag, returning 0 if the method was successful, and a -1 if there was a problem. The code for this method is provided in Listing 29.3.

**Listing 29.3   BCKORDRS.CLS—The *ChangeNumBackOrders* Method Updates the Requisition Table in a Similar Manner to the *ChangeInv* Method in the Inventory Maintenance Module**

```
Public Function ChangeNumBackOrders(aiPrdID As Long, _
                    aiChange As Integer, _
                    ByRef aiBackOrder As Integer) As Integer
    Dim ctxObject As ObjectContext
    Dim rdoConn As rdoConnection
    Dim strSQL As String
    Dim rdoRS As rdoResultset

    'Get our object context
    Set ctxObject = GetObjectContext()
'Set up error handling
    On Error GoTo ErrorHandler
'Obtain the RDO environment and connection
```

*continues*

**Listing 29.3    Continued**

```
    Set rdoConn = rdoEngine.rdoEnvironments(0).OpenConnection("", _
                        rdDriverNoPrompt, False, strConnect)
'Set up error handling for the record update (this probably
    'won't be called, and we'll have to perform our own error triggering)
    On Error GoTo ErrorCreateRecord
'Update the current back order count
    strSQL = "UPDATE Requisition SET Req_Count = Req_Count + " + _
                    Str$(aiChange) + " WHERE Prd_ID = " + Str$(aiPrdID)
    rdoConn.Execute strSQL, rdExecDirect
'Get resulting count
    strSQL = "SELECT Req_Count FROM Requisition WHERE Prd_ID = " + _
                        Str$(aiPrdID)
    Set rdoRS = rdoConn.OpenResultset(strSQL, rdOpenForwardOnly, _
                    rdConcurReadOnly, rdExecDirect)
    'Did we retrieve any records?
    If rdoRS.EOF <> True Then
        'Yes, let's get the current back order count
        aiBackOrder = rdoRS.rdoColumns("Req_Count")
    Else
        'No, let's jump to the ErrorCreateRecord section
        GoTo ErrorCreateRecord
    End If
'Close the database connection
    rdoConn.Close
'Tell Transaction Server that we have successfully
    'completed our task
    ctxObject.SetComplete
'Return a 0 to signal that we were successful
    ChangeNumBackOrders = 0
Exit Function
ErrorCreateRecord:
    'Set up error handling
    On Error GoTo ErrorHandler
'Did we have any new back orders to add?
    If aiChange > 0 Then
        'Create a new back order record
        strSQL = "INSERT INTO Requisition (Prd_ID, Req_Count) values (" _
                    + Str$(aiPrdID) + ", " + Str$(aiChange) + ")"
        rdoConn.Execute strSQL, rdExecDirect
        'Return the number changed as the current number of back orders
        aiBackOrder = aiChange
    Else
        'There are no new back orders, so we have nothing to do
        aiBackOrder = 0
    End If
'Close the database connection
    rdoConn.Close
'Tell Transaction Server that we have successfully completed our task
    ctxObject.SetComplete
'Return a 0 to signal that we were successful
    ChangeNumBackOrders = 0
Exit Function
ErrorHandler:
```

```
        'Have we connected to the database yet?
        If Not rdoConn Is Nothing Then
            'If so, then close the connection
            rdoConn.Close
        End If
    'Tell Transaction Server that we had problems
        ctxObject.SetAbort
        'Indicate that an error occurred
        ChangeNumBackOrders = -1
End Function
```

**Adding the Back Order Module to Transaction Server**   Once we have built the BackOrdrs project into a DLL, we can register it with Transaction Server by following the same series of steps that we followed in the previous chapter, including setting the Transaction attribute to Requires a Transaction. At this point, the Transaction Server Explorer should look like Figure 29.3. We are now ready to begin building the Merchandise Movement Control component.

**FIG. 29.3**

After the Back Order component has been built and registered with Transaction Server, the component should be visible in the Transaction Server Explorer.

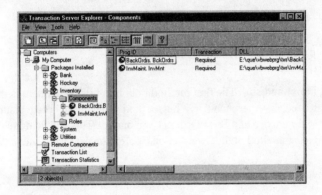

## Merchandise Movement Control

For our Merchandise Movement Control component, things will begin to look a little different. Begin by creating an ActiveX DLL project, which you should name MvMrch, with a single class named MerchMv, and mark the project for unattended execution, just as in the previous two components built. This control does not contain any database interaction, so no reference to the Remote Data Object need be included, and there are no additional database tables that need to be added. However, this component will be interacting with both the Inventory Maintenance component, and the Requisition Maintenance component, so include references to both of these components that have already been built, as in Figure 29.4.

Since you aren't connecting to the database with this module, the declaration section can be limited to just the error number that will be raised in the event of an error, as in Listing 29.4.

**FIG. 29.4**

Include references to our previous two components in the Merchandise Movement Control component.

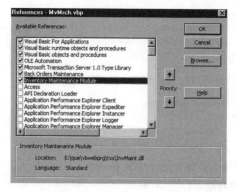

---

**Listing 29.4 MERCHMV.CLS—We Are Not Connecting to the Database with This Component, so All that Goes into the Declarations Section Is the Error Number that We Will Raise in the Event of a Problem**

```
Option Explicit

'We always return the same error number
Private Const ERROR_NUMBER = vbObjectError + 0
```

---

**Receiving Merchandise**    The first method built into this component is the method that is called when receiving merchandise. This method will need to create instances of both the Inventory Maintenance and Back Orders components. This will be done using the CreateInstance method of the Transaction Context object, using the following code:

```
Dim ctxObject As ObjectContext
Dim objInventory As InvMaint.InvMnt

Set ctxObject = GetObjectContext()
Set objInventory = ctxObject.CreateInstance("InvMaint.InvMnt")
```

By using the CreateInstance method, the new instance of the object is created within the context of the current transaction, assuming that the component is registered as supporting transactions. If the new object requires a new transaction, then it is created with a new transaction context.

Once you have the two objects, check to see if there are any outstanding requisitions for the product you are receiving. If there are any, and you are receiving a positive number of the items, then reduce the number of outstanding requisitions by the number of items you are receiving, or the number of outstanding requisitions, whichever is less.

The next thing to do is adjust the current inventory count to reflect the number of items being received (or shipping out in the case of a negative number). If this change results in new back orders, then the number of outstanding requisitions is adjusted once again. This method can be seen in Listing 29.5.

### Listing 29.5 MERCHMV.CLS—The *ReceiveMerch* Method Is Used to Receive Merchandise, and Adjusts the Current Inventory and Outstanding Requisitions as Appropriate

```
Public Function ReceiveMerch(aiPrdID As Long, aiNumRecv As Integer, _
            ByRef aiBackOrder As Integer, _
            ByRef aiStockRemain As Integer) As Integer
    Dim ctxObject As ObjectContext
    Dim objInventory As InvMaint.InvMnt
    Dim objRequisition As BackOrdrs.BckOrdrs
    Dim iiNumRemainToRecv As Integer
    Dim iiNumToRecv As Integer

    'Get our object context
    Set ctxObject = GetObjectContext()
'Set up error handling
    On Error GoTo ErrorHandler
'Create the inventory object using our context
    Set objInventory = ctxObject.CreateInstance("InvMaint.InvMnt")
    If objInventory Is Nothing Then
        Err.Raise ERROR_NUMBER, "Could not create inventory object"
    End If
'Create the requisition object using our context
    Set objRequisition = ctxObject.CreateInstance("BackOrdrs.BckOrdrs")
    If objRequisition Is Nothing Then
        Err.Raise ERROR_NUMBER, "Could not create requisition object"
    End If
'Get the current number of back orders
    iiNumRemainToRecv = objRequisition.GetNumBackOrders(aiPrdID)
    'Are there any existing back orders?
    If iiNumRemainToRecv > 0 Then
        'Is the number of back orders greater than the number
        'that we are receiving?
        If iiNumRemainToRecv > aiNumRecv Then
            'Yes, set number to change back orders to the number
            'we have received
            iiNumToRecv = aiNumRecv
        Else
            'No, set the number to change back orders to the
            'current number of back orders. This will prevent
            'us from having a negative number of back orders.
            iiNumToRecv = iiNumRemainToRecv
        End If
        'Update the current number of back orders
        ReceiveMerch = objRequisition.ChangeNumBackOrders(aiPrdID, _
                    (0 - iiNumToRecv), iiNumRemainToRecv)
        If ReceiveMerch <> 0 Then
            Err.Raise ERROR_NUMBER, _
                "Could not change the number of outstanding orders"
        End If
    End If
'Change the current number in inventory
```

*continues*

**Listing 29.5 Continued**

```
    ReceiveMerch = objInventory.ChangeInv(aiPrdID, aiNumRecv, _
                            aiBackOrder, aiStockRemain)
    If ReceiveMerch <> 0 Then
        Err.Raise ERROR_NUMBER, _
                "Could not change the number of items in inventory"
    End If
'Did the inventory change cause us to have additional back orders?
    If aiBackOrder > 0 Then
        'If so, then add the new back orders to the existing back orders
        ReceiveMerch = objRequisition.ChangeNumBackOrders(aiPrdID, _
                            aiBackOrder, iiNumRemainToRecv)
        If ReceiveMerch <> 0 Then
            Err.Raise ERROR_NUMBER, _
                "Could not change the number of outstanding orders"
        End If
    End If
'Return the current number of back orders
    aiBackOrder = iiNumRemainToRecv
'Tell Transaction Server that we have successfully completed our task
    ctxObject.SetComplete
'Return a 0 to signal that we were successful
    ReceiveMerch = 0
Exit Function
ErrorHandler:
'Tell Transaction Server that we had problems
    ctxObject.SetAbort
    'Indicate that an error occurred
    ReceiveMerch = -1
End Function
```

**Shipping Merchandise** Although you won't be using it for a while, you will need to be shipping merchandise with the system being built. In order to support this functionality, add a method to the Merchandise Movement Control component for shipping merchandise. This method, named `RequestMerch`, is almost the same as the `ReceiveMerch` method, with a couple of key differences.

The first difference is that, because this method will be used for shipping merchandise supposedly already in stock, you don't have to worry about updating the current number of outstanding requisitions for the specified product. You'll only be updating this amount if the request generates new back orders.

The second difference is that you'll reverse the sign on the number of items being passed to the Inventory Maintenance component, so that you can pass this method a positive number of items being shipped, and it will automatically translate the number into a number of items being removed from the inventory. The code for this method can be found in Listing 29.6.

## Listing 29.6  MERCHMV.CLS—The *RequestMerch* Method Is Very Similar to the *ReceiveMerch* Method, with a Couple of Key Differences

```
Public Function RequestMerch(aiPrdID As Long, aiNumReqst As Integer, _
                    ByRef aiBackOrder As Integer, _
                    ByRef aiDelivered As Integer) As Integer
    Dim ctxObject As ObjectContext
    Dim objInventory As InvMaint.InvMnt
    Dim objRequisition As BackOrdrs.BckOrdrs
    Dim iiStockRemain As Integer
    Dim iiNumRemainToRecv As Integer

    'Get our object context
    Set ctxObject = GetObjectContext()
'Set up error handling
    On Error GoTo ErrorHandler
'Create the inventory object using our context
    Set objInventory = ctxObject.CreateInstance("InvMaint.InvMnt")
    If objInventory Is Nothing Then
        Err.Raise ERROR_NUMBER, "Could not create inventory object"
    End If
'Create the requisition object using our context
    Set objRequisition = ctxObject.CreateInstance("BackOrdrs.BckOrdrs")
    If objRequisition Is Nothing Then
        Err.Raise ERROR_NUMBER, "Could not create requisition object"
    End If
'Change the current number in inventory
    RequestMerch = objInventory.ChangeInv(aiPrdID, (0 - aiNumReqst), _
                                    aiBackOrder, iiStockRemain)
    If RequestMerch <> 0 Then
        Err.Raise ERROR_NUMBER, _
                "Could not change the number of items in inventory"
    End If
'Did the inventory change cause us to have any back orders?
    If aiBackOrder > 0 Then
        'If so, then add the new back orders to the existing back orders
        RequestMerch = objRequisition.ChangeNumBackOrders(aiPrdID, _
                                    aiBackOrder, iiNumRemainToRecv)
        If RequestMerch <> 0 Then
            Err.Raise ERROR_NUMBER, _
                "Could not change the number of outstanding orders"
        End If
    End If
'Return the number of back orders generated
    aiDelivered = aiNumReqst - aiBackOrder
'Tell Transaction Server that we have successfully completed our task
    ctxObject.SetComplete
'Return a 0 to signal that we were successful
    RequestMerch = 0
```

*continues*

**Listing 29.6   Continued**

```
Exit Function
ErrorHandler:
'Tell Transaction Server that we had problems
    ctxObject.SetAbort
    'Indicate that an error occurred
    RequestMerch = -1
End Function
```

**Registering the Merchandise Movement Control**   Once built, the Merchandise Movement control will need to be registered with Transaction Server with the same steps used to register the previous two components built. Once you've registered this component, the Transaction Server Explorer should look like Figure 29.5.

**FIG. 29.5**
The Transaction Server Explorer should display the three components built and registered with it at this time.

## Updating the User Interface

In order to update our user interface to make use of the Merchandise Movement control component instead of going directly to the Inventory Maintenance component, you will need to change the cmdReceived_Click subroutine to instantiate the Merchandise Movement control, and call its ReceiveMerch method, as in Listing 29.7.

**Listing 29.7   RECVNG.FRM—By Changing the Object We Are Instancing and the Method Being Called, We Can Adapt Our User Interface to Use the Merchandise Movement Control Component**

```
Private Sub cmdReceived_Click()
    Dim ProgID As String
    Dim obj As Object
    Dim iBackOrder As Integer
    Dim iCurInventory As Integer

    'Set up the error handling
    On Error GoTo ErrorHandler
'Decide which component to use
```

```
    ProgID = "MvMrch.MerchMv"
'Create the appropriate object
    Set obj = CreateObject(ProgID)
    'Were we able to create the object?
    If obj Is Nothing Then
        MsgBox "Create object " + ProgID + "failed."
        Exit Sub
    End If
'Call the object method
    If obj.ReceiveMerch(iiProductID, CLng(txtCount.Text), _
                    iBackOrder, iCurInventory) = -1 Then
        Err.Raise ERROR_NUMBER
    End If
'Release the object
    Set obj = Nothing
'Display for the user what the current inventory is
    MsgBox "New Inventory received, current backorder count = " + _
                    Str$(iBackOrder) + " and current inventory = " _
                    + Str$(iCurInventory)
    Exit Sub
ErrorHandler:
    'Show the user the error message
    MsgBox "Error " + Str$(Err.Number) + " : " + Err.Description
    Exit Sub
End Sub
```

After these changes to the user interface form, run the project and watch in the Transaction Server Explorer as the components are instantiated and called, as in Figure 29.6.

**FIG. 29.6**
With the Transaction Server Explorer showing the component status, watch as each of the components are instantiated and called.

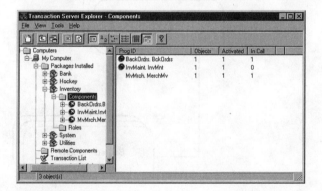

# Using Shared Objects

Often within large applications there is information that must be maintained and shared between all instances of the application that may be running. Some of this information can be freely accessed by all copies of the application that may be running simultaneously, but there are other types of information that the various copies of the application will be needing to change and update. Usually, client/server applications maintained this information in the database, and used various techniques to try to limit access to the information such that only one instance of the application may update the information at any point in time. Now Transaction Server provides a way to maintain and safely update these "shared properties" through its Shared Property Manager.

## The Shared Property Manager

The Transaction Server Shared Property Manager is implemented as a series of three objects, as shown in Figure 29.7. The first object is the Shared Property Group Manager. There is only one of these at any time in Transaction Server, and it manages all of the shared property groups. A reference to the Shared Property Group Manager is created in the following manner:

```
Dim spmMgr As SharedPropertyGroupManager
Set spmMgr = CreateObject("MTxSpm.SharedPropertyGroupManager.1")
```

The CreateObject function that creates the reference to the Shared Property Group Manager is always guaranteed to succeed, so there is no reason to check the returned reference to see if the call might have failed.

**FIG. 29.7**

The Transaction Server Shared Property Manager is implemented as a family of three objects.

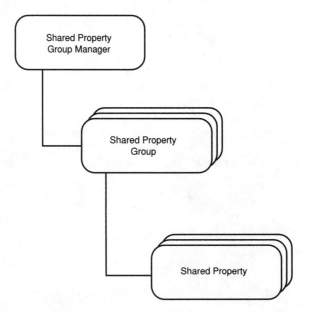

The second object is the Shared Property Group. This object contains a group of shared properties that are related and can be considered a single object. The Shared Property Group is created by the CreatePropertyGroup method of the Shared Property Group Manager, as in the following example:

```
Dim spmGroup As SharedPropertyGroup
Set spmGroup = spmMgr.CreatePropertyGroup("OrderNum", LockSetGet, _
                                 Process, bResult)
```

The first parameter to this method is a name for the property group. If the group hasn't been created, then a new group will be created with this name. If a group already exists with this name, then a reference to that existing group will be returned instead. If the group already existed before this call, the last parameter is set to TRUE to indicate that the property group that was returned already existed, and that the second and third parameters were ignored. If the property group was created with this call, then the last parameter is set to FALSE, and the second and third parameters were used in creating the property group.

The second parameter specifies the isolation mode of the properties in the group. There are two possible values for this parameter, as specified in Table 29.2.

**Table 29.2 The Isolation Mode Properties for a Shared Property Group**

| Constant | Value | Description |
|---|---|---|
| LockSetGet | 0 | This is the default value for this parameter. This specifies that only one client can access any one shared property at a time. This applies for both reading and writing the value of the property, but has no effect on the accessibility of other properties in the same group. |
| LockMethod | 1 | This value specifies that all properties are locked and only the caller process can access any of the properties in the group until the calling process exists the current method. |

The third parameter tells the Shared Property Group Manager how long to maintain the Shared Property Group. There are two possible values for this property as well, listed in Table 29.3.

**Table 29.3 The Release Mode Properties for a Shared Property Group**

| Constant | Value | Description |
|---|---|---|
| Standard | 0 | The shared property group is automatically destroyed once all clients have released their references to the property group. |
| Process | 1 | The shared property group is not destroyed until the process in which the group was created has terminated. All SharedPropertyGroup objects must still be released by setting them to Nothing. |

Finally, the third object in this family is the SharedProperty. This object is created by the SharedPropertyGroup object using the CreateProperty method, as in the following example:

```
Dim spmPropNextOrder As SharedProperty
Set spmPropNextOrder = spmGroup.CreateProperty("Next", bResult)
```

As you can see, the `CreateProperty` method is much simpler than the method used to create a `SharedPropertyGroup`. The `CreateProperty` method takes two parameters. This first parameter is the name for the shared property, and the second is a flag that is returned to indicate whether a new shared property was created, or if a reference to an existing shared property with the specified name was returned. If the second parameter is set to `FALSE`, then a new shared property was created. If the second parameter is set to `TRUE`, then a shared property already existed in this shared property group with the specified name, and the `CreateProperty` method returned a reference for the existing property.

The `SharedProperty` object is a Variant data type, and can contain any value that can be held in a Variant variable. There may be any number of shared properties in a shared property group. Once we have created the shared property, we can freely access and update its value property without worrying about how to protect it from simultaneous manipulation by other instances of the same or other applications.

## Creating a Next Number Generator Using Shared Properties

Use the shared property manager to create a component that will generate the next numbers, which will be used for shipping invoice numbers. Once again, this project will be implemented as an ActiveX control, with unattended execution set to `TRUE`. Name this project `OrderNum`, and create two classes, the first named `NextOrder`, and the second named `OrdUpdate`. Create an empty method in the second class called `Update`, which takes no parameters and returns a long, and we'll come back to fill in this method later. The last thing to do is include references to the Remote Data Object, the Transaction Server Type library, and the Shared Property Manager Type library, as in Figure 29.8.

**FIG. 29.8**

Include a reference for the Shared Property Manager in our next number generator project.

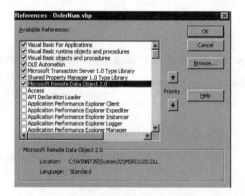

**Building the Next Number Generator**  The design to take for the next number generator will use two shared properties. The first property will be the actual next number that we are generating. The second number will be the current maximum number that we will increment to before updating the next number value in the database. By updating the database every 100 numbers, you can gain a bit of a performance boost by limiting the amount of database interaction that these objects will have to perform.

In the `NextOrder` class, since there is no database interaction, limit the declarations to the error number that will be raised in the event of a problem, just as in the Merchandise Movement Control, back in Listing 29.4. Now create a method called `GetNextOrderNum`, which will perform all of the next number generation.

The first thing to do in this method is to create all shared properties, along with the shared property group and group manager. Create two properties, the first named `Next`, and the other named `MaxNum`, in a group named `OrderNum`. If these already have been created, then you'll have references to the existing ones, so don't worry about initializing them.

The next thing to do is check to see if you have reached the maximum number to reach before updating the database. If so, then create an instance of the `OrdUpdate` class and call its `Update` method to perform this update. Set the next maximum number to 100 greater than the current value stored in the database. Once sure that the database is as up to date as it needs to be, increment the next number shared property, mark this transaction as complete, and return the generated next number. By using the current value of the shared property in updating itself, you have guaranteed that you were using the most current value of the shared property, and that no one else could update the property between the time that you read the value and the time the value was last updated. The code that performs all of this is in Listing 29.8.

**Listing 29.8   NEXTORDER.CLS—The *GetNextOrderNum* Method Generates
Next Numbers Using the Shared Property Manager**

```
Public Function GetNextOrderNum() As Long
    Dim ctxObject As ObjectContext
    Dim spmMgr As SharedPropertyGroupManager
    Dim spmGroup As SharedPropertyGroup
    Dim bResult As Boolean
    Dim spmPropNextOrder As SharedProperty
    Dim spmPropMaxNum As SharedProperty
    Dim objOrderUpdate As OrderNum.OrdUpdate

    'Get object context
    Set ctxObject = GetObjectContext()
'Set up error handling
    On Error GoTo ErrorHandler
'If Shared property does not already exist it will be initialized
    Set spmMgr = CreateObject("MTxSpm.SharedPropertyGroupManager.1")
    Set spmGroup = spmMgr.CreatePropertyGroup("OrderNum", LockSetGet, _
                            Process, bResult)
    Set spmPropNextOrder = spmGroup.CreateProperty("Next", bResult)
    Set spmPropMaxNum = spmGroup.CreateProperty("MaxNum", bResult)
'Do we need to update the current order number in the database?
    If spmPropNextOrder.Value >= spmPropMaxNum.Value Then
        Set objOrderUpdate = ctxObject.CreateInstance("OrderNum.OrdUpdate")
        spmPropNextOrder.Value = objOrderUpdate.Update()
        spmPropMaxNum.Value = spmPropNextOrder.Value + 100
    End If
'Get the next order number and update property
```

*continues*

---

**Listing 29.8 Continued**

```
    spmPropNextOrder.Value = spmPropNextOrder.Value + 1
'Tell Transaction Server that we have successfully completed our task
    ctxObject.SetComplete
'Return the next order number
    GetNextOrderNum = spmPropNextOrder.Value
Exit Function
ErrorHandler:
'Tell Transaction Server that we had problems
    ctxObject.SetAbort
    'Indicate that an error occurred
    GetNextOrderNum = -1
End Function
```

---

**Providing Next Number Persistence**  Now that you can use the shared property manager in Transaction Server to build a next number generator, you must provide a way of maintaining the next number in the database. Seeing as how you will be interacting with the database with the OrdUpdate class, use the same declaration section used in the Requisition component, back in Listing 29.1. Also, you'll need to add a new table to the database called OrderNum with a single column, NextOrder which is declared as an int data type.

In the Update method, query the database to retrieve the current value stored for the next order number, and then update the database by adding 100 to the current value. If the query doesn't return any rows, assume that the record doesn't exist yet, and insert a new record initializing the table with the value of 100. The code to perform this is provided in Listing 29.9.

---

**Listing 29.9  ORDUPDATE.CLS—The *Update* Method Will Be Used to Update the Next Number in the Database Every 100 Increments**

```
Public Function Update() As Long
    Dim ctxObject As ObjectContext
    Dim rdoConn As rdoConnection
    Dim rdoRsOrder As rdoResultset
    Dim lngNextOrder As Long
    Dim strSQL As String

    'Get object context
    Set ctxObject = GetObjectContext()
'Setup RDO connection
    Set rdoConn = rdoEngine.rdoEnvironments(0).OpenConnection("", _
                            rdDriverNoPrompt, False, strConnect)
    rdoConn.QueryTimeout = 60 ' 1 minute
'Get result set and then update table with new receipt number
    strSQL = "Select * from OrderNum"
    Set rdoRsOrder = rdoConn.OpenResultset(strSQL, rdOpenForwardOnly, _
                            rdConcurReadOnly, rdExecDirect)

    If rdoRsOrder.EOF <> True Then
        lngNextOrder = rdoRsOrder.rdoColumns("NextOrder")
        strSQL = "Update OrderNum set NextOrder = " & (lngNextOrder + 100)
    Else
```

```
            lngNextOrder = 100
            strSQL = "Insert into OrderNum (NextOrder) values (100)"
        End If
        rdoConn.Execute strSQL, rdExecDirect
    'Close the database connection
        rdoConn.Close
    'Tell Transaction Server that we have successfully completed our task
        ctxObject.SetComplete
    'Return the new maximum order number value
        Update = lngNextOrder
    Exit Function
    ErrorHandler:
        'Have we connected to the database yet?
        If Not rdoConn Is Nothing Then
            'If so, then close the connection
            rdoConn.Close
        End If
    'Tell Transaction Server that we had problems
        ctxObject.SetAbort
        'Indicate that an error occurred
        Update = -1
    End Function
```

## Configuring Transactions

Once you build the OrderNum project into an ActiveX DLL, and register it with Transaction Server, update the transaction attributes of both components. Leave the NextOrder components transaction attribute as Does not support transactions, while updating the OrdUpdate's transaction attribute to Requires a new transaction. This should have the properties display of the Transaction Server Explorer looking like Figure 29.9.

**FIG. 29.9**
After configuring the OrderNum component transaction attributes, the Transaction Server Explorer should reflect the appropriate transaction attribute settings.

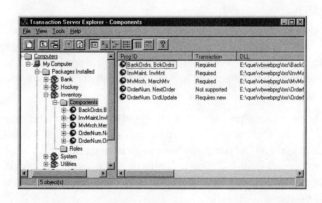

With the transaction attributes as you currently have them configured, the three components built for moving merchandise will all maintain a consistent transaction, where if any one of the three encounters a problem, the entire transaction will be rolled back. Whereas the NextOrder

Part
VIII

Ch

29

component will never be part of a transaction, and will not contribute to the success or failure of any transaction. Meanwhile, the OrdUpdate component will always execute within its own transaction, completely independent of any other transaction that might have triggered its actions. This implements our transaction configuration for these objects much like that in Figure 29.10.

**FIG. 29.10**
The current transaction configuration will keep the next number generator executing outside of any transaction, and the number update component executing in its own transaction, much like objects D and E.

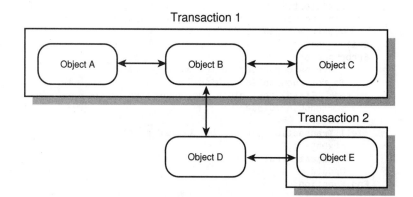

# Understanding Role-Based Security

Transaction Server provides for a couple of options on security, which are intertwined with regular NT security and providing access to various resources. These are all controlled via the Transaction Server administration. However, there is one aspect of security that is important to understand for programming purposes, and that is the use of roles in the Transaction Server security model.

## Defining Roles

As a developer, you can go into the Transaction Server Explorer and create any number of roles into which the users of your application should be grouped. These roles should be included as part of the package that you have built for your application. You don't need to worry about placing users into these roles; that will be the job of the system administrator when your application is deployed.

When you begin defining package roles, you need to spend some time planning how the roles will be used in your application. You need to determine what each role will be allowed or prevented from doing. The last thing you need to do is begin defining a large number of roles just for the sake of creating roles. This is probably one of the quickest ways to get your system administrator to not like you, by making him or her determine into which of all the roles each user should be placed.

To define a role for use in building security into your application, follow these steps:

1. Select the Roles folder in the package for which you want to define one or more security roles.

2. Select File ¦ New from the main menu.

3. Type in the name to be used for the role, as in Figure 29.11, and click OK.

**FIG. 29.11**
Specify a name that describes the access level that the role will have in your application.

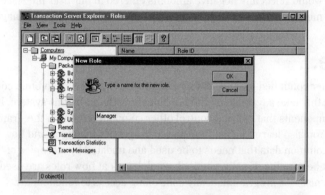

4. The Transaction Server Explorer should display the newly created role in the roles folder, as in Figure 29.12. Repeat steps 2 and 3 for every role that you need defined for your application.

**FIG. 29.12**
The Transaction Server Explorer should update the display to include the role you just defined.

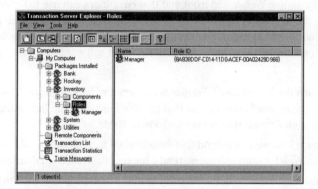

## Checking User Roles

Checking to see whether the user is in a specific role that is necessary for certain actions is simply a matter of calling the `IsCallerInRole` method of the context object. This method takes one parameter, the role name, and returns a `TRUE/FALSE` condition to let you know if the user is in the role specified. For instance, if we wanted to modify the Merchandise Movement class that we built earlier in the chapter such that `ReceiveMerch` method would allow only a manager to enter negative amounts of merchandise to receive, then before we have created the Inventory Maintenance object, we could include the following code:

```
If (aiNumRecv < 0) Then
    If Not ctxObject.IsCallerInRole("Manager") Then
        Err.Raise ERROR_NUMBER, _
```

```
        "Only Managers are allowed to enter negative merchandise amounts."
    End If
End If
```

This code would reject any negative amounts entered in our user interface that we were using to receive merchandise, unless the user is specified as being in the Manager role.

# From Here...

This chapter continued looking at Transaction Server, and how to build components with Visual Basic that take advantage of the functionality offered by this system. It also showed how to create components that call and control other components within the Transaction Server environment. You also learned about the shared properties manager, and how it can be used to maintain common data that needs to be used and updated by all copies of the same application that might be running. Finally, you took a quick look at how roles are used to provide a security mechanism for programmatically controlling access to functionality.

From here you might want to expand on our fictional catalog order company system by adding automatic purchase order generation functionality, or building in additional functionality to automatically order additional merchandise when the current inventory drops below a certain minimum threshold. In the meantime, you'll continue adding to the system in the next chapter by building a simple Web-based front end that customers can use to enter their own order, and integrating this Web interface with the system that is already in place. At this time, use the next number generator built in this chapter to generate shipping invoice numbers that are assigned to the orders received over the Web. From here you will want to check out the following chapters:

- To learn the basics about Transaction Server, what it does and how it provides a facility for building small components that provide business rule functionality, see Chapter 28, "Microsoft Transaction Server and Visual Basic."

- To learn how we can extend this system even further and provide an order entry system on the Web for our customers, read Chapter 30, "Building Distributed Web Applications."

- To learn about some of the security systems that we would want to put in place before opening up our integrated order entry system for all Web surfers, check out Chapter 31, "Internet Security and Web Applications."

# Building Distributed Web Applications

**In** the previous two chapters, we have seen how Transaction Server allows us to build small components that can interact with each other to provide functionality for a large distributed application that is integrated with several systems. We learned the basic concepts behind this new technology from Microsoft, and saw how it could be used to provide all of the "wiring" to connect all of these small simple components with a minimal programming effort on our part. We learned how Transaction Server provides a facility for defining shared information that is to be used by all running instances of an application, and how we can build components that take advantage of this functionality. We also learned how we could call and control components that are running within the Transaction Server environment from a stand-alone Visual Basic application, as well as from other Transaction Server components.

**Integrate Web Applications with Transaction Server**

Components registered with Transaction Server can be called from Active Server Pages and OLEISAPI2 applications, as well as WinCGI applications. We'll look at how this can be done on each of these platforms.

**Build and Integrate Shipping Order Maintenance**

We'll be building three new components that are part of our catalog order company for maintaining customer orders and moving merchandise from the warehouse inventory to the shipping dock.

**Web-Based Customer Order Entry Catalog Orders**

We'll be building a Web-based front end to our catalog order company system, and integrate it into the inventory and requisition systems that we built in the previous chapters.

In this chapter, we will extend our distributed system to the Web, with a Web-based front-end application that allows customers of our catalog order company to place their orders from the Web, and have the orders filled automatically, with any out of stock items being back ordered, all while the customer is online, so that the customer gets a copy of his or her shipping invoice as the response to their order. In implementing this front end, we'll build an OLEISAPI2 application that is integrated with Transaction Server, and calls a new Shipping Order component that we will also be building in this chapter. We'll also take the time to look at what would be involved in building this Web front-end using Active Server Pages and a WinCGI application. ■

# Integrating Transaction Server with the Web

By integrating Transaction Server with a Web server, whether IIS or another vendor Web server, the majority of the processing logic of the Web-based application can be moved off of the Web server computer and onto other computers. If you have a very busy Web site, this is an important capability. The more of the number crunching that can be moved to another computer, the more hits your Web server will be able to service. This is true both for public Internet Web applications like virtual stores, and internal Intranet business applications.

Transaction Server can be easily integrated with any Visual Basic Server-side programming technology, whether WinCGI, OLEISAPI2, or Active Server Pages, through the use of the CreateObject method. In each of these server-side programming technologies, the Web server application is acting as the front-end for the Transaction Server process. The Web server application is no different from the simple Visual Basic window that we built for receiving new merchandise at the receiving dock in the previous two chapters. As long as the object that is being created is registered with Transaction Server, and Transaction Server is installed and configured on the Web server, the Web server application will interact with Transaction Server no differently from any other front-end application. This makes it easy to move the majority of your Web application logic off of the Web server computer and onto other computers in your site.

**N O T E** Since OLEISAPI2 applications are built as ActiveX DLLs, you might think that you could register them with Transaction Server and move the interface to the Web server one step closer to the Web server process. Unfortunately, this approach does not work, in part because of the Active Request Object that the OLEISAPI2 interface passes to the Visual Basic DLL. Your OLEISAPI2 Visual Basic DLL has to be the Transaction Server client, and cannot be registered with Transaction Server.

If you do try to register an OLEISAPI2 DLL with Transaction Server, you will have to re-register the DLL with the registry database before you will be able to use it outside of Transaction Server. When Transaction Server registers an ActiveX DLL, it alters the registry database information about that DLL, so that all calls to the DLL are routed through Transaction Server. Once you delete a component from Transaction Server, you will need to re-register the DLL either by recompiling or by using regsrv32.exe. ■

# Building the Shipping Order Components

Before we can begin to build our Web-based front-end for our catalog company, we still have three more components to build. We will be expanding our system with three components that handle the building and maintenance of the shipping order, pulling the information that's necessary from the other components that we have built in the previous two chapters. When we are finished, our catalog store system will look like the diagram in Figure 30.1.

**FIG. 30.1**
Our completed catalog store system will include three new components that create and maintain shipping invoices by interacting with other components.

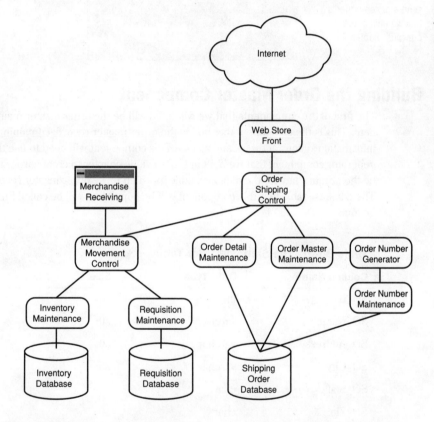

Since these three components all are logically part of the same functional component, we'll be building them as a single project. We'll call our project "ShipOrdr," and it will contain three classes, "MstrOrder," "DtlOrder," and "ShpOrder." We'll need to include in the references the Remote Data Object, the Transaction Server Type library, and the Order Number Generator that we built in the previous chapter, and the Merchandise Movement component we built in the previous chapter, as in Figure 30.2.

Part
VIII

Ch
30

**FIG. 30.2**

Along with the Remote Data Object and the Transaction Server Type library, you need to be sure to include the merchandise movement and order number generator components that we built in the previous chapter.

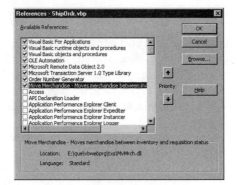

# Building the Order Master Component

The first of the components that we will build will be the order master maintenance component. This is the component that builds the order master record, containing the customer information (name, address, and so on). This component will need to use the next number generator component that we built in the previous chapter to create order numbers, which will be the primary key for the database table in which these order master records will be placed. The database table that this component will be populating will be called ShippingOrder and can be found in Table 30.1.

### Table 30.1   The ShippingOrder Table

| Column Name | Data Type | Size |
|---|---|---|
| SO_ID | int | |
| SO_Name | varchar | 30 |
| SO_Address | varchar | 30 |
| SO_City | varchar | 25 |
| SO_State | char | 2 |
| SO_Zip | char | 10 |
| SO_Phone | char | 15 |

We'll be connecting to the database, so we'll use the same declaration section as we used in the components that we built earlier that also connected to the database, as seen in Listing 30.1.

### Listing 30.1   MSTRORDER.CLS—The Class Declaration Section Containing the Database Connection String

```
Option Explicit
'We always return the same error number
```

```
Private Const ERROR_NUMBER = vbObjectError + 0
'The database connect string
Private Const strConnect = "DSN=InvMntDB;UID=TxsVB;PWD=vbtxs;"
```

We'll add only one method to our class, for inserting new shipping orders. In order for this class to be functionally complete, we would also need to add methods for updating, querying, and possibly deleting records from this table. The method we'll build will be called NewOrder, and the code is provided in Listing 30.2.

## Listing 30.2  MSTRORDER.CLS—The NewOrder Method Creates the Order Master Record for New Orders

```
Public Function NewOrder(asName As String, asAddr As String, _
                    asCity As String, asState As String, _
                    asZip As String, asPhone As String) As Long
    Dim ctxObject As ObjectContext
    Dim rdoConn As rdoConnection
    Dim objOrderNo As OrderNum.NextOrder
    Dim lngOrderNo As Long
    Dim strSQL As String
    'Get our object context
    Set ctxObject = GetObjectContext()

    'Set up error handling
    On Error GoTo ErrorHandler

    'Obtain the RDO environment and connection
    Set rdoConn = rdoEngine.rdoEnvironments(0).OpenConnection("", _
                        rdDriverNoPrompt, False, strConnect)

    'Get Order Number for the transaction
    Set objOrderNo = ctxObject.CreateInstance("OrderNum.NextOrder")
    lngOrderNo = objOrderNo.GetNextOrderNum
    If lngOrderNo <= 0 Then
        Err.Raise ERROR_NUMBER, "Error. Unable to generate order number."
    End If

    'Insert the new order record
    strSQL = "INSERT into ShippingOrder (SO_ID, SO_Name, _
        SO_Address, SO_City, SO_State, SO_Zip, SO_Phone) values (" + _
        Str$(lngOrderNo) + ", '" + asName + "', '" + asAddr + _
        "', '" + asCity + "', '" + asState + "', '" + asZip + "', '" + _
        asPhone + "')"
    rdoConn.Execute strSQL, rdExecDirect
    'Close the database connection
    rdoConn.Close

    'Tell Transaction Server that we have successfully completed our task
    ctxObject.SetComplete
```

*continues*

**Listing 30.2   Continued**

```
        'Return the new order number
        NewOrder = lngOrderNo

  Exit Function
ErrorHandler:
        'Have we connected to the database yet?
        If Not rdoConn Is Nothing Then
            'If so, then close the connection
            rdoConn.Close
        End If

        'Tell Transaction Server that we had problems
        ctxObject.SetAbort
        'Indicate that an error occured
        NewOrder = -1
End Function
```

# Building the Order Detail Component

The next component that we'll build in this project is the order detail maintenance component. This component will add the product records into the database in an order detail table named "Shipping." This table will consist of the order number, product ID, and the number of items being shipped and back ordered. The table specification can be found in Table 30.2.

**Table 30.2   The Shipping Database Table**

| Column Name | Data Type |
| --- | --- |
| Prd_ID | int |
| SO_ID | int |
| Shp_Count | smallint |
| Shp_BackOrder | smallint |

**N O T E**   The *int* and *smallint* data types in SQL Server are a fixed size, and thus do not require a column size to be specified. An *int* data type is defined as four bytes, and a *smallint* is defined as two bytes. The available number range that can be stored in each of these data types is completely dependent on what range of numbers can be represented by each of these storage allocations.   ▇

Because the order detail component will be connecting to the database, it'll be using the same declaration section as the order master component, as seen in Listing 30.1. The order detail component will contain a single method called NewDetail. This method will be passed to all order detail information, and the component will add a single record to the database containing this information. The code that performs this can be found in Listing 30.3.

**Listing 30.3   DTLORDER.CLS—The NewDetail Method Adds Order Detail
Records to the Database**

```
Public Function NewDetail(aiPrdID As Long, aiSOID As Long, _
                    aiCount As Integer, aiBackOrder As Integer) As Long
    Dim ctxObject As ObjectContext
    Dim rdoConn As rdoConnection
    Dim strSQL As String
    'Get our object context
    Set ctxObject = GetObjectContext()

    'Set up error handling
    On Error GoTo ErrorHandler

    'Obtain the RDO environment and connection
    Set rdoConn = rdoEngine.rdoEnvironments(0).OpenConnection("", _
                    rdDriverNoPrompt, False, strConnect)

    'Insert the order detail record
    strSQL = "INSERT into Shipping (Prd_ID, SO_ID, Shp_Count, " + _
                " Shp_BackOrder) values (" + _
            Str$(aiPrdID) + ", " + Str$(aiSOID) + ", " + _
            Str$(aiCount) + ", " + Str$(aiBackOrder) + ")"
    rdoConn.Execute strSQL, rdExecDirect
    'Close the database connection
    rdoConn.Close

    'Tell Transaction Server that we have successfully completed our task
    ctxObject.SetComplete

    'Return a 0 to signal that we were successful
    NewDetail = 0

  Exit Function
ErrorHandler:
    'Have we connected to the database yet?
    If Not rdoConn Is Nothing Then
        'If so, then close the connection
        rdoConn.Close
    End If

    'Tell Transaction Server that we had problems
    ctxObject.SetAbort
    'Indicate that an error occured
    NewDetail = -1

End Function
```

# Building the Order Shipping Component

The third and final component for this project is the order shipping control component. This is
the component that will be interfaced with the Web server. It will control the other two components in this project, as well as interact with the merchandise movement component that we
built in the previous chapter.

Our plan for this component will be to build two methods. The first method will be called for all new orders, and will build the order master and first detail record. The second method will add order detail records to an existing order record. With both methods, the component will be requesting the specified merchandise from the merchandise movement component, using the RequestMerch method, which will return the number of items that will be shipped, and the number of items being back ordered.

Because we will not be connecting this component to the database, we will only be defining the error number that we will be raising in the event of a problem in the class declarations section, as seen in Listing 30.4.

**Listing 30.4   SHPORDER.CLS—The Declaration Section of the Order Shipping Component Contains only the Error Number Definition**

```
Option Explicit
'We always return the same error number
Private Const ERROR_NUMBER = vbObjectError + 0
```

**Creating the Order Detail Record**   We'll build the method to add the order detail records first, as we'll be calling it from the other method to add the initial detail record. We'll call this method "AddItemToOrder," and it will be passed the order number, product ID, and the quantity ordered. This method will call the RequestMerch method of the merchandise movement component, from which it will receive back the number of items available for shipping, and the number of items back ordered. The method will then call the NewDetail method of the order detail maintenance component to insert the detail record into the database. The code to perform these tasks can be found in Listing 30.5.

**Listing 30.5   SHPORDER.CLS—The AddItemToOrder Method Moves Merchandise from the Inventory to the Shipping Dock**

```
Public Function AddItemToOrder(aiSOID As Long, aiPrdID As Long, _
                                 aiCount As Integer) As Long
    Dim ctxObject As ObjectContext
    Dim iiRemain As Integer
    Dim iiBackOrdered As Integer
    Dim objMveMerch As MvMrch.MerchMv
    Dim objOrdDtl As ShipOrdr.DtlOrder
    'Get our object context
    Set ctxObject = GetObjectContext()
    'Set up error handling
    On Error GoTo ErrorHandler
    'Request the merchandise ordered
    Set objMveMerch = ctxObject.CreateInstance("MvMrch.MerchMv")
    If objMveMerch Is Nothing Then
        Err.Raise ERROR_NUMBER, "Could not create merchandise object"
    End If
    If objMveMerch.RequestMerch(aiPrdID, aiCount, iiBackOrdered, _
                                 iiRemain) < 0 Then
```

```
          Err.Raise ERROR_NUMBER, "Could not order requested merchandise"
     End If

     'Create the order detail object
     Set objOrdDtl = ctxObject.CreateInstance("ShipOrdr.DtlOrder")
     If objOrdDtl Is Nothing Then
          Err.Raise ERROR_NUMBER, "Could not create order detail object"
     End If
     If objOrdDtl.NewDetail(aiPrdID, aiSOID, iiRemain, iiBackOrdered) _
                                                           < 0 Then
          Err.Raise ERROR_NUMBER, "Could not insert order detail records"
     End If

     'Tell Transaction Server that we have successfully completed our task
     ctxObject.SetComplete

     'Return a 0 to signal that we were successful
     AddItemToOrder = 0

     Exit Function
ErrorHandler:
     'Tell Transaction Server that we had problems
     ctxObject.SetAbort
     'Indicate that an error occured
     AddItemToOrder = -1
End Function
```

**Creating the Order Master Record**   Our final method for this component, which we'll name "NewOrder," will pass the customer's name, address, and phone number along with the first item on the purchase. This method will first call the NewOrder method of the order master maintenance component to create the order master record, and to generate an order number. Once this method has the order number, it'll call the previous method to create the initial order detail record, passing the order number, product ID, and quantity ordered. The code for this method can be found in Listing 30.6.

**Listing 30.6   SHPORDER.CLS—The NewOrder Method Creates the Order Master Record then Calls the AddItemToOrder Method to add the Initial Detail Record**

```
Public Function NewOrder(asName As String, asAddr As String, _
                         asCity As String, asState As String, _
                         asZip As String, asPhone As String, _
                         aiPrdID As Long, aiCount As Integer) As Long
     Dim ctxObject As ObjectContext
     Dim objMstrOrd As ShipOrdr.MstrOrder
     Dim ilOrderNum As Long
     Dim iiRemain As Integer
     Dim iiBackOrdered As Integer
     Dim objMveMerch As MvMrch.MerchMv
```

*continues*

Part
VIII

Ch
30

**Listing 30.6    Continued**

```
    Dim objOrdDtl As ShipOrdr.DtlOrder
    'Get our object context
    Set ctxObject = GetObjectContext()
    'Set up error handling
    On Error GoTo ErrorHandler
    'Create the order master object using our context
    Set objMstrOrd = ctxObject.CreateInstance("ShipOrdr.MstrOrder")
    If objMstrOrd Is Nothing Then
        Err.Raise ERROR_NUMBER, "Could not create master order object"
    End If

    'Create the shipping order record
    ilOrderNum = objMstrOrd.NewOrder(asName, asAddr, asCity, _
                                     asState, asZip, asPhone)
    'Did we receive back a valid order number?
    If ilOrderNum < 0 Then
        Err.Raise ERROR_NUMBER, "Could not create master order record"
    End If

    'Create the order detail object
    If AddItemToOrder(ilOrderNum, aiPrdID, aiCount) = -1 Then
        Err.Raise ERROR_NUMBER, "Could not insert the detail record"
    End If

    'Tell Transaction Server that we have successfully completed our task
    ctxObject.SetComplete

    'Return the new order number
    NewOrder = ilOrderNum

    Exit Function
ErrorHandler:
    'Tell Transaction Server that we had problems
    ctxObject.SetAbort
    'Indicate that an error occured
    NewOrder = -1

End Function
```

At this point, we can build the project and register the DLL with Transaction Server. Once we have registered the components, we will want to set the transaction attributes for each of the components in this DLL to "Requires a Transaction." At this point the Transaction Server Explorer should look like Figure 30.3.

**FIG. 30.3**
Once the ShipOrdr DLL has been registered with Transaction Server, the Explorer should reflect the new components with their transaction attribute configuration.

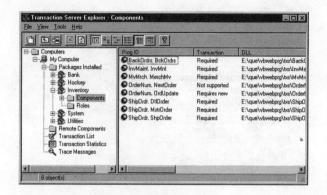

# Adding the Virtual Store Front

Now that we have the entire back-end system built, it's time to turn our attention to the Web-based order entry system. This system has to provide the customer with a form to fill out for shipping information (e.g., name, address, phone), and provide them with a list of products from the database.

Ideally, we would implement this with a shopping basket, so that the customer could browse through the merchandise and select the individual items to purchase, one at a time. This would involve tracking the customer through the Web site, and maintaining a session identifier, either through use of a cookie, or added to the URL, or through the TCP/IP address of the user. For brevity's sake, we will not be implementing our store front in this manner. Just like everything else about our catalog order corporation, the store front will be greatly simplified from what it would be in an actual, real-world, system.

## Initializing the Project

We'll be building this project as an OLEISAPI2 application. We could just as easily have built this as a WinCGI or Active Server Pages application, as the means of calling the Transaction Server components is the same in all three (with one slight deviation in the ASP implementation). We'll name our project "StrFrnt," and include the General.bas and Paramtrs.cls files from our earlier OLEISAPI2 projects. As with the previous OLEISAPI2 applications, we will be building this project as an ActiveX DLL, and will need to include references to the Remote Data Object and the OLEISAPI2 Type library, as seen in Figure 30.4.

**N O T E** We do not need to include the Transaction Server Type library, or any reference to Transaction Server in our project. Transaction Server does need to be installed on the same computer as your Web server, and configured so that it can see the objects that we built in this and the previous two chapters. If these are installed on the same machine as the Web server, they should appear in a package just as in Figure 30.3. If these components are on another system, then they should appear in the *Remote Components* folder in the Transaction Server Explorer. ∎

**FIG. 30.4**

We need to include references to the Remote Data Object and the OLEISAPI2 Type library in our project.

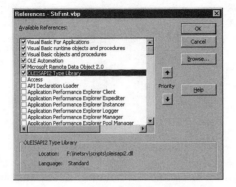

We'll start a new class called "PlaceOrder," and place the database connect string, along with the rest of our typical OLEISAPI2 declarations in the declaration section, as in Listing 30.7. We'll also copy the RemoveCharacter, RemoveFormatting, RetrieveParameters, Class_Initialize, and Class_Terminate methods from our earlier OLEISAPI2 project in Chapter 23.

---

**Listing 30.7   PLACEORDER.CLS—We will Include the Standard OLEISAPI2 Constants and Object in our Declaration Section**

```
Option Explicit
'Declare a constant for the error number that we will be generating
Private Const PLACEERR = 501
'Database variable and path
Private dbWebDB As New rdoConnection
Private Const strConnect = "DSN=InvMntDB;UID=TxsVB;PWD=vbtxs;"
'The OLEISAPI and class path for insertion into HTML forms
Private Const OLEISAPI_PATH = "/scripts/oleisapi2.dll/StrFrnt.PlaceOrder."
```

---

## Building the Purchase Form

Before our customers can place an order for the merchandise we are selling, we have to provide them with a form that they can fill out to specify their name and address, along with how many of each item are desired. We'll build a method into our OLEISAPI2 application called BuildForm that will provide the user with a simple HTML form for providing this information. The upper part of the form will be for the customer's name and address. The bottom part of the form will be a list of items pulled from the Products table, so that the customer can place a number beside any of the items listed. We'll be showing the customers the full item description, so our customers don't have to interpret any of our product codes. The code to perform this can be found in Listing 30.8, and the resulting HTML form can be seen in Figure 30.5.

# Part VII

**Listing 30.8  PLACEORDER.CLS—The BuildForm Method Builds an Order Form for the Customer to use to Order Widgets from our Catalog Order Site**

```
Public Sub BuildForm(aReq As Request)
    Dim dbrsWebRS As rdoResultset
    Dim lNumRecs As Long
    Dim strHTML As String
    Dim strSQL As String
    'Build the SQL to select the product IDs and descriptions from
    'the database
    strSQL = "Select Prd_ID, Prd_Desc from Products order by Prd_Desc"
    'Open the record set using the SQL statement built earlier
    Set dbrsWebRS = dbWebDB.OpenResultset(strSQL, rdOpenStatic)
    'Determine how many records were retrieved
    If Not dbrsWebRS.EOF Then
        With dbrsWebRS
            .MoveLast
            lNumRecs = .RowCount
            .MoveFirst
        End With
    Else
        lNumRecs = 0
    End If

    'Build the HTML document
    strHTML = strHTML & "<HTML><HEAD><TITLE>"
    strHTML = strHTML & "Transaction Server Example"
    strHTML = strHTML & "</TITLE></HEAD><BODY BGCOLOR=#C0C0C0>"
    strHTML = strHTML & "<H1>Transaction Server Example</H1><HR><P>"
    strHTML = strHTML & "Please fill in your name, address, and the number"
    strHTML = strHTML & " of each item that you wish to order.</P>"
    'Build the form for the customer to enter the delivery information
    strHTML = strHTML & "<FORM ACTION=" & Chr(34) & OLEISAPI_PATH
    strHTML = strHTML & "MakeOrder" & Chr(34) & "METHOD=" & Chr(34)
    strHTML = strHTML & "POST" & Chr(34) & ">" & vbCrLf & "<PRE>" & vbCrLf
    strHTML = strHTML & "          Name : <INPUT TYPE=" & Chr(34) _
                    & "TEXT" & Chr(34)
    strHTML = strHTML & " NAME=" & Chr(34) & "Name" & Chr(34)
    strHTML = strHTML & " SIZE=30 MAXLENGTH=30>" & vbCrLf
    strHTML = strHTML & "          Address : <INPUT TYPE=" & Chr(34) _
                    & "TEXT" & Chr(34)
    strHTML = strHTML & " NAME=" & Chr(34) & "Address" & Chr(34)
    strHTML = strHTML & " SIZE=30 MAXLENGTH=30>" & vbCrLf
    strHTML = strHTML & "City, State, Zip : <INPUT TYPE=" & Chr(34) _
                    & "TEXT" & Chr(34)
    strHTML = strHTML & " NAME=" & Chr(34) & "City" & Chr(34)
    strHTML = strHTML & " SIZE=25 MAXLENGTH=25>, <INPUT TYPE=" _
                    & Chr(34) & "TEXT" & Chr(34)
```

*continues*

**Listing 30.8   Continued**

```
        strHTML = strHTML & " NAME=" & Chr(34) & "State" & Chr(34)
        strHTML = strHTML & " SIZE=2 MAXLENGTH=2>, <INPUT TYPE=" _
                        & Chr(34) & "TEXT" & Chr(34)
        strHTML = strHTML & " NAME=" & Chr(34) & "ZipCode" & Chr(34)
        strHTML = strHTML & " SIZE=10 MAXLENGTH=10>" & vbCrLf
        strHTML = strHTML & "                  Phone : <INPUT TYPE=" & Chr(34) _
                        & "TEXT" & Chr(34)
        strHTML = strHTML & " NAME=" & Chr(34) & "Phone" & Chr(34)
        strHTML = strHTML & " SIZE=15 MAXLENGTH=15>" & vbCrLf _
                        & "</PRE>" & vbCrLf
    'Build a table of the items that may be purchased
    strHTML = strHTML & "<TABLE BORDER=0>"
    strHTML = strHTML & "<TR><TH>Product</TH><TH>Number Desired</TH></TR>"
    'Are there any records to place in the table?
    If lNumRecs > 0 Then
        'Loop through each of the records
        With dbrsWebRS
            Do While Not .EOF
                'Place the description in the first column
                strHTML = strHTML & "<TR><TD>" & .rdoColumns!Prd_Desc _
                                & "</TD>"
                'Put a input field in the second column
                strHTML = strHTML & "<TD><INPUT TYPE=" & Chr(34) _
                                & "TEXT" & Chr(34)
                strHTML = strHTML & " NAME=" & Chr(34) _
                                    & .rdoColumns!Prd_ID & Chr(34)
                strHTML = strHTML & " SIZE=5 MAXLENGTH=5>"
                strHTML = strHTML & "</TD></TR>"
                'Loop to the next record
                .MoveNext
            Loop
        End With
    End If
    'Close the HTML table and document and add the submission and
    'reset buttons.
    strHTML = strHTML & "</TABLE><BR><INPUT TYPE=SUBMIT VALUE=" _
                    & Chr(34) & "Submit Order"
    strHTML = strHTML & Chr(34) & "><INPUT TYPE=RESET VALUE=" & Chr(34)
    strHTML = strHTML & "Reset Order Information" & Chr(34) & ">"
    'Close the HTML Form and document
    strHTML = strHTML & "</FORM></BODY></HTML>"
    'Set the result code
    aReq.ResponseStatus = "200 OK"
    'Set the content-type header line
    aReq.ResponseType = "text/html"
    'Return the HTML document to the calling routine
    aReq.WriteResponse strHTML
End Sub
```

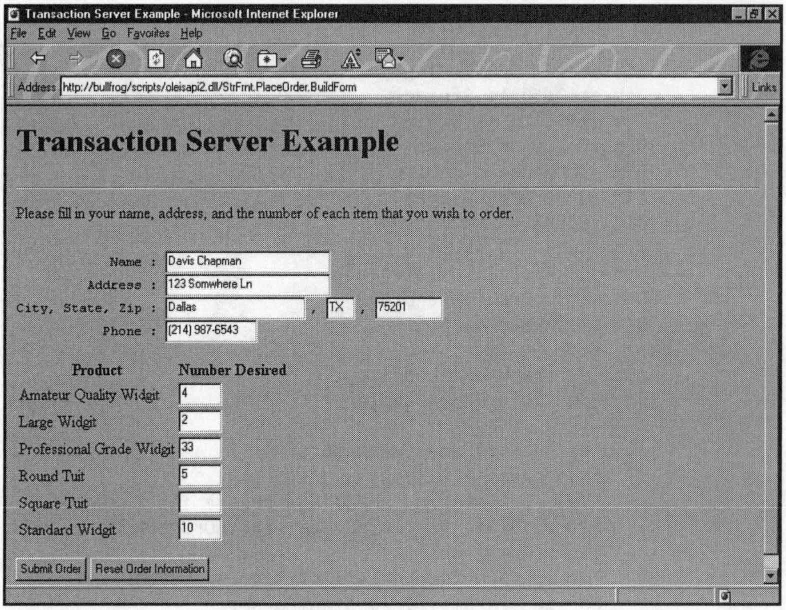

**FIG. 30.5**

We have to provide our customers with an HTML form for them to enter what they want to purchase and where they want it shipped.

## Calling the Shipping Order Component

We'll build a private function called SendOrder, which will call the shipping order component. This function will be called after the parameters have been parsed from the incoming data, and stored in the Parameters class that is a member of the calling method. We'll loop through all of the parameters, putting together the entire name, address, and phone into local variables. Once we have found the first product with a non-negative (and non-blank) quantity, we'll call the NewOrder method of the Shipping Order component. Once this method has returned, we'll loop through each of the subsequent product values, calling the AddItemToOrder method for each product that has a quantity value. At the end of the function, we'll return the order number to the calling method, so that the shipping order information may be retrieved from the database to build the customer a shipping receipt. The code for this function can be found in Listing 30.9.

---

**Listing 30.9  PLACEORDER.CLS—The SendOrder Method Calls the Transaction Server Components to Pass the Order Through the Catalog Company System**

```
Private Function SendOrder(pcParams As Parameters, _
                         aiNumParams As Integer, asMsg As String) As Long
     Dim objOrder As Object
     Dim strName As String
```

*continues*

**Listing 30.9 Continued**

```
Dim strAddr As String
Dim strCity As String
Dim strState As String
Dim strZip As String
Dim strPhone As String
Dim lOrderNum As Long
Dim iCurParam As Integer
Dim iCurPrdID As Long
Dim iCurPrdOrd As Integer
Dim strCurPrdOrd As String
Dim strCurKey As String

'Set up the error handling
On Error GoTo ErrorHandler

'Did we receive any parameters?
If aiNumParams > 0 Then
    'Yes, so let's go ahead and create the ShipOrdd object
    Set objOrder = CreateObject("ShipOrdr.ShpOrder")
    lOrderNum = 0
    'We'll loop through all of the parameters
    For iCurParam = 1 To aiNumParams
        'Get the parameter key name
        strCurKey = pcParams.GetKeyNameByNum(iCurParam)
        'Place the parameter value into the appropriate variable
        Select Case strCurKey
            Case "Name"
                strName = pcParams.GetKeyValueByNum(iCurParam)
            Case "Address"
                strAddr = pcParams.GetKeyValueByNum(iCurParam)
            Case "City"
                strCity = pcParams.GetKeyValueByNum(iCurParam)
            Case "State"
                strState = pcParams.GetKeyValueByNum(iCurParam)
            Case "ZipCode"
                strZip = pcParams.GetKeyValueByNum(iCurParam)
            Case "Phone"
                strPhone = pcParams.GetKeyValueByNum(iCurParam)
            Case Else
                'All that's left are the product orders
                strCurPrdOrd = pcParams.GetKeyValueByNum(iCurParam)
                'Do we have valid product IDs and quantities?
                If IsNumeric(strCurPrdOrd) And IsNumeric(strCurKey) Then
                    'Convert the product ID and quantity into numbers
                    iCurPrdOrd = CInt(strCurPrdOrd)
                    iCurPrdID = CLng(strCurKey)
                    'Do we have an order number yet?
                    If lOrderNum = 0 Then
                        'No, so we need to start a new order
                        lOrderNum = objOrder.NewOrder(strName, _
                                           strAddr, strCity, _
```

```
                                                  strState, strZip, _
                                                  strPhone, iCurPrdID, _
                                                  iCurPrdOrd)
                    If lOrderNum < 0 Then
                        Err.Raise PLACEERR
                    End If
                Else
                    'Yes, so we need to add to the order
                    If lOrderNum > 0 Then
                        If objOrder.AddItemToOrder(lOrderNum, _
                                      iCurPrdID, iCurPrdOrd) _
                                      < 0 Then
                            Err.Raise PLACEERR
                        End If
                    End If
                End If
            End If
        End Select
    Next
End If
'Return the order number to the calling routine
SendOrder = lOrderNum
'Free the Shipping Order object
Set objOrder = Nothing
'We have no message that needs returning
asMsg = ""
Exit Function
ErrorHandler:
'Format the error message as a string to be returned
asMsg = "Error " + Str$(Err.Number) + " : " + Err.Description
'Return an invalid order number
SendOrder = -1
'Free the Shipping Order object
'If Not (objOrder = Nothing) Then
    Set objOrder = Nothing
'End If
End Function
```

# Building the Shipping Invoice

Our final method that we'll be implementing in our OLEISAPI2 application is the method that receives the order that was submitted by our customer. We'll call this method "MakeOrder." The first thing this method will do is call the RetrieveParameters function to retrieve the submitted data and load it into the Parameters class. Next, it'll call the SendOrder function, which will pass all of the submitted information to the Transaction Server components, placing the customer's order into the database. Once the SendOrder function has returned control to the MakeOrder method, we'll retrieve the new order from the database and format it into an HTML document which will be returned to the customer as the confirmation of their order. This document will show the customer how many of each item are being shipped and how many are being back ordered. The code that performs this is in Listing 30.10.

**Listing 30.10  PLACEORDER.CLS—The MakeOrder Method Receives th Order Information, Calls SendOrder, and then Returns a Shipping Invoice to the Customer**

```
Public Sub MakeOrder(aReq As Request)
    Dim pcParams As New Parameters
    Dim dbrsWebRS As rdoResultset
    Dim dbrsOrderRS As rdoResultset
    Dim iNumParams As Integer
    Dim lNumRecs As Long
    Dim strHTML As String
    Dim strSQL As String
    Dim lOrderNum As Long
    Dim strMsg As String


    'Pass the parameters sent from the HTML form
    'to the local instance of the Parameters class
    iNumParams = RetrieveParameters(aReq, pcParams)
    'Pass the parameters received to the SendOrder function
    'to be placed into the database.
    lOrderNum = SendOrder(pcParams, iNumParams, strMsg)
    'Did we receive back a valid order number?
    If lOrderNum > 0 Then
        'Yes, begin selecting the information from the database
        'so that we can display for the user the information that
        'we received.
        strSQL = "Select SO_Name, SO_Address, SO_City, SO_State, " _
                & "SO_Zip, SO_Phone from ShippingOrder where SO_ID = " _
                & Str$(lOrderNum)
        'Open the record set using the SQL statement built earlier
        Set dbrsWebRS = dbWebDB.OpenResultset(strSQL, rdOpenStatic)
        'Determine how many records were retrieved
        If Not dbrsWebRS.EOF Then
            With dbrsWebRS
                .MoveLast
                lNumRecs = .RowCount
                .MoveFirst
            End With
        Else
            lNumRecs = 0
        End If
        'Build a HTML document to return to the user.
        strHTML = strHTML & "<HTML><HEAD><TITLE>"
        strHTML = strHTML & "Order Accepted"
        strHTML = strHTML & "</TITLE></HEAD><BODY BGCOLOR=#C0C0C0>"
        strHTML = strHTML & "<H1>Your order was accepted</H1><HR><P>"
        strHTML = strHTML & "Displayed below is the shipping information "
        strHTML = strHTML & " we received from your order.</P><PRE>" _
                        & vbCrLf
        'Include the shipping information that we received
        strHTML = strHTML & "             Name : <B>" _
                        & dbrsWebRS.rdoColumns!SO_Name & "</B>" & vbCrLf
        strHTML = strHTML & "          Address : <B>" _
                        & dbrsWebRS.rdoColumns!SO_Address & "</B>" _
                        & vbCrLf
```

```
strHTML = strHTML & "City, State, Zip : <B>" _
                  & dbrsWebRS.rdoColumns!SO_City
strHTML = strHTML & ", " & dbrsWebRS.rdoColumns!SO_State & " " _
                  & dbrsWebRS.rdoColumns!SO_Zip & "</B>" & vbCrLf
strHTML = strHTML & "            Phone : <B>" _
                  & dbrsWebRS.rdoColumns!SO_Phone & "</B>" & vbCrLf
'Select the product information
strSQL = "Select a.Prd_Desc Prd_Desc, b.Shp_Count Shp_Count, " _
       & "b.Shp_BackOrder Shp_BackOrder from Products a, " _
       & "Shipping b where b.SO_ID = " & Str$(lOrderNum)
strSQL = strSQL & " and a.Prd_ID = b.Prd_ID"
'Open the record set using the SQL statement built earlier
Set dbrsOrderRS = dbWebDB.OpenResultset(strSQL, rdOpenStatic)
'Determine how many records were retrieved
If Not dbrsOrderRS.EOF Then
    With dbrsOrderRS
        .MoveLast
        lNumRecs = .RowCount
        .MoveFirst
    End With
Else
    lNumRecs = 0
End If
'Build a table of the products that were ordered
strHTML = strHTML & "<TABLE BORDER=2>"
strHTML = strHTML & "<TR><TH>Product</TH><TH>Number Shipping</TH>" _
                  & "<TH>Back Ordered</TH></TR>"
'Are there any records to place in the table?
If lNumRecs > 0 Then
    'Loop through each of the records
    With dbrsOrderRS
        Do While Not .EOF
            strHTML = strHTML & "<TR><TD>" _
                              & .rdoColumns!Prd_Desc & "</TD>"
            strHTML = strHTML & "<TD>" & .rdoColumns!Shp_Count _
                              & "</TD>"
            strHTML = strHTML & "<TD>" _
                              & .rdoColumns!Shp_BackOrder _
                              & "</TD></TR>"
            'Loop to the next record
            .MoveNext
        Loop
    End With
End If
'Close the HTML table and document.
strHTML = strHTML & "</TABLE></BODY></HTML>"
'Set the result code
aReq.ResponseStatus = "200 OK"
Else
    'Build the HTML document
    strHTML = "<HTML><HEAD><TITLE>"
    strHTML = strHTML & "Order Not Accepted"
    strHTML = strHTML & "</TITLE></HEAD><BODY BGCOLOR=#C0C0C0>"
```

*continues*

**Listing 30.10 Continued**

```
        strHTML = strHTML & "<H1>Order Not Accepted</H1><HR><P>"
        'Include the context error message
        strHTML = strHTML & "There was a problem with your order. "
        strHTML = strHTML & "Please call your service representative " _
                            & "to correct the problem.</P>"
        strHTML = strHTML & "<HR><P>" & strMsg & "</P>"
        strHTML = strHTML & "</BODY></HTML>"

        'Set the result code
        aReq.ResponseStatus = "501 OK"
    End If
    'Set the content-type header line
    aReq.ResponseType = "text/html"
    'Return the HTML document to the calling routine
    aReq.WriteResponse strHTML
End Sub
```

Once you build this module, and call it from a Web browser using the URL **http://<your server>/scripts/oleisapi2.dll/StrFrnt.PlaceOrder.BuildForm**, you can fill in the form and submit an order. While the order is being processed, you can watch the Transaction Server Explorer (in View|Status mode) and see as the various components are activated and called, as seen in Figure 30.6. Once the system is finished processing the request, your order confirmation will be returned to your Web browser, as in Figure 30.7.

**FIG. 30.6**

You can watch as each of the components are activated and executed in the Transaction Server Explorer.

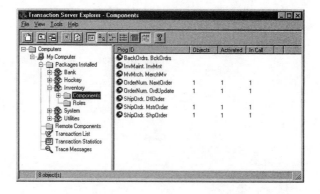

**N O T E** If you are wanting to use Transaction Server with Active Server Pages, you would instantiate your Transaction Server components with either the New or Server.CreateObject() methods, just as you would instantiate custom components, as specified in Chapter 17, "Constructing Your Own Server Components." Working with custom components on the server is no different than working with Transaction Server components. The operating system, along with Transaction Server, knows which components are Transaction Server components, and which are not. When a Transaction Server component is created in a Visual Basic application, or in an Active Server Page, Transaction Server is automatically handed the work to be performed. ■

**FIG. 30.7**
Once all order processing has been completed, the order confirmation will be returned showing the quantity of each product that is being shipped, and the quantity being back ordered.

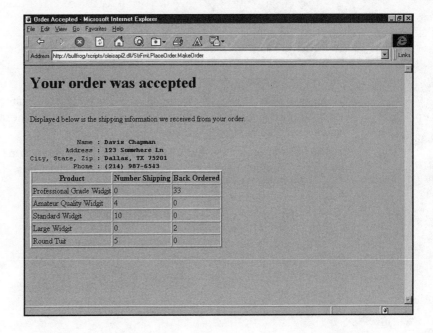

# Part VIII

# From Here...

In this chapter we completed our vastly simplified catalog order system that allows customers to place orders through the Web, and have the merchandise automatically moved from the warehouse to the shipping dock, and back ordered if there was insufficient quantities of the product in stock. As simple as we made our example of this system, this was not an insignificant system that we built over the past three chapters. We integrated what would normally be three separate systems, and would likely be spread out over at least three servers, using three separate databases. By allowing us to focus on what is called the business logic of each of our components, and not have to worry about the wiring that connects the components together, we were able to integrate these systems with relative ease.

While there is a lot that we can do with Transaction Server to build large, distributed, integrated applications, there are some shortcomings. All processing in Transaction Server is synchronous in nature. If you want to trigger another process to start because of some combination of events, but you don't want to have to wait for this new process to finish before continuing with your process, you have to write your own code to spawn off this second process. Once Microsoft releases their message queuing server product (code named Falcon) later this year (or early next), it should be able to relieve most of the Transaction Server shortcomings. The combination of Transaction Server and the message queuing server will provide a powerful combination of technologies, enabling large, powerful, distributed, integrated applications to be built with relative ease.

From here you might want to check out the following chapters:

■ To learn the basics about Transaction Server, what it does and how it provides a facility for building small components that provide business rule functionality, see Chapter 28, "Microsoft Transaction Server and Visual Basic."

■ To see how we can extend the example we began in Chapter 28 further, by adding the automatic ordering of new inventory when we have exhausted the inventory in the warehouse, see Chapter 29, " Building Multi-Tier Applications."

■ To learn about some of the security systems that we would want to put in place before opening up our integrated order entry system for all Web surfers, check out Chapter 31, "Internet Security and Web Applications."

# CHAPTER 31

# Internet Security and Web Applications

The Internet was originally designed as a means for sharing research and information. Even today, the prevailing attitude is that "information wants to be free." With this general attitude, it's no wonder that the Internet is a very insecure place. The Internet was never designed to be secure, and all efforts to make it secure are hacks at best.

Even so, a lot of businesses want to conduct business over the Internet. To do so, these businesses need some way of guaranteeing the security of sensitive information that has to travel between any two locations. These businesses also need to make sure that any information on their own computers that is not intended for public consumption be securely locked away from prying eyes wandering the Internet, and surfing the Web.

Most business conducted over the Internet falls into one of two categories: Virtual Store Fronts, where Web-browsing users can go to purchase things, and intranet applications being run over the Internet, in which the entire Web application consists primarily of internal corporate information. Both of these Web-based applications have specific yet unique security requirements. It is your job, as a Web developer, to understand the security requirements of each and, while not necessarily having to implement the security yourself, know how to avoid opening up any holes in the site security through your Web applications. ■

## Security needs of a corporate site connected to the Internet

We'll examine the security needs of corporate networks, and see what technologies are currently in common use to provide this security, including learning what firewalls and proxy servers are, and how they work.

## Security needs of a Virtual Store Front

We'll look at commercial store fronts on the Web, learn about some of the technologies available for use in conducting financial transactions over the Internet, and how these stores need to protect the financial information of the shoppers that make purchases.

## Symmetrical and asymmetrical encryption

We'll look at both of these encryption methods, learn how each performs encryption, and how each is used in the DES and RSA encryption standards.

## Digital Signatures and Certificates

We'll look at how these are constructed, and how they are used to guarantee security of messages and software.

# Types of Internet Security

The security needs of a corporate intranet Web site are different from those of a public store front on the Web. While the first needs to make sure that all corporate business information be kept secure from its competitors, the second needs to make sure that only customer financial information is kept secure, and that it provides its customers with the impression that their financial information is being securely protected. Because of the different natures of these two situations, they can be referred to as *network* and *transaction* security.

## Network Security

Corporate needs for Internet and Web site security are twofold:

- Prevent unauthorized access to corporate systems connected to the Internet for purposes of internal access to outside resources or authorized access from external sources.
- Secure communications over unsecured connections on the Internet.

Access to internal resources is achieved through the use of two technologies, firewalls and proxy servers. These two technologies perform different tasks, and achieve seemingly similar results with these different approaches. Secure communications are achieved through a combination of encryption and authentication technologies, which work together to achieve a single goal.

**Firewalls**   Firewalls are a network device that sits between two networks (such as between a corporate internal network and the Internet) and decides which network traffic is passed from one network to the other. There are several different ways that firewalls can perform this task, and the type of firewall is determined by which of these methods of operation is performed by the firewall. The types of firewalls are:

- Screening Router or Packet Filter
- Bastion Host
- Dual-Homed Gateway

In general, a firewall can be programmed to determine whether any particular packet should be allowed through. The firewall can make this determination based on information in any level of the OSI model, as can be seen in Figure 31.1. A firewall can be programmed to accept network packets going to a Web server on the other side of the firewall, while denying network packets from certain TCP/IP addresses.

**FIG. 31.1**

Basic Firewall operation consists of filtering out unwanted packets at any level in the OSI network communications model.

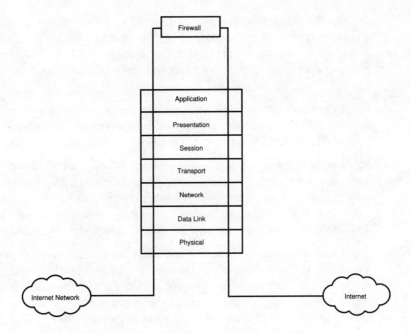

***Screening Router or Packet Filter***   A screening router (or packet filter) is a commercial router that can screen packets based on criteria such as the type of protocol, the source or destination address, and control fields that are part of the protocol. Screening routers are limited in making their determinations of which packets to let through based on the network layer because they are limited to operating at Level 3 of the OSI model. This makes screening routers a powerful mechanism to control the type of network traffic flowing into and out of an internal network.

However good screening routers are at controlling network traffic based on the network level, they cannot control traffic based on the application being used. In order to allow network traffic through based on the application being used, the screening router would need to operate at Level 7 of the OSI model. This means that you cannot use a screening router to allow access to a Web server inside the firewall, while limiting all other outside access.

Screening routers are vulnerable to spoofing, where an intruder fools the screening filter into thinking that the attacker is an authorized user, by using an authorized TCP/IP address or network protocol. If an attacker can successfully spoof past the screening router, all application and data files on the internal network are wide open for abuse and misuse.

***Bastion Host***   A bastion host works on the application level of the OSI model, allowing access based on what applications are being accessed. A bastion host can also be configured to allow or deny access based on authorized user lists, thus allowing configuration so that authorized users can have full access to all applications. Under this system, unauthorized users can be allowed access to a single application (such as a Web server) or denied all access.

Since bastion host firewalls operate on the application level, there is a strong possibility that they will slow network traffic considerably. Configuring a bastion host to operate on an authorized-user-list basis is not much better, as the bastion host has to maintain a database with the authorized user and current network address for checking each passing packet against.

Bastion host firewalls are vulnerable to impersonation, where an intruder is impersonating an authorized user. If an attacker is successful in impersonating an authorized user, full access can be gained to the internal network, placing all internal resources at risk.

**Dual-Homed Gateway**   A dual-homed gateway is a computer that has two or more network cards, each connected to a separate network. In normal operations, this computer would route network traffic between each of the separate networks, but for firewall purposes, this routing capability is disabled. Instead, the dual-homed gateway runs applications that access shared data, allowing access to a common set of data from each of the networks.

A dual-homed gateway can be configured where the applications perform routing between the separate networks, and thus allow access to internal applications from external network connections. Since there is a large amount of flexibility in what the nature of the applications running on the computer are, the routing can be programmed to operate on just about any layer of the OSI model, and follow any set of rules that the applications can be programmed to follow. This provides the dual-homed gateway the most flexibility of all firewall configurations, but it also can have the most overhead, slowing network traffic considerably.

A dual-homed gateway is vulnerable to direct login access by an attacker. If an attacker is able to log in to the gateway as an administrative user, the attacker can alter the basic operation of the firewall, reconfiguring it to allow complete and open access to the internal network the firewall is supposed to be protecting.

**Proxy Servers**   Proxy servers act as a go-between to control Internet access from a private corporate network and the Internet. A proxy server will often transpose server addresses and ports on either side so that clients and servers do not know the real address of the computer with which they are interacting. The primary reason for this is to control internal access to the Internet.

All Web requests travel to the proxy server, which replaces its own address with the real server address, and then returns the resulting objects (HTML Pages, images, and so on) to the client computer that originally made the request. The proxy server will often cache Web pages and frequently requested objects, to enhance response speed and to limit outgoing requests onto the Internet (a real concern for a large corporate network with a limited bandwidth Internet connection). A proxy server can be configured to prevent access to certain sites, so that employees can visit only Web sites deemed appropriate business usage sites.

A proxy server performs its job by interacting with the client browsers, as illustrated in Figure 31.2:

- A client Web browser (or FTP client) sends a request for a file from a specific server to the proxy server.

■ The proxy server searches its cache to see if it already has a copy of the requested file, and if so, returns it to the client.

■ If the proxy server does not have a cached copy of the file, it passes the request on to the server originally specified by the client.

■ When the server returns the requested file to the proxy server, the proxy server saves a copy in its cache, and then passes the file along to the client that made the request.

**FIG. 31.2**

An example of a typical proxy server operation, showing the steps each Web request follows that goes through a proxy server.

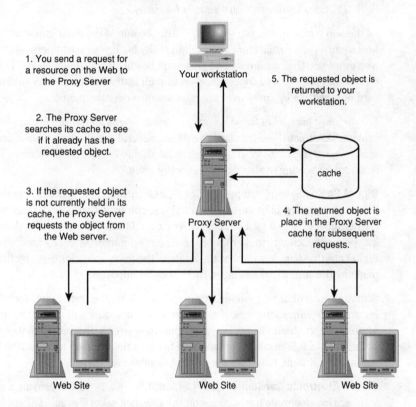

1. You send a request for a resource on the Web to the Proxy Server

Your workstation

5. The requested object is returned to your workstation.

2. The Proxy Server searches its cache to see if it already has the requested object.

3. If the requested object is not currently held in its cache, the Proxy Server requests the object from the Web server.

4. The returned object is place in the Proxy Server cache for subsequent requests.

Proxy Server

cache

Web Site        Web Site        Web Site

Part
**VIII**

Ch
**31**

**Secure Communications**   If a corporate intranet application is running on a Web server accessible from the Internet, the users will need to be guaranteed that the proprietary corporate information they are receiving and inputting into the application cannot be seen by just anybody with a packet sniffer hooked up to the Internet. In short, all communications need to be encrypted, so that only the Web server and the end user can see what information is really being sent between the two. This can be a simple matter of installing secure sockets on the Web server. Most Web servers are capable of using secure sockets, and it is usually a matter of generating the public and private keys, and applying for and receiving a site certificate from an authorized certificate-issuing organization.

# Transaction Security

For financial transactions on the Web, security takes on a different set of needs:

- Validate the identity of the buyer.
- Secure identification numbers (for example, credit card, account numbers, and so on).
- Verify available credit.
- Provide customers with a sense of security.

Of these security issues, the last could easily be one of the most important. It doesn't matter how secure your virtual store front might really be, if your customers don't feel secure, they won't give you their business, and you won't be able to stay in business. This is an issue high on Internet users' list of concerns, even though statistically, it is safer to provide your credit card number to a business over the Internet than over the phone.

For the most part, all of these security issues are dealt with in a few complete packages that provide a complete Web-transaction system. Several digital or electronic cash systems are available, but the majority of vendors are looking to the Secure Electronic Transaction (SET) standard for solving the transaction security issue.

**Digital Cash**   Several competing digital or electronic cash systems operate on the Internet. These systems are all based around a holding company that provides customers with an account number backed by a cash deposit or a credit card. This provides the customer with an independent account number that cannot be used if intercepted by another person. With each digital cash system, it is the responsibility of the system vendor to verify that the purchase was made by the authorized customer and not by an impostor.

Although each of these systems works well at solving the transaction security issues, all are incompatible with each other. If a customer uses one digital cash system, and the virtual store at which the customer wants to make a purchase uses a different digital cash system, they are both out of luck. The customer will have to make the decision to subscribe to an additional digital cash system, or to take his or her business elsewhere.

**Secure Electronic Transaction (SET) Standard**   In an effort to provide a single, accessible standard for electronic transactions on the Internet, several organizations, including Microsoft, Netscape, Mastercard, and VISA, got together and developed the Secure Electronic Transaction (SET) standard. The SET specification provides for encrypting of credit card numbers in a form that the vendor from whose store front a customer is making a purchase can't decrypt the purchaser's credit card number. Instead, the vendor forwards the encrypted credit card number on to the vendor's bank. The bank then decrypts the credit card number and returns a purchase authorization or purchase decline back to the vendor. The overall SET procedure can be seen in Figure 31.3.

The SET protocol uses a combination of symmetric and asymmetric encryption with digital signatures and certificates to encrypt the customer's purchase and credit card information within a "digital envelope."

**FIG. 31.3**

The basic SET transaction protocol steps are designed to provide the ease and convenience of a single means of making purchases over the Internet, while securing sensitive personal information such as credit card numbers from vendors and other unessential parties.

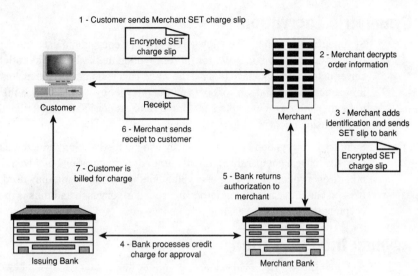

1 - Customer sends Merchant SET charge slip

Encrypted SET charge slip

Customer

Receipt

6 - Merchant sends receipt to customer

7 - Customer is billed for charge

Merchant

2 - Merchant decrypts order information

3 - Merchant adds identification and sends SET slip to bank

Encrypted SET charge slip

5 - Bank returns authorization to merchant

Issuing Bank

4 - Bank processes credit charge for approval

Merchant Bank

# DES and RSA Encryption

Two primary encryption standards are used for the majority of secure communications and information transfer, Data Encryption Standard (DES) and RSA encryption. These standards are complementary, and are often used in conjunction with each other (as in the SET standard digital envelope).

**N O T E**  The RSA encryption standard is named for its three inventors—Ron Rivest, Adi Shamir, and Leonard Adleman. The algorithm is owned by Public Key Partners (PKP) of Sunnyvale, California, and was patented in 1983. Anyone in North America must obtain a royalty-based license from PKP to use the RSA algorithm for commercial purposes, but written permission can often be obtained for free noncommercial use for personal, academic, or intellectual purposes. The RSA algorithm was originally developed at the Massachusetts Institute of Technology (MIT) with government funding, so the United States government can use RSA algorithms without a license.  ■

The DES encryption standard uses secret-key or symmetric encryption, while the RSA standard uses public-private key or asymmetric encryption. Because of these different approaches, the approach most commonly used (and used in the SET standard) is as follows:

1. Generate a random DES key, and use it to encrypt the message.

2. Encrypt the DES key with the public RSA key of the message recipient.

3. Send the combined DES/RSA document to the recipient.

4. The recipient uses the private RSA key to decrypt the DES key.

5. The recipient uses the DES key to decrypt the message.

This allows for greater security and flexibility than using only one of the two encryption methods.

## Symmetric Encryption

Symmetric encryption, also known as secret-key encryption, uses the same key to encrypt and decrypt the message. In order for this encryption method to work, both the sender and receiver of the message have to have the same encryption key. This makes symmetric encryption impractical for the millions of users on the Internet by itself, because the secret key would have to be transmitted unencrypted, making it easily stolen. This would effectively defeat the purpose of using encryption in the first place.

Symmetric encryption is already heavily used in the banking industry, as well as other industries that have a comparatively small number of organizations that would need to know each other's encryption keys. This encryption method is also commonly used to encrypt PIN numbers on banking cards. Symmetric encryption is very fast, and thus is more suitable for encrypting large files than asymmetric encryption.

## Asymmetric Encryption

Asymmetric encryption, also known as public-key or public/private-key encryption, uses two closely related keys to encrypt and decrypt messages. Either key can be used to encrypt the message, but the other key has to be used to decrypt the message. This makes asymmetric encryption ideal for use over the Internet.

By transmitting a public key to another user, messages can be passed back and forth between two users in an encrypted form. The first user can encrypt the messages by using the public key of the second user, and the second user can decrypt the message by using his or her private key. Likewise, the second user can encrypt messages to the first user by using the first user's public key, which the first user would then decrypt by using his or her private key. As long as the private keys are kept private, messages can be securely sent in an encrypted form.

If both users are passing messages by using a single key pair, then the public key could be intercepted, and messages from the key owner could be decrypted. Because of this danger, both users normally transmit their public keys to each other, so that the other user can use these public keys to encrypt their messages to the other. This method ensures that the messages can be decrypted only by the owner's private key, which is what makes asymmetric encryption a very secure form of communication.

# Certification and Digital Signatures

A key piece of ensuring security of messages, identity of users, and safety of software downloaded from the Internet is accomplished through the use of digital signatures and digital certificates. A digital signature is a file checksum encoded by using the sender's private key. The user's public decryption key is encoded by using the private key of a certification authority (such as VeriSign). This allows the recipient of the message or software to decode your public key by using the public key of the certificate authority, assuming that the authority is on the trusted list of the user (or the user has the option of adding the authorizing vendor to his or her list of trusted authorizing vendors). Once your public key has been decoded, it can be used to decode the unique 160-bit checksum, which can be used to verify that the message or software has not been tampered with.

**N O T E** The latest versions of browsers from Netscape and Microsoft, among others, ship with several certificates already installed for various Certificate Authorities. ■

# Acquiring a Certificate

To acquire a certificate, visit a certificate authority, such as VeriSign (at **http://www.verisign.com/**), and follow the instructions for acquiring the desired type of certificate. You will need to be prepared to provide the certificate authority with information such as your social security number, date of birth, and other identifying information if you are applying for an individual certificate, and corporate information if you are applying for a corporate certificate. Also, if you are applying for a corporate certificate, you will need to be able to provide proof that you are authorized to apply for a certificate on behalf of the company and provide corporate financial information so that the corporate identity can be verified.

Cost for an individual certificate ranges from around $6 annually for an e-mail address certification certificate, to $20 annually for a software signature certificate. For a corporate certificate, the price ranges from around $300 annually for a Web server certificate, to $400 annually for a software signature certificate. The certificate that is right for your needs depends on what you want the certificate for, and how you are going to be using it.

# Signing Your Controls

Once you have built your own ActiveX controls and want to place them on a Web page, you will need to sign them unless you want your controls to be rejected by the majority of Internet Explorer users (the only viewers will be those users willing to take risks by setting IE security to low). In order to sign your controls by using Microsoft's Authenticode control-signing technology, you will need to follow these steps:

1. Make sure that you have the latest version of Internet Explorer (3.0 or higher).

2. Apply for a control-signing certificate from a certificate authority (a list of available authorities can be found at **http://www.microsoft.com/intdev/security/authcode/certs.htm**). It may take up to a week for the certificate authority to verify your identity and issue your certificate, but by now most certificate authorities can issue your certificate within a matter of minutes.

3. Download the latest ActiveX Software Development Kit (SDK) from Microsoft at **http://www.microsoft.com/intdev/sdk/** (these first three steps should only need to be followed once per computer on which you are signing controls).

4. Build your control. You can sign only executable controls; you do not sign source or uncompiled code.

5. Sign your controls by using the signcode.exe application found in the ActiveX SDK.

6. Test your control signature by using the chktrust.exe application found in the ActiveX SDK.

If you make changes to your controls, you will need to resign them, using steps 4, 5, and 6.

Part
VIII

Ch
31

**Using Signcode.exe to Sign Your Controls** The signcode.exe code-signing application can be run from the DOS prompt, or as a Windows application. If signcode is run as a windows application, either from the Start|Run menu selection, or from a shortcut, it will prompt you with a control-signing wizard to walk you through the signing process. Likewise, you can provide all of the required information on the command line, and run the application as a DOS application. The command line syntax is as follows:

```
signcode [-prog <filename> -spc <credentials file> -pvk
➥<private key file> [-name <control description> [-info
➥<Company information URL>]]]
```

In the preceding command, the *filename* is the name of your control. The *credentials file* is the certificate file received from the certificate authority. The *private key file* is the private key file that was generated during the certificate application process. The *control description* is the description of the control that will show up in the certificate that is displayed for users. The *Company information URL* should be an URL that the user can visit in order to get more information on the control. If you leave out all of these values, the wizard will prompt you for each of these information elements.

**Using ChkTrust.exe to Check Your Controls** The chktrust.exe application is run only from the DOS command line. The chktrust application name is followed by the name of the control or application that you want to check, as in the following example:

```
chktrust <control name>
```

If the control was properly and successfully signed, the chktrust application should show you the control's signature certificate, just as it should appear to a user when downloading your control for use within a Web page.

# From Here...

In this chapter, we learned about the basic security concerns of corporations that have internal networks connected to the Internet, as well as the security concerns of businesses that have stores on the Web. Along with learning about the security issues surrounding each of these, we looked at some of the basic approaches being taken to overcome each of these security concerns. We also looked at the basic types of encryption used on the Internet today, and how they differ from each other. Finally, we looked at digital signatures and certificates, and how they can be used to guarantee that a message or software control has not been tampered with since it left the creator's computer. Along with this, we learned how we can acquire our own digital certificates and use them to sign the ActiveX controls that we create.

This is an area that, even though the standards are still emerging and developing, will be of increasing importance in the months and years to come, as more and more business is done on the Internet. At the same time, as this area of communication technology is growing, the federal government is coming under pressure from the business community to loosen the current export laws that restrict the type of encryption and security technology that can be exported out of the United States (these technologies are considered to be munitions, and as a result fall under the domain of the National Security Council, which is reluctant to loosen current restrictions). If you are interested in this area of technology and want to learn more, check out the following Web sites for more information.

- RSA Data Security at **http://www.rsa.com/**
- The National Computer Security Association at **http://www.ncsa.com/**
- The Internet Engineering Task Force at **http://www.ietf.cnri.reston.va.us/ home.html**
- The IBM home page at **http://www.ibm.com/**
- The Microsoft Internet Development area at **http://www.microsoft.com/intdev/ default.htm**
- The Netscape Development area at **http://developer.netscape.com/index.html**
- The Internet Documentation area of InterNIC at **http://ds.internic.net/ds/ dspg0intdoc.html**
- The VeriSign home page at **http://www.verisign.com/**
- Raptor Systems Security at **http://www.raptor.com/**
- Haystack Labs, Inc. at **http://www.haystack.com/**

Now that you have a high-level view of Internet security as it relates to the Web and Web-based applications, you might want to check out some of the following chapters:

- To learn how to build ActiveX controls, see Chapter 3, "Building ActiveX Controls with VB."
- To see inside the Authenticode technology, learn how it works, and go through the steps of getting your own certificate and signing your own controls, read Chapter 6, "Making Your ActiveX Controls Web-Friendly."
- To understand how to incorporate ActiveX controls into your Web pages, read Chapter 8, "Interacting with ActiveX Controls and VBScript."

Part
VIII

Ch
31

# Web-Related Topics

# Web-Enabling Visual Basic Applications

A matter of months ago, had you wanted to build a Web-enabled VB application, or FTP client, you needed to be well versed in WinSock programming, as well as the HTTP or FTP protocol. Thanks to Microsoft, this is no longer the case. With the introduction of ActiveX technology to the Web, Microsoft also added the Internet extensions to the Win32 API. Normally referred to as the INetAPI, the Internet API extensions are a series of functions that enable a Windows-based application to use regular API calls to perform all HTTP, FTP, and Gopher client functions, all without any WinSock programming.

## The Internet Extensions to the Win32 API (INetAPI)

The Internet extensions to the Windows API makes Web functionality available to any Windows application, and it greatly simplifies Internet application development.

## The Internet Transfer Control

The Internet extensions to the Win32 API have been encapsulated into an ActiveX control. Look at how this control works and how it can be used in building Web-enabled VB applications.

## The Hypertext Transport Protocol (HTTP) and File Transfer Protocol (FTP)

Look at how these two Internet protocols work, and how the Internet Transfer Control can be used to implement both of these Internet application protocols.

## The Uniform Resource Locator (URL)

Learn how it is constructed, and how to break it down into its components.

## A brief overview of Hypertext Markup Language

Learn what tags contain URLs and how HTML can be parsed to pull out the URLs that are embedded within a document.

---

**WinSock**

WinSock is short for Windows Socket. Sockets are the standard programming interface for network communications and, therefore, are the foundation upon which all Internet applications are built. The WinSock API is a fairly straightforward port of the Berkeley UNIX implementation of sockets with Windows-specific extensions that enable it to work in a more Windows-oriented (event-driven) fashion.

---

With the introduction of Visual Basic 5, Microsoft has taken this addition to the Windows API one step further and encapsulated it into an ActiveX control that can be plugged into any Visual Basic application. This control, called the Internet Transfer Control, enables you to build HTTP and FTP functionality into any Visual Basic application that needs to interact with Web and FTP servers, on the Internet or an internal network. ■

# The Microsoft Internet API (INetAPI)

When the Internet took off like wildfire, Microsoft turned its entire corporation around and began heading full-force in the Internet's direction. Microsoft management issued a decree to its developers that all Microsoft applications be "Internet-enabled" quickly and that all of its applications—especially those aimed at the business market—be built around the Internet. The Internet was no longer a side effort, which a Microsoft application user could plug into and browse at his or her convenience. Instead, the Internet was to be a core foundation to all of Microsoft's products, including its platforms and operating systems.

## Programming for the Internet

Along with the surging interest in using the Internet and the Web was a corresponding interest that programmers be able to build applications that used the Web and could interact with various Internet application servers. The only problem with this idea is that, to build applications that interact with Internet-based application services, you have to learn and understand socket programming. On the Windows platform, this means WinSock programming.

While a very straightforward port of the Berkeley UNIX sockets implementation, the WinSock programming interface with Windows-oriented extensions seems to be one of the more difficult areas of application development for average programmers to learn (not to say that the UNIX implementation is any easier to learn). The majority of information about this programming interface is aimed at C/C++ programmers and not developers working in other programming languages. As a result, this became a big stumbling block for many Windows programmers.

Another stumbling block is the protocols used to provide application functionality for most Internet-based applications. These protocols can be found in large, hard to read and understand documents called RFCs (Request For Comment). These RFC documents are a part of the Internet standards process and document all of the established Internet application standards, as well as many that have faded away into Internet history. To build an FTP client application, you need to find the RFC that documents the FTP protocol, as well as any RFCs that document any extensions to the FTP protocol, and learn how the FTP protocol works (which you will look at later in this chapter). You can then use that information to design and build your own FTP client.

Microsoft recognized that the combination of learning WinSock programming and the Internet application protocols discouraged many programmers; so it made the decision to do something to make building Internet-based applications easier. The solution Microsoft came up with was the Internet extensions to the Win32 API.

# Retrieving Files

When Microsoft designed the Internet extensions to the Win32 API, what it was really designing were Web extensions to the Win32 API. Originally, there were few HTTP servers running on the World Wide Web. Instead, there were a large number of Web sites that were using FTP or Gopher servers in the place of HTTP servers. All of these protocols perform one basic task: They request and retrieve files. Because, in the beginning, the Web consisted mostly of static files (mostly HTML and graphic images), all three of these Internet services (HTTP, FTP, and Gopher) worked just as well. It has only been in the more recent past—as more sites started using more of the functionality offered specifically by HTTP servers—that the use of FTP and Gopher servers has slowly died off.

---

### What Is Gopher?

Gopher is an Internet service that is very similar in nature to the World Wide Web. It provides the user with an index of files and links in a directory, with additional information provided to describe each item. If a file is selected, the file is returned to the user. If a link is selected, the user is taken to that link location, either in another directory on the same Gopher server or on another Gopher server. Because of the way in which Gopher works, it is very similar to the Web, only much more limited in functionality.

---

Because each of these three Internet services (HTTP, FTP, and Gopher) perform basically the same tasks—providing a means of requesting, sending, and receiving files—it made sense to build support for all three into the Internet extensions to the Win32 API. This means that all HTTP, FTP, and Gopher functionality is included as functions that are more consistent with the rest of the Win32 API. Having these protocols embedded in the Win32 API relieves Windows programmers from having to struggle through learning WinSock programming, as well as the application protocols for these Internet services.

**N O T E**  Microsoft has also included a WinSock control with Visual Basic 5, so if you want to learn the application protocols, you can still build your own Internet applications without having to spend an extensive amount of time learning WinSock programming. ■

# The Internet Transfer Control

With the Internet extensions to the Win32 API, Microsoft knew it had taken care of most programmers but wanted to make it even easier for Visual Basic programmers. So Microsoft decided to wrap the Internet extensions in an ActiveX control that could be used in Visual Basic applications, as well as just about any other ActiveX enabled application built using any other programming language. The Internet Transfer Control is this ActiveX control wrapper around the Internet extensions.

The Internet Transfer Control allows you to think, not in terms of the INetAPI calls, but more in terms of what commands you need to send to the host with which your application is communicating. If you are pulling HTML documents from a Web server, you can tell the Internet Transfer Control to execute the GET command on a specific URL and then sit back and wait for the HTML document to be retrieved. If you are maintaining a connection to a FTP server, you can issue each individual FTP command to be executed by the Internet Transfer Control and wait for the results to be returned to you.

**N O T E**   The Internet Transfer Control is completely self-contained and, in order to work, doesn't require any other controls to be placed in a Visual Basic application. It doesn't require the WinSock control, as it uses the Internet extensions to the Win32 API, which contains all of the WinSock functionality needed by the Internet Transfer Control. ▪

## Properties

Most of the properties of the Internet Transfer Control can be left alone, as the control sets the properties itself if you are passing complete URLs into the control. However, there are two properties that you want to be sure to make available to the user of your applications through application configuration settings.

**Using a Proxy Server**   If a user is running an application that uses the Internet Transfer Control in a setting where all of the user's Internet requests travel through a proxy server, then, to get the Internet Transfer Control to work properly, there are two properties that need to be set by the user:

- The AccessType property needs to be set to icNamedProxy (3).
- The Proxy property needs to be set to point to the proxy server.

Setting these two control properties enables the Internet Transfer Control to make proper use of the proxy server, and work correctly.

▶ **See** Chapter 31, "Internet Security and Web Applications," on **p. 759**

**Setting Other Properties**   If the Internet Transfer Control will be connecting to servers that require a user login, then the user needs to be able to set the UserName and Password properties through some form of text entry fields, either on the main application window or some form of dialog box. If these properties are left blank, the Internet Transfer Control automatically fills them in for anonymous access to FTP servers (that is, "anonymous" as the user name and the user's e-mail address as the password).

**CAUTION**

If you are allowing the user to enter values into these two properties, you need to guard against the user filling in the password property while leaving the user name blank. This results in an error condition and prevents the Internet Transfer Control from working properly.

## Methods

There are five methods for the Internet Transfer Control, and these methods are key to working with this control. These methods are provided in Table 32.1.

**Table 32.1   The Internet Transfer Control Methods**

| Method | Description |
| --- | --- |
| OpenURL | This method opens a connection to the specified URL. The URL can be passed as an argument to this method; or, if no URL is passed as an argument, the method uses the URL in the URL property. |
| Execute | This method executes a single command. If the control is connected to an FTP server, this command can be any (Microsoft) FTP command (for example, DIR, GET, SEND, and so on); or, if the control is not connected to a server, it can be an HTTP command (for example, GET, POST, HEAD), which causes the control to establish a connection, pass the command to the Web server, retrieve the results, and disconnect. If this method is being used to establish a connection with a server— either an HTTP, FTP, or Gopher server—it behaves the same as the OpenURL method, in that, if an URL is not provided as a method argument, it uses the URL in the URL property on the control. If the command being executed requires that data or an object be sent to the server, this data has to be included as an argument to the method. |
| GetHeader | This method can be used to retrieve either the entire header that was returned with a file from a Web server or any specific header entry. If no arguments are passed to this method, the entire header is returned. If a specific header entry (for example, Date, Content-type, Server, and so on) is specified, then only that header entry is returned. |
| GetChunk | This method is used to retrieve the object that was returned from the server. This method requires two parameters: the first to specify how large a chunk to retrieve, the second to specify what data type to return it as. This is the only method that can be used to extract the returned object from the control, and it is intended to be called from the controls StateChanged event after the entire object has been retrieved. |
| Cancel | The Cancel method is used to interrupt and cancel any ongoing operation. If the control is retrieving a large file and the user makes the decision to cancel the retrieval, the Cancel method should be used to end the retrieval. |

Part
IX

Ch
32

**N O T E**  The Microsoft FTP commands are slightly different from the standard FTP commands. FTP
originated as a UNIX utility, and the standard commands are very similar to the UNIX
commands that perform a similar task. LIST is used to get a directory listing, STOR is used to send a
file, RETR is used to retrieve a file.

With its first version of FTP for DOS and Windows, Microsoft made the decision to use more DOS-
oriented commands to make the user-interface more familiar to DOS users. As a result, the Microsoft
FTP uses DIR to get a directory listing, SEND to send a file, and GET to retrieve a file. Internally,
Microsoft FTP is translating these commands into the standard FTP commands so that the FTP client
works with all FTP servers. ▩

# Events

There is only one event for the Internet Transfer Control, and that is the StateChanged event.
This event passes in an argument that specifies which state the control has entered. The states
of the Internet Transfer Control are provided in Table 32.2.

**Table 32.2   The Event States of the Internet Transfer Control**

| State | Description |
| --- | --- |
| icNone | No state to report. |
| icHostResolvingHost | The control is looking up the TCP/IP address of the server computer it will be connecting to. |
| icHostResolved | The control has found the TCP/IP address of the server computer it will be connecting to. |
| IcConnecting | The control is connecting to the server computer. |
| icConnected | The control is connected to the server computer. |
| icRequesting | The control is sending the specified request to the server computer to which it is connected. |
| icRequestSent | The control has completed sending the request to the server computer and is waiting for the response from the server. |
| icReceivingResponse | The control has started receiving the response from the server. |
| icResponseReceived | The response has been completely received from the server. |
| icDisconnecting | The control is disconnecting from the server. |
| icDisconnected | The control has disconnected from the server. |
| icError | An error has occurred that prevents the control from completing the request. |
| icResponseCompleted | The entire request has been completed. |

It is unlikely that you want to have code executing on each and every one of these `StateChanged` events. More likely, you want to use a `Switch Case` statement in the `StateChanged` event script to have code executing on one or more specific state events.

## Adding the Internet Transfer Control to the Toolbox

Before you can use the Internet Transfer Control in a Visual Basic project, you need to add it to the Toolbox. This is done by selecting Project|Components and placing a check beside the Internet Transfer Control in the list of available controls, as shown in Figure 32.1.

**FIG. 32.1**

Add the Internet Transfer Control to the Visual Basic Toolbox through the project Components dialog box.

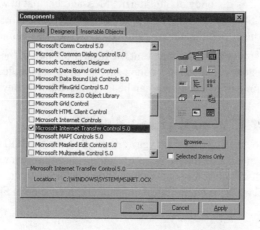

# The Hypertext Transport Protocol (HTTP) and File Transfer Protocol (FTP)

While the functionality of the current implementations of both the Hypertext Transport Protocol (HTTP) and the File Transfer Protocol (FTP) are very similar in nature, the way they actually work is very different. Both allow you to make requests for a file from a server, and, if the file is found in the place you specified, the server sends you the file. This is where most of the similarity ends.

## How the Hypertext Transport Protocol (HTTP) Works

The Hypertext Transport Protocol (HTTP) is a very simple communications and transaction protocol. There are only four steps in any HTTP transaction:

1. The client connects to the Web (HTTP) server.
2. The client sends a command to the server.
3. The client receives the response from the server.
4. The client disconnects from the server.

This single transaction model used by the HTTP consists of the following three basic commands (with a few recent extensions):

- GET—Sends the server an URL (Uniform Resource Locator), which designates a file to be returned. GET can call a CGI application (or other extension to the server), and all data that is passed is formatted as part of the URL being sent to the server. The length of the URL is limited, so the GET command is very limited in the amount of data that can be sent to the CGI application.

- POST—Similar to GET, only any data being passed to the server with the command is passed separately, as the body of the Internet Message Format in which the command is being passed. With the data being passed in the message body, the length limitations associated with the GET command are removed from the POST command.

- HEAD—Tells the server that you only want the header portion of the response to be returned. The header contains information such as the last modification date, so that the client can determine if a cached copy can be used instead of retrieving the entire file.

## How the File Transfer Protocol (FTP) Works

The File Transfer Protocol (FTP) operates very differently from the HTTP. With FTP, two socket connections are used: one that remains open the entire time, over which commands are passed, and a second that is used for sending files and directory listings, and is open only while the transfer is taking place. This communications model can be seen in Figure 32.2.

**FIG. 32.2**
The FTP communications model uses two connections between the client and server, one for passing commands and the other for sending files and data.

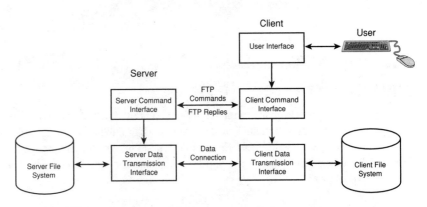

The FTP has a complete set of commands not for just sending and receiving files, but also for directory navigation and management. Files on the server can be moved, renamed, deleted, copied, and more, all under the control of the FTP client (assuming that the user has sufficient authorization on the server to perform these tasks). An FTP connection can be kept open indefinitely and can issue as many commands as desired within a single session.

The FTP does not directly understand URLs; therefore, URLs are interpreted instead by the FTP client, broken down into the server, the directory, and the file that is being requested. The FTP also does not use the Internet Message Format. Instead, it uses a simple command/reply format with specific response codes for each command, which communicates to the client the specific response to each command—whether it succeeded, failed, requires more information, or is in progress.

# Understanding URLs

Uniform Resource Locators (URLs), also known as Web page addresses, are the mechanism by which World Wide Web users find various Web pages, as well as many other Internet and internal network resources. This addressing and identifying scheme is very generalized, flexible, and complete.

The original design for URLs came from the European Laboratory for Particle Physics (CERN) as the World Wide Web project was starting back in 1990. The original designers needed and came up with a way to embed within an HTML document the address of another document that the current document referenced in some way. This addressing scheme had to identify the following several elements to enable the browser to link correctly to the referenced document:

- The protocol used by the server on which the referenced document is located. (Originally, about a dozen Internet protocols were used over the Web, but most have been phased out as the demand for full HTTP functionality has increased.)
- The server on which the document resides. This includes the Transmission Control Protocol (TCP) port to which to connect and, possibly, the user name and password to use when connecting.
- The directory in which the document can be found (relative to the service's root directory).
- The document file name.

The following is the format for this scheme:

```
protocol://[username[:password]][@]host[:port]/[directorypath/][filename]
```

The only truly required portions in this format are the protocol and host. If you don't specify a port, the default port of the specified protocol is assumed. If you don't specify a file name, the default file configured on the server is assumed (often named index.html or default.html).

Part

**IX**

Ch

**32**

---

### What Is a Port?

A TCP port is a mechanism used by TCP/IP to identify separate applications running on a single computer, all performing network communications. Each socket is assigned a unique port number (unless specified that the socket will be sharing a port with another socket). When a client application requests a connection to an application using a socket on a specific port, the server searches through the applications with open sockets that are listening for connection requests until it finds the application using the port specified by the client. Upon identifying the appropriate application, the connection request is passed to that application. Most server applications have specific, well-known port numbers that are assigned to them. This allows a Web browser to know that, unless another port is specified, it should try to connect to a Web server on port 80, or an FTP server on port 21, and so on.

---

The URL specification includes information being added onto the end of the URL so that, if the URL specifies an application to be run instead of a file to be retrieved, additional information can be passed as arguments to that application.

# The Internet Message Format

The Internet Message Format is a simple format in which information needed for transporting and delivering a message or other object is embedded in the message header, which is separated from the message body by an empty line. This message format is used by several Internet applications, including Internet mail, UseNet News, and Hypertext Transport Protocol (HTTP). The header section includes several lines that consist of a field title followed by a colon, a space, and the value. As is typical in most Internet messages, a carriage-return/newline character combination (vbCrLf) terminates the lines of text. A header field uses the following basic syntax:

```
Header Field Name: Value<vbCrLf>
```

HTTP servers and clients use the information in the header section to determine the type of object being sent (and thus how to display or process it), the last modification of the object, the size of the object, and what the capabilities are of the client or server with which each is communicating. The HTTP usage of the Internet Message Format is extended by placing a single line in front of the standard header fields. This leading header line does not follow the format of the rest of the header fields. If the message is being sent from a client to a server, this first line consists of the command (GET, POST, or HEAD), an URL being requested, and the protocol being used (normally HTTP/1.0) as follows:

```
GET /thisfile.html HTTP/1.0
```

If the message is being sent from the server to a client, this first line consists of the protocol being used, a response status code, and a textual message, as follows:

```
HTTP/1.0 200 OK
```

Among other responses, the response code can tell the client that the request was serviced with no problems, the requested resource has been moved, or the requested resource cannot be found. A listing of the common response codes can be found in Table 32.3.

**Table 32.3 The Common HTTP Response Codes**

| Code | Meaning |
|------|---------|
| 200 | OK |
| 201 | Created |
| 202 | Accepted |
| 204 | No content |
| 301 | Moved permanently |

| Code | Meaning |
|------|---------|
| 302 | Moved temporarily |
| 304 | Not modified |
| 400 | Bad request |
| 401 | Unauthorized |
| 403 | Forbidden |
| 404 | Not found |
| 500 | Internal server error |
| 501 | Not implemented |
| 502 | Bad gateway |
| 503 | Service unavailable |

These codes follow a pattern where the first digit has significance in indicating the type of response being received, as listed in Table 32.4.

**Table 32.4    The Significance on the First Digit in HTTP Response Codes**

| Code | Meaning |
|------|---------|
| 1 | Informational. The HTTP 1.0 specification does not use informational response code. Therefore, there are no 100 series response codes. |
| 2 | Success. The command was received, understood, and accepted. |
| 3 | Redirection. You have to take further action to complete the request. |
| 4 | Client error. The request contains bad syntax or otherwise cannot be fulfilled. |
| 5 | Server error. The server failed to fulfill an apparently valid request. |

# Building a Web-Enabled VB Application

For your Web-enabled application, you will build a link-checking bot application. This application retrieves an HTML document specified by the user, scans the document to extract all URLs referenced in the document, either as links, images, or active objects (either Java or ActiveX), and then verifies that each of those URLs is still valid. The user ends up with a list of the URLs in the HTML document that cannot be verified by the bot, either because the object specified by the URL does not exist on the server specified by the URL or because of any other reason that the bot could not verify the URL.

---

**What Is a Bot?**

A bot application is any Web-oriented application that performs maintenance or other nonbrowsing tasks. A bot might search through the Web, finding information on subjects of interest, or it might build indexes for a search engine. Most often, you find bot applications for maintaining a Web site, checking for broken links in HTML documents, finding unreferenced documents, validating addresses, finding and eliminating duplicate files, and so on.

---

For your bot application to perform its duties, it should follow these steps:

1. Upon the user typing in an URL for an HTML document to be checked, the bot enables the command button to trigger the document retrieval.

2. When the user presses the command button that triggers the document retrieval, the bot places the entered URL into the URL property of the Internet Transfer Control and then calls the control's execute method.

3. Upon the document retrieval being completed, the bot extracts the entire HTML document from the Internet Transfer Control and places it in a Text Box control, so the user can examine the document.

4. Upon placing the HTML document in a Text Box control, the bot proceeds to scan the document, looking for HTML elements containing URLs.

5. Upon finding an HTML element, the bot searches the element for three attributes, any one of which indicates the presence of an URL in the element. These attributes are HREF (links), SRC (images), and CODEBASE (Java Applets and ActiveX controls).

6. If one of the preceding three attributes are found, the URL isparsed from the HTML element and placed into the List Box control for URLs to be tested.

7. The bot continues scanning for HTML elements, repeating steps 5 and 6 until the entire document has been scanned.

8. After the entire document has been scanned, the list of URLs is scanned to remove any duplicates, and the command button that triggers the URL verification is enabled.

9. After the command button that triggers the URL verification is pressed, the bot begins looping through the URLs in the first list box. The bot also sets a flag to indicate that the bot is verifying links and not retrieving an HTML document to be checked.

10. Each URL is examined to determine if it is an absolute or relative URL. If the URL is a relative URL, the original URL entered by the user is used to provide the base URL for the link. Any file names are removed from the base URL so that it provides no more than a starting directory on the server, and the relative URL is added on the end to provide a complete absolute URL.

11. The Internet Transfer Control's execute method is called, passing it the HEAD command and the URL to be verified.

12. After the Internet Transfer Control has completed its retrieval, the entire header is extracted from the control, and the HTTP response code is examined.

13. If the response code indicates that the link could not be verified, the URL is copied from the first list box to a second list box of URLs that could not be verified.

14. If the flag indicating that the last URL has been reached has not been set, the current entry in the first list box is incremented to the next entry, and steps 10 through 13 are repeated.

15. After the final URL has been reached, a flag is set to indicate that, after this URL has been verified, there are no more to be checked.

16. After the final URL has been checked, the bot returns to an idle state, waiting for the user to close the application or enter another URL to be checked, starting the process all over again.

This is a single form application with the Internet Transfer Control being the only nondefault control to be used. The files used in this example are those listed in Table 32.5.

**Table 32.5   Web-Enabled Visual Basic Project Files**

| File | Description |
| --- | --- |
| INetExpl.frm | The Web-bot Visual Basic Form file |
| chap34ex.vbp | The Visual Basic project file |

# Declaring the Two Flags

The previous listing of the steps your bot application takes specified that you will be using two flags in performing the link verifications, so let's begin by declaring those two flags. Because they are used as simple, yes/no flags, you can declare them as Booleans. This gives you the form declaration section as shown in Listing 32.1.

**Listing 32.1   INETEXPL.FRM   Web-Bot Example Variable Declarations**

```
Option Explicit

'Flag to tell INetAPI Control whether we are retrieving the
'initial HTML page, or are verifying the links within the
'initial HTML page.
Private mbTestingLinks As Boolean
'Flag to tell the INetAPI control that we are at the last link
'to be verified.
Private mbEndOfLinks As Boolean
```

Next you need to lay out your form with all of the controls that you will be using in this application. The controls that you add to the window are as follows in Table 32.6, and are shown in Figure 32.3.

**Table 32.6    Controls Added to the Form for Your Bot Application**

| Control Type | Name | Purpose |
| --- | --- | --- |
| Text Box | txtURLToVerify | This is the text box into which the user enters the URL of the HTML document on which you perform your link checking. |
| Command Button | cmdRetrieveURL | This is the command button that triggers the retrieval of the original HTML document. |
| Command Button | cmdTestLinks | This is the command button that triggers the link verification process on all of the URLs extracted from the original HTML document. |
| Text Box | txtData | This is the display area for the original HTML document specified by the URL entered by the user. |
| List Box | lstURLsToTest | This is the list box into which all of the URLs are placed that are extracted from the original HTML document. |
| List Box | lstUnresolvedURLs | This is the list box into which the URLs are placed that are not found or return some other error condition. |
| Internet Transfer Control | InetRetvControl | This is the Internet Transfer Control that performs all of the Web document retrievals. |
| Labels | <default names> | There are several labels used to indicate to the user what is in each of the text and list boxes. |

Other than setting the captions on, and initially disabling the command buttons, the only other property settings that you really need to be sure to set is on the list boxes. These need the Sorted property set to TRUE. You are now ready to jump into the code behind this form.

**FIG. 32.3**

The Visual Basic form as seen in the designer environment, showing the controls placed on the form.

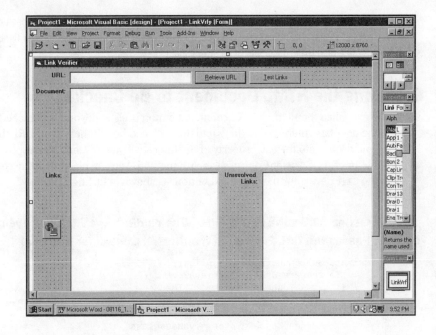

# Enabling the Retrieve URL Command Button

The first step (listed previously in the chapter) is to enable the command button to retrieve the original HTML document after the user enters an URL to retrieve. This is a simple matter of placing two lines of code, shown in Listing 32.2, into the Change event on the URL text box.

**Listing 32.2  INETEXPL.FRM—The *txtURLToCheck Change* Event Procedure, Enabling the Command Button to Retrieve the Document**

```
Private Sub txtURLToCheck_Change()
    'Is there a URL to retrieve?
    If txtURLToCheck.Text <> "" Then
        'Enable the "Retrieve URL" command button
        cmdRetrieveURL.Enabled = True
    End If
End Sub
```

All this routine does is check to see that something has been typed into the text box before enabling the command button. In reality, the user might have typed in garbage instead of a document URL. In checking for an URL in this text box, both here and in the clicked event for the command button, a more thorough checking should be performed to verify that it is indeed a valid URL that has been entered, and not some incomprehensible garbage.

**N O T E**   The most that you can verify is that the URL looks like a valid URL. You can't really verify that it is indeed valid until you try to retrieve it, and the Internet Transfer Control either returns a valid HTML document or an error condition. ■

## Retrieving the HTML Document to Be Checked

Next, when the Retrieve URL command button is clicked, you need to check to make sure that the user has entered something into the URL text box. If there is an URL there to be retrieved, you place it into the URL property of the Internet Transfer Control, clear the list boxes, and call the Internet Transfer Control's Execute method. You can place all of the code to do this into the Click event for the command button, as shown in Listing 32.3.

**Listing 32.3   INETEXPL.FRM—The *cmdRetrieveURL Click* Event Procedure Passes the URL Entered to the INetAPI Control for Retrieval**

```
Private Sub cmdRetrieveURL_Click()
    'Is there a URL to retrieve?
    If txtURLToCheck.Text <> "" Then
        'Set the mouse pointer to an hour glass, so the user
        'knows that something is going on
        Screen.MousePointer = vbHourglass
        'Copy the entered URL to the INetAPI Control's URL
        'property
        InetRetvControl.URL = txtURLToCheck.Text
        'Set the "Testing Links" flag to false
        mbTestingLinks = False
        'Clear the list boxes
        lstURLsToTest.Clear
        lstUnresolvedURLs.Clear
        'Call the INetAPI Control's Execute method to retrieve the
        'HTML Document specified by the URL entered by the user.
        InetRetvControl.Execute
    End If
End Sub
```

After you have called the Internet Transfer Control's Execute method, you sit back and wait for the document to be retrieved.

## Extracting the HTML Document from the Internet Transfer Control

You place your code to extract the HTML document that has been retrieved from the Internet Transfer Control in the control's StateChanged event. You use a Switch Case statement to make sure that you have reached the icResponseCompleted state. After you have reached that state, you loop, extracting 1024 byte chunks of the retrieved document, until you have extracted the entire document. After you have the whole thing, you copy it to the txtData text box so the user can see and examine it. Next, you call a subroutine, ParseHTMLDocument, that you write to find all of the URLs in the document. All of this is shown in Listing 32.4.

**Listing 32.4   INETEXPL.FRM—The Initial *InetRetvControl_StateChanged*
Event Procedure, Placing the HTML Document in the Text Box**

```
Private Sub InetRetvControl_StateChanged(ByVal State As Integer)
    'Which state has the control entered?
    Select Case State
        'Has the complete response been received?
        Case icResponseCompleted
            'We are retrieving the initial HTML document
            Dim vtData As Variant
            Dim strData As String: strData = ""
            Dim bDone As Boolean: bDone = False

            'Get the first chunk of the HTML document from
            'the INetAPI control
            vtData = InetRetvControl.GetChunk(1024, icString)
            'Is there nothing in the document?
            If Len(vtData) = 0 Then
                'If so, then we are done here
                bDone = True
            End If
            'Loop until we have extracted the entire document
            'from the INetAPI Control
            Do While Not bDone
                'Add the newly extracted chunk to the previously
                'extracted portion of the document
                strData = strData & vtData
                'Extract the next portion of the document from
                'the INetAPI Control
                vtData = InetRetvControl.GetChunk(1024, icString)
                'Have we reached the end of the document?
                If Len(vtData) = 0 Then
                    'If so, set the flag to indicate that we are
                    'done
                    bDone = True
                End If
            Loop
            'Copy the HTML document to the display for the user
            'to see and examine
            txtData.Text = strData
            'Parse out the URLs from the document
            ParseHTMLDocument
            'Reset the command buttons so that the "Test Links"
            'button is now the default button
            cmdTestLinks.Enabled = True
            cmdRetrieveURL.Default = False
            cmdTestLinks.Default = True
            'Reset the mouse pointer to an arrow to
            'indicate to the user that there is no longer
            'anything going on
            Screen.MousePointer = vbArrow
    End Select
End Sub
```

Part

**IX**

Ch

**32**

Notice that you have not placed any error handling in this routine to make sure that a valid HTML document was retrieved. It assumes that a valid document was found and retrieved. It really should have some error checking added, both for any error conditions that might arise and to verify that a successful HTTP response code was returned.

## Parsing URLs from the HTML Document

Parsing the URLs from the HTML document is broken down into simple steps and contained in the subroutine ParseHTMLDocument, which was called from the StateChanged event of the Internet Transfer Control. You set up a loop, calling a function GetNextURL, that you will build in the next section, and loop until it no longer returns any more URLs. As each URL is returned to your routine, you add it to the list box of URLs to be verified. After all URLs have been found, you scan the list box to remove any duplicate URLs from the list using another subroutine, RemoveDuplicateURLS, that you will build in the "Removing Duplicate URLs" section. The code for the ParseHTMLDocument subroutine is shown in Listing 32.5.

> **Listing 32.5   INETEXPL.FRM—The *ParseHTMLDocument* Subroutine, Which Scans the Document for HTML Elements Containing URLs**

```
Public Sub ParseHTMLDocument()
    Dim strHTMLDoc As String
    Dim strURL As String

    'Copy the HTML document from the display
    strHTMLDoc = txtData.Text
    'Get the first URL from the HTML document
    strURL = GetNextURL(strHTMLDoc)
    'Loop as long as we are finding URLs in the HTML document
    Do While strURL <> ""
        'Add the extracted URL to the list box
        lstURLsToTest.AddItem strURL
        'Get the next URL from the HTML document
        strURL = GetNextURL(strHTMLDoc)
    Loop
    'All URLs have been extracted, scan the list box to remove
    'duplicates
    RemoveDuplicateURLS
End Sub
```

## Finding the HTML Elements that Contain URLs

The function that finds the URLs in the HTML document, GetNextURL, looks for the starting and ending markers for HTML elements (< and >). After these have been found, the HTML element between them is parsed out, and everything through the element ending marker is truncated from the HTML document. (This is so that scanning for the next element can always begin at the beginning of the document. This is a copy of the document being held in variables, so you are not affecting the copy in the text box that the user sees.)

The HTML element is then passed to a function, DoesElementContainURL, that scans it for any of the three element attributes that indicates the presence of an URL. If that function finds any of these attributes, the element is passed to another function, ExtractURL, that parses out the URL from the HTML element. After an URL has been found or the end of the document has been reached, this function stops scanning and returns the URL found or an empty string to indicate that the end of the document has been reached. The code that performs all of this is shown in Listing 32.6.

**Listing 32.6    INETEXPL.FRM—The *GetNextURL* Function, Which Scans the HTML Document Until an HTML Element Containing an URL Is Found**

```
Public Function GetNextURL(strHTMLDoc As String) As String
    Dim lStartPos As Long
    Dim lEndPos As Long
    Dim strElement As String
    Dim bFoundURL As Boolean: bFoundURL = False

    'Loop until the URL Found flag is set to TRUE
    Do While Not bFoundURL
        'Find the beginning of the next HTML tag
        lStartPos = InStr(1, strHTMLDoc, "<", vbTextCompare)
        If lStartPos > 0 Then
            'Find the end position of the HTML tag
            lEndPos = InStr(lStartPos, strHTMLDoc, ">", _
                vbTextCompare)
            If lEndPos > 0 Then
                'Copy the tag into the strElement variable
                strElement = Mid(strHTMLDoc, (lStartPos + 1), _
                    (lEndPos - (lStartPos + 1)))
                'Chop off all of the HTML document through the
                'end of the HTML tag that has been found
                strHTMLDoc = Mid(strHTMLDoc, (lEndPos + 1))
                'Check to see if the element contains a URL
                If DoesElementContainURL(strElement) Then
                    'If so, set the URL Found flag to true
                    bFoundURL = True
                    'Extract the URL from the element and return
                    'it to the calling routine
                    GetNextURL = ExtractURL(strElement)
                End If
            End If
        Else
            'No more tags to be found in the HTML document, we
            'must be at the end of the document. Set the URL
            'Found flag to true to end the loop, and return an
            'empty string to the calling routine.
            bFoundURL = True
            GetNextURL = ""
        End If
    Loop
End Function
```

Part
IX

Ch
32

# Checking an HTML Element

The function DoesElementContainURL, which scans the HTML element to determine if it contains an URL, looks for any one of three attributes that the element might contain. These attributes are the following:

- HREF—Usually used in links and anchors
- SRC—Usually points to image and sound files that are to be displayed in the Web page
- CODEBASE—Points to where the Java applets or ActiveX controls can be found

If any one of these three attributes is found, the function returns TRUE; otherwise, it returns FALSE to the calling routine, signifying that no URL is contained in the element. The code that looks for these URLs is in Listing 32.7.

---

**Listing 32.7   INETEXPL.FRM—The *DoesElementContainURL* Function, Which Determines Whether or Not an HTML Element Contains an URL that Needs to Be Parsed Out**

```
Public Function DoesElementContainURL(strElement As String) _
        As Boolean
    'Initialize the flag indicating whether the element contains
    'a URL to false, so we only have to change its value if we
    'find that the element does contain a URL
    Dim bHasURL As Boolean: bHasURL = False

    'Does the element contain the "HREF" attribute?
    If InStr(1, strElement, "HREF", vbTextCompare) > 0 Then
        'If so, then it contains a URL
        bHasURL = True
    Else
        'If not, does it contain the "SRC" attribute?
        If InStr(1, strElement, "SRC", vbTextCompare) > 0 Then
            'If so, then it contains a URL
            bHasURL = True
        Else
            'If not, does it contain the "CODEBASE" attribute?
            If InStr(1, strElement, "CODEBASE", vbTextCompare) _
                    > 0 Then
                'If so, then it contains a URL
                bHasURL = True
            End If
        End If
    End If
    DoesElementContainURL = bHasURL
End Function
```

---

The reason that this function scans for the element attributes instead of the element tags is that these three attributes are used in many more HTML elements, and the elements in which these attributes are used do not have to use these attributes. If the elements do not use one of these attributes, the element does not contain an URL, even though it might be an HTML element that you would expect to contain an URL.

## Parsing the URL from the HTML Element

After an HTML element has been determined to contain an URL, the ExtractURL function is called to parse out the URL from the element. This function locates the attribute that identified this element as containing an URL and then finds the first quote character following the attribute (which should be one character before the URL) and the following quote character (which should be one character after the end of the URL). The portion of the element between these two quote characters is parsed out and returned as the URL, as seen in Listing 32.8.

### Listing 32.8   INETEXPL.FRM—The *ExtractURL* Function, Which Parses Out the URL from the HTML Element

```
Public Function ExtractURL(strElement As String) As String
    Dim lStartPos As Long
    Dim lEndPos As Long
    Dim lURLStart As Long
    Dim strURL As String: strURL = ""

    'Find the attribute that indicates the presence of a URL
    lStartPos = InStr(1, strElement, "HREF", vbTextCompare)
    If lStartPos = 0 Then
        lStartPos = InStr(1, strElement, "SRC", vbTextCompare)
        If lStartPos = 0 Then
            lStartPos = InStr(1, strElement, "CODEBASE", _
                vbTextCompare)
        End If
    End If
    'Search for the opening quote character
    lURLStart = InStr(lStartPos, strElement, Chr(34), _
        vbTextCompare)
    If lURLStart > 0 Then
        'Search for the closing quote character
        lEndPos = InStr((lURLStart + 1), strElement, Chr(34), _
            vbTextCompare)
        If lEndPos > 0 Then
            'Extract the URL from between the quote characters
            strURL = Mid(strElement, (lURLStart + 1), (lEndPos - _
                (lURLStart + 1)))
        End If
    End If
    'Return the URL
    ExtractURL = strURL
End Function
```

Part
IX

Ch
32

This routine can take this process further and examine the URL that has been extracted from the HTML element to verify that it is indeed a valid URL and not some garbage that has gotten mixed up in the document. It can also make the determination whether the URL is a positional URL that only causes the Web browser to reposition itself within this document. There is no need to verify positional URLs for the document in which they are found. There is still a need to verify positional URLs that are for positions in other HTML documents.

# Removing Duplicate URLs

After you have extracted all of the URLs from the HTML document, you need to scan the list of URLs to remove any duplicates. It's common for HTML documents to reuse the same URL several times. The URL could be links to another document being referenced several times within the document, or the URL could be for a simple section divider graphic. Either way, you only need to verify the link once. If it's valid one time, it will be valid all times. If the link isn't valid the first time, it's unlikely that it will become valid the second or third time it's checked, unless it is on an extremely overloaded server.

You remove the duplicate URLs with the RemoveDuplicateURLS subroutine. This subroutine depends on the Sorted property of the list box to be set to TRUE, so that duplicate URLs can dependably be next to each other. This routine starts with the last URL in the list box and sequentially compares each URL to the previous entry. If a duplicate URL is found, it is removed, and the routine continues with the next entry. By traversing from the last entry to the first, this routine does not have to worry about performing any convoluted logic to prevent skipping any URLs as it is deleting duplicates. The code for this subroutine is shown in Listing 32.9.

> **Listing 32.9  INETEXPL.FRM—The *RemoveDuplicateURLs* Subroutine, Which Scans the List Box of URLs to Be Tested and Removes Any Duplicates**

```
Private Sub RemoveDuplicateURLS()
    Dim strPrevURL As String: strPrevURL = ""
    Dim strCurURL As String: strCurURL = ""
    Dim lCurEntry As Long

    'Get the number of entries in the list box of URLs to be
    'checked
    lCurEntry = lstURLsToTest.ListCount
    'We will loop through the list box, going from last to first,
    'until all entries have been checked.
    Do While lCurEntry > 0
        'Copy the current URL into the current URL variable
        strCurURL = lstURLsToTest.List((lCurEntry - 1))
        'Is the current URL the same as the previous URL?
        If strCurURL = strPrevURL Then
            'If so, the remove the current URL
            lstURLsToTest.RemoveItem (lCurEntry - 1)
```

```
    Else
        'If not, copy the current URL to the previous URL
        strPrevURL = strCurURL
    End If
    'Move down one position in the list box
    lCurEntry = lCurEntry - 1
    Loop
End Sub
```

## Beginning the URL Testing

You now have a list box full of URLs to be verified, and the application is sitting idle waiting for the user to begin testing by clicking the Test Links command button. After this command button is clicked, you need to select the first entry in the list box containing the URLs to be checked, set the flag indicating that you are verifying URLs, and then call the TestLinks subroutine to verify the currently selected URL. This can all be placed in the Click event for the cmdTestLinks command button, as shown in Listing 32.10.

**Listing 32.10    INETEXPL.FRM—The *cmdTestLinks Click*ed Event Routine, Which Begins the Process of Verifying URLs**

```
Private Sub cmdTestLinks_Click()
    'Set the mouse pointer to an hour glass, so the user knows
    'that something is going on
    Screen.MousePointer = vbHourglass
    'Select the first entry in the list box of URLs to be checked
    lstURLsToTest.ListIndex = 0
    'Set the "Testing Links" flag to TRUE
    mbTestingLinks = True
    'Set the flag indicating that the last URL to be tested has
    'been reached to FALSE
    mbEndOfLinks = False
    'Test the first URL
    TestLinks
End Sub
```

## Testing the Currently Selected URL

By selecting the next URL to be tested upon completing testing on the previous URL, you can assume that the currently selected URL in the list box of URLs is the one that you need to work with in the TestLinks subroutine. The first thing you do is check to see if the current URL is the last URL. If it is, then you need to set the flag that indicates you are on the final URL to be tested. Next, you call the BuildTestURL function, which returns URL to you an absolute, that you can pass directly to the Internet Transfer Control. You pass the URL to the Internet Transfer Control by calling its Execute method, passing the URL as the first parameter, and specifying that you want to send the HEAD command to the HTTP server as the command. This causes the Web server to only send the header information, which should be sufficient to verify the link in most cases. The code to do all of this is shown in Listing 32.11.

**Listing 32.11 INETEXPL.FRM—The *TestLinks* Subroutine, Which Creates an Absolute URL for the Currently Selected URL, Then Calls the INetAPI Control's Execute Method**

```
Private Sub TestLinks()
    Dim lNumLinks As Long
    Dim lCurLink As Long
    Dim strURLToTest As String

    'Grab the current List Box entry number
    lCurLink = lstURLsToTest.ListIndex
    'Grab the number of entries in the list box (minus one for
    'comparing with the current entry number)
    lNumLinks = lstURLsToTest.ListCount - 1
    'Compare the current entry to see if it is the last entry
    'in the list box
    If lCurLink = lNumLinks Then
        'If the current entry is the last entry, set the
        'mbEndOfLinks flag to true to indicate that there are
        'no other entries to be checked after this one.
        mbEndOfLinks = True
    End If
    'Call the BuildTestURL function to get an absolute URL
    strURLToTest = BuildTestURL()
    'Call the INetAPI Control Execute method, specifying that
    'the header information for the specified URL be retrieved
    InetRetvControl.Execute strURLToTest, "HEAD"
End Sub
```

 Although it is not included in this example, a full functioning version of this application would check for certain response codes indicating that the request could not be fulfilled and would retry with the GET or POST command. If the URL was for a CGI application or other Web server extension instead of a file, it could be that the server could not respond properly to a HEAD command and could only respond to a GET or POST command. This would have the benefit of limiting the usage of GET and POST to only those URLs that required these commands and not having to tie up the servers and network with transferring unnecessary files.

# Building an Absolute URL

The BuildTestURL function checks the currently selected URL to determine if it is an absolute or relative URL. If the URL contains the protocol separator ://  then it is considered to be an absolute URL and is returned to the calling routine as is. If it is a relative URL, then the original URL entered by the user is used as a base URL. This original URL has to be scanned to remove any file names from the end, so that it provides nothing more than the protocol, server, and directory, and the URL to be tested is added to the end. This new URL is then returned to the calling routine. This entire process is shown in Listing 32.12.

**Listing 32.12 INETEXPL.FRM—The *BuildTestURL* Function, Which Builds an Absolute URL from the Current Test URL and the Original URL**

```
Private Function BuildTestURL() As String
    Dim strNewURL As String
    Dim strBaseURL As String
    Dim lProtoPos As Long
    Dim lStartPos As Long
    Dim lNextPos As Long

    'Get the current URL to be checked
    strNewURL = lstURLsToTest.List(lstURLsToTest.ListIndex)
    'Check to see if it contains a protocol separator marker
    lProtoPos = InStr(1, strNewURL, "://")
    'if there is no protocol separator marker, or it's too far
    'from the front of the URL to be an absolute URL, we will
    'need to build an absolute URL using the HTML page URL as
    'the base
    If (lProtoPos = 0) Or (lProtoPos > 10) Then
        'If the first character in the URL is a slash, then
        'remove it (we'll make sure that the base URL ends
        'in a slash)
        If Left(strNewURL, 1) = "/" Then
            strNewURL = Mid(strNewURL, 2)
        End If
        'Grab the URL of the HTML page being checked to use as
        'the base URL
        strBaseURL = txtURLToCheck.Text
        'Does the Base URL end with a slash?
        If Right(strBaseURL, 1) = "/" Then
            'If so, then we can just concatenate the two together
            strNewURL = strBaseURL & strNewURL
        Else
            'If not, the we need to find the ending slash, so
            'that we are not using the name of an HTML page as
            'a directory name in our URL
            'We start by finding the protocol separator
            lStartPos = InStr(1, strBaseURL, "://", vbTextCompare)
            'Move our starting position past the protocol
            'separator
            lStartPos = lStartPos + 3
            'Now let's look for the next slash
            lNextPos = InStr(lStartPos, strBaseURL, "/", _
                    vbTextCompare)
            'Did we find another slash?
            If lNextPos > 0 Then
                'If so, then let's keep looking and looping until
                'we find the last slash in the URL
                Do While (lNextPos > 0) And (lNextPos < _
                        Len(strBaseURL))
                    'Set the starting position to one past the
                    'slash
                    lStartPos = lNextPos + 1
```

*continues*

Part
**IX**
Ch
**32**

**Listing 32.12  Continued**

```
                        'Check to make sure that we are not past the
                        'end of the base URL
                        If lStartPos < Len(strBaseURL) Then
                            'If not, then find the next slash
                            lNextPos = InStr(lStartPos, strBaseURL, _
                                        "/", vbTextCompare)
                        Else
                            'Otherwise, set the next slash to 0 to
                            'break out of this loop
                            lNextPos = 0
                        End If
                    Loop
                    'Set the last slash position to one behind the
                    'last starting position
                    lNextPos = lStartPos - 1
                    'Extract the URL up to the last slash, and tack
                    'on the URL to be checked onto the end
                    strNewURL = Left(strBaseURL, lNextPos) & strNewURL
                Else
                    'If there are no slashes in the URL, let's
                    'concatenate the Base URL with the URL to be
                    'checked, placing a slash between them
                    strNewURL = strBaseURL & "/" & strNewURL
                End If
            End If
        End If
        'Return the new URL to be checked
        BuildTestURL = strNewURL
End Function
```

# Determining Whether the Current URL Is Valid

You determine whether the URL being checked is valid in the StateChanged event for the Internet Transfer Control. You expand the routine to include checking for an error response, in which case the URL is copied into the Unverified URLs list box, as you were unable to verify that it was a valid URL. If the icResponseCompleted state is reached, you request the entire response header and pass it to the CheckHeaderReturnCode function to check the response code returned with the header. If the response code indicates that the URL is invalid, it is copied into the Unverified URLs list box. If the last URL has not been reached, the next URL in the list box is selected, and the TestLinks subroutine is called again. This continues until all links have been checked, at which point the application returns to the idle state, waiting for the user to decide what to do next. The code that performs this can be seen in Listing 32.13.

**Listing 32.13  INETEXPL.FRM—The Full *InetRetvControl_StateChanged* Event Routine, Which Processes the Results from Both the Initial Document Retrieval and the URL Verifications**

```
Private Sub InetRetvControl_StateChanged(ByVal State As Integer)
    'Which state has the control entered?
    Select Case State
        'Did an error occur?
        Case icError
            'Are we testing links?
            If mbTestingLinks Then
                'If so, the copy the current URL to the unresolved
                'URLs list box
                lstUnresolvedURLs.AddItem (lstURLsToTest.List(_
                        lstURLsToTest.ListIndex))
                'Have we reached the end of the URLs to be tested?
                If Not mbEndOfLinks Then
                    'No, select the next URL in the list box
                    lstURLsToTest.ListIndex = _
                            lstURLsToTest.ListIndex + 1
                    'Test the currently selected URL
                    TestLinks
                Else
                    'Yes, reset the mouse pointer to an arrow to
                    'indicate to the user that there is no longer
                    'anything going on
                    Screen.MousePointer = vbArrow
                End If
            End If
        'Has the complete response been received?
        Case icResponseCompleted
            'Are we testing links?
            If mbTestingLinks Then
                'Yes, we are testing links
                Dim strHeader As String

                'Get the complete header for the requested URL
                strHeader = InetRetvControl.GetHeader()
                'Check the response code in the header
                If Not CheckHeaderReturnCode(strHeader) Then
                    'The response code indicated that we requested
                    'an invalid URL, add the current URL to the
                    'unresolved URLs list box
                    lstUnresolvedURLs.AddItem (_
                        lstURLsToTest.List(lstURLsToTest.ListIndex))
                End If
                'Have we reached the end of the URLs to be tested?
                If Not mbEndOfLinks Then
                    'No, select the next URL in the list box
                    lstURLsToTest.ListIndex = _
                            lstURLsToTest.ListIndex + 1
                    'Test the currently selected URL
                    TestLinks
```

*continues*

**Listing 32.13   Continued**

```
        Else
            'Yes, reset the mouse pointer to an arrow to
            'indicate to the user that there is no longer
            'anything going on
            Screen.MousePointer = vbArrow
        End If
    Else
        'No, we are retrieving the initial HTML document
        Dim vtData As Variant
        Dim strData As String: strData = ""
        Dim bDone As Boolean: bDone = False

        'Get the first chunk of the HTML document from
        'the INetAPI control
        vtData = InetRetvControl.GetChunk(1024, icString)
        'Is there nothing in the document?
        If Len(vtData) = 0 Then
            'If so, then we are done here
            bDone = True
        End If
        'Loop until we have extracted the entire document
        'from the INetAPI Control
        Do While Not bDone
            'Add the newly extracted chunk to the
            'previously extracted portion of the document
            strData = strData & vtData
            'Extract the next portion of the document from
            'the INetAPI Control
            vtData = InetRetvControl.GetChunk(1024, _
                        icString)
            'Have we reached the end of the document?
            If Len(vtData) = 0 Then
                'If so, set the flag to indicate that we
                'are done
                bDone = True
            End If
        Loop
        'Copy the HTML document to the display for the
        'user to see and examine
        txtData.Text = strData
        'Parse out the URLs from the document
        ParseHTMLDocument
        'Reset the command buttons so that the "Test
        'Links" button is now the default button
        cmdTestLinks.Enabled = True
        cmdRetrieveURL.Default = False
        cmdTestLinks.Default = True
        'Reset the mouse pointer to an arrow to
        'indicate to the user that there is no longer
        'anything going on
        Screen.MousePointer = vbArrow
    End If
    End Select
End Sub
```

# Checking the HTTP Header Response Code

The CheckHeaderReturnCode function parses out the response code from the header by looking for the first space in the header (which should be just before the response code), looking for the next space character (which should be just after the response code), and parsing out the code from between those two characters. The response code is then passed through a Switch Case statement, checking against codes that indicate an invalid or uncheckable URL. If any of the cases are triggered, a FALSE is returned to the calling routine, indicating an invalid URL. If none of the cases are triggered, a TRUE is returned, indicating that it is a valid URL. The code for this function is shown in Listing 32.14.

**Listing 32.14   INETEXPL.FRM—The *CheckHeaderReturnCode* Function, Which Checks the Response Code from the HTTP Response Header**

```
Private Function CheckHeaderReturnCode(strHeader As String) _
        As Boolean
    Dim bGoodResponse As Boolean: bGoodResponse = True
    Dim strRespCode As String: strRespCode = ""
    Dim iSpacePos As Integer

    'Find the first space in the header, this should be just
    'before the response code
    iSpacePos = InStr(1, strHeader, " ", vbTextCompare)
    If iSpacePos > 0 Then
        'Move the entire header forward, so that the response
        'code is the first thing in the header
        strHeader = Mid(strHeader, (iSpacePos + 1))
        'Find the space immediately following the response code
        iSpacePos = InStr(1, strHeader, " ", vbTextCompare)
        If iSpacePos > 0 Then
            'Parse out the response code
            strRespCode = Left(strHeader, (iSpacePos - 1))
        End If
    End If
    'Check for an invalid response code. The default function
    'return is true, so we only need to check for response codes
    'that would cause us to return FALSE
    Select Case strRespCode
        Case "204"
            bGoodResponse = False
        Case "301"
            bGoodResponse = False
        Case "302"
            bGoodResponse = False
        Case "304"
            bGoodResponse = False
        Case "400"
            bGoodResponse = False
        Case "404"
            bGoodResponse = False
```

Part
**IX**

Ch

**32**

*continues*

**Listing 32.14   Continued**

```
        Case "500"
            bGoodResponse = False
        Case "501"
            bGoodResponse = False
        Case "502"
            bGoodResponse = False
        Case "503"
            bGoodResponse = False
    End Select
    CheckHeaderReturnCode = bGoodResponse
End Function
```

This completes the coding for our link-verifying Web-bot. The running application is shown in Figure 32.4.

**FIG. 32.4**

The running Link-Verifier Web-bot application.

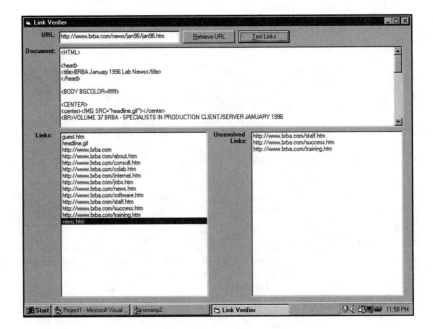

# From Here...

In this chapter, you learned about Microsoft Internet extensions to the Win32 API and how they encapsulated this functionality within a new ActiveX control that comes with Visual Basic 5. You looked at how this new control works, how to use it, and then used that knowledge to build a working application using the control. To build your application, you also looked at how URLs are constructed, so that you can build routines to examine and assemble URLs as needed.

Now, you can extend the functionality of this Web-bot application by building in more robust error checking and handling, as well as more thorough analysis of the URLs entered by the user and extracted from the HTML document. You can enhance the application by allowing the user to load an HTML document from a file instead of an URL, make updates to that file to correct the invalid URLs, provide automatic updating of URLs that have moved and return a 301 or 302 response code, and include FTP functionality (through the Internet Transfer Control) to place the corrected HTML document back on the Web server.

To learn about integrating Visual Basic with other Web-based and Web-oriented technologies, check out the following chapter:

■ To learn about integrating Visual Basic and Java, read Chapter 34, "Integrating Visual Basic with Java."

Part
**IX**

Ch
**32**

# Building Web Design-Time Controls

There is a new class of ActiveX controls used entirely at design time when creating a Web application. These controls are called design-time ActiveX controls. They are called design-time controls because most of the power of the control is used during the design process of a Web page. These controls can be edited to modify the text (code) it generates into the Web page it is placed on. By using design-time controls, you can take advantage of all the OLE design-time capabilities, such as, in-place editing and property sheets. This allows you to extend the capability of the editor that you are using with the functionality of the design-time control. ▪

**A Note from the Author**

The ability to create ActiveX controls is available only in the Professional and Enterprise versions of Visual Basic 5. However, if you want to create controls, but do not own Visual Basic or only have the Learning edition, you can get the Visual Basic 5 Control Creation Edition off the CD in the back of this book or directly from the Microsoft Web site at **www.microsoft.com/Vbasic/Controls**.

# Defining Web Design-Time Controls

In Chapter 27, you learned how to use Visual InterDev to create a Web application. During that process you used several different types of objects that were added to the Web pages. On one of those pages you added a table that displayed data from a database (see Figure 33.1). Design-time controls were used as the tool to assist you in adding to the database support to that Web page.

**FIG. 33.1**

The final result of using design-time controls when creating a database Web page.

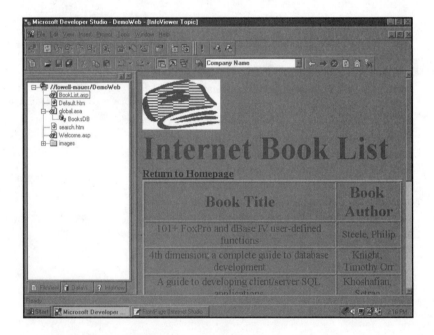

What you will see in this chapter is exactly what design-time controls are, what they can do, and finally, how to build a design-time control of your own. HTML editors use design-time controls to place custom code into an HTML Web page. Design-time controls are actually standard ActiveX controls with a special interface that allows them to generate separate HTML code that is executed when the Web page is processed and displayed. They are used at design-time just like any other ActiveX control. What this really means is that any type of process that you can design as an ActiveX control can be converted to a design-time control with just a little effort and programming.

The biggest difference between a standard ActiveX control and the design-time version is that a design-time control is never used when the Web page is being run. Instead, a design-time control generates the code executed by the client browsers or a server component running on a Web server. This allows for easy creation and editing of HTML or Active Server Pages that will contain VBScript. They allow you to automate complicated code creation or give you the ability to set HTML tag properties using a standard Windows interface (see Figure 33.2).

**FIG. 33.2**
A Standard Windows Properties page showing how many properties can be entered for a control.

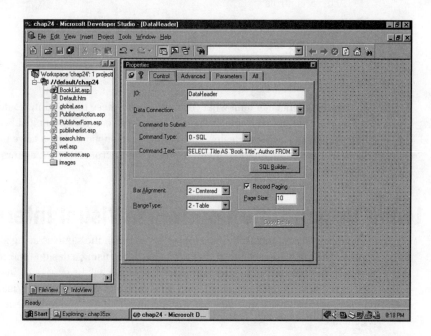

When a design-time control is used to add functionality to a Web page, the design-time control information is included in the HTML text as a comment, while the run-time text from the control is inserted as HTML text immediately after the commented text as shown in the following:

```
<!--METADATA TYPE="DesignerControl" startspan
    <OBJECT ID="Bgsound1" WIDTH=343 HEIGHT=23
    CLASSID="CLSID:ED016809-B8F3-11D0-9021-444553540000">
        <PARAM NAME="_ExtentX" VALUE="9049">
        <PARAM NAME="_ExtentY" VALUE="609">
        <PARAM NAME="Source" VALUE="E:\SOUNDS\Thatsit.wav">
        <PARAM NAME="Repeat" VALUE="2">
    </OBJECT>
-->
<BGSOUND SRC="file:///E:\SOUNDS\Thatsit.wav" LOOP="2">
<!--METADATA TYPE="DesignerControl" endspan-->
```

If the Web page the control is on is an Active Server page, then the commented text will be stripped from the file before it is sent to the browser for execution. The above HTML code is very simple. However, the design-time control used to create it presents the user with a property sheet to set the needed parameters.

Part
IX

Ch
33

Because HTML files are basically text-oriented command files interpreted by either the server or the browser they are running on, design-time controls can be used to create any text-based solution to an application problem. The range of what design-time controls falls into is very wide. A design-time control can be used to create the following:

- HTML tags and content
- ActiveX controls
- ActiveX Server components
- Server scripting in any language
- Client scripting in any language
- Java applets

The only things that can limit what you can do with these design-time controls are the software on your PC and your imagination. To use these controls, you must be using an HTML editor that supports them. Design-time controls are supported by a large number of HTML editors that are on the market, including all of the Microsoft HTML editors (that is, Visual InterDev and FrontPage).

# Using Design-Time Controls in Visual InterDev

Using design-time controls in Visual InterDev is much the same as using any other ActiveX control. The difference between the two is that when using a design-time control, you can interact with that control to affect the HTML text that will be generated into the HTML text file. To see how to make use of a design-time control, we will be using Visual InterDev to insert one of the available design-time controls into an HTML file and then see how it works and what it generates.

Begin by starting Visual InterDev and creating a new Web application by using the Web Project Wizard. Choose File, New from the menu, then select the Web Project Wizard and name the new Web project "CHAP35." When you get to Step 2 of the wizard process, do not enable the full text search Web page. As seen previously, this will create a Web site on whichever Web server you are using to build Web applications.

**N O T E** Make sure that the Web server you are using is already started or you are connected to it, before starting Visual InterDev. For this chapter, the Microsoft Personal Web Server is used. ▓

Next, add a new HTML page to the application by selecting File, New from the menu and then selecting HTML Page from the Files tab. Name the HTML page "DTDemo" and click OK to finish the process. At this point, you should be looking at the HTML text generated for the default page (see Figure 33.3).

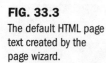

**FIG. 33.3**
The default HTML page
text created by the
page wizard.

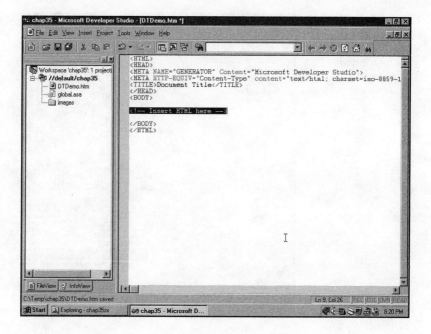

To really see the difference between the two types of ActiveX controls, we will do two things.
First, insert a standard ActiveX control into the HTML page and look at how it works and the
text it will generate in the HTML file. Second, create another HTML page and insert a design-
time control into it to see what it generates and how it works. For the first example, an ActiveX
control that comes with Visual Basic 5 will be used to insert the control into the HTML page.

## Adding a Standard ActiveX Control

To add a standard control to a Web page by using Visual InterDev is easy. Place the cursor in
front of the comment

```
<!-- Insert HTML here -->
```

Next, from the menu, select Insert, Into HTML, ActiveX Control. This will display a dialog box
with two tabs (Controls, Design-Time Controls). Locate the new MSFlexGrid control and select
it. Figure 33.4 shows you what your screen should now look like with the ActiveX control displayed with its properties sheet.

Close this display to go back to the HTML text editor and look at what was generated by the
control. The following text was inserted into your HTML file:

```
<OBJECT ID="MSFlexGrid1" WIDTH=428 HEIGHT=228
    CLASSID="CLSID:6262D3A0-531B-11CF-91F6-C2863C385E30">
        <PARAM NAME="_ExtentX" VALUE="11324">
        <PARAM NAME="_ExtentY" VALUE="6033">
        <PARAM NAME="_Version" VALUE="327680">
    </OBJECT>
```

Part

IX

Ch

33

**FIG. 33.4**

Using the standard
Microsoft Grid control in
a Web page to display
data information.

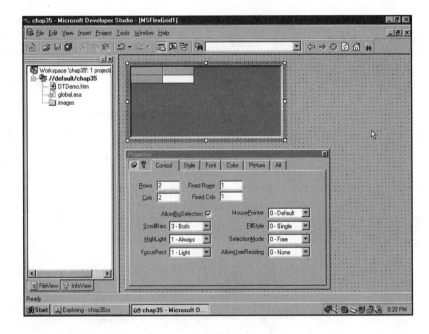

This text is executed by the client when the Web page is displayed. If you preview this page now, what you will see is an empty grid. To make use of this grid, you must add VBScript by using the Visual InterDev Script Wizard. For the purposes of this demo, a single line of code as shown below was added to the Window_OnLoad routine. When previewing this now, it will display "Hello" in the grid (see Figure 33.5).

```
MSFlexGrid1.Text = "Hello"
```

Of course, if this control does not exist on the client's PC, then it needs to be downloaded. When using standard ActiveX controls you must set up the Web application to download the controls to the client if they do not exist there before the first page is displayed.

▶ **See** Chapter 6, "Making Your ActiveX Controls Web-Friendly," **p. 115**

## Adding a Design-Time Control

Four design-time controls come with Visual InterDev. The one that you will be using in this section is the Include control. This control allows you to include another HTML text file into the HTML page that you are currently working with. The first thing that you need to do is create the text file that will be included in the HTML page. Normally, the file(s) that you will include contain sections of HTML code that you want to use in multiple Web pages. Of course, you can use the old fashioned way of "cut-and-paste." But, by using the Include control to "copy" this file into the HTML page that you will create, you will be automating the process.

**FIG. 33.5**
The MSGrid ActiveX
Control when displayed
by the browser.

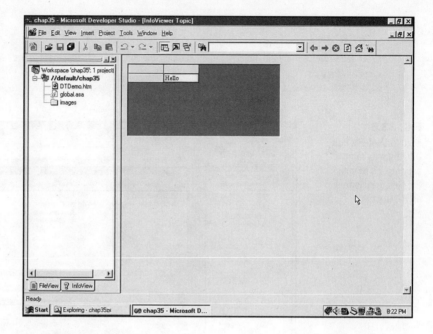

You might be asking yourself, "Why am I doing this? Can't I just enter this text into the HTML page directly?" Well, yes, you can. However, if you need the same HTML text in different HTML pages, then you would have to make any changes needed to every one of the pages that have this text in it. The Include control allows you to "copy" this HTML text into any HTML page you want. Now, when you make changes to the Include file, the HTML pages will automatically get these changes when the page is refreshed. Let's keep this HTML file simple. Create a new HTML text file and name it, `"IncludeCode"`. Then, in the HTML editor, enter the following HTML code:

```
<Font Size=5>
<p>Welcome to ActiveX Programming</p>
```

This code will be included in the Web page you create next. Save this file and close the editor. Now, create a new HTML page called `"IncDemo"` and insert the Include control within the `<body> ... </body>` tags. This control will display a properties sheet that requests an URL for the included file. Click the URL Builder button to display the Edit URL form (see Figure 33.6).

This property sheet allows you to select a file on the Web site you are developing or a standard file that exists on the server PC. Select the text file that you created (you should see it listed) and click OK. Because the Include control is processed by the server, you must rename the HTML file from `"IncDemo.Htm"` to `"IncDemo.asp"`. This enables the Active Server Page processing on the Web server.

Preview this new Web page to see how the text file is included and how the HTML code in it is executed. Now, to see how the automatic process works, go back and edit the text file by changing the string that will be displayed and save it. Switch back to the browser and refresh the Web page. You will see that the change you just made was incorporated into the Web page.

Part
IX

Ch

**WARNING**

An HTML file used by the Include control should only contain HTML text that can be used in the section you have placed it.

**FIG. 33.6**

Include Control's Edit URL property form allowing the selection of the files to include into an HTML page.

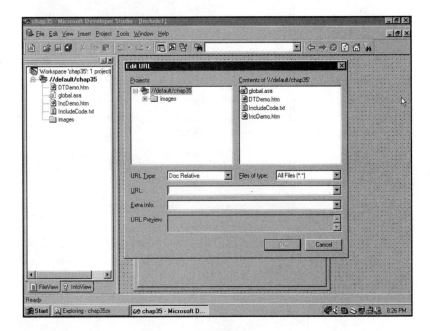

# Looking at the Future of Web Design-Time Controls

Because design-time controls are still fairly new to the industry, there are only a few controls available to the developer. However, just as there was an explosion of OCX and then ActiveX controls as the third-party companies started developing new controls, there will be many design-time controls coming on the market in the coming months. These controls are actually split into two separate groups—server-side and client-side processed controls.

Server-side processed controls, as the name suggests, will execute on the server before any HTML code being sent to the browser for a given Web page. This allows large amounts of server-side processing to be completed and added to the Web page before it's sent. A good example of a complex server-side design-time control is the Data Header control included with Visual InterDev. This control connects to a database and starts the data retrieval process. Another example of server-side controls is the Include control that you have just used in the previous section. However, these controls do require that the server contains the required programs, OCXs, or databases to be processed properly.

Client-side processed controls will generate HTML code that will execute on the client browser. They can also contain object references to ActiveX controls that reside on the client. If the ActiveX control is not on the client, then it would need to be downloaded to the client before the Web page can be displayed. This process requires the ActiveX control to be packaged for download, including registration information and licensing files if needed. This will open up a variety of controls that a developer can include in a Web site.

▶ For more information about Packaging ActiveX controls for Internet download, see the Visual Basic 5 Setup Wizard Help documentation.

# Building a Sample Web Design-Time Control

As you have seen, a design-time control consists of an ActiveX interface that the developer interacts with to set runtime parameters and the runtime text actually inserted into the HTML page when completed. The best way to understand how a design-time control works is to create one. In this section, you will be building a relatively simple design-time control. This control will generate the HTML tags needed to have a Wav, Mid, or Au file played when the Web page is displayed by the client browser.

On the CD

The Visual Basic source files for this design-time control can be found on the CD-ROM included with this book.

Good Web developers can create the HTML tags themselves; however, they would need to type in the complete code, including the path and file name for the Web page. But, if they need this code on many pages, or intend to use the same functionality in different Web pages or sites, it could get a little tiresome.

This control will give developers a property sheet that allows them to specify the number of times to repeat the sound file and the computer location for the file (server or a downloaded file). It will also make use of the Visual Basic 5 common dialog control to allow selection of the sound file without any typing. Because the common file open control is standard in Windows, this design-time control can be used by any developer using a 32-bit Windows environment. The steps needed to build this control are as follows:

1. Create an ActiveX control.
2. Use the ActiveX Control Interface Wizard.
3. Add a Property page.
4. Add Active Designer references and required code.
5. Compile and test the New control by using Visual InterDev.

## Creating an ActiveX Control

Begin by starting Visual Basic 5 and selecting the ActiveX control from the New Project form (see Figure 33.7). This will create a new project specifically for an ActiveX control.

Part
IX

Ch
33

**FIG. 33.7**

Starting an ActiveX control project from the New project Selection dialog in Visual Basic.

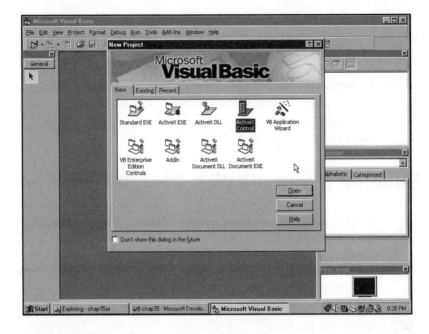

**FIG. 33.8**

User Control Form showing the Labels Inserted to describe the text boxes on the form.

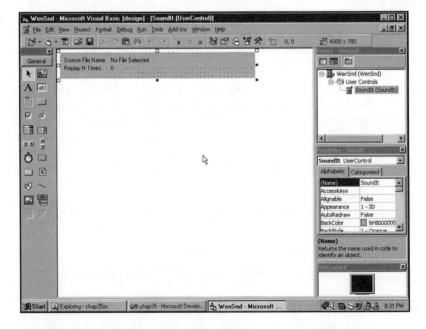

By selecting the ActiveX control project, you are telling Visual Basic 5 that this project will be an executable program by itself. It must be included in a standard Visual Basic project as a control or made into a design-time control to be used by an HTML editor. As we create this control, you will see a few differences between the building and testing of a standard ActiveX control and a design-time control.

The controls that you place on the displayed form will be visible only to the developer. The client browser will not display these forms to the user. So that the developer will know what settings were picked, insert four labels on the form, two labels on one line and the other two below them as shown in Figure 33.8. At the same time, reduce the overall size of the form.

Set the Name and Caption properties of the controls as listed in Table 33.1.

**Table 33.1    Property Settings for Labels on Design-Time Control**

| Name | Caption |
| --- | --- |
| LblSrc | Source File Name |
| LblSource | No File Selected |
| LblRpt | Replay N Times |
| LblRepeat | 0 |

**N O T E**   Name the project `"WebSnd"` and the user control `"SoundIt"`. When you save the project, it will be named WebSnd.vbp and the user control will become SoundIt.ctl. Although you have created a control, it doesn't do anything yet.

# Using the ActiveX Control Interface Wizard

The next step is to create the *public* interface for the ActiveX control. Visual Basic 5 comes with the ActiveX Control Interface Wizard to assist you in this process. To use this wizard, you must first add it to the add-ins menu by using the Add-In manager to select the wizard.

The wizard helps you create the code for the public interface of your control. However, it does not create the user interface. You must create the ActiveX control with the elements that you want before you use the wizard. ▉

Start the wizard by selecting it from the Add-In menu. An introduction form is displayed that explains the purpose of the wizard. Click the Next button to continue. If you had more than one user control defined in this project, you would need to select the control you want to work with (see Figure 33.9).

Since we are working with only one control, the next form displays the properties, methods, and events that you can select for use in the user control (see Figure 33.10).

The names initially listed are those commonly supported by controls. If your control already has code in its Code Window, the items shown in the list box are those properties, methods, and events which already exist in your control. For this example, remove all of the selected Names and click Next. The next form displays so you can add your own custom property, method, and event names to your user control. Click the New button to add a custom member to the list (see Figure 33.11).

**FIG. 33.9**

Choosing the Control to create properties, events, and methods.

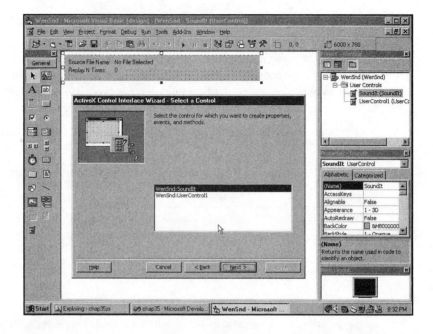

**FIG. 33.10**

Selecting the Interface Members.

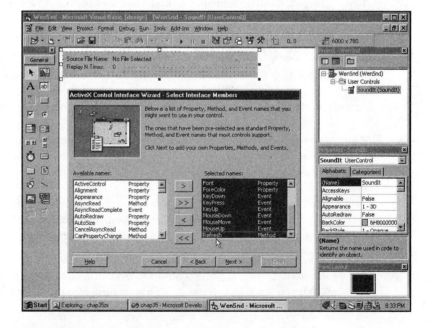

Enter "Source" as the Name and ensure that the type is property. Click OK and then repeat the process for "Repeat". When finished, the My Custom Members list should have both of the names listed in it. Click Next to proceed. This next step in the process allows you to map the functions of the *public* property, method, or event names to the underlying *private* property, method, or event names on your user control. To map a property, you have to select a public name, then in the Maps To frame, choose the control and the required member (see Figure 33.12).

**FIG. 33.11**
Adding any Custom Interface Members that the control might need to operate properly.

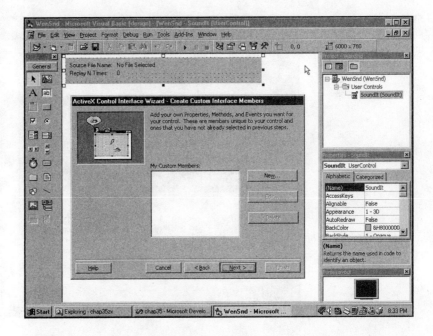

**FIG. 33.12**
Assigning the public properties to the internal control elements on the form.

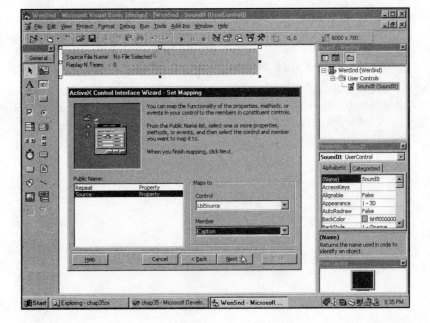

For the control to work, you have to map the source property to the `LblSource` control and its `Caption` member. Do not map the `Repeat` property to any private control. Click <u>N</u>ext to set the attributes of the `Repeat` property (see Figure 33.13).

**FIG. 33.13**

Setting the attributes of the new properties.

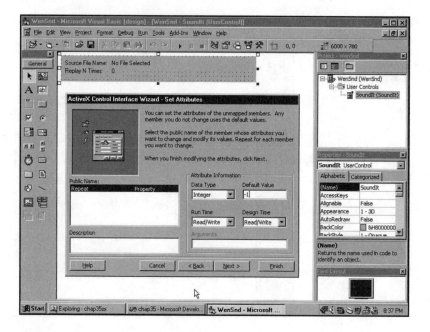

This allows you to control what is entered by the developer. Set the `Repeat` datatype to `Integer` and the default value to `-1`. You can also enter a description of this member at this time. When you are satisfied with what you have entered, click <u>F</u>inish to complete the process. The wizard will generate a summary file that is displayed (see Figure 33.14). This file will list the steps needed to test and debug the control you created. After browsing this list, close the form.

Because a design-time control will generate HTML code, you can test only the developer interface portion of the control in the Visual Basic IDE. Now that all of the properties have been defined, you can create the Property Page the user will work with.

**FIG. 33.14**

The Summary To Do List File from the wizard helps you to know what to do next.

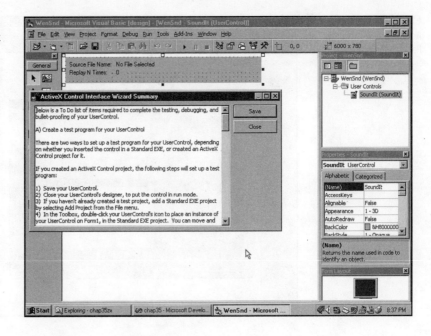

## Adding a Property Sheet to the Control

The property page is really a standard Visual Basic form that interacts with the HTML developer (see Figure 33.2). To design a property page, you must first add one to the project. Right-click anywhere in the project windows and select Add, Property Page to display the "Add Property Page" dialog box. Select the VB Property Page Wizard to help you add the property page to the control. This will display the information form for the wizard; click Next to go to the next step. You can have many property pages defined in a project and you can then select a particular page to use with a given user control. Add a New Property Page and name it, "SoundProp". This new page is automatically added to the list and selected (see Figure 33.15).

Click Next to select the properties that will be displayed on the property page you are creating. Move both displayed properties to the SoundProp list on the left side of the form (see Figure 33.16). Then click Finish to complete the wizard.

Browse the To Do list before closing it. Display the finished property page form so that you can make some changes to it (see Figure 33.17).

Add a square command button named "cmdOpen" to the right side of the source label and put '...' in its Caption property. This button will be used to display the common dialog file open box to allow the user to select a sound file to use. At this moment, you are back to standard Visual Basic programming techniques. Add the Miscrosoft Common Dialog Control 5.0 reference to the Components list to allow you to access it. Next, add the control to the form by double-clicking the control button in the toolbar, then name the control "CmDlg1" and add the following code to the cmdOpen_Click routine:

```
CmDlg1.Filter = "Sound Files (*.wav;*.mid)|*.wav;*.mid"
CmDlg1.ShowOpen
txtSource.Text = CmDlg1.filename
```

Part

IX

Ch

33

**FIG. 33.15**

Adding a new Property Page to the project.

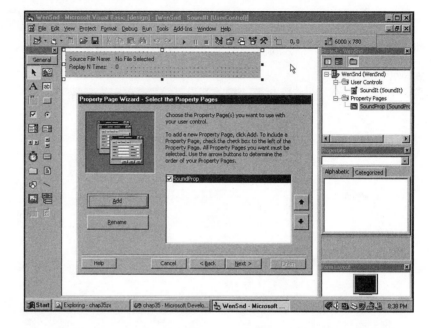

**FIG. 33.16**

Moving Properties to the page.

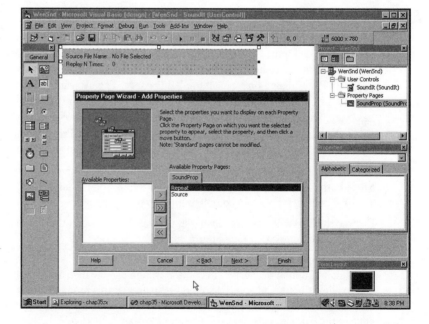

**FIG. 33.17**
Wizard-created
Property Page form.

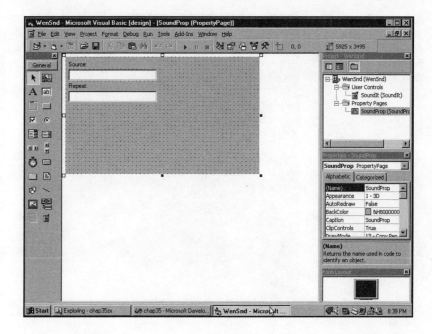

This code will set the filter property and then display the File Open dialog box. When the user selects a file and closes this dialog box, the file name is placed in the LblSource control on the user control form and in the Source property that was defined. Then in the SoundIt controls "Let Repeat" routine, add the following line of code to assign the value entered for the Repeat control to be displayed in the LblRepeat control on the main user control form.

```
LblRepeat.Caption = Repeat
```

You can then test the property page by adding a standard project to the open workspace you are in. This allows you to add the new control, "SoundIt" to the standard form and select "Custom Properties" from the properties windows in Visual Basic (see Figure 33.18). Click the '...' button to display the FileOpen dialog box, select a file, then close the dialog windows and enter a repeat value. Now close the property page and you should see the values you entered displayed in the controls labels.

Part
**IX**

Ch
**33**

**FIG. 33.18**

The ActiveX controls Property Pages, being displayed in Visual Basic.

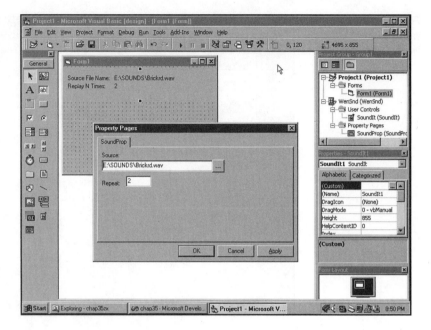

## Adding the Design-Time References and Code

In order for design-time controls to pass runtime text to the HTML page, it needs to have some additional, special handling done by the host server. Design-time controls implement an interface called IActiveDesigner that allows the container to retrieve the runtime text of the control. This interface gives the ActiveX control you have just created the ability to set HTML text and have it inserted into the HTML page that the control is placed.

To have Visual Basic 5 be able to use this interface, you need to add the reference to the "Microsoft Web Design-Time Control Type Library." To add this reference, open Project, References, and scan the list of available references. If this type library is listed, select it and then click OK.

> **N O T E**  If you do not find it, you should install the design-time control SDK that comes on the Visual InterDev product disk in client/vintdev/misc/sdk. ▓

Once you have the references set properly, you need to have the control *implement* the interface that you need. To do this, you would add the following line of code to the General Declarations section of the user controls code.

```
Implements IProvideRuntimeText
```

The Implements statement is new to Visual Basic 5 and allows you to add a class in a type library to a Visual Basic program. Visual Basic would then implement the class's methods with the corresponding methods in Visual Basic.

When you add this statement, there will be a new control called `IProvideRuntimeText` added to your control. The only event that it has is the `GetRuntimeText` event. In this event enter the code as shown in the following:.

```
Private Function IProvideRuntimeText_GetRuntimeText() As String
    Dim strText As String, strQuote As String
    strQuote = Chr$(34)
    strText = "<BGSOUND SRC=" & strQuote & "file:///" & _
              lblSource.Caption & strQuote
    strText = strText & " LOOP=" & strQuote & Repeat & strQuote & ">"
    IProvideRuntimeText_GetRuntimeText = strText
End Function
```

This code is what actually builds the HTML tag code for the BGSOUND tag. As you can see, it uses the input from the property page and includes this input in the strings being created. Finally, it sets a special variable called `IProvideRuntimeText_GetRuntimeText` to that string. This is the variable accessed by the HTML editor when it needs to build the HTML code in the Web page.

You are now ready to compile the control as an OCX. You use the same process as you would when compiling a standard Visual Basic application. From the menu choose File, Make SoundIt.Ocx. Once the control is compiled successfully there is one last thing that you need to do before you can use it in Visual InterDev as a design-time control.

Design-time controls need to be registered on the PC where they are to be used. The registration is done the same way any other ActiveX control would be registered. Unfortunately, Visual Basic 5 does not provide a way to write code that runs when a control is registered. This means that your design-time control is not set up automatically when it is used the first time. Until there is a way to do this from within the Visual Basic code, you will need to use a program called Regsvrdc.exe that registers the design-time control. This program is run from the DOS interface and can be run from the setup program that will install your control. The syntax for this program is as follows:

REGSVRDC [/U] [/S] control [+ control]

where *Control* specifies the control(s) to register as design-time controls. The two parameters that can be used are:

/U    Unregisters the control as design-time control.

/S    Silent. Outputs no messages.

An example of the use of this program is:

```
Regsvrdc websnd.SoundIt
```

Once you have registered your control, continue on to test your control.

## Testing the Completed Design-Time Control

To test the control you just created, you need to start Visual InterDev and open the Workspace that you created earlier in this chapter. To add the design-time control follow these steps:

Part
IX

Ch
33

1. Add a new HTML page to the Web application and name it `'SoundOff'`.

2. Place the cursor in the HTML text to set the location for the design-time control to be inserted.

3. From the menu, select <u>I</u>nsert, Into <u>H</u>TML, Active<u>X</u> Control.

4. From the Insert ActiveX Control dialog box (see Figure 33.19) click the Design-Time tab and select the `websnd.soundit` control that should be listed there and click OK.

**FIG. 33.19**

ActiveX Control Insert dialog box showing the newly created design-time control.

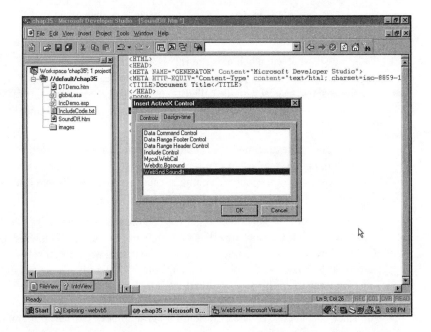

5. This will display the design-time control and its property page (see Figure 33.20). The property page will respond the same way it did when you tested it in Visual Basic.

6. Select a sound file from your PC and then close the control to see the HTML text that is added to your HTML page (see Figure 33.21).

> **WARNING**
>
> Although you can modify the text that is generated, any changes you might make will be blown away the next time the design-time control is edited.

Preview the HTML page you have created, but make sure that you have your speakers turned on so you can hear the results of your efforts.

**FIG. 33.20**

The new control showing the property page associated with it.

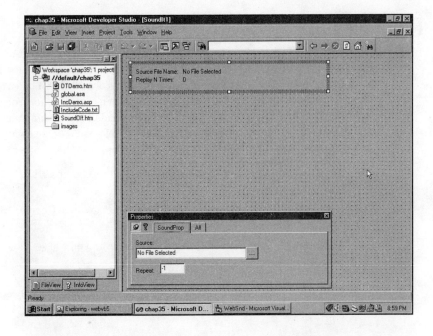

**FIG. 33.21**

The HTML text that is generated by the design-time control.

Part

**IX**

Ch

**33**

**TIP** If you want to prevent the design-time control from being shown in the text, you must use Active Server Pages (.ASP) that will be processed by the Active Server. When the Active Server sees a METADATA comment, it will strip it from the file before processing. This leaves behind just the runtime text of the design-time control. This step occurs before any other logic so the run-time text is fully active.

# From Here...

This chapter showed you how to meld your knowledge of Visual Basic, ActiveX control design, and the desire to create Web application tools. What you have seen is how to build a simple ActiveX control by using Visual Basic. You have also learned what it takes to make an ActiveX control into a design-time control that can be used in an HTML editor. You can take what you have learned in this chapter to build more complex and useful design-time controls for use by yourself or to distribute to other Web application developers. The following chapters will help you understand some of the concepts that were discussed in this chapter.

- For more information on creating your own ActiveX controls, see Chapter 3, "Building ActiveX Controls with VB."

- To get a better understanding of Active Server Pages, see Chapter 13, "Active Server Pages and Server-Side Scripting."

- In Chapter 34, "Integrating Visual Basic with Java," you will see how to integrate Visual Basic with Java.

# Integrating Visual Basic with Java

**A**lthough I agreed to write this chapter, it was odd to find it included in a book on Web programming with Visual Basic. To me, Java and Visual Basic seemed an unlikely pair. It is true that the Java programming language and the World Wide Web are made for each other. It is also true that this book is on Web programming. So it makes some sense to include the chapter, but I was not completely convinced. However, by the time I had finished writing the sample programs for it I was more than convinced that the book would not be complete without this chapter.

What changed my mind? The answer to this question is not as straightforward as you would expect. The marriage of Visual Basic and Java did not unleash in me an unrealized creative potential; on the contrary, it was at times frustrating. When you look over the examples covered in this chapter you might look at the number of steps needed to access a Java class from Visual Basic and scream derogatory comments about Microsoft. I sure did. You might be disappointed to find that Java's ability to create ActiveX Controls is not what you expected. I sure was. But if you look past the present limitations and forward a release or so you will see the possibilities of leveraging hard-won Visual Basic skills with Java and Microsoft's ActiveX technologies, such as ActiveX Documents and ActiveX Controls, to produce applications that will run on multiple platforms. All without the hassles of the machine-dependent issues encountered with languages such as C++.

This will not come overnight. The potential will be realized, I suspect, over the next year or so. The first step is for Microsoft to provide a wizard that is more seamlessly integrated within Visual J++, to allow for the quick creation of ActiveX Controls, as well as expand the type of controls that can be created with it. Currently, only automation servers can be created. More on these limitations later in the chapter. The second step, which is the more crucial and admittedly more uncertain, is for Microsoft and other companies such as Netscape, Sun, and Apple, to provide support for the full suite of ActiveX technologies within their respective Java environments. This remains to be seen and has a long way to go from the current position where Internet Explorer, Visual J++, and Microsoft's Java Virtual Machine are the only ones in their respective categories supporting the ActiveX technologies.

Having discussed the motivation of this chapter and the potential future, let's look at the present because there are still useful things that can be accomplished even with the current state of technology. There are presently two major ways for Visual Basic to execute Java source code, both of which rely on ActiveX. One uses Visual J++'s support for the creation of ActiveX Controls. The other uses Visual Basic support for ActiveX Documents to launch a Java applet. Both will be covered, as you can see from the following list of major topics discussed within this chapter. ■

# Understanding Java

You need to understand the Java programming language to get the most out of this chapter. Since Java is a relatively new language, and for many users may be their first exposure, I have included this quick overview. It is intended to give just enough background from which to follow the discussions in the chapter.

## A Very Short History of Java

The Java language has taken the programming world by storm. It seems that overnight it has captivated the industry's imagination. Although it is true that Java as a language for the World Wide Web is a recent arrival, the core language dates to the early 90s. At that time a team at Sun Microsystems developed a language to facilitate communication among consumer electronics devices. Sun tried unsuccessfully a number of times to license this language, named OAK, and related technologies. In 1994, Sun added a few features to OAK and repositioned it as a language ideal for the World Wide Web. They decided to distribute the language and a Web browser with an OAK interpreter for free. This time things worked out well; Sun made a licensing agreement with Netscape Communications Corporation to include OAK support within its browser. With Java as its new name, the language was officially released May 23, 1995. Since then, Java continues to gain momentum in the industry with companies such as Apple, IBM, and Microsoft making it a cornerstone of their strategic planning.

# What Is Java?

With the short history lesson behind us, this brings us to the question: What really is Java? In a nutshell it is an interpreted, object-oriented programming language, strongly influenced by C++ that is intended to run in environments with limited hardware capabilities. It is ideal for Web-based programming because of built-in support for networking, extensive security features, such as the elimination of pointer data types, portability, and CPU independence. Since Java source code is compiled into an intermediate form known as bytecode an application written in Java can run on any machine in which a Java Virtual Machine exists.

Java is like most modern languages. It has a rich set of operators, data types, and flow control statements. See Table 34.1 for some comparisons with those found in Visual Basic. It supports object-oriented design concepts such as encapsulation, inheritance, and polymorphism via the class mechanism like C++ and Visual Basic. However, unlike Visual Basic it has no limitation on its support of inheritance and polymorphism. The other major difference between Visual Basic and Java, with regard to this chapter, is that Java does not support global data objects or global functions. This may seem strange but neither feature is needed in Java to support the object-oriented design paradigm. This, by the way, is the only paradigm it was designed to support. This is different from Visual Basic, which has strong procedural roots that can be traced back to the language, BASIC, developed at Dartmouth University. The concept of classes is just a recent addition to Visual Basic, added in release 4.0. Many applications rich with features have been designed and implemented with Visual Basic without using either the object-oriented design paradigm or the class mechanism. This is in contrast to Java, which forces you to use classes because no function can exist out of the class structure, and through their use leads you to adopt object-oriented design methodology for your application.

**Table 34.1  Select Operators, Data Types, and Flow Control Statements**

| Java | Visual Basic |
| --- | --- |
| && | And |
| >= | >= |
| \| | Xor |
| int | Integer |
| boolean | Boolean |
| float | Single |
| if…else… | If…Then…Else…End If |
| while… | While…Wend |
| for… | For…Each…Next |

Part
IX

Ch
34

The last thing we need to cover before we move on to our first example is the structure of a Java program. Java applications come in two forms, *applications* and *applets*. The applet is intended to run within a Web browser such as Microsoft Internet Explorer. It has restricted access to the resources of the local machine with no file access capabilities whatsoever. A Java application on the other hand has no such restrictions and is no different from any other application created with C++ except that it needs the Java Virtual Machine to execute. The language specification does support Just In Time compilation of Java bytecode, but for the most part, Java applications and applets still use the interpreter. With a little luck, this will change in the future.

# Combining Visual Basic and Java via ActiveX Controls

Finally, the meat of this chapter. In this section, we introduce the first of the two mechanisms that allow Visual Basic to access source code written with Java. The first covered in this section leverages Visual J++'s support for the creation of ActiveX Controls to expose public members of a Java class to Visual Basic and the second covered towards the end of the chapter uses Visual Basic support for ActiveX Documents to launch a Java applet. We will start this section with a short discussion of ActiveX Controls produced with Visual J++, then move on to cover the steps necessary to create them and end by presenting a sample application.

## Visual J++'s Variety of ActiveX Controls

Someone at Microsoft must really love ActiveX technologies. They seem to come out of the woodwork. We have ActiveX Controls, ActiveX Documents, and ActiveX Objects. To help me gain a handle on ActiveX, I developed two rules. The first is that most ActiveX technologies are OLE technologies with a new name plus or minus a few interfaces. For example, ActiveX Documents are Office Binder Documents plus a few interfaces, and ActiveX Controls are OLE or OCX controls minus a few interfaces. The second rule is that the definitions of ActiveX technologies are subject to change. Again as an example, take ActiveX Controls whose definition has expanded to include OLE Automation, now known as Automation. This can be very confusing to the developer but beneficial to Microsoft since by expanding the definition they can claim support for the creation of ActiveX Controls where previously there was only support for Automation. Since Visual J++ supports the creation of automation servers, Microsoft can now state that by definition it also supports the creation of ActiveX Controls. This was not quite what I expected and imposes the following limitation on ActiveX Controls created with Visual J++:

- They are unable to expose a user interface.
- They are unable to send notification events to their container.
- They are unable to communicate with other automation servers.

It should be noted that the first two limitations are inherent in being an automation server and the last is imposed by the Java language since the language is unaware of OLE.

# Exposing a Java Class via Automation

If you have ever created an automation server before using another language, you are well aware of the number of steps necessary to do so. Creating an automation server with Visual J++ is no different. There are a number of steps as you can see from the following list:

1. Create an ODL (Object Description Language) description of the interface.
2. Build the type library.
3. Create a Java description of the interface.
4. Implement the interface in Java.
5. Register the Java class.

I will do my best to walk you through each one to explain the mechanics of the step, as well as to try to convey its purpose. I have chosen not to use Visual J++'s ActiveX Wizard for this example for two reasons. The first is I found the ActiveX Wizard not as seamlessly integrated within the IDE as Visual C++'s wizard and consequently a little confusing. The second is by eliminating the need to integrate into the discussion ActiveX Wizard, I am in a better position to focus on the current details. Afterward I will come back to the ActiveX Wizard and provide an example on how to use it.

**Step 1: Create an ODL Description of the Interface**   My previous attempt at listing the preceding steps had "Create an ODL description of the interface" as the second step after "Implement the interface in Java." The choice of what to put first reminds me of the old question; which came first, the chicken or the egg? It does not matter in what order you write, the Java Class or the ODL file; the end result is a Java Class that is an automation server. However, to focus on the relationship between the COM interface specified in the ODL file and the Java class which implements it, I have chosen to discuss creating the ODL description first. This is an important relationship because it is how Microsoft adds Automation support to Java without extending the language. In short, Microsoft has overloaded Java's "implements" keyword by expanding it to indicate that the class implements not only interfaces created in Java but those created within an ODL file. What does this mean? Well, a class can inherit from its parent either an interface or an interface and its implementation. Unlike C++, Java distinguishes between the two with a separate keyword for each. When a class inherits an interface the keyword "implements" is used to indicate that the class will provide an implementation for each function contained within the interface, as the following code shows:

Part
**IX**

Ch
**34**

```java
interface MyInterface
{
     void Greeting(String g);
}

class MyGreeting implements MyInterface
{
     public void Greeting(String g)
     {
          System.out.println(g);
     }
}
```

Microsoft realized that they could use the keyword to also indicate that the Java class is implementing a COM interface. So Java source code will look the same as before, except "MyInterface" will no longer be defined as earlier but will be specified within an ODL file.

Now for the specifics, an ODL file used by an automation server created with Visual J++ has three sections: the Library, CoClass, and Interface sections. See Listing 34.1 for an example.

The library section specifies the name of the type library and its attributes. The following is a segment of the ODL file found in Listing 34.1 which describes the type library ExposeJavaClassesViaCOM.odl:

```
[
    uuid (D9B15DA0-720F-11d0-A85B-444553540000),
    version (1.0),
    helpstring("LExposeJavaClassesViaCOM Type Library")
]
library LExposeJavaClassesViaCOM
{
    // Both the CoClass and Interface section are contained within the braces
}
```

The name of the library in this case is LExposeJavaClassesViaCOM. It is a convention to prefix the name of a type library with the letter 'L' just as it is a convention to prefix the name of each interface with 'I' and each CoClass with 'C'. The library has three attributes: a UUID, a version number, and a help string. Of the three attributes UUID is the only mandatory one. See the side bar "Globally and Universal Unique Identifiers" for a discussion of what UUIDs are and how to generate one.

---

### Globally and Universal Unique Identifiers

A Globally Unique Identifier (GUID) and a Universal Unique Identifier (UUID) serve the same purpose; they are used as names for COM interfaces. They are generated from a time-stamp and a machine-specific identifier such as the MAC address of a network card. GUID is the name used with ODL (Object Description Language), and UUID is the name used with IDL (Interface Definition Language). ODL was created to support OLE Automation but since has been merged into IDL, which is a more general language used to create type libraries for COM objects that support other interfaces besides OLE Automation.

To generate a GUID, run the program guidgen.exe by selecting the Create GUID menu item found under Visual J++'s Tools menu. The program appears as shown in Figure 34.1. You'll see four radio buttons, each with a GUID in a different format. Select the fourth radio button to generate the format found in the system registry and used within ODL files. When the application is launched a GUID is automatically generated. To copy the GUID to the clipboard, click the Copy button. To generate another GUID, press the New GUID button. A help file, GUIDGEN.HLP, gives more detail on the different formats each radio button produces and can also be found in the bin directory with guidgen.exe.

---

> **N O T E** For the record, a MAC address is unique to each network card and used by the media
> access control layer of the IEEE 802.2 network protocol specification to reference the
> network card. ■

**FIG. 34.1**
Guidgen.exe, which
ensures that your COM
interface has a
completely unique
name.

A library can contain multiple interfaces. In ExposeJavaClassesViaCOM.odl there are three.
Here's one of them:

```
[
    odl,
    uuid(D9B15DA1-720F-11d0-A85B-444553540000),
    helpstring("IFactorial Interface"),
    oleautomation,
    dual
]
interface IFactorial : IDispatch
{
    // The methods exported by the interface
    [helpstring("Describes the Java class method recursive")]
    HRESULT recursive([in] int posIntOrZero, [out, retval] double *retval);

    [helpstring("Describes the Java class method iterative]
    HRESULT iterative([in] int posIntOrZero, [out, retval] double *retval);
}
```

The name of the interface is IFactorial. It is derived from IDispatch. This is required for all dual
interfaces whose definition we will come back to shortly. Each interface description has a
UUID and a help string, as well as three other attributes that are required and specific to an
interface description. The first, odl, identifies the interface as an Object Description Language
interface. The second, oleautomation, indicates that the return types, parameters, and such of
the interface's methods are compatible with OLE Automation. The third, dual, indicates that
the interface exposes its properties and methods through IDispatch, as well as directly
through a Vtabel.

Until recently, Visual Basic required OLE Automation servers to expose their interfaces
through IDispatch. Please refer to an OLE technologies reference for a more detailed

**Part**
**IX**

**Ch**
**34**

discussion. I have found the discussion in Chapter 4 of David Chappell's book, *Understanding ActiveX and OLE*, by Microsoft Press a good starting point, although it is not a technical reference. The body of the interface section is the description of the methods exposed by the interface. Each method can also have attributes. I have decided to supply a help string attribute for each method that is straightforward. The tricky part is how to specify the return type and parameters. Let's take a closer look at one of IFactorial's methods and the corresponding Java function that implements it.

```
// ODL file entry
HRESULT iterative([in] int posIntOrZero, [out, retval] double *retval);

// Java function that implement it
double iterative(int posIntOrZero)
```

Notice that the ODL file entry has iterative returning an HRESULT, but the Java function returns a double. How can this be you ask? It is required that all OLE Automation interface methods return an HRESULT, and every method in the ExposeJavaClassesViaCOM.odl file does so.

To allow for different return types, ODL provides the ability to pass the return value as a function parameter retval, as shown in the preceding example. The next item that we need to cover is the distinction between parameters marked with the "in" attribute, such as posIntOrZero, which are passed by value and cannot be modified, and those marked with the "out" attribute, which are passed by reference with the intent of being modified. The last item we need to cover is the differences between an ODL type and a Java type. For example, if you need to pass or return a Java String class, its equivalent ODL type is BSTR. This by far is the most difficult part of creating a Java automation server. I have listed more Java types and their equivalent ODL types in Table 34.2. I have also tried to use different types throughout the sample application for you to use as a reference.

### Table 34.2   Select Java Data Types and Their ODL Equivalents

| ODL | Java |
| --- | --- |
| boolean | boolean |
| short | short |
| int | int |
| int64 | long |
| long | int |
| float | float |
| double | double |
| void | void |
| BSTR | class java.lang.String |
| IDispatch | class java.lang.Object |

| ODL | Java |
|-----|------|
| IUnknown | interface com.ms.com.IUnknown |
| VARIANT | class com.ms.com.Variant |
| SAFEARRAY (*typename*) | class com.ms.com.SafeArray |

For each interface specified, a coclass entry needs to be provided as done for the following IFactorial interface:

```
// The coclass that implements the CFactorial interface
[
    uuid (D9B15DA4-720F-11d0-A85B-444553540000),
    helpstring("Class that calculates the factorial of a number using Java"),
    appobject
]
coclass CFactorial
{
    interface IFactorial;
};
```

The purpose of the coclass is to specify the name of the class that will implement each interface. In this case, if you search the Java source file for the sample application (see Listing 34.1) you will find that the Java class CFactorial implements the IFactorial Automation interface. The appobject attribute makes the functions and properties of the coclass globally available in the type library.

---

**Listing 34.1** *ExposeJavaClassesViacom.odl*: **ODL for Sample Application**

```
// Filename: ExposeJavaClassesViaCOM.odl
// Copyright (c) 1997 by Robert K. Amenn

// This describes the library LExposeJavaClassesViaCOM
[
    uuid (D9B15DA0-720F-11d0-A85B-444553540000),
    version (1.0),
    helpstring("LExposeJavaClassesViaCOM Type Library")
]
library LExposeJavaClassesViaCOM
{
    // Imports various predefined interfaces like IDispatch
    importlib("stdole32.tlb");

  [
    odl,
    uuid(D9B15DA1-720F-11d0-A85B-444553540000),
    helpstring("IFactorial Interface"),
    oleautomation,
    dual
  ]
interface IFactorial : IDispatch
```

*continues*

**Listing 34.1   Continued**

```
{
    // The methods exported by the interface
    [helpstring("Describes the Java class method recursive")]
    HRESULT recursive([in] int posIntOrZero, [out, retval] double *retval);

    [helpstring("Describes the Java class method iterative")]
    HRESULT iterative([in] int posIntOrZero, [out, retval] double*retval);
}

// The coclass that implements the CFactorial interface
[
    uuid (D9B15DA4-720F-11d0-A85B-444553540000),
    helpstring("Class that calculates the factorial of a number using Java"),
    appobject
]
coclass CFactorial
{
    interface IFactorial;
};

}
```

**Step 2: Build the Type Library**   Before we get into the details of creating a *type* library, I would like to discuss what type libraries are and what their purpose is. In the previous section, you learned about how to describe a COM interface using ODL. A type library is a binary form of that description. It is used by an automation client, such as a Visual Basic application, to bind to the server. It is created with the mktyplib.exe command-line utility distributed with Visual J++. To generate a type library for the ExposeJavaClassesViaCOM.odl, run the following from a command prompt:

```
mktyplib.exe ExposeJavaClassesViaCOM.odl /nocpp
```

The /nocpp switch is used to prevent the C pre-processor from being called. This is a required switch on machines that do not have a recent version of Visual C++ installed. One note before we move on. If a development environment is currently using a type library that you wish to modify, you need to free it by closing the development environment. Otherwise, mktyplib.exe will fail, reporting error M0003.

**N O T E**   All command-line utilities discussed in this chapter can be found in the bin subdirectory of
Visual J++. On my system, the full path to the subdirectory would be C:\Program Files\
DevStudio\Vj\bin. ■

**Step 3: Create a Java Description for the Interface**   The description contained within an ODL file specifies a COM interface, which we will implement shortly by using Java. Before this can happen, however, we need to generate a Java class file for each COM interface contained within the ODL. These class files will contain information needed by the Java compiler. They are created with the javatlb.exe command-line utility distributed with Visual J++. To do this for ExposeJavaClassesViaCOM.tlb, type the following at the command prompt:

```
javatlb ExposeJavaClassesViaCOM.tlb
```

All the Java class files generated will be placed in the Java\TrustLib\ ExposeJavaClassesViaCOM directory, which is created by javatlb.exe if necessary. The full path to this subdirectory on my local machine is C:\Windows\Java\TrustLib\ ExposeJavaClassesViaCOM. The Java directory and the subdirectory TrustLib were created when I installed the Java Virtual Machine that comes with Microsoft Internet Explorer. This may be different for your machine, it depends on the directory in which you installed Windows.

 I have found it helpful to add to the Visual J++ Tools menu a menu item for both the mytylib.exe and javatlb.exe command-line utilities. This is done by selecting the Tools tab of the dialog box displayed and by selecting the Customize menu item under the Tools menu. Make sure that the Prompt For Arguments check box is checked, so when you run either utility you will be prompted for the corresponding input file.

**Step 4: Implement the Interface in Java**    With Steps 1-3 completed we are now ready to concentrate on writing a Java implementation for the IFactorial COM interface. The following code is an abridged version of the CFactorial class. For clarity of discussion I removed the body of each function since they are not needed here. See the CD-ROM packaged with this book for a complete version. This class implements both functions specified by the IFactorial interface described in ExposeJavaClassesViaCOM.odl.

```
import exposejavaclassesviacom.*;

class CFactorial implements Ifactorial
{

    public double recursive(int posIntOrZero)
    {
        // Calculates the factorial of posIntOrZero using recursion
    }

    public double iterative(int posIntOrZero)
    {
        // Calculates the factorial of posIntOrZero using iteration
    }
}
```

To indicate to the Java compiler that CFactorial implements the IFactorial interface, use the following:

```
class CFactorial implements IFactorial
```

Looking at the Java source, it does not seem any different from how you would implement an interface specified with Java; to be precise, it is identical. The only noticeable difference is the addition of the following at the top of the source file, which contains the implementation of the CFactorial class:

```
import exposejavaclassesviacom.*;
```

Here again Microsoft is overloading an existing Java keyword to provide a mechanism for its compiler to locate the Java class, which we generated in Step 3. This contains, as mentioned previously, a description so that the compiler can understand the IFactorial interface. On my machine, this file would be in the C:\Windows\Java\TrustLib\ExposeJavaClassesViaCOM directory. Notice that the import keyword takes a relative path to the class files with the root of the path specified in the HKEY_LOCAL_MACHINE\SOFTWARE\Microsoft\Java VM\ TrustedLibsDirectory system registry setting and the * is used to indicate to import all of the classes in that directory. Now wasn't that easy. We have one more step to go.

---

### For the Java Programmer

When designing classes to be accessed with OLE Automation please keep the following in mind:

- Since Automation servers cannot reside in a Web browser any class that implements one can not extend the Applet class contained within the package java.applet.

- The current implementation will not allow member functions of classes declared public to be accessed with Automation.

- The OLE naming convention calls for class names to have the uppercase "C" as a prefix.

- You are unable to access data members directly; they must be accessed via a get and put method. For an example, please see the class CFrameWindow in exposejavaclassesviacom.java. Both these functions have been specified so the count data member of CFrameWindow can be accessed by an automation client.

---

**Step 5: Register the Java Class**   The last step before the Java automation server can be accessed by Visual Basic is to register it. This needs to be done for each Java class that implements a COM interface. The purpose for this is to store in the system registry all the information needed to bind the COM interface to its implementation. This is done with the javareg.exe command-line utility distributed with Visual J++ as follows:

> javareg /register /class: CFactorial /clsid:{D9B15DA4-720F-11d0-A85B-444553540000}

When the preceding line is executed, the Java class CFactorial will be registered. The command switches are straightforward and do not need much explanation:

- /register registers the class
- /unregister will do the opposite
- /class specifies the Java class to be registered
- /clsid specifies the UUID for the Java class. This is the same UUID used in ExposeJavaClassesViaCOM.odl

## The Sample Application

Figure 34.2 is a sample application VBCallsJavaClassesViaCOM.exe.

**FIG. 34.2**

A look at this section's sample, VBCallsJava-ClassesViaCOM.exe.

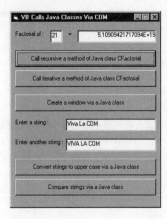

Its sole purpose is pedagogical in nature. When creating it, I tried to add functionality that provided clear examples of passing different data types between Visual Basic and Java. I will not cover the sample application in any detail; please refer to the CD-ROM packaged with the book for all of the source code. But before we leave this section, I would like to go over just how to access public member functions of a Java class from Visual Basic. The first step is to select the type library from Visual Basic's reference dialog as shown in Figure 34.3.

**FIG. 34.3**

Visual Basic's reference dialog allows you to include within the Visual Basic environment the necessary information to access COM objects.

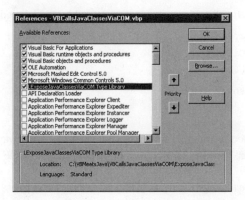

This dialog box can be accessed from the menu item References under Visual Basic's Project menu. This will load the type library and create a reference to objects contained within it. The second step is to declare a variable to hold a reference to the Java class. This can be done with Visual Basic's Dim statement as follows:

```
Dim MyFactorial As IFactorial
Dim MyFrameWindow As IFrameWindow
```

You will notice that here we do not refer to the Java class name but the name of the COM interface that the class implements. We want these variables to have global scope and so we declare them in the general section of the project.

The last step is to create an instance of the Java class with the new statement and assign it to the reference variable with the set statement as follows:

```
Private Sub Form_Load()
    Set MyFactorial = New CFactorial
    Set MyUsingJavaStrings = New CUsingJavaStrings
    Set MyFrameWindow = New CFrameWindow
End Sub
```

A good place to do this is in the Form_Load method of the application's main form. That's all there is to it. Three easy steps. Now you are ready to use methods or access data members from a Java class. I have included two examples to see how this is done. They both come from the sample application on the CD-ROM. The first is the click method for the command button labeled, "Call iterative a method of Java class CFactorial."

```
Private Sub Command2_Click()
    Dim d As Double
    Dim number As Integer

    number = CInt(MaskEdBox1.Text)
    d = MyFactorial.iterative(number)

    Label5.Caption = CStr(d)
End Sub
```

The second comes from the click method of the command button labeled "Create a window via a Java class."

```
Private Sub Command3_Click()
Dim count As Integer
count = MyFrameWindow.count
Call MyFrameWindow.display
count = MyFrameWindow.count
End Sub
```

Notice how easy it is to access member functions. It is done the same way as any other method from a Visual Basic object. This goes for accessing member data as well.

**N O T E**  If you have trouble running the sample applications in this chapter, please read the readme.txt file on the CD-ROM packaged with this book. ▪

# A Brief Tour of Visual J++'s ActiveX Wizard

In the previous section we covered in detail all of the steps necessary to expose a Java class via Automation. As promised, I will now provide an example of how to use Visual J++'s ActiveX Wizard to do the same. To have a point of reference, I will expose the CFactorial class. We need to perform most of the same steps as before except this time in a different order as outlined in the following list:

1. Implement the interface in Java.
2. Create an IDL (Interface Definition Language) description of the interface.
3. Register the Java class.
4. Build the type library.
5. Modify the Java implementation.

If you look carefully at the preceding list, you will notice, besides the different order, that there are three other differences from the list in the previous section. The first is the elimination of the Step titled "Create a Java Description of the Interface." This is no longer needed because the wizard will automatically generate this information behind the scenes. The second is the addition of the Step "Modify the Java Implementation." This is required because the Java source file will need to be updated to reflect the wizard's output. The last is the replacement of the Step titled "Create an ODL Description of the Interface," with the Step titled "Create an IDL Description of the Interface." This was done to reflect the fact that the wizard uses IDL instead of ODL to describe the interfaces it generates. This is perfectly legal because IDL is a super-set of ODL and will eventually replace the latter.

**Step 1: Implement the Interface in Java**    Previously, we specified the COM interface first and then implemented the Java class. To use the wizard we need to first create and compile the Java class, which we wish to expose via Automation. Listing 34.2 is a file that just contains the CFactorial class used in the previous section. Notice, however, that initially the definition of the CFactorial class does not use the implements keyword. We will need to add it later after we use the ActiveX Wizard to generate an IDL description of the interface.

**Listing 34.2    *CFactorialViaActiveXWizard.java*: Java Source Which Will Become an Implementation of the IFactorail interface**

```
// Filename: CFactorialViaActiveXWizard.java
// Copyright (c) 1997 by Robert K. Amenn

// Java allows for classes to be grouped into what in Java terminology
// is referred to as a package. To access these classes the import
// declaration is used.
import java.awt.*;

class CFactorialViaActiveXWizard
{
    public double recursive(int posIntOrZero) throws IllegalArgumentException
      {
          if(posIntOrZero < 0)
          {
              throw new IllegalArgumentException("Function does not accept
➥negative numbers");
          }
```

Part
IX

Ch
34

*continues*

**Listing 34.2 Continued**

```java
        if(posIntOrZero == 0)
        {
            return 1;
        }
        else
        {
            // Call myself until posIntOrZero equals 0 in which I return 1
            // and then unwind the stack returning finally the factorial of
            // posIntOrZero.
            return posIntOrZero * recursive(posIntOrZero-1);
        }
    }

    public double iterative(int posIntOrZero) throws IllegalArgumentException
    {
        if(posIntOrZero >= 0)
        {

            // Set factorial to 1 so if posIntOrZero is zero we can return 1
            double factorial = 1;

            for(int i = posIntOrZero; i > 0; i--)
            {
                factorial = factorial * i;
            }

            // If posIntOrZero is zero we return 1
            return factorial;
        }
        else
        {
            throw new IllegalArgumentException("Function does not accept
  negative numbers");
        }
    }
```

Since we borrowed the implementation from the previous section, the first step is nearly complete. All that is left to do is compile CFactorialViaActiveXWizard.java to generate the file CFactorialViaActiveXWizard.class and we can move on to the next step.

**Step 2: Create an IDL Description of the Interface**    Start the ActiveX Wizard by selecting the menu item ActiveX Wizard for Java found under Visual J++'s Tools menu. A window appears, as shown in Figure 34.4.

**FIG. 34.4**

ActiveX Component
Wizard for Java - Page 1
of 4: It allows for the
specification of the file
which contains the
bytecode for the Java
class whose functions
need to be exposed, as
well as indicated which
IDL file to use.

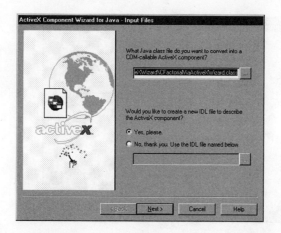

You have two choices for this page. The first is used to indicate the class file that contains the bytecode for the Java class whose functions you wish to expose. The second is whether or not to specify an IDL file or have one generated for the Java class file. For this example, please select the defaults of CFactorialViaActiveXWizard.class and "Yes" to have an IDL file generated. In order for CFactorialViaActiveXWizard.class to be the default you must have CFactorialViaActiveXWizard.java open and selected as the current source file within Visual J++'s IDE. It does seem strange that the wizard needs to access Java byte code instead of source and as of yet I have been unable to come up with a satisfying reason why.

**N O T E** When you request that the ActiveX Wizard generate an IDL file; each public member function of the Java class will become a member of the COM interface contained with the generated file. ■

**Step 3: Register the Java Class** Pressing the "Next" button brings you to the page as shown in Figure 34.5. This page gives you two choices as well. The first is whether you want to specify a CLSID for the COM component or have it generated. For the purpose of this example, allow the CLSID to be generated. The second choice will determine if the class will be registered or not. Select "Yes" since this needs to be done in order to access the Java class' public functions.

**Step 4: Build the Type Library** Pressing the "Next" button this time brings you to the page shown in Figure 34.6.

Part

**IX**

Ch

**34**

**FIG. 34.5**

ActiveX Component Wizard for Java - Page 2 of 4: It allows for the specification of a CLSID and whether or not to register the COM component generated by the wizard.

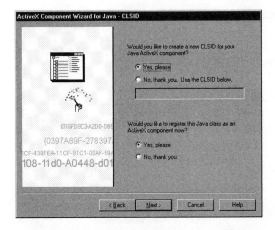

**FIG. 34.6**

ActiveX Component Wizard for Java - Page 3 of 4: It allows for the selection of the type of interface generated as well as determines whether or not you want to generate a type library for the COM component generated by the wizard.

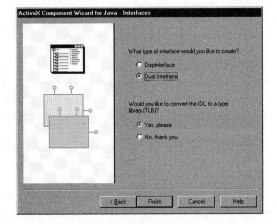

On this page you have the choice of whether you want the COM interface to be a dual interface or just a dispinterface. Select dual interface to be consistent with the previous section. The second choice is to determine whether or not you want to generate a type library. Again select "Yes," since we need it to continue.

**Step 5: Modify the Java Implementation**    Pressing the "Finish" button causes the wizard to generate all the necessary files and then display the final page as shown in Figure 34.7.

We are almost done; the last step is to select the text displayed with the textbox and paste it into the Java source file. For this example, the following text needs to be pasted into CFactorialViaActiveXWizard.java:

```
import cfactorialviaactivexwizardlib.*;

public class CFactorialViaActiveXWizard
    implements cfactorialviaactivexwizardlib.ICFactorialViaActiveXWizard
{
    private static final String CLSID =
        "9896b7c0-c1b5-11d0-8769-00aa00c08146";
```

**FIG. 34.7**

ActiveX Component
Wizard for Java - Page 4
of 4: It contains the
Java source that needs
to be added to the Java
source file which
contains the class
whose functions are
being exported.

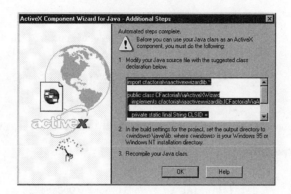

Listing 34.3. shows CFactorialViaActiveXWizard.java with this step completed.

---

**Listing 34.3** *Modified CFactorialViaActiveXWizard.java*: **A Java Implementation of the IFactorial Interface**

```
// Filename: CFactorialViaActiveXWizard.java
// Copyright (c) 1997 by Robert K. Amenn

// Java allows for classes to be grouped into what in Java terminology
// is referred to as a package. To access these classes the import
// declaration is used.
import java.awt.*;
import cfactorialviaactivexwizardlib.*;

public class CFactorialViaActiveXWizard
    implements cfactorialviaactivexwizardlib.ICFactorialViaActiveXWizard
{
    private static final String CLSID =
        "3fe8a9a0-c1b8-11d0-8769-00aa00c08146";

    public double recursive(int posIntOrZero) throws IllegalArgumentException
        {
            if(posIntOrZero < 0)
            {
                throw new IllegalArgumentException("Function does not accept
➥negative numbers");
```

*continues*

Part

IX

Ch

34

**Listing 34.3 Continued**

```
        }

        if(posIntOrZero == 0)
        {
            return 1;
        }
        else
        {
            // Call myself until posIntOrZero equals 0 in which I return 1
            // and then unwind the stack returning finally the factorial of
            // posIntOrZero.
            return posIntOrZero * recursive(posIntOrZero-1);
        }
    }

    public double iterative(int posIntOrZero) throws IllegalArgumentException
    {
        if(posIntOrZero >= 0)
        {

            // Set factorial to 1 so if posIntOrZero is zero we can return 1
            double factorial = 1;

            for(int i = posIntOrZero; i > 0; i--)
            {
                factorial = factorial * i;
            }

            // If posIntOrZero is zero we return 1
            return factorial;
        }
        else
        {
            throw new IllegalArgumentException("Function does not accept
➥negative numbers");
        }
    }
}
```

With this last step, we completed the process. One final note before we move on. If you now
look at the definition of the CFactorial class, it is as follows:

```
public class CFactorialViaActiveXWizard
    implements cfactorialviaactivexwizardlib.ICFactorialViaActiveXWizard
```

It is now using the implements keyword to indicate that the class implements the COM interface ICFactorialViaActiveXWizard.

# Combining Visual Basic and Java via ActiveX Documents

In this section, we will provide another example of how to combine Java and Visual Basic. This time we will launch a Java applet by taking advantage of the support for ActiveX Documents provided by Visual Basic and Microsoft Internet Explorer. Figure 34.8 is a screen shot of this section's sample, ActiveX Document StartJavaApplet.vbd, loaded in Microsoft Internet Explorer. Very unimpressive to say the least. I did not want to spend a lot of time on discussing how to create ActiveX Documents with Visual Basic; Microsoft provides good documentation and a wizard to help you to accomplish this. I wanted to focus on how Visual Basic can launch a Java applet.

**FIG. 34.8**

A screen shot of this section's sample, ActiveX Document StartJavaApplet.vbd, loaded in Microsoft Internet Explorer.

To generate the sample application, I started the ActiveX Document EXE wizard from Visual Basic's New Project dialog box and accepted all default setting as I transversed through the successive dialog boxes present to me. I then added one command button to the ActiveX Document, labeled it "Press to start Java applet," and entered the following code in its click method:

```
Private Sub Command1_Click()
' Create path to SpinningWorld.html

' Need to do this because in the version I used to write this chapter
' Hyperlink.NavigateTo did not support a relative path. This may change
' in future releases.

' Assumes that the path to SpinningWorld.html is relative to StartJavaApplet.vbd
' c:\VbMeetsJava\StartJavaApplet\StartJavaApplet.vbd
' c:\VbMeetsJava\StartJavaApplet\SpinningWorld\SpinningWorld.html
```

```
Dim htmlFile$
htmlFile$ = App.Path
htmlFile = htmlFile & "\SpinningWorld\SpinningWorld.html"

' Load HTML page that contains a reference to Java applet SpinningWorld.java
' This will cause the applet to be executed
UserDocument.Hyperlink.NavigateTo htmlFile
End Sub
```

That is it for the Visual Basic side of the project. It was even easier generating the Java applet for the sample application. I used Developers Studio's wizard to generate a Java applet, again selecting all default settings. This time I was not required to write a single line of code. The applet packaged on the CD-ROM was all generated by Visual J++. That is all there is to it. We are now ready to open the ActiveX Document StartJavaApplet.vbd from within Internet Explorer. Please see readme.txt file contained on the CD-ROM for all necessary details.

# From Here...

In this chapter, we presented two mechanisms that allow Visual Basic to access Java code. The first relied on the support of OLE Automation contained within Microsoft's Java VM to expose public member functions of various Java classes to Visual Basic. The second used an ActiveX Document to execute a Java applet contained within an HTML page. I have tried to give a sense of current possibilities with the current state of technology. I just barely touched on the possibilities that can be realized with a Java automation server. Currently, it is now possible to access most public member functions of a Java class. In the future, hopefully, Microsoft will expand its support of ActiveX technologies within its Java VM, binding code written with Visual Basic and Java that much more closely.

# Appendixes

# Standard CGI, WinCGI, and Visual Basic

**Learn about the Common Gateway Interface**

This appendix shows you the fundamentals of CGI and how to make Internet applications using CGI.

**Learn how to create CGI applications**

Learn how to use streams and environmental variables to make responsive server side applications.

**Make a Guest Book with CGI by using Visual Basic**

Use fundamental CGI concepts and methods to make a Guest Book application in Visual Basic.

The ability to accept and respond to user input is an important feature of any World Wide Web site. HTML technology such as hypertext jumps allow visitors to your Home Page to easily go to other pages and sites on the Internet. Without this ability, your page would be just a dead end on the Information SuperHighway. However, responding to user input using the HTML <HREF> tag, the tag denoting a hypertext jump, has limitations. The only way a visitor can send input to an Internet server is by clicking on hypertext. They cannot enter text or numeric data, such as a search phrase, password, or items for calculation. Also, the response to a hypertext click is "hard coded." The response to the click is the same, no matter who you are or when you click. When you click a piece of HTML hypertext, the hypertext cannot make a decision whether to take you to a given site if you click in the morning or a different one if you click in the evening.

One way to overcome these fundamental limitations of HTML is to have your Web pages accept text and numeric input and then send this data to "data processing" applications that reside on Internet servers. These "data processing" applications then process the submitted data and return it to your site's visitor.

This is what CGI programming is all about— creating applications that reside on an Internet server, that can receive data sent from an Internet client, process that data, and return a response to the sending client. ■

# Understanding CGI

CGI is an acronym for the Common Gateway Interface. The Common Gateway Interface is a specification that defines a standardized data structure and methodology that act as an intermediary between applications that reside on the server and any given Internet client. Applications that reside on an Internet server and use these data structures and methods are called CGI applications. CGI applications are also known as CGI scripts.

Think of it this way. Imagine you are at a food court at your local shopping mall. One booth serves ice cream, one booth serves pizza, and one sells hat and gloves. (The last one used to sell baked potatoes, but baked potatoes didn't go over, so they're now trying apparel.) All booths accept credit cards, your favorite form of payment. You go to order a sundae from the ice cream booth and pay by credit card. At the pizza booth you order a slice of pepperoni and a soda pop. There, you also pay by credit card. Finally, at the hat and glove stall you buy a pair of mittens. Again, you pay by plastic. One form of payment suits all!

Here's how the analogy plays out. The food court is akin to an Internet server, a place where lots of applications can run and can be accessed by the general public. Each booth in the food court is an application on the Internet server. Your activity in the food court is similar to your activity on the Internet. You browse the food court as you would a Web Page and if you see something that interests you, you interact with it.

Finally, your credit card is akin to the Common Gateway Interface. All credit cards have a standardized data structure. All credit cards have an account number, your name, your issuing bank, and expiration date. And, when you run your card for authorization there will be even more standardized data fields generated—purchase amount, time of purchase, place of purchase, and so on. Just by showing up at a booth in the food court and using your card, a standardized structure of information is generated. Now, different vendors will do different things with this information. The ice cream booth will make you a sundae for this information, the pizza booth a slice and a pop, and the hat and glove booth will package a pair of mittens. However, the data structure is identical regardless of who is using it or what they are using it for.

In the Common Gateway Interface some of the information fields that are generated just by calling a CGI application are the name of the server upon which the CGI application resides, the type of server software the Internet server is running, the Internet address of the computer contacting the site and using the CGI application, and the name of the browser being used to access the Internet site. There is more. You can also pass information specific to the interaction between the client and the Internet server, analogous to telling the ice cream booth you want a sundae and the pizza booth you want a slice of pepperoni. Or, asking the guy in the hat and glove booth if he knows where the restrooms are.

The point here is to understand that the Common Gateway Interface is a standardized data structure and methodologies that enable you to invoke and pass data to applications that reside on Internet servers from Internet clients. These applications can perform tasks, make conditional decisions, and can communicate back to the calling client. Also, because the CGI specification support is determined by the Internet server software running on your physical server, any given CGI application can run on a number of platforms, if that server supports CGI, which, by the way, almost all do. Thus, the CGI application that you write for a UNIX system can be run on server software running Windows NT or the MAC OS.

---

### Not all interfaces are graphical

Most people think of an interface as the collection of graphic elements that allows users to interact with modern operating systems such as Windows, the MacOS, or XWindows. These elements are windows, menus, and buttons. However, the word *interface* has a much broader meaning. An interface is a set of data and methods by which objects "expose" themselves for manipulation. Objects can have multiple interfaces, where each interface has different types of access.

For example, a car exposes its steering mechanism to the end user through the steering wheel. However, it also exposes its steering mechanism to a mechanic through its power steering unit. The mechanic has lower level access to the steering mechanism through the power steering unit because he or she has the knowledge and tools to access that particular interface.

An operating system such as Windows 95 works much the same way. It has many different interfaces. There is the graphical interface that shows you graphical elements by which you interact with the functionality and data of the operating system—using the Date/Time dialog box to set the system time, for example. However, there is also a non-graphical interface, the functions and data that the operating system exposes to the programmer that he or she uses when making the functionality of the Date/Time dialog box. The Windows API functions, GetSystemTime() and SetSystemTime(), are two low-level functions that a programmer would use to get or set the system time. These functions are considered part of an interface of the operating system, though not a graphical interface, nor one made available to the end user.

---

# Using CGI

Now that you have a general conceptual overview of CGI, let's take a look at the specific CGI elements: scripts, environmental variables, standard input, standard output, and HTML forms. The set of instructions that make up your CGI application is called a CGI script. Information about the status of the Internet server upon which your script is running and information about the relationship between that server and the calling client is stored in environmental variables. Lastly, the manner by which a client calls and sends information to a CGI script is through URL Encoding and HTML forms.

Figure A.1 shows a diagram of the elements of a CGI interaction between Internet clients and an Internet server. The following sections will take a look at these elements in detail.

**FIG. A.1**

The Elements of the Common Gateway Interface.

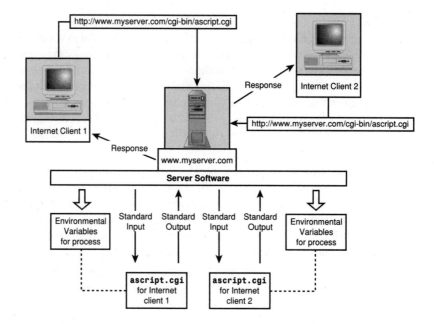

## Scripts

The CGI specification allows CGI scripts on your server to receive and process information sent from a client-side Internet browser such as Netscape Navigator or Internet Explorer. Usually, a CGI script is a program of limited functionality. It is very unusual to use CGI to write an expansive application such as a word processing program. Usually, CGI scripts are used to do things such as search and retrieval, calculation, or data entry.

The early implementations of CGI programs were hosted on UNIX servers. Given such roots, scripts were usually written in languages common to that platform, Perl, C, or a flavor of a UNIX shell language.

Perl is similar to Visual Basic in that it is an interpreted language that requires a runtime module. However, unlike Visual Basic, Perl is character-based, without a graphical development environment. Perl is very fast, making it very popular on UNIX sites that have to process a lot of traffic. Perl is also supported by Windows NT.

C is a compiled language that also offers very fast execution. One of the nice advantages of C is that it is *portable*. That is, CGI source code written in C can be compiled to work on different operating systems. For the most part, all you need to do to make your CGI script operative on various platforms is to compile your script's source code using a compiler native to the operating system. Thus, the source code you write to run on a UNIX server will run on a Windows NT server or on a Macintosh.

> **CAUTION**
>
> Carefully consider the low-level, OS specific requirements of your script before you compile and deploy it!
>
> Though C is considered a portable language, when re-compiling your source code to a specific operating system, you can run into problems. For instance, when you compile C code in VC++ 5.x to run under Windows, the compiler will only issue a warning for variables that are created but not initialized and used. However, uninitialized variables will cause fatal memory errors when running under Internet server software.

Writing a CGI script in a UNIX shell language is similar to writing a batch file in DOS. A shell program is little more than a text file containing a collection of shell commands that are executed by the operating system. Shell scripts can be quite efficient and effective.

### Daemons

In the UNIX world, the program an Internet server uses to invoke CGI scripts and pass data to and from the scripts is called a *daemon*. In the Windows NT environment it is called a *service*. Daemons run continuously, but "out of sight." There are different daemons for different protocols. The most common are HTTP daemons and FTP daemons. HTTP daemons take care of handling Web pages. FTP deamons handle file transfers using the File Transfer Protocol.

## Environmental Variables

When an Internet client calls your CGI script, the daemon (see note) on the server upon which your script resides invokes your script and creates a process space in memory for it. In addition to invoking the script, the daemon creates a set of environmental variables that pertain to the server, your script, and the method and means by which your script was called. These environmental variables are similar to the environmental variables that you've encountered in DOS. By querying the environmental variables of your CGI script's process, you can find out things such as the name or address of your Internet server, the browser being used by your client, the address of the calling Internet client, the length of the data stream sent to the standard input, and much, much more. Environmental variables are a very important and powerful tool that will enable you to write some very effective and robust CGI programs.

**N O T E**    A call to your CGI script is also called a *request*. ∎

Table A.1 shows the server specific environmental variables that you can put to use in your CGI programs. These variables contain information about the state of the server, regardless of what client is calling it or what script is being run.

### Table A.1  Environmental Variables Specific to the Server

| Variable | Purpose |
| --- | --- |
| GATEWAY_INTERFACE | CGI version used by server. |
| SERVER_NAME | Server's IP address or host name. |
| SERVER_PORT | Port from which the HTTP request was received. |
| SERVER_PROTOCOL | Name and version of protocol used by server to process requests. |
| SERVER_SOFTWARE | Name of Internet server software being used. |

The variables in the table above are useful for sending information about the server back to the calling client. Suppose you want to write a CGI script that created a Web page that allowed the user to call another script that resided on the same server as your script. To send the address of the server, you simply get the address assigned to the SERVER_NAME variable and pass it back to the calling client.

Table A.2 shows the environmental variables specific to accommodating a particular HTTP request.

### Table A.2  Environmental Variables Specific to the Request

| Variable | Purpose |
| --- | --- |
| AUTH_TYPE | Authentication scheme used by the server. |
| CONTENT_FILE | File used to pass data to a CGI program, typically used in WinCGI (see Chapter 18). |
| CONTENT_LENGTH | The size of the data, in terms of bytes passed to your CGI script when a POST request is used. |
| CONTENT_TYPE | Type of data being sent to the server. |
| OUTPUT_FILE | File name for the output file, typically used in WinCGI. |
| PATH_INFO | Additional path information passed to server after the script name, but before the query data. |
| PATH_TRANSLATED | Same as PATH_INFO, but with relative paths translated to absolute paths. |
| QUERY_STRING | In the URL, all the data after the question mark symbol (?). |
| REMOTE_ADDR | End user's IP address. |
| REMOTE_USER | User name if authorization was used. |

| Variable | Purpose |
|---|---|
| REQUEST_LINE | The full HTTP request line provided by the server. |
| REQUEST_METHOD | Specifies if data was sent to your script using either the GET method or the POST method. (See the section, HTTP Methods in this appendix for more on the GET and POST methods.) |
| SCRIPT_NAME | The name of your CGI script. |

Most of the work of your CGI script will be done by manipulating the data in the request specific environmental variables, especially the variable QUERY_STRING. QUERY_STRING contains custom data sent to your script by the Internet client. Using the data in the QUERY_STRING variable, you can do things such as determine the criteria for database entry and queries.

▶ For more information about environmental variables, **see** the Que publication, *Special Edition, Using CGI*, ISBN 0-7897-0740-3, Chapter 3, "Standard CGI Environmental Variables" on **p. 57-60**

# URL Encoding

So far we have talked about the role and functionality of scripts and environmental variables. However, we haven't really addressed the question of how data is passed to and from your CGI script. Let's do that now.

Data is sent to your CGI script by the Internet client's browser. Data processed by your CGI script is returned to the client's browser by the HTTP daemon (or service for you NT folks) on the Internet server.

Take a look at how a standard Web page is called in HTML. Listing A.1 shows a portion of HTML code that calls a Web page, www.whitehouse.gov/index.htm.

### Listing A.1  Using the < A HREF> Tag to Call a Web Page

```
<A HREF="http://www.whitehouse.gov/index.htm">Click here to go to the White
House</A>
```

The <A HREF> HTML tag tells the client's browser to request that the Internet server at www.whitehouse.gov send back the page, index.htm when the user clicks the words, "Click here to go to the White House." The HTTP daemon finds that file and sends the .htm file back to the calling client.

Now, lets take a look at the <A HREF> tag in Listing A.2.

---

### Listing A.2    The <A HREF> Tag Used to Call a CGI Script

```
<A HREF="http://www.mysite.com/cgi-bin/fruit.cgi?buy=apples&sell=peaches+plums">
Click here to invoke a CGI script at My Site.</A>
```

---

Listing A.2 shows an <A HREF> tag that requests a CGI script, fruit.cgi. Notice that the calling convention is similar to calling a Web page. As with the Web page request, the tag indicates a request to the Internet server, www.mysite.com. However, things are a little different in the URL after the call to the site. Instead of requesting an .htm file, the tag references a .file in the /cgi-bin directory of the Internet server, www.mysite.com. This file has an extension of .cgi. The HTTP daemon on the Internet server knows that files in the /cgi-bin directory of the server, with an extension, .cgi are CGI scripts and should be invoked as such. How does the daemon know to invoke files with a .cgi extension? When the Internet server was configured, the Webmaster, the person that administers the server, set it up that way. In this case, the CGI script fruit.cgi will be invoked.

---

### HTTP

HTTP stands for Hypertext Transport Protocol. HTTP is the specification that describes how Web pages work on the Internet.

---

Before the daemon invokes that .cgi script, it looks for a "?" symbol. Anything after the question mark is interpreted by the HTTP daemon to be a query string. The question mark separates the query string from the script path. A query string is instance specific information that is passed to the CGI script. In Listing A.2 the query string is "buy=apples&sell= peaches+plums." When the daemon finds data after the question mark, it takes the data and sends it to either the environmental variable, QUERY_STRING, or directly to STDIN (see the side bar, Streams, for a discussion of STDIN) depending on the action method.

**N O T E**    We will discuss action methods later in the section, HTML Forms.    ■

---

### Streams

A way that data is sent to and from a CGI script is by *streams*. Streams have been around for quite a while, back to the prehistoric days of character-based C. One of the advantages of streams is that they were a device independent way of managing data input and output before Windows made device independent programming de riguer. When you are programming using streams, you are really only concerned with receiving data from "input" or sending data to "output." You really don't know or care whether data is coming from a mouse, keyboard, or other computer, or if you are sending it to a monitor or another computer such as an Internet client. It is the operating system's job to negotiate where the data is coming from and where it is going.

The input stream is called standard input, and the output stream is called standard output. In the C/C++ programming environment these are referred to as *stdin* and *stdout*, respectively.

When an Internet client calls your CGI script, it is actually asking the Internet server software to invoke your script. When your script is invoked, it is given its own area of memory in which to run. This memory area is called a *process*. When your script is invoked, its process is given its own standard input and standard output stream. Thus, the Internet server passes data sent by a calling Internet client to the standard input of your script's process. When your script sends data out, it is passing the data though the standard output of that process to the Internet server software via standard output. The Internet server software then passes that data onto the Internet client.

There are other types of streams. There is *stderr*, which is a stream for error messages, *stdprn*, the stream for sending data to a printer, and *stdaux*, which is used for serial communication.

In many ways this stuff really is a bit of a throw back to pre-graphical programming. Object oriented languages such as C++, Delphi, and Java have replaced streams with objects that can still handle data I/O devices independently, but with more power and versatility. However, streams are still applicable and extremely useful, especially for CGI programming.

You construct a query string following a very explicit format described in the HTTP 1.0 Specification. This format is called *URL Encoding*.

The key to using URL Encoding is understanding the form and function of the symbols "?", "=", &" and "+". Table A.3 shows the standard URL Encoding symbols with their associate functionality.

## Table A.3  The URL Encoding Symbols

| Symbol | Function |
|--------|----------|
| ? | Separates URL from query string. |
| = | Separates a variable's name from a variable's value (such as, myvalue=foo). |
| & | Separates one variable name/value pair from another (such as, fruit=apple&vegetable=pea). |
| + | Used to denote a space character (such as, name=Dick+Tracy). |
| % | Used to indicate that the next two characters are the HEX of a given character (such as, the quotation mark character would be sent to a server as, %22). |

**CAUTION**

Keep in mind that URL Encoding is only a specification. You can encode script bound data anyway you want provided the Internet server software can negotiate your convention. However, it is rarely done and not at all advised.

Once a query string has been passed by the HTTP daemon to your script, it is up to your script to parse the string. In most cases you will have to separate each variable into name/value pairs and then separate each name/value pair into usable variables specific to your code. In addition, you'll need to convert "+" symbols to space characters. This is a lot of parsing— dry programming, but nonetheless very necessary.

In the <A HREF> example for requesting a CGI script as shown in Listing A.2, the query string is, buy=apples&sell=peaches+plums. Therefore, once our CGI script gets the string from the QUERY_STRING environment variable or from stdin, to make the data in the string useful, you need to parse the string into the variable name/value pairs, buy=cherries and sell=peaches+plums by removing the ampersand between the pairs. Then, you substitute the space character for the "+" sign between "peaches" and "plums" which results in "sell=peaches plums." From here, you assign the values to variables internal to your script.

# HTTP Methods

When a browser sends data to your CGI script, it isn't just arbitrarily thrown out into cyberspace with the hope that the Internet server can figure things out. Rather, the data is first collected and assembled in an HTML <FORM>. Then the data is sent to your script as specified in the HTTP protocol. The manner by which data is passed to your CGI script is called the *method*. The methods that are most commonly used in CGI programming are GET and POST.

> **N O T E**   In addition to GET and POST, there are other methods such as PUT and HEAD, but they are rarely used.

> **N O T E**   Take a look at the section, HTML Forms for a detailed discussion of the HTML <FORM> tag.

You set the HTTP method as an argument within the HTML <FORM> tag as shown in Listing A.3.

### Listing A.3   Using the METHOD= Argument in an HTML Form

```
<FORM METHOD=POST ACTION="http://www.mysite.com/cgi-bin/fruit.cgi">
 .
 .
 .
</FORM>
```

The HTTP method by which data is sent to your CGI script is reported in the environmental variable, REQUEST_METHOD.

**GET**   By default, all requests that a browser sends to an Internet server use the GET method. When you send data to an Internet server using the GET method, the data gets tacked onto the end of the URL and sent to the QUERY_STRING environment variable by the HTTP daemon.

You poll the environmental variable, QUERY_STRING to get incoming data. However, be advised, the QUERY_STRING environment variable has a maximum size of 255 characters. If you need to pass data to your CGI script that may exceed 255 characters, you need to use the POST method.

**POST**   The POST method is more commonly used for passing data to CGI scripts. The difference between the GET and POST methods is that while the GET method tells the HTTP daemon to send the incoming data to the environment variable, QUERY_STRING, the POST method tells the HTTP daemon to send the URL encoded data directly to Standard Input.

With the POST method your CGI script accesses that data by first setting up an area in memory, the size of which is defined in the environmental variable, CONTENT_LENGTH. Then, once the memory has been allocated, your script polls STDIN for its contents and copies that data over to the allocated memory for further manipulation. The advantage of using POST is that you can send data that exceeds 255 bytes in size to the Internet server.

There is a small inconsistency in the way in which various Internet servers respond to the POST method. Some Internet servers may respond to the POST method by not only sending data to STDIN but also by sending the incoming data to the environmental variable, QUERY_STRING. But don't depend on it. Some servers do and some servers don't.

Figures A.2 and A.3 show the return values from the CGI program methods.cgi. (method.cgi comes on the disk that accompanies this appendix). The program returns the value of the REQUEST_METHOD variable. In both figures the script was sent the query string, fname=Bob&lname=Reselman. Figure A.2 shows that when the data was sent via the GET method, the QUERY_STRING environment variable contained the data sent from the Internet client and the value of Standard Input is an empty string. Figure A.3 shows when data was sent using the POST method, the data was sent to STDIN and the value of the QUERY_STRING is an empty string.

**FIG. A.2**
The GET method sends
data to QUERY_STRING.

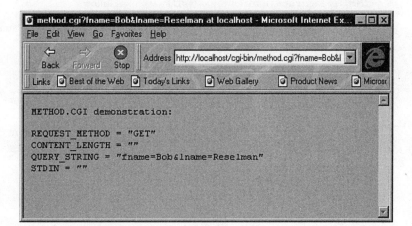

**FIG. A.3**
The POST method sends data to STDIN.

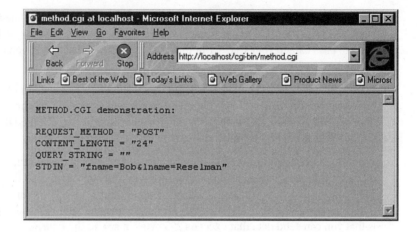

```
METHOD.CGI demonstration:

REQUEST_METHOD = "POST"
CONTENT_LENGTH = "24"
QUERY_STRING = ""
STDIN = "fname=Bob&lname=Reselman"
```

# HTML Forms

A Web page collects, assembles, and then sends data to your CGI scripts using HTML Forms. An HTML Form begins with a <FORM> tag and ends with a </FORM>. The syntax of the <FORM> tag is as follows:

> <FORM METHOD="type of method" ACTION="path to your CGI script">
>
> </FORM>

Listing A.3, a few lines above, shows an example of the <FORM> tag syntax.

You enter data in a <FORM> using HTML input elements. An input element creates a field on the <FORM> in which an end-user enters data to be sent to your CGI script. You place HTML input elements between the <FORM> and </FORM> tags. Input elements are denoted with the <INPUT> tag. The syntax for the <INPUT> tag is as follows:

> <INPUT TYPE="field type" NAME="name of field" [VALUE="default value"]>

Where:

TYPE denotes that type of Input device, such as, TEXT, RADIO, SELECT, SUBMIT.

NAME is the unique name for the element, such as, text1, text2, firstname, lastname. The NAME attribute of TEXT, TEXTAREA, PASSWORD, SELECT, RADIO, and CHECKBOX can also be thought of as variable names to which data entered or selected in the element will be assigned.

VALUE is the default value assigned to the element.

Table A.4 lists the different types of input fields.

## Table A.4   The Various Types of Input Fields

| Type | Description | Visual Basic Equivalent |
|------|-------------|------------------------|
| TEXT | For inputting a single line of text. | TextBox |
| TEXTAREA | For inputting multiple lines of text. | TextBox |
| PASSWORD | Similar to a textbox except that inputted characters appear as *, with password property set TRUE. | TextBox |
| SELECT | A selection item in a list of items. | ListBox |
| CHECKBOX | A box that you can check on and off. More than one check box can be checked at one time. | CheckBox |
| RADIO | A circle that you can click on and off. Only one radio can be selected at one time. | Option |
| HIDDEN | Invisible, holds a predefined value. | None |
| SUBMIT | Button used for submitting data from all input fields. | CommandButton |
| RESET | Button that clears the value of all input fields. | CommandButton |
| IMAGE | A graphic with the behavior of a SUBMIT input type. | PictureBox, Image |

Listing A.4. shows the HTML for a simple Form element. Figure A.4 shows what the Form code looks like in a browser.

## Listing A.4   Chtm04.HTM—HTML Code for a TEXT Input Field

```
<FORM METHOD="GET" ACTION="http://www.fruit.com/cgi-bin/myscript.cgi">
I am a TEXT input element <INPUT TYPE="text" NAME="mydata"><P>
I am another TEXT input element <INPUT TYPE="text" NAME="moredata"><P>
<INPUT TYPE="SUBMIT" NAME=submit VALUE="Send in the data">
</FORM>
```

**FIG. A.4**

A simple HTML Form.

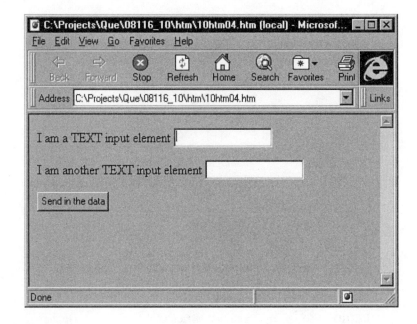

You'll notice that the code uses two types of input elements, two TEXT elements, and a SUBMIT element. The name of the first TEXT element is mydata. When the user enters data in the TEXT element via the Web page, the data that he or she enters is assigned to the input name, mydata. The same is true of the second TEXT element except that the data entered in that field will be assigned to the input name, moredata.

The input element, SUBMIT, also has a VALUE attribute, "Send in the data." The SUBMIT element assigns its VALUE attribute to be the caption of SUBMIT button. Why? Because that's the way the SUBMIT elements work. They were born that way.

Say that the end user enters the string "Fred" into the TEXT element with the name mydata and enters the string "Flintstone" into the TEXT element with the name moredata. When the enduser clicks the SUBMIT button the following URL is sent by the browser:

**www.fruit.com/cgi-bin/myscript.cgi?mydata=Fred&moredata=Flintstone**

Thus, the environmental variable QUERY_STRING for the scripts www.fruit.com/cgi-bin/ myscript.cgi is mydata=Fred&moredata=Flintstone&submit=Send+in+the+data. The last variable name/value pair, submit=Send+in+the+data might seem a little odd. This pair is the value associated with the SUBMIT button. Though the primary functionality of the SUBMIT element is to encode and transmit the data in the Form, it also passes its name and value along *if the NAME keyword has a value assigned to it*. You really don't have to do anything with the value other than be aware that this is happening and prepare for it when you do your string parsing.

For as long as you do CGI programming, you will be creating HTML forms. They can get quite complex, particularly as you learn to use the <TABLE> and <FRAME> elements. The point here is to give you a basic overview of the construction of simple forms and to demonstrate the relationship between HTML Forms and your CGI scripts.

▶ For more information about using HTML forms, **see** the Que publication, *Special Edition, Using CGI*, ISBN 0-7897-0740-3, Chapter 5, "Integrating CGI into you HTML Pages" on **p. 90-112**

## Installing Your Script on an Internet Server

Once you have your script written and compiled, you install your script on an Internet server. This is usually a pretty straight forward operation, but sometimes, you can encounter a glitch or two.

Most Internet servers have a special directory in which to place binary executable files, which is what your CGI script is. The convention that has evolved among Webmasters and Internet server manufacturers is to name this directory, /cgi-bin. Sometimes the Webmaster will create other directories for your CGI scripts. They might have the name /scripts or /cgi-shl. These directories might be mapped to a virtual directory, \cgi-bin. These directories are special because all files in this directory are set to have "executable" permission. Remember, Internet servers are like any other server. Therefore, all files and directories have a collection of permissions which can be set to accommodate the access level of a given user.

**N O T E** Virtual Directory

A virtual directory is a "pretend" name for a directory or set of directories. They don't really exist on your server's hard drive. For instance, you might have a directory on your server named c:\programs\users\bob\myapps. Though this is useful if you are working directly on the server, it is quite a long confusing URL if you are trying to get to that directory on the Internet. To solve this problem you would configure your server to have c:\programs\users\bob\myapps map to a virtual directory, /webapps. As a result, if your server's Internet address is www.fruit.com, you could get to that directory by calling http://www.fruit.com/webapps/. This address is just a "made up" name for the world outside of you server to see. ▪

On an Internet server is an abstract user, the HTTP daemon. When a browser requests that a CGI script be invoked, it is the HTTP daemon that does the invocation. However, if the CGI script does not grant "execute" permissions to the daemon, the script will not work. And, if one of the features of the CGI script is that it read or write data to or from another file, and that other file does not grant read/write permissions to the daemon, the daemon will not be able to open the file for reading or writing.

Figure A.5 shows a screen shot of a UNIX server displaying the permissions of a /cgi-bin directory.

**FIG. A.5**

The UNIX command, ls -l, shows you the permissions of a directory.

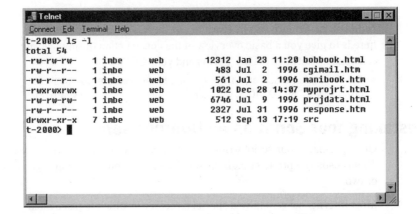

```
t-2000> ls -l
total 54
-rw-rw-rw-   1 imbe     web        12312 Jan 23 11:20 bobbook.html
-rw-r--r--   1 imbe     web          483 Jul  2  1996 cgimail.htm
-rw-r--r--   1 imbe     web          561 Jul  2  1996 manibook.htm
-rwxrwxrwx   1 imbe     web         1022 Dec 28 14:07 myprojrt.html
-rw-rw-rw-   1 imbe     web         6746 Jul  9  1996 projdata.html
-rw-r--r--   1 imbe     web         2327 Jul 31  1996 response.htm
drwxr-xr-x   7 imbe     web          512 Sep 13 17:19 src
t-2000>
```

Generally the read, write, and execute permissions are granted to given directories on the Internet server by the Webmaster. As a result, all you really need to be certain of is that you are placing your scripts in a directory that has been granted executable permission, as well as read/write permissions, should your script write to an external file.

## The Limitations of CGI

Though CGI is powerful, portable, and versatile, it does have limitations. For programmers coming to CGI from a visual programming paradigm such as Visual Basic, getting the hang of character-based, graphic-less programming using Standard Input and Output can be a bit of a chore. You cannot easily do CGI in a programming environment such as Visual Basic, Delphi, or non-console Visual C++. Windows does not accommodate CGI well at all. This is not to say that you can't do CGI programming in these language environments. It's just that it is hard. In the section, Using CGI with Visual Basic: The Guest Book, that you'll encounter later in this appendix, you'll see an example of making a CGI application in Visual Basic. But in the real world, making direct access of the CGI interface in the manner shown is rarely done. More often than not, WinCGI (discussed in Chapter 18) is used. But, you can do it if you really, really want to.

Picking up the lower-level programming skills necessary to do string parsing in C (one of the more preferred languages for old fashioned CGI programming) requires a bit of patience and fortitude. Visual Basic string parsing functions operate at a pretty high level. The language does most of the grunt work, hiding the lower-level complexities of parsing and memory allocation from the programmer. Typically, Visual Basic programmers have a formidable learning curve when trying to do low-level string parsing. You should expect that you will have to make a certain investment of time to conquer this learning curve.

Also, though doing CGI in a language such as C is supposed to be portable, in the real world portability is a matter of degrees. Though similar in most respects, C does vary from platform to platform. You can encounter some gotchas. Compound this with the effort to learn C in the first place and you could be in for some pretty frustrating late night sessions.

However, the biggest limitation of CGI programming is the nature of CGI itself. CGI is *stateless*. When a browser calls a CGI script, the only thing that the CGI script knows about is that specific call.

It's similar to the relationship the information operator at the phone company has with any given caller. You call the operator to ask for a phone number for your friend, Shemp. The operator gives you the number that you asked for. But say you forget the number. You call right back and get the same operator. You ask him or her for the number you asked for a few minutes ago. At that point the information operator has no idea what you are talking about. All he or she can do is give you a number that is associated with a name at the time you call. He or she has no possible way of knowing that you called before or when.

The same is true of CGI. The only thing the CGI interface knows about is the specific connection of the given moment. When you call a script, the daemon opens a process, invokes the script, pours values into the environmental variables, and sends some data to Standard Input for that connection only! When the script terminates, the process is closed, the values in the environmental variables vanish into thin air as do the variables themselves. If you call the script again, the same procedures start all over again with no knowledge of the previous call. As a result, if you plan to write scripts that have a number of interactions between the client and the server and needs to retain information about the prior connection, you will have to find yourself some workarounds, such as client-side cookies, to store state data.

▶ For more information about Client-Side Cookies, **see** Chapter 23, "Using Remote Data Objects with the OLEISAPI2 Interface" on **p. 541**

# Using CGI with Visual Basic: The Guest Book

Now, it's time to put the CGI concepts and skills that we have been discussing to work. To demonstrate writing a CGI application the "original web programming way," a Guest Book application will be developed. A Guest Book is typically put on a Web page to allow visitors to record personal specifics about themselves. Usually a Guest Book provides text fields for visitors to enter their name, address, and e-mail address. After the information has been entered, the visitor clicks a submit button and the data entered on the page is written back to a file that resides on the Internet server. Webmasters then use the recorded information to get back in contact with the visitor at a later date.

The project for the Guest Book is named VB_GBOOK.VBP and can be found on the CD-ROM disk that accompanies this book.

## Planning your Guest Book

The Guest Book needs to have two parts: a Web Page upon which to enter data and send data, and a CGI script to receive that data, write it to a file, and then send an acknowledgment back to the Internet client. When you do a task analysis detail of the requirement, you get an instruction set that looks like this:

1. Send a Web page that contains an HTML Form for data entry to client.

2. When the client clicks the Submit button, send the data to the CGI script.

3. Have the CGI script receive the data.

4. Check the REQUEST_METHOD.

5. If it is GET, read the value in QUERY_STRING. If it is POST, get the length of STDIN from the environmental variable, CONTENT_LENGTH. Then read the value of STDIN.

6. Parse the data in to variable name/value pairs.

7. Assign each value in a name/value pair to a variable internal to the script.

8. Construct a time stamped output with the internal variable values.

9. Open a file with error check.

10. Append the output to the file.

11. Close the file.

12. Create another output acknowledging receipt and write of data.

13. Send that data back to the calling Internet client.

## Creating your Guest Book

Before you can create the actual CGI script, you need to create the HMTL form in which the end user will enter the data to be sent to the script. Listing A.5 shows the HTML code for the form. Figure A.6 shows the form that results from the code.

---

**Listing A.5   Clist05.HTM—HTML Code for Entering Data in a Guest Book**

```
<HTML>

<HEAD><TITLE>
A Guest Book
</HEAD></TITLE>
<BODY BGCOLOR="white">

<CENTER>
<FONT FACE=arial SIZE=5><B>VB Guest Book</B></FONT><BR>
<FONT FACE=arial SIZE=4><B>Using CGI</B></FONT>
</CENTER>
<P>
<P>
<FORM METHOD="POST" ACTION="http://localhost/cgi-bin/vb_gbook.exe">

<FONT FACE=arial SIZE=3>Enter your First Name: </FONT>
<INPUT TYPE="text" NAME="First"><BR>


<FONT FACE=arial SIZE=3>Enter your Last Name: </FONT>
<INPUT TYPE="text" NAME="Last"></FONT><BR>
<P>
<P>
```

```
<FONT FACE=arial SIZE=3>Enter your E-mail: </FONT>
<INPUT TYPE="text" NAME="E-mail"></FONT><BR>
<P>
<P>
<INPUT TYPE="submit" VALUE="Submit">
</FORM>

<CENTER>
<FONT SIZE=3 COLOR=BLUE>
Copyright &copy; 1997<BR>
Macmillan Publishing
by Bob Reselman
</FONT></CENTER>

</BODY>
</HTML>
```

**FIG. A.6**

The Guest Book data entry form.

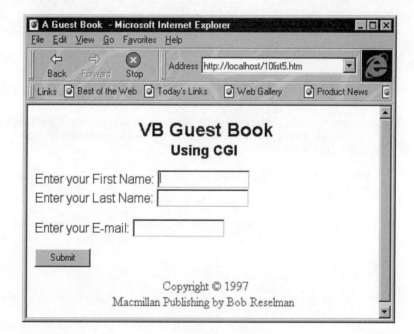

**Accessing Standard Input/Output**   As we described earlier, the basic structure of the Guest Book script is that you get the data, parse the data, write the data, and send back a confirmation. Though our intention is simple enough, there is a fundamental problem: Visual Basic has no direct way to access data from standard input. This is unfortunate because manipulating standard input and output is the heart of CGI programming. We can retrieve data from the CGI environmental variables using the environ() function. However, getting to standard input is going to require a bit of help from the Windows API.

Using standard input and standard output in day-to-day Windows programming is pretty rare. Most of the time you get your input from KeyPress or MouseMove events, and if you have to send output, you tend to send it to the Screen or Printer objects. However, there is a way to access Standard Input and Output. You do this using a combination of three API functions, GetStdHandle(), ReadFile() and WriteFile().

Standard Input and Standard Output work like files—mystical files, but files nonetheless. To talk to them, you need to get their file handle. You get a handle to Standard Input or Standard Output by using the API function, GetStdHandle(). GetStdHandle() takes one argument which is a constant that indicates the handle type, Standard Input, Standard Output, or Standard Error. These constants are STD_INPUT_HANDLE, STD_OUTPUT_HANDLE, and STD_ERROR_HANDLE, respectively.

Once you have a handle to the data stream, you use the API function, ReadFile() to get data from Standard Input or WriteFile() to send data to Standard Output. One of the argument values required by ReadFile() and WriteFile() is the handle returned by GetStdHandle(). Listing A.6 shows the Visual Basic declarations for GetStdHandle(), ReadFile(), and WriteFile(), as well as the associated constants.

### Listing A.6  modCGI.bas—The API Functions Necessary for CGI

```
'API functions needed to access CGI
Declare Function ReadFile Lib "kernel32" (ByVal hFile As Long, ByVal lpBuffer _
As String, ByVal nNumberOfBytesToRead As Long, lpNumberOfBytesRead As Long, _
ByVal lpOverlapped As Long) As Long

Declare Function WriteFile Lib "kernel32" (ByVal hFile As Long, ByVal lpBuffer _
As String, ByVal nNumberOfBytesToWrite As Long, lpNumberOfBytesWritten As Long, _
ByVal lpOverlapped As Long) As Long

Declare Function GetStdHandle Lib "kernel32" (ByVal nStdHandle As Long) As Long

'API constants
Public Const STD_INPUT_HANDLE = -10&
Public Const STD_OUTPUT_HANDLE = -11&
Public Const INVALID_HANDLE_VALUE = -1&
```

Listing A.7 shows the function, GetStandardInput(). GetStandardInput, which is an integral part of the Guest Book code, is a wrapper function for the GetStdHandle() and ReadFile() API functions. GetStandardInput() returns a string which reflects the data that is in the Standard Input stream of the Guest Book's process.

## Listing A.7    modCGI.bas—GetStandardInput() Gets Standard Input

```
Public Function GetStandardInput() As String
'''''''''''''''''''''''''''''''''''''''''''''''''
    'Function: GetStandardInput
    '
    'Arguments: none
    '
    '
    'Return:    The a string containing the data in the
    '           Standard Output of the application process
    '
    'Comments:  This function is a wrapper for the API functions,
    '           GetStandardHandle() and ReadFile(). GetStandardHandle()
    '           returns a handle to the standard output and input stream
    '           for the application's process. ReadFile() reads the data
    '           from Standard Input once a handle is retreived.
    '
    'Author/Programmer:    Bob Reselman
    'Copyright, Macmillian Publishing,  1997
'''''''''''''''''''''''''''''''''''''''''''''''
    Dim hStdIn As Long 'variable for the standard input handle
    Dim lResult As Long 'variable to hold return of value of ReadFile()
    Dim lBufferSize As Long 'variable for buffer size
    Dim strInBuff As String 'buffer to hold the string returned by ReadFile
    Dim lBufferSizeRead As Long 'bytes actually read by ReadFile()

    'Make sure that the method is POST
    If Environ("REQUEST_METHOD") <> "POST" Then
        'There is a problem, leave town
        GetStandardInput = "Method Not Supported!!"
        Exit Function
    End If

    'Get a handle to standard in
    hStdIn = GetStdHandle(STD_INPUT_HANDLE)

    'Get the size of the standard output from
    'the evnironment variable, "CONTENT_LENGTH"
    lBufferSize = CLng(Environ("CONTENT_LENGTH"))

    'Do an error check
    If hStdIn <> INVALID_HANDLE_VALUE Then
        'Pad the string
        strInBuff = String(lBufferSize, 0)
        'Read the data
        lResult = ReadFile(hStdIn, strInBuff, lBufferSize, lBufferSizeRead, 0&)

        If lResult <> 0 Then
            'Return the data
            GetStandardInput = Left(strInBuff, lBufferSizeRead)
```

*continues*

---
**Listing A.7   Continued**

```
        Else
            GetStandardInput = ""
        End If
    Else
        GetStandardInput = ""
    End If

End Function
```
---

**Parsing CGI Data**   Once you get data from Standard Input, you have to parse it to make it useful. Remember, all the data assembled on the HTML form will be sent to the Guest Book in one long string. However, the string will be URL encoded. Thus, the logic of URL Encoding can be incorporated to parse the string into coherent and related data.

Listing A.8 shows the function, SetGlobalUserTuples(). SetGlobalUserTuples takes the string returned from Standard Input as an argument. It goes through the string figuring out how many ampersands are in strings. Based on how many ampersands the function finds, it breaks the string up into name/value pairs. Within this program a name/value pair is called a tuple assigned to a user defined type of the same name. The term tuples is borrowed from Robert Denny, the creator of WinCGI. (You can learn about WinCGI in Chapter 18, "The WinCGI Interface and Visual Basic.") The Guest Book code makes tuples global in scope.

Once the function has determined and parsed all of the tuples within the string passed from Standard Input, it returns the number of tuples found.

---
**Listing A.8   modCGI.bas— SetGlobalUserTuples() Parses Standard Input**

```
Public Function SetGlobalUserTuples(QString As String) As Integer

    '*******************************
    'Function:   SetGlobalUserTuples
    '

    'Arguments: QString      The passed in string that contains the
    '                        extra command line parameters to be
    '                        converted into tuples
    '

    'Returns:   An integer representing the number of created tuples
    '

    'Comment:   A tuple is a group of two strings that is analogous to the
    '           URL encoding convention of:
    '

    '           var1name=var1val&var2name=var2value.
    '

    '           Where, tuple.key = var_name
    '                  tuple.value = var_value
    '
```

```
'              These groups are created by parsing the string that is
'              returned from either standard input or from the
'              environmental variable, QUERY_STRING.
'
'              This function does that parsing, making an array of global
'              tuples, each tuple array element containing a KEY and a VALUE.
'Author/Programmer:     Bob Reselman
'Copyright, Macmillian Publishing,    1997
'******************************
Dim i%
Dim sQString$          'local variable for the passed in
                       'string from which to extract the
                       'tuples

Dim TupleStrings()     'array to hold the parsed, but unseparated
                       'tuple strings
Dim TupleTakenOut$     'parsing variable
Dim TupleKey$          'key buffer
Dim TupleValue$        'value buffer

Dim NumOfTuples%       'Number of tuples to make
Dim NumOfAmpersands%   'Number of ampersand found
Dim AmpersandPos%      'position of the ampersand
Dim EqualPos%          'position of the equal sign

'Initialize the ampersand counter
NumOfAmpersands% = 1
'Initialize the local string
sQString$ = QString

For i% = 0 To Len(sQString$)
        'Find out how many ampersands are in the string.
        'This will tell you how many tuples there are.
        'For example, if there are no ampersands, then you
        'know that there is only one tuple. Thus, the number
        'of tuples is one more than the number of ampersands.
        If Mid(sQString$, i + 1, 1) = "&" Then
            NumOfAmpersands% = NumOfAmpersands% + 1
        End If
Next i%

NumOfTuples% = NumOfAmpersands%
'Make an array of tuple strings
ReDim TupleStrings(NumOfTuples)
'Make an array of Tuples to hold the parsed
'tuple strings
ReDim gUserTuple(NumOfTuples%)
'Initialize the 'working tuple string"
TupleTakenOut$ = sQString$
'Set the extracted TupleString to their respective array
For i% = 0 To NumOfTuples% - 1
    'If there are no plus signs left, assign
```

*continues*

**Listing A.8   Continued**

```
            If InStr(TupleTakenOut$, "&") = 0 Then
                TupleStrings(i%) = TupleTakenOut$
            Else
                AmpersandPos% = InStr(TupleTakenOut$, "&")
                'Doing this: (AmpersandPos% - 1) removes the "&" from the string.
                'Keep doing this until there are not ampersands left.
                TupleStrings(i%) = Left$(TupleTakenOut$, AmpersandPos% - 1)
                'Reset the string to get another tuple.
                TupleTakenOut$ = Right$(TupleTakenOut$, Len(TupleTakenOut$) -
➥AmpersandPos%)
            End If
        Next i%
        'Fill up the gUserTuples() array

        'Find the transaction string
        For i% = 0 To NumOfTuples% - 1
            EqualPos% = InStr(TupleStrings(i%), "=")
            'Take out the left side of the string and assign it
            'to the Key buffer
            TupleKey$ = Trim$(Left$(TupleStrings(i%), EqualPos% - 1))
            TupleValue$ = Trim$(Right$(TupleStrings(i%), Len(TupleStrings(i%)) -
➥EqualPos%))
            gUserTuple(i%).key = TupleKey$
            gUserTuple(i%).value = TupleValue$
        Next i%

        SetGlobalUserTuples = NumOfTuples%
    End Function
```

After the Standard Input has been parsed and assigned to the tuple name/value structure, the Guest Book script writes the data to a file, GBOOK.HTM, and sends the calling Internet client a file write confirmation. The function SetBookString() prepares and formats HTML output that will be written to the data file, GBOOK.HTM. The function transverses all the tuples and makes continuous string output of each variable name with its associated value. The function, SetBookEntry() opens the file, GBOOK.HTM, and append writes the output created in SetBookString() to it.

Listing A.9 shows the outputted text of the Guest Book data file, GBOOK.HTM. Figure A.7 shows the Guest Book data file, GBOOK.HTM, in an Internet browser after a write has been made.

**Listing A.9   gbook.htm—The Guest Book Data File**

```
<HR>
1/28/97 8:03:02 PM<BR>
<B>First: </B>Fred<BR>
<B>Last: </B>Flintstone<BR>
<B>E-mail: </B>fred@rock.com<BR>
```

```
<HR>
1/28/97 8:04:50 PM<BR>
<B>First: </B>Barney<BR>
<B>Last: </B>Rubble<BR>
<B>E-mail: </B>barney@rock.com<BR>

<HR>
1/28/97 8:05:22 PM<BR>
<B>First: </B>Dick<BR>
<B>Last: </B>Tracy<BR>
<B>E-mail: </B>dtracy@nynews.com<BR>

<HR>
1/28/97 8:05:44 PM<BR>
<B>First: </B>Bob<BR>
<B>Last: </B>Reselman<BR>
<B>E-mail: </B>reselbob@pionet.net<BR>

<HR>
1/28/97 8:06:25 PM<BR>
<B>First: </B>Bill<BR>
<B>Last: </B>Clinton<BR>
<B>E-mail: </B>president@whitehouse.gov<BR>
```

**FIG. A.7**

A portion of the Guest Book data file, gbook.htm viewed in a browser.

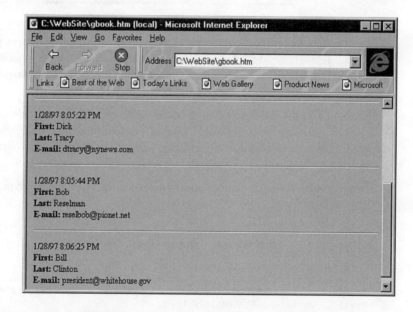

If a write to the data file, GBOOK.HTM, was successful, the Guest Book application sends a confirmation to the client using the functions, SetStandardOutput in conjunction with SetConfirmation(). Figure A.8 shows the confirmation that is sent back to the Internet client after a successful write to the Guest Book data file.

**FIG. A.8**

The Guest Book confirmation page.

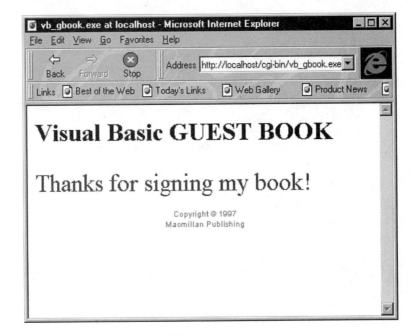

**The Complete Code: The Guest Book**   In the previous sections you were given an overview of the critical programming items necessary to do the Guest Book (vb_gbook.exe) transactions by using Standard Input and Standard Output within the Visual Basic programming paradigm. Now, let's take a look at the complete body of code for this project.

First, take a look at the program declarations as described in the module, modCGI.bas (Listing A.10). The program declares the API functions GetStdHandle(), ReadFile(), and WriteFile(). As you read above, GetStdHandle() will get a handle to Standard Input/Output. ReadFile() will retrieve Standard Input, and WriteFile will send data to Standard Output.

The program also declares some constants and creates a user defined type, TUPLE, and declares a global array of type TUPLE, gUserTuple().

**Listing A.10   modCGI.bas— Guest Book: Declarations**

```
'API functions needed to access CGI
Declare Function ReadFile Lib "kernel32" (ByVal hFile As Long, ByVal lpBuffer _
As String, ByVal nNumberOfBytesToRead As Long, lpNumberOfBytesRead As Long, _
ByVal lpOverlapped As Long) As Long

Declare Function WriteFile Lib "kernel32" (ByVal hFile As Long, _
ByVal lpBuffer As String, ByVal nNumberOfBytesToWrite As Long, _
lpNumberOfBytesWritten As Long, ByVal lpOverlapped As Long) As Long
```

```
Declare Function GetStdHandle Lib "kernel32" (ByVal nStdHandle As Long) As Long

'API constants
Public Const STD_INPUT_HANDLE = -10&
Public Const STD_OUTPUT_HANDLE = -11&
Public Const INVALID_HANDLE_VALUE = -1&

'A Tuple is a structure that holds URL encoded
'name\value pairs
Public Type Tuple
    key As String
    value As String
End Type

Public gUserTuple() As Tuple 'an array of tuples
Public giNumOfUserTuples As Integer 'number of global tuples
```

Figure A.9 shows a flowchart of the Sub Main() of The Guest Book project. When the program, vb_gbook.exe is invoked by the calling client, the program assigns the Guest Book output file and determines the request method as shown in Listing A.11. If the request method is "POST," the program calls the function, GetStandardInput (a wrapper function for all the functions necessary to write to Standard Input using VB). If the request method is not "POST," the program assumes a "GET" request method and calls GetQueryString() which is a wrapper function for the VB function, Environ(). These functions return the input sent from the calling client, particular to the request method.

Once the input has been determined, it is sent to the function, SetGlobalUserTuples(). SetGlobalUserTuples() parses the input string (passed a paramenter of the function) into an array of NAME/VALUE pairs (gUserTuple() of type,TUPLE) and returns an integer that indicates the of NAME/VALUE array size.

After the NAME/VALUE pair array size has been determined, the program calls, SetBookString(). SetBookString will set NAME/VALUE array into valid "Guest Book" HTML code for later viewing. After the function does the reformatting, it writes the newly created string of HTML to a file on the server disk by using the function, SetBookEntry().

If the file write is successful, (a return of TRUE by SetBookString()), a confirmation message is sent to the calling client by the function, SetStandardOutput(). SetStandardOutput takes the string to output as an argument. If the write fails, an error message is sent by the same function. However, the function, SetConfirmError(), which returns an error string, is passed as an argument to SetStandardOutput. SetStandardOutput() is a wrapper function for the Win32 API functions necessary to write to standard output from within Visual Basic.

**FIG A.9**

The flow chart of Sub Main() of the Guest Book project, vb_gbook.vbp.

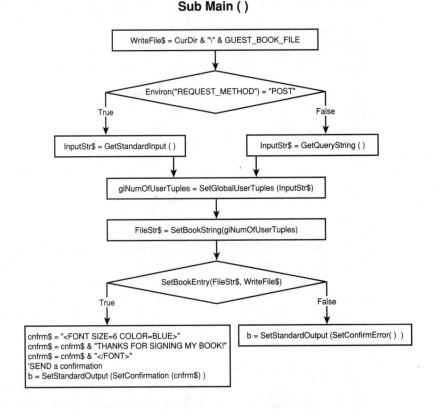

**Sub Main ( )**

## Listing A.11 modGBook.bas— Guest Book function: Sub Main()

```
Option Explicit

'Constants
'File to which to write the guest book data
Global Const GUEST_BOOK_FILE = "gbook.htm"

Public Sub Main()
    'Project: Guest Book
    'Project File: G_BOOK.VBP
    Dim InputStr$
    Dim FileStr$
    Dim WriteFile$
    Dim b As Boolean
    Dim cnfrm$ 'Confirmation variable

    WriteFile$ = CurDir & "\" & GUEST_BOOK_FILE
    'Check the request method
    If Environ("REQUEST_METHOD") = "POST" Then
        'Get the data from standard input
        InputStr$ = GetStandardInput()
    Else
```

```
        'Get the data for the QUERY_STRING
        InputStr$ = GetQueryString()
    End If

    'Parse the data into name/value pairs (tuples)
    giNumOfUserTuples = SetGlobalUserTuples(InputStr$)

    'Prepare it to be written to a file
    FileStr$ = SetBookString(giNumOfUserTuples)
    'Write to file
    If SetBookEntry(FileStr$, WriteFile$) Then
        'Set the confirmation text
        cnfrm$ = "<FONT SIZE=6 COLOR=BLUE>"
        cnfrm$ = cnfrm$ & "Thanks for signing my book!"
        cnfrm$ = cnfrm$ & "</FONT>"
        'Send a confirmation
        b = SetStandardOutput(SetConfirmation(cnfrm$))
    Else
        'Send an error
        b = SetStandardOutput(SetConfirmError())
    End If
End Sub
```

Listing A.12 shows the code for GetStandardInput(). GetStandardInput() is the function that you create to "wrap" the Win32 API functions, GetStdHandle() and ReadFile(). Within the logic of the Guest Book code, GetStandardInput() is used in response to a POST method.

### Listing A.12    modGBook.bas— Guest Book Function: GetStandardInput()

```
Public Function GetStandardInput() As String
    ''''''''''''''''''''''''''''''''''''''''''''''

    'Function: GetStandardInput
    '

    'Arguments: none
    '

    '

    'Return:     The a string containing the data in the
    '            Standard Output of the application process
    '

    'Comments:   This function is a wrapper for the API functions,
    '            GetStandardHandle() and ReadFile(). GetStandardHandle()
    '            returns a handle to the standard output and input stream
    '            for the application's process. ReadFile() reads the data
    '            from Standard Input once a handle is retrieved.
    '

    'Author/Programmer:      Bob Reselman
    'Copyright, Macmillian Publishing,   1997
    ''''''''''''''''''''''''''''''''''''''''''''''


    Dim hStdIn As Long 'variable for the standard input handle
    Dim lResult As Long 'variable to hold return of value of ReadFile()
    Dim lBufferSize As Long 'variable for buffer size
```

*continues*

**Listing A.12  Continued**

```
Dim strInBuff As String 'buffer to hold the string returned by ReadFile
Dim lBufferSizeRead As Long 'bytes actually read by ReadFile()

'Make sure that the method is POST
If Environ("REQUEST_METHOD") <> "POST" Then
    'There is a problem, leave town
    GetStandardInput = "Method Not Supported!!"
    Exit Function
End If

'Get a handle to standard in
hStdIn = GetStdHandle(STD_INPUT_HANDLE)

'Get the size of the standard output from
'the evnironment variable, "CONTENT_LENGTH"
lBufferSize = CLng(Environ("CONTENT_LENGTH"))

'Do an error check
If hStdIn <> INVALID_HANDLE_VALUE Then
    'Pad the string
    strInBuff = String(lBufferSize, 0)
    'Read the data
    lResult = ReadFile(hStdIn, strInBuff, lBufferSize, lBufferSizeRead, 0&)

    If lResult <> 0 Then
        'Return the data
        GetStandardInput = Left(strInBuff, lBufferSizeRead)
    Else
        GetStandardInput = ""
    End If
Else
    GetStandardInput = ""
End If

End Function
```

GetQueryString() (see Listing A.13) shows the code that you use if data is passed to the Guest Book via the "GET" method. The function is a wrapper for the Visual Basic function, Environ(). You pass the string, "QUERY_STRING," to the VB function and that function returns the value of the HTTP environmental variable, QUERY_STRING. The return is then passed back as a return value for GetQueryString().

**Listing A.13  modGBook.bas— Guest Book Function: GetQueryString g()**

```
Public Function GetQueryString() As String
'''''''''''''''''''''''''''''''''''''''''''''''''''''''
'Function: GetQueryString
'
'Arguments: none
'
'
```

```
'Return:     The data in the environmental variable, QUERY_STRING
'
'Comments:   This function is a wrapper for the VB function, Environ()
'            It returns the value of QUERY_STRING. QUERY_STRING
'            is the environmental variable to which a HTTP server
'            assigns Internet client data that is passed using
'            the GET method.
'
'Author/Programmer:     Bob Reselman
'Copyright, Macmillian Publishing,   1997
'''''''''''''''''''''''''''''''''''''''''''''''''''''''

    GetQueryString = Environ("QUERY_STRING")
End Function
```

Listing A.14 shows the function, GetGlobalUserTuples(). GetGlobalUserTuples() takes the input string as an argument. You use this function to redimension the global array of NAME/VALUE pairs (TUPLE) and then to populate that redimensioned array. The function returns the number of TUPLEs (size of the global NAME/VALUE pair array).

**Listing A.14   modCGI.bas— Guest Book Function: SetGlobalUserTuples()**

```
Public Function SetGlobalUserTuples(QString As String) As Integer

    '*******************************
    'Function:   SetGlobalUserTuples
    '

    'Arguments: QString    The passed in string that contains the
    '                      extra command line parameters to be
    '                      converted into tuples
    '
    'Returns:   An integer representing the number of created tuples
    '
    'Comment:   A tuple is a group of two strings that is analogous to the
    '           URL encoding convention of:
    '
    '           var1name=var1val&var2name=var2value.
    '
    '           Where, tuple.key = var_name
    '                  tuple.value = var_value
    '
    '           These groups are created by parsing the string that is
    '           returned from either standard input or from the
    '           environmental variable, QUERY_STRING.
    '
    '           This function does that parsing, making an array of global
    '           tuples, each tuple array element containing a KEY and a VALUE.
    '
    'Author/Programmer:     Bob Reselman
    'Copyright, Macmillian Publishing,   1997
    '*******************************
```

*continues*

---

**Listing A.14   Continued**

```
Dim i%
Dim sQString$          'local variable for the passed in
                       'string from which to extract the
                       'tuples

Dim TupleStrings()     'array to hold the parsed, but unseparated
                       'tuple strings
Dim TupleTakenOut$     'parsing variable
Dim TupleKey$          'key buffer
Dim TupleValue$        'value buffer

Dim NumOfTuples%       'Number of tuples to make
Dim NumOfAmpersands%   'Number of ampersand found
Dim AmpersandPos%      'position of the ampersand
Dim EqualPos%          'position of the equal sign

'Initialize the ampersand counter
NumOfAmpersands% = 1
'Initialize the local string
sQString$ = QString

For i% = 0 To Len(sQString$)
        'Find out how many ampersands are in the string.
        'This will tell you how many tuples there are.
        'For example, if there are no ampersands, then you
        'know that there is only one tuple. Thus, the number
        'of tuples is one more than the number of ampersands.
        If Mid(sQString$, i + 1, 1) = "&" Then
            NumOfAmpersands% = NumOfAmpersands% + 1
        End If
Next i%


NumOfTuples% = NumOfAmpersands%
'Make an array of tuple strings
ReDim TupleStrings(NumOfTuples)
'Make an array of Tuples to hold the parsed
'tuple strings
ReDim gUserTuple(NumOfTuples%)
'Initialize the 'working tuple string"
TupleTakenOut$ = sQString$
'Set the extracted TupleString to their respective array
For i% = 0 To NumOfTuples% - 1
    'If there are no plus signs left, assign
    If InStr(TupleTakenOut$, "&") = 0 Then
        TupleStrings(i%) = TupleTakenOut$
    Else
        AmpersandPos% = InStr(TupleTakenOut$, "&")
        'Doing this: (AmpersandPos% - 1) removes the "&" from the string.
        'Keep doing this until there are not ampersands left.
        TupleStrings(i%) = Left$(TupleTakenOut$, AmpersandPos% - 1)
        'Reset the string to get another tuple.
        TupleTakenOut$ = Right$(TupleTakenOut$, Len(TupleTakenOut$) -
➥AmpersandPos%)
```

```
        End If
    Next i%
    'Fill up the gUserTuples() array

    'Find the transaction string
    For i% = 0 To NumOfTuples% - 1
        EqualPos% = InStr(TupleStrings(i%), "=")
        'Take out the left side of the string and assign it
        'to the Key bugger
        TupleKey$ = Trim$(Left$(TupleStrings(i%), EqualPos% - 1))
        TupleValue$ = Trim$(Right$(TupleStrings(i%), Len(TupleStrings(i%)) -
➥EqualPos%))
        gUserTuple(i%).key = TupleKey$
        gUserTuple(i%).value = TupleValue$
    Next i%

    SetGlobalUserTuples = NumOfTuples%
End Function
```

Listing A.15 shows the code for the function, SetBookString(). SetBookString() takes the size of the global NAME/VALUE array, gUserTuple, as an argument. The function parses the array into HTML code, later be appended onto the Guest Book file on the server. The function returns the string of HTML code that it creates.

### Listing A.15  modGBook.bas— Guest Book Function: SetBookString()

```
Public Function SetBookString(NumOfTuples As Integer) As String
    ''''''''''''''''''''''''''''''''''''''''''''''''''

    'Function: SetBookString
    '

    'Arguments: NumOfTuples,  The number of name/value pairs (tuples)
    '           as defined in the function, SetGlobalUserTuples.
    '

    '

    'Return:    The string to be written to the Guest Book
    '           data file.
    '

    'Comments:  This function transverses all the name/value pairs
    '           (tuples), the number of which is passed in NumOfTuples.
    '           As the tuples are transversed, a string is created with
    '           the write date, a tuple name and a tuple value, for all
    '           tuples.
    '

    '

    'Author/Programmer:    Bob Reselman
    'Copyright, Macmillian Publishing,  1997
    ''''''''''''''''''''''''''''''''''''''''''''''''''
    Dim s$  'string to build
    Dim i%  'counter variable
    Dim j%  'local variable for number of tuples

    'Set the number of tuples to a local variable
```

*continues*

**Listing A.15 Continued**

```
    j% = NumOfTuples

    'Put in line break HTML char, <HR>
    s$ = s$ & "<HR>" & vbCrLf

    'Add a time stamp
    s$ = s$ & CStr(Now) & "<BR>" & vbCrLf

    'Transverse the tuples
    For i% = 0 To j% - 1
        s$ = s$ & "<B>" & gUserTuple(i%).key & ": </B>"
        s$ = s$ & gUserTuple(i%).value & "<BR>" & vbCrLf
    Next i%
    'Return the string
    SetBookString = s$
End Function
```

SetBookEntry() (see Listing A.16) writes data sent by a calling client to the Guest Book file on the server. As described earlier, SetBookEntry() takes two arguments, strEntry as String and strFile as String. The argument, strEntry is the data to write to a file. The argument, strFile, is the file you write to.

**Listing A.16 modGBook.bas— Guest Book Function: SetBookEntry()**

```
Public Function SetBookEntry(strEntry As String, strFile As String) As Boolean
'''''''''''''''''''''''''''''''''''''''''''''''''''
    'Function: SetBookEntry
    '
    'Arguments: strEntry  The entry to write to a the Guest Book File
    '           strFile   Name of the Guest Book data file
    '
    '
    'Return:    True if write was successful
    '
    'Comments:  This function appends the data passed in strEntry
    '           to a file passed in strFile. If the file does
    '           not exist, the function will create it.
    '
    '
    'Author/Programmer:     Bob Reselman
    'Copyright, Macmillian Publishing,   1997
'''''''''''''''''''''''''''''''''''''''''''''''''''
    Dim i%
    Dim FileNumber%
    Dim entry$
    Dim f$

    On Error GoTo SetBookEntryErr
    'set the string to write to a file to a local variable
    entry$ = strEntry
    'set the file to a local variable
```

```
    f$ = strFile

    For i% = 1 To 255
        FileNumber% = FreeFile(0)
        If FileNumber% <> 0 Then Exit For
    Next i%
    'open the file
    Open f$ For Append As #FileNumber%
    'Print the data to the file
    Print #FileNumber%, entry$
    'Print in a blank line
    Print #FileNumber%,
    'Close the file
    Close #FileNumber%
    'Things are good, set the function to true
    SetBookEntry = True

SetBookEntryErr:
    Exit Function
End Function
```

SetStandardOutput() is a wrapper function for the Win32 API functions, GetStdHandle() and WriteFile(). You use SetStandardOutput() to access an Internet server's Standard Output and pass data back to the calling client, as shown in Listing A.17.

## Listing A.17  modCGI.bas— Guest Book Function: SetStandardOutput()

```
Public Function SetStandardOutput(strOutput As String) As Boolean
''''''''''''''''''''''''''''''''''''''''''''''''''''
    'Function: SetStandardOutput
    '
    'Arguments: strOutput,  The string to send to the process's
    '                       Standard Output
    '
    '
    'Return:    True, if successful.
    '
    'Comments:  This function is a wrapper for the API functions,
    '           GetStandardHandle() and WriteFile(). GetStandardHandle()
    '           returns a handle to the standard output and input stream
    '           for the application's process. WriteFile() writes the data
    '           to Standard Output once a handle is retrieved.
    '
    'Author/Programmer:     Bob Reselman
    'Copyright, Macmillian Publishing,   1997
''''''''''''''''''''''''''''''''''''''''''''''''''''
    Dim hStdOut As Long 'variable for the standard output handle
    Dim lResult As Long 'variable for API result
    Dim lBytesWritten As Long   'varible reporting bytes written
    Dim s$ 'local variable for the string to output

    'Assign the output to a local variable
    s$ = strOutput
```

*continues*

**Listing A.17   Continued**

```
    'Get a handle to standard out
    hStdOut = GetStdHandle(STD_OUTPUT_HANDLE)
    'Do an error check
    If hStdOut <> INVALID_HANDLE_VALUE Then
        'Write the data out
        lResult = WriteFile(hStdOut, s$, Len(s$), lBytesWritten, 0)
        'Do another error check, to make sure things are right
        If lResult <> 0 Or lBytesWritten <> Len(s$) Then
            SetStandardOutput = False
        Else
            SetStandardOutput = True
        End If
    Else
        SetStandardOutput = False
    End If
End Function
```

The function, SetConfirmation(), takes as an argument a string indicating a confirmation message. The argument is then formatted into a snippet of HTML and returned, as shown in Listing A.18.

**Listing A.18   modGBook.bas— Guest Book Function: SetConfirmation()**

```
Public Function SetConfirmation(strConfirm As String) As String
    '''''''''''''''''''''''''''''''''''''''''''''''''''''
    'Function: SetConfirmation
    '
    'Arguments: strConfirm   String that contains the phrase to
    '                        pass into the confirmation return.
    '
    '
    'Return:     A string containing the completed confirmation message,
    '            including the confirmation phrase, to send to the
    '            Internet Client
    '
    'Comments:   This function creates a string that is passed to
    '            Standard Output, upon successful write to the Guest
    '            Book file.
    '
    '
    'Author/Programmer:     Bob Reselman
    '
    '''''''''''''''''''''''''''''''''''''''''''''''''''''

    Dim s$
    Dim c$
    'Set the confirmation text to a local variable
    c$ = strConfirm
    'Get an HTML header
    s$ = GetPlainHeader()
    'Make the confirmation string
    s$ = s$ & "<HTML>"
```

```
    s$ = s$ & "<BODY BGCOLOR=WHITE>"
    s$ = s$ & "<H1>Visual Basic GUEST BOOK </H1><BR>"

    'Add the string holding the confirmation phrase
    s$ = s & c$ & "<BR><P><P>"

    'Add copyright and closing HTML
    s$ = s$ & "<CENTER><FONT SIZE=1 FACE=Arial COLOR=808080>"
    s$ = s$ & "Copyright &copy; 1997<BR>"
    s$ = s$ & "Macmillan Publishing</FONT></CENTER>"
    s$ = s$ & "</BODY></HTML>"

    SetConfirmation = s$
End Function
```

The function, SetConfirmationError(), returns a snippet of HTML code to be passed to Standard Output as an error message, as shown in Listing A.19.

### Listing A.19    modGBook.bas— Guest Book Function: SetConfirmation()

```
Public Function SetConfirmError() As String
    '''''''''''''''''''''''''''''''''''''''''''''''
    'Function: SetConfirmError
    '
    'Arguments: none
    '
    '
    'Return:      An HTML formated string
    '
    'Comments:    This function returns a string containing an error
    '             message that is to be passed to Standard Output
    '
    '
    'Author/Programmer:      Bob Reselman
    'Copyright, Macmillian Publishing,   1997
    '''''''''''''''''''''''''''''''''''''''''''''''
    Dim s$   'variable to hold constructed string
    Dim c$   'variable to hold the error text

    'Set the error text to a local variable
    c$ = "Application Error! Please notify Webmaster"
    'Get an HTML header
    s$ = GetPlainHeader()

    'Make the HTML text
    s$ = s$ & "<HTML><BODY BGCOLOR=WHITE>"
    s$ = "<HEAD>Guest Book Error</HEAD>"
    s$ = s$ & "<FONT COLOR=RED SIZE=6>GUEST BOOK ERROR!</FONT><BR>"
    s$ = s & c$ & "<BR>"
    s$ = s$ & "</BODY></HTML>"

    'Return the string
    SetConfirmError = s$
End Function
```

`GetPlainHeader()` is a utility function (see Listing A.20) that takes no arguments and returns a standard HTTP header line, "Content-type: text/html" with the obligatory NULL line afterwards. This function is used by functions that create HTTP output. The HTTP protocol specifies that all text sent to a browser to be interpreted as HTML have these two lines at the beginning of the data stream. If you do not send these lines, the browser will NOT interpret the text as HTML. It will think that the data stream is a regular text file and display it as such.

**Listing A.20    modCGI.bas— Guest Book Function: GetPlainHeader()**

```
Public Function GetPlainHeader()
    '******************************
    'Function:  GetPlainHeader
    '
    'Arguments: none
    '
    '
    'Return:    a string with the HTTP initialization
    '           string
    '
    '
    'Comment:   All HTML files to be dynamically returned
    '           require this string to be the first line
    '           prior to the <HTML> tag.
    '
    'Author/Programmer: Bob Reselman
    '
    'Copyright (c) 1997 Macmillan Publishers
    '
    '******************************

    Dim s$ 'local string variable
    s$ = s$ & "Content-type: text/html"
    s$ = s$ & vbCrLf
    s$ = s$ & " "
    s$ = s$ & vbCrLf
    GetPlainHeader = s$
End Function
```

# Summary

In this appendix, you learned about the fundamentals of the Common Gateway Interface. You've learned about the conceptual underpinnings of CGI specification. You've learned about environmental variables, standard input and output, scripts and scripting languages, submit methods, and HTML forms. You've observed the results of sending data to a CGI script using the GET method and the POST method. Finally, you put these concepts to work making a CGI application in Visual Basic. ●

# What's on the CD?

The CD included with this book contains all of the source code from each of the examples in this book. Having this code allows you to immediately compile and run each of the examples. This also allows you to examine, modify, and enhance each of the examples. The goal of having the code is to enable you to get up and running immediately with each of the technologies discussed in this book.

The CD also contains numerous ActiveX controls, and Visual Basic tools and utilities. The reason for this is to allow you to experiment with the numerous ways in which you can extend your Visual Basic applications into new areas of functionality. The tools and utilities enable you to extend your development environment and improve the quality of your Visual Basic applications.

If you examine the CD, you'll also find a collection of shareware utilities and applications, including Web browsers, Web servers, HTML editors, and others. These tools can be used to build, test, and deploy your own Web applications, although most of them will not allow you to take advantage of most of the tools and techniques you've read about in this book. ■

## Visual Basic Control Creation Edition

The Control Creation Edition of Visual Basic enables you to build your own ActiveX controls by using Visual Basic. The controls you create with this version of Visual Basic can be used in Web pages, Visual Basic applications, and applications built by using any other ActiveX-enabled languages like Visual C++, Delphi, and others.

## HTML Reference

A complete HTML reference book is included on the CD in HTML format, viewable by using any Web browser.

## Requests For Comments and Other Internet Standard Documents

The RFC documents that specify the Internet application standards such as FTP, HTTP, SMTP, POP3, and NNTP. These documents specify how each of these applications need to communicate, and commands they should recognize, and how they should respond to each of the commands.

## InstallShield Express

InstallShield has become the Windows install utility by which all other install utilities are measured.

# Source Code

The source code, HTML files, database, and other necessary files for building and running every one of the examples in this book are located in a series of directories on the CD. The root directory of the CD where you will be able to find all of the book examples is \CODE, under which you will find a number of subdirectories named after the chapter for which the directory contains the examples.

For any of the examples that you want to compile and run, modify, extend, and experiment with, make a directory on your hard drive and copy that set of example code to your directory. You can now make any changes desired to the example applications, and extend them as far as you possibly want, knowing that you can go back to the original code on the CD at any time and start again.

# On Shareware

Many of the applications, tools, utilities, and controls found on the CD are what is known as *shareware*. Shareware is what makes it possible for us to include what is literally hundreds of dollars of software on a CD that comes with a book costing much less. It is also a model for marketing software that, although well established before the Internet began its popularity explosion, has become the primary software marketing model for the majority of software corporations in the world today.

Several years ago, the majority of shareware applications were written by one- or two-person development teams (with an occasional larger team), and owned by small software companies. Shareware was considered an alternative for marketing an application to a respectable number of computer users for a minimal cost. Within the past couple of years, the profile of a typical shareware software company has changed dramatically. Now, it's not just the domain of small software companies, but also of some of the largest, with Microsoft, Symantec, Borland, and Lotus joining the ranks of shareware, and sometimes even freeware, software manufacturers.

So what is shareware? Shareware is based on the "try before you buy" principle. The idea is that once you try the software, if you like it, you'll pay for it. If you don't like it, you will stop using it. Just about all shareware is based on a 30-day trial period, during which you should have a chance to work with the software enough to make the determination whether you like it or not. A large amount of shareware will allow you to continue using the software after the evaluation period is up, but a growing number of shareware vendors are building their software such that it will disable itself after 30 days, only reenabling itself after you have entered a valid registration ID.

**N O T E**  Upon installing and first using any shareware software, you are legally agreeing to the license agreement that accompanies the software. After the evaluation period is up, if you continue to use the software, you are legally obligated to register the software, and pay whatever license fees are specified by the software manufacturer. ■

Upon registering your copy of the software, many shareware manufacturers bestow various benefits upon you including:

- A clean conscience, knowing that you have paid the author for the many hours that he or she spent to create such a useful program.
- Inclusion on the author's mailing list, informing you of updates, and maintenance releases of the product, often including free updates to the next full version.
- Often you will be provided with some degree of technical support and documentation, and often additional functionality that is only enabled for registered versions of the software.

**N O T E**  All of the software packages on the CD should contain information about where and how to register the product. For the few that have specific expiration dates, they will include information about where you can get a newer evaluation copy, with a future expiration date, so you will have time to take it for a test drive. ■

# ActiveX Controls

A number of ActiveX controls have been included on the CD, many of which can be used to build Web pages as well as standard Visual Basic applications. Most of these controls fall into the category of shareware, although there are a few freeware controls mixed in. All of the controls on the CD are included as samples of the controls that are available from various ActiveX Control developers who would be more than happy to sell you fully licensed versions of the controls included on the CD, but also their other controls that they have available for your use. Keep in mind that this is little more than a small sampling of the ActiveX controls available for your purchase and use. For every control you find on the CD, there are probably a hundred other controls that you can purchase and use in building applications.

In addition to the ActiveX controls, you will also find some DLLs that can provide your Visual Basic applications with various kinds of new functionality. Some of these DLLs enable you to build Visual Basic applications that work with various other technologies, or perform specialized functionality that are more suited for encapsulating into a DLL rather than an ActiveX control. As far as building Web applications are concerned, most of the DLLs will be more practical when building server-side functionality, but you can also use them in regular and Web-enabled Visual Basic applications.

# Visual Basic Tools and Utilities

Also included on the CD are several tools and utilities that can enhance your Visual Basic applications. These include application documentation tools, installation utilities, license protection utilities, and others. While these don't provide you with new functionality that you can use to build a better application, they can help to improve the total impression that your product makes on your customers and clients.

Just about all of the versions of these products are demonstration or very reduced functionality versions of the products. These are all commercial products that are used by some of the biggest software companies in the industry. These products enable you to put together a complete and very professional package for the software you develop, all the while allowing you to focus on what you enjoy and do best, build software.

# Finding Updates

All of the software on the CD should have some form of documentation accompanying it. The documentation should provide you with the address, URL, and other information where you can get updated versions of the software. For the shareware and freeware software, there are some other easily accessible locations on the Internet that you can go to find updated versions of software, as well as other shareware and freeware software that you can check out. While not all of the software on the CD can be found at each of these Web sites, you can find many of them plus many more at the following sites:

- Que's FTP site at **ftp.mcp.com** maintains up-to-date copies of many shareware programs and utilities. As soon as Que receives updated versions of shareware programs, it is placed on their FTP site for anonymous downloading from the Internet. You can use your Web browser by typing in the URL **ftp://ftp.mcp.com/pub/que/inetapps/** and drilling down into the various directories based on what type of application you are looking for.

- The Ultimate Collection Of Winsock Shareware (TUCOWS) is one of the largest sites on the Internet to find shareware and freeware. TUCOWS is so popular that it has established over 140 mirror sites around the world. It is organized by platform and type of application. Every application has a brief description and is rated on a five-cow rating system. To go to TUCOWS, start at the main site at **http://www.tucows.com/**, then select a mirror site closest to you.

- Another great location to check out is EarthWeb. EarthWeb started out by creating the Gamelan directory at **http://www.gamelan.com/**, which became the central resource for finding all sorts of Java applets and resources on the Web. EarthWeb has built on the success of Gamelan by creating EarthWeb.Net at **http://www.earthweb.net/**, which includes not just the Gamelan Java resource center, but also an ActiveX resource center, a VRML resource center, and a JavaScript resource center.

- A large amount of credit for the boom in popularity of the Internet in the last few years has to go to the fact that the Internet is based on open, publicly available, application standards. These standards are not based on any particular operating system, or programming language, but more on how applications talk to each other. This covers both the commands and replies that are passed between client and server applications, but also to the format used for passing messages and files back and forth. It is this nature of the Internet application standards that allow anyone to build the client and server applications for each of these Internet applications, on any platform, using just about any programming language.

Most, if not all of the Internet application protocols are documented in an ASCII text file known as a *Request For Comment*, or RFC. The RFCs document working application protocols that have been submitted to the Internet Engineering Task Force (IETF) for consideration as a standard. These RFCs are reviewed by the IETF, and once approved, are assigned an RFC number and placed in the public domain for peer review by the entire Internet community. If all goes well, the RFC is eventually accepted as a standard, and the RFC document number is added to the list of standards. These documents can be found at **http://www.internic.net/ ds/dspg0intdoc.html**, along with Internet Drafts, For Your Information (FYI) documents, IETF meeting minutes, and other documents of interest. ●

App

B

# Index

## Symbols

## A

# B

**B tags, Minimal Database application example,** 517

**Back Order component,** 717

**BACK.HTM file, History object Back method,** 154

**BackColor property**
AXYESNO control, 59-60
text boxes, 354

**bastion hosts,** 761

**BCKORDRS.CLS file**
Back Orders component, 718
ChangeNumBackOrders method, 719-721
GetNumBackOrders method, 718-719

**bin directory, CGIs,** 865

**BinaryWrite method, Response Object,** 343

**BINDINGS property, AdvancedDataControl object,** 637

**book listing Web application example,** 642

**BOOKLIST.ASP file, DataHeader and DataFooter controls HTML code,** 667-670

**bookmarks,** 620

**Boolean subtype, Variant data type,** 260

**Border attribute, OBJECT tags,** 167

**bots, link-checking application,** 783
absolute URL resolution, 796
checking document for URLs, 792
checking HTTP response codes, 801
form controls, 786
parsing URLs, 790
removing document for URL check, 788
removing duplicate URLs, 794-795
Retrieve URL button, 787-788

retrieving URL for checking, 788
testing URLs, 795-796
validity checking for URLs, 798-800
verifying URLs, 795

**BOTTOM property, Java applets,** 193

**browsers**
ActiveX Document options, 206-211
CGI scripts, 854-855
types and technological overview, 252-253
uniform data handling, 22
Visual Basic programming options, 21
*see also* Web browsers

**browsing**
files, 25
Web pages, 26

**Buffer property, Response Object,** 340

**BuildForm method, PLACEORDER.CLS file,** 749-750

**building**
ActiveX controls with Visual Basic, 49, 52-57
ActiveX Document applications, 211-216
AXYESNO control, 52-57
design-time ActiveX controls, 813-825
OLEISAPI2 interface applications, 453-459
Web applications with Visual InterDev, 646

**BuildTestURL function, INETEXPL.FRM file,** 797-798

**Button type, INPUT tag (ELEMENTS.HTM file),** 136

**bws.INI file, request processing (Minimal Database application),** 517-518

**byte codes, Java,** 191

**BytesReceived property, Winsock Control,** 98

# C

**C programming**
CGIs, 854-855
string parsing, 866

**CAB files, creating with DIANTZ.EXE program,** 118

**CAB files (cabinet files), mime types,** 117

**caching tasks, Guestbook Pro application,** 334-335

**caching user data with Session Objects,** 304

**CalculatePayment function,** 354

**Calendar Control**
adding to Web pages, 676
user input option, 678
NewMonth event example, 181
updating textbox, 183
Visual InterDev example, 176

**calling**
OLEISAPI applications, 413-414
OLEISAPI methods via POST method, 414

**CallObject function, OLENSAPI.C file,** 488-492

**Cancel method, Internet Transfer Control,** 777

**CancelUpdate method, Advanced Data Connector,** 635

**caption properties, AXYESNO control,** 54

**cbAvailable field, ISAPI structure,** 410

**cboIncentive combo box, PropertyBag application,** 220

**cboMembershipLevel combo box, PropertyBag application,** 220

**cbSize field, ISAPI structure,** 409

**cbTotalBytes field, ISAPI structure,** 410

# R

RADIO (CGI form input field), 863

Radio type, INPUT tag, 137

Raise method, Err object, 356

RDOs (Remote Data Objects), 553-557
objects, 554
corresponding DAOs, 555
OLEISAPI interaction example, Contact Database application, 557-580

ReadClient() function, ISAPI, 411

ReadFile() function, CGIs, 870

reading client-submitted data, OLEISAPI2 interface, 444-445

reading request headers, OLEISAPI2 interface, 445-446

ReadProperties event
ActiveX Documents, 205
PropertyBag object, 226

ReceiveMerch method, MERCHMV.CLS file, 723-724

record editing forms, Contact Database application, 563-566

RecordSet Object, 614-617

recordsets, 612
ADC, 634
creating with Connection Object, 614

recursive programming, 332-334

RECVNG.FRM file
Merchandise Movement interface updates, 726-727
obtaining product ID, 710
product ID form example, 710
referencing Transaction Server object, 711

Redirect method, Response Object, 343

redirection with Request Object, LOGONVALIDATE.TXT file, 306-308

Refresh method, Advanced Data Connector, 635

registering
design-time controls, 823
Transaction component, 368

registering Java classes, 838

registering VB DLLs with Transaction Server, 703-707

Registry, file association keys, 586

Regsvrdc.exe program, registering design-time controls, 823

relational database management, 619-621

remote access checking, WebSite server, 379

REMOTE_ADDR (CGI environmental variable), 856

REMOTE_USER (CGI environmental variable), 856

RemoteHost property, Winsock Control, 98

RemotePort property, Winsock Control, 99

RemoveDuplicateURLs Subroutine, INETEXPL.FRM file, 794-795

RemoveFormatting function, Contact Database application, 574

repaint() function, 196

repetitive processing statements, VBScript, 263

ReplaceChars() function, 424

replacing characters in strings, 424

ReportTime sub, TIME.HTM file example, 33-34

Requery method, ADO, 618

request headers, reading, OLEISAPI2 interface, 445-446

request methods, HTTP, 319

Request Object, 318-323
Active Request object methods, 442
Form collection, 322
methods, 320
QueryString collection, 319, 321
redirection, LOGONVALIDATE.TXT file, 306-308

Request structure, NSAPI, 471

Request.Cookies, 337-338

Request.Form command, ASP file default values, 333

REQUEST_LINE (CGI environmental variable), 857

REQUEST_METHOD variable, CGIs, 861

REQUEST_METHOD (CGI environmental variable), 857

RequestMerch method, MERCHMV.CLS file, 725-726

requests
CGI, environmental variables, 855-857
processing
Netscape servers, 463-464
section, Netscape server config files, 467
with bws.INI file, Minimal Database application, 517-518

requisition maintenance component, 716-721

RESET (CGI form input field), 863

## X-Y-Z

# Complete and Return this Card
# for a *FREE* Computer Book Catalog

Thank you for purchasing this book! You have purchased a superior computer book written expressly for your needs. To continue to provide the kind of up-to-date, pertinent coverage you've come to expect from us, we need to hear from you. Please take a minute to complete and return this self-addressed, postage-paid form. In return, we'll send you a free catalog of all our computer books on topics ranging from word processing to programming and the internet.

☐ Mrs. ☐ Ms. ☐ Dr. ☐

ne (first) [ ][ ][ ][ ][ ][ ][ ][ ][ ][ ][ ] (M.I.) [ ] (last) [ ][ ][ ][ ][ ][ ][ ][ ][ ][ ][ ][ ][ ][ ]

ress [ ][ ][ ][ ][ ][ ][ ][ ][ ][ ][ ][ ][ ][ ][ ][ ][ ][ ][ ][ ][ ][ ][ ][ ][ ][ ]

[ ][ ][ ][ ][ ][ ][ ][ ][ ][ ][ ][ ][ ][ ][ ][ ][ ][ ][ ][ ][ ][ ][ ][ ][ ][ ]

[ ][ ][ ][ ][ ][ ][ ][ ][ ] State [ ][ ] Zip [ ][ ][ ][ ][ ] [ ][ ][ ][ ]

ne [ ][ ][ ][ ][ ][ ][ ] Fax [ ][ ][ ][ ][ ][ ][ ]

pany Name [ ][ ][ ][ ][ ][ ][ ][ ][ ][ ][ ][ ][ ][ ][ ][ ][ ][ ][ ][ ][ ][ ][ ][ ][ ]

ail address [ ][ ][ ][ ][ ][ ][ ][ ][ ][ ][ ][ ][ ][ ][ ][ ][ ][ ][ ][ ][ ][ ][ ][ ][ ]

**lease check at least (3) influencing factors for urchasing this book.**

t or back cover information on book ....................... ☐
cial approach to the content ........................................ ☐
pleteness of content ................................................... ☐
hor's reputation ........................................................... ☐
isher's reputation ....................................................... ☐
k cover design or layout .............................................. ☐
x or table of contents of book .................................... ☐
e of book ..................................................................... ☐
cial effects, graphics, illustrations ........................... ☐
er (Please specify): _____ ☐

**ow did you first learn about this book?**

in Macmillan Computer Publishing catalog .......... ☐
ommended by store personnel .................................... ☐
the book on bookshelf at store .............................. ☐
ommended by a friend ................................................ ☐
eived advertisement in the mail ................................ ☐
an advertisement in: _____ ☐
d book review in: _____ ☐
er (Please specify): _____ ☐

**ow many computer books have you urchased in the last six months?**

book only ....... ☐      3 to 5 books ..................... ☐
oks .................. ☐      More than 5 ..................... ☐

**4. Where did you purchase this book?**

Bookstore ................................................................ ☐
Computer Store ....................................................... ☐
Consumer Electronics Store .................................. ☐
Department Store .................................................... ☐
Office Club ............................................................. ☐
Warehouse Club ..................................................... ☐
Mail Order .............................................................. ☐
Direct from Publisher ............................................ ☐
Internet site ............................................................ ☐
Other (Please specify): _____

**5. How long have you been using a computer?**

☐ Less than 6 months      ☐ 6 months to a year
☐ 1 to 3 years               ☐ More than 3 years

**6. What is your level of experience with personal computers and with the subject of this book?**

|  | With PCs | With subject of book |
|---|---|---|
| New | ☐ | ☐ |
| Casual | ☐ | ☐ |
| Accomplished | ☐ | ☐ |
| Expert | ☐ | ☐ |

Source Code ISBN: 0-7897-0811-6

## 7. Which of the following best describes your job title?

Administrative Assistant .................................. ☐
Coordinator ..................................................... ☐
Manager/Supervisor ....................................... ☐
Director .......................................................... ☐
Vice President ................................................ ☐
President/CEO/COO ....................................... ☐
Lawyer/Doctor/Medical Professional ............. ☐
Teacher/Educator/Trainer ............................... ☐
Engineer/Technician ....................................... ☐
Consultant ...................................................... ☐
Not employed/Student/Retired ....................... ☐
Other (Please specify): _____ ☐

## 8. Which of the following best describes the area of the company your job title falls under?

Accounting ..................................................... ☐
Engineering .................................................... ☐
Manufacturing ............................................... ☐
Operations ..................................................... ☐
Marketing ...................................................... ☐
Sales .............................................................. ☐
Other (Please specify): _____ ☐

## 9. What is your age?

Under 20 ........................................................
21-29 ..............................................................
30-39 ..............................................................
40-49 ..............................................................
50-59 ..............................................................
60-over ...........................................................

## 10. Are you:

Male ...............................................................
Female ............................................................

## 11. Which computer publications do you read regularly? (Please list)

_____
_____
_____
_____
_____
_____
_____
_____
_____

**Comments**: _____
_____
_____

Fold here and scotch-tape to

# Licensing Agreement

By opening this package, you are agreeing to be bound by the following:

This software product is copyrighted, and all rights are reserved by the publisher and author. You are licensed to use this software on a single computer. You may copy and/or modify the software as needed to facilitate your use of it on a single computer. Making copies of the software for any other purpose is a violation of the United States copyright laws.

This software is sold *as is* without warranty of any kind, either expressed or implied, including but not limited to the implied warranties of merchantability and fitness for a particular purpose. Neither the publisher nor its dealers or distributors assumes any liability for any alleged or actual damages arising from the use of this program. (Some states do not allow for the exclusion of implied warranties, so the exclusion may not apply to you.)